T0230741

Enterprise System Architectures

Building Client/Server and Web-based Systems

Mark Goodyear
Hugh W. Ryan
Scott R. Sargent
Stanton J. Taylor
Timothy M. Boudreau
Yannis S. Arvanitis
Richard A. Chang
John K. Kaltenmark
Nancy K. Mullen
Shari L. Dove
Michael C. Davis
John C. Clark
Craig Mindrum

CRC Press
Taylor & Francis Group
Boca Raton London New York

CRC Press is an imprint of the
Taylor & Francis Group, an **informa** business

CRC Press
Taylor & Francis Group
6000 Broken Sound Parkway NW, Suite 300
Boca Raton, FL 33487-2742

First issued in hardback 2017

© 2000 by CRC Press, LLC
CRC Press is an imprint of Taylor & Francis Group, an informa business

No claim to original U.S. Government works

ISBN-13: 978-0-8493-9836-0 (pbk)
ISBN-13: 978-1-1384-6851-1 (hbk)

Visit the Taylor & Francis Web site at
http://www.taylorandfrancis.com

and the CRC Press Web site
http://www.crcpress.com

Library of Congress Cataloging-in-Publication Data

Enterprise system architectures : building client/server and Web-based systems / Mark Goodyear ... [et al.].
    p. cm.
    ISBN 0-8493-9836-3 (alk. paper)
      1. Client/server computing. 2. Web pages--Design. I. Goodyear, Mark.

QA76.9.C55 E68 1999
005.2'76 21--dc21
                                          99-044954

Table of Contents

Table of Contents

SECTION IV
SPECIAL TOPICS

Introduction

A fundamental shift is occurring today in the business capabilities of organizations — in the power that they are able to exercise in their marketplace. At the technical heart of this shift is a new form of client/server computing called "netcentric computing." This book is a comprehensive and practical guide to netcentric computing: what it is, what it means, and how organizations today can design and deliver netcentric computing solutions that result in new business capabilities.

NEW TECHNOLOGIES AND NEW BUSINESS CAPABILITIES

When most people are trying to understand the revolutionary development of netcentric computing, an example from the Internet often suffices. Try this one: using your favorite Internet search engine, type in the word *shopping*. How many hits did you get? Probably well over one million.

Success stories about doing business on the Internet will also soon number over a million. Consider, for example, the cookie company located in Newcastle, in the United Kingdom. When the company built its Web site, it was suddenly selling cookies 5,000 miles away in Newcastle, Wyoming, and 10,000 miles away in Newcastle, New South Wales. Profits doubled in 4 months.

What happened to the Newcastle cookie company was not just that new technology became available, but that the technology enabled a new business capability: selling to an international market.

The real power of netcentric computing, however, cannot be captured by a mere Internet story. Consider another example: a consumer is redesigning the back sun room on his house. He goes to a nearby home supply store and works with a salesperson at a computer kiosk to design a certain configuration of windows for the new room. Another customer with similar needs decides not even to drive to the store but works instead from home on a similar window design application offered through the window company's Web site. When processed, the design and ordering application automatically triggers a chain of operations at the company's headquarters. Supplies are ordered from inventory, and order-entry and billing applications are triggered.

At some point in the process, a certain critical material needed for the window is depleted, and one of the window company's suppliers is automatically notified by e-mail of the urgent need for delivery of this material. Each order is captured in reports available in real time by the company's strategy group, as well as by the marketing and advertising groups. One of the orders placed by a customer involves a complicated custom design; the designers at company headquarters place a call to one of their freelance designers located on the other side of the continent. A groupware application allows all of them to work on-line simultaneously to resolve the problems involved with this customer's design. The designers at headquarters realize that this solution will affect many other designs currently in process at the company, so they notify their supervisor by e-mail of the need for an urgent meeting. The supervisor, on site with a client, is automatically paged by the e-mail message through her personal digital assistant, which has scheduled her for a meeting based on her previous availability.

This story begins to capture both the amazing power and the amazing complexity of netcentric computing — a world in which computing, communications, and knowledge have converged into a business solution with a seemingly infinite array of possibilities. Although IT professionals have acknowledged for years that in current computing solutions, the network is everywhere, recent developments have — as the name *netcentric* implies — shifted the center of focus of computing solutions to the network of computing resources that characterize the core of new technology solutions.

THE NEXT STAGE IN EXTENDING HUMAN POWER

Computing has always been about extending human capabilities. We can still see the original extensions of human power in the name *computer.* Those first primitive business machines computers extended, through automation, the computational abilities of humans. As that computational power was transferred into the world of business, computing first focused primarily on business transactions. The advent of the personal computer broadened that sense of extension by dramatically heightening the rich world of content available to the human mind. It allowed us to create information in new ways and allowed information to be presented *to* us in new ways.

Beginning in the 1980s, when client/server computing models began to rise in prominence, information technology became not just about transactions and not just about content but about *connecting* an organization's processes. Computing suddenly connected people together in new ways; the distinctions between computing, communications, and content — or knowledge — began to blur. Client/server computing brought with it new kinds of business solutions, new ways of organizing companies, and new ways to serve companies. Again, the technology turned out really to be about new kinds of business capabilities.

Today, we are in the midst of another generational shift in the business capabilities enabled by information technology: what we call netcentric computing (sometimes also referred to as "network-centric" computing). As client/server technologies broke down organizational barriers and put knowledge into the hands of knowledge workers, so the new era of ubiquitous computing and communications is putting knowledge into everyone's hands. Netcentric computing — the convergence of computing, communications, and knowledge — is the era we are now shaping.

We are only just now beginning to understand completely the new business capabilities of netcentric computing. However, those who understand them first will reap the most benefits. Netcentric technology has incredible potential. It makes it possible to extend reach *within* an enterprise, among its departments, business units, or its globally dispersed groups; it enables the sharing of information and allows everyone to tap into the company's brain power. Netcentric technology also reaches *outside* an enterprise, to a company's suppliers, customers, and business partners wherever they are situated on our planet, creating new business capabilities for everyone. It can enable new content, in multiple media, to feed automated processes, to inform decision makers, or to bring knowledge to a new network of collaborating colleagues.

To be here at a time of technological change such as this is truly challenging.

DEFINING NETCENTRIC COMPUTING

Consider the previously discussed example of the window company. Several features of the example are particularly important. First, it is clear that in this particular computing solution, many different people are users of the system: not just company employees, but also consumers, business partners, and suppliers. Second, multiple information sources are at work, as well as multiple ways in which to access that information. Finally, although it is not immediately apparent, the solution would not work if it were not built on a common architecture and did not employ open standards.

These features form the basis of our definition of netcentric computing. Netcentric is an emerging architecture style and an evolutionary stage of client/server computing that

- Expands the reach of computing both within and outside the enterprise
- Enables sharing of data and content between individuals and applications
- Uses applications that provide capabilities to publish, interact, or transact
- Uses Internet technologies to connect employees, customers, and business partners

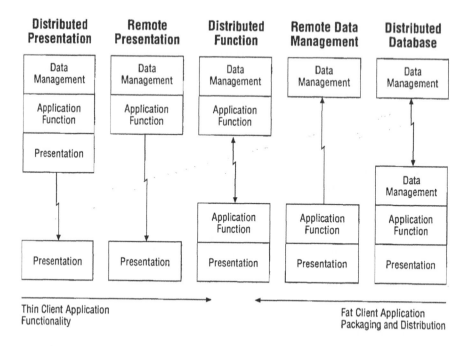

Exhibit 1. Gartner Group's Five Stages of Client/Server Computing.

In other words, netcentric computing is a common architecture built on open standards that supports

- Many different ways for
- Many different kinds of people to collaborate and to reach
- Many different information sources

Although netcentric computing sounds new and some analysts and vendors may want people to believe that it is new, netcentric represents, in fact, an *evolution* from what we already know about client/server computing. We can represent this evolution in the following mathematical equation:

$$\text{Netcentric} = \text{Client/Server} + \text{Reach} + \text{Content}$$

This equation helps communicate the evolutionary nature of the new style. Netcentric is a form of client/server. At the same time, the equation shows that netcentric brings with it a new capability: reaching, interacting, communicating, transacting, and partnering with more entities in more locations, and there are new and richer forms of content being published, interacted with, or transacted.

We can also use the Gartner Group's well-known five stages of client/server (depicted in Exhibit 1) to illustrate how netcentric computing fits into a technical model.

The Gartner Group continuum plots the distribution of processing and data on either side of a network. (Gartner's various reports on network computing models demonstrate how emerging forms of distributed applications can implement these five styles using technologies such as Web-based terminals, HTML, applets, servlets, intelligent dynamic platform adjustment mechanisms, and proxies.) On the far left-hand side of the five-styles diagram, there are almost no distributed processes or data, so there are very thin clients — the thinnest used to be the old dumb 3270 terminal. Everything went across from the network to the terminal. As we move to the right, we progressively get more intelligence, more processing, more function, and more data close to the end user. So at the far right-hand side of the continuum are the richest and fattest of the clients; that is where the distribution of function, data, and presentation logic is maximized.

Using the Gartner model, netcentric computing is somewhere in the middle. What netcentric does with these five stages, however, is to add a way of interconnecting these system components, characterized by a set of open, common standards that the Internet has legitimized. HTML, Java, and Java database connectivity enable the coexistence of applications that will let the desktop become the universal client capable of connecting to multiple servers and the recipient of an enterprise server reaching out to touch it.

To take another viewpoint on this different world, consider the new kind of complexity involved in building netcentric infrastructures. When we were in the mainframe world, we may have had three or four major infrastructure components: the database, the CPU, a network, and some terminals. Two or three suppliers provided all those major components, so life was relatively simple ... or at least constrained. Because there were only six to eight combinations of all of components and vendors, the complexity was manageable.

When we went to client/server, we had five or six infrastructure components, made up of maybe three tiers of the client/server model, a database, and a couple of networks. Each of these has five or seven possible suppliers. So instead of 6 to 8 combinations, we are now looking at up to 40 — about 5 times as many. The size of the problem was bigger and the nature of the problem got more complex.

With netcentric computing, if we add only 20% more components and, let us say, 30% more providers we go from some 40 combinations to up to 100, and to make things even more exciting, the components and providers change practically by the day. The vendors are more numerous, and the products are younger.

It is not just the infrastructure that changes; almost every other aspect of systems delivery is different to varying degrees. Think what it is like to implement and test an application that runs on multiple platforms through a universal network. Think about what it means when most of the people in the world and potentially many of the computers are connected to the network. It makes user testing rather different, does it not? If from these various points you sense that the integration challenge can be greater, and that there is more complexity to manage — then you are right. Demonstrating how organizations today can address that challenge and manage that complexity is a key purpose of this book.

CLIENT/SERVER IS NOT DEAD

Some followers of the technology press may have heard claims over the past few years that the Internet has rendered the client/server computing model obsolete. Charles Babcock's 1996 article, "Client/server is dead. Long live the intranet," (*ComputerWorld*, 3/11/96) was one of the first to make such a claim. However, statistics show something quite different. That same year, a research report by Datapro Information Services reported that only 46% of information systems managers had implemented even traditional client/server applications.

Today, it is becoming increasingly important to view netcentric computing in its evolutionary context. Again: netcentric equals client/server plus new kinds of reach and new kinds of content. Understood as the next phase of client/server computing, the move to netcentric appears inevitable. Projections today indicate that the netcentric adaptation of client/server has begun a steep ascent, and will pass traditional client/server by the year 2001.

It is best, however, to think of these technology movements, again, as a move toward new business capability. A recent survey of the banking industry, for example, revealed that 75% of financial institutions, regardless of asset size, will offer on-line banking by the year 2000. These companies know that the capability of interacting directly with customers is vital to their success.

All these statistics confirm the inexorable move of computing from the mainframe platform, to the client/server model, and confirm the belief that the evolution to netcentric will be at least as fast as that of client/server. As systems-building models evolve into netcentric, we will see the creation of new systems with netcentric capabilities, as well as the extension of existing client/server systems to provide greater reach to new users and new classes of user, and to provide greater content to these newly-connected business users.

INTEGRATING STRATEGY, PROCESS, TECHNOLOGY, AND PEOPLE

Advances in information technology often expose certain flaws in the way organizations operate. Client/server computing, for example, exposed as never before the silos that had developed within companies — silos that restricted the optimal flow of information. Because netcentric computing is so all-encompassing and involves such an array of players, it is also likely

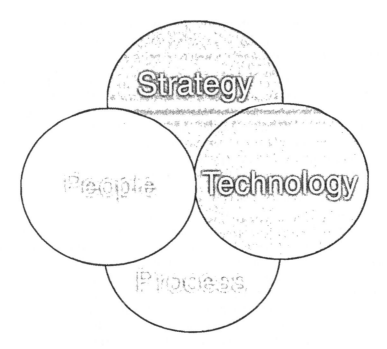

Exhibit 2. The Business Integration Model.

to expose limitations within business structures that few people have yet thought about. Organizations would benefit from a model that would help them deal with these changes.

Netcentric computing cannot be considered apart from the organizational, economic, and commercial system of which it is a part. Although the system here must be understood organically, organizational theory has rarely stressed this organic dimension. It may speak of the interaction of various components, but the image has generally been more mechanistic than organic.

In our experience, Exhibit 2 is extremely useful in understanding what Accenture calls "business integration" — a way to make all the component parts of an organization work together toward the same goals.

The exhibit depicts the organization as an integrated whole, comprising its people, strategy, processes, and technology. None of these elements can be understood if isolated from any of the others. People perform processes, enabled by technology. Processes and technology arise from strategic intent, yet technology also enables new kinds of strategies. Strategy arises from people and then helps to direct them. The list of interconnections is long and complex.

Using the business integration model, we can better understand how organizations are likely to be affected as they move from a more basic client/server model of computing toward a netcentric model.

From the end-user perspective, for example, client/server provided a way to take systems with powerful front ends and link them up to back-end systems. The main impact of the technology in that case was more productive, empowered individuals. Rather than supporting individuals or single processes, however, netcentric computing connects *collections* of people, both inside and outside the enterprise. Suddenly, it is the communication and the information sharing among these people that creates the difference.

Client/server supported the reengineering of processes, because it took the technology closer to the point at which the business process was actually being executed. However, with netcentric computing, the technology allows the enterprise to reach outside itself and allows others to reach in. For example, when Federal Express provided the means for its customers to track their own packages on its company Web site, it saved 5 million dollars a year in customer service costs, simply because customers no longer had to talk with a person. Customer satisfaction on call tracking also increased. As well as providing new business capabilities, the technology was used for competitive advantage. Obviously, this kind of ability to change how business is conducted has profound implications for how a business thinks about what it does, why it does it, how it does it, and how it should change its people and processes to exploit the new capabilities created by the technology.

EMERGING NETCENTRIC INITIATIVES

In the emerging field of netcentric, we should expect to see companies take a wide range of approaches to implement new solutions using the netcentric model. Three in particular appear to be emerging:

1. Publishing: a basic, read-only, nonspecific service, which is essentially advertising
2. Interacting: a targeted read-only inquiry service, with some personalization
3. Transacting: a fully commercial service

Publishing

With this first type, a company is basically publishing or advertising, as the Newcastle cookie maker did. But even something as simple as that — a new, free, outward flow of information such as "our cookies are delicious and here's how to order by phone or mail" — can dramatically change a business. Remember, the cookie company doubled its sales.

Interacting

The next type of solution involves inquiries and simple interaction. A classic example is the utility company that offers its customers a Web site where they can inquire about their electricity use, usage pattern, and account status. These specific, inquiry-only types of transactions can be a potentially powerful marketing and client-satisfaction tool with a real business case.

Transacting

The third type of solution creates a one-to-one interactive relationship with the enterprise and its employees, customers, or business partners so that they can hold virtual meetings, place orders, pay bills, or customize requests. Companies can even share supply-chain information, as competitors GM, Ford, and Chrysler hope to do when they pilot a system linking the three manufacturers with their suppliers through an Internet service for a projected savings of 1 billion dollars a year.

THINK NOW ABOUT THE FUTURE

A critical point for companies today is this: even if their current business solutions do not involve netcentric computing, it is vital to maintain the flexibility in technical architecture that will permit a move to netcentric computing in the future.

Case in point: our firm has been working on a systems development project for a large automotive manufacturer. Recently we were reviewing the technical infrastructure for the system — a stand-alone dealer system to be integrated with local dealer systems. We asked the company executives this question: what if, at some point in the future — 1 or 2 years from now — the way in which the business is transacted changes? What if, for example, somebody walked into a dealership on a Thursday or Friday, interacted with the system (that is, created a customized car, selected the color, looked at the finance or lease package) but then said, "I want to go away and think about this for the weekend."

Then suppose the company had a 24-hour call center. That same customer could call and, by speaking to a customer service representative about the details of the package designed at the dealership, talk through the deal on a Sunday afternoon. Right there, the customer could make some adjustments and close the transaction over the phone. Of course, being a 24-hour operation, the call center could be based anywhere in the world.

Now this would be a new way to buy cars. It may not be dramatically different, but it would have a big impact on the technology infrastructure. All of a sudden, all of the context of the transaction from the showroom conversation on Thursday or Friday would have to be made available to a call center three days later, potentially on the other side of the world.

We asked our client if this scenario was within the realm of possibility. It was. Was it being considered? No.

This brings us back to the organizational impact of netcentric computing. From the point of view of business integration, the technology has a major impact on the dealer's business process; it is a new strategy for the automotive manufacturer. It is a perfect example of business integration: blending strategy, process, people, and technology. No particular aspect of the change by itself is earth shattering. But taken together in the perspective of the business integration framework, the new solution could have a major effect on the company's position in the marketplace.

HOW TO USE THIS BOOK

This book represents a combination and significant update of two books also written by Accenture and published by Auerbach: *Practical Guide to Client/Server Computing* and *Netcentric Computing: Computing Communications and Knowledge.*

The book reflects the experience and expertise of Accenture, the premier global management consulting firm, which helps its clients with insights, practical know-how, and global, integrated capabilities to help them achieve far-reaching change. Acknowledged for many years as a leader in the application of information technology to business solutions, our approach helps companies translate the full potential of technology into improved business performance today and in the future.

The authors of this book represent over 90 years of experience in the application of technology to business and of over 100 completed industrial-strength netcentric implementations which are delivering business value as you read these words. The Accenture Netcentric Architecture Framework is proven to help understand and manage the technology complexity that businesses face today. Our intent in this book is to distill from these experiences and approaches the essentials of what it takes to get netcentric right.

If our take-up projections are correct, it is increasingly vital for all organizations to get it right. The IS specialist today must understand and work with mainframe and client/server systems and networks, netcentric implementation complexities, and business strategists.

Many publications, books, and training materials about this subject are available. In our estimation, however, there has been no satisfactory, comprehensive, and yet practical guide to understanding and implementing this new technology. This book was written to help fill that void.

The book is not designed to be read from cover to cover — not just because of its length but because it was written so that different parts would support the work of different groups of people within contemporary organizations. The book is organized into four major sections so that readers may dip in to parts of the book most appropriate to their work and easily access helpful support for their development projects. Occasionally, there is some overlap; material covered in one section may be briefly summarized in another so that each section can continue to stand alone.

Readers will glean specific information from this book and its four sections. We start with an overview of the technical and business issues relating to netcentric computing. In the middle sections, we introduce a comprehensive netcentric architecture and discuss the many factors affecting netcentric implementation. A final section of the book looks at some emerging technologies and issues that are certain to affect the evolution of netcentric solutions throughout the coming years.

WHO SHOULD READ WHAT?

Section I: Overview of Netcentric Computing Solutions

Section I covers the big picture of what netcentric is and why it is important. It looks at the subject from the perspective of the CIO or the head of a business unit who wants to grasp the basic steps in moving to netcentric computing.

Section II: Architectures and Frameworks for Netcentric Solutions

Section II discusses the key architectural components and technologies of client/server and netcentric computing. It contains information for chief information officers, chief technology officers, project leaders, or lead architects.

Section III: Designing and Implementing Netcentric Solutions

Section III contains practical implementation details. It covers design specifics for architectures, applications, and networks; rollout strategies; and ongoing management of distributed operations. Project leaders will find detailed suggestions on how to structure a project and complete critical tasks and steps.

Section IV: Special Topics in Netcentric Computing

Section IV discusses a number of critical issues, such as security, data warehousing, data mining, and componentware. It answers questions that CIOs, project leaders, and project team members may have about the future direction of technologies, so they can plan their strategies accordingly.

Plus ça change

A French proverb runs, "Plus ça change, plus c'est la même chose": "the more things change, the more they remain the same." We are fortunate that, in the midst of great technology and business change, there are a set of underlying principles of technology that help us decipher the clues hidden in the latest jargon, and also help us create frameworks to navigate the ever-changing route toward greater business results. As implementers of solutions, we must strive to balance the often-conflicting demands that the individual parts of the system impose on the overall design. As those parts grow in number and complexity, as they do with netcentric, our juggling acts must become even more professional as we take the pragmatic steps towards that business vision.

Can a single book guarantee you success? Certainly not. Individual success depends on many factors including insight, timing, hard work, experience and a commitment to quality. It is the same with cooking — having the recipe of the best chef in the world does not mean you will make a living in the restaurant business. We try here to contribute to your recipe book with our understanding and insight of implementing new technology. The timing, hard work, and commitment is up to you. My father once told me "A wise person learns from experience, a wiser person learns from other people's experiences."

If us wise folk can make you a bit wiser on the steps to your own successes, then our writing and your reading have been worthwhile.

Mark Goodyear, Accenture

Acknowledgments

This book represents the accumulated knowledge and experience of many individuals and groups within Accenture, in addition to the named authors. We would like to thank, in particular, the following people who made substantive contributions to the information in this book:

Michael W. Alber

Prem N. Mehra

William M. Gilliland

Anthony Roby

Chris M. Degiorgio

David A. Antoniolli

David K. Black

James P. Behling

William W. Westerman

Anatole V. Gershman

Glover T. Ferguson

David K. Black

Jennifer L. Wilson

John P. Jordan

Sharon K. Dietz

Bill G. Chang

David Chen

Jeff A. Goldberg

Stephen A. Barlock

Section I
Overview of Netcentric Computing Solutions

Chapter 1

Netcentric: The Evolution of Computing, Frameworks, and Architectures

To understand client/server and netcentric computing, it is important to look at the context of prior technologies and prior solutions based on those technologies. This perspective helps to locate the differences as well as what is important about them. It can also help business users recognize the impact of these differences on future solutions.

In this chapter we will track the development of client/server and then see how it has evolved to provide the foundation for the capabilities that have been described for netcentric computing.

WHAT IS CLIENT/SERVER? WHAT IS NETCENTRIC?

Client/server computing is a style of computing involving multiple processors, one of which is typically a workstation and across which a single business transaction is completed. We can better understand the term "netcentric" (which is actually a shortened version of "network centric") by considering what client/server meant to businesses. Client/server computing recognized that business users, and not a mainframe, were the real center of a business. Therefore, client/server was also "client-centric" computing. Today, the concept of "business users" has expanded greatly, thanks to the linkages made possible by a near-universal network. Today's business computing solutions are network centric or netcentric. Netcentric takes the technological next step. Netcentric is "an evolution of client/server that expands the reach of computing both within and outside the enterprise, and that enables sharing of data and content between

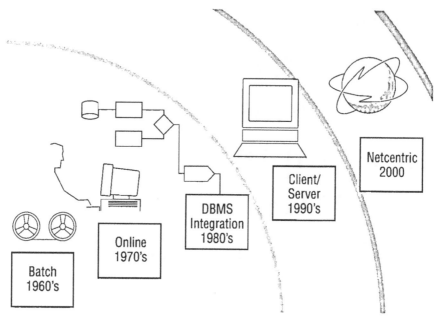

Exhibit 1. Evolution of Computing Solutions.

individuals and applications." The many variations and implications of these definitions are explored and explained later, but these definitions are adequate for the following discussion.

Consider the case of an insurance program used to validate and evaluate the risk of an application for coverage. A client/server implementation might have the validation and risk-evaluation logic run on the workstation. A netcentric application might have the prospective policy holder complete the application form using a browser. Policy details might be built up on a server in the local office. Finally, when the policy is complete and accepted, the bound (agreed-to) policy could be stored on the central file server where it would be available to the company as a whole. In a netcentric application the policy holder may then have access to it.

Consider this example now in the context of the business computing solutions that have evolved over the last 30 years (see Exhibit 1).

THE EARLY YEARS: BATCH PROCESSING

The majority of business solutions delivered in the mid- to late 1960s focused on the use of batch technology. There are many variations in this style of computing.

In batch processing, the business user would present a file of transactions to the application. The system would then run through the transactions, processing each one, essentially without user intervention. The system would provide reporting at some point in the batch processing. Typically, the reports would be batch printed. These in turn would be used by the business user to correct the input transactions that were resubmitted along with the next night's batch transactions.

THE 1970S: ON-LINE TRANSACTIONS

In the 1970s, businesses began a transition to on-line, interactive transactions. Once again, there are many variations to on-line processing. However, at a conceptual level this processing opened up the file of transactions found in batch transactions and allowed the user to submit them one at a time, receiving either immediate confirmation of the success of the transaction or else feedback on the nature of the transaction error.

The conceptually simple change of having the user interact with the machine on a transaction-at-a-time basis caused huge changes in the nature of business computing. Those who were present at the beginning of this era can remember long discussions on such questions as what good screen design was and whether the concept of a dialog was a good thing.

More important, users saw huge changes in what they could do on a day-to-day basis. A transaction was processed when it happened, and the impact of the transaction was known to all concerned. Customers were no longer forced to wait for a batch run to process the application. In essence, the machine had an impact on the entire flow of work for the business user. Technological impact became human impact and business impact.

With the advent of on-line interactive systems, it was equally significant that the systems provided a means for the business user to communicate with others in the business as the day-to-day business went along. This capability was provided on the backbone of a wide area network (WAN). The WAN was in itself a demanding technology; because of these demands, telecommunications groups emerged within organizations, charged with the responsibility to maintain, evolve, and manage the network over time.

THE 1980S: DATABASES

The theme of the 1980s was database and database management systems (DBMSs). Organizations used and applied database technology in the 1970s, but in the 1980s they grew more confident in the application of DBMS technology. They began to focus more on the sharing of data across organizational and application boundaries.

Curiously, database technology did not change the fundamental way in which business processing was done. DBMS made it more convenient to access the data and to ensure that it could be updated while maintaining the integrity of the data. In the long term it became apparent that DBMS was more about the business changing than about the technology changing. If the organization was willing to share information across organizational boundaries, DBMS could and did provide extraordinary benefits. If not, it was a rather machine-intensive way to achieve what could be done using more traditional access routines.

THE 1990S: THE COMING OF CLIENT/SERVER

In the 1990s, technology began to shift toward client/server computing. In this style of computing, once again, there were fundamental changes in technology.

First, there was another shift in the level of processing. Using the workstation, the transaction entered by the user could now be processed on a keystroke-by-keystroke basis. This was a change, again, in the level of interaction. This change led to a whole new set of discussions on how to do good window design, how to place widgets, and when and how to do processing driven off the keystrokes of the business.

Furthermore, there was a change in the communications. With client/server, users could communicate with others in the work group via a local area network (LAN). The LAN permitted workstation-to-workstation communications at speeds of 100 to 1,000 times what was typically available on a WAN area network. The LAN was a technology that could be grown and evolved in a local office with little need for direct interaction from the telecommunications group. This meant the local site could begin to evolve its own answer to the changing demands of the local business.

THE NEXT EVOLUTIONARY STEP: NETCENTRIC COMPUTING

Netcentric computing has brought new technologies to the forefront, especially in the area of external presence and access, ease of distribution, and media capabilities. Some of these are

- *Browsers, which provide a "universal client."* The browser-centric application style offers a new option in distributing functionality to both internal and external users. In the traditional client/server environment, distributing an application internally or externally for an enterprise requires that the application be recompiled and tested for all specific workstation operating systems. It also usually requires loading the application on each client machine. The browser-centric application style offers an alternative to this traditional problem. Today the Web browser provides a universal client that offers users a consistent and familiar user interface. Using a browser, a user can launch many types of applications and view many types of documents. This can be accomplished on different operating systems/platforms and is independent of where the applications or documents reside. The browser technology is also changing the traditional desktop as companies such as Netscape and Microsoft, leading Web browser vendors, continue to evolve their products (such as Internet Explorer and Netscape Communicator) and to redefine the structure and style of the traditional desktop.

- *Direct supplier-to-customer relationships.* The external presence and access enabled by connecting a business node to the Internet has opened up a series of opportunities to reach an audience outside a company's traditional internal users. Consequently, the Internet is becoming another vehicle for companies to conduct business with their customers through broadcasting of product and service descriptions, exchanging interactive information and conducting actual business transactions.

- *Richer documents.* The ability to digitize, organize, and deliver textual, graphical, and other information in addition to traditional data to a broader audience enables new ways for people and enterprises to work together. Netcentric technologies (such as HTML documents, plug-ins, and Java) and standardization of media information formats enable support for these types of complex documents, applications, and even nondiscrete data types such as audio and video. Network bandwidth remains a performance issue; however, advances in network technologies and compression continue to make richer media-enabled applications more feasible on the Web.

- *Application version checking and dynamic update.* Configuration management of traditional client/server applications, which tend to be stored on both the client hard disk and on the server, is a major issue for many corporations. The distribution and update problems of such applications that are packaged as one large or a combination of a few large executables makes minor updates difficult for even a small-scale user population because, every time an update is made, a process must be initiated to distribute new code to all client machines.

Advances in netcentric technologies are allowing applications to be packaged differently. For instance, ActiveX technology (from Microsoft) introduced version checking and dynamic install and update. The need for this had long been recognized; however, it was typically at best a custom effort, often bypassed due to its difficulty and cost. The introduction of this capability into core system software changes its implementation cost and makes it a more feasible option to implement.

This brief history suggests that there have been four fundamental shifts in technology over the years that have changed how the business user can do various business tasks.

1. The shift in the manner in which the business user interacted with the computer changed how business was transacted.
2. The shift or augmentation in the ability to communicate by increasing connectivity or the speed of connection made other fundamental business changes.
3. The shift to connect business processes outside the traditional enterprise boundaries.
4. The shift to the sharing of new data types among new participants.

The first two changes played a significant part in client/server computing and, as a result, laid the technological foundation for the netcentric evolution, which is characterized by the second two changes.

WORKING DEFINITIONS: CLIENT/SERVER

The insurance example discussed earlier is one powerful application corresponding to the working definition of client/server used in this book: "a style of computing in which multiple processors, one of which is typically a workstation, complete a business transaction."

As another example, consider the case of an order entry application for an organization that builds and delivers very complex electronic products. The application accepts the order from the sales engineer and validates that the proposed product configuration is one that actually can be built. Then the application checks central databases for availability of the product in inventory. The databases are found on servers at various places in the company. If the product is not available the application then goes through an allocation effort in real time, controlled from the workstation, to determine where and when the product can be assembled. This is returned to the sales engineer, who builds up the order initially as a confirmation of order acceptance.

This example illustrates most of the characteristics of our client/server definition:

- There are multiple processors: the workstation for the entry and then various servers to check availability of parts and assembly line for manufacturing.
- There is a complete business transaction processed across multiple servers: the entry of the order.
- Various databases are updated to reflect the existence of the order.

Although the client/server definition here is straightforward, it contains some implicit subtleties that are worth elaborating on further.

- *Why are multiple processors important?* Client/server and netcentric processing, as defined here, means that developers are dealing with multiple processors in making decisions about where processing and data are located. The processors are distinct and connected through some form of a network.
- *Why is one of the processors "typically" a workstation?* Workstations are not a requirement for client/server or netcentric computing. Indeed, there are excellent examples of both where the business user input device has limited processing capability. Typically, applications using X-terminals, NC devices or very thin front end devices have very limited processing capability in comparison to the typical workstation, but they can still provide excellent solutions in certain cases.
- *What is a "business transaction"?* A business transaction can cover a wide range of concerns. It can be no more than a simple update for a change of address, for example. It can also be a longer-running transaction such as the addition of an insurance policy that may occur in stages over several days. Generically, a business transaction means a business event that is recorded as a part of the user interacting with the system. The recording typically is done in real time or near real time. It is also typically done by storing the information in data files that are used by the business.

The key factor within this concept of a business transaction is that it must have the integrity that is required by the business. Thus, if it is essential that the transaction have exclusive control of all related data when the update occurs, the impact often is that the update occurs in one data record under the exclusive control of a DBMS. Conversely, if integrity constraints can be relaxed, the update may occur in a delayed fashion at other distributed sites where the data have been replicated. Most important here, the level of integrity required is a business decision and needs to be evaluated on a case-by-case basis. In a client/server or netcentric solution, it is not a given that all updates must occur in real time.

Client/Server: Hardware, Data, and Processing

Client/server computing must be viewed not only in terms of its hardware and network configuration but also in terms of the allocation of data and processing to the levels of the architecture.

Exhibit 2 suggests a typical three-level hierarchy of servers found in client/server computing. The first level is the workstation, the device with which the business user interacts to record the business events. Typically, these devices are connected to each other and to the next level by a a LAN. The intermediate level is the work group server, a server that is shared by a group of individuals. These may be linked with other devices and to the next level by a LAN or through the use of a WAN and some form of bridges

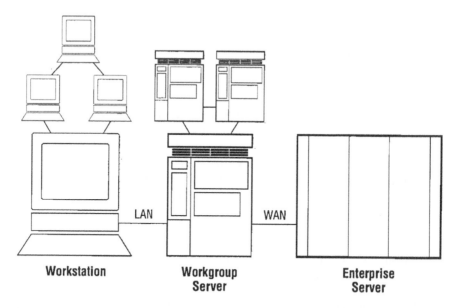

LAN   WAN

Workstation   **Workgroup Server**   **Enterprise Server**

Exhibit 2. Three-Level Client/Server Hardware and Network Configuration.

and routers. The highest level shown in the exhibit is the enterprise server. This level of server is used to share information and processing across the entire company.

Although the exhibit shows a three-level hierarchy, there may in fact be multiple servers with which the individual on the workstation interacts. Client/server systems are either "two-tier" or "three-tier" solutions, that is, while many client/server applications use devices at all three levels or tiers, others consist of only two tiers; in this case the workstation interacts directly with a server — often, an enterprise server. This type of solution has been common in an IBM environment, where the workstation interacts directly with the mainframe. In the full three tier solution, all three levels are present.

The notion of an "n-tiered" architecture is often discussed today, the implication being that there is no real limit to the number of tiers of a systems architecture. However, the phrase "n-tier" is not entirely accurate. The "n" actually means that the number of servers can be extended horizontally, as it were, at a particular level. There may be many servers, but they will still be clustered in either a two-tier or three-tier framework.

Designers of client/server systems make decisions about the allocation of data and processing to these levels based on the specifics of the business needs, hardware, network, and available software. Exhibits 3 and 4 are

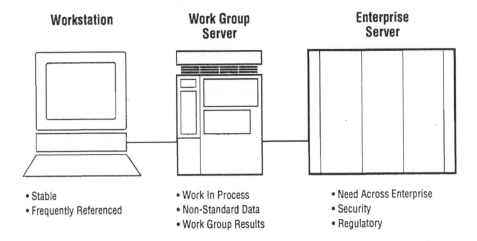

Exhibit 3. Allocation of Data in a Client/Server Environment.

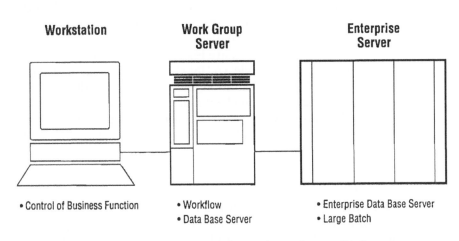

Exhibit 4. Allocation of Processing in a Client/Server Environment.

summaries of one approach to this allocation and represent a conceptual, not a physical, allocation.

DISTINGUISHING NETCENTRIC FROM TRADITIONAL CLIENT/SERVER

Both netcentric as well as traditional client/server systems are tiered architectures. In both cases, there is a distribution of presentation services, application code, and data across client and server. In both cases, there is a networking protocol that is used for communication between clients and servers.

There are, of course, also a number of important differences between client/server systems and netcentric systems:

- For netcentric systems, the way in which the application logic is distributed to clients differs from traditional client/server systems. In netcentric systems, application logic can be packaged into components and distributed from a server machine to a client machine over a network. In traditional client/server systems, the application logic is split between the client and the server on a permanent basis; there is normally no dynamic distribution of application logic.
- The client in netcentric systems also differs. The client in this case has standardized interfaces so that an application can execute within a client that can run on multiple operating systems and hardware platforms. In traditional client/server systems, the client is custom-made for a specific operating system and hardware platform.
- The way in which netcentric and traditional client/server systems can be extended and adapted is different. Components enable netcentric systems to be adaptable to a variety of distribution styles, from a "thin client" to a "fat client." In comparison, traditional client/server systems, once designed and built, are less easily adapted for use with more than one computing style. (A "fat client" application is one that typically has all of the presentation logic and most of the business logic and data resident on the client machine. In contrast, a "thin client" application has very little application logic on the client; it primarily supports the display of information stored and managed on the server.)

A Netcentric Application in Action

Consider now the order entry application example used previously as it would play out in a netcentric environment. In this case, the organization allows end customers to access the product catalog on-line — with explanatory video descriptions showing how some of the products function. The browser application used by the customers on their own terminals accepts the order detail and validates that the proposed product configuration is one that actually can be built. If any problems are not easily resolved by the application, the customer can call or e-mail a sales engineer, who will call back to help with the configuration. The application checks central databases for availability of the product in inventory. The databases are found on servers at various places in the company. If the product is not available the application then goes through an allocation process in real time, controlled from the server, to determine where and when the product can be assembled. This is returned to the customer, with a follow up e-mail as a confirmation of order acceptance.

This example illustrates the additional characteristics of our netcentric definition.

- The boundaries of the business process are now extended to include the end customer.
- New data types are exchanged as part of the processes — in this case catalog pictures, video, and e-mail.
- Without the existence of a set of common interconnection standards, such a solution would be excessively costly and inflexible, demanding a standard level of client hardware.
- The solution is an evolution — an extension of the client/server solution.

The new extensions of reach and content that characterize netcentric computing have implications for the traditional client/server components:

- A greater and more complex network traffic
- A broader base of end users, who may need to use the application with little or no training
- An increased level of reliance on a greater number of production system components, some of which are outside the host enterprise's boundary

These challenges are an unavoidable part of the challenge in providing netcentric solutions.

TIERS IN NETCENTRIC COMPUTING

As with traditional client/server architectures, netcentric architectures support a style of computing where processes on different machines communicate using messages. In this style, "client" processes delegate business functions or other tasks (such as data manipulation logic) to one or more server processes. Server processes respond to messages from clients.

Business logic can reside on both client and server. Clients are typically PCs or workstations with a graphical user interface running in a Web browser. Servers are usually implemented on UNIX, NT, or mainframe machines.

A key design decision for a client/server system, as already mentioned, is whether it should be two-tiered or three-tiered (or multitiered within the three-level model) and how business logic is distributed across the tiers. In netcentric architectures there is a tendency to move more business logic to the server tiers, although "fatter" clients result from newer technologies such as Java and ActiveX.

Two-Tiered Architectures

Two-tiered architecture describes a distributed application architecture in which business applications are split into front ends (clients) and back ends (servers). Such a model of computing began to surface in the late 1980s and is the prominent configuration in use today by companies that have migrated to client/server based computing.

There are some advantages to the two-tiered approach. At a minimum, a two-tiered client/server architecture assumes that an application's presentation logic resides on the client and its data management logic resides on the server. This style of computing became attractive to early adopters of client/server because it clearly addresses the inadequacies of a character-based interface, that is, it allows PC-based clients to introduce a graphical user interface (GUI) into the application environment.

In addition a two-tiered approach results in decreased communication overhead because of a direct connection (for a small number of users) and also allows the distribution of the program's logic (application, presentation, and data management).

The two-tiered approach has limitations, however. The use of two-tier tools has resulted in a de facto "client-heavy" or "fat-client" two-tiered model, where the presentation and application logic resides on the client and data management resides on the server. In fact, the use of these tools "out-of-the-box" assumes the adoption of such a model. Unfortunately, such an architectural model falls short of addressing many important issues required of an enterprise-wide information architecture. This model of computing was actually developed for less-demanding PC environments where the database was simply a tool for decision support.

Three-Tiered (Multitiered) Architectures

Three-tiered architecture describes a distributed application architecture in which business applications are separated into three logical components: presentation and control, application logic, and data management. These logical components are "clean layered" such that each runs on a different machine or platform and communicates with the other components via a network.

A three-tiered architecture is often enhanced by the integration of distributed transaction processing middleware. This model of computing is often termed the "enhanced" client/server model. Most netcentric architectures use an approach with a Web server and potentially a separate application server layer.

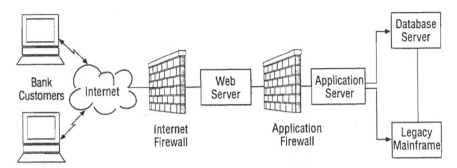

Exhibit 5. A Home Banking Netcentric Solution.

In the enhanced client/server model, all presentation and control logic reside on the client, all application logic resides on multiple back-end application servers, and all data management logic resides on multiple back-end database servers.

There are advantages to the three-tiered approach. In contrast to mainframe and two-tiered client/server computing models, a three-tiered enhanced client/server architecture provides the benefits of a GUI application, but also provides a level of integrity and reliability found in mainframe centralized computing, that is, it will evolve to serve high-volume, high-integrity, and high-availability environments. On the other hand, the three-tiered approach is more complex to implement, involving longer implementation times, higher development costs, additional developer skills, more complex planning, and additional hardware.

Example of a Three-Tiered Netcentric Solution

Exhibit 5 shows how the three-tiered netcentric architecture played out in an actual solution built for a major bank to provide its customers with home banking capabilities.

At a functional level, the architecture of this solution is made up of seven components: Client, Internet Firewall, Web Server, Application Firewall, Application Server, Database Server, and Host. The remote clients connect via the Internet to the Web server. The Web server is connected to the application server which accesses the host (centralized legacy system). The mainframe acts as the application server where business information is stored and maintained and where the business transactions are processed. The database server caches data that flows from the mainframe to the communications server to speed up further transactions. It also logs the transaction history for utilization analysis.

- *Client.* Customers' personal computers are the client machines of the home banking system. Customers can use their Web browser to access the site and conduct banking transactions. Both Netscape Navigator and Microsoft Internet Explorer are supported by the architecture. In addition to the browser, customers are required to use special security software supplied by the bank. The security software allows their browser to talk securely with the Web server to reduce the potential of fraudulent transactions.
- *Internet Firewall.* The Internet firewall is used to isolate internal systems from unwanted intruders. In the architecture, it is used to isolate the Web server from all the Internet traffic that is not relevant to the system. The only requests allowed through the firewall are for services on the Web server. All requests for other applications (e.g., FTP, Telnet) and other IP addresses are blocked. The firewall not only services the home banking system but also allows the security architecture to provide Internet access for the bank's employees.
- *Web Server.* The Web server is the primary interface to the client for all interactions with the applications. The main task of the Web server is to authenticate the client, establish a secure path from the client to the server using encrypted messages, and to allow the client application to transparently access the provided resources. The Web server is responsible for accepting incoming HTTP messages and fulfilling the requests. For dynamic HTML page generation, requests are forwarded to the application server. Static HTML pages, such as help pages of the home banking system, are directly invoked from the Web server. The Web server in this architecture only houses information specific to the home banking system. The bank does have a more substantial Web presence, which is outsourced to a content provider. Links to the home banking system are made from the bank's Web homepage.
- *Application Firewall.* An application firewall is interposed between the Web server and application server to increase the security of the system. Its purpose is to check the information that flows between the two servers, allowing communication only via well defined communications services. This is an important security measure; in the case of a security breach in the Web server, the application server cannot be directly reached with standard remote access applications such as Telnet.
- *Application Server.* The primary logical function of the application server is to provide a link through which the Web server can interact with the host, trigger business transactions, and send back resulting data to the user. A fundamental role of the application server is to manage the logical flow of the transactions, keeping track of the state of the sessions. The application server is also responsible for managing all sessions.

- *Database Server.* The main purpose of the database server is to handle the application log. All requests (i.e., account queries and transfer requests) sent to the mainframe as well as all responses are logged into the application log. The application log is used for traceability. Requests are logged in the application log directly by the application server. Responses corresponding to transfer requests (asynchronous messages sent by the host) are handled by the database server and logged. The log files are replicated to a help desk database so advocates can trace events through the system.
- *Host.* The host, which is represented by the existing bank mainframe, stores all data and performs all the logic related to the business transactions. As the business logic and the technical infrastructure already exist on the host, the services provided are aimed at accessing these functions. A thin interface layer has been developed on the host to allow access to the business application functions.

THE GARTNER GROUP MODEL OF CLIENT/SERVER COMPUTING

There are, of course, other models for looking at client/server computing. One model that has received widespread attention is the Gartner Group's "Five Styles of Client/Server Computing" (Exhibit 6) Because so many people in the information technology field are aware of this model, there is some value in discussing it and extending it into a netcentric environment.

The Gartner Group model is based on dividing business processing into three distinct layers: database, application logic, and presentation.

The first layer is the presentation layer. This layer is involved with collecting and returning information from the user. It presents the windows and collects the keystrokes and other events that the business user provides to the application.

The next layer is the application logic of the business process. This is the processing logic needed to meet particular business needs. In the insurance application, for example, the logic to rate the risk of a policy would be an example of application logic.

The data layer is the third layer in the model. For most business processing there is a need to access and store data to support and reflect the processing done by the application logic. The role of the data layer is to access and store information.

Client/server computing involves, in part, introducing processors and networks over which these layers can be allocated. One way to view client/server is to define possible allocations of presentation, application, and data on processors across the network. This is the graphic depiction

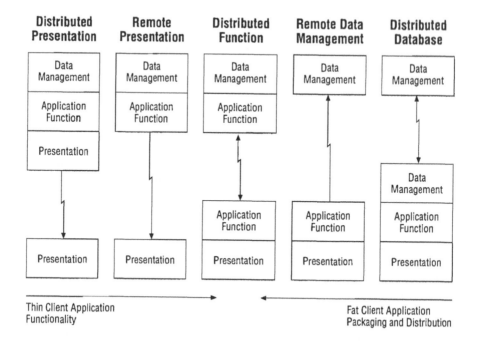

Exhibit 6. Gartner Group's Five Stages of Client/Server Computing.

in the Gartner model. The solid line labeled "Network" shows which of the five layers are allocated to client and which are allocated to server.

The Gartner Group has given the names shown at the top of the exhibit to the proposed allocations of presentation, application logic, and data. Following is a brief summary of the processing approach implied by the allocation.

Distributed Presentation

In this style of processing, presentation is split between the client and the server. One example of this style of computing is referred to as screen scraping. It is found when a traditional 3270 application has its user interface presented on a workstation rather than on the 3270 terminal for which it was implemented. Usually this means that a window is presented to the user and the input is captured and sent to the application on the server. This style is often used to place a new improved terminal and a consistent user interface onto an existing character terminal application. This style of computing alone generally does not justify a move to client/server computing.

Remote Presentation

In this style of client/server computing, presentation logic is placed on the client. The workstation is used primarily to put windows in front of the users and to perform basic input processing.

Examples of such processing might include checking that numeric fields are numeric and that required fields are entered. Application processing remains on the server. The model is not explicit about when the information from presentation is provided to the application logic. However, this style may be adopted to allow for the continued use of legacy systems with a new front end with extended capability. In this case, it often happens that, as a window is filled out, it is provided to the legacy application as a completed screen. In this case, such processing as numeric checks may be done redundantly in the window and the legacy application.

Distributed Logic

In the third style of client/server computing, some of the application processing logic and presentation logic is moved to the client. Some application logic remains on the server. In this style of processing, the workstation takes on a significant portion of the processing load of the application. Data accessing is found only on the server. Experience suggests that this is the most prevalent style of client/server processing.

Remote Data Management

In the next style of client/server computing, the application logic is placed entirely on the workstation. The server has only data management logic.

Distributed Database

In the final style of processing, all application logic, presentation logic, and some data accessing logic are placed on the client. In this case, the client may have local servers that provide information to the client. In addition, data used across multiple clients are placed on a common server.

Evolution to Netcentric

Using the Gartner model, netcentric computing adds a new way of interconnecting and extending these processing layers, characterized by a set of open, common standards that the Internet has legitimized. The key evolutionary differences relating to reach and content differences have greater impact on how such a model is used and what it is used for. The Gartner model is therefore of value when implementing a client/server or a netcentric solution.

Considerations Regarding the "Five Styles"

The Gartner Group model of client/server computing has had wide exposure in the industry, and many organizations have considered the implications of the model for planning and designing client/server solutions. The models have helped frame many issues and concerns. At the same time, experience suggests that organizations must keep in mind a number of things during implementation:

- Any conceptual model must be supplemented with working criteria to help select the appropriate design for implementation. First-time client/server and netcentric developers need to be aware of the difference between conceptual models and physical implementations.
- Remember that data design and allocation is as important a part of client/server design as processing allocation. Designers must begin with what data and information various business users need to do their work.
- Actual implementations are often a mix of the five styles, based on business need. Taking a hybrid approach is vital.

FRAMEWORKS AND ARCHITECTURES FOR IMPLEMENTING NETCENTRIC SOLUTIONS

By this time, an important theme of this book should be clear: netcentric computing must be talked about both in terms of its business impact and in terms of the new demands placed on client/server architectures and technologies. Chapter 2 is devoted to the business value discussion. The remainder of this chapter examines the architectural impact of netcentric solutions — the effects on the major structure and components of systems in the enterprise.

These components, based on repeated experience, are found in one form or another in most client/server implementations. Because they are repeated, there is value in abstracting the components and identifying them. "Architecture" here is an abstraction of components found across multiple applications. When the architecture appears to be usable across a wide net of applications, it is a "technical architecture."

One of the values of having frameworks and architectures is that they distill numerous experiences over a wide variety of implementations. Thus they can reduce the learning curve of the designer trying to decide what the pieces are and how they fit together. For a site just moving into client/server, or evolving to netcentric, an application framework or a technical architecture can be of real value. Otherwise, the site may simply be learning what others have already learned, thus incurring greater costs and effort.

How does one distinguish a "framework" from an "architecture"? In this book, frameworks are presented as something to aid with understanding and structuring a problem. They are not necessarily prescriptive. By contrast, architectures are aimed at delivery and are more prescriptive. They are about breaking up what is potentially a large problem, helping to understand and deliver the parts, and integrating the whole to provide something of even greater value. The architecture is how this magical feat of integration is performed and how the risk of the delivery processes are managed. In summary, frameworks help us to understand; architectures help us deliver.

The framework discussion that makes up the rest of this chapter is divided into two primary sections, (1) the Netcentric Application Framework and (2) the Netcentric Technical Architecture, which includes the execution, development, and operations architectures.

NETCENTRIC APPLICATION FRAMEWORK

Netcentric means reaching out to customers and partners with computing and knowledge over a communications backbone. This means that one will need components in a future architecture that address the communications and computing dimensions and that allow the organization to share knowledge and processes with customers and partners.

To define such an architecture, we begin with a framework to describe the applications in a netcentric environment (Exhibit 7). If we consider the types of business activities or types of business needs that need support, these can be broken down into three primary levels. The top level of the exhibit depicts organizations' needs support for their dealings with customers and business partners. The middle layer contains support for internal processes and the work of both individual knowledge workers as well as teams of workers. At the bottom of the diagram is the traditional layer of transactions, data, and knowledge.

Given these primary activities in the netcentric application environment, a conceptual framework can be mapped against them (Exhibit 8).

The following sections introduce the major components of the netcentric application framework. Subsequent chapters in the book provide more detail about what these components are and how one creates and uses them.

Knowledge Handling

Knowledge management applications capture, store, and make available the knowledge capital of a company. In doing this, applications can turn data and information into knowledge. In addition, they provide richer

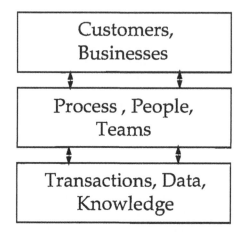

Exhibit 7. Business Activities in a Netcentric Environment.

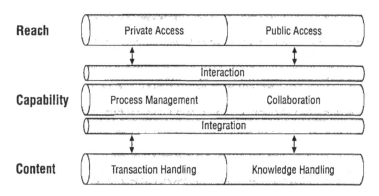

Exhibit 8. Netcentric Application Framework.

forms of information, including such media as image, voice, and video. They can provide information and knowledge in rich mixtures based on the needs and interests of the individuals working with them. To this end, the applications have indexing and accessing schemes to find knowledge, simulating the means of finding knowledge in a library. Unlike a library, however, these applications can create new forms of knowledge from underlying knowledge sources based on the specifics of the requester.

Simple examples of these capabilities include supplying customers with a custom catalog based on their needs and concerns. Another is the ability to provide to suppliers very rich data types, such as CAD/CAM-based data, so that business partners can extend, revise, or even move designs to computer-driven manufacturing machines to control manufacturing.

At Accenture, the Knowledge Xchange® knowledge management system, built on Lotus Notes, is becoming the backbone of the organization. Currently over 40,000 of Accenture's professionals have access to the Knowledge Xchange®, and they are getting information from over 3,000 databases. Very little traditional transaction data reside in those 3,000 "databases."

Knowledge management is a burgeoning area. The types of knowledge contained in these applications will broaden, and the applications will move beyond capturing, storing, and displaying knowledge. They will begin to provide more and richer ways to organize knowledge so that even a vague request is met by a high-quality response of useful knowledge. In addition, sources of knowledge will expand far beyond the boundaries of the enterprise. In an Internet-like style, users will be able to reach into the world to find the knowledge they need. In addition, the knowledge component will have the ability to detect similarities and patterns in knowledge and provide analogs and related knowledge components based on these patterns.

One example of leveraging knowledge effectively is the Department of Defense (DoD). In the United States, the DoD's logistic command has developed a system called Trans-ASK, which helps train officers. It puts at the user's fingertips the answers to over 12,000 questions; the answers come from lessons learned from Desert Storm. For a distributed team such as the U.S. Army, this has a huge benefit. Trans-ASK provides knowledge around the world, just in time, at the point of need. It makes the knowledge of the most experienced people available to those who need it.

Experience suggests that the components to manage and process transaction data, when compared to those to manage and process the extended data types of knowledge described in this chapter, are quite distinct. Obviously, they can and do have a high level of interaction that must be managed. To this end, the netcentric architecture contains distinct applications to manage transaction data.

Transaction Handling

Transaction handling and data management — data processing — is the foundation of information technology, and transaction and data management still includes the majority of today's applications. These applications — order entry and billing, to name two — primarily deal with individual transactions and clerical tasks.

During the past decade, organizations have been moving these applications beyond transaction accounting to providing operational support. Over the last several years, these applications have been moved from the mainframe to client/server architectures.

A U.S. telecommunications company provides an example of transaction and data management within the netcentric architecture. The telecommunications company supports its customer service representatives through new, sophisticated transaction and data management. The system analyzes customer call patterns and then recommends changes to the customer's call packages to save them money. The system prompts the representative, who then makes the call.

As one would expect in the age of convergence, these applications are increasingly distributed and moving closer to the customer. For example, if customers can enter sales transactions whenever and wherever they need to, this component can capture the sale as it is made. In addition, organizations may be able to capture market data about customers, such as when they are likely to place orders, and perhaps correlate marketing activities with order placement as the customers act.

The size and complexity of these applications will continue to grow rapidly. They will contain larger and larger databases of potentially valuable data. The recent interest in data warehousing and data mining to draw more useful information out of these databases will grow more critical in these systems as netcentric computing provides the opportunity to know more as it happens.

Integration

Integration applications provide a bridge between existing systems and new systems for the integration of data and knowledge. They help leverage legacy system assets as organizations move from one set of technologies and applications to the next generation. These applications also shield the application from the tools used to access and store data and knowledge, which provides a level of flexibility and future proofing, which is always desirable.

Screen scrapers and database interface architecture components are current examples of these applications. The database interface components, for example, may allow one to access legacy databases and connect together sets of physical records into a logical record that meets specific application needs.

Building interfaces between old and new systems is vital. Organizations moving to such software packages as SAP, for example, spend up to 50% of the total effort building interfaces to legacy systems. Processes and supporting tools are being developed to automate the creation of these interfaces.

A second kind of integration application involves building new systems so they are easier to integrate with future systems. One utility company, for example, is building a new customer system using object technology. Given the size of the database, it decided to use DB2. The company is, however, building an object layer or wrapper around the DB2 database. This will help enable a smooth integration with future object-oriented applications and technologies.

Finally, integration applications will increasingly support companies as they team with other enterprises. If alliances are to be successful, companies must share data and information stored in a wide variety of systems. Integration and interface support applications will help companies connect and integrate with their external partners and customers.

Process Management

Process management can be compared to transaction and data management applications. These latter forms deal with clerical functions and individual transactions. Process management applications, on the other hand, support knowledge workers and address entire processes. They provide front-to-back management of critical processes such as customer service or product development.

Many of the initial process management applications in this area have involved imaging, document management, and workflow management technologies. These applications can significantly improve business process performance. They improve quality, reduce elapsed time, and lower costs. The applications found in process management are those that are based on well-defined processes; although flexible, they nonetheless follow a set of well-defined and predictable steps. For example, entering an order or checking on inventory stock or setting up an insurance claim are examples of applications found in process management.

For example, a large U.S. insurance company has been working on its customer service processes. The goal was to automate 95% of the new business and renewal processes. For these customers, new applications and renewals are not seen or worked on by employees. For the remaining 5%, a workflow automation system routes the case files to underwriters for personal attention.

In the netcentric environment, these applications are extended out to customers and partners, taking advantage of the automation that such extensions offer. For example, the business partner would be able to check on-hand stock and the volume of usage and, on this basis, automatically restock on-hand inventory. Customers in their homes will be able to complete the insurance policy application and get a quote and an indication of acceptance of the risk.

The first important trend here is not only to manage the process but to perform it as well. The ultimate goal is for the application to do everything except what requires human intelligence or physical transport.

Second, these applications make it easier to adjust processes as business conditions or strategies change. For these applications, document management and workflow technologies continue to be important. Object technology holds promise relative to tailorable business processes.

Collaboration

Whereas process management applications support the execution of well-defined processes, collaboration applications support less-defined processes that involve teamwork. These applications arise when the steps and sequence of doing the work are unclear. They also arise when the process is complex and requires the interaction of people to see that a job is done well.

The following cases are contrasting examples. The application for a simple loan to cover the costs of a new piece of furniture could well be completed by a bank customer from home using a well-defined process found in process management. Conversely, settling on a home loan with complex interest arrangement and the use of stocks for collateral could well require human interaction and would be managed out of the collaboration component.

Collaboration applications are increasingly adding computing value to what has initially been primarily a communications solution. One Japanese consumer goods manufacturer, for example, is working on improving innovation and time to market. By setting up a global research and development (R&D) team linked with teamware, it has flattened its R&D organization and accelerated new product development. These applications help organizations respond quickly and cohesively to changing market conditions.

Collaboration support is critical in the netcentric environment, but it is a challenge as well. It is critical because collaboration is a way to ensure that the "human touch" is still present for the customer or partner, when needed. Also, it is central to avoiding automating things that are just too complex to automate. For example, a consumer trying to set up a home loan will need help to understand all the financial and legal implications of such a transaction.

Collaboration support is also a challenge because many people with an IT background believe that anything less than the 100% solution is not enough. IT experts tend to view the unstructured nature of collaborative systems as a failure. Another challenge is that some of the key technologies to deliver collaborative applications are not widely available and tend to be incompatible. Further, they make demands on the telecommunications component that it cannot always handle.

Interaction

Interaction applications improve the performance of knowledge workers, teams, partners, and customers. In the past, these applications have supported the unique needs of employees, especially system users. They help workers learn and use systems that have become increasingly complex. They also help workers get up to speed more quickly and enable them to achieve higher levels of performance.

Performance support features are often mandatory in the applications that organizations make available to their customers and partners. These applications need to reach out and pull in customers who are highly intolerant users and are unwilling to learn an organization's systems. For the customer, application usage revolves around performance support. Customers must find it easy to buy and to develop relationships with companies.

Several trends are important here. First, organizations are increasingly emphasizing learning, not just training. Performance support applications are becoming more self-directed, allowing knowledge workers to find what they need instead of what managers think they need. This is clearly key in the netcentric environment, where a system user such as the customer really has little interest in being "trained" on the organization's systems.

Most interaction applications today are standalone systems. The trend will be to build integrated applications with embedded performance support. These applications will sense, based on customer or partner activities and prior interactions, when the person needs help in doing the work. Letting customers, partners, and employees learn just in time, at the point of need, and providing them with advice and direction enable significant improvements in performance and acceptance of systems by those engaging them.

Public Access

Public access applications address the needs of public users — specifically, consumers — and narrow the gap between the company, its products, and the consumer. Effective applications give customers what they want, when they want it. They will let the customer participate directly in such processes as order entry and product design. For example, Andersen Windows has a kiosk system called "Window of Knowledge." Using the kiosk, customers can enter a drawing of their floor plan and try out standard window options. However, they can go beyond that and design their own custom windows. The system tells them what can be built and what cannot. When they have made a final decision, the system automatically generates parts lists, prices, and places the order.

One important trend in public access is integration with home devices. Moving these applications into the home is having a tremendous impact on business, education, and entertainment. Another trend is mobility — making an organization available wherever and whenever a customer wants it to be. Smart cards are one way mobility is achieved today. Wireless communications and PDAs will be the way this is done in the near future. Mobility will extend the reach and power of the enterprise, which eliminates barriers and becomes closer and more direct with its customers.

Private Access

Applications dealing with private access are also called business-to-business applications. With these applications, the enterprise establishes and maintains its links with other organizations, such as suppliers, distributors, alliance partners, and the government. The first stage of these applications has primarily been a communications link for transaction exchange. Electronic Data Interchange (EDI) is one well-known example.

The direction in this application area is to take full advantage of the convergence of computing, communications, and knowledge. These applications provide more direct links with business partners and allow them to coordinate more effectively their response to changes in customer demand.

Eventually, private access applications will enable almost total supply chain integration. The window design application noted earlier is already part way there. Parts lists are generated for contractors, and orders are placed. For some products, information is sent right to the shop floor, where windows are built to specification. In that case, the glass suppliers are also connected into the process.

Applications that manage and perform business-to-business processes enable the ultimate virtualization of business, bringing together strategy, people, process, and technology in a unique configuration across multiple companies to serve the customer in a more powerful way than any one company could on its own. The final convergence will be one in which barriers between companies and their customers have been removed.

Netcentric Application Framework Summary

At an overview level, these are the components of the netcentric application framework. As the saying goes, however, the whole is greater than the sum of the parts. The whole, in this case, is an organization that is not constrained by time, by place, or by physical form. Its information technology is indispensable, integral, and invisible.

The netcentric application framework shows how technology will be applied to enable exceptional business results. With these applications, enterprises can deliver astounding solutions.

A TECHNICAL ARCHITECTURE FOR NETCENTRIC SOLUTIONS

A key value of having a technical architecture is that it provides a standard, consistent approach. With mainframe computing, architectures were often identified too late. Done correctly and consistently, client/server and netcentric implementations provide the opportunity to get things right the first time because they are environments many organizations have not worked in before. Having a technical architecture provides many benefits to this consistency, including

- A common background for information systems personnel
- More rapid delivery of solutions
- Reduced impact of change

An architecture, then, is a set of processing components that represents a common approach. Typically, these components are presented in a graphical format. The format attempts to portray the major components and their interaction.

Experience suggests that such architectures have three primary manifestations:

- An *execution* architecture, which describes the components required when an application executes
- A *development* architecture, which describes the components required to create the execution architecture
- An *operations* architecture, which describes the components required to operate and manage the system

EXECUTION ARCHITECTURE

The critical architecture to understand is the execution architecture. Exhibit 9 illustrates the execution architecture that will be referenced throughout this volume: the Netcentric Architecture Framework (NCAF). It is an evolution and extension of the client/server framework that has been used widely by Accenture in a variety of industries and applications over the past several years.

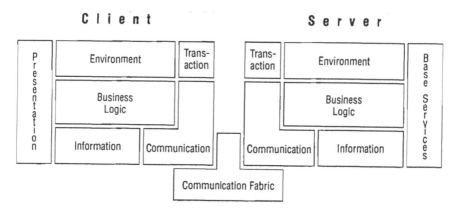

Exhibit 9. Netcentric Execution Architecture.

A brief word about the graphical depiction itself may be worthwhile. Discussions of architectures frequently seem to hit a snag when graphical notations or depictions of the architecture do not make sense. First, each of the shapes in the graphical depiction of the netcentric execution architecture represents a processing component. These are divided into client-side and server-side components. The name within the shape provides a notion of what the component is about. The components are recursive in the sense that one component can and will be broken out into other, lower-level components.

The way the components are drawn suggests the degree of interface that exists between components. For example, the business logic component is in close proximity to the information access component. Thus, users can expect the frequent execution of interfaces or application programming interfaces (APIs) between these components. Also, information access services are in close proximity to communications services. This close proximity suggests how information access services request data from a remote server. However, the business logic client component has to interface with other components on the server over the network.

Despite all this, the components are not strictly limited to the interactions implied in the exhibit. For example, the presentation component may have some reason to interact directly with communications components. This is not prohibited by the architecture; it is simply less common. The size of the boxes is unimportant and does not carry any special meaning. The boxes are sized based partly on aesthetics and partly on the words that need to fit inside them.

Finally, it is worthwhile to note in the diagram the focus on the separation of components. The intent of an architecture is to separate distinct functions. Doing so benefits the development process by separating development concerns. It also makes it feasible to organize and deliver components as they are needed by teams focused on specific, well-defined pieces of the whole problem.

The following discussion provides a high-level look at each of the components of the execution architecture. More detail on each of them is found in Section II of this book.

Client-Side Components

The following discussion presents a first level of detail about what is found in the components on the client side. If the component is repeated in the server side, the description found at this level of detail also stands for the server side. When components differ, the section "Server-Side Components" describes the differences.

Presentation Services. Presentation services enable an application to manage the human–computer interface, including capturing user actions and generating resulting events, presenting data to the user, and assisting in the management of the dialog flow of processing. Typically, presentation services are required only by client workstations.

Information Services. Information Services manage information assets and enable applications to access and manipulate data stored locally or remotely from documents, databases, or external data sources. They minimize an application's dependence on physical storage and location within the network. Information services may also be used directly by the end user when ad hoc data and document access are integral to the application work task.

Communication Services. Communication services enable an application to interact transparently with other applications regardless of whether they reside on the same computer or on a remote computer. Communication services include core messaging, specialized messaging, communications security, virtual resource services, and directory services.

Communications Fabric Services. As communications networks become increasingly complicated and interconnected, the services provided by the network itself have by necessity increased as well. Clients and servers are rarely directly connected to one another but are commonly separated by a network of routers, servers, and firewalls, providing an ever-increasing number of network services such as address resolution, message routing, and security screening. The Communications Fabric extends the client/server computing model by placing intelligence into the physical network, acknowledging the network as a sort of standalone system that provides intelligent shared network services.

Environment Services. Environment Services provide miscellaneous application and system level services that do not deal directly with managing the user interface, communicating to other programs, or accessing data. They include runtime services, system services, and application services.

Transaction Services. Transaction Services provide the transaction integrity mechanism for the application. This allows all data activities within a single business event to be grouped as a single, logical unit of work.

Business Logic. Business Logic is the core of any application, providing the expression of business rules and procedures (e.g., the steps and rules that govern how a sales order is fulfilled). As such, the Business Logic includes the control structure that specifies the flow for processing business events and user requests.

Server-Side Components

The server components of the technical architecture are on the whole similar to the client components. One difference is a new component, Base Services, which exists only on the server side. Also, a presentation services component cannot be found on the server because the server does not interact directly with the user.

Base Services. Base Services provide support for delivering applications to a wide variety of users over the Internet, intranet, and extranet. Base Services include Web Server Services, Push/Pull Services, Batch Services, Report Services, and Workflow Services.

DEVELOPMENT ARCHITECTURE

In the client/server and netcentric environments, it is vital to get the development environment right the first time. Changing the development environment when construction is fully staffed may entail serious disruptions and expensive loss of productivity. The purpose of the development architecture is to support the tasks involved in the analysis, design, construction, and maintenance of business systems as well as the associated management processes. A comprehensive framework for understanding the requirements of the development environment is shown in Exhibit 10. It is discussed in detail in Section II.

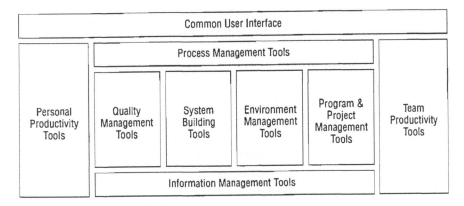

Exhibit 10. Development Architecture.

OPERATIONS ARCHITECTURE

The operations architecture, the third part of the technical architecture, is a combination of tools, support services, procedures, and controls required to keep a production system up and running well. It differs from an execution architecture in that its primary users are systems administrators and production support personnel. Exhibit 11 shows the framework used throughout this book to illustrate the operations architecture, shown in the exhibit as supporting the work of both the execution and development architectures. The operations architecture is also discussed in detail in Section II.

CONCLUSION

A critical success factor for the implementation of client/server and netcentric solutions is that the various architectures be established and agreed-upon prior to starting work on the first application. This architecture should be employed by all systems developers as a framework for their design efforts. Further, they should be expected to prove why they cannot work within the confines of the architecture. This process is one of the few ways that one can contain the potential for chaos in going to a new technology.

This chapter began by noting that organizations often spend too much time on formal definitions and not enough time building their first applications. The purpose of this chapter has been to map out a range of systems development in which there is real benefit and also real difficulty in building successful systems. As the book proceeds, it builds a case for why an organization wants to do this and then provides a good deal of material on how to build this next generation of systems solutions.

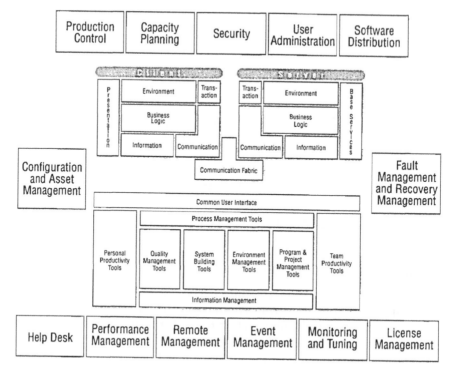

Exhibit 11. Operations Architecture.

Chapter 2
Netcentric Computing and New Business Capabilities

One of our firm's research scientists enjoys illustrating today's amazing business and technological environment by telling his "water softener" story. After moving to a new condominium in the Chicago suburbs, he and his wife found that a very nice man from a water softener company kept showing up every couple of months to replace the salt supply in the softener. One day, they kidded the man that it was almost like he knew exactly when the softener needed refilling. In fact, the man did know. There was a chip in the softener that monitored the salt level. The condominium telephone system was rigged so that when the level of the softener fell below a certain level, a call went to the company letting them know it was time to deliver salt.

It's a great story of what we call "convergence"; it's not a computing story and it's not a communications story. It's both, and more.

The dominant forms of information technology — computing and communications — developed for years independent from one another. Today, however, these technologies are converging, producing new capabilities that are far greater than a mere sum of the parts. Today's information systems based on a client/server model, for example, cannot even really be called computing solutions because the computer is in fact the entire communications network. The phenomenal ascent of the Internet as a market force is another expression of convergence. We will see most business solutions in the future built upon a converged sense of computing and communications.

The complete "convergence model," shown in Exhibit 1, contains a third component: *knowledge*. Without that component, there is no point to the computing and communications — nothing for them to do. Knowledge is the "blood" running through the veins of today's business. It includes both raw content as well as the logical schemata for interpreting that content,

Exhibit 1. The Convergence of Computing, Communications, and Knowledge.

that is, it can include traditional data as well as rules and procedures that capture people's expertise. It can include simple digitized raw video as well as complex representations that combine multiple points of view and extensive cross-indexing. It can include kinds of captured objective reality such as photographs and transactional data as well as subjective interpretations such as opinions and problem-solving heuristics. It can be static and waiting to be used, like a photograph or a movie, or it can be dynamic, like an expert or an intelligent agent.

Finally, the convergence model shows the ultimate point of it all: the ability to focus on the customer in new ways and the ability to partner and form alliances in new ways. The convergence model is also the most basic model of netcentric computing.

Netcentric computing is making new kinds of capabilities possible — for individuals and for businesses. For companies around the world, netcentric computing means new business solutions, new ways of organizing companies, and new ways to serve customers. As client/server technologies broke down organizational barriers and put knowledge into the hands of knowledge workers, so the new netcentric era — an era of ubiquitous computing and communications — is putting knowledge into everyone's hands. That is the promise of netcentric. However, there is a threat as well.

THE MYTH OF THE SUSTAINABLE ADVANTAGE

The age of netcentric computing promises to restructure entire industries. That restructuring is simply an affirmation of what has been happening already in the information age. Exhibits 2 through 5 demonstrate the impact of new business and technology solutions on major businesses over the past 17 years.

Airlines

1980

Rank	Company	Revenues (Millions)
1	United Airlines	$4,373
2	American Airlines	$3,675
3	Pan Am	$3,639
4	Eastern	$3,453
5	Delta	$3,302
6	TWA	$3,278
7	Northwest	$1,628
8	Braniff	$1,444
9	Western	$996
10	Continental	$988

1997

Rank	Company	Revenues (Millions)
1	United Airlines	$16,316
2	American Airlines	$15,136
3	Delta	$13,317
4	Northwest	$ 9,751
5	US Airways	$ 7,704
6	Continental	$ 5,487
7	TWA	$ 3,554
8	Southwest	$ 3,407
9	America West	$ 1,751
10	Alaska	$ 1,306

Exhibit 2. Airline Industry Rankings.

Banking

1980

Rank	Company	Assets (Millions)
1	Citicorp	$109,551
2	Bank America Corp.	$106,803
3	Credit Agricole Mutuel	$106,646
4	Banque Nationale de Paris	$105,584
5	Credit Lyonnais	$98,833
6	Societe Generale	$90,794
7	Barclays Group	$88,474
8	Deutsche Bank	$88,242
9	National Westminster Bank Ltd.	$82,447
10	Da-Ichi Kangyo Bank Ltd.	$79,451

1997

Rank	Company	Assets (Millions)
1	Bank of Tokyo-Mitsubishi	$690,461
2	Deutsche Bank	$579,992
3	Sumitomo Bank Ltd.	$482,707
4	Credit Suisse	$472,767
5	Hsbc Holdings	$471,256
6	Barclays Bank	$451,948
7	Dai-Ichi Kangyo Bank Ltd.	$432,189
8	Sanwa Bank	$427,077
9	Credit Agricole	$417,973
10	Fuji Bank	$413,296

Exhibt 3. Banking Industry Rankings.

These lists are striking because they reveal the absolute lack of permanence in industry leadership. In 1980, Dai-Ichi Kangyo Bank, Ltd. brought up the end of the Top 10, with a full 25% fewer assets than Citicorp, the clear leader. Over course of the next years, Dai-Ichi moved up to a number 2 ranking in 1994, settling back to number 7 by 1997. By contrast, Citicorp is not even ranked in the top 10. In discount retailing, Wal-Mart, which decided to compete on both price and service, came from the back of the pack to take the lead. Southwest is succeeding in the airline industry with a business model that was all "wrong," at least in theory. In a time of spokes and hubs and an industry built on elegance, Southwest followed the obsolete route model and bargain-basement prices and performed beyond all expectations.

Discount Retailing

1980

Rank	Company	Revenues (Millions)
1	Kmart	$11,208
2	Woolco Department Stores	$1,710
3	Gamco Department Stores	$1,266
4	Zayre Corp.	$1,223
5	Gibson's Discount Stores	$1,125
6	The Fed-Mart Corp.	$975
7	Wal-Mart Stores Inc.	$961
8	Target Stores Inc.	$899
9	Two Guys	$702
10	Korvettes, Inc.	$638

1997

Rank	Company	Revenues (Millions)
1	Wal-Mart Stores Inc.	$58,000
2	Kmart	$27,559
3	Target Stores Inc.	$20,368
4	Dollar General	$ 2,627
5	ShopKo	$ 2,577
6	Caldor	$ 2,497
7	Ames	$ 2,325
8	Family Dollar	$ 1,995
9	Hills	$ 1,768
10	Bradlees	$ 1,392

Exhibit 4. Discount Retailing Rankings.

Computers, Office Equipment

1980

Rank	Company	IT Sales (Millions)
1	IBM	$26,213
2	Honeywell	$4,925
3	Sperry Corp.	$4,785
4	NCR	$3,322
5	Burroughs	$2,857
6	Rank Xerox	$2,840
7	Control Data	$2,766
8	Olivetti	$2,551
9	Digital Equipment Corp.	$2,368

1997

Rank	Company	IT Sales (Millions)
1	IBM	$78,508
2	Hewlett-Packard	$42,895
3	Fujitsu Limited	$40,613
4	Compaq	$24,584
5	Canon	$22,812
6	Xerox	$18,166
7	Digital	$13,046
8	Dell	$12,327
9	Ricoh	$11,432

Exhibit 5. Computer Industry Rankings.

A great deal of ink has been spilled trying to determine why these companies succeeded or failed. Deregulation had a huge impact in airlines. Technology and market segmentation made a difference for retailing. Banking was hit by consolidation related to deregulation and investments. The computing industry was tremendously affected by new technologies, especially the Internet. Even though several factors can be identified, it is extremely difficult to learn many replicable lessons from either the successes or the failures because there are so many ways to fail and so many ways to flourish. The ultimate lesson from these lists is that over time, there is no sustainable competitive advantage.

Whatever advantage a company gains today is fleeting. Either competitors adopt the advantage or they find a better alternative. Certainly they do not give up. For example, every airline today is focused on reducing costs following the Southwest Airlines model. Retailers are following the Wal-Mart model, reducing money in the supply chain by shifting inventory and delivery to suppliers.

If competitors cannot improve on the company's basic process, they will invent a new process, a better way of doing things. The story of the microprocessor vs. the mainframe is one example. The winning companies did not try to make a better or cheaper mainframe; they decided to do something completely different. They came up with a processor that behaved and worked in ways a mainframe could not, at prices the mainframe could not meet. That difference totally restructured the computer industry over the last 15 years.

Finally, if no one can come up with a better or different answer and one company becomes dominant in an industry, a regulator may step in. Today, discussions about the computing and communications industries often include what role the government should play in ensuring open and free competition. In a sense, however, government regulation is another way of saying, "No winners," or at least, "No massacres." Today's headlines about Microsoft are evidence that companies that do find competitive advantage may find themselves face to face with regulators whose actions may render that advantage unsustainable in the future.

The inability to sustain competitive advantage can be seen in the story of Tom Peters's well-known book, *In Search of Excellence*. This book profiled a number of companies that had emerged as clear leaders in their industries. It implied that, by following certain principles of excellence, one could not fail. A relatively short time after the book was published, most of the companies profiled were out of business or in serious difficulty. Peters himself began his next book with the admission that "there are no excellent companies." There is no such thing, Peters wrote later in *Thriving on Chaos,* as a "solid, or even substantial, lead over one's competitors. Excellent firms do not believe in excellence — only in constant improvement and constant change. That is, excellent firms of tomorrow will cherish impermanence — and thrive on chaos." [Tom Peters, *Thriving on Chaos: Handbook for a Management Revolution* (New York: Alfred A. Knopf, 1987), 3–4.]

Can the challenge of unsustainable competitive advantage be addressed? Perhaps it can. For example, an insurance company gains a clear edge in the marketplace by creating a customer focus that provides very high levels of service, reduces costs, and increases sales. As with information processing over the last 30 years, the next step is to drain the costs of doing the business. Often, information technology is the means to achieve those cost reductions, but cost reduction is not just an IT strategy.

Over the past few years, numerous companies have announced extensive layoffs, even in the face of sound financial results. Although occasionally the reductions have been tied to reengineering initiatives, often the goal was simple cost reduction to stay competitive.

Many methods can achieve cost reduction. IT is one, but another, surprisingly, is the creation of bureaucracy. The word "bureaucracy" has negative connotations today; however, before it became a bad word, it meant simply a system for making routine decisions. Bureaucracy ensured that the least expensive person gave just the right amount of attention to the problem at hand before moving on. In this sense, it was a way to standardize a process to make it predictable and well controlled. Therefore, the principles of bureaucracy can be applied to the problem of reducing costs.

This process of concentrating first on what people know how to do says much about human beings. It is entirely natural for people to prefer working with what they know rather than wanting to start all over. Therefore, people focus on reducing costs within the processes they know how to perform. They can quantify the impact of change so that risk is reduced.

Then, there comes a point at which cost reduction is not very impressive anymore. When all the heads have rolled, there are no more costs to reduce. By illustration, 50% of 50% of 50% of anything is not much.

Next, the systems put in place to reduce costs — IT and bureaucracy — become a barrier to leaping to the next competitive advantage. They become the legacy that prohibits change. The systems cannot be changed to provide a view of the customer. The bureaucracy has measures and rewards that focus on an efficient current process, and the new process means new measures and rewards. The cost reduction process becomes a hindrance to the development of the "next astounding solution."

The Role of the Next Astounding Solution

Of course, the most obvious reason the next astounding solution is so difficult to achieve is that it never walks in and introduces itself as an astounding solution. Sometimes, the solution may appear at first to be insignificant or even suspect, or it may just be something at the right place at the right time. An often-cited example is the Sabre airline system, which was devised just to facilitate the reservations process; only later did people realize that it was changing the rules of competition. Another example is the study done by IBM that concluded that the PC would never amount to much. As IBM and countless other organizations have proved, one of the functions of a bureaucracy is to stamp out anything threatening to the bureaucracy. *Fumbling the Future,* the story of Xerox's failure to capitalize on its development of the first personal computer, asks the key question, "Why do corporations find it so difficult to replicate earlier successes in new and unrelated fields?"[Douglas K. Smith and Robert C. Alexander, *Fumbling the Future* (New York: William Morrow and Company, Inc., 1988), 19.]

The answer to this question is both obvious and difficult to accept. Companies must

- Find and deliver an astounding solution.
- Manage the costs out of the solution until the company finds the next astounding solution.
- Obliterate all the bureaucracy, process, and procedure that the company has built to deliver the old astounding solution.

This unending cycle is called the "competition cycle." The cycle sounds exhausting, and it certainly is, but the only other alternative is to be among those three fourths of your friends who are no longer around.

Have any companies succeeded at the competition cycle? With the obvious caveat that one can only speak about the present moment, the growth of Microsoft is one example. Microsoft has grown from a compiler company to an operating system company to a company providing entertainment and information content in the Internet age. If one looks at the change in the core technology, all of these transitions were huge, but the company seemed to achieve them with relatively little trauma. Conventional wisdom said that Microsoft waited too long and missed the World Wide Web phenomenon. However, as current ventures such as MS/NBC and CarPoint indicate, Microsoft continues to have the ability to reinvent itself.

Another example of finding new sources of competitive advantage is Dell. Dell's original operating model was to sell through channels and to target corporate customers. Today they are leaders in the direct sales of computers to consumers. Such a drastic shift in focus could not be achieved unless a company were nimble, both in terms of its strategy and its technology infrastructure that enables such rapid change.

Could one begin to forecast where the source of the next astounding solutions might lie? The next section examines this question from two standpoints. One is to think of where the solutions have focused in the past. Wherever they are, the assumption is that they ceased to be astounding long ago and have become the target of cost reduction. Looking past these solutions may reveal the opportunity for the next astounding solution. The other is to look at technology today and ask what solutions the technology can enable. What comes out of this discussion is a remarkable situation in which the next business opportunity is aligned exactly with what the technology can do.

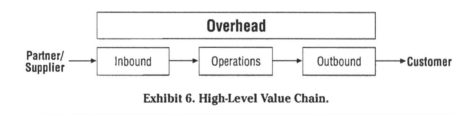

Exhibit 6. High-Level Value Chain.

TRADITIONAL COMPETITIVENESS: INTERNAL OPERATIONS

Exhibit 6 represents, at a very high level, the value chain for a typical enterprise.

The typical enterprise must manage its inbound flows of resources and its relationships with partners and suppliers. The enterprise must provide internal operations that deliver the services and products its brings to market and then manage the outbound flow of these services to customers. In addition to all this are the typical overhead activities, such as human resources or accounting, which must be done to survive in the market. At this very high level, the diagram applies across a wide range of industries and businesses.

Over the last 30 years, most companies have devoted most of their attention to internal operations and overhead activities. For example, in insurance, many companies have set up and revised claims systems as the technology progressed from IBM 360 architecture to on-line to database architectures. Many companies have gone back and addressed their internal processes as they participated in total quality management (TQM) and business process reengineering initiatives. However, in spite of these changes, many claims systems today still primarily reflect internal processes for management and actuarial evaluation, that is, the company is thinking in new ways, but its technology still reflects old thinking. This is a problem, given the fact that, in the insurance industry, the customer's view of the company is primarily defined by experience with the claims process, not with the policy sales process. The technology continues, in this case, to impede the progress of a company in getting closer to its customers.

In manufacturing, the focus over the years has been on material requirements planning (MRP), shop floor control, inventory management, cost accounting, and quality control. Even with order entry, which is dependent on customer contact, much of the focus is on reserving inventory and feeding MRP efforts for smooth shop floor operations. These, again, reflect a focus on internal operations and overhead activities, not on the customer.

In banking, the focus over the years has been on "back-office" operations, including check clearing, account updating and reporting, loan processing, and statement issues. Over time, these processes and supporting automation have become increasingly efficient. For example, check clearing at a large bank is something to behold from both an automation and process standpoint. Once again, in each of these cases the work has focused on internal operations and overhead activities, with the result that the processes have become very efficient.

The point here, again, is that, over the last 30 years, much of the work with design and automation of business processes has focused on the internal operations and the overhead activities. Furthermore, in our experience, much of this work has been done and redone as industries moved from batch processing in the 1960s to on-line processing in the 1970s to database architectures in the 1980s. Many of the processes are being reinvented because of client/server capabilities. This is not to say, however, that the work has been fruitless. Many of these systems were redone with clear and evident bottom-line impact and were well worth the investment. With all the iterations, however, companies may be increasingly dealing with big percentages of small percentages — 50% of 50% of 50%. It is now time to look elsewhere.

The New Competitiveness: Innovative Distribution Channels

Exhibit 6 may also suggest an area to focus on: the inbound and outbound channels. There is opportunity outside the enterprise at the boundaries between business partners and customers. This opportunity depends on obliterating the traditional inbound logistics channels and the outbound distribution channels, by implementing new kinds of channels — electronic or otherwise — that are in themselves astounding solutions. In this obliteration there is an opportunity and a challenge to rethink the entire structure of industries. The next astounding solutions lie at the boundaries of the traditional enterprise.

ATMs as an Electronic Distribution Channel

Identifying the next astounding solution may seem both obvious and highly questionable. As noted earlier, astounding solutions can be characterized in their early days by being almost invisible. One example of change in a distribution channel is banking with an ATM machine. Originally, the view was that this was a means to displace bank clerks and reduce head count and costs. The impact has been far wider. ATMs have indeed reduced clerk head count, but, more importantly, they have convinced many customers that they do not need to interact directly with a banker to do business. At the same time, ATM use has allowed bankers to realize that a bank branch does not need to be a large capital investment of brick and mortar; it may only need a wire and a programmable vault. From this realization has come the growth of on-line, home-banking tools. In the end, it is clear that banking can and will become a virtual enterprise. The greatest impediments to this evolution are regulatory concerns rooted in brick-and-mortar banking institutions and current banking laws based on geographic boundaries. For anyone who has begun to bank through such a tool as Quicken™ or Money™, the relevance of either concern is increasingly questionable.

Data Warehousing

Another example of reaching out to customers is the increasing use of data warehousing approaches to segment and understand customer interest and behaviors. Although data warehousing is not an example of expanding direct interaction with the customer, it does reflect a step in the direction to understand the customer better by understanding what the customer is doing. Also, as the capability grows, it allows the organization to understand more clearly the impact that its actions are having on the customer. Some commentators have viewed this as trying to manipulate the customer. However, more often the sellers change their behaviors based on the actions that the customer takes. In this sense, convergence through the channels is making the seller change and adapt to meet customer needs more effectively, based on the feedback they obtain.

Antiquated Distribution Channels

Financial services and retailing are industries where obliterating distribution channels has already made a big difference. Other industries are following, among them, insurance. The traditional distribution channel for insurance is the local agent. Today that distribution channel is in need of renewal. Agents represent challenges in terms of cost, training, and turnover. High turnover rates disrupt the connection to the customer or even sever the connection when the customer follows the agent to another company. Because agents tend to sell what they know, they often represent a hindrance when bringing new products to market.

In addition, the insurance industry is currently redefining its very identity. An insurance company today no longer considers itself simply the provider of coverage of loss against unexpected risk. Today they are providing financial security. The products devised to provide this service are complex and difficult to sell. Many agents will not take on the demands to sell these products. This means that the typical distribution channel for insurance can, on occasion, contribute to customer distance rather than customer closeness. At the same time, because consumers appear willing to move to in-home banking, it is feasible to expect them to be able and willing to undertake some of their own product evaluation if they have the right tools and capabilities. As a result, many insurance companies are looking at alternative distribution channels to make the connection to the customer.

The Risks of Changing Distribution Channels

The insurance example illustrates why altering distribution channels can be difficult. Many people argue that the distribution channel is the single most difficult thing to change in an organization. There are a number of examples that illustrate the challenges in either adding to or changing from existing channels.

To illustrate, imagine a fictional example of General Motors deciding to sell something really different: spaghetti. It could readily purchase the means of production for spaghetti and begin pumping GM spaghetti into its sales channel, but there it would encounter problems. It would find a distribution channel of hundreds of thousands of sales people who would simply say, "I sell cars, not spaghetti." Over time, GM could create alternative channels, but that is not changing the channel; rather, it is creating a parallel channel. If GM grew insistent on the change, it would probably find its sales people leaving to go to companies where they could sell cars again.

Losing the Existing Channels Too Soon

In insurance, a fairly common conclusion is that there is no way to go past the current agent network to the customer without risking having all the agents stop selling. This is clearly the case for companies that deal with independent agents, who sell from a variety of sources and can simply avoid a source that is threatening to become a competitor in the customer's home. Captive or tied agents are also a problem, as they typically have a fairly high turnover. These agents can easily anticipate that, before too long, their annual sales will begin to decline as a customer goes directly to the company. The result is that companies with captive agents will suffer increased agent turnover and difficulty in attracting new agents simply because the agents' future may be limited, at least in their current roles.

Companies have attempted to deal with this problem in a number of ways. One is to encourage the agents to move to more complex products, where they can continue to add value. These products continue to need the agent's assistance in selling and provide potentially higher margins. However, the difficulty is that agents often are reluctant to learn and sell such products. Another approach to the problem is to continue to have the agents participate in the revenue stream from the customer, even if they are not directly involved with the sale. The issue in this case is that a significant portion of the cost of distribution remains in the sales channel.

Risking Competitiveness by Not Building Alternative Channels

The result of these concerns is that many insurance companies have looked at this astounding solution and said, "Not astounding enough." By doing so, however, they place themselves at risk. The competition cycle demonstrates that, if the legacy insurance companies do not address the issue, other companies that do not have an established distribution channel and a bureaucracy will do so very quickly. Without the baggage of an existing distribution channel, a new company can quickly seize significant market share. For example, Microsoft seized the encyclopedia market, eventually bankrupting the old and venerable Encyclopedia Britannica, because it could more easily go directly to the consumer with CD-ROM versions of Encarta™. Banking is also beginning to move into the markets traditionally held by the insurance industry. The combination of home banking and ATMs could mean that banking could pursue this route very quickly.

This example goes beyond the insurance industry and seems to be a characteristic of any industry with a traditional sales channel. One manufacturer, for example, wanted to sell over the Internet. It encouraged its sales people to inform customers that they could buy products over the Internet and that they would be able to do so at reduced costs resulting from the elimination of sales peoples' take. Not surprisingly, not many salespeople did much to encourage this new distribution channel. The Web site is now a product catalog site while the company rethinks its approach.

Distribution Channels and Customer Appeal

A second challenge to changing the sales channel, or adding a new one, is getting customers to use it. Companies frequently make the mistake of assuming that its customers will use the new sales channel simply because it is so much easier for the company. The fact is that there must be some benefit to the consumer to use the new channel, such as faster delivery, more customized products, or less expensive products. "Cheaper and easier for the company" is not a customer benefit.

The challenge in this case is to deliver on the promise. How can the customer's willingness to work with the sales program result in quicker delivery? Can it cut the time to get the order back? Can it cut the time to assure the customer that the stock is available? Can the process by which customers work through the order make the product better suited to their needs? This can be a complex problem simply because one may need to package the knowledge of the talented sales person in a set of programs — an example of knowledge management — and then make the programs attractive to use. The distribution channel can account for as much as 60% of the cost of a product. [Robert Benjamin and Rolf Wigand, "Electronic Markets and Virtual Value Chains on the Information Superhighway," *Sloan Management Review* (Winter 1995), 62–72.] Is a company willing to share some of the savings with a customer?

Can the sales effort be made a transparent part of the business process? In insurance, companies could tie the entry of purchases into the insurance process. For example, in a package such as Quicken™, an account is named "Automobiles," and new entries are monitored in the account. When a large new entry is made in the account, a pop-up window asks, "There seems to have been a large change in the Auto account. Should you look at your current auto insurance to see if it needs changing?" Obviously, such an approach is not foolproof, but, done correctly and improved over time, it could be much better than hoping the customer remembers to call or expecting the agent to drive by the house looking for new cars in the driveway.

Facilitating Change in Distribution Channels

Converging on the customer through new sales channels is not for the faint of heart. Most companies that undertake the challenge either are desperate and have no other option or are outsiders who have no legacy of culture, regulation, or systems to hinder the change. In a few other cases, the enterprise has a visionary leadership that simply wills the change to happen and drives the process forward.

To address the sales side of the business, one needs some special mix of characteristics to succeed. At the same time, the cycle of identifying an astounding solution, draining the costs from the processes, and moving to the next astounding solution suggests that, if one organization does not take on the change demands, another will. At some point, a company can be certain that it will be desperate enough to make such a change. One of the key themes of this book is how to make these changes easier to accomplish.

NEW COMPETITIVENESS: INNOVATIVE PARTNER CHANNELS

Similar issues may be seen with the business partner channel, which supplies raw materials or services so that the enterprise can operate. One well-known example of innovation on this side of the business equation is Wal-Mart. Some years ago, Wal-Mart recognized the significant costs tied up in inventory on the inbound side to stores. Further, this inventory tended to be an impediment to responding to changes in buyer patterns. If there was a shift in popularity from GI-Jeff to Bean Bag Babies and one had a huge inventory of GI-Jeffs, costs were involved in selling the inventory at discount, and time was involved in getting the Bean Bag Babies through the distribution channel. To address this problem, Wal-Mart began working with its suppliers. It moved the inventory back to the suppliers. Further, it worked with the suppliers on predicting demand so that stores needing restocking got the products when they needed them. These types of actions significantly reduced costs for the product on the shelf. For an industry in which margins are often near zero, the effect was to bring Wal-Mart to the top of the retailing lists.

In essence, a change in partner channels can mean a great many things based on industry, product, and life cycle. In the auto industry, it has meant moving much of design and assembly to suppliers. Similarly, in the aircraft industry, it has meant moving design of major components to partners on a worldwide basis. In property and causality insurance, it has meant contracting with repair offices, agreeing to use bids as submitted, and directing customers to preferred providers.

In each case, these were difficult transitions. Internal groups watched "their work" go outside to other companies, some of which had been or continued to be competitors. In each case, the new ties provided benefits in terms of better time to market, less ongoing cost, or access to local markets. In addition, as the first technology connections were made, it soon became apparent that more synergy can be found by extending the reach and insight of the network. As this continues to happen, the virtual enterprise will begin to emerge. Such an enterprise is very much a network on which the events of the business are communicated and shared among the components. In this case, the network becomes the enterprise. That, in itself, is an astounding solution.

TECHNOLOGY'S NEW ROLE: HELPING PUT INTELLIGENCE AT ORGANIZATIONAL BOUNDARIES

To bring about successful change at the boundaries of the traditional enterprise, where it meets its customers and partners, an organization needs to put intelligence at the boundary. Part of this intelligence must be delivered by human beings, simply because human intelligence is necessary to handle nonroutine and variable processes. The intelligence, however, cannot all be provided by humans. Any one organization has too many partners and customers; the company cannot possibly have a staff member available to all partners and customers whenever they need help. To meet this need, part of the intelligence must be computer based, responding to and interacting with the partner or customer in a highly responsive and intelligent manner, providing access to needed information, and at the same time communicating what is happening within the enterprise.

The primary client and server split, which is still inherent in netcentric solutions, gives us another view of how intelligence is managed. The client side corresponds to the need to put intelligence and/or access to information where the partner or customer is doing the work and then to manage the communications side of the work. The server side provides a place to summarize and share the contents of events that are happening with many partners and customers. This mixture of computing and communications allows management of the process at a macro level. The company can know where the business is, based in part on what is happening at the partner and customer sites as it happens. The communications core is essential to make all this happen. Finally, the material that needs to be shared is the knowledge of what is happening in the business.

The ability to put access to information where the events are happening is key to making the vision of netcentric computing a reality. Readily accessible information allows people to sense and respond to things around them. For example, as a large airplane component moves through the assembly process, the bar coding of individual assemblies gives one an atomic view of the process. When these various atomic views are assembled, they provide a holistic view of when the aircraft component will be available. This view is provided, however, only if it can be communicated to everyone concerned in the process. The netcentric system provides the intelligence to decide who needs to know what and to communicate on that basis.

As events occur in these types of systems, such as a sale or an addition to inventory that a supplier needs, the data, information, and knowledge of what is happening must be shared with the right people. An example of this knowledge transfer is the on-line catalog that is made available to customers as they enter their own sales. Another example is the posting of a change to a design component that a supplier must have in order to build the component.

From a business point of view, as noted earlier, many companies are reaching maximum efficiency in overhead and internal operations, which leads them to netcentric technologies and the opportunities at the boundaries of the enterprise — in the inbound and outbound channels. From the technological point of view, netcentric computing presents new business opportunities with customers and suppliers. In short, the business opportunities today are being enabled in part by the technology opportunities. From this point of view, convergence or netcentric is the natural, inevitable solution. The competition cycle now needs the next astounding solution, and someone will take advantage of the technology that wants to make the business solution happen.

The business/technology scene today is more crowded than ever. The public is reading about the Internet every day. Major newspapers and popular news magazines now have regular columns and sections on IT. Consumers and employees take for granted today computing capabilities that were expensive options only a few years, such as video, voice, and image. IT vendors are increasingly aggressive and creative in their solutions.

These are not independent events, nor are they simply technology events. Rather, they are reflections that the business enterprise must converge on its customers and suppliers, not because of some plan or conscious effort, but because most businesses have drained much of the opportunity from the current processes and now must find new ones. The new opportunities will be found in new connections to the customer and partner.

THE CHALLENGES OF NETCENTRIC SOLUTIONS

Netcentric computing presents two key challenges discussed earlier. One is the problem of how to transition to new distribution channels while not destroying the current ones, which would cut off the business. There are several possible methods to avoid a crippling dip in business volumes during this transition. One is to provide incentives to the current sales channel so that the new channel is seen as a source of revenue rather than a source of competition. For example, a company could pay sales people for all sales in their region, whether they make the sale or whether it is made through the direct efforts of the customer. Another method is to track customers that have moved to alternate channels and provide compensation to sales personnel based on the moved customers and on expected sales going forward. There are certainly other methods, but all must begin with the recognition that the natural concerns of the old channel during such a transition must be addressed.

The second challenge is to make a business case, as it were, for the customer to participate in the newly defined channel. Once again, organizations must realize the obvious fact that customers will not use the channel simply to help the company out. Customers must see tangible benefits in terms of better products or sales, quicker delivery, cheaper products, or the potential to participate in broader markets.

Similarly, new partner channels must be instituted only after serious forethought about incentives for partners to participate. Here again, they will not participate just to "be nice" to the company; customers must see something in their own self-interest. Perhaps working with the company will ensure a shorter cycle to delivery. Possibly the value can be found in assurances that cooperation will decrease the tendency to have competitors bid on price. In any case, there must be a value to the vendor that makes the proposition attractive.

The word "coopetition" has been coined to describe this approach to business. Although the concern in working with partners may not be as great as when working with the sales channel, the fact is that forming tighter partnerships is often a difficult transition, particularly for internal groups. The idea of giving up on the annual bid and evaluation processes and accepting a vendor for a period of years may just seem wrong to some people. Internal groups may see a possible loss of independence in partnerships. Having partners take over work that has been done internally is always a concern because internal people may be displaced, giving jobs to always a concern because internal people may be displaced, giving jobs to competitors. Developing trust is also a major issue, and rightfully so. Competitors yesterday may be partners today, and then competitors again tomorrow. Partners have access to information that could be of great value if they then become competitors. Each of these issues must be confronted and addressed.

SUCCESSES

Netcentric success stories are growing every day. As the two cases described in this section demonstrate, netcentric computing offers new business value whether a company looks outside, to its customers and other businesses, or inside, to its employees.

NBTel

NBTel, the telecommunications provider for the eastern Canadian province of New Brunswick, has a policy of serving customers 24 hours a day, 7 days a week. NBTel will hook up a new phone line at 4 A.M. Tuesday morning, for example, if a customer so desires. In fact, around 40% of NBTel's customers contact the company during nontraditional work hours.

This tradition of "anytime" customer service led NBTel to launch NBTel Express™ in 1993, which enabled customers to interact with the company on an automated, self-service basis. Customers could use a touch-tone or screen phone to add or remove custom-calling features, inquire about account balances, and pay utility bills. Continuing to expand and upgrade the self-service options for customers, NBTel asked Accenture to help it move NBTel Express to a richer multimedia environment accessible through various interactive channels, including the Internet. The result was "The Interactive Phone Store™."

With the creation of the Interactive Phone Store, customers are able to use their PCs to learn about new products and services, add or remove custom calling features, and inquire about account balances. NBTel customers can connect to customer service representatives if they need further explanation. They can add or change reward programs and review toll call particulars. Customers are also able to pay bills using preauthorized checking accounts or credit cards.

Access is now available to customers over NBTel's broadband network, which provides services at speeds up to 150 times faster than a 28.8 modem. NBTel added Internet access in August 1997, thereby making the new service available to thousands of its customers already on-line. Access by interactive television is also planned. The robust architecture has the ability to evolve as new channels and functionality become available.

The Interactive Phone Store has proven to be a vital NBTel business strategy; they have some impressive statistics on the business benefits they have achieved. The compelling tangible benefits are the reductions in transactional costs in customer service, the creation of incremental revenues, and protecting market share and revenue. NBTel estimates that its transactional costs, which were over $11 in 1992, will be around $2.30 in the year 2000.

There are also broader benefits to this new capability. NBTel has extended its brand image, enhanced customer service, and preempted the competition. NBTel's advanced electronic infrastructure has helped to bring employees to the province. Job growth is important for the economic development of the region because this, in turn, generates incremental revenues for NBTel.

Motorola

One thinks of netcentric computing, first, as an enabler of interchanges among businesses or between a business and its customers. However, it can also be applied to a company's internal customers — a perspective that helped Motorola develop an innovative human resources solution.

Motorola, located in Chicago, Illinois, is one of the world's leading providers of wireless communications, semiconductors, and advanced electronic systems, components, and services. The company maintains sales, service, and manufacturing facilities throughout the world, conducts business on six continents, and employs more than 139,000 people worldwide.

For companies such as Motorola, people are a continuing source of competitive advantage. The new emphasis today on the workforce as "capital" means that increased attention is being paid to the human resources (HR) function, which is charged with ensuring that this capital grows in value. To compete effectively, HR departments need to become strategic business partners, relationship managers, builders of competencies within the organization, and stewards of the company's human capital.

Historically, HR personnel at Motorola spent the majority of their time following up on personnel administration change requests, researching employee salary histories for managers, and answering frequently asked questions about benefits plans. Motorola recognized the need to reduce the time HR personnel spent processing paperwork to free those resources to address higher value-added work, such as consulting and business advocacy. Consistent with its history of combining the best of technology and people, Motorola established Global HR Systems, a group dedicated to implementing the HR systems required to support organizational goals. The group concentrated on issues such as maintaining data integrity, reducing cycle time, and improving process quality.

Motorola took the view that an "internal electronic commerce" strategy — where information is the currency being exchanged — was the solution of choice because it would allow them to meet the functional objectives of today while providing the flexibility to adapt to the unforeseen requirements of tomorrow and beyond. In addition, the solution presented an effective interface to their existing SAP HR backend system as well as an architectural framework that would support future intranet- and Internet-based solutions.

Together with Accenture, Motorola designed the Employee Self-Service Network, or Enet, an application that would be accessible through Motorola's intranet and through stand-alone corporate kiosks. Whereas previous interaction with HR personnel was restricted by working hours and availability, this system would allow access to information and services at any time of any day and by people at all levels in the organization.

With Enet, HR stakeholders — employees, managers, HR personnel, and Service Center representatives — use a simple, interactive, graphical interface to initiate, approve, and track the progress of personnel administration change requests such as merit increases, leaves of absence, and department or job changes. Based on the user's login data, the system tailors the available features to match the user's role. For example, employees can view and edit their own personal profiles, and managers have access to initiate personnel administration changes for the employees they supervise. Once a change request is launched, managers and HR representatives are notified via e-mail of items that are awaiting their approval and progress of the request can be checked at any time. Once a change request has been reviewed and approved by HR, records are then updated in the SAP HR system.

A model for HR service delivery was created around the Enet application that effectively reduces the demand on the HR representative, enabling faster customer service and addressing most concerns through the least costly channels. In the new technology filter model, it was estimated that the greater majority of inquiries and transactions could be addressed through the self-service of Enet, while remaining questions and requests would be referred to a Call Center. Only those issues requiring further attention, such as hands-on planning and policy resolution, would be handled by HR representatives who are available to serve as employee advocates in meeting their needs.

Motorola recognized that deploying a self-service application could have a dramatic impact on the way employees think about HR processes and the HR department. To help manage this change, the project team created a pilot application of Enet and distributed it to approximately 100 managers, HR representatives, and Service Center representatives for

100 managers, HR representatives, and Service Center representatives for technical and functional feedback. The team then incorporated the suggestions and developed a phased rollout approach that begins with the training and enabling over 25,000 U.S.-based users. Next, Motorola plans to implement Enet on a global scale, following closely on the heels of a global SAP HR rollout.

SUMMARY

In today's environment, businesses must begin to cope with the absence of a sustainable competitive advantage. In place of competitive advantage is the competition cycle: a business delivers an astounding solution, manages the costs out of the solution, and then moves to the next astounding solution.

Many opportunities for the next astounding solution reside at the boundaries of the enterprise where it meets its customers and partners — more specifically, in eliminating some of these boundaries through direct ties to the customer and to partners.

With this shift, the focus of IT attention, which has been moving from the IT department to the business user, is now starting to move to the ultimate customer — at the boundary of the enterprise. This can dramatically change the nature of the implementation challenge.

Converging on one's customers and partners opens up many opportunities but also presents many challenges and issues. This convergence is breaking down old boundaries, creating new visions of the enterprise and what it means to do business. The notion of the virtual enterprise becomes real, in this context. Customer loyalty, fiercely guarded, is challenged as customers can now "vote with their fingertips."

Although the virtual enterprise will mean many things, it will increasingly mean that the distinctions between customer, enterprise, and suppliers will become less clear, and the relationships between them will change and evolve.

Clearly, huge challenges and opportunities are part of this environment, but careful thought, planning, and determination are the ingredients to meet the challenges and maximize the opportunities. One cannot meet today's business challenges without IT, but the technology must be part of a larger scheme of vision, leadership, and expertise.

Section II
Architectures and Frameworks for Netcentric Computing

Chapter 3
Architecture Frameworks for Client/Server and Netcentric Computing

THE NEED FOR ARCHITECTURES: INSURANCE AGAINST RISK

At the heart of systems development, the use of architectures provides *insurance*: insurance against the complexities of development and maintenance, against the obsolescence of technologies, against the possibility that all the parts of a solution may not work together. Architectures are the master plans that ensure that the solution will work.

This notion implies that risk is involved, and that is so. In client/server and netcentric environments, a number of risks are generally present.

More Complex Development and Maintenance

A number of factors contribute to the complexity of client/server and netcentric solutions:

- Client/server applications incorporate sophisticated graphical user interfaces (GUIs). GUIs are usually event driven rather than hierarchical. They are interactive and require more complex logic than traditional terminal (e.g., 3270) style interfaces.
- Client/server and netcentric applications have to "cooperate" with other applications. Communication code must establish communication connections, ensure that messages are sent and received correctly, manage errors, and handle any required data translation. Care must be taken that programmers and designers have these skill sets.
- The skills required for development, installation, and support of netcentric systems may be difficult to find.

More Difficult Operations Support

Operations support for netcentric solutions is more difficult than for traditional systems. The increased complexity of operations support, including hardware and software configuration management, is directly related to the number and location of distributed nodes. If a system has 100 remote nodes, it is more difficult to ensure that they are at the same software and hardware versions than it is with two local nodes.

In addition, data backup/restore must now occur at multiple locations, and support for hardware, software, and communications problems must also be provided locally at multiple sites.

More Complex Data Security

When data are distributed, protecting that data becomes more difficult. Intelligent workstations are inherently less secure than minicomputers and mainframes. The effort required to maintain an equivalent level of data security, therefore, increases.

New Distributed Data Update and Refresh Strategies

Most client/server systems incorporate multiple copies of the same data. This requires logic to ensure that data values in each of those copies are consistent. For example, if a user working off server A wants to change a "balance due" field, how and when will this change be reflected on servers B and C?

Increased Susceptibility to Viruses and Malicious Users

Again, this risk is directly proportional to the number of nodes in a distributed system. Each workstation is a potential point of entry for a virus or a malicious hacker.

Higher Communications Loads

Netcentric applications must communicate with each other and with other applications, typically legacy systems. This is accomplished over communications networks. For a networked system to work well, accurate estimates of the amount of network traffic must be determined. This is often difficult because, as the knowledge and popularity of newly released applications increase, application use (and network traffic) increases. Applications designed with communication speeds in mind may, therefore, end up being "communications bound." In addition, there are not many tools available that model new-age computing communication loads.

Missed Opportunities

Because netcentric systems are comprised of hardware and software that are continually being improved, it is often difficult to stop waiting for enhancements. Many development teams become paralyzed, waiting for the next release of some component that promises to facilitate the installation process or enhance the final product.

Lack of a Standard Operating Environment

There are many popular operating system and window manager options that can be used to develop workstation applications. The risk is in choosing a combination that ends up with little or no support in the long run and requires future migrations of applications and data.

Increased Complexity of User ID and Password Strategies

Because netcentric solutions require the use of multiple computers, user ID and password strategies become more complex. For example, a security system on one computer may require password changes more frequently than another, or maximum and minimum password lengths may conflict on different systems. Even if these issues are not present, the maintenance of security information on multiple platforms is difficult.

THE BENEFITS OF ARCHITECTURES

The risks just discussed illustrate the need for architectures as crucial aspects of client/server and netcentric systems development. What is an architecture?

An architecture is a proven mechanism and an approach that can be used to isolate and mitigate the risks of delivering applications now and into the future.

According to the Gartner Group, an architecture is "a formal specification of how a computer solution will be organized." Gartner sets forth seven characteristics of a successful architecture:

1. Delimitation of the problem to be addressed.
2. Decomposition of the solution to components with clearly assigned responsibilities.
3. Definition of interfaces, formats, and protocols to be used between the components. These should be sufficiently clear and robust to permit asynchronous development and ongoing reimplementation of the components.
4. Adequate documentation to permit compliance by implementers.
5. An auditing mechanism that exercises the specified interfaces to verify that specified inputs to components yield specified results.
6. An extendibility mechanism to enable response to changing requirements and technologies.
7. Policies, practices, and organizational structures that facilitate adoption of the architecture.

In the netcentric environment, an architecture is used to define how a system is structured and how the various components of the system interact. In a netcentric computing environment, there are more components and many more interactions that make an architecture even more important.

Organizations that have carefully implemented, delivered, and utilized these architectures have realized some of the following benefits:

1. *Better productivity, and less "reinvention of the wheel."* Architectures can abstract common requirements and approaches from applications and can eliminate having to identify, analyze, and implement them for each application. This improves developer productivity and the quality of the final product.

2. *Consistent, reliable, high-quality applications.* The framework provided by an architecture encourages applications to be built in a consistent fashion or structure, to deliver consistent behavior, and to work with a consistent interface (both to users and other applications), resulting in a system easier to build, use, and maintain.

3. *Rapid delivery of business solutions.* By providing a consistent external interface, an architecture simplifies integration of applications and facilitates rapid delivery of new solutions. This is achieved through the use of standard architecture components, adherence to standards, and the availability of the necessary tools, techniques, and training.

4. *Reduced impact of changes to underlying products and tools.* Because an architecture incorporates "layers of isolation," new products and tools can be more easily integrated into a system. Changes in one element of the architecture are less likely to affect other architecture elements.

5. *Better integration of business applications within and between organization business units.* By providing consistency of architecture components within and across an organization, the opportunity to build applications that have a higher degree of integration is greater. This should facilitate the exchange of critical information across the company.

6. *Isolation of users and applications developers from the complexities of the underlying technologies.* By having a standard architecture that includes a standard set of tools with a consistent interface, users and developers are not required to know the details of the platform technologies (i.e., the operating system, database, and network). Additional technology components could be added in the future with minimal additional training for the users.

7. *A consistent, standard development framework.* An architecture provides a framework for analyzing the requirements of a system or application. It can help business applications developers by providing

a structure from which to work. In a netcentric environment, the requirements of a GUI, distributed data, and distributed processing contribute to the complexity of the solution. Moreover, these requirements have many interdependencies. Without an architecture to help structure the problem, it is easy for applications developers to become overwhelmed by technical issues and spend insufficient time on the business problems they are there to solve.

8. *A common background for IS personnel.* In addition to providing a common approach for building systems, an architecture provides a common means of describing systems and a common language. As a result, IS personnel are more easily interchanged and cross-trained, providing more flexibility in the management of the organization.

This chapter will move from a high-level description of an overall architecture — what is called an Enterprise Information Architecture — to a summary of the primary technical architectures discussed in this book: the execution, development, and operations architectures for client/server and netcentric computing solutions. More detail on each of these architectures — their services and subservices — is provided in subsequent chapters of Section II.

THE ENTERPRISE INFORMATION ARCHITECTURE (EIA)

What are the components of an effective architecture? The Enterprise Information Architecture (EIA) framework provides a starting point for understanding what is meant by the various architectures under consideration. The EIA framework contains seven layers (Exhibit 1).

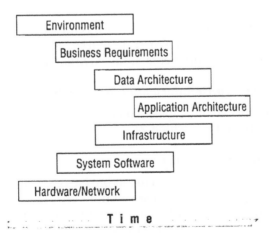

Exhibit 1. Enterprise Information Architecture (EIA).

- The *environment* layer includes those factors that influence the business requirements and technical layers. These factors may be either internal (e.g., profitability) or external (e.g., government regulation and market competition).
- The *business requirements* layer addresses the business needs of the organization. Both the environment layer and the business requirements layer are mainly concerned with business-level processes, strategies, and directions. The layers below are mainly concerned with the information technology to support the business. The business requirements give key input and guidelines on how to define the lower layers. The link from business requirements to the information technology layers is crucial to a successful EIA.
- The *data architecture* layer consists of a high-level data design that describes the structure of an enterprise's data needs in terms of entities and relationships between entities. The structure and relationships of data entities can be used to define the basic relationships of business functions and applications.
- The *applications architecture* layer defines the applications that must exist to support the business functions and their relationships. It also addresses any issues about distributed data processing.
- The *infrastructure* layer deals with those components of an architecture that can be used by multiple applications and that are developed and maintained within the enterprise. Usually, these common technical components help support the applications architecture. This layer also includes the infrastructure of the organization that manages the architecture definition and design and its technical components.
- The *systems software* layer encompasses the software and standards obtained from and maintained by outside vendors (e.g., a database management system.)
- The *hardware/network* layer deals with central processing units, local area network (LAN), wide area networks, and other hardware and physical network components of the environment.

Redefining the Enterprise Information Architecture

For purposes of this volume, these components can be grouped into four categories of architecture (Exhibit 2).

Business Solutions Architecture

Because this chapter does not focus on business specifics, the top three levels can be grouped into a business solutions architecture. It is important to remember, however, that, when it comes time to decide what technical architecture to use, many of the answers are found by looking at the business solutions architecture. The decisions made for the application and data architectures drive the requirements of the technical architecture and

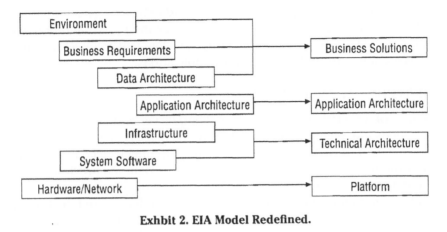

Exhbit 2. EIA Model Redefined.

platform. At the same time, the constraints of the technical architecture and platform can also shape the application architecture and the business solutions that are possible.

Applications Architecture

The applications architecture layer can be defined here as those services that perform business functions on the computer. It represents the components that provide the automation support for a business function or activity in the business process (but does not include the platform and cross-application architecture). For example, a manufacturer's sales and marketing system application architecture could include sales tracking applications and the distributed data architecture to support both networked sales offices and mobile sales people.

Technical Architecture

The Infrastructure and System Software layers are combined to form the technical architecture. The technical architecture is where the buy decisions of the system software marketplace are combined with the build decisions for the needs of specific applications. We treat these as one architecture by incorporating these two concepts. The technical architecture is comprised of the execution, development, and operations architectures, which are discussed subsequently.

Platform Architecture

The final layer in the EIA model is the platform architecture layer. It is often described as "the things you can see." The netcentric platform architecture provides a framework for selecting the platform components required: the servers, workstations, operating systems, and networks. This framework represents the overall technology platform for the implementation and deployment of the execution architecture, development architecture, operations architecture, and, of course, the applications.

THE TECHNICAL ARCHITECTURE

Because of its relative importance in client/server and netcentric implementations, the technical architecture will be discussed in some detail in the remainder of this chapter. The technical architecture consists of the infrastructure and systems software layers, as discussed previously. The differentiation between them is primarily a question of make vs. buy, that is, a key decision for organizations intent on "building an architecture" is how much they want to build vs. how much they can simply buy from preexisting sources. An organization can choose to build a great deal, thereby making the architecture very close to what it wants. That means that there is a great deal of logic being built by the shop.

Alternatively, the organization can choose to buy most of what it wants. To the extent that business or application demands make it necessary for the tools to be integrated, developers can then do simple assembly, or gluing together, of the pieces. The decision for most organizations depends on balancing demands. On the one hand, the organization has a large front-end commitment to build and an ongoing commitment to maintain an infrastructure architecture; on the other hand, the organization has a tool that is exactly what it wants.

Over the years there has been a tendency to buy rather than make. This is especially the case as the market matures with more technical entrants. It is practical for IS organizations to build technical architecture components only when essential. By purchasing rather than building, they can then more easily apply their strong skills in the applications architecture business.

Components of the Technical Architecture

The technical architecture layer can in turn be broken into three primary components, execution, development, and operations (Exhibit 3).

- An *execution* architecture describes the components required when an application executes.
- A *development* architecture describes the components required to create the execution architecture.
- An *operations* architecture describes the components required to operate and manage the system.

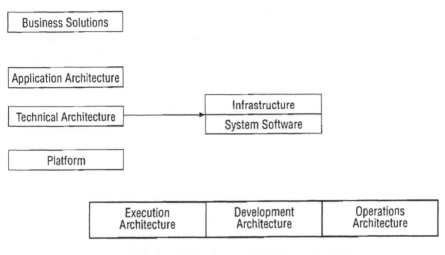

Exhibt 3. Three Components of a Technical Architecture.

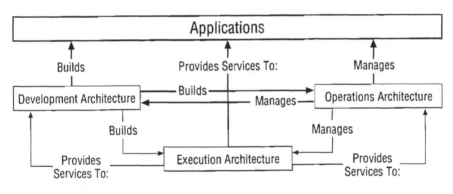

Exhibit 4. Relationships Among the Technical Architectures.

These architectures must be flexible enough to accommodate a wide range of technologies, but they must also be structured enough to provide valuable guidelines and to ensure that interoperability is available where it is required. Exhibit 4 illustrates the relationships among the execution, development, and operations architectures.

The remainder of this chapter will provide an overview of these technical architectures. Because of its relative importance in the design and delivery of netcentric solutions, the execution architecture will be discussed last, and in a great deal more detail.

DEVELOPMENT ARCHITECTURE

The development environment is the production environment for one or several systems development projects as well as for the maintenance efforts. Thus, it requires the same attention as a similarly sized end-user execution environment.

The purpose of the development architecture is to support the tasks involved in the analysis, design, construction, and maintenance of business systems as well as the associated management processes. It is important to note that the environment should adequately support *all* the development tasks, not just the code/compile/test/debug cycle. Given this, a comprehensive framework for understanding the requirements of the development environment should be used.

Another reason for the comprehensive framework is that it is important to get the development environment right the first time. Changing the development environment when construction is fully staffed may entail serious disruptions and expensive loss of productivity.

Experience has shown that, within the same medium- to large-size project, with the same people, moving from a poor to a good development environment, productivity can be improved by a factor of ten for many tasks. The improvements come in two categories:

- The elimination of redundant and non-value-added tasks
- The streamlining of useful tasks

While it seems intuitive that most tasks can be streamlined, the following list gives a few examples of redundant tasks that must be eliminated:

- Analysis to determine how to merge the uncoordinated changes applied by two programmers to the same module.
- Reentry of the source code for and retesting of a module, which was accidentally deleted.
- Recurring discussions about "what a design packet should contain" or "what constitutes good programming style in a particular context."
- Repeated design, coding, testing, and maintenance of very similar logic (e.g., error handling, date conversion and manipulation, main structure of a module).
- Searching for the manuals of a particular productivity tool to find information.
- Remigration to system test of a cycle because the impact analysis for a change request was incomplete.
- Requesting support from another team (e.g., environment support, information management) and waiting unnecessarily for a response.

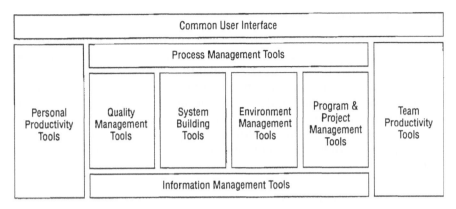

Exhibit 5. Development Architecture.

On a smaller project, these problems can be solved using a brute force approach. This becomes very expensive as the project grows, and finally, impossible. A well-designed development environment becomes important as the project team reaches 20 to 30 people and is absolutely critical with a project size of more than 50 people.

The investment needed to design, set up, and tune a comprehensive, good development and maintenance environment is typically several hundred man days. Numbers between 400 and 800 days are commonly seen, depending on the platforms, target environment complexity, amount of reuse, and size of the system being developed/maintained. This investment warrants the following considerations:

- *This effort is large enough to justify work that will make it more efficient.* Among the factors that affect the effort, reuse is the most apparent. These guidelines, together with the parallel project to instantiate the model, constitute a step toward greater reuse.
- *The effort is large enough to require a cost/benefit analysis.*

Exhibit 5 is the model used throughout this book to describe the development architecture. The components of the development architecture include the following.

Common User Interface Tools

Common user interface tools provide a common launching place for all the tools in the development environment to make it appear more integrated and consistent. This is the simplest level of integration, in that all the tools are presented to the developer via a single view of the entire environment. Tools that support the common user interface are known as window managers (e.g., Microsoft Windows, Presentation Manager, and Motif).

Process Management Tools

Process management tools integrate the development environment by providing tool-to-tool communication and workflow management. Tool-to-tool communication integrates tools by enabling information in the form of short messages to be passed from one tool to another. Workflow management integration builds the development methodology and process into the tool environment. Workflow management enforces the correct sequencing of tasks and tools. Process integration is often implemented through the use of integration frameworks or through custom coding of interfaces.

Personal Productivity Tools

Personal productivity tools are a collection of software applications that enhance the development environment for the individual developer. These applications are typically integrated suites of PC software that allow the developer to work on the workstation independent of the development server or mainframe to complete tasks such as analysis and documentation. These tools are basic office automation software and include spreadsheet software, word processing software, graphics software (e.g., drawing, diagramming, and presentation), and personal calendar software.

Quality Management Tools

Quality management is a management discipline that promotes a customer satisfaction focus and continuous improvement. Quality management tools support the planning and measurement of quality. These tools include quality function deployment tools, measurement and metrics tools, statistical process control tools, and continuous improvement tools.

System Building Tools

System Building tools comprise the core of the development architecture and are used to design, build, and test the system. All the system building tools must be integrated and share development objects appropriately. These include

- Analysis and Design tools
- Reverse Engineering tools
- Construction tools
- Testing tools
- Configuration management tools

Environment Management Tools

A netcentric development environment is complex and sophisticated. It supports many different functional and technical requirements (illustrated by the Execution Architecture), many different development teams, and tools from many different product vendors and often must support projects in different stages of the development life cycle. These tools monitor performance, provide help desk support, manage and distribute changes to the development environment, administer the environment, and track and plan development environment capacity.

Environment Management tools include

- Service Management tools
- Systems Management tools
- Managing Change tools
- Service Planning tools

Program and Project Management Tools

Program and project management are usually differentiated by the size of the effort; programs are typically composed of more than one project. Similarly, the program and project management tools are differentiated by the ability to support multiple projects, complex functions, and adequate performance when supporting multiple concurrent projects.

Program and project management tools provide many key features that assist project planners in planning, scheduling, tracking, and reporting on project segments, tasks, and milestones.

These tools include

- Planning tools
- Scheduling tools
- Tracking tools
- Reporting tools

Team Productivity Tools

Team productivity tools are used to make the work cell and project team as a whole more productive. Instead of the software residing on the individual's PC or workstation, these tools typically are LAN based and shared by the project members. These tools are focused on enhancing communication and information sharing.

These tools include

- E-mails
- Teamware
- Publishing tools
- Group calendars
- Methodology browsing tools

Information Management

Information management of the development architecture is provided through an integrated development repository. At this level of integration, tools share a common repository of development objects, design documents, source code, and test plans and data. Ideally, the repository would be a single database with an all-encompassing information model. Practically, the repository must be built by integrating the repositories of the different development tools through interfaces. Tool vendors may also build part of the integrated repository by integrating specific products.

The repository includes

- Folder management
- Repository management

OPERATIONS ARCHITECTURE

An operations architecture is a combination of tools, support services, procedures, and controls required to keep a production system up and running well. It differs from an execution architecture in that its primary users are systems administrators and production support personnel. Exhibit 6 shows the framework used throughout this book to illustrate the operations architecture. It depicts a set of tools supporting the execution and development architectures.

The major tool categories of the operations architecture include the following.

Software Distribution

Software distribution is the automated delivery to, and installation of, applications and systems software on servers and end user devices (e.g., workstations, kiosks, etc.). This can be for an organization's internal computing environment as well as for its extended one, i.e., its business partners and customers. The architectural support required to support software distribution is largely driven by the numbers of workstations, servers, and geographic locations to be served.

Configuration and Asset Management

To manage a netcentric environment successfully, one must have a solid understanding of *what* is *where*, and one must maintain rigor in the change control procedures that govern modifications to the environment. Configuration and asset management information that may need to be tracked includes such details as product licensing information, warranty information, vendor names, logical and physical device information (such as total capacity and current utilization), product configuration tracking, software

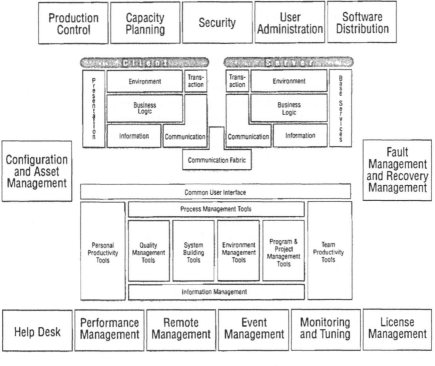

Exhibit 6. Operations Architecture Framework.

and data version levels, network configuration parameters, physical location, and perhaps accounting information.

Fault Management and Recovery Management

The fault management services of an operations architecture assist in the diagnosis and correction of system faults. Faults may include network-, server-, workstation-, or even application-level faults. Fault diagnosis may require services for isolation; viewing of host, server, and workstation error logs; and determining the software and data versions and configurations of affected machines.

Capacity Planning

Capacity planning tools focus on components of an environment such as the network, physical space, and processing power to understand the need to change the capacity of those components based on organizational changes. The tools typically focus on components that are considered to be heavily sensitive to changes in computing resource usage. The tools may use historical management data combined with estimates for growth or changes to configuration to simulate the ability of different system configurations to meet capacity needs.

Performance Management

Performance management is more difficult because of the lack of tools to assist with performance in heterogeneous environments. Performance is no longer confined to the network or to the central processing unit. Performance needs to be viewed in an end-to-end manner, accounting for all the factors that affect the system's performance relative to a user request.

License Management

In addition to guaranteeing compliance with software licensing agreements, license management provides valuable information about which people and how many people are actually using a given software product.

Remote Management

Remote Management tools allow support personnel to "control" a user's desktop over a network so that they do not need to be physically present at a workstation to diagnose problems. Once control of the desktop is established, screen updates for the controlled desktop are displayed at both locations. The support person is then effectively sitting at the workstation he/she controls and can do necessary diagnostics.

Event Management

In addition to hardware devices, applications and systems software also generates events. Common event-handling mechanisms are required to provide information to management in a simple, consistent format and to forward information on important events for management purposes.

Monitoring and Tuning

The number of devices and the geographic disparity of devices in a netcentric environment increase the effort required to monitor the system. The number of events generated in the system rises due to the increased complexity. Devices such as client machines, network components, and servers generate events on startup or failure to periodically report device status.

Security

The security concerns of netcentric environments have been widely publicized. Although requirements for netcentric security architectures are constantly evolving as new security breaches are discovered, there are many tools categories that can help provide reasonable levels of security.

User Administration

The netcentric environment introduces many new challenges to the task of user administration. The majority of these stem once again from the dramatically increased number of system components. Adding a user to the system may require adding a user to the network, one or more server operating systems, one or more database systems (so that the user can access data), an e-mail system, and an existing host-based system.

Production Control

Scheduling processes across a distributed environment can be quite complex, requiring significant management effort to ensure that the processes run smoothly. Many other day-to-day activities become more difficult in a distributed environment, including print management, file transfer and control, mass storage management, backup and restore, archiving, and system startup and shutdown.

Help Desk

As netcentric computing puts the operations Help Desk closer to the "end user" in terms of visibility and influence, the Help Desk will need to become integrated with the business processes being supported through netcentric. Unless the operations Help Desk is well integrated with the business process, there is risk that the user may be given information that is incorrect, forwarded to the wrong department, or otherwise mishandled. It is also important that the information collected by the Help Desk about a user be properly shared with other stakeholders in the business process.

EXECUTION ARCHITECTURE

The netcentric Execution Architecture Framework identifies those common, run-time services required when an application executes in a netcentric environment. The services can be broken down into logical areas: Presentation Services, Information Services, Communication Services, Communication Fabric Services, Transaction Services, Environment Services, Base Services, and Business Logic (Exhibit 7).

As shown in the figure, the netcentric execution architecture is best represented as an extension to a client/server execution architecture. The figure shows the logical representation of a requester and a provider, designated by the "Client" and the "Server." Although the figure shows only one "Client" and one "Server," a physical implementation of an execution architecture typically has many clients and many servers. Thus, the services described here can be located on one physical machine, but most likely will span many physical machines, as shown in Exhibit 8.

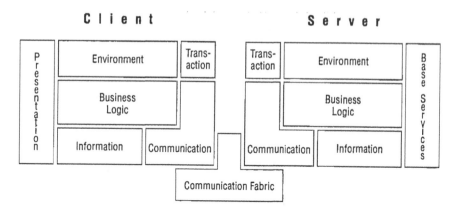

Exhibit 7. Netcentric Execution Architecture.

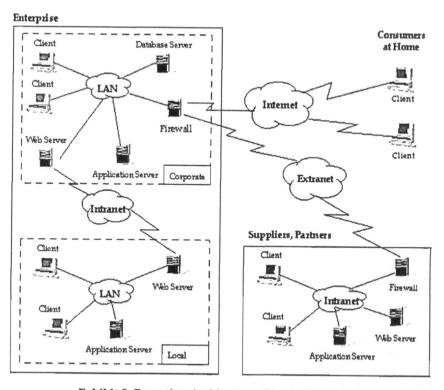

Exhibit 8. Execution Architecture: Physical Picture.

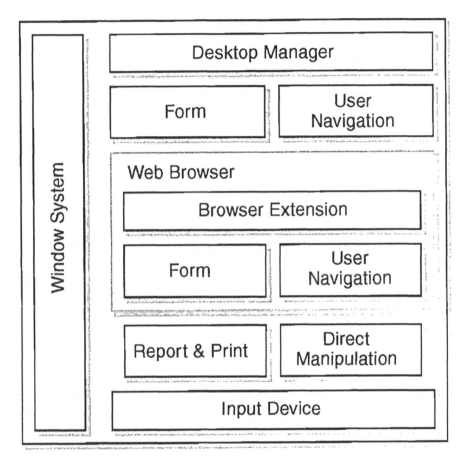

Exhibit 9. Presentation Services.

This section provides an overview of the services and subservices within the execution architecture. More detailed information is provided in the chapters devoted to each of these services in Section II.

PRESENTATION SERVICES

Presentation services (Exhibit 9) enable an application to manage the human–computer interface, including capturing user actions and generating resulting events, presenting data to the user, and assisting in the management of the dialog flow of processing. Typically, presentation services are required only by client workstations.

The major Presentation Services are

- Desktop Manager Services
- Direct Manipulation Services
- Form Services
- Input Devices Services
- Report and Print Services
- User Navigation Services
- Web Browser Services
- Window System Services

Desktop Manager Services

Desktop Manager Services provide for implementing the "desktop metaphor," a style of user interface that tries to emulate the idea of a physical desktop. It allows the user to place documents on the desktop, launch applications by clicking on a graphical icon, or discard files by dragging them onto a picture of a wastebasket. Desktop Manager Services include facilities for launching applications and desktop utilities and managing their integration.

Direct Manipulation Services

Direct Manipulation Services enable applications to provide a direct manipulation interface (often called "drag & drop"). A direct manipulation interface allows users to manage multiple "application objects" by manipulating visual representations of those objects. For example, a user may sell stock by dragging "stock" icons out of a "portfolio" icon and onto a "trading floor" icon. Direct Manipulation Services can be further divided into Display and Input/Validation.

Form Services

Form services enable applications to use fields to display and collect data. A field may be a traditional 3270-style field used to display or input textual data, or it may be a graphical field, such as a check box, a list box, or an image. Form services provide support for display, input/validation, mapping support, and field interaction management.

Input Devices

Input devices detect user input from a variety of input technologies, such as pen based, voice recognition, touch-screen, mouse, and digital camera.

Report and Print Services

Report and Print Services support the creation and on-screen previewing of paper or photographic documents, which contain screen data, application data, graphics, or images.

User Navigation Services

User Navigation Services provide a user with a way to access or navigate between functions within or across applications. Historically, this has been the role of a text-based menuing system that provides a list of applications or activities for the user to choose from. However, client/server technologies introduced new navigation metaphors. A common method for allowing a user to navigate within an application is to list available functions or information by means of a menu bar with associated pull-down menus or context-sensitive pop-up menus.

Web Browser Services

Web Browser Services allow users to view and interact with applications and documents made up of varying data types, such as text, graphics, and audio. These services also provide support for navigation within and across documents no matter where they are located through the use of links embedded into the document content. Web Browser Services retain the link connection, i.e., document physical location, and mask the complexities of that connection from the user.

Web Browser services can be further subdivided into

- Browser Extension Services
- Form Services
- User Navigation Services

Browser Extension Services

Browser Extension Services provide support for executing different types of applications from within a Browser. These applications provide functionality that extend Browser capabilities. The key Browser Extensions are plug-ins, helper/application viewers, Java applets, Active/X controls, and Java beans.

Form Services

Like Form Services outside the Web Browser, Form Services within the Web Browser enable applications to use fields to display and collect data. The only difference is the technology used to develop the Forms. The most common type of Forms within a browser is Hypertext Markup Language (HTML).

User Navigation Services

Like User Navigation Services outside the Web Browser, User Navigation Services within the Web Browser provide a user with a way to access or navigate between functions within or across applications. These User Navigation Services can be subdivided into three categories: Hyperlink, Customized Menu, and Virtual Reality.

Window System

Typically, part of the operating systems, Window System Services provide the base functionality for creating and managing a GUI: detecting user actions, manipulating windows on the display, and displaying information through windows and graphical controls.

INFORMATION SERVICES

Information Services (Exhibit 10) manage information assets and enable applications to access and manipulate data stored locally or remotely from documents, databases, or external data sources. They minimize an application's dependence on physical storage and location within the network. Information services may also be used directly by the end user when ad hoc data and document access are integral to the application work task. Information Services are grouped into two primary categories:

- Database Services
- Document Services

Database Services

Database services are responsible for providing access to a local or remote database as well as maintaining integrity of the data within the database. These services also support the ability to store data on either a single physical platform or in some cases across multiple platforms. These services are typically provided by database management system (DBMS) vendors and accessed via embedded or call-level SQL variants and supersets. Depending upon the underlying storage model, non-SQL access methods may be used instead.

Database Services include

- Storage Services
- Indexing Services
- Security Services
- Access Services
- Replication/Synchronization Services

Storage Services

Storage Services manage data physical storage. These services provide a mechanism for saving information so that data will live beyond program execution. Data are often stored in relational format (an RDBMS) but may also be stored in an object-oriented format (OODBMS) or other structures such as IMS and VSAM.

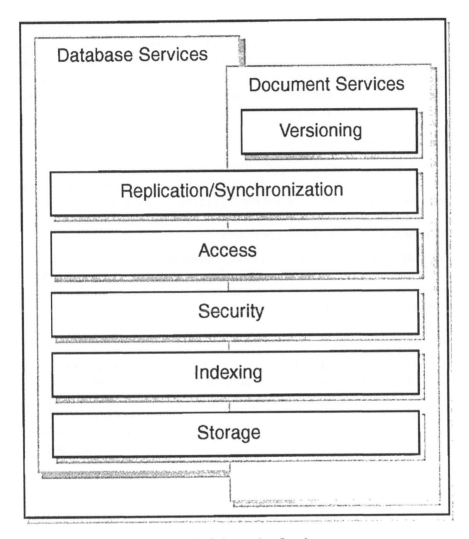

Exhibit 10. Information Services.

Indexing Services

Indexing Services provide a mechanism for speeding up data retrieval. In relational databases one or more fields can be used to construct the index. Therefore, when a user searches for a specific record rather than scanning the whole table sequentially the index is used to find the location of that record faster.

Security Services

Security Services enforce access control to ensure that records are only visible or editable by authorized people for approved purposes. Most DBMSs provide access control at the database, table, or row levels to specific users and groups as well as concurrency control. They also provide execution control for such things as stored procedures and database functions.

Access Services

Access Services enable an application to retrieve data from a database as well as manipulate (insert, update, or delete) data in a database. SQL is the primary approach for accessing records in today's DBMSs.

Replication/Synchronization Services

Replication Services support an environment in which multiple copies of databases must be maintained. Synchronization Services perform the transactions required to make one or more information sources that are intended to mirror each other consistent.

Document Services

Document Services provide similar structure and control for documents that DBMSs apply to record-oriented data. A document is defined as a collection of objects of potentially different types (e.g., structured data, unstructured text, images, or multimedia) that a business user deals with. Regardless of the software used to create and maintain the component parts, all parts together constitute the document, which is managed as a single entity.

Document Services include

- Storage Services
- Indexing Services
- Security Services
- Access Services
- Replication/Synchronization Services
- Versioning Services

Storage Services

Storage Services manage the physical storage of documents. Generally, the documents are stored in a repository using one of the following methods: proprietary database, industry standard database, or industry standard database and file system.

Indexing Services

Locating documents and content within documents is a complex problem and involves several alternative methods. Most document management products provide index services that support searching document repositories by the methods of attribute search, full-text search, context search, or Boolean search.

Security Services

Documents should be accessed exclusively through the document management backbone. If a document is checked in, checked out, routed, viewed, annotated, archived, or printed, it should be done only by authorized users. Security services controls access at the user, role, and group levels.

Access Services

Access Services support document creation, deletion, maintenance, and retrieval. These services allow users to capture knowledge or content through the creation of unstructured information, such as documents. Access Services also allow users to effectively retrieve documents that were created by them and documents that were created by others.

Replication/Synchronization Services

Replication Services support an environment in which multiple copies of documents must be maintained. Synchronization Services perform the transactions required to make one or more information sources that are intended to mirror each other consistent.

Versioning Services

These services maintain a historical record of the changes to a document over time. By maintaining this record, versioning services allow for the recreation of a document as it looked at any given point in time during its evolution.

COMMUNICATION SERVICES

Communication Services enable an application to interact transparently with other applications regardless of whether they reside on the same computer or on a remote computer.

There are five primary communications services categories (Exhibit 11):

- Core Messaging Services
- Specialized Messaging Services
- Communications Security Services
- Virtual Resource Services
- Directory Services

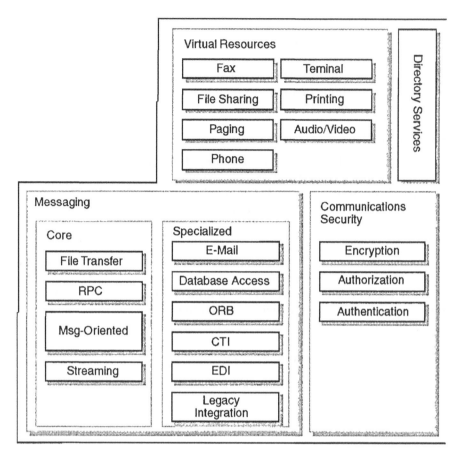

Exhibit 11. Communication Services.

Core Messaging Services

Broadly defined, messaging is sending information or commands between two or more recipients. Recipients may be computers, people, or processes within a computer. To send this message, a protocol (or in some cases, multiple protocols) is used that both the sender and receiver can understand. A protocol is a set of rules describing, in technical terms, how two end points should exchange information. Protocols exist at several levels during the exchange of information. Protocols facilitate transport of the message carrying the information. Both end points must recognize and observe the protocol. As an example, a common protocol in today's networks is the TCP/IP protocol.

Core messaging services can further be divided into the following services:

- *File Transfer Services.* File Transfer Services enable the copying and receiving of files or other large blocks of data between two resources.
- *Remote procedure call (RPC) services.* RPCs are a type of protocol by which an application sends a request to a remote system to execute a designated procedure using the supplied arguments and return the result.
- *Message-Oriented Services.* Message-Oriented Services refers to the process of distributing data and control through the exchange of records known as messages. Message-Oriented Services provide the application developer with a set of simple verbs (e.g., connect, send, receive, and disconnect) that are used to exchange information with other distributed applications.
- *Streaming Services.* Streaming is the process of transferring time-sensitive data streams (e.g., video and/or audio) in real time. Streaming differs from the other types of Core Messaging services in that it delivers a continuous, one-way stream of data, rather than the relatively short messages associated with RPC and Message-Oriented messaging or the large, batch transfers associated with File Transfer. Streaming may be used to deliver video, audio, and/or other real-time content across the Internet or within enterprise networks.

Specialized Messaging Services

Specialized Messaging Services extend the Core Messaging Services to provide additional functionality. Specialized Messaging Services may extend Core Messaging Services in the following general ways:

- Provides messaging among specialized systems by drawing upon basic messaging capabilities
- Defines specialized message layouts
- Defines specialized intersystem protocols
- Suggests ways in which messaging draws upon directory and security services to deliver a complete messaging environment

Specialized Messaging Services is comprised of the following subservices:

- *E-Mail Messaging.* E-Mail Messaging services reliably exchange messages using the store-and-forward messaging style. E-Mail message systems traditionally include a rudimentary form of directory services
- *Computer-Telephone Integration (CTI) Messaging.* CTI integrates computer systems and telephone systems to coordinate data and telephony activities. CTI Messaging has two primary functions: device-specific communication and message mapping.

- *EDI (Electronic Data Interchange) Messaging.* EDI supports system-to-system messaging among business partners by defining standard message layouts. Companies typically use EDI to streamline commercial transactions within their supply chains.
- *Object Request Broker (ORB) Messaging.* ORB Messaging enables objects to transparently make requests of and receive responses from other objects located locally or remotely. Objects communicate through an ORB. An ORB enables client objects to access server objects either locally or remotely over a network and invoke operations (i.e., functions and methods) on them.
- *Database Access Messaging.* Database Messaging services (also known as Database Access Middleware or DBAM) provide connectivity for clients to access databases throughout the enterprise.
- *Legacy Integration Messaging.* Legacy services provide gateways to mainframe legacy systems.

Communications Security Services

Communications Security Services control access to network-attached resources. Combining network Security Services with security services in other parts of the system architecture (e.g., application and database layers) results in robust security.

Communications Security Services are broken down into the following three categories:

- *Encryption Services.* Encryption services encrypt data prior to network transfer to prevent unauthorized interception.
- *Authorization Services.* When a user requests access to network resources, Authorization Services determines if the user has the appropriate permissions and either allows or disallows the access.
- *Authentication Services.* Authentication services verify network access requests by validating that users are who they claim to be. For secure systems, one or more authentication mechanisms can be used to validate authorized users and to verify which functions and data they have access to.

Virtual Resource Services

Virtual Resource Services proxy or mimic the capabilities of specialized, network-connected resources. This allows a generic network node to emulate a specialized physical device. In this way, network users can interface with a variety of specialized resources.

A common example of a Virtual Resource service is the capability to print to a network printer as if it were directly attached to a workstation.

Virtual Resource services include

- *Terminal Services.* Terminal services allow a client to connect to a non-local host via a network and to emulate the profile (e.g., the keyboard and screen characteristics) required by the host application.
- *Print Services.* Print services connect network workstations to shared printers.
- *File Sharing Services.* File Sharing Services allow users to view, manage, read, and write files that may be located on a variety of platforms in a variety of locations.
- *Phone Services.* Phone virtual resource services extend telephony capabilities to computer platforms.
- *Fax Services.* Fax Services provide for the management of both inbound and outbound fax transmissions.
- *Audio/Video Services.* Audio/Video Services allow nodes to interact with multimedia data streams. These services may be implemented as audio only, video only, or combined audio/video.
- *Paging Services.* Paging virtual resource services provide the message formatting and display functionality that allows network nodes to interface with wireless paging systems.

Directory Services

Managing information about network resources involves a variety of processes ranging from simple name/address resolution to the logical integration of heterogeneous systems to create a common view of services, security, etc. This breadth of functionality is discussed as part of Directory Services.

Because of their ability to unify and manage distributed environments, Directory Services play a key role in locating and accessing resources in a network, including Internet/intranet architectures.

COMMUNICATIONS FABRIC SERVICES

As communications networks become increasingly complicated and interconnected, the services provided by the network itself have by necessity increased as well. Clients and servers are rarely directly connected to one another but are commonly separated by a network of routers, servers, and firewalls, providing an ever-increasing number of network services such as address resolution, message routing, and security screening.

The Communications Fabric extends the client/server computing model by placing intelligence into the physical network, acknowledging the network as a sort of standalone system that provides intelligent shared network services. There is certainly overlap between services typically

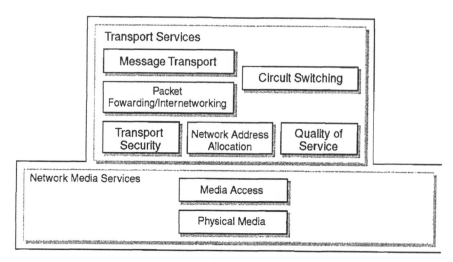

Exhibit 12. Communications Fabric Services.

thought of as part of a client/server architecture and services increasingly provided by the network itself.

Communications Fabric Services is comprised of two subservices: Transport Services and Network Media Services (Exhibit 12).

Transport Services

Transport Services are responsible for establishing, maintaining, and terminating end-to-end communications between users and processes. Connection management provides transfer services that ensure the delivery of data from sender to receiver, which support the transferring of messages from a process running on one machine to a process running on another machine. In addition, connection management provides services that initiate a connection, gracefully terminate a connection, and handle abrupt termination. These services take place for application before and after the data are formatted for transport over the network.

Transport Services include

- *Message Transport Services.* These are responsible for the end-to-end delivery of messages. They can include functionalities such as end-to-end data transfer, connection control, reliable transfer, flow control, and multiplexing.
- *Packet Forwarding/Internetworking Services.* The Packet Forwarding/Internetworking Service transfers data packets and manages the path that data take through the network. It includes functionalities

such as fragmentation/reassembly, addressing, routing, switching, and multicasting.

- *Circuit Switching Services.* Where Message Transport Services and Packet Forwarding/Internetworking Services support the transfer of packetized data, Circuit Switching Services establish physical circuits for the transfer of such things as circuit-switched voice, fax, and video.
- *Transport Security Services.* Transport Security Services (within the Transport Services layer) perform encryption and filtering.
- *Network Address Allocation Services.* Network Address Allocation Services manage the distribution of addresses to network nodes. This provides more flexibility compared to having all nodes assigned static addresses.
- *Quality of Service (QoS) Services.* QoS Services deliver a defined network throughput for designated traffic by allocating dedicated bandwidth, prioritizing data traffic, etc.

Network Media Services

The Network Media layer provides the following capabilities:

- Final framing of data for interfacing with the physical network
- Receiving, interpreting, and acting on signals from the communications fabric
- Transferring data through the physical network

Network Media Services performs two primary service functions:

- *Media Access Services.* Media Access Services manage the low-level transfer of data between network nodes. These services provide functions such as physical addressing, packet transfer, shared access, flow control, error recovery, and encryption.
- *Physical Media Services.* The Physical Media includes both the physical connectors and the the physical media (wired or wireless).

ENVIRONMENT SERVICES

Environment Services provide miscellaneous application and system level services that do not deal directly with managing the user interface, communicating to other programs, or accessing data (Exhibit 13).

Runtime Services

Runtime Services convert noncompiled computer languages into machine code during the execution of a program. Two subservices comprise Runtime Services: language interpreter and virtual machine.

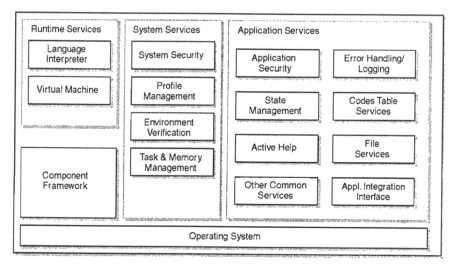

Exhibit 13. Environment Services.

- *Language Interpreter Services.* Language Interpreter Services decompose a fourth generation and/or a scripting languages into machine code (executable code) at runtime.
- *Virtual Machine Services.* Typically, a Virtual Machine is implemented in software on top of an operating system and is used to run applications. The Virtual Machine provides a layer of abstraction between the applications and the underlying operating system and is often used to support operating system independence.

System Services

System Services are services that applications can use to perform system-level functions. These services include

- System Security Services allow applications to interact with the operating system's native security mechanism. The basic services include the ability to login, logoff, authenticate to the operating system, and enforce access control to system resources and executables.
- Profile Management Services are used to access and update local or remote system, user, or application profiles. User profiles, for example, can be used to store a variety of information such as the user's language and color preferences to basic job function information that may be used by Integrated Performance Support or Workflow Services.
- Task and Memory Management Services allow applications and/or other events to control individual computer tasks or processes and

manage memory. They provide services for scheduling, starting, stopping, and restarting both client and server tasks (e.g., software agents).

- Environment Verification Services ensure functionality by monitoring, identifying, and validating environment integrity prior and during program execution. (e.g., free disk space, monitor resolution, and correct version).

Application Services

Application Services are miscellaneous services that applications can use for common functions. These common functions can apply to one application or can be used across applications. They include

- *Applications Security Services.* Besides system level security such as logging into the network, there are additional security services associated with specific applications, including user access services, data access services, and function access services.
- *Error Handling/Logging Services.* Error Handling Services support the handling of fatal and nonfatal hardware and software errors for an application. Logging Services support the logging of informational, error, and warning messages.
- *State Management Services.* State Management Services enable information to be passed or shared among windows and/or Web pages and/or across programs.
- *Codes Table Services.* Codes Table Services enable applications to utilize externally stored parameters and validation rules.
- *Active Help Services.* Active Help Services enable an application to provide assistance to a user for a specific task or set of tasks.
- *File Services.*
- *Application Integration Interface Services.* An Application Integration Interface provides a method or gateway for passing context and control of information to an external application.
- *Other Common Services.* This is a catch-all category for additional reusable routines useful across a set of applications (e.g., Date Routines, Time Zone Conversions, and Field Validation Routines).

Component Framework Services

Component Framework Services provide an infrastructure for building components so that they can communicate within an application and across applications, on the same machine or on multiple machines across a network, to work together. COM/DCOM and CORBA are the two leading component industry standards. These standards define how components should be built and how they should communicate.

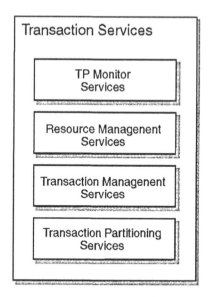

Exhibit 14. Transaction Services.

Operating System Services

Operating System Services are the underlying services such as multitasking, paging, memory allocation, etc., typically provided by today's modern operating systems. Where necessary, an additional layer or APIs may be provided to gain either operating system independence or a higher level of abstraction for application programmers.

TRANSACTION SERVICES

Transaction Services provide the transaction integrity mechanism for the application. This allows all data activities within a single business event to be grouped as a single, logical unit of work.

In small- to moderate-scale environments of fewer than 150 simultaneous users on a single server, this service may be provided by the DBMS software with its restart/recovery and integrity capabilities. For larger client/server environments, an emerging class of software, referred to as "distributed on-line transaction managers," might be more applicable. These transaction managers provide sharing of server processes across a large community of users and can be more efficient than the DBMSs.

Transactions Services include (Exhibit 14):

- TP Monitor Services
- Resource Management Services

- Transaction Management Services
- Transaction Partitioning Services

TP Monitor Services

The Transaction Monitor Services are the primary interface through which applications invoke Transaction Services and receive status and error information. Transaction Monitor Services, in conjunction with Information Access and Communication Services, provide for load balancing across processors or machines and location transparency for distributed transaction processing.

Resource Management Services

A Resource Manager provides for concurrency control and integrity for a singular data resource (e.g., a database or a file system). Integrity is guaranteed by ensuring that an update is completed correctly and entirely or not at all. Resource Management Services use locking, commit, and rollback services and are integrated with Transaction Management Services.

Transaction Management Services

Transaction Management Services coordinate transactions across one or more resource managers either on a single machine or multiple machines within the network. Transaction Management Services ensure that all resources for a transaction are updated or, in the case of an update failure on any one resource, all updates are rolled back. This service allows multiple applications to share data with integrity.

Transaction Partitioning Services

Transaction Partitioning Services provide support for mapping a single logical transaction in an application into the required multiple physical transactions. For example, in a package or legacy-rich environment, the single logical transaction of changing a customer address may require the partitioning and coordination of several physical transactions to multiple application systems or databases. Transaction Partitioning Services provide the application with a simple single transaction view.

BASE SERVICES

Base Services provide support for delivering applications to a wide variety of users over the Internet, intranet, and extranet. Web Services include: Web Server Services, Push/Pull Services, Batch Services, Report Services, and Workflow Services (Exhibit 15).

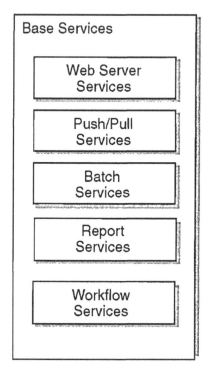

Exhibit 15. Base Services.

Web Server Services

Web Server Services enable organizations to manage and publish information and deploy netcentric applications over the Internet and intranet environments. These services support

- Managing documents in most formats such as HTML, Microsoft Word, etc.
- Handling of client requests for HTML pages
- Processing scripts such as Common Gateway Interface (CGI) or Active Server Pages (ASP)
- Caching Web pages

Push/Pull Services

Push/Pull Services allow for interest in a particular piece of information to be registered and then changes or new information to be communicated to the subscriber list. Depending upon requirements, synchronous or asynchronous push/pull services may be required. Synchronous push/pull services provide a mechanism for applications to be notified in real time if a subscribed item changes (e.g., a stock ticker). Asynchronous push/pull services do not require that a session-like connection be present between the subscriber and the information.

Batch Services

Batch processing is used to perform large-scale repetitive processing where no user involvement is required as well as reporting. Areas for design attention include scheduling, recovery/restart, use of job streams, and high availability (e.g., 24-hour running). In addition, close attention must be paid to performance as batch systems usually must be processed within strict batch windows.

Batch Services are comprised of the following subservices:

- *Driver Services*. These services provide the control structure and framework for batch programs. They are also referred to as Batch Scheduling Services.
- *Restart/Recovery Services*. These services are used to automatically recover and restart batch programs if they should fail during execution.
- *Batch Balancing Services*. These services support the tracking of run-to-run balances and totals for the batch system.
- *Report Services*. Project reporting tools are used to summarize and communicate information, using either printed paper or on-line report.

Report Services

Report Services are facilities for simplifying the construction and delivery of reports or generated correspondence. These services help to define reports and to electronically route reports to allow for on-line review, printing, and/or archiving. Report Services also support the merging of application data with predefined templates to create letters or other printed correspondence. Report Services include

- Driver Services
- Report Definition Services
- Report Built Services
- Report Distribution Services

Workflow Services

Workflow Services control and coordinate the tasks that must be completed to process a business event. Workflow enables tasks within a business process to be passed among the appropriate participants, in the correct sequence, and facilitates their completion within set times and budgets. Task definition includes the actions required as well as work folders containing forms, documents, images, and transactions. It uses business process rules, routing information, role definitions, and queues.

Workflow provides a mechanism to define, monitor, and control the sequence of work electronically. These services are typically provided by the server as they often coordinate activities among multiple users on multiple computers.

Workflow can be further divided into the following components:

- *Role Management Services.* These provide for the assignment of tasks to roles that can then be mapped to individuals.
- *Route Management Services.* These enable the routing of tasks to the next role.
- *Rule Management Services.* Rule Management Services support the routing of workflow activities by providing the intelligence necessary to determine which routes are appropriate given the state of a given process and knowledge of the organization's workflow processing rules.
- *Queue Management Services.* These services provide access to the workflow queues that are used to schedule work.

BUSINESS LOGIC

Business Logic is the core of any application, providing the expression of business rules and procedures (e.g., the steps and rules that govern how a sales order is fulfilled). As such, the Business Logic includes the control structure that specifies the flow for processing business events and user requests.

The execution architecture services described thus far are all generalized services designed to support the application's Business Logic. How Business Logic is to be organized is not within the scope of the execution architecture and must be determined based upon the characteristics of the application system to be developed. This section is intended to serve as a reminder of the importance of consciously designing a structure for Business Logic that helps to isolate the impacts of change and to point out that the underlying netcentric architecture is particularly well suited for enabling the packaging of Business Logic as components.

There are many ways in which to organize Business Logic, including rules-based, object-oriented, components, and structured programming. However, each of these techniques include common concepts, which we can group as Interface, Application Logic, and Data Abstraction (Exhibit 16).

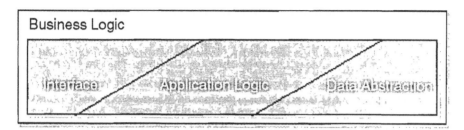

Exhibit 16. Business Logic.

Interface

Interface logic interprets and maps the actions of users into business logic processing activities. With the assistance of Presentation Services, Interface logic provides the linkage that allows users to control the flow of processing within the application.

Application Logic

Application Logic is the expression of business rules and procedures (e.g., the steps and rules that govern how a sales order is fulfilled). As such, the Application Logic includes the control structure that specifies the flow for processing for business events and user requests. The isolation of control logic facilitates change and adaptability of the application to changing business processing flows.

Data Abstraction

Information Access Services isolate the Business Logic from the technical specifics of how information is stored (e.g., location transparency, RDBMS syntax, etc.). Data Abstraction provides the application with a more logical view of information, further insulating the application from physical information storage considerations.

The developers of business logic should be shielded from the details and complexity of other architecture services (e.g., information services or component services), and other business logic for that matter.

It is important to decide whether the business logic will be separate from the presentation logic and the database access logic. Today, separation of business logic into its own tier is often done using an application server. In this type of an environment, although some business rules such as field validation might still be tightly coupled with the presentation logic, the majority of business logic is separate, usually residing on the server. It is also important to decide whether the business logic should be packaged as components to maximize software reuse and to streamline software distribution.

Another factor to consider is how the business logic is distributed between the client and the server(s) — where the business logic is stored and where the business logic is located when the application is being executed. There are several ways to distribute business logic:

1. Business logic can be stored on the server(s) and executed on the server(s).
2. Business logic can be stored on the server(s) and executed on the client.
3. Business logic can be stored and executed on the client.
4. Some business logic can be stored and executed on the server(s), and some business logic can be stored and executed on the client.

Having the business logic stored on the server enables developers to centrally maintain application code, thereby eliminating the need to distribute software to client machines when changes to the business logic occur. If all the business logic executes on the server, the application on the client will make requests to the server whenever it needs to execute a business function. This could increase network traffic, which may degrade application performance. On the other hand, having the business logic execute on the client may require longer load times when the application is initially launched. However, once the application is loaded, most processing is done on the client until synchronization with the server is needed. This type of an architecture might introduce complexities into the application that deal with the sharing of and reliance on central data across many users.

If the business logic is stored and executed on the client, software distribution options must be considered. Usually the most expensive option is to have a system administrator or the user physically install new applications and update existing applications on each client machine. Another option is to use a tool that performs automatic software distribution functions. However, this option usually requires the software distribution tool to be loaded first on each client machine. Another option is to package the application into ActiveX controls, utilizing the automatic install/update capabilities available with ActiveX controls — if the application is launched from a Web browser.

Currently, Internet applications house the majority of the business processing logic on the server, supporting the thin-client model. However, as technology evolves, this balance is beginning to shift, allowing business logic code bundled into components to be either downloaded at runtime or permanently stored on the client machine. Today, client-side business logic is supported through the use of Java applets, JavaBeans, Plug-ins and JavaScript from Sun/Netscape, and ActiveX controls and VBScript from Microsoft.

CONCLUSION

To operate optimally in the world of architectures, it is vital to remember a key point: one should not dwell too long at the abstract level. One can get mired in representations, in logical arguments. Pictures are important, but an architecture must be looked at pragmatically. It lives and breathes. It may evolve as the organization evolves. Yet, without the common understandings, common terminology, and common direction provided by architecture frameworks, project teams are putting their entire organization at risk.

Chapter 4
Presentation Services

Presentation services is the component of the client/server execution architecture that controls how users interact with the system. If the user requires a style or form of interaction with an application, the presentation services layer has a function that prescribes how that interaction should be implemented.

Presentation services is vital to effective systems design, in part because it is the most obvious part of the system to the common system user. "You don't get a second chance to make a good first impression" is an adage that applies well to interface design. Indeed, to the new types of users working in the client/server and netcentric environments, *the interface is the system*.

THE INTERFACE CONTINUUM

System interfaces should be considered on a continuum, arranged by the degree of human/machine integration that each possesses (Exhibit 1). Toward one end of the continuum are the early computing machines, where interaction took place on the machine's terms, in the form of punch cards. Toward the other end of the continuum are the interfaces designed with a bias toward more natural or more human communication methods. Here users interact with computers using methods that are natural to them simply because they are human beings (e.g., speech, gestures, writing, and movement). Ultimately, these interfaces move toward virtual reality interfaces where the computer simulates a natural human sensory environment.

Today, in the era of very sophisticated, we may forget the value of interfaces at the lower end of the continuum. Exhibit 2 illustrates an example of a character-based interface for an airline reservationist making seat assignments. The interface is not pretty, but its main strength is permitting high-quantity use. For so-called heads-down, high-volume, or specialized jobs, a character- or code-based interface allows users to work quickly and efficiently — provided they have the time to learn how to use the system and the ability to remember a large set of commands and codes and do not make mistakes.

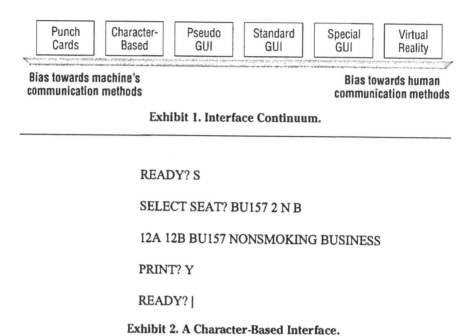

Punch Cards	Character-Based	Pseudo GUI	Standard GUI	Special GUI	Virtual Reality

Bias towards machine's
communication methods

Bias towards human
communication methods

Exhibit 1. Interface Continuum.

READY? S

SELECT SEAT? BU157 2 N B

12A 12B BU157 NONSMOKING BUSINESS

PRINT? Y

READY? |

Exhibit 2. A Character-Based Interface.

Users, however, seldom view this type of system as a source of job satisfaction. From management's point of view, the fatal weakness of systems with character-based interfaces is that great amounts of training are required to use them. Generally, the user has to remember codes even to have basic proficiency, and more sophisticated navigation through the system takes a great deal of experience.

A large number of codes that must be memorized can totally undermine the performance of the workers at the system. One U.S. utility company, for example, introduced two new systems for its customer service representatives. Using the old system, representatives only had to remember codes to access about 30 different 3270-type screens. The new system required more than 250 screens. Here, a continued reliance on character-based interfaces might pose a real bottom-line threat to the enterprise because representatives would be hampered in providing high-quality service to customers.

The interface continuum illustrates character-based interfaces with many of the desirable qualities of graphic interfaces but without some of the costs. Some graphical user interfaces (GUIs), often the result of conversions of legacy systems, are actually character-based interfaces in attractive new wrappings. These interfaces are called pseudo-GUIs, to distinguish them from applications that were originally developed as GUIs.

Netcentric applications typically are in the Pseudo to Standard GUI range of the Interface Continuum depending on their use of HTML forms or Java applets.

WHAT IS A GUI?

Today, as users find themselves moving up the continuum toward natural interaction with computers, the state of the market has rapidly become the GUI.

A GUI is an interface that takes advantage of a high-resolution display to present a great amount of meaningful information to the user, grouped and organized graphically. Because of the increased resolution, a graphic interface is able to display more bytes of information at any given time than a character-based interface. The GUI is presented on a bit-mapped display monitor, which enables the software to address each display pixel individually. (A standard bit-mapped display monitor has more than 300,000 pixels; a 3270 screen consists of 1,920 displayable characters.) The GUI has more separately distinguishable parts visible and thus can more easily take advantage of the strengths of the human brain: *to recognize and associate, generalize, and deduce.*

Because of increased processing capacity provided by workstations, it is easy to change the information presented on any part of the screen in response to user actions. The appearance of the GUI responds to actions by users who interact via a mouse, keyboard, touch-sensitive monitors, voice recognition, pen stylus, or any other input device. The sensitivity of the interface to user actions means feedback can be provided quickly and in the most appropriate context.

For example, if a user types in an invalid date, the field could immediately change color to indicate this (compared to the traditional approach of waiting until a PF key is pressed to validate all data), or, as a user cursors across cells in a spreadsheet, the cell's contents or formula are instantly displayed in an edit field. This type of interface is not possible without the ability to respond to events much smaller than the PF key.

The most important result of GUI flexibility is that the user experiences the system as responsive. When people get immediate feedback from almost any action, they learn more quickly and experience greater satisfaction and a sense of control. Both visually and in terms of responsiveness, GUIs seem to increase rapport or emotional satisfaction and reduce anxiety or alienation. Although these factors are more difficult to quantify, they may still determine the ultimate acceptability of an interface to today's computer user.

More Than Just a Pretty Face

The visual appeal of a GUI is certainly the most obvious facet of today's systems. However, the presence of color and effective design is not merely a matter of esthetics. Mere prettiness is not the point; indeed, it is hardly a justification for the cost of such a system. What is the primary *business* benefit of the new GUIs?

To understand this, people need to step back a minute and consider what the introduction of computers did to the manner in which they go about performing their work. Previous forms of office technology — the telephone, the typewriter, and the dictation machine — augmented the work they did but did not take it over. They came to their jobs focused on the tasks at hand: x amount of sales to make a quota, y number of products to manufacture, z number of customer service inquiries to answer.

For better and for worse, the computer altered that understanding of their work. The computer made those tasks more efficient, but it also put blinders on people. No longer could they look at the whole picture of their work but only that slice of it that a particular system application let them see. Too often, the tasks of workers became oriented around using a system rather than performing work; instead of transacting business, workers were processing transactions. The system was in charge, and that affected the manner in which interfaces were designed.

Over the past few years, systems designers have begun a gradual paradigm shift: from a machine-oriented perspective on design to a user- or human-centered perspective. The shift may have started when people began to suspect that most difficulties they had using a computer system might be the computer's fault, not their fault. However, it is being driven home by the netcentric revolution. If a system being used by your customers or business partners isn't usable, they may very likely go somewhere else.

Before GUIs, the notion of designing for usability was somewhat alien to a designer because there was not much the designer could do to make the system usable. The ability to provide clues and quick feedback was limited or impractical. GUIs have given designers new tools and techniques for making systems easier to use. Beyond just looking good, GUIs allow designers to focus on the user as the center of the design process. User-centered design emphasizes the needs of the system user above the needs of the system.

According to Donald A. Norman, in his book *Design of Everyday Things*, there are four important facets of user-centered design:

- Make it easy for the user to know which actions are possible at any moment.
- Make visible to the user such things as the entire conceptual model of the system, the alternative actions, and the results of actions.

- Make it easy to evaluate the current state of the system.
- Make natural to the user the manner in which intentions are linked to required actions as well as the link between actions and results and between the visible information and the interpretation of the state of the system.

In short, simply make sure that users can figure out what to do and that they can also track easily what is going on at any given moment.

Why should designers operate now on these principles? There are three principal reasons:

1. Training costs for organizations can be drastically reduced if users can reach proficient performance levels quickly. Overall training costs, beyond systems training, can also be reduced eventually as so-called performance support systems become more accepted, delivering training to workers on demand, at their point of need.
2. The success of applications designed for the new computer users — professionals and executives — largely depends on their acceptance and satisfaction with the new system. This in turn demands principles of advanced usability. Minimizing the adverse impacts of technological change is vital for users because they have the influence to reject the system if it does not have a positive impact on their work rather quickly.
3. Organizations are increasingly "hiring the customer" and discovering new ways to move technology beyond the walls of the organization and let the customer control part of the business process. The World Wide Web offers the most obvious examples, but there are also self-service airline ticketing terminals, shop-at-home services through interactive television, and a wide array of other opportunities for letting customers interact directly with an organization's computer systems. The primary interface of the system must be effective and allow customers to intuitively transact their business via the system.

ICONS

An icon is a small, simplified picture. Icons are important in GUI design because they take advantage of a human's superior ability to recognize symbols rather than placing demands on the individual's ability to remember. Icons and other pictures are often used in GUIs for the following reasons:

- Two icons are easier to distinguish from each other than are two words.
- Icons and pictures can carry more information in less space than words can.

- When the users are partially familiar with an application, icons help them remember functions and select them quickly and correctly. "Partially familiar" is important to remember here. Icons are not usually meant to be 100% self-explanatory. They take their meaning from their context and one's cultural experience. Pictures are less ambiguous.
- In seldom-used applications, icons may be more self-explanatory and more easily recalled.

The following section discusses two other important aspects of GUIs: metaphors and interaction styles. Both are critical to the successful design of a usable application, and both have been given significantly more flexibility in delivery with the advent of GUIs.

INTERFACE METAPHORS

"Metaphor" has become the word of choice for describing the overall communicative symbolism of the interface. Communication between human beings is filled with metaphorical references.

"The way we think, what we experience, and what we do every day is very much a matter of metaphor," G. Lakoff and M. Johnson, both linguists, write in their book *Metaphors We Live By*. Consider the manner in which people consider arguments to be a kind of war: "Arguments have *sides* that can be *defended* and *attacked*. If a position is *indefensible*, one can *retreat* from it. Arguments can be right on *target*; arguments can be *shot down*." Speech built on metaphors is the rule, not the exception.

As with speech, so it is with the visual world. Metaphors function as common and natural models, which allow people to extend their familiarity with concrete objects and experiences to the level of abstract concepts. The central metaphor of the system interface is the most crucial one for systems designers, one that must be selected with particular attention to the unique needs and work views of the primary user.

In the user interface, metaphors allow people to "talk about" parts of the system as if they were parts of the more familiar physical world. Using a metaphor endows a part of the computer system with a whole set of characteristics belonging to its metaphorical comparison.

Within the more general category of the human metaphor, however, several other types of metaphors are increasingly found in GUIs. Perhaps the most powerful is the workplace metaphor.

Workplace Metaphor

The concept of a workplace metaphor is built on the premise that the worker's electronic work environment should mirror his or her physical environment. This allows applications developers to leverage off what is sometimes called the user's real-world knowledge.

If the person works at a desk, the electronic workplace should resemble a desk. For example, it may contain a calculator, inbox and outbox assorted filing cabinets, and folders. Workers should be able to manipulate electronic objects, such as files and papers, in the same way they manipulate physical objects. Therefore, instead of physically putting a memo in the outbox, an individual would use the mouse to drag and drop an electronic memo onto an image of the outbox. Because well-designed electronic environments behave similarly to physical environments, users can interact with their electronic tools more naturally.

The physical desk is a common interface metaphor. Recently, however, other interface metaphors are becoming available. One of them is the notebook metaphor.

In this case, the user's electronic environment resembles a notebook with tabbed sections. By selecting a tab, the user can flip to that section of the notebook. Users can organize and use their electronic notebooks just as they would a paper version (although with the added benefit of electronic sorting and searching capabilities). A similar result is often achieved in a netcentric user interface through the use of frames and navigation bars. The navigation bars act as the tabs for selecting the section a user desires.

Workplace metaphors transcend application design. An individual business application is only one of the items users may work with. They may need to work with other business applications, personal productivity tools, or utility applications, such as calculators, or address books. All these applications should conform to the workplace metaphor, whatever it may be.

Another point to note about metaphors is that, technically, they could be separated from the operating system. Many operating systems, however, come bundled with presentation services that already implement a particular metaphor. Microsoft Windows and Macintosh interfaces, for example, present desktop metaphors.

Metaphors create expectations for the user because of their "affordances." All objects have affordances — clues as to what we are supposed to do with them. Most chairs are clearly intended to be sat on; the most prevalent type of light switch is clearly supposed to be moved up or down. However, everyone has come across examples of objects with unclear affordances, objects that apparently were designed by someone more interested in aesthetics than function. People push on a door that they are supposed to pull or hit the flight attendant call button instead of the light switch. It is essential that there be a good match between the expectations created by an interface metaphor and the actual functions that the system has to offer.

For example, most people occasionally find that they have tossed an important paper into the waste basket. In the real world, they simply retrieve — and possibly uncrumple — the paper. When Apple and other manufacturers introduced the wastebasket or bin metaphor for the delete function, there was a potential mismatch. Delete did not necessarily allow undelete. Various implementations of a metaphor for delete have solved this in various ways:

- On the Macintosh, the wastebasket (called a Recycle Bin in Microsoft Windows) is actually a buffer. Things are not truly deleted until the user gives a command to empty it. This solves the problem by adding both function and complexity. As visual feedback, the wastebasket bulges as it gets full to remind the user to empty it.
- In Lotus Organizer, things placed in the wastebasket are seen to go up in flames. This is not reversible, and it adjusts user expectations in a memorable way.
- In OS/2 2.0, the wastebasket was replaced with the metaphor of a paper shredder. This solution adjusted user expectations to the fact that a delete was not reversible.

Thus, selecting the appropriate metaphor for a particular application is extremely important.

Following are some tips for systems developers in choosing a metaphor:

1. Select function(s) to be represented by metaphor(s). Which functions are expected to be difficult for users to understand in the abstract? Which functions are essential?
2. Understand the function to be modeled. What does it do, and how?
3. List possible metaphors that have comparable functions. Try to find several.
4. Evaluate the possibilities. Look for the choice that is most concrete, is most familiar to users, and creates the best match between user expectations and function. Look for one that is easy to represent visually.
5. Test the selected metaphor, and possibly an alternative, with the target user community.

Finally, the use of metaphors is not limited only to functions. Applications can have metaphors, too. For instance, a flight planning application might use a graphical map as its metaphor. The map would reflect the charts typically used by pilots for flight planning and would display landmarks, navigational aids, and restricted airspace, for example.

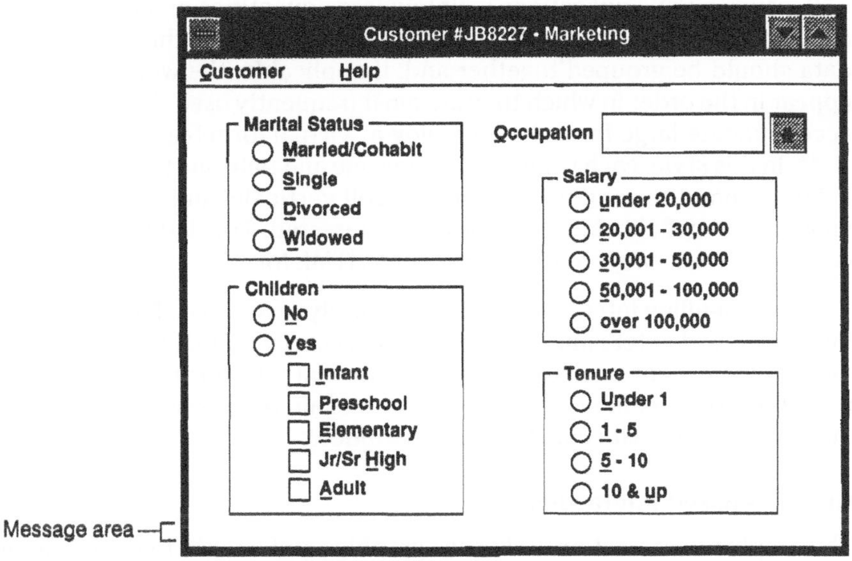

Exhibit 3. Example of a Form-Filling Window.

Alternatively, it could use a flight planning form as its metaphor. Which metaphor is most appropriate depends on the user community and is a further example of the need to follow the previous five steps in selecting an appropriate metaphor.

INTERACTION STYLES IN A GUI ENVIRONMENT

Once a appropriate metaphor has been defined for the application being designed, interaction styles must be chosen for performing the various activities and functions within the application. The most common interaction styles in GUI applications are form filling, graphics based, and direct manipulation. These styles are not mutually exclusive and are often incorporated in the same application and sometimes in the same window.

Form Filling

A windowed form-filling application is similar to its traditional on-line counterpart. Essentially, users perform their work by completing an electronic form (as opposed to a paper form). Because it is electronic, however, the form has a "behavior."

For example, it may prevent the user from changing protected data, it may verify that the user enters valid information, it may prompt the user to save changes, and it may dynamically indicate which fields are required. Exhibit 3 depicts a sample form-filling window.

Because many applications maintain large quantities of data, it is often necessary to break up a "form" into multiple windows. In this case, related data should be grouped together and, if applicable, the windows should appear in the order in which they are most frequently used. Another way to accommodate large forms is to employ a "virtual form-based" interaction style. In this style, each window contains one and only one form. If the form is larger than the window, users can scroll vertically and horizontally to view the entry fields in which they are interested. This latter approach is common in netcentric applications using HTML forms.

The form-filling interaction style is primarily text based. The user reads, interprets, and enters information that is primarily textual (although there may be some icons used to supplement the textual information). Form filling is the most common interaction style, and almost every GUI application incorporates at least some form-filling windows.

Graphics-Based Interaction

The graphical interaction style uses graphics and images to convey information. These can be in the form of drawings, photographs, charts, and video.

In its simplest form, the graphics-based style can be used to provide similar functions as the form-filling style. For example, it can allow users to select from a group of related images or can present a list of numbers as a graph. The graphics-based style can also be used to extend form-filling capability to incorporate photographs and full-motion video. For example, product images can be incorporated into an on-line catalog or product information database. Another example could include an auto insurance application, where it could be beneficial to store a photographic image of a claim form or of a damaged vehicle. Exhibit 4 depicts a window with a graphics-based interaction style.

Although they are much more common today, graphics-based interfaces were initially slow to gain acceptance because of the complexity of developing them and the high volume of memory and disk space they required for image and video. The World Wide Web accelerated the use of graphics-based interfaces and, as a result, the tools for developing these interfaces have become more powerful. The biggest limitation to such interfaces today is the storage space and communications time required for dealing with extensive collections of graphics, audio, or video.

Direct Manipulation

Direct manipulation is a style of interaction that allows the user to employ drag-and-drop techniques to manipulate data. Direct manipulation differs from graphics-based and form-filling styles in that it is not typically

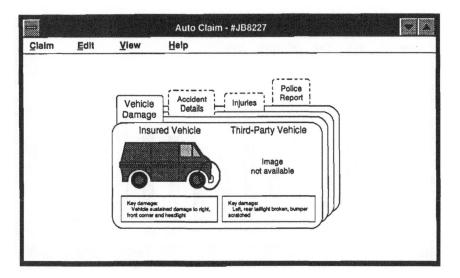

Exhibit 4. Example of a Graphics-Based Window.

independent, and it must be used in conjunction with either a graphics-based or a form-filling interface.

As the name suggests, direct manipulation allows the user to directly manipulate objects on the screen. For example, if the user is viewing a bar chart that indicates projected inventory levels by month, he or she could change the June inventory level by dragging the top of the June bar up or down (Exhibit 5).

Direct manipulation is often used in conjunction with icons. For example, if users want to open a new purchase order (PO) for an existing customer, they could drag a customer icon over the PO application icon. This action would open a new PO, which already contains all the customer's header information.

Direct manipulation can also be employed in a form-filling window. For example, if users want to populate a field with an item from a list, they could just drag that item from the list to the field, or, if they want to delete a line item from a list, they could select that line and drag it to the Trash icon.

Having introduced the concepts behind the new graphical interfaces, the next section looks in more detail at the component parts of GUIs and at what is going on behind the scenes technologically within a GUI environment.

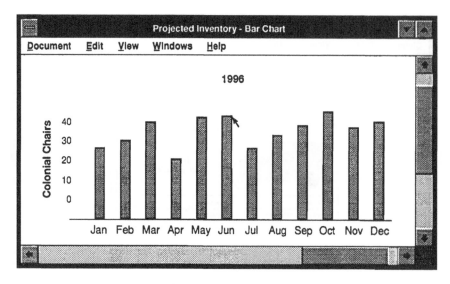

Exhibit 5. Example of a Window that Employs Direct Manipulation.

GUI APPLICATIONS

This section provides some context with which to better understand the capabilities and challenges of GUI applications, beginning with a simple example of how GUIs work, contrasting GUI systems to traditional, host-based systems, and discussing the most commonly encountered components and terms in a GUI environment. Finally, the discussion focuses on both the key advantages and the primary challenges of GUIs.

Although GUIs have many potential benefits, these benefits do not come cheaply. In general, client/server and GUI solutions are more expensive than traditional solutions. As a result, it is important that the organization is motivated by more than just the desire for a nicer look or a newer technology. The technology must also be a sound business decision.

The list of challenges is intentionally long to help ensure that the subtleties of GUI development are not overlooked when planning and justifying such an effort. By no means are systems developers to be dissuaded from undertaking GUI development. On the contrary, they are more likely to be successful when diving into GUI development if they know where the rocks and shallows are in these new technological waters.

A GUI AT WORK

To provide context, this section discusses the typical layers found in a GUI system and traces an event from its generation by the user, through the layers

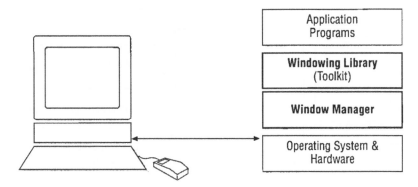

Exhibit 6. Software Layers in a GUI Environment.

into the application, and back out to the user in the form of visual feedback. Exhibit 6 depicts the different layers found in most windowed environments.

Operating System and Hardware

The operating system and hardware appear at the lowest level. This level is no different than in a character-based environment except for the higher-resolution, graphics-ready display and input that incorporates a mouse or other pointing device.

Window Manager

The next component, the Window Manager, is the core of the windowing system. It is the system software that really delivers the capabilities and characteristics of the GUI, including the display of windows, the interaction with the user and menus, icons, the mouse, and so on. This is where the look and feel of the GUI are implemented.

Windowing Library

The Windowing Library, or "toolkit," sits on top of the Window Manager. This is the interface between the applications programs and the Window Manager. The toolkit provides applications programs with the services necessary to display windows, update the contents of a window, set up menus, display icons, and receive input from the mouse and keyboard.

Behind the Scenes

In a GUI environment, the Window Manager is the software that is able to display images on the screen. This means that, while it is executing, a GUI application is continually making "service requests" from the Window Manager. In

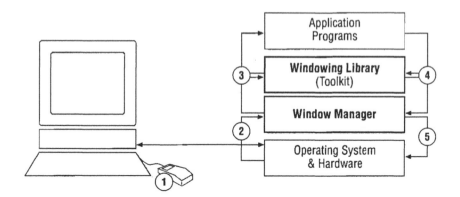

Exhibit 7. Steps in Working with a GUI Application.

addition to displaying screen images, the Window Manager also is responsible for routing messages between applications. In some ways, it behaves like a traffic cop; it determines where messages are coming from and routes them to the appropriate application.

The following brief scenario describes what happens when a user interacts with a GUI application, in this case, a word-processing application. It may be helpful to map the events that occur to their numbered counterparts in Exhibit 7. In the example, plain text indicates actions performed by system, hardware driver, or Window Manager software. Italic text indicates actions performed by business applications software.

Word-Processing Scenario

1. Users double-click the mouse over a word they would like to select.
2. The mouse clicks are passed from the hardware and operating system up to the Window Manager so it can interpret the action.
3. The Window Manager determines where on the screen the mouse pointer is and which window that corresponds to. The mouse clicks are translated to mouse "messages" that are sent to the appropriate application window.
4. The applications program receives the mouse messages and uses the coordinates in the messages to determine where the double-clicks occurred. Because double-clicking is a request for selecting a complete word, the word processor requests the Window Manager to display the text of the word as selected (inverted video). This request is made through the toolkit, which provides applications

programming interfaces (APIs) for the functions typically required by applications programs (e.g., create windows and display text/graphics).

5. The Window Manager determines which pixels on the screen need to change and updates them through the operating system or by directly interacting with the hardware.

This scenario describes only one iteration of a repetitive process that occurs in hundredths of a second. Every time the user invokes an action with an input device, a message is sent to the Window Manager. The Window Manager then routes this message to the appropriate application, and the application usually responds by requesting a service from the Window Manager. Note that, because of the granularity of the user–interface events (e.g., mouse movements and keyboard activity), the result can be hundreds of messages per second that the application receives and can act on.

Note that this scenario describes the model used by client/server GUI applications. Netcentric applications are similar, but the functions of the Operating System, Window Manager, and Windowing Library are effectively combined and handled by the browser (i.e., Netscape Navigator or Microsoft Internet Explorer). In such cases, mouse movements and keyboard events may be handled completely by the browser without application involvement (e.g., clicking on a field, typing data into it) or through a combination of the browser and application logic (e.g., use of JavaScript to handle events within an HTML page or clicking on a button that sends a request to the Web server for processing).

DIFFERENCES BETWEEN GUI APPLICATIONS AND TRADITIONAL ON-LINE APPLICATIONS

Program Structure

Traditional on-line applications are "screen exchange oriented," that is, an application displays a screen and then processes a user's changes against the screen. The user can see and act on only one screen at a time; the application responds to screen-level events, for example, it is not aware of such things as field entry and exit. Exhibit 8 depicts what happens in such an environment.

On the other hand, event-driven programs or "message-based architectures" are structured in an entirely different way. The code may be executed in a nonsequential order, and the events can be as small as the movement of the mouse or the pressing of a key.

Exhibit 9 depicts what happens when an event-driven program executes. It takes approximately 1 to 5 seconds for the system to process a

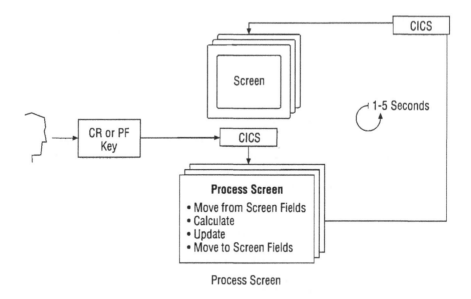

Exhibit 8. Processing Loop in a Traditional On-line Application.

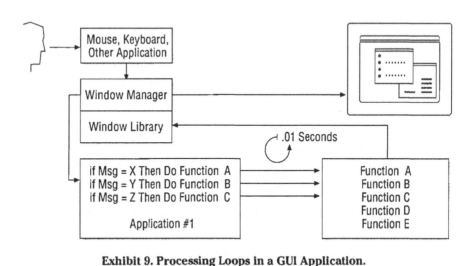

Exhibit 9. Processing Loops in a GUI Application.

user's actions in a traditional environment. In a GUI environment, on the other hand, users may expect to see the system respond to their actions in a fraction of a second. (Imagine waiting 2 seconds for the cursor to change shapes every time the mouse moved.)

Application Responsiveness

GUI applications are much more responsive to user input than traditional systems. For example, on detecting a keystroke (e.g., the letter A or the Tab key), a GUI application can selectively make options available to the user or immediately format data fields.

Application Composition

In most GUI applications, more code is devoted to the user interface than in traditional on-line applications. When coding to the native windowing toolkit, GUI applications require more code to process the complex message routing that is an integral part of window-based applications. With more sophisticated tools or libraries, much of this code is hidden from the applications programmer. However, even in these cases, more code is likely to be required than in a traditional application because of the interactive nature of the GUI and the user expectations of clear and immediate feedback. For example, when a field is invalid, the OK button should be disabled.

GUI COMPONENTS

This section discusses the most commonly encountered GUI components and terminology. These apply to client/server GUI applications and netcentric GUI applications developed with Java. Netcentric applications using HTML forms have a different structure and components and are not covered in this edition of the book.

Windows

Windows are the key component of GUIs. A window is normally defined as an area on the display screen used to present a view of an object or to conduct a dialog with a user. Windows are used to present objects, action options, and messages. Typically, windows have many, if not all, of the components shown in Exhibit 10.

Border

The border is a rectangular outline denoting the limits of the window. It can often be moved to alter the size and shape of the window.

Title Bar

This is the top bar of the window. It is composed of several different areas: the system menu symbol, the window title, and the window sizing buttons.

- *System menu.* The icon in the upper-left-hand corner of the window contains choices that affect the window and other operating environment specific functions. By selecting this icon, a pull-down menu appears with a list of choices.

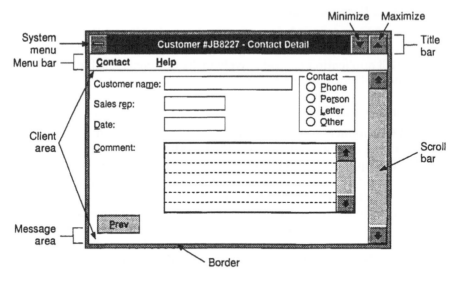

Exhibit 10. A Typical Window.

- *Window title.* This text area in the title bar identifies the window.
- *Minimize button.* This button contains either a small rectangle or an inverted triangle. When it is selected, it reduces the window to an icon.
- *Maximize/restore button.* This button contains a large rectangle, a triangle, or two triangles pointing up and down, depending on the state of the window. It is used to restore the window to its previous size or to the size of the work space.

Menu Bar

This area is just below the title bar and contains routing and action choices. When a choice is selected, a pull-down menu is displayed. A menu bar is sometimes called an action bar.

Scroll Bars

This window component informs a user that more information is available than fits in the window's viewable area. If the object being viewed is wider than the client area, a horizontal scroll bar is provided. If the object being viewed is longer than the client area, a vertical scroll bar is provided. Users can manipulate the scroll bars to change the view currently visible in the scrollable area.

Client Area

The client area is where the user works. It is just below the menu bar and inside the scroll bars. This area can contain graphics, text, and controls.

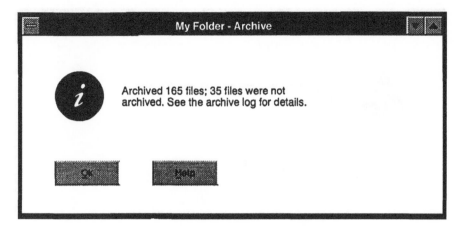

Exhibit 11. An Information Message Box.

Message Area

Some windows contain a message area. The message area is a rectangular region just above the bottom window border. This area can be used to display nondisruptive messages. Often, these messages relate to the status of objects and actions.

Message Box Windows

Message box windows (or message boxes) indicate that an unexpected event has occurred or that additional action is required by the user. To distinguish between these events, three distinct message boxes are commonly used. An icon is usually placed on the window to indicate the type of message being displayed. When a message box is displayed, the user must act on it before continuing to work on any other window within the application.

Information

An information message appears when some situation occurs that the user can do nothing about (Exhibit 11). Often, this window displays a status message concerning the original request. Users can usually request more information about the situation from the help option.

Warning

A warning message is displayed when the user can continue with the original request but should be made aware of some situation (Exhibit 12). Users can continue the request without modification or can choose to stop processing.

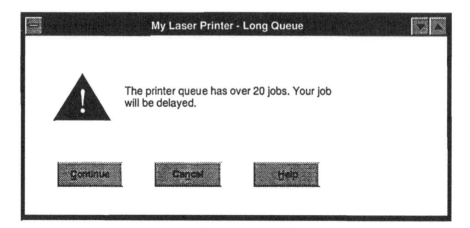

Exhibit 12. A Warning Message Box.

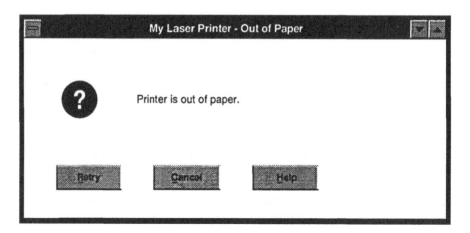

Exhibit 13. An Action Message Box.

Action

An action message is displayed when the user must take some action for processing to continue (Exhibit 13). Users can correct the situation or choose to retry the original request.

Parent and Child Windows

Typically, when a window opens another window, the opening window is called a parent and the opened window is called a child. (There are exceptions to this in which a window opens a "peer" window, but this is less common.) A child window can, in turn, have its own child windows. In fact, any number of child windows can be opened, but the depth of nested windows should be limited to minimize the complexity of the program and the user interface.

From a user's perspective, parent/child relationships define how windows behave. Although this behavior is platform dependent, the following is typically true:

- When a parent is iconized, children are iconized.
- When a parent is closed, children are closed.
- When a parent is moved on the display, children are not moved.

In some environments, such as Microsoft Windows, a child window can be drawn within the borders of its parent. If the user attempts to move the child beyond these borders, only the portion of the child that is still visible within the parent window is displayed. This is called clipping.

Modal and Modeless Windows

Windows can be either "modal" or "modeless" (sometimes called non-modal). These terms refer to the manner in which the user interacts with the window.

A modeless window allows the user to activate other windows within the same application before closing the current window. Users are free to determine sequence and can work with many windows simultaneously. Modeless windows allow users to take full advantage of the GUI.

A modal window, on the other hand, requires users to respond before working in another window. "System modal" behavior locks all windows in the *system*. "Application modal" behavior locks all windows in an *application*. Because modal windows restrict users to working with only one window at a time, they can be used to implement a sequenced processing in a windowed environment.

Active and Inactive Windows

A window is considered active if it has the input "focus." Several windows may be visible, but, if the user types on the keyboard, which window reflects that input? The one with input focus, or the active window. The active window is set apart from other windows with some sort of visual emphasis. The title bar may be highlighted, for example. If a window does not have the input focus, it is considered inactive.

From a user's perspective, only one window may be active at a time. Technically, however, in many modern windowing environments, logic for "inactive" windows may be executing in the background (e.g., spreadsheet recalculation and chart plotting).

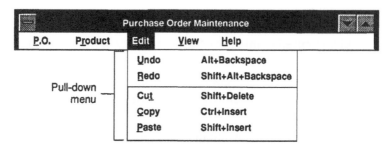

Exhibit 14. Pull-Down Menu.

Menus

Menus are window components that provide users a list of options for making an action, routing, or setting choice. An action choice immediately begins to perform an action, such as Find.

A routing choice displays a menu or window that contains additional choices used to further specify or clarify the routing choice. A setting choice allows a user to change a property of an object. The choices on a menu typically vary depending on the state of the object or application; for instance, charting options only appear when a chart object is selected. Separator lines are used to visually divide groups of choices within a single menu.

There are three menu types that may be combined to meet application requirements.

Pull-Down Menus

Pull-down menus are accessed from the menu bar or the system menu icon (Exhibit 14). These menus typically have action or routing choices that relate to the contents of the window but may also have settings choices.

Cascaded Menus

When a menu choice routes the user to another menu, the resulting menu is called a cascaded menu. These secondary menus usually have settings choices but may have action or routing choices as well. They are used to reduce the length of a menu.

Pop-Up Menus

Pop-up menus provide choices specific to an object. These menus, often displayed next to an object, are not visible until the user requests that the pop-up be displayed (usually with a specific mouse button).

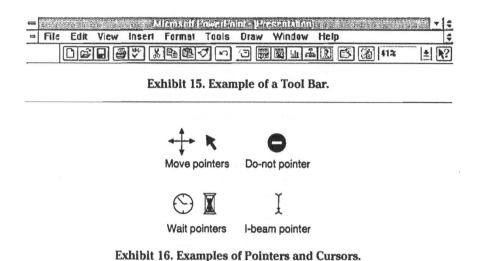

Exhibit 15. Example of a Tool Bar.

Move pointers   Do-not pointer

Wait pointers   I-beam pointer

Exhibit 16. Examples of Pointers and Cursors.

Tool Bars

A tool bar is a graphical area at the top of the window just below the menu bar that contains icons for commonly used functions in the application (Exhibit 15). The action can be invoked by clicking on the toolbar icon instead of pulling down a menu and selecting it from there. Depending on the application, the toolbar may be hard coded or fully customizable.

Client Area Components

The user works in the client area — the area just below the menu bar but inside the scroll bars. This area can contain graphics, text, and controls. Controls (also called "widgets") are predefined graphical images that allow users to enter or select data elements. Often, a control visibly changes appearance to indicate its state. For example, the label of the control may be gray, not black, indicating that the control is currently inactive.

This section lists many of the common controls.

Pointers and Cursors

A pointer is a symbol, often in the shape of an arrow, that is displayed on the screen and is moved by a pointing device. It is used to point or select choices or to otherwise interact with objects (Exhibit 16).

The GUI often comes with a set of predefined pointers to convey specific information. For example, an arrow is used to select or move objects. An hourglass or watch is used to indicate that the user must wait while the

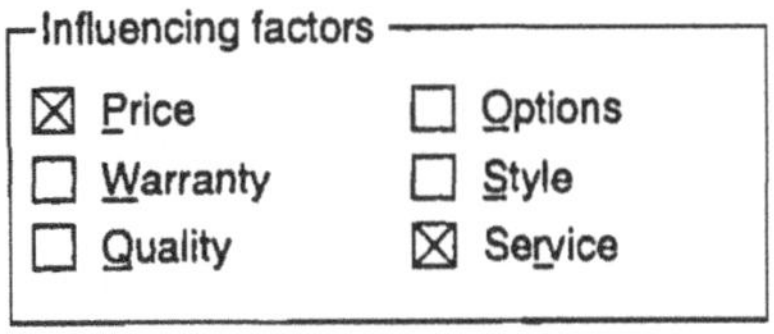

```
┌─Influencing factors ──────────────────┐
│  ☒ Price            ☐ Options          │
│  ☐ Warranty         ☐ Style            │
│  ☐ Quality          ☒ Service          │
└────────────────────────────────────────┘
```

Exhibit 17. Check Boxes.

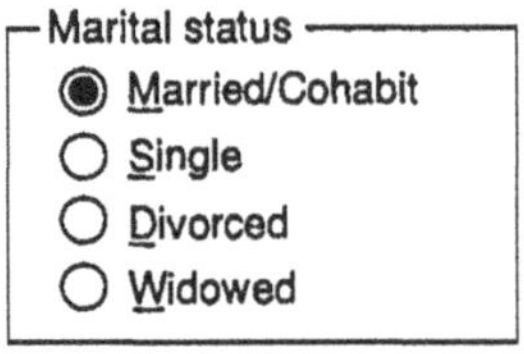

```
┌─Marital status ──────────┐
│  ◉ Married/Cohabit        │
│  ○ Single                 │
│  ○ Divorced               │
│  ○ Widowed                │
└───────────────────────────┘
```

Exhibit 18. Radio Buttons.

computer performs some function. An l-beam pointer indicates that the area in which the pointer currently appears is used for text entry.

Check Box

This control is a simple rectangle with two clearly distinguishable states: checked and not checked (Exhibit 17). It is used to capture and display data of a binary nature (yes/no and on/off). When organized into groups, several of the options can be selected (checked) at once.

Radio Buttons

This control is a simple circle with two clearly distinguishable states: on or off (Exhibit 18). Radio buttons derive their name from the radios of older cars. On these radios, only one button could be pressed at a time. With GUIs, radio buttons are always used in a group to provide a set of mutually exclusive choices. Only one button within a group may be on at a time.

List Box

This control displays a list of objects or settings that a user can view and select (Exhibit 19). List boxes can support single or multiple selection of items in the list. In some environments, this control may be editable.

Single-Line Entry Field

This control is used for the entry of a single line of text. An entry field can be allowed to scroll horizontally if more information is available than is currently visible.

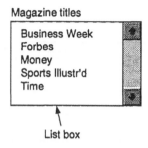

Magazine titles

List box

Exhibit 19. List Box.

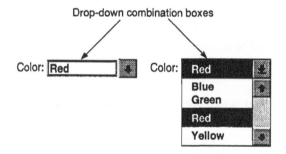

Drop-down combination boxes

Exhibit 20. Drop-Down Combination Box.

Multiple-Line Entry Field

This control is used for the entry of more than one line of text. A multiline entry field can be scrolled horizontally or vertically if more information is available than is currently visible.

Drop-Down Combination Box

This control combines the functions of an entry field and a list box (Exhibit 20). The combination box contains a list of objects or settings that a user can scroll through and select. Alternatively, the user can merely type text into the entry field. The entered text need not match the choices provided in the list.

Group Box

This rectangular box is drawn around a group of fields to indicate that the fields are related (Exhibit 21). It has no behavior of its own. Group boxes usually contain labels or titles.

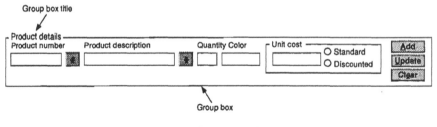

Exhibit 21. Group Box.

Push Button

This control contains text, graphics, or both, representing an action choice or routing choice (e.g., Cancel, Help, Add, Update, and Clear) that is activated when a user selects it. Push buttons and menus are generally the only controls used to invoke an action.

Scroll Bar

This control indicates to a user that more information is available than fits in the scrollable area. If the information being viewed is wider than the specified area, a horizontal scroll bar should be provided. If the information being viewed is taller than the area, a vertical scroll bar should be provided. These bars (see Exhibit 10) are often used in conjunction with other controls such as entry fields, combination boxes, and list boxes.

Having discussed the various components of GUIs, the next section takes a frank look at the challenges facing designers in a GUI environment.

ADVANTAGES OF GUIS

There are at least three advantages of GUIs:

1. They are easier and more satisfying to use, which often leads to reduced training costs.
2. They allow for the integration of different data types.
3. They facilitate business process reengineering

Ease of Use and Reduced Training Costs

Although the benefit that comes from ease of system use is difficult to quantify, it is generally agreed that training costs are lower for GUI applications than for traditional on-line applications. This may be especially important to organizations that have high staff turnover rates and high training costs.

In addition, most people would agree that well-designed GUIs are easier and more satisfying to use. There are many reasons for this belief.

1. *Recognition, not recall.* GUI interfaces allow users to recognize, rather than recall, data (i.e., codes).
2. *Faster response.* GUI applications provide a new, lower level of interaction (keystroke or mouse movement), which allows them to respond more quickly to the user. This responsiveness can reduce errors and enhance user satisfaction.
3. *More intuitive.* GUI interfaces can be more intuitive and can provide visual cues to the user as to operations that are valid, available, and expected.
4. *Better help facilities.* The more robust on-line help available in many GUI applications allows a user to read help text and to simultaneously view the windows he is working in. Moreover, help is often made available through a hypertext mechanism that allows users to select successively more detailed help topics. This gives users faster access to a greater volume of help information.
5. *Support for multiple applications.* Because a windowed environment allows users to view and work on multiple applications simultaneously, it is well suited to professional users who need to switch between applications and tasks more frequently. In addition, GUI applications often make it easy to share text and images between applications and to create new, hybrid documents.

Together, these features make the system easier to learn and use. When designed correctly, a GUI can significantly help the novice or casual user and, at the same time, not penalize the experienced user. In the netcentric world, ease of use and delivery of a positive and effective user–interface experience is critical because the users are customers or business partners.

Integration of Different Data Types

Because GUIs run on graphical displays and utilize a local processor, the platform inherently is suited for the display and manipulation of other types of data types. Video, voice, and many other types of information can be integrated into a GUI application to assist the user in learning about a task, marketing a product or service, or eliminating the handling and routing of information that would otherwise require paper (e.g., a picture of a damaged auto filed with an insurance claim).

Facilitation of Business Process Reengineering

Because GUI applications allow users to do things they were previously unable to do, they can change the type and quality of work produced by their users. For example, GUIs allow auto insurance claims processors to view photographic images of damaged vehicles on-line; office workers can create professional quality documents and presentations without the help of a graphics department; developers, designers, and customers can view and "walk through" a three-dimensional representation of a building's interior before construction actually begins.

In addition, by providing automated support for professionals, it is often possible to reduce or eliminate the need for transcription processes. The insurance agent may now choose to enter information directly into a computer system, eliminating the need for a back office "middle man." Furthermore, with mobile personal computers, the entered information can be used to print a contract instantly in a potential customer's location (e.g., home or office), thus eliminating wasted time and effort otherwise involved in mailings and corrections.

In these examples, GUI technology changes the business process by allowing unnecessary or non-value-added steps to be eliminated and by providing better information and feedback at the point of need. As a result, GUIs are often key enablers in reengineering the business. In many cases, the costs of a GUI are often justified by the value derived from changing the business process rather than from savings in ease of use.

CLIENT/SERVER AND NETCENTRIC GUI CHALLENGES

In addition to these advantages, GUIs also present a number of challenges for designers.

Need for Intelligent Workstation

Because many GUI applications require a substantial amount of local processing, they can run only on intelligent workstations or on network computers. (Network Computers are intelligent devices, usually without disk drives, that download their software from a network — intranet or Internet.) Although the cost of these workstations continues to fall, it is still higher than the cost of standard dumb terminals. As a result, the costs associated with deploying a GUI to first-time users are typically several thousand dollars per user, above and beyond the cost of the development alone. For a small number of users this is probably nothing to worry about. For large-scale implementations, however, the additional cost can be much more significant.

Demanding Design and Usability Testing

Although an effective GUI design makes an application easy for the user, executing an effective design takes considerable time and energy on the part of the developers.

Efficient GUI designs are typically the result of an effort that involves significant participation from users, systems builders, and usability or human factors experts. Discipline and analysis are required to balance the flexibility offered by GUIs with the cost of development and those capabilities that are really useful to users. For example, imagine an airline reservation system for dedicated reservation agents that was based on drag-and-drop GUI techniques. The interface would be wonderful to look at but hardly productive to use 8 hours a day every day.

Allowing sufficient time and budget for usability testing is also more critical for GUI applications than for traditional on-line applications. This is because the GUI interface is more likely to be different from what mainframe applications users are accustomed to.

When users first see a prototype of the system, they are often distracted by the colors and glitz of the new system, and they may not notice any shortcomings in the interface design. It is not until users sit down and actually try to use the system several times to perform an activity that they realize how useful or obstructive the design really is. It is advisable to perform usability tests (using realistic mockups or prototypes) early in the design and construction process so that any significant problems are identified in time to be corrected before release.

Expensive to Develop and Maintain

There are three primary contributors to the high cost associated with GUI applications development. Each of these increases the complexity of the application logic and, correspondingly, the cost of development and maintenance.

GUIs Are Event Driven. GUIs are continually sending, receiving, and responding to messages. In some cases, while processing one message the application may take an action that causes another message to be generated that gets processed immediately, thus invoking another piece of application code before the current function has completed processing.

Moreover, GUI applications typically manage a great number of messages because it is possible to send messages at very low levels of interaction (e.g., when a user presses a character key). This combination of nested messages and the number of possible messages can result in subtle interactions that must be identified and accounted for in the applications design.

Managing Windows and Data Is Complex. Many GUI applications allow users to work in multiple windows simultaneously. Managing these windows and the data they share is complex. For instance, if one window is allowing the user to maintain a customer's address and another window is displaying the shipping address for the same customer, when the customer address is changed and committed to the database, the shipping address window must be updated to reflect this change. Typically, implementing this capability requires custom mechanisms.

There Are More Unit and System Testing Conditions. Development is further complicated by the increased number of unit and system testing conditions that exist in a GUI environment. For example, data validation logic must be tested to ensure that it is invoked when the user exits a field. Similarly, there may be many conditions for enabling and disabling buttons (the OK button, the Add button) that must also be tested. All these conditions must be identified, tested, and verified. Even with automated testing tools, the test planning effort is substantial and should not be overlooked.

Netcentric Performance Challenges

In addition to the challenges discussed, netcentric applications have a unique performance challenge associated with them. Netcentric applications, by their nature, require most (if not all) of the application components to be downloaded at the time a user is interacting with them. Because users of netcentric applications are likely to be using a low-bandwidth connection (probably 28,800 bps or less, although higher speeds are now available) rather than attached to a local area network (10 megabits per second or more), netcentric user interfaces need to take this into account and limit the number of components or their size to ensure the performance of the interface is acceptable. The World Wide Web has occasionally been called the "World Wide Wait" as a result of applications that embed too many graphics or too much complexity (such as large Java applets) into them. Typically, their developers are running these over a local area network and don't see the response times a more typical user will encounter. In addition to limiting graphics and complexity, it is a good practice to test netcentric applications under conditions that more realistically reflect those of an end user's (i.e., over a dialup connection).

APPLICATION STRUCTURE AND SERVICES

Although GUI applications may need to perform the same basic business logic as a traditional application, the way this logic is structured and supported can be substantially different. Some of the greatest differences will be discussed.

Validation

GUI applications usually validate a user's entries at the character or field level. Cross-field dependencies within a window are usually performed on field exit and must take into account the state of each field involved in the validation (e.g., some fields may still be invalid, in which case the cross-field validation cannot be performed). Field dependencies across windows must take into account whether data have been entered in the other windows.

For instance, totaling an order requires that sales tax be calculated, but, if the user has not yet entered customer information (e.g., the state of residence), the tax rate is not available; thus, the calculation is meaningless and probably should not be performed.

Window Flow

Although GUI application window flow is determined to a great degree by the user, for some types of applications it is usually necessary to control the user's flow in some way. For example, in an order entry system, it may be desirable to allow a user to specify the customer information first or go directly to the order entry window. However, the order cannot be completed until the order information *and* the customer information are valid. In this case, the order confirmation window could not be opened until the previous conditions were met.

Essentially, the control is indirect; the user is not forced to take actions but is prevented from taking invalid actions. This type of control is enforced through selective enablement of controls and action choices.

Restart and Recovery

Although restart and recovery strategies are desirable in a GUI environment, they are difficult to implement. At the point of failure, an application may have multiple windows open. Moreover, multiple applications may be open. It can be extremely complex to return all these windows and applications to their exact states before failure. The more typical approach is to allow work in process to be saved periodically during lengthy tasks and to rely on the database management system for data recovery and integrity.

MAKING APPLICATION DEVELOPMENT EASIER

As noted earlier, a number of challenges face the GUI developer. Fortunately, in the past few years, the market for development tools has come a long way in terms of providing common capabilities and services required by GUI applications that allow applications developers to focus more on the business problem than on the basic mechanics expected of any effective GUI application.

Painting the Actual GUI

In today's development environment, designers are likely to paint the actual windows and components of the GUI with a GUI tool such as Visual

Basic, PowerBuilder, or Symantec's Cafe. Following are the primary steps in GUI development:

1. *Lay out the window.* Designers should lay out, or "paint," the window and its various controls (menus, buttons, etc.). Thanks to the GUI tool, designers can rapidly paint the window by selecting types of controls from the basic graphical palette provided by the development software.

2. *Specify display attributes.* Designers should specify the display attributes of the particular controls chosen. For example, the designer might specify the type of field (numeric? alphanumeric?) and the background and foreground colors for entry fields. He or she might select an icon for a label rather than text. For list boxes, the designer might specify different columns and data that would appear within them.

3. *Specify behaviors.* Designers should begin to specify behaviors, that is, how the controls should respond to user input. For example, when the user clicks on a button that reads OK, what should happen? If the user types a valid entry into a field, how should the cross-field validation be invoked?

4. *Run and test.* Run and test the window. Some tools may require a code generation step here. However, most are ready to run the window after it has been painted. At this point, the designer should run the window to test whether it works correctly and then iterate back to step 1 or 2 for new functions and new windows.

The presentation services model has been extremely useful in the establishment of a productive development environment. The model describes the basic functions and features that an application requires to provide the minimum levels of expected GUI behavior.

Systems designers should purchase tools and libraries that provide as many as possible of the features noted subsequently and then supplement them when necessary to provide a base architecture on which GUI applications can be developed. The model and a description of its various components follows.

NETCENTRIC PRESENTATION SERVICES MODEL

The presentation services component of the netcentric architecture enables an application to manage the human–computer interface. This includes capturing user actions and generating events, presenting data to the user, and assisting in the management of the window flow. Typically, presentation services are only required by client workstations.

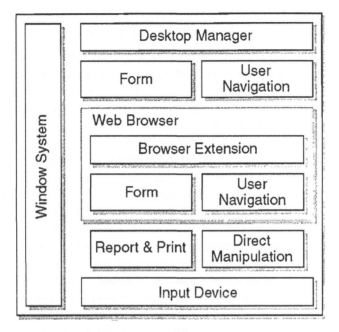

Exhibit 22. Presentation Services.

Exhibit 22 portrays the detailed subservices of Presentation Services:

- Desktop Manager Services
- Direct Manipulation Services
- Form Services
- Input Devices Services
- Report and Print Services
- User Navigation Services
- Web Browser Services
- Window System Services

Desktop Manager Services

Desktop Manager Services provide for implementing the "desktop meta-phor," a style of user interface that tries to emulate the idea of a physical desktop. It allows the user to place documents on the desktop, launch applications by clicking on a graphical icon, or discard files by dragging them onto a picture of a wastebasket. Desktop manager services include facilities for launching applications and desktop utilities and managing their integration. Most windowing systems contain elementary desktop manager functionality (e.g., the Windows 95 desktop), but often more user-friendly or functional desktop manager services are required. Some representative of products that provide desktop manager services include

- *Norton Navigator.* Targeted at users who often interact with the Windows 95 desktop, Norton Navigator provides multiple virtual desktops, enhanced file management, including direct FTP connectivity, long file-name support for some Windows 3.x applications, file unerase, and other features.
- *Microsoft Windows 95 Task Bar.* The user shell environment in Microsoft's Windows 95 interface extends the desktop metaphor by introducing graphical elements such as the launch bar, which allows user to access recently used documents, to launch applications, or to switch between active applications. The Windows 95 desktop and launch bar are programmable, allowing developers to extend and customize the desktop manager for their specific application or user. For example, the desktop can be extended with icons or Start Menu options for creating a new customer account or finding an order.
- *Xerox Tabworks.* This utility presents the user with a notebook metaphor for application and document access; allows creation of tabbed sections that contain related files (e.g., a "Winston Account" or "New Product Launch") for easier access.
- *Starfish Software Dashboard.* This desktop utility is designed to simplify application and system management. It provides quick launch buttons, system resource gauge, drag-and-drop printing and faxing, and a calendar.

Direct Manipulation Services

Direct Manipulation Services enable applications to provide a direct manipulation interface (often called "drag & drop"). A direct manipulation interface allows users to manage multiple "application objects" by manipulating visual representations of those objects. For example, a user may sell stock by dragging "stock" icons out of a "portfolio" icon and onto a "trading floor" icon. Direct Manipulation Services can be further divided into Display and Input/Validation.

- *Display.* These services enable applications to represent application objects as icons and control the display characteristics (color, location, etc.) of these icons.
- *Input/Validation.* These services enable applications to invoke validation or processing logic when an end user "acts on" an application object. "Acting on" an object may include single clicking, double clicking, dragging, or sizing.

Form Services

Form Services enable applications to use fields to display and collect data. A field may be a traditional 3270-style field used to display or input textual data, or it may be a graphical field such as a check box, a list box, or an image. Form Services provide support for

- *Display* — support the display of various data types (e.g., text, numeric, date, etc.) in various formats (e.g., American/European date, double-byte characters, icons, etc.).
- *Input/Validation* — enable applications to collect information from the user, edit it according to the display options, and perform basic validation such as range or format checks.
- *Mapping Support* — eliminate the need for applications to communicate directly with the windowing system; rather, applications retrieve or display data by automatically copying the contents of a window's fields to a copybook structure in memory. These services may also be used to automate the merging of application data with predefined electronic form templates.
- *Field Interaction Management* — coordinate activity across fields in a window by managing field interdependencies and invoking application logic based on the state of fields and user actions. For example, the Field Interaction Manager may disable the "OK" button until all required input fields contain valid data. These services significantly reduce the application logic complexity inherent to an interactive windowed interface.

Input Devices Services

Input devices detect user input from a variety of input technologies, such as pen based, voice recognition, touch-screen, mouse, and digital camera.

Voice response systems are used to provide prompts and responses to users through the use of phones. Voice response systems have scripted call flows, which guide a caller through a series of questions. Based on the user's key pad response, the voice response system can execute simple calculations, make database calls, call a mainframe legacy application, or call out to a custom C routine. Leading voice response system vendors include VoiceTek and Periphonics.

Voice recognition systems are becoming more popular in conjunction with voice response systems. Users are able to speak to the phone in addition to using a keypad. Voice recognition can be an extremely powerful technology in cases where a key pad entry would be limiting (e.g., date/time or location). Sophisticated voice recognition systems have been built that support speaker independence, continuous speech, and large vocabularies.

Report and Print Services

Report and Print Services support the creation and on-screen previewing of paper or photographic documents that contain screen data, application data, graphics, or images.

Printing services must take into consideration varying print scenarios common in netcentric environments, including varying graphics/file types (Adobe .PDF, .GIF, .JPEG), page margins and breaks, HTML constructs including tables and frames, headers/titles, extended character set support, etc.

Buy vs. Build Considerations

There are numerous packaged controls on the market today that support basic report and print capability. However, a careful evaluation of both functions and features and vendor viability must be completed before a decision can be made. Architects must additionally be sure to evaluate that controls will support all required environments and are small in size and extensible as requirements demand.

User Navigation Services

User Navigation Services provide a user with a way to access or navigate between functions within or across applications. Historically, this has been the role of a text-based menuing system that provides a list of applications or activities for the user to choose from.

Client/server technologies introduced new navigation metaphors. A common method for allowing a user to navigate within an application is to list available functions or information by means of a menu bar with associated pull-down menus or context-sensitive pop-up menus. This method conserves screen real estate by hiding functions and options within menus but for this very reason can be more difficult for first time or infrequent users. This point is important when implementing electronic commerce solutions where the target customer may use the application only once or very infrequently (e.g., purchasing auto insurance).

Additionally, client/server development tools such as Visual Basic and PowerBuilder do not provide specific services for graphical navigation, but the effect can be recreated by selecting (i.e., clicking on) graphical controls, such as picture controls or iconic push buttons, programmed to launch a particular window.

Web Browser Services

Web Browser Services allow users to view and interact with applications and documents made up of varying data types, such as text, graphics, and audio. These services also provide support for navigation within and across documents no matter where they are located through the use of links embedded into the document content. Much of the appeal of the Web browsers is the ability to provide a "universal client" that offers users a consistent and familiar user interface from which all types of applications can be executed and all types of documents can be viewed, regardless of the type of operating system or machine as well as independent of where these applications and documents reside. Browsers employ standard protocols, such as Hypertext Transfer Protocol (HTTP) and File Transfer Protofocol (FTP) to provide seamless access to documents across machine and network boundaries.

Examples of products that provide browser services include

- *Netscape Navigator.* One of the original browsers, Navigator currently has a large share of the installed browser market and strong developer support.
- *Microsoft Internet Explorer (IE).* Leveraging the market strength of Windows, Internet Explorer is tightly integrated with Windows and supports the major features of the Netscape Navigator as well as Microsoft's own ActiveX technologies.

It should be noted that the distinction between desktop and Web browser may well disappear with the release of products that integrate Web browsing into the desktop and give a user the ability to view directories as though they were Web pages. Web browser, as a distinct entity, may even fade away with time.

Browsers require new or at least revised development tools for working with new languages and standards such as HTML and Java. Many browser content development tools have flooded the market recently. The following are several representative products that provide browser services:

- *Netscape LiveWire and LiveWire Pro* — visual tool suite designed for building and managing complex, dynamic Web sites and creating live on-line applications.
- *Symantec Visual Café* — the first complete Rapid Application Development (RAD) environment for Java. With Visual Café one can assemble complete Java applets and applications from a library of standard and third party objects, without writing source code, for very simple applications. Visual Café also provides an extensive set of text based development tools.
- *Microsoft FrontPage* — provides an integrated development environment for building Web sites, including WebBots, which provide services for implementing common features such as search engines and discussion groups.

- *Microsoft Visual J++* — a product similar to Visual C++, VJ++ allows the construction of Java applications through an integrated graphical development environment.

Web Browser services can be further subdivided into

- Browser Extension Services
- Form Services
- User Navigation Services

Browser Extension Services

Browser Extension Services provide support for executing different types of applications from within a Browser. These applications provide functionality that extend Browser capabilities. The key Browser Extensions are

- *Plug-in* — a term coined by Netscape, a plug-in is a software program that is specifically written to be executed within a browser for the purpose of providing additional functionality that is not natively supported by the browser, such as viewing and playing unique data or media types. For example, early browsers did not natively support multimedia data types such as sound. Sound plug-ins were used by the browser to play back the sound component of a document. Other plug-ins allow mainframe 3270-based applications to be viewed directly or mapped into a more friendly form style interface. Plug-ins cover everything from streaming video to interactive conferencing, and new ones are being released every week. Typically, to use a plug-in, a user is required to download and install the plug-in on his/her client machine. Once the plug-in is installed, it is integrated into the Web browser. The next time a browser opens a Web page that requires that plug-in to view a specific data format, the browser initiates the execution of the plug-in. Special plug-in APIs are used when developing plug-ins. Until recently plug-ins were only accessible from the Netscape browser. Now, other browsers such as Microsoft's Internet Explorer are beginning to support plug-in technology as well. However, plug-ins written for one browser will generally need to be modified to work with other browsers. Also, plug-ins are operating system dependent. Therefore, separate versions of a plug-in are required to support Windows, Macintosh, and Unix platforms.
- *Helper Application/Viewer* — is a software program that is launched from a browser for the purpose of providing additional functionality to the browser. The key differences between a helper application (sometimes called a viewer) and a plug-in are
  How the program is integrated with the Web browser — unlike a plug-in, a helper application is not integrated with the Web browser, although it is launched from a Web browser. A helper application generally runs in its own window, contrary to a plug-in, which is generally integrated into a Web page.

How the program is installed — like a plug-in, the user installs the helper application. However, because the helper application is not integrated with the browser, the user tends to do more work during installation specifying additional information needed by the browser to launch the helper application.

How the program is initiated — the user tends to initiate the launching of the helper application, unlike a plug-in where the browser does the initiation.

From where the program is executed — the same helper application can be executed from a variety of browsers without any updates to the program, unlike a plug-in, which generally needs to be updated for specific browsers. However, helper applications are still operating system dependent.

- *Java applet* — a program written in Java that runs within or is launched from the client's browser. This program is loaded into the client device's memory at runtime and then unloaded when the application shuts down. A Java applet can be as simple as an animated object on an HTML page or can be as complex as a complete windows application running within the browser.

- *ActiveX control* — is also a program that can be run within a browser, from an application independent of a browser, or on its own. ActiveX controls are components, developed using Microsoft's standards that define how software components should be built. Although Microsoft is positioning ActiveX controls to be language and platform independent, today they are limited to the Intel platforms. Within the context of a browser, ActiveX controls add functionality to Web pages. These controls can be written to add new features such as dynamic charts, animation, or audio. Plug-ins and ActiveX controls are functionally similar, but ActiveX controls provide more functionality, such as a self-installing capability.

- *JavaBeans* — JavaSoft's (i.e., Sun's Java development and marketing unit) counterpart to ActiveX controls, based on CORBA standards. JavaBeans can also be anything from small visual controls, such as a button or a date field, to full-fledged applications, such as word processors, spreadsheets, browsers, etc.

Viewers and plug-ins are some of the most dynamic segments of the browser market due to quickly changing technologies and companies. What was yesterday's plug-in or viewer add-on often becomes a built-in capability of the browser in its next release.

The following are examples of plug-in execution products:

- *Real Audio* — a plug-in designed to play audio in real-time on the Internet without needing to download the entire audio file before you can begin listening.

- *VDOLive* — a plug-in designed to view real-time video streams on the Internet without needing to download the entire video file before you can begin viewing; similar in concept to Real Audio.
- *Macromedia Shockwave* — a plug-in used to play back complex multimedia documents created using Macromedia Director or other products.
- *Internet Phone* — one of several applications that allow two-way voice conversation over the Internet, similar to a telephone call.
- *Information Builder's Web3270* — a plug-in that allows mainframe 3270-based applications to be viewed across the Internet from within a browser. The Web3270 server provides translation services to transform a standard 3270 screen into an HTML-based form. Interest in Web3270 and similar plug-ins has increased with the Internet's ability to provide customers and trading partners direct access to an organization's applications and data. "Screen scraping" viewers can bring legacy applications to the Internet or intranet very quickly.

Form Services

Like Form Services outside the Web Browser, Form Services within the Web Browser enable applications to use fields to display and collect data. The only difference is the technology used to develop the Forms. The most common type of Forms within a browser are HTML Forms. The HTML standard includes tags for informing a compliant browser that the bracketed information is to be displayed as an editable field, a radio button, or other form-type control. Currently, HTML browsers support only the most rudimentary forms, basically providing the presentation and collection of data without validation or mapping support. When implementing Forms with HTML, additional services may be required such as client side scripting (e.g., VB Script or JavaScript).

Additionally, Microsoft has introduced ActiveX documents that allow Forms such as Word documents, Excel spreadsheets, and Visual Basic windows to be viewed directly from Internet Explorer just like HTML pages.

Today different technologies are used to create Forms that are accessible outside of the browser from those that are accessible within the browser. However, with the introduction of ActiveX documents, these differences are getting narrower.

User Navigation Services

Like User Navigation Services outside the Web Browser, User Navigation Services within the Web Browser provide a user with a way to access or navigate between functions within or across applications. These User Navigation Services can be subdivided into three categories:

1. *Customized Menu.* A common method for allowing a user to navigate within an application is to list available functions or information by means of a menu bar with associated pull-down menus or context-sensitive pop-up menus. This method conserves screen real estate by hiding functions and options within menus, but for this very reason it can be more difficult for first time or infrequent users. This point is important when implementing electronic commerce solutions in which the target customer may use the application only once or very infrequently (e.g., pricing and purchasing auto insurance). Also, browsers themselves can be programmed to support customized menus. This capability might be more applicable for intranet environments where the browsers need to be customized for specific business applications.

2. *Hyperlink.* The Internet has popularized the use underlined key words, icons, and pictures that act as links to additional pages. The hyperlink mechanism is not constrained to a menu but can be used anywhere within a page or document to provide the user with navigation options. It can also take a user to another location within the same document or a different document altogether or even a different server or company for that matter. There are three types of hyperlinks: hypertext, icon, and image map.

   • *Hypertext* is very similar to the concept of "Context Sensitive Help" in Windows, where the reader can move from one topic to another by selecting a highlighted word or phrase.

   • *Icon* is similar to the hypertext menu above, but selections are represented as a series of icons. The HTML standard and popular browsers provide hyperlinking services for nontext items such as graphics.

   • *Image Map* is also similar to the hypertext menu, but selections are represented as a series of pictures. A further evolution of image map menu is to display an image depicting some place or thing (e.g., a picture of a bank branch with tellers and loan officers).

Client/server development tools such as Visual Basic and Power-Builder do not provide specific services for image map navigation, but the effect can be recreated using graphical controls (such as picture controls or iconic push buttons) programmed to launch a particular window when clicked on. The hyperlink metaphor makes it possible for the user to jump from topic to topic instead of reading the document from beginning to end. For many types of applications, this can create a more user-friendly interface, enabling the user to find information faster. An image map menu can be useful where all users share some visual model for how business is conducted and can be very engaging but also painfully slow if a slow or even moderate speed communications connection is required. Additional Image Map services are required to map the location of user mouse clicks within the image to the corresponding page or window which is to be launched.

3. *Virtual Reality.* A virtual reality or virtual environment interface takes the idea of a graphical map to the next level by creating a three-dimensional environment for the user to "walk" around in. Popularized by such PC games as Doom, the virtual environment interface can be used for business applications. The consumer can walk through a shopping mall and into and around virtual stores or "fly" around a three-dimensional (3D) virtual version of a resort complex being considered for holiday.

To create sophisticated user navigation interfaces such as these requires additional architectural services and languages. The Virtual Reality Modeling Language (VRML) is one such language gaining in popularity. Additionally, many tool kits and code libraries are available to speed development. The following are representative products that provide or can be used to implement virtual environment services:

- *Silicon Graphics Open Inventor.* This object-oriented 3D toolkit is used to build interactive 3D graphics using such objects as cameras, lights, and 3D viewers and provides a simple event model and animation engines.
- *VREAM VRCreator.* This is a toolkit for building interactive virtual reality environments. It supports gravity, elasticity, and throwability of objects, textured and colored 3D objects, and construction of networked multiparticipant worlds. It provides support under Windows for DDE and ActiveX.
- *Dimension X Liquid Reality.* This set of Java class libraries comprise a VRML toolkit that can be used to build VRML viewers and tools and is extensible using Java to create custom virtual reality (VR) environment viewers.

Window System

Typically, part of the operating systems, the Window System contains the base functionality for creating and managing a GUI: detecting user actions, manipulating windows on the display, and displaying information through windows and graphical controls. Examples of windowing systems include Microsoft Windows, Windows 95/98 and Windows NT, Macintosh OS, Presentation Manager for OS/2, and X-Windows/Motif.

Window Systems expose their functionality to application programs through a set of APIs. For the Microsoft windowing platforms, this API is called Win32, a documented set of over 400 C functions that allow developers to access the functionality of the windowing system as well as various other operating system functions. Developers are able to call the Win32 API or its equivalent on other platforms directly, using a C language compiler; however, most development is done using higher-level development languages, such as Visual Basic or PowerBuilder, which make the lower level calls to the operating systems on behalf of the developer.

Chapter 5
Information Services

"Information" in today's client/server and netcentric environment is much broader and diverse in nature than traditional data, that is, data that were understood as characters. Information, or "knowledge," as we characterized it in the introduction to this book, can consist of many things in today's computing solutions, including graphics, image, voice, and full-motion video. This information is extremely complex and difficult to manage, control, and deliver.

The information challenge of the workplace today is the "feast-or-famine" syndrome: workers often cannot find information when they need it, or they may be confronted by too much information at any given time. Information is of no use unless we know where it is and how to get at it. Information Services are where that access is achieved. (Note that, although there are many useful distinctions to be made between the words "data," "information," and "knowledge," this chapter will use both the words data and information to refer to the knowledge or content being managed in a netcentric environment.)

In a traditional computing environment, an organization's information is usually centralized in a particular location, or it may be fragmented across multiple locations. In a netcentric environment, however, information is most often distributed because distribution of processors and data is an inherent part of the new styles of and netcentric computing.

Exhibit 1 presents an example of how information may be distributed in a netcentric computing environment. In this example from an airline information system, the reservations are centralized in Dallas. Each region has a server to maintain its own flights and maintenance information (horizontally segmented by region), and each workstation at each region maintains replicated airport and plane data. In general, the following may be said about the information within this system:

- Information that is stable or static is often found on all clients.
- Information that is volatile or specific to particular locations or groups is on the server.
- Information that is accessed and updated throughout the organization is on the central system, or enterprise system.

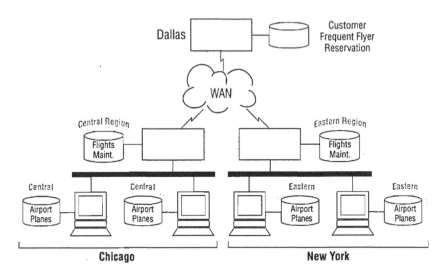

Exhibit 1. Example of Distribution of Information.

- Most information (except, perhaps, for some static codes tables) is stored on the server, although the processing may be distributed across client and server.
- Putting information on a client may require information replication across clients (usually limited to codes tables) and could lead to synchronization and integrity issues.

CHARACTERISTICS OF INFORMATION IN NETCENTRIC COMPUTING

The example illustrates the primary characteristics of information in a client/server and netcentric computing environment.

Information Is Distinct from Processes

The most important characteristic of information is that it is kept distinct from the processes that access and use it. The chief function of the netcentric architecture is to isolate the business logic from the technology itself. Within the Information Services component of the architecture, this isolation is achieved by maintaining two layers, a logical layer and a physical layer.

- From a logical viewpoint, an application issues a request for information, and elements of that information (e.g., location, formats, and management mechanisms) are transparent to the user. A single information request is all that is necessary to retrieve the information, potentially from multiple sources, to support a business function.

- From a physical viewpoint, the information may actually be stored on, and retrieved from, many different sources that are being managed by many different database managers on many different platforms.

Information Is Usually Distributed

Distributed information can be defined formally as "information that is physically separated between locations or platforms." Netcentric computing does not imply distributed information nor does distributed information imply netcentric computing. However, most client/server and netcentric systems rely on some form of distributed information.

Client/server and netcentric computing implies more processing locations (geographic and platform) with local disk storage capabilities. Because information should reside close to the users who need to access that information, information distribution offers important advantages, discussed subsequently.

Information Is Spread Across Multiple Environments

Because of the distributed nature of information in a netcentric computing environment, organizations often have to deal with a multivendor environment. This places demands on the networking and communications aspects of the netcentric architecture.

Information Is in Multiple Forms

The graphical environment of today's applications and the ability to send different types of information (e.g., data, graphic, image, voice, or video) directly to the desktop have made the information environment of client/server and netcentric computing much more complex.

Information May Be Replicated or Duplicated

Because information is generally distributed in the netcentric architecture, it often means that information must be replicated across multiple locations. The existence of multiple copies of information means that users must be especially concerned with keeping them synchronized and accurate.

Replication of information implies methods to perform the replication, additional disk resources, possible integrity problems because of multiple copies, and information management and ownership issues. These issues are addressed later in this chapter.

Information Is Often Fragmented or Segmented

Because information accessed by an application is heterogeneous and dispersed, it is often fragmented. The information may be recombined in various ways, and so the Information Services component of the netcentric architecture must have a way of ensuring the integrity of the information in its various combinations.

ISSUES IN THE DISTRIBUTION OF INFORMATION

The ultimate goal of distributed information processing is to give every user transparent access to dispersed, disparate information. With client/server and netcentric computing, developers seek to isolate applications from knowledge of information location, information access methods, and information management products. At the same time, they seek to ensure that the information is reliable, i.e., that it has integrity.

When to Consider a Distributed Database Strategy

When particular business functions have certain characteristics, distributed information and distributed information processing may be considered:

1. *Geographical distribution.* The business functions are spread over several different sites, making it impractical to support some (or all) of the processing requirements from a central site.
2. *Local decision making and independence.* The organizational structure is distributed and the business has several local sites with the authority to make local decisions as to how to process and act upon its information.
3. *Performance.* The response time at the local site becomes unacceptable due to the transfer of data between the central and local sites.
4. *Scalability.* Business growth has caused the volume of data to expand, the volume of processing to increase, or has resulted in expansion to new sites.

Potential Benefits

The potential benefits for a distributed database strategy apply both to true distributed database management systems and to implementations that incorporate distributed data management strategies.

Organization. A distributed system may better reflect an organization's structure, which often is logically distributed (e.g., into divisions, departments, and projects) as well as physically distributed (e.g., into plants, warehouses, and branch offices).

Ease of Growth. Once installed, a distributed system is able to expand more gracefully than a nondistributed system. For example, if significant business growth has caused the volume of information to expand or the volume of processing to increase, it may be easier to expand the system by adding a new site to an existing distributed system than by replacing or extending an existing centralized system with a larger one.

Lower Costs. It may be less expensive for organizations to add another server or to extend the server than to add or extend a mainframe.

Local Autonomy. Distributing a system allows individual groups within an organization to exercise control over their own information while still being able to access information at remote locations when necessary.

Increased Availability. A distributed system may offer greater availability than a centralized system in that it can continue to function (though at a reduced level) even if an individual site or communication link has failed. Also, with the support of replicated information, availability is improved in that a replicated information object remains available as long as at least one copy of that object is available.

Increased Efficiency. Response times can be reduced because information in a distributed system can be stored close to its point of use, enabling most information accesses to be local.

Increased Flexibility. Information can be dynamically moved or replicated, existing copies can be deleted, or new information types can be added to accommodate changes in how the information is used.

Potential Challenges

Although distribution of information throughout a system has many benefits, it must overcome a number of challenges, as well.

Complex Architectural-Level Communications. In these systems, messages containing information, processing requests, and acknowledgments of previous requests are passed continuously among various remote sites. Coordinating this message flow is complex and can be costly.

Complex Update Control. If two users update the same piece of information, a method must be found to mediate conflicts. One way to ensure information integrity is to employ a locking mechanism. However, the locking strategy becomes more challenging as machines are added; network failure must be taken into consideration. Added complexity also arises with distributed transactions, where one user updates two data sources simultaneously, and both updates must occur in synch.

Network Dependency. When data are distributed across the network, reliable communications between sites are required or processing may be halted. This increased reliability may require expensive duplication of network resources to provide an acceptable amount of system availability for the users.

Complexity of "Location Transparency." In the ideal distributed information environment, the end user or application programmer has access to all required information without having to know where that information is physically located. This feature is known as location transparency and it is supported by some of the database management system (DBMS) products currently available. This places a substantial burden on the architecture and its designers to locate the information efficiently and to transport the information to the application on request, without excessive processing delays.

Location Transparency also Complicates User Support. A user problem within a single application may originate from any number of remote sites that are transparent to the user, making the problem more difficult to identify and resolve.

Information Synchronization. Maintenance of redundant information over multiple sites and processors increases the complexity of information synchronization routines. Complex time synchronization between separate machines may be required.

Organizations must be aware of what their synchronization requirements are. Timing is one example of a synchronization challenge. When does information need to be synchronized? In real time? Overnight? Several techniques for performing information synchronization efficiently are discussed later.

Changes in Organizational Structure. Changes in the existing organizational structure could invalidate the information design. With distributed information, one must build in flexibility to change as the organization changes.

Security. Managing access to information and preventing unauthorized access are greater challenges in client/server and netcentric computing than in a centralized environment. Complexity here is a result of the distributed nature of system components (hardware, software, and data).

Information Transformation. Because information is on multiple platforms and multiple management environments, the information must be transformed from one format or type to another. Some information types may be supported in one environment and not in another.

Information Management. Distributed information is more difficult to manage, creating challenges for backup and recovery of information and for overall information integrity.

Heterogeneous Environments. Client/server and netcentric information may be on multiple databases, file systems, and hardware platform, connected by multiple network protocols.

Rules for Design

"Location transparency" is a key to successful information design in client/server and netcentric computing. Database expert C.J. Date puts this principle another way: To a user, a distributed system should look exactly like a nondistributed system. The user or programmer who accesses and manipulates information should be able to do so logically through a single access, as if it were all managed by a single DBMS on a single machine.

From this underlying principle, Date sets forth 12 related rules for distributed data design, or distributed information design. Date's guidelines are helpful in designing overall information access in a netcentric architecture, although it is unlikely that any system will conform to all 12 of these rules. Most organizations focus on the need to achieve local autonomy and the need for information independence.

The 12 rules follow.

Local Autonomy. All operations at any particular site should be controlled by that site and not dependent on another site to function. Each local site owns and manages its own information, and each site is therefore responsible for the accuracy, security, and integrity of that information.

No Reliance on a Central Site. A corollary of rule 1, this rule is necessary to prevent bottlenecks and the potential vulnerability of relying on a central site.

Continuous Operation. Planned system shutdowns should never be necessary. Good design means that maintenance, database administration and operations, and upgrades should take place without shutting down the system.

Location Independence. Users and applications should be able to access remote information as if it were local. This simplifies application design and permits information to be moved around without causing changes to existing applications.

Segmentation Independence. If an information relation can be separated into segments for physical storage and access, the distributed database design should support storing the segments at the location where they are used most frequently. Users should be able to access any information logically as if it were not segmented at all.

Replication Independence. Replication of information should be transparent to the users and to the application. Access proceeds logically as if there is only one copy of the information.

Distributed Query Processing. Users should be able to make a single query across multiple physical information locations.

Distributed Transaction Management. The system should provide a single point of entry for the transaction, even if the transaction involves information from multiple sites to complete the business function.

Hardware Independence. Client/server and netcentric systems include a variety of machines. The system must be able to present a "single-system image" of the database to the user, while allowing different hardware systems to participate as partners in the system.

Operating System Independence. Systems with heterogeneous hardware may use more than one operating system. The information should be able to allow all operating systems to participate in the same distributed system.

Network Independence. In a client/server or netcentric system, multiple communications systems must be able to operate together, transparently to users and application designers.

DBMS Independence. Many system installations have different types of DBMSs. Thus, it is vital that they all support the same interface and that they can interoperate.

Meeting these challenges of distributed information is the function of the Information Services component of the netcentric architecture.

INFORMATION SERVICES FRAMEWORK

A two-layer approach is useful to keep information distinct from the processes that access and use it: a logical layer and a physical layer. Within the netcentric architecture, the Information Services component maintains this logical/physical distinction (Exhibit 2).

Logical Layer

The logical layer acts to isolate the physical aspects of information (e.g., location, storage format, and access language) from applications and applications developers. This layer provides all the detail services associated with information and with access to or from that information.

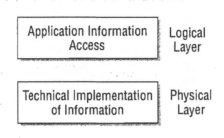

Exhibit 2. Logical and Physical Layers.

Physical Layer

The physical layer can be used within a netcentric architecture to isolate the detailed technical implementations of information. This layer insulates an organization and its applications from the rapid pace of change in information management technology. This layer can also be used to position legacy information sources into the netcentric computing environment, independent from migrating applications and implementing new applications.

DATABASE SERVICES

Database Services are responsible for providing access to a local or a remote database, maintaining integrity of the data within the database, and supporting the ability to store data on either a single physical platform, or in some cases across multiple platforms. These services are typically provided by DBMS vendors and accessed via embedded or call-level SQL variants and supersets. Depending upon the underlying storage model, non-SQL access methods may be used instead.

Many netcentric applications today are broadcast-type applications, designed to market a company's products and/or publish the company's policies and procedures. Furthermore, there is now a growth of netcentric applications that are transaction-type applications used to process a customer's sales order, maintenance request, etc. Typically, these types of applications require integration with a database manager. Database Services include Replication/Synchronization Services, Access Services, Security Services, Indexing Services, and Storage Services.

Replication/Synchronization Services

Replication Services support an environment in which multiple copies of databases must be maintained. For example, if ad hoc reporting queries or operational data stores can work with a replica of the transaction database, these resource intensive applications will not interfere with mission-critical transaction processing. Replication can be either complete or partial. During complete replication all records are copied from one destination to another; during partial replication, only a subset of data is copied, as specified by the user or the program. Replication can also be done either real time or on demand (i.e., initiated by a user, program, or scheduler). The following might be possible if databases are replicated on alternate server(s):

- Better availability or recoverability of distributed applications
- Better performance and reduced network cost, particularly in environments where users are widely geographically dispersed
- Improved access to wider ranges of data, as data replicas may be more readily available

Synchronization Services perform the transactions required to make consistent one or more information sources that are intended to mirror each other. This function is especially valuable when implementing applications for remote users or users of mobile devices because it allows a working copy of data or documents to be available locally without a constant network attachment. The emergence of applications that allow teams to collaborate and share knowledge (e.g., the Knowledge Xchange® at Accenture) has heightened the need for Synchronization Services in the execution architecture.

The terms Replication and Synchronization are used interchangeably, depending on the vendor, article, book, etc. For example, when Lotus Notes refers to Replication, it means both a combination of Replication and Synchronization Services described previously. When Sybase refers to Replication, it only means copying data from one source to another.

Access Services

Access Services enable an application to retrieve data from a database as well as manipulate (insert, update, and delete) data in a database. SQL is the primary approach for accessing records in today's DBMSs.

Client–server and netcentric systems often require data access from multiple databases offered by different vendors. This is often due to integration of new systems with existing legacy systems. The key architectural concern is in building the application where the multivendor data problem is transparent to the application needing the data. This provides future portability and flexibility and also makes it easier for application developers to write to a single database access interface. Achieving database access transparency requires the following.

Standards-Based SQL API. This approach uses a single, standards based set of APIs to access any database and includes the following technologies: Open Database Connectivity (ODBC), Java Database Connectivity (JDBC), and Object Linking and Embedding (OLE DB).

SQL Gateways. These provide a mechanism for clients to transparently access data in a variety of databases (e.g., Oracle, Sybase, or DB2) by translating SQL calls written using the format and protocols of the gateway server or primary server to the format and protocols of the target database. Currently there are three contending architectures for providing gateway functions.

Distributed Relational Data Access (DRDA). This is a standard promoted by IBM for distributed data access between heterogeneous databases. In this case the conversion of the format and protocols occurs only once. It supports SQL89 and a subset of the SQL92 standard and is built on top on APPC/APPN and TCP/IP transport stacks.

IBI's EDA/SQL and the Sybase/MDI Open Server. These use SQL to access relational and nonrelational database systems. They use API/SQL or T-SQL, respectively, as the standard interface language. A large number of communication protocols are supported, including NetBIOS, SNA, DecNET, and TCP/IP. The main engine translates the client requests into specific server calls. It handles security, authentication, statistics gathering, and some system management tasks.

Security Services

Security Services enforce access control to ensure that records are only visible or editable by authorized people for approved purposes. Most DBMSs provide access control at the database, table, or row level as well as concurrency control. However, there may be severe limitations in the DBMS's ability to pass data needed for security authentication across a network, forcing the architect to build those services into the Security Services layer.

Indexing Services

Indexing Services provide a mechanism for speeding up data retrieval. In relational databases, one or more fields can be used to construct the index. Therefore, when a user searches for a specific record, the index is used to find the location of that record, which is faster scanning the whole table sequentially. Revolutionary advances in indexing techniques — such as bitmapped indexing, context indexing, and star indexes — provide rich capabilities for netcentric computing.

Storage Services

Storage Services manage the physical storage of data. These services provide a mechanism for saving information so that data will live beyond program execution. Data are often stored in relational format (an RDBMS) but may also be stored in an object-oriented format (OODBMS) or other formats such as IMS or VSAM.

DOCUMENT SERVICES

Document Services provide similar structure and control for documents that DBMSs apply to record-oriented data. A document is defined as a collection of objects potentially of different types (e.g., structured data, unstructured data, images, multimedia) a business user deals with. An individual document might be a table created using a spreadsheet package, a report created using a word processing package, a Web page created using an HTML authoring tool, unstructured text, or a combination of these object types. Regardless of the software used to create and maintain the component parts, all parts together constitute the document, which is managed as a single entity.

Netcentric applications that are executed from a browser are particularly well suited for serving up document style information. If the Web application consists of more than just a few HTML documents, integration with a document management system should be considered. Document Services include Replication/Synchronization Services, Access Services, Indexing Services Security Services, Storage Services, and Versioning Services (see Exhibit 3).

Replication/Synchronization Services

Replication Services support an environment in which multiple copies of documents must be maintained. A key objective is that documents should be shareable and searchable across the entire organization. Therefore, the architecture needs to *logically* provide a single repository, even though the documents are *physically* stored in different locations. Replicating documents on alternative server(s) may have some benefits: better availability or recoverability of a distributed application, better performance, reduced network cost, or increased information access and availability.

Synchronization Services perform the transactions required to make consistent one or more information sources that are intended to mirror each other. They support the needs of intermittently connected users or sites. As with databases, these services are especially valuable for users of remote or mobile devices that need be able to work locally without a constant network connection and then be able to synchronize with the central server at a given point in time.

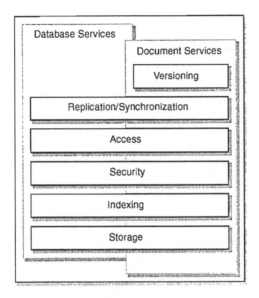

Exhibit 3. Information Services Framework.

Access Services

Access Services support document creation, maintenance, and retrieval. These services allow users to capture knowledge or content through the creation of unstructured information, i.e., documents. Access Services allow users to effectively retrieve documents that were created by them and documents that were created by others. Documents can be comprised of many different data types, including text, charts, graphics, or even audio and video.

Indexing Services

Locating documents, as well as content within documents, is a more complex problem and involves several alternative methods. The Windows file manager is a simplistic implementation of a hierarchical organization of files and collections of files. If the user model of where documents should be stored and found can be represented in this way, the use of structure and naming standards can be sufficient. However, a hierarchical document-filing organization is not suitable for many types of document queries (e.g., retrieving all sales order documents for over $1,000).

Therefore, most document management products provide index services that support the following methods for searching document repositories:

- *Attribute Search.* Scans short lists (attributes) of important words that are associated with a document and returns documents that match the search criteria. For example, a user may query for documents written by a specific author or created on a particular date. Attribute search brings the capabilities of the SQL-oriented database approach to finding documents by storing in a database the values of specially identified fields within a document and a reference to the actual document itself. To support Attribute Search, an index maintains document attributes, which it uses to manage, find, and catalog documents. This is the least complicated approach of the searching methods.
- *Full-text Search.* Searches repository contents for exact words or phrases and returns documents that match the search criteria. To facilitate Full-text Search, full-text indexes are constructed by scanning documents once and recording in an index file which words occur in which documents. Leading document management systems have full-text search services built-in, which can be integrated directly into applications.
- *Context Search:* Searches repository contents for exact words or phrases. It also searches for related words or phrases by using synonyms and word taxonomies. For example, if the user searches for *auto*, the search engine should look for *car, automobile, motor vehicle*, etc.
- *Boolean Search:* Searches repository contents for words or phases that are joined together using boolean operators (e.g., AND, OR, or NOT). The same type of indexes are used for Boolean Search as for Full-Text Search.

Security Services

Documents should be accessed exclusively through Document Services. If a document is checked in, checked out, routed, viewed, annotated, archived, or printed, it should be done only by users with the correct security privileges. Those access privileges should be able to be controlled by user, role, and group. Analogous to record locking to prevent two users from editing the same data, document management access control services include check-in/check-out services to limit concurrent editing.

Storage Services

Storage Services manage the physical storage of documents. Most document management products store documents as objects that include two basic data types: attributes and content. Document attributes are key fields used to identify the document, such as author name or created date. Document content refers to the actual unstructured information stored within the document. Generally, the documents are stored in a repository using one of the following methods:

- *Proprietary database.* Documents (attributes and contents) are stored in a proprietary database, one that the vendor has specifically developed for use with its product.
- *Industry standard database.* Documents (attributes and contents) are stored in an industry standard database such as Oracle or Sybase. Attributes are stored within traditional database data types (e.g., integer or character); contents are stored in the database's BLOB (Binary Large Objects) data type.
- *Industry standard database and file system.* Documents' attributes are stored in an industry standard database, and documents' contents are usually stored in the file system of the host operating system. Most document management products use this document storage method today because this approach provides the most flexibility in terms of data distribution and also allows for greater scalability.

Versioning Services

Versioning Services maintain a historical record of the changes to a document over time. By maintaining this record, these services allow for the recreation of a document as it looked at any given point in time during its evolution. Additional key versioning features record who made changes when and why they were made.

DDBMS FRAMEWORK

The rest of this chapter discusses a critical component of managing information in a netcentric application: the distributed DBMS (DDBMS). The DDBMS promises a number of benefits for organizations, including the ability to expand a system more gracefully in an incremental fashion, local autonomy, increased availability and reliability of information, and increased efficiency and flexibility. With a DDBMS, users located in different geographical locations will be able to retrieve and update information from one or more locations in a network, transparently, and with full integrity and security.

CHARACTERISTICS OF DDBMS IN CLIENT/SERVER AND NETCENTRIC COMPUTING

Client/server and netcentric computing allow information to be kept distinct from the processes that use that information. Any DDBMS product used in a netcentric environment must be able to maintain this distinction. This section discusses a number of crucial characteristics of DDBMS products:

- Stored procedures
- Triggers
- Support for referential integrity
- Two-phase commit

- Support for nontextual or multimedia information
- Information replication
- Information gateways
- Disk mirroring

Stored Procedures

A stored procedure is a set of named SQL statements defined within a function, which is compiled within the DDBMS for runtime execution by name. Essentially, it is information access logic coded into the database server for use by all clients.

Stored procedures can be compared to third-generation language (3GL) routines, but they are executed by DDBMS software and contain SQL statements. At runtime, the stored procedure is accessed through a 3GL or 4GL call.

Advantages of Stored Procedures. Stored procedures have a number of important advantages:

- *Information transfer volume is minimized.* Because the stored procedure can execute all SQL statements and information access logic, only required information is returned to the requesting process.
- *Speeds execution.* Stored procedures are usually compiled into the database engine (not the application) for fast execution, which generally improves DDBMS and information access performance.
- *Decreases lines of code.* Applications can have less code, and they do not need to include, within each application, information integrity or reused information access logic.
- *Eases some maintenance activities.* Applications have less data structure information; therefore, it is easier to change table sizes, column names, and so forth.
- *Promotes code reusability.* Stored procedures can be thought of as object processing for information tables; they modularize and encapsulate information operations into a library-like area. Each stored procedure can be reused when accessed by any application that has permission to use it.
- *Enforces distinctions between information and process.* All information access, location, format, and so forth can be addressed within the stored procedure and therefore removed from the application logic that processes that information.

Potential Drawbacks of Stored Procedures. However, the use of stored procedures has a number of potential drawbacks:

- *Each DDBMS vendor's implementation is different.* Once an organization chooses a particular DDBMS and uses that vendor's stored procedures, it may be locked in to that vendor, or, at a minimum, those stored procedures have to be reimplemented.

- *Changes in a stored procedure can affect many applications.* The balance of application processing between the application and stored procedure must be understood. Like any library routine, changes require a test of all users.
- *System performance may be degraded by the inappropriate use of a stored procedure.* For example, a stored procedure that must return multiple information types from multiple sources to respond to a single request.

When to Use Stored Procedures. Stored procedures should be used in the following cases:

- *When a set of SQL calls should be grouped logically for a single business operation.* A logical set of data operations, which perform a single business function and are executed frequently (such as "make reservation"), provide a good base for a stored procedure.
- *When the same set of SQL calls are used in many applications.* As soon as the same SQL statements are used by more than one application, stored procedures are valuable for avoiding problems in updating several applications when changes are made and for improving the consistency of SQL use within an organization or project.
- *When one wants to decrease information transfer from client to server in complicated information requests.* A stored procedure call often is a smaller information message from a client to a server than a complex SQL statement(s). However, when there is less information transfer, there are more MIPS used on the server.
- *When one wants to maximize processing on a server platform, balancing client processing.* Stored procedures add central processing unit usage on the server and should be balanced against application processing on the client.

Triggers

Triggers are convenient "start" mechanisms to initiate a stored procedure or SQL command. Triggers can be based on either clock events or data events. A clock-based trigger might be, "At 1:00 A.M. each night, replicate the AIRPORT entity to sites New York, Chicago, and Dulles with the AIRPORT_REP stored procedure." A data-based event might be, "When a new row is inserted into the RESERVATION table, initiate the RESERVATION_ACCOUNTING stored procedure."

Triggers have a number of advantages. They permit applications developers to remove event-based logic from applications or the infrastructure software, and they tie a data-driven event to the actual data that drives the event. However, it is difficult to know what will happen to the database if many triggers cascade on and on. Infinite loops may be possible if designers are not careful and do not conduct thorough testing.

Referential Integrity

Referential integrity is the correctness and consistency of relationships among data tables and the correctness of information content. These are crucial issues in a relational database environment. The most important question with regard to referential integrity is whether it should be handled by the DDBMS or by the applications.

If the DDBMS enforces the integrity rules, integrity is centralized and not maintained in all application programs; integrity can be changed without modifying applications. However, DDBMS integrity enforcement, used indiscriminately, generates high overhead. Too much integrity checking slows down the system considerably.

In general, DDBMS-enforced referential integrity should be used when possible. The advantage to using DDBMS-enforced referential integrity is that the DDBMS enforces integrity more effectively than application logic. Furthermore, applications do not have to design and code the logic, and the logic can be centralized in the DDBMS. However, applications still have to test it.

There are two reasons to avoid DDBMS-enforced referential integrity:

1. The business rule that needs to be enforced is not a rule available from the DDBMS.
2. Using DDBMS-enforced referential integrity forces awkward constraints on application programs or on database maintenance processes.

It is vital to define all the business rules between tables before deciding how the relationship should be maintained. There are 4 ways to alter a referential relationship (insert a child, update the primary key of a child, update a foreign key of a parent, and delete a parent), and there are 4 possible business rules for how to retain referential integrity in each situation, for a total of 16 options. Most DDBMSs offer only six options. When you need one of the missing options, the application must enforce it.

DDBMS-enforced referential integrity should not make program structures awkward or less maintainable. However, complex links between tables may force difficult management, loading, and unloading scenarios. For example, a credit card company wanted a 24x7 application to allow new credit card products to be defined on-line, in such a way that the new products were not available to customers until all rules regarding the new product were fully defined. Credit card products have many complex rules, which were to be split across many child tables under the main Product table. The simplest way to guarantee that the Product could not be used until it was complete was to insert all the children first and insert the parent only when all the child rows were entered and validated. DDBMS-enforced referential integrity would not permit such a scenario, so application-enforced integrity was used instead.

Similarly, if too many tables are linked together through DDBMS-enforced referential integrity, backup/restore scenarios may become excessively difficult, so it is wise to keep referentially linked sets of tables below about 15.

When bulk-loading information into the database, referential integrity constraints should ensure that the database is consistent and accurate after loading. Some DDBMS products have a "backdoor" load that bypasses integrity constraints.

In general, DDBMS-enforced integrity should be used whenever it is justified by business events. However, the DDBMS should not be used to perform application integrity, for example, to validate codes against code tables. These values usually do not change often, and the constant validation is simply unnecessary overhead.Also, developers should not put more than a manageable number of tables into a single connected referential tree structure that must be maintained by the DDBMS. Developers must understand the characteristics of the specific DDBMS they are working with to determine what that manageable number is.

Two-Phase Commit

Two-phase commit (sometimes abbreviated 2PC) is a protocol used when a logical unit of work updates information in two or more recovery managers or "nodes." 2PC ensures integrity of information between nodes. It has been used for many years to ensure integrity between a transaction monitor and a DBMS, running on the same processor.

In a client/server or netcentric environment, distributed 2PC is a technique for guaranteeing integrity across distributed processors. Exhibit 4 shows a timeline of activities associated with two-phase commit.

Phase 1. Phase 1, or the prepare phase, queries all the recovery managers to verify that they are ready to commit, that is, ready for updating. This phase initiates the clean-up tasks of the memory management facilities at each node.

If a participating node (not the coordinating node) is unable to receive the prepare message (and any subsequent rollback), it checks periodically for unreleased locks (or checks when communication/processing is restored) and queries the coordinator about the status of the transaction.

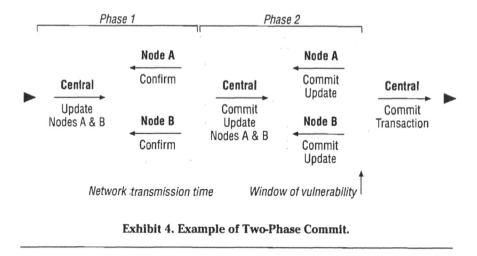

Exhibit 4. Example of Two-Phase Commit.

The coordinator responds that the transaction was rolled back because all sites could not participate, and the participating site also rolls back, releasing all locks.

Phase 2. Phase 2, or the commit phase, tells each participating node to write a commit log record. If the commit is successful at all the remote nodes involved in the transaction, and the originating node receives a successful acknowledgment from each of the remote nodes, the transaction at the originating node is committed. If confirmation is not received from all nodes involved, the transaction is rolled back.

Advantages and Disadvantages. Two-phase commits have several advantages. A 2PC approach can ensure that multiple databases remain synchronous. If some other approach is used to guarantee synchronization, it must incorporate similar synchronization logic and could mean building a custom 2PC architecture.

Two-phase commits are DDBMS supported; the DDBMS product can enforce and control the protocol (e.g., sending the messages, waiting for receipt, confirming, committing, and rolling back). Also, 2PCs are application independent. Because they are controlled by the DDBMS, applications do not need to control the execution of the protocol.

However, the 2PC implementation does leave a window of vulnerability: there are gaps in transmission between the central/coordinating node and the nodes involved in the transaction. If the participating node commits but the initiating node does not receive acknowledgment of the commit, the initiating node does not know whether to commit or to roll back. As a result, the initiating node does not know what to do and data integrity may be lost, defeating the entire objective of 2PC. The probability of this occurring increases with the number and distance of sites involved in the transaction. It works extremely well between CICS and DB2 running on the same mainframe box, where the distance between nodes is negligible. However, it is a different matter when the commit message must travel through space to a satellite and back, en route between nodes. Two-phase commit can also affect overall system and application performance.

Distributed two-phase commit is a complicated strategy — time consuming and costly. It relies on complex synchronous messaging over the network. Communications failures can have a substantial impact on the practicality of this technique.

In addition, the common approach requires participation and success from all sites involved in the transaction. If one site cannot complete the transaction, the entire transaction fails. Some observers have described 2PC as a protocol that guarantees that failure at one node will be replicated to all nodes.

So, when is two-phase commit appropriate? Developers should avoid two-phase commits by designing applications so that information updated during a single logical unit of work is located within the same node. If they cannot avoid it, designers should use two-phase commits when they need to have some form of synchronization of information between nodes. However, they must remember that inconsistencies in information integrity are still possible, so they must either control the integrity problems with a "data check" program or with regular off-line downloads or synchronizations.

Multimedia or Nontextual Information Storage

Support for more complex types of information is an important DDBMS capability to evaluate. This information goes by a number of different names: unstructured information, nontextual information, multimedia, and extended information. By whatever name, this information consists of such things as digital images, graphics, video images, voice, word processing documents, and spreadsheets.

The DDBMS has two primary methods by which it can handle these kinds of information: either defined within the database in data types called binary large objects (BLOBs) or defined outside the database structure with a pointer containing the file name where the information is contained within the DDBMS. The decision to use a BLOB or a file should be reviewed to determine application requirements, data administration requirements, and network impact.

BLOB storage has several advantages. The integrity of information is maintained by the DDBMS. Also, BLOBs are logically equivalent to other data types, which makes retrieval easier. However, a BLOB is a nonstandard SQL data type, so the designer must be careful to ensure that the DDBMS supports it. Current performance levels may be poor as a result of the large size of the BLOBs.

An advantage of storing extended data types outside the database is that the file can be accessed independently of the DDBMS, through operating system services. This may lead to better retrieval performance. Disadvantages to this type of storage include the fact that the integrity of the pointer to the file, and of the information itself, must be maintained by the application. Also, backup and restore operations must use both the DDBMS and file procedures.

Information Replication

Information replication is a critical function of most mission-critical distributed information architectures. Replication is the synchronization of a database or subset of a database from one location to another. Replication can occur regularly or irregularly, automatically or manually. Replication works well for information that does not change frequently and for data that need to be synchronized but not in real time. This is the case most of the time.

Replication provides faster access to information and less transfer of information across the network. However, a challenge to replication is keeping multiple copies of information synchronized. If the DDBMS cannot provide automatic synchronization, additional development time is necessary to provide and maintain this synchronization.

Hands-on experience to date suggests that recovery is very complex. In addition, replication can throw unpredictable loads on the network, such that network administration groups are reluctant to allow the feature into the network.

Information Gateways (Middleware)

Information gateways (also referred to as DBMS middleware) are mechanisms that allow applications to access information from a variety of DDBMSs, without extensive platform-specific or DDBMS-specific programming.

An information gateway may be a part of the DDBMS or it may be a separate product. The primary functions of the gateway include transparent routing of SQL calls and translating between various dialects of SQL. Gateways are particularly valuable when there is an existing installed base using a variety of DDBMSs.

An information gateway accepts an SQL statement from the client application and translates it into a format understandable by the target DDBMS(s). The gateway then sends the statement to be processed. After processing, the information gateway receives the results, translates them into a form that can be understood by the client, and then returns the information and status to the client.

Gateways allow access to information across multiple database management systems. The applications can use a consistent interface for all information, which saves development time and cost as well as training time for application designers and end users. However, gateways may result in a slower response time to queries because of the time required for formatting, protocol conversion, and other activities of the gateway. Some gateways offer read-only access, so updates must be processed differently. There are also potential information accuracy and integrity issues associated with the use of information gateways.

Disk Mirroring

Disk mirroring is a DDBMS-enforced "hot backup" disk capability within a single platform. It ensures that information is not lost in cases of disk failure. Generally, in a disk failure or disk crash, all information inserted since the last tape backup is lost. With disk mirroring, the backup disk is always up-to-date with respect to the primary disk. Disk mirroring also increases the availability of the DDBMS.

With disk mirroring, the DDBMS automatically transfers to the backup disk if the primary disk fails. It then automatically synchronizes the primary disk after the failure is cleared.

Disk mirroring provides obvious advantages to information security; in addition, it is transparent to applications controlled by the DDBMS. However, more disks are required in disk mirroring, and mirroring cannot be done over a LAN. Also, some minor performance decreases may result from mirroring.

MATCHING FUNCTIONS AND FEATURES

In any particular client/server or netcentric system, some features and functions of DDBMSs may be critical and others may not. When evaluating a DDBMS, it is important to find one appropriate for the specific system and business requirements. A matrix, such as the one in Exhibit 5, is a worksheet for matching functions and features to products under consideration.

CONCLUSION

Maximizing the benefits of client/server and netcentric computing presents some of the greatest challenges to designers and developers. One of

	Product A	Product B	Product C
Stored Procedures			
Triggers			
Two-Phase Commit			
Referential Integrity			
Multimedia			
Replication			
Gateways			
Mirroring			

Exhibit 5. Matrix of Features.

the primary business benefits of netcentric computing is that knowledge workers have access to more and better types of information, located throughout the enterprise. However, that access requires a methodical approach to enabling applications to access and manipulate information, whether it is stored locally or remotely in files or databases. Even the fact that we refer to this part of the netcentric architecture as information access (rather than its traditional name, data access) reveals an important part of the information challenge of netcentric systems.

In addition, a key technology in client/server and netcentric computing is the DDBMS. Although theoretically a distributed DBMS does not have to be relational, the relational model does provide a simpler and more practical vehicle to support DDBMS functions than hierarchical or network models.

A relational DDBMS also tends to provide better support for the flexible, dynamic information requirements found in most netcentric applications. The major DDBMS products in the marketplace today are built on a relational framework, and the success of relational DBMSs has had a direct effect in spurring the development of DDBMS products. More and more, organizations will see distributed DBMS as a practical technology component that is needed to support their growing business needs.

Chapter 6
Communications Architectures

Netcentric computing is an outgrowth of the increased importance and capabilities of the network as well as the associated communications that the network enables between computing environments and access devices. Netcentric computing implies being connected anywhere, anytime. It transforms the common phrase "The network is the computer" into "The network is everywhere." The popular and academic journals, professional gatherings, and our firm's work with organizations all bear witness to the fact that people have now realized the scope of communications issues in developing business solutions today.

In netcentric computing, the network is no longer simply a pipe that moves data from point A to point B. Instead, networks provide a rich set of services that are increasingly more sophisticated to keep pace with the requirements of netcentric applications.

This chapter explores an architectural framework that categorizes and defines the services that are provided by the network and discusses areas in which these services are evolving. Specific networking technologies that are evolving to support netcentric applications are discussed in Section III of this book.

WHAT IS A COMMUNICATIONS ARCHITECTURE?

The evolving role of a network can be seen in the advent of such concepts as "electronic commerce" and the "virtual enterprise." The network continues to support traditional types of data traffic in an individual corporate enterprise, (i.e., local area networks (LANs) and wide area networks (WANs). However, nontraditional business flows (video, graphics, voice, etc.) also need to be supported as well as the new relationships created in the virtual enterprise. Companies that produce the final packaged product or service interact with their suppliers through a seamless information infrastructure. In addition, the need to support an ever-increasing base of public access from home and mobile locations further stretches and redefines the old network boundaries. As computing becomes more distributed and pervasive, the role of the network will grow to support and enable this exchange of content between any point that generates or uses information. Exhibit 1 illustrates these key characteristics of the network.

What is a network? The domain of the network may be defined as the portion of the overall enterprise technology architecture that supports the movement of knowledge in a digital, electronic format between different locations. To provide this capability, the network is composed of communications hardware, software, and services. The network does not include the computing platforms, knowledge technologies, or business logic and applications. However, all network components must provide well-defined services and interfaces to interact effectively with these other technology components.

COMMUNICATIONS ARCHITECTURE GUIDING PRINCIPLES

How is this definition of a network any different from the way the role of the network has been perceived in the past? At first glance, the answer may be, "Not much." However, some fundamental concepts are introduced here that are key to how network architectures will be viewed in the foreseeable future. While the following guiding principles affect all aspects of near-term computing architectures, they will have some very specific impacts to the network domain that will guide the characteristics of future communication architectures.

Netcentric Computing

A netcentric architecture is a standard architecture that allows internal users, customers, and business partners to use multiple electronic access devices (e.g., PCs, mobile computers, kiosks, telephones, etc.) to access disparate sources of information. Netcentric architectures employ open, commonly accepted standards for the network, client, and associated components (e.g., Internet, TCP/IP, Web Browser, ActiveX, COM, CORBA, Java, etc.). Web-based solutions are examples of netcentric architectures. A netcentric architecture requires an intelligent, flexible, standards-based network.

Individuals

The physical network infrastructure is shifting to support more dynamic human-to-human communications styles instead of the traditional, precise computer-to-computer communications. Until now, application requirements were the sole driver for network designs. Now, with interaction styles mimicking more human traits, networks must incorporate multimedia, workflow, collaboration, and other qualities that better support how different individuals use the network.

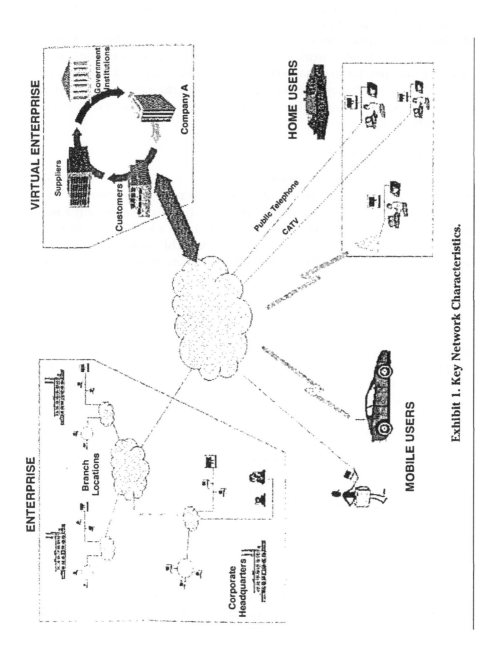

Exhibit 1. Key Network Characteristics.

Mobility

As individuals drive out new requirements, an "anywhere, anytime" computing paradigm must be addressed to support new classes of personal devices. These new devices no longer follow the "bigger, better, faster" characteristics of legacy workstations and servers and hosts but rather the "smaller, cheaper, faster" characteristics of phones, personal digital assistants (PDAs), and laptop computers. This forces the network to support more devices, more variety of devices, and the added overhead of intermittent connectivity.

Distributed Computing

Although most enterprises are still hierarchical, some are flattening their processes by introducing more autonomy. This requires systems to support distributed data, applications, and infrastructure. Because the network is the only part of the infrastructure that has a logical and physical end-to-end view of all resources, the network architecture must provide services to help manage processes that transcend central implementation.

Public Access

Just as enterprise networks are extended to business partners to create virtual enterprises, the enterprise network may also be opened to interaction with the general public (customers, potential customers, etc.). Supporting public access (e.g., internet access, access via public kiosks, etc.) and the resulting virtual communities requires specialized network services relating to security, directories, heterogeneous platforms, etc.

Open Network Services and Interfaces

The communication architecture must support common, open network services and interfaces that are easily shared. Not only must there be well defined standards that can be shared between the client and server, but an "intelligent network" role will need to exist to help proxy capabilities as well. This will allow more rapid expansion of enterprises as they take advantage of virtualization.

The Virtual Enterprise

As more enterprises begin to partner and cooperate, networks will need to support relationships with services that never had to exist before. The challenge to the communication architecture is not in providing the connections but in enabling the end-to-end processes associated with them. Many of these processes will require the network to provide secure, independent, reliable, dynamic services that transcend organizational boundaries.

Enterprise

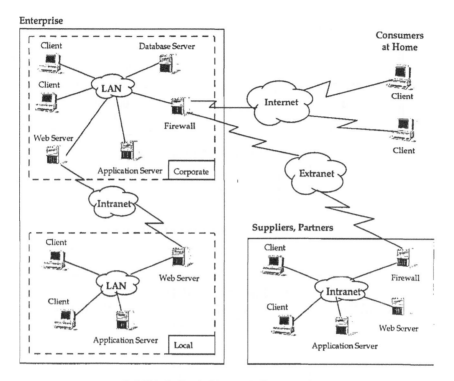

Exhibit 2. Basic Network Components.

THE COMMUNICATIONS ARCHITECTURE

Exhibit 2 is a representation of the physical networking environment of net-centric solutions.

This physical environment is supported by a logical representation of a netcentric execution architecture, discussed in Chapter 3 (Exhibit 3). The components of the architecture that represent the network architecture have been colored gray.

The Communication Services component on the client and server and the communication fabric component represent a high-level view of the communications architecture. The remainder of this chapter focuses on a description of the communication services and the communications fabric portions of the Netcentric Execution Architecture. Exhibit 4 illustrates a further breakdown of the network-specific layers of a netcentric communication architecture.

Each layer (e.g., communication services layer, transport service layer, and the network media layer) contains specific network-related services

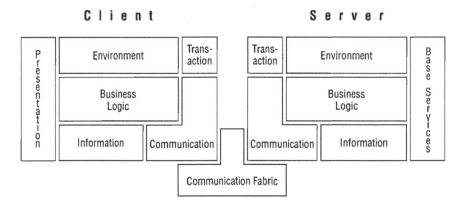

Exhibit 3. Netcentric Execution Architecture.

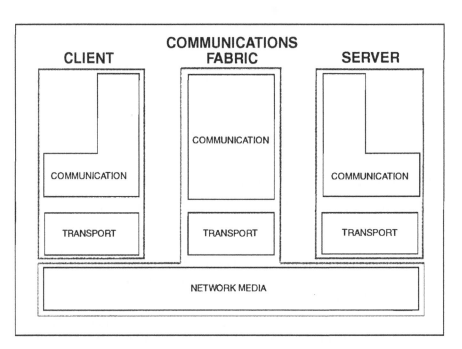

Exhibit 4. Network-Specific Layers of the Communications Architecture.

that are needed to deliver the necessary functionality. To be fully functional, a netcentric architecture requires services from each of the three layers. Within a layer, individual services are selected to deliver the necessary functionality. The services provided in these three layers enable the applications and higher level services to be isolated from the intricacies of the low-level network (e.g., developing application interfaces directly with complex communications protocols).

Communication Services Layer

The Communication Services layer manages the interaction of distributed processes over the network. This layer enables an application to interact transparently with other applications regardless of whether they reside on the same computer or on a remote computer. The Communication Services layer performs four distinct functions:

- Manages communications between applications
- Initiates and manages the transfer of information between processes over the network
- Provides specialized interface and communication management capabilities based on the type of resource accessed so that network nodes can intelligently interact with distributed resources
- Provides interfacing and translation to ensure that information received is in a readable format for the local system

Transport Services Layer

The Transport Services layer provides capabilities for transferring data through the network to the ultimate destination. Its primary functions include transporting data (including reliability, security, and quality of service) and transporting voice calls.

Network Media Services Layer

The Network Media Services layer performs the low-level transfer of data between network nodes, using physical media such as wiring. Its primary functions include

- Performing low-level transfer of data between network nodes
- Managing low-level signaling across physical media
- Physical wiring, cabling and radio frequency spectrum

Each of these layers plays a distinctive role in the delivery of information from one computing device to another. An analogy might better clarify their distinctive roles. Consider a passenger train moving toward its destination.

The tracks, railroad switches, lights, and stations are performing similar functions as Network Media Services in a Communications Architecture.

The train itself — including engine, cars, and conductor — provides the Transport Services.

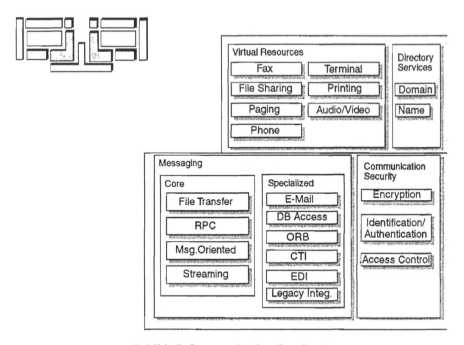

Exhibit 5. Communication Services.

Additionally, at the station, passengers have various services to choose from: the express train, dinner train, destination, and so forth. These services at the station are analogous to the communication services component of the architecture.

The rest of this chapter looks at each of these layers in more detail.

COMMUNICATION SERVICES

There are five primary communications services categories (Exhibit 5):

- Core Messaging services
- Specialized Messaging services
- Communications Security services
- Virtual Resource services
- Directory services

CORE MESSAGING SERVICES

Broadly defined, messaging is sending information or commands between two or more recipients. Recipients may be computers, people, or processes in a computer. To send this message, a protocol (or in some cases, multiple protocols) is used that both the sender and receiver can understand. A protocol is a set of rules describing, in technical terms, how two end points should exchange information. Protocols exist at several levels during the exchange of information. Protocols facilitate transport of the message carrying the information. Both end points must recognize and observe the protocol. As an example, a common protocol in today's networks is the Transmission Control Protocol/Internet Protocol (TCP/IP). TCP/IP is the principle method for transmitting data over the Internet today. This protocol is responsible for ensuring that a series of data packets sent over a network arrives at the destination and is properly sequenced.

Messaging services transfer formatted information from one process to another. By drawing upon messaging services, applications can shield themselves from the complexity of the low-level Transport services. There are three key messaging styles used to support Interprocess Communication (IPC): Store and Forward and Synchronous and Asynchronous Messaging.

Store and forward messaging provides deferred message processing. For example, store and forward messaging may use an e-mail infrastructure upon which to build applications. Common uses would be for forms routing and e-mail.

Synchronous messaging allows an application to send a message to another application and wait for a reply before continuing. Synchronous messaging is typically used for update and general business transactions. It requires time-out processing to allow the application to reacquire control in the event of failure.

Asynchronous messaging allows an application to send a message to another application and continue processing before a reply is received. Asynchronous messaging is typically used for larger retrieval type processing, such as retrieval of larger lists of data than can be contained in one message.

Messaging styles are important because they serve as the primary link to the application and business requirements. For example, suppose a business process requiring a series of processing steps needs to be automated. Additionally, each step needs to be performed in sequence at real time. Before continuing to the next step of the process, an application must know if the previous step was successful. Because of the send, receive, continue nature of the business process, the more appropriate messaging style for this application is synchronous messaging.

In addition to the messaging styles, interprocess messaging is typically implemented in one of two ways:

- *Function based:* uses the subroutine model of programming. The message interface is built upon the calling program passing the appropriate parameters and receiving the returned information.

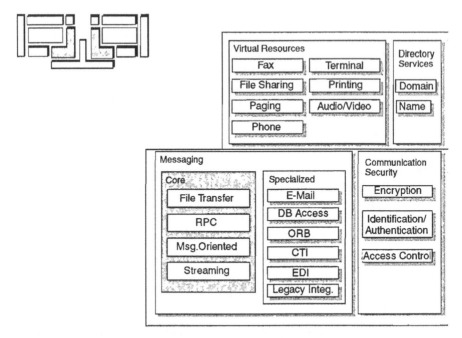

Exhibit 6. Core Messaging Services.

- *Message based:* uses a defined message format to exchange information between processes. While a portion of the message may be unstructured, a defined header component is normally included. A message-based approach is not limited to the call/return structure of the function-based model and can be used in a conversational manner.

Core messaging services can be divided into the following services (Exhibit 6):

- File transfer services
- RPC (Remote procedure call) services
- Message-Oriented services
- Streaming services

File Transfer Services

File Transfer services enable the copying and receiving of files or other large blocks of data between two resources. Exhibit 7 depicts File Transfer, in which a bulk data transfer occurs (possibly in either direction). Note that a file transfer copies a file, resulting in a copy on both machines.

The following are examples of File Transfer protocols and standards.

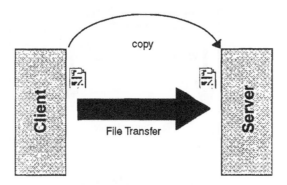

Exhibit 7. File Transfer.

File Transfer Protocol (FTP). Allows users to upload and download files across the network. FTP also provides a mechanism to obtain file name, directory name, attributes, and file size information. Remote file access protocols such as Network File System (NFS) also use a block transfer method but are optimized for on-line read/write paging of a file.

Hyper-Text Transfer Protocol (HTTP). Within a Web-based environment, Web servers transfer HTML pages to clients using HTTP. HTTP can be thought of as a lightweight file transfer protocol optimized for transferring small files. HTTP reduces the inefficiencies of the FTP protocol. HTTP runs on top of TCP/IP and was developed specifically for the transmission of hypertext between client and server.

Secure Hypertext Transfer Protocol (S-HTTP). A secure form of HTTP, mostly for financial transactions on the Web. S-HTTP has gained a small level of acceptance among merchants selling products on the Internet as a way to conduct financial transactions (using credit card numbers or passing sensitive information) without the risk of unauthorized people intercepting this information. S-HTTP incorporates various cryptographic message formats such as DSA and RSA standards into both the Web client and the Web server.

File Transfer and Access Management (FTAM). The OSI (Open Systems Interconnection) standard is used for file transfer, file access, and file management across platforms.

Remote Procedure Calls (RPC) Services

RPCs are a type of protocol by which an application sends a request to a remote system to execute a designated procedure using the supplied arguments and return the result.

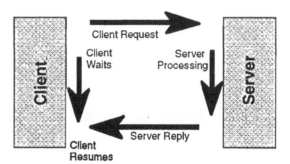

Exhibit 8. RPC Messaging.

RPCs emulate the function call mechanisms found in procedural languages (e.g., the C language). This means that control is passed from the main logic of a program to the called function, with control returning to the main program once the called function completes its task. Because RPCs perform this mechanism across the network, they pass some element of control from one process to another, for example, from the client to the server. Because the client is dependent on the response from the server, it is normally blocked from performing any additional processing until a response is received. This type of synchronous data exchange is also referred to as blocking communications.

Exhibit 8 depicts RPC messaging, in which the message originator stops processing while waiting for a reply.

Message-Oriented Services

Message-Oriented Services refers to the process of distributing data and control through the exchange of records known as "messages." Message-Oriented Services provide the application developer with a set of simple verbs (e.g., connect, send, receive, and disconnect) that are used to exchange information with other distributed applications.

For example, to send data to a remote process, the application developer uses a send verb. This verb along with the appropriate parameters (e.g., data to be sent and the process's logical name) are included as part of the application code.

Once the verb is called, the Message-Oriented Services are responsible for managing the interface to the underlying communications architecture via the communications protocol APIs and ensuring the delivery of the information to the remote process. This interface may require that Message-Oriented Services have the following capabilities:

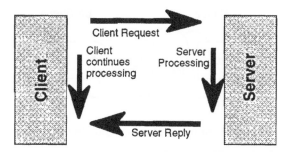

Exhibit 9. Message Passing.

- Translating mnemonic or logical process names to operating system compatible format
- Opening a communications session and negotiating parameters for the session
- Translating data to the proper format
- Transferring data and control messages during the session
- Recovering any information if errors occur during transmission
- Passing results information and status to the application

An application continues processing after executing a Message-Oriented Services verb, allowing the reply to arrive at a subsequent time. Thus, unlike RPCs, Message-Oriented Services implements a "nonblocking" messaging architecture.

Message-Oriented Services products typically support communication among various computing platforms (e.g., DOS, Windows, OS/2, Macintosh, UNIX, and mainframes).

There are three types of Message-Oriented Services commonly implemented:

- Message Passing
- Message Queuing
- Publish and Subscribe

Message Passing. This is a direct, application-to-application communication model. An application request is sent in the form of a message from one application to another. The communication method can be either synchronous (in this case the sending applications waits for a response back from the receiving application, like RPCs) or asynchronous (through callback routines). In a message-passing model, a direct link between two applications that participate in the message exchange is always maintained (Exhibit 9).

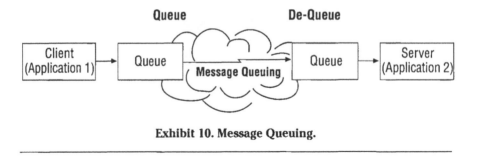

Exhibit 10. Message Queuing.

Exhibit 11. Publish and Subscribe Messaging.

Message Queuing. Message Queuing (also known as Store and Forward) is an indirect application to application communication model that allows applications to communicate via message queues rather than by calling each other directly (Exhibit 10). Message queuing is asynchronous by nature and connectionless, meaning that the recipient need not be directly available when the message is sent. Moreover, it implies support for reliable, guaranteed, and assured (nonduplicate) message delivery.

Publish and Subscribe. Publish and Subscribe (also known as Push messaging) is a special type of data delivery mechanism that allows processes to register an interest in (i.e., subscribe to) certain messages or events (Exhibit 11). An application then sends (publishes) a message, which is then forwarded to all processes that subscribe to it.

Streaming Services

Streaming is the process of transferring time-sensitive data streams (e.g., video and/or audio) in real time. Streaming differs from the other types of Core Messaging services in that it delivers a continuous, one-way stream of data rather than the relatively short messages associated with RPC and

Functionality	Sample Protocol options	Architecture Service
Controlling media delivery	RTSP or proprietary	Streaming messaging service
Monitoring data stream	RTCP or proprietary	Streaming messaging service
End-to-end delivery of stream	RTP or proprietary	Streaming messaging service
Message transport	UDP, Multicast UDP, TCP	Message transport service
Packet forwarding/Internetworking	IP, IP multicast	Packet forwarding/Internetworking service

Exhibit 12. Streaming Architecture Options

Message-Oriented messaging or the large, batch transfers associated with File Transfer. (While the media stream is one-way from the server to the client, the client can issue stream controls to the server.) Streaming may be used to deliver video, audio, and/or other real-time content across the Internet or within enterprise networks.

Streaming is an emerging technology. While some multimedia products use proprietary streaming mechanisms, other products incorporate standards. Data streams are delivered using several protocols that are layered to assemble the necessary functionality. The following are examples of emerging standards for streaming protocols.

Real-Time Streaming Protocol (RTSP). RTSP is the proposed Internet protocol for establishing and controlling on-demand delivery of real-time data. For example, clients can use RTSP to request specific media from a media server, to issue commands such as play, record and pause, and to control media delivery speed. Because RTSP simply controls media delivery, it is layered on top of other protocols, such as the following.

Real-Time Transport Protocol (RTP). Actual delivery of streaming data occurs through real-time protocols such as RTP. RTP provides end-to-end data delivery for applications transmitting real-time data over multicast or unicast network services. RTP conveys encoding, timing, and sequencing information to allow receivers to properly reconstruct the media stream. RTP is independent of the underlying transport service, but it is typically used with UDP. It may also be used with Multicast UDP, TCP/IP, or IP Multicast.

Real-Time Control Protocol (RTCP). RTP is augmented by the RTCP. RTCP allows nodes to identify stream participants and communicate about the quality of data delivery.

Exhibit 12 summarizes the protocol layering that supports Streaming.

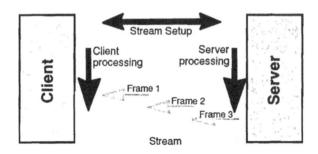

Exhibit 13. Streaming.

A key attribute of any streaming architecture is the adherence to a flow of time-sequenced data packets. Each series of packets contains the necessary information to play the next segment in a sound or video clip. Exhibit 13 highlights the one-way, time-sequenced nature of the flow of data packets for a Streaming architecture.

SPECIALIZED MESSAGING SERVICES

Specialized Messaging services extend the Core Messaging services to provide additional functionality. Specialized Messaging services may extend Core Messaging services in the following general ways:

- Providing messaging among specialized systems by drawing upon basic messaging capabilities
- Defining specialized message layouts
- Defining specialized intersystem protocols
- Suggesting ways in which messaging draws upon directory and security services to deliver a complete messaging environment

An example of a specialized messaging service is E-Mail Messaging. E-Mail Messaging is an implementation of a store-and-forward Message-Oriented Services, in that E-Mail Messaging defines specialized, mail-related message layouts and protocols that utilize store-and-forward messaging.

Specialized Messaging services is comprised of the following categories (Exhibit 14):

- E-Mail Messaging
- CTI Messaging
- EDI Messaging
- Object Request Broker Messaging
- Database Access Messaging
- Legacy Integration Messaging

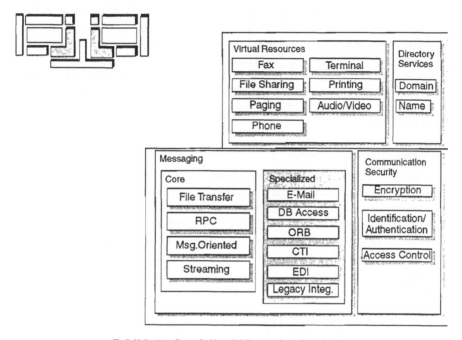

Exhibit 14. Specialized Messaging Services.

E-Mail Messaging Services

E-Mail Messaging services reliably exchange messages using the store-and-forward messaging style. E-Mail message systems traditionally include a rudimentary form of directory services (discussed later). While some e-mail products use proprietary protocols, the following are examples of E-Mail-related standards:

X.400. The X.400 message handling system standard defines a platform independent standard for store-and-forward message transfers among mail servers. X.400 is often used as a backbone E-Mail service, with gateways providing interconnection with end-user systems.

Simple Mail Transfer Protocol (SMTP). SMTP is a UNIX/Internet standard for transferring E-Mail among servers.

Multi-Purpose Internet Mail Extensions (MIME). MIME is a protocol that enables Internet users to exchange multimedia E-Mail messages.

Post Office Protocol (POP). POP3 is used to distribute E-Mail from an SMTP server to the actual recipient.

Internet Message Access Protocol, Version 4 (IMAP4). IMAP4 allows a client to access and manipulate E-Mail messages on a server. IMAP4 permits manipulation of remote message folders, called "mailboxes," in a way that is functionally equivalent to local mailboxes. IMAP4 also provides the capability for an off-line client to resynchronize with the server. IMAP4 includes standards for message handling features that allow users to download message header information and then decide which E-Mail message contents to download.

Database Messaging Services

Database Messaging services (also known as Database Access Middleware, or DBAM) provide connectivity for clients to access databases throughout the enterprise. Database messaging software draws upon basic interprocess messaging capabilities (e.g., RPCs) to support database connectivity. DBAM can be grouped into one of three categories:

- Open
- Native
- Gateway

Open database messaging services typically provide single applications seamless access to multiple data sources, both relational and nonrelational, through a standard application programming interface (API) set. Examples include ODBC (Open Database Connectivity) and JDBC (Java Database Connectivity). ODBC is considered an industry de facto standard.

By contrast, *native* database messaging services are those services, usually proprietary, provided by the DBMS vendor. Examples include SQL*Net for Oracle DBMS and DB-LIB for Sybase DBMS.

Additionally, *gateway* database messaging services can be used to facilitate migration of data from one environment to another. For example, if data in a DB2 environment needs to be integrated with data in a Sybase environment, Gateway DBAM can enable the integration.

Object Request Broker (ORB) Messaging Services

ORB Messaging enables objects to transparently make requests of, and receive responses from, other objects located locally or remotely. Objects communicate through an ORB. An ORB enables client objects to access server objects either locally or remotely over a network and invoke operations (i.e., functions and methods) on them. ORBs typically provide interoperability between heterogeneous client and server environments across languages and/or operating systems and/or network protocols. In that respect, some have said that ORBs will become a kind of "ultimate middleware" for truly distributed processing. A standardized Interface Definition Language (IDL) defines the interfaces that applications must use to

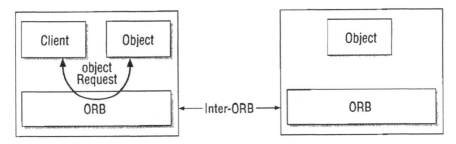

Exhibit 15. CORBA-Based Object Request Broker Messaging.

access the ORB Services. The two major Object Request Broker standards/implementations are

- Object Management Group's Common Object Request Broker Architecture (CORBA) (www.omg.org)
- Microsoft's (Distributed) Component Object Model (COM/DCOM) (www.microsoft.com)

CORBA. Common Object Request Broker Architecture (CORBA) is a standard for distributed objects being developed by the Object Management Group (OMG). The OMG is a consortium of software vendors and end users. Many OMG member companies are developing commercial products that support the CORBA standards and/or are developing software that use these standards. CORBA provides the mechanism by which objects transparently make requests and receive responses, as defined by OMG's ORB. The CORBA ORB is an application framework that provides interoperability between objects, built in different languages, running on different machines in heterogeneous distributed environments.

The OMG's Internet Inter-Orb Protocol (IIOP) specifies a set of message formats and common data representations for communication between ORBs over TCP/IP networks. CORBA-based Object Messaging is summarized in Exhibit 15.

Component Object Model. Component Object Model (COM) is a client/server object-based model, developed by Microsoft, designed to allow software components and applications to interact with each other in a uniform and standard way. The COM standard is partly a specification and partly an implementation. The specification defines mechanisms for creation of objects and communication between objects. This part of the specification is paper based and is not dependent on any particular language or operating system. Any language can be used as long as the standard is incorporated. The implementation part is the COM library that provides a

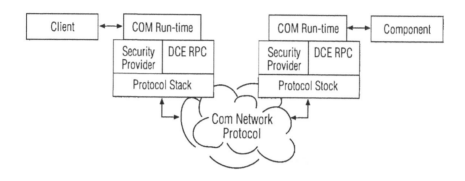

Exhibit 16. Microsoft COM/DCOM Messaging.

number of services that support a mechanism that allows applications to connect to each other as software objects (Exhibit 16).

COM is not a software layer through which all communications between objects occur. Instead, COM serves as a broker and name space keeper to connect a client and an object, but, once that connection is established, the client and object communicate directly without having the overhead of passing through a central piece of API code. Originally conceived of as a compound document architecture, COM has been evolved to a full object request broker including recently added features for distributed object computing. DCOM (Distributed COM) contains features for extending the object model across the network using the DCE RPC mechanism. In sum, COM defines how components should be built and how they should interact. DCOM defines how they should be distributed. Currently COM/DCOM is only supported on Windows-based machines. However, third-party vendors are in progress of porting this object model to other platforms such as Macintosh, UNIX, etc.

CTI Messaging Services

Computer-Telephone Integration (CTI) integrates computer systems and telephone systems to coordinate data and telephony activities. For example, CTI can be used to associate a customer's database entry with the customer's telephone call and route the call accordingly.

CTI Messaging supports communication among clients, CTI servers, PBXs/ACDs, hybrid platforms, networks, and external telephony devices. CTI Messaging relies upon proprietary PBX/ACD APIs, CTI vendor-specific APIs or message sets, and industry-standard APIs.

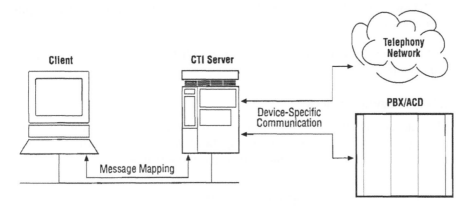

Exhibit 17. CTI Messaging.

CTI Messaging has two primary functions (Exhibit 17):

1. Device-specific communication
    Manages direct communications between telephony devices and
    data devices.
    Allows applications to control PBXs, key telephone systems, ISDN,
    analog PSTN, cellular, Centrex, etc. and supports features such as
    address translation, call setup, call answering, call dropping, and
    caller ID.
    Provides interface to carrier networks for call delivery and call-
    related messaging.
2. Message mapping
    Translates device-specific communication to generic API and/or
    message set

CTI products can be divided into the following categories.

CTI Platform-Specific Products. These can only be implemented on the
hardware of a specific vendor.

CTI Telephony-Based API Products. These include proprietary PBX/ACD-
based messaging sets, which permit external devices to interface with the
vendor's PBX/ACD call and station control logic.

CTI Server/Workstation-Based or Host-Based API Products. These operate
on a particular computer vendor's hardware platform and provide call control and messaging functionality.

CTI Cross-Platform Vendors. These products have been ported to multiple hardware platforms/operating systems.

CTI Enabling Solutions. These focus solely on call control and call/application synchronization functions.

CTI Enterprise Solutions. These provide all CTI business functions to varying degrees.

EDI Messaging Services

EDI (Electronic Data Interchange) supports system-to-system messaging among business partners by defining standard message layouts. Companies typically use EDI to streamline commercial transactions in their supply chains.

EDI standards (e.g., EDIFACT, ANSI X12) define record layouts for transactions such as "purchase orders." EDI services include the generation and translation of EDI messages according to the various public message layout standards.

EDI messaging can be implemented via electronic mail or customized message-oriented architectures.

Legacy Integration Services

Legacy services provide gateways to mainframe legacy systems. Design techniques for integration with existing systems can be grouped into two broad categories:

- Front end access: access of information through screens/windows (this will be further discussed in the Terminal Emulation section in Virtual Resources later in this chapter).
- Back end access: this approach tends to be used when existing data stores have information that is needed in the client/server environment, but accessing the information through existing screens or functions is not feasible. Legacy messaging services typically include remote data access through gateways. A database gateway provides an interface between the client/server environment and the legacy system. The gateway provides an ability to access and manipulate the data in the legacy system.

COMMUNICATION SECURITY SERVICES

As organizations open up their computing resources to business partners, customers, and a broader audiences of employees, security becomes one of the hottest topics in most discussions. This section focuses on network communications-related security. For a broader perspective on security in netcentric environments, refer to Chapter 28. This chapter will introduce some of the key communications architecture security concepts.

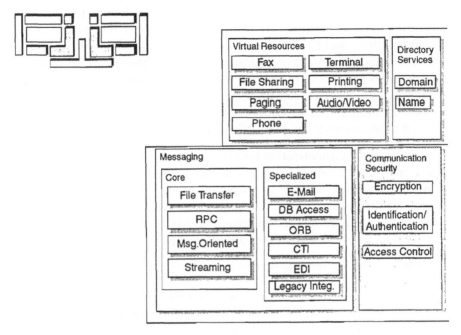

Exhibit 18. Communication Security Services.

Communications security services can be broken down into the following three categories (Exhibit 18):

- Encryption Services
- Identification and Authentication Services
- Access Control Services

Encryption Services

Encryption services encrypt data prior to network transfer to prevent unauthorized interception. (Note that encryption can occur within the Communication Services layer, the Transport Services layer, or the Network Media Services layer.) Within the Communication Services layer, encryption occurs at the top of the protocol stack and is typically performed in an application (e.g., in an e-mail application). This is an end-to-end approach that can leave the remainder of the protocol stack (i.e., the Transport services and the Network Media services) unaffected. Refer to Transport Security topic in the Transport Services section for more information on security.

Identification/Authentication Services

Identification/Authentication services verify network access requests by validating that users are who they claim to be. For secure systems, one or more Identification/Authentication mechanisms can be used to validate authorized users and integrated with Access Control Services to verify which functions and data they have access to. Within the corporate network, Identification/Authentication services are often included in directory services products like Novell's NDS (NetWare Directory Services) or Microsoft's Windows NT Domain Services. These products require the user to have an established account and supply a password before access is granted to resources through the directory.

Identification/Authentication for accessing resources across an Internet or intranet is not as simple and is a rapidly evolving area. Web sites need to restrict access to areas of information and functionality to known customers or business partners. More granular Identification/Authentication services are required where sensitive individual customer account information must be protected from other customers.

Identification/Authentication can occur through various means.

Basic ID/Authentication. This requires that the Web client supply a user name and password before servicing a request. Basic ID/Authentication does not encrypt the password in any way, and thus the password travels in the clear over the network where it could be detected with a network sniffer program or device. Basic ID/Authentication is not secure enough for banking applications or anywhere where there may be a financial incentive for someone to steal someone's account information. It is, however, the easiest mechanism to set up and administer and requires no special software at the Web client.

ID/Password Encryption. This offers a somewhat higher level of security by requiring that the user name and password be encrypted during transit. The user name and password are transmitted as a scrambled message as part of each request because there is no persistent connection open between the Web client and the Web server.

Digital Certificates or Signatures. These are encrypted digital keys that are issued by a third party "trusted" organization (i.e., Verisign). They are used to verify a user's authenticity.

Hardware Tokens. These are small physical devices that may generate a one-time password or that may be inserted into a card reader for ID/Authentication purposes.

Virtual Tokens. These are typically a file on a floppy or hard drive used for ID/Authentication (e.g., Lotus Notes ID file).

Biometric Identification. This involves the analysis of biological characteristics (such as fingerprints, voice recognition, or retinal scans) to verify
an individual's identify.

Access Control Services

When a user requests access to network resources, the Access Control service determines if the user has the appropriate permissions or privileges
and either allows or disallows the access. (This occurs after the user has
been properly identified and authenticated.)

The following are examples of ways to implement Access Control services.

Network Operating Systems. Access Control services are bundled with all
network operating systems to control user access to network resources.

Application Proxies. An application-level proxy, or application-level gateway, is a robust type of firewall. (A firewall is a system that enforces an
access control policy between a trusted internal network and an untrusted
external network.) The application proxy acts at the application level
rather than the network level. The proxy acts as a go-between for the end
user by completing the user-requested tasks on its own and then transferring the information to the user. The proxy manages a database of allowed
user actions, which it checks prior to performing the request.

Filters. World Wide Web filters can prevent users from accessing specified content or Internet addresses. Products can limit access based on key-
words, network addresses, time-of-day, user categories, etc. Filters are
typically implemented on a firewall.

Servers, Applications, and Databases. Access Control can occur locally on
a server to limit access to specific system resources or files. Applications
and databases can also authorize users for specific levels of access within
their control. (This functionality is within the Environment Services grouping in the execution architecture.)

DIRECTORY SERVICES

Directory services will play a major role in the future of netcentric computing, primarily because of the increasingly distributed and dynamic nature
of netcentric environments. Directory services manage information about
resources on the network and perform a variety of processes. These processes range from simple name-to-address resolution (e.g., when
www.ac.com is typed in a browser connected to the Internet, that name
resolves to IP address 204.167.146.195.) to the logical integration of heterogeneous systems to create a common view of resources.

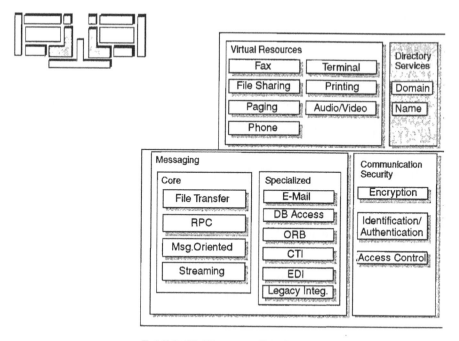

Exhibit 19. Directory Services.

Directory Services typically perform one or many of the following functions

- Store information about network resources and users, and track relationships
- Organize resource access information in order to aid in the location of and access to other resources throughout the network
- Provide location transparency, because resources are accessed through a directory rather than based on their physical location
- Convert between logical resource names and physical resource addresses
- Interact with Security services such as identification/authentication and access control services to maintain necessary access permissions and privileges
- Provide single network logon to file and print resources; in certain cases, provide single network logon for network applications integrated with the directory services
- Distribute and synchronize directory information throughout the environment (for reliability and location-independent access)

Directory Services is comprised of two subservices: Name Services and Domain Services (Exhibit 19).

Name Services

The Name service creates a logical "pronounceable" name in place of a binary machine number. These services could be used by other communications services such as File Transfer, Message Services, and Terminal Services. A Name service can be implemented on its own or as part of a full-featured Directory service.

Domain Services

A network domain is a set of network nodes under common control (i.e., common security and logins, unified addressing, coordinated management, etc.). Domain services manage these types of activities for the network nodes in a domain. Domain services may be limited in their ability to support heterogeneous systems and in the ability to scale to support the enterprise.

Most Directory services running today tend either to provide limited functionality or to be highly proprietary. In fact, many organizations maintain multiple directories from e-mail to printer and host information. In a netcentric environment, it is crucial to provide seamless location of, and access to, resources, individuals, and applications. Emerging directory service technologies such as the Lightweight Directory Access Protocol (LDAP) may prove key in providing integrated, open Directory services for netcentric applications.

VIRTUAL RESOURCE SERVICES

Virtual Resource Services proxy or mimic the capabilities of specialized, network-connected resources. This allows a generic network node to emulate a specialized physical device. In this way, network users can interface with a variety of specialized resources.

A common example of a Virtual Resource service is the capability to print to a network printer as if it were directly attached to a workstation.

Virtual Resource Services include the following (Exhibit 20):

- Terminal Services
- Print Services
- File Sharing Services
- Phone Services
- Fax Services
- Audio/Video Services
- Paging Services

Terminal Services

Terminal Services allow a client to connect to a nonlocal host via a network and to emulate the profile (e.g., the keyboard and screen characteristics)

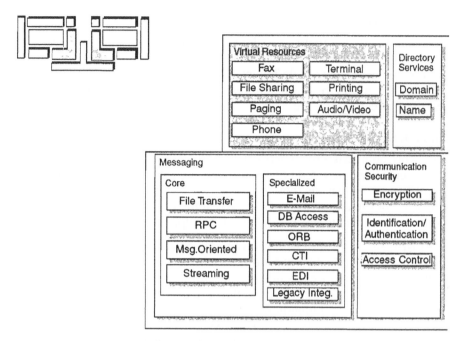

Exhibit 20. Virtual Resource Services.

required by the host application. For example, when a workstation application logs on to a mainframe, the workstation functions as a dumb terminal. Terminal Services receive user input and send data streams back to the host processor. If connecting from a PC to another PC, the workstation might act as a remote control terminal (e.g., PC Anywhere).

The following are examples of Terminal services.

Telnet: a simple and widely used terminal emulation protocol that is part of the TCP/IP communications protocol. Telnet operates establishing a TCP connection with the remotely located login server, minicomputer, or mainframe. The client's keyboard strokes are sent to the remote machine while the remote machine sends back the characters displayed on the local terminal screen.

3270 emulation: emulation of the 3270 protocol that is used by IBM mainframe terminals.

tn3270: a Telnet program that includes the 3270 protocol for logging onto IBM mainframes; part of the TCP/IP protocol suite.

X Window System: allows users to simultaneously access applications on one or more UNIX servers and display results in multiple windows on a local display. Recent enhancements to XWS include integration with the Web and optimization of network traffic (caching, compression, etc.).

Remote control: while terminal emulation is typically used in host-based environments, remote control is a sophisticated type of client/server Terminal service. Remote control allows a client computer to control the processing on a remote desktop computer. The GUI on the client computer looks as if it is the GUI on the remote desktop. This makes it appear as if the remote applications are running on the client.

rlogin: a remote terminal service implemented under BSD UNIX. The concept behind rlogin is that it supports "trusted" hosts. This is accomplished by having a set of machines that share common file access rights and logins. The user controls access by authorizing remote login based on a remote host and remote user name. This service is generally considered a security risk and avoided in most business system configurations.

Print Services

Print services connect network workstations to shared printers. The administration of Print Services is usually handled by a print server. Depending on the size of the network and the amount of resources the server must manage, the print server may run on a dedicated machine or on a machine that performs other server functions. Print servers queue print jobs sent to network printers, which are stored in the server's print buffer and then sent to the appropriate network printer as it becomes available. Print services can also provide the client with information, including print job status, and can manage in-progress print jobs.

File Sharing Services

File Sharing Services allow users to view, manage, read, and write files that may be located on a variety of platforms in a variety of locations. File Sharing services enable a unified view of independent file systems. This is represented in Exhibit 21, which shows how a client can perceive remote files as being local.

File Sharing services typically provide some or all of the following capabilities:

Transparent access: access to remote files as if they were local.

Multiuser access: distribution and synchronization of files among multiple users, including file locking to manage access requests by multiple users.

File access control: use of Security services (user authentication and authorization) to manage file system security.

Multiplatform access: access to files located on various platforms (e.g., UNIX, NT, etc.).

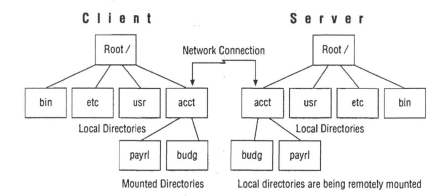

Exhibit 21. UNIX File Sharing Services Example.

Integrated file directory: a logical directory structure that combines all accessible file directories, regardless of the physical directory structure.

Fault tolerance: use of primary and replica file servers to ensure high availability of file system.

Scalability: ability to integrate networks and distributed file systems of various sizes

Phone Services

Phone virtual resource services extend telephony capabilities to computer platforms. For example, an application on a desktop computer can place and receive telephone calls for the user. Phone virtual resource services may be used in customer care centers, help desks, or any other environment in which it is useful for a computer to replace a telephone handset.

Phone services enable clients, servers, and specialized telephony nodes (PBXs, ACDs, etc.) to control the telephony environment through the following telephony controls:

- Call control
- Controls telephone features
- Controls recorded messages
- Manipulates real time call activities (e.g., make call, answer, transfer, hold, conference, mute transfer, release, route call, call treatments, and digits collected)
- Telephone status control
- Controls telephone status functions

- Logs users in and out of the system
- Sets ready, not ready, and make busy statuses for users

The following are examples of uses of Phone virtual resources.

PC Telephony. PC telephony products allow desktop computers to act as conduits for voice telephone calls.

Internet Telephony. Internet telephony products enable voice telephone calls (and faxing, voice mail retrieval, etc.) through the Internet. For example, an Internet telephony product can accept voice input into a workstation, translate it into an IP data stream, and route it through the Internet to a destination workstation, where the data is translated back into audio.

Desktop Voice Mail. Various products enable users to manage voice mail messages using a desktop computer.

Fax Services

Fax Services provide for the management of both inbound and outbound fax transmissions. If fax is used as a medium for communicating with customers or remote employees, inbound fax services may be required for centrally receiving and electronically routing faxes to the intended recipient. Outbound fax services can be as simple as supporting the sharing on the network of a single fax machine or group of machines for sending faxes.

Examples of Fax service functionality include the following:

- Managing incoming faxes
- Receiving faxes via the telephone network
- Queuing faxes
- Routing and distributing faxes
- Displaying or printing faxes
- Managing outgoing faxes
- Generating faxes
- Queuing faxes
- Transferring faxes via the telephone network

Fax services can provide centrally managed faxing capabilities, thus eliminating the need for fax modems on every workstation. A fax server generally provides fax services to clients, such as receiving, queuing, and distributing incoming faxes and queuing and sending outgoing faxes. Clients can view faxes and generate faxes to be sent.

Applications may compose and transfer faxes as part of notifying users or delivering information. For example, an application may use Fax services to add customer-specific information to a delivery receipt form and fax the form to a customer.

Audio/Video Services

Audio/Video services allow nodes to interact with multimedia data streams. These services may be implemented as audio only, video only, or combined audio/video.

Audio Services. Audio services allow components to interface with audio streams such as the delivery of music or radio content over data networks.

Video Services. Video services allow components to interface with video streams such as video surveillance. Video services can add simple video monitor capabilities to a computer, or they can transform the computer into a sophisticated video platform with the ability to generate and manipulate video.

Combined Audio/Video Services. Video and audio content is often delivered simultaneously. This may be accomplished by transferring separate audio and video streams or by transferring a single interleaved stream. Examples include video conferencing and television (traditional or interactive).

Audio/Video services can include the following functionality:

- Streaming content (audio, video, or both) to end users
- Managing buffering of data stream to ensure uninterrupted viewing/listening
- Performing compression and decompression of data
- Managing communications protocols to ensure smooth delivery of content
- Managing library of stored content and/or manages generation of live content

Audio/Video services draw upon lower-level services such as streaming (see Streaming Messaging services) and IP Multicast (see Packet Forwarding/Internetworking services) to efficiently deliver content across the network.

Paging Services

Wireless short messaging (i.e., paging) can be implemented through wireless systems such as paging networks, GSM voice/data networks, PCS voice/data networks, and dedicated wireless data networks.

Paging virtual resource services provide the message formatting and display functionality that allows network nodes to interface with wireless paging systems. This service emulates the capabilities of one-way and two-way pagers (Exhibit 22).

Exhibit 22. Use of a Paging Virtual Resource.

Paging systems allow pages to be generated in various ways:

- E-Mail messages to a specified mailbox
- DTMF (touch tone) signaling to a voice response system
- Encoded digital messages transferred into a paging provider gateway
- Messages transferred to a locally attached two-way wireless pager

COMMUNICATION SERVICES LAYER SUMMARY

Overall, the communication services layer provides the foundation for net-centric applications enabling client/server and virtual resource communications. Selecting the appropriate Communication Services, services that meet the business and applications requirements, is a key step to ensuring a successful Communications Architecture. In addition, ensuring the required Transport Services support the selected Communication Services is important. Transport Services are the subject of the next section.

TRANSPORT SERVICES

Transport Services are the portion of the Communications Architecture that provides the movement of information across a network. While the Communications Fabric includes all the hardware, software, and services between the client and server nodes, the Transport Services play a key role

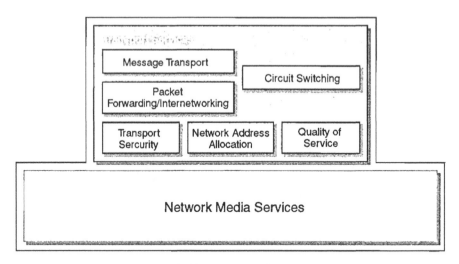

Exhibit 23. Transport Services.

performing network functions across the enterprise or between enterprises. Transport Services include the following (see also Exhibit 23):

- Message Transport services
- Packet Forwarding/Internetworking services
- Circuit Switching services
- Transport Security services
- Network Address Allocation services
- Quality of Service services

Message Transport Services

Message Transport Service are responsible for the end-to-end delivery of messages. They can include the following functionality.

End-to-End Data Transfer. The Message Transport Service formats messages for sending and confirms the integrity of received messages.

Connection Control. The Message Transport service may establish end-to-end (client–server) connections and track addresses and other associated information for the connection. The service also tears down connections and handles hard connection failures.

Reliable Transfer. The Message Transport service may manage reliable delivery of messages through the use of acknowledgments and retransmissions.

Flow Control. The Message Transport service may allow the receiver to govern the rate at which the sender transfers data.

Multiplexing. The Message Transport service may define multiple addresses or ports within a single network node, allowing multiple processes on the node to have their own communications paths.

It is important to note that some transport services do not implement all of the listed functionalities. For example, the UDP protocol does not offer connection control or reliable transfer.

The following are examples of protocols that provide message transport:

- SPX (Sequenced Packet eXchange)
- TCP (Transmission Control Protocol)
- UDP (User Datagram Protocol)
- NetBIOS/NetBEUI (Network Basic Input/Output System/NetBIOS Extended User Interface)
- APPC (Advanced Program-to-Program Communications)
- AppleTalk

Packet Forwarding/Internetworking Services

Packet Forwarding/Internetworking Services transfer data packets and manage the path that data takes through the network. They includes the following functionalities.

Fragmentation/Reassembly. The Packet Forwarding/Internetworking service divides an application message into multiple packets of a size suitable for network transmission. The individual packets include information to allow the receiving node to reassemble them into the message. The service also validates the integrity of received packets and buffers, reorders, and reassembles packets into a complete message.

Addressing. The Packet Forwarding/Internetworking service encapsulates packets with addressing information.

Routing. The Packet Forwarding/Internetworking service can maintain routing information (a view of the network topology) that is used to determine the best route for each packet. Routing decisions are made based on the cost, percent utilization, delay, reliability, and similar factors for each possible route through the network.

Switching. Switching is the process of receiving a packet, selecting an appropriate outgoing path, and sending the packet. Switching is performed by routers and switches within the communications fabric. Switching can be implemented in several ways.

- For some network protocols (e.g., TCP/IP), routers draw upon dynamic routing information to switch packets to the appropriate path. This capability is especially important when connecting independent networks or subnets.
- For other network protocols (e.g., Ethernet, Token Ring), switching simply directs packets according to a table of physical addresses. The switch can build the table by "listening" to network traffic and determining which network nodes are connected to which switch port. Some protocols such as Frame Relay involve defining permanent routes (permanent virtual circuits, or PVCs) within the network. Because Frame Relay is switched based upon PVCs, routing functionality is not required.

Multicasting. The Packet Forwarding/Internetworking service may support multicasting, which is the process of transferring a single message to multiple recipients at the same time. Multicasting allows a sender to transfer a single copy of the message to the communications fabric, which then distributes the message to multiple recipients.

The following are examples of protocols that provide Packet Forwarding/Internetworking:

- IP (Internet Protocol)
- IP Multicast (emerging standard that uses a predefined set of IP addresses to instruct network routers to deliver each packet to all users involved in a multicast session)
- IPX (Internetwork Packet Exchange)
- ATM (Asynchronous Transfer Mode)
- Frame Relay
- X.25

The following are examples of network components that perform Packet Forwarding/Internetworking:

- Routers
- Switches
- ATM switches, Frame Relay switches, IP switches, Ethernet switches, etc.

The following are examples of protocols that maintain routing information tables within routers:

Distance Vector Protocols. Each router periodically informs neighboring routers as to the contents of routing table (destination addresses and routing metrics); routing decisions are made based on the total distance and other "costs" for each path:

- IP and IPX Routing Information Protocols (RIP)
- AppleTalk Routing Table Management Protocol (RTMP)
- Cisco's Interior Gateway Routing Protocol (IGRP) and Enhanced IGRP

Link-State Protocols. Each router periodically broadcasts changes to the routers directly on adjacent networks:

- Open Shortest Path First (OSPF)
- ISO's Intermediate System to Intermediate System (IS-IS)
- Novell's NetWare Link Services Protocol (NLSP)

Policy Routing Protocols. These allow Internet backbone routers to accept routing information from neighboring backbone providers on the basis of contracts or other nontechnical criteria; routing algorithms are Distance Vector:

- Border Gateway Protocol (BGR)
- Interdomain Routing Protocol (IDR)

Circuit Switching

While Message Transport services and Packet Forwarding/Internetworking services support the transfer of packetized data, Circuit Switching services establish physical circuits for the transfer of circuit-switched multimedia- and image-oriented content such as voice, fax, video.

Circuit Switching Packetized uses an end-to-end physical connection between the sender and the receiver that lasts for the duration of the "call" transferred through brief, temporary, logical connections between nodes.

Circuit Switching services include the following functionality:

- Establishing end-to-end path for circuit (may involved multiple inter-mediate nodes/switches)
- Managing end-to-end path (quality, billing, termination, etc.)

The following are examples of Circuit Switching services:

- Analog dial-up telephone circuit
- Cellular telephone circuit
- ISDN (Integrated Services Digital Network)

Transport Security

Transport Security services (within the Transport Services layer) perform encryption and filtering.

Transport-Layer Encryption. Encryption within the Transport Services layer is performed by encrypting the packets generated by higher level services (e.g., Message Transport) and encapsulating them in lower level packets (e.g., Packet Forwarding/Internetworking). (Note that encryption can also occur within the Communications Services layer or the Network Media Services layer.) Encryption within the Transport Services layer has the advantage of being independent of both the application and the transmission media, but it may make network monitoring and troubleshooting activities more difficult.

The following standards support transport-layer encryption:

- Point to Point Tunneling Protocol
- Layer 2 Tunneling Protocol

Transport-layer Filtering. Network traffic can be controlled at the Transport Services layer by filtering data packets based on source and/or destination addresses and network service. This ensures that only authorized data transfers can occur. This filtering is one of the roles of a packet filtering firewall. (A firewall is a system that enforces an access control policy between a trusted internal network and an untrusted external network.)

The IETF standard IPSec supports interoperability among security systems. IPSec allows two nodes to dynamically agree on a security association based on keys, encryption, authentication algorithms, and other parameters for the connection before any communications take place; operates in the IP layer and supports TCP or UDP. IPSec will be included as part of IPng, or the next generation of IP (IPv6).

Network Address Allocation Services

Network Address Allocation services manage the distribution of addresses to network nodes. This provides more flexibility compared to having all nodes assigned static addresses. This service assigns addresses to nodes when they initially power-on and connect to the network.

The following are examples of standards that implement Network Address Allocation and allow a network node to ask a central resource for the node's network address (e.g., IP address):

- DHCP (Dynamic Host Configuration Protocol)
- BootP (Bootstrap Protocol)

Quality of Service Services

Different types of network traffic (e.g., data, voice, and video) have different quality of service requirements. For example, data associated with video conferencing sessions is useless if it is not delivered "on time." On the other hand, traditional best-effort data services, such as file or e-mail transfer, are not affected by variations in latency. Quality of Service (QoS) services deliver a defined network throughput for designated traffic by allocating dedicated bandwidth, prioritizing data traffic, etc. (Note that, as an alternative to predefined throughput, some QoS protocols can also offer a best effort, i.e., variable) throughput QoS based on available network capacity.)

Exhibit 24. Quality of Service Parameters

Parameter	Description
Connection establishment delay	Time between the connection request and a confirm being received by the requester
Connection establishment failure probability	Chance that the connection will not be established within the maximum establishment delay
Throughput	Bits per second of transmitted data
Transit delay	Time elapsed between when sender transfers packet and recipient receives packet
Residual error rate	Number of lost or corrupted messages compared to total messages in the sampling period.
Transfer failure probability	The fraction of the time when the throughput, transit delay, or residual error were not those agreed upon at the start of the connection.
Connection release delay	Time between when one node initiates a release and the other node performs the release
Connection release failure probability	Fraction of release attempts which do not succeed
Protection	Specifies a secure connection
Priority	Indicates traffic priority over the connection
Resilience	Probability that the transport layer spontaneously terminates

Exhibit 24 provides a description of various Quality of Service parameters.

Quality of Service can be achieved in various ways.

Specialized QoS Communications Protocols. These provide guaranteed QoS.

Asynchronous Transfer Mode (ATM). ATM is a connection-oriented wide area and local area networking protocol that delivers QoS on a per-connection basis. QoS is negotiated as part of the initial connection set up and as network conditions change. Because of the small size of ATM data cells, QoS can be better managed, compared to protocols such as Ethernet that have large frames that can tie up network components. For ATM to deliver QOS to applications, ATM must be used end to end.

Resource Reservation Protocol (RSVP). The emerging RSVP specification, proposed by the Internet Engineering Task Force (IETF), allows applications to reserve router bandwidth for delay-sensitive IP traffic. With RSVP, QoS is negotiated for each application connection. RSVP enables the network to reserve resources from end to end, using Frame Relay techniques on Frame Relay networks, ATM techniques on ATM, and so on. In this way, RSVP can achieve QoS across a variety of network technologies, as long as all intermediate nodes are RSVP capable.

IP Stream Switching. This improves network performance but does not guarantee QoS.

IP Switching. IP Switching is an emerging technology that can increase network throughput for streams of data by combining IP routing software with ATM switching hardware. With IP Switching, an IP switch analyzes each stream of packets directed from a single source to a specific destination and classifies it as short or long lived. Long-lived flows are assigned ATM Virtual Channels (VCs) that bypass the IP router and move through the switching fabric at the full ATM line speed. Short-lived flows continue to be routed through traditional store-and-forward transfer.

Tag Switching. Like IP Switching, emerging Tag Switching technology also improves network throughput for IP data streams. Tag Switching aggregates one or more data streams destined for the same location and assigns a single tag to all associated packets. This allows routers to more efficiently transfer the tagged data. Tag Switching is also known as Multiprotocol Label Switching.

Data Prioritization. This improves network performance for prioritized application traffic but does not guarantee QoS.

Although not an example of end-to-end QoS, various network components can be configured to prioritize their handling of specified types of traffic. For example, routers can be configured to handle legacy mainframe traffic (SNA) in front of other traffic (e.g., TCP/IP). A similar technique is the use of prioritized circuits within Frame Relay, in which the Frame Relay network vendor assigns different priorities to different permanent virtual circuits.

Prioritization techniques are of limited effectiveness if data must also pass through network components that are not configured for prioritization (e.g., network components run by third party network providers).

TRANSPORT SERVICES SUMMARY

Transport Services continue to improve and evolve to new levels. Through enhanced quality, tighter security, improved management and control, and increased speeds, transport services play an important role in moving key business information to an intended destination quickly, safely, and accurately. As netcentric computing continues to evolve, transport services should continue to converge to an infrastructure based on open industry standard technologies that integrate the many physical networking options available today. The next section discusses these physical networking options in more detail.

NETWORK MEDIA SERVICES

The Network Media layer, which provides the core of the communication fabric from the overall communications architecture framework, provides the following capabilities:

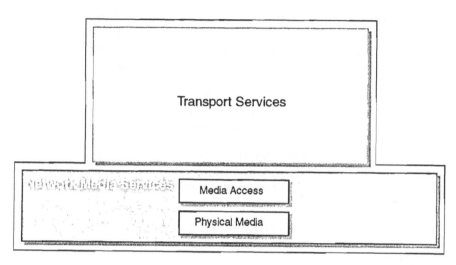

Exhibit 25. Network Media Services.

- Final framing of data for interfacing with the physical network
- Receiving, interpreting and acting on signals from the communications fabric
- Transferring data through the physical network

Network Media services (Exhibit 25) performs two primary service functions:

- Media Access services
- Physical Media services

Media Access Services

Media Access services manage the low-level transfer of data between network nodes. Media Access services perform the following functions.

Physical Addressing. The Media Access service encapsulates packets with physical address information used by the data link protocol (e.g., Ethernet and Frame Relay).

Packet Transfer. The Media Access service uses the data link communications protocol to frame packets and transfer them to another computer on the same network/subnetwork.

Shared Access. The Media Access service provides a method for multiple network nodes to share access to a physical network. Shared Access schemes include the following.

CSMA/CD (Carrier Sense Multiple Access with Collision Detection). A method by which multiple nodes can access a shared physical media by "listening" until no other transmissions are detected and then transmitting and checking to see if simultaneous transmission occurred.

Token passing. A method of managing access to a shared physical media by circulating a token (a special control message) among nodes to designate which node has the right to transmit.

Multiplexing. A method of sharing physical media among nodes by consolidating multiple, independent channels into a single circuit. The independent channels (assigned to nodes, applications, or voice calls) can be combined in the following ways.

Time division multiplexing (TDM) — use of a circuit is divided into a series of time slots, and each independent channel is assigned its own periodic slot.

Frequency division multiplexing (FDM) — each independent channel is assigned its own frequency range, allowing all channels to be carried simultaneously.

Flow Control. The Media Access service manages the flow of data to account for differing data transfer rates between devices. For example, flow control would have to limit outbound traffic if a receiving machine or intermediate node operates at a slower data rate, possibly due to the use of different network technologies and topologies or due to excess network traffic at a node.

Error Recovery. The Media Access service performs error recovery, which is the capability to detect and possibly resolve data corruption that occurs during transmission. Error recovery involves the use of checksums, parity bits, etc.

Encryption. The Media Access service may perform encryption. (Note that encryption can also occur within the Communications Services layer or the Transport Services layer.) Within the Network Media Services layer, encryption occurs as part of the data link protocol (e.g., Ethernet, frame relay). In this case, all data are encrypted before it is placed on the wire. Such encryption tools are generally hardware products. Encryption at this level has the advantage of being transparent to higher level services. However, because it is dependent on the data link protocol, it has the disadvantage of requiring a different solution for each data link protocol.

The following are examples of Media Access protocols:

- Ethernet
- Token Ring

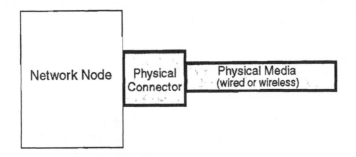

Exhibit 26. Subcomponents of Physical Media.

- FDDI (Fiber Distributed Data Interface)
- Portions of the ATM (Asynchronous Transfer Mode) standard
- HDLC (High-level Data Link Control)/SDLC (Synchronous Data Link Control)
- LAP-B (Link Access Procedure — Balanced)
- T-carrier, E-carrier (e.g., T1, T3, E1, E3)
- TDM and FDM (Time Division Multiplexing and Frequency Division Multiplexing; used on T-carriers, etc.)
- SONET (Synchronous Optical Network), SDH
- PPP (Point-to-Point Protocol), SLIP (Serial Line Internet Protocol)
- V.32, V.34, V.34 bis, etc.
- RS-232, EIA-232
- TDMA and FDMA (Time Division Multiple Access and Frequency Division Multiple Access; used on wireless links)

Specialized services convert between addresses at the Media Access level (i.e., physical addresses like Ethernet) and the Packet Forwarding/Internetworking level (i.e., network addresses like IP). The following protocols are examples of this functionality.

Address Resolution Protocol (ARP). ARP allows a node to obtain the physical address for another node when only the IP address is known.

Reverse Address Resolution Protocol (RARP). RARP allows a node to obtain the IP address for another node when only the physical address is known.

Physical Media Services

The Physical Media are divided into two categories (Exhibit 26):

- Physical connectors
- Physical media (wired or wireless)

Physical Connectors. The following are examples of wiring connectors used to connect network nodes to physical media:

- RJ-11, RJ-45
- BNC
- DB-9, DB-25
- Fiber optic connectors

Physical Media. Physical Media may be wired or wireless. Wired Physical Media includes wiring and cabling, while wireless Physical Media includes antennas, connectors, and the radio frequency spectrum.

The following are examples of wired physical media:

- Twisted pair wiring
- Shielded twisted pair wiring
- Coaxial cable
- Fiber optic cable
- Four-pair voice-grade wiring

The following are examples of wireless physical media:

- Cellular antennas and the associated radio frequencies
- Wireless local area network antennas and the associated radio frequencies
- Satellite antennas and the associated radio frequencies

NETWORK MEDIA SERVICES SUMMARY

Without the Network Media Services (which we compared earlier to the interconnected train tracks, signals, and switches), information would not be capable of traveling to its intended destinations. While this infrastructure is a complex network of numerous interconnected copper wires, fiber optics cables, and radio antennas, continued change in Network Media Services is likely to be slow. We are more likely to continue to see new technologies evolve to adapt and bridge the various physical network options. These technologies make up the essense of netcentric computing, which continues to expand the reach of client/server while delivering rich new content.

CONCLUSION

Today's advanced communications architectures permit organizations to take full advantage of the convergence of computing, communications, and knowledge. Netcentric computing applications provide more direct links with business partners and allow companies to respond quickly to fluctuations in customer demand. As communications architectures grow in sophistication, one should expect the network to enable almost total supply chain integration. Applications that manage and perform business-to-business processes will enable the ultimate virtualization of business: bringing together strategy, people, process, and technology in a unique configuration across multiple companies to serve the customer in a more powerful way than any one company could on its own. That will be the final convergence, one in which most barriers between companies and their customers have been removed.

Chapter 7
Transaction Services

Today, as organizations are becoming more comfortable with client/server and netcentric computing and as related technologies continue to stabilize, there has been an increase in distributed transaction processing. Networks are becoming more stable, operating systems are proving themselves, relational databases have been used successfully, and tools are now being produced to help manage distributed systems. With stabilization and increased confidence in client/server and netcentric technology, systems building can move from conservative applications (decision support systems and departmental systems) to more mission-critical systems (transaction processing systems and enterprisewide systems).

MISSION-CRITICAL SYSTEMS

Mission-critical client/server and netcentric systems can have different requirements than other types of systems.

- Users in many locations share data and resources.
- Complex transactions (sometimes spanning multiple data sources) need to be managed to guarantee completion and data integrity.
- System availability and reliability become more critical.
- Performance needs to be predictable and controllable as more users and locations are added to systems.

Distributed transaction processing (DTP) is a vital element in managing transactions in mission-critical client/server and netcentric systems. Many information technology departments today want to increase the price/performance of their systems by moving mainframe applications to smaller operating systems platforms, where the processing is distributed among several platforms. This distribution of processors is what distributed transaction processing refers to. A transaction is considered distributed if it accesses more than one resource manager, processor, database, file system, printer, or any other shared resource.

WHAT IS A TRANSACTION?

A transaction is a logical unit of work; it consists of the logic and the processing needed to perform an individual, unique business function. When a transaction consists of multiple steps of processing and those steps occur simultaneously, each step must be completed successfully before the entire transaction is completed.

A transaction must exhibit what are sometimes referred to as "ACID" qualities, an acronym standing for atomicity, consistency, isolation, and durability:

- Atomicity guarantees that, in case of error or rollback, no partial transaction data remains to corrupt the database. For example, a transfer of funds consists of two parts: a debit and a credit. Atomicity makes sure that a $20 transfer from savings to checking does not debit a savings account without crediting a checking account.
- Consistency means that the execution of a transaction maintains the interrelationships of all data. Consistency of data is the end result of the other three properties. The work done by a transaction must take resources from one consistent state to another consistent state. Continuing the example, the $20 debited from the savings account must match the $20 credited to the checking account. If a transaction is repeated many times in an identical manner, the results should be identical.
- Isolation means transactions are separated from one another so they can execute concurrently. In other words, the execution of one transaction has no effect on other transactions. In effect, concurrent transactions must behave as if they are executed serially.
- Durability reduces the likelihood of a failure and protects the transaction data in case the system does fail, that is, when a transaction succeeds, the effects remain in the database after a system failure.

In a client/server or netcentric environment, the logical units of work may not be neatly defined and may span multiple processes and resources. Ensuring that these transactions maintain their ACID qualities is the challenge of distributed transaction processing in a client/server or netcentric environment.

WHAT IS DISTRIBUTED TRANSACTION PROCESSING MANAGEMENT?

In small- to moderate-scale environments of less than 150 simultaneous users on a single server, management of transactions may be provided by the database management system (DBMS) software with its restart/recovery and integrity capabilities. For larger client/server environments, a class of software is starting to appear, referred to as Distributed Transaction Processing (DTP) managers.

These transaction managers share server processes across a large community of users and can be more efficient and effective than DBMSs alone. Example products include Tuxedo and TopEnd (formerly NCR) from BEA

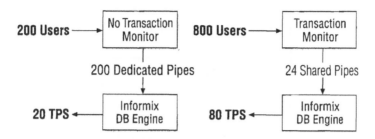

Exhibit 1. Comparison of Performance with and without a TP Monitor.

Systems (formerly AT&T), Microsoft Transaction Server, and Encina from Transarc (owned by IBM).

Performance Improvements

What are the advantages of DTP? One estimate is that the cost of processing a transaction in a distributed environment is about one fifth what it would be in a mainframe environment.

In a client/server or netcentric environment, TP monitors can increase the performance of systems. Exhibit 1 compares a database engine on a server running Tuxedo. The TP monitor increased the transactions-per-second benchmark fourfold.

Not every situation results in this kind of improvement, however. The potential for throughput or performance improvement depends on the nature of both the application and the hardware/systems software being used (e.g., DBMS product). TP monitors can also be used to control and monitor tasks and processes distributed across a network of processors.

Two-Phase Commit in DTP

In a traditional mainframe environment, ensuring the ACID properties was simpler to achieve. If one piece of the transaction failed, the entire transaction failed. In a distributed environment, on the other hand, distributed transactions may be found running on multiple components. The DTP architecture achieves this through the use of two-phase commit. Any component of the system could falter while the remaining pieces continue working to complete a transaction that should have been canceled. Two-phase commit makes sure that a transaction is either committed correctly or aborted in all systems.

In the first phase, the prepare phase, all participants in a transaction (e.g., a database or other resource manager) are polled to see whether they are prepared to commit a transaction. A travel agent trying to make plane,

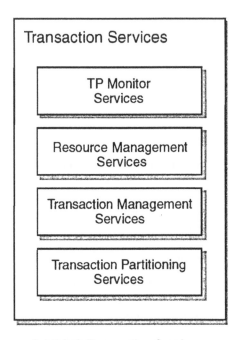

Exhibit 2. Transaction Services.

hotel, and rental car reservations at once provides an analogy. The agent does not want to book a flight if a hotel room cannot be reserved or request a car rental on Tuesday if the passenger cannot get a plane until Wednesday, so the agent finds out whether all the reservations can be made before committing to any of them.

The second phase is called the commit phase. In the same example, if all three participants respond affirmatively, the transaction is committed. If any or all the participants respond negatively, the transaction is rolled back.

TRANSACTION SERVICES IN THE NETCENTRIC EXECUTION ARCHITECTURE

Transaction Services (Exhibit 2) provide the transaction integrity mechanism for the application. This allows all data activities within a single business event to be grouped as a single, logical unit of work.

TP Monitor Services

TP monitor services are the primary interface through which applications invoke transaction services and receive status and error information. TP monitor services, in conjunction with information access services and communication services, provide for load balancing across processors or platforms and location transparency for DTP architectures.

The TP monitor is a critical component of the DTP architecture. TP monitors provide many services, including

- Providing resource management (e.g., load balancing)
- Scheduling transactions for efficient, high-volume execution
- Scheduling tasks across heterogeneous resource managers
- Providing priority-based transactions
- Providing location transparency of servers
- Transaction recovery

Two key features separate TP monitors from systems using a database engine without a TP monitor: multithreading and load balancing. Multithreading permits an application to perform more than one function simultaneously, such as collecting multiple files from a database that does not already support multithreading. Because more than one activity is being completed, multithreading typically speeds up transaction throughput.

Load balancing examines which application functions have to be completed and what the work load is on each resource so that needed tasks are shifted to lower-utilized resources. Load balancing can be either equitably based or priority based. With equitably based load balancing, all transactions have the same importance: they are executed in the order received. Priority-based load balancing assigns certain priorities to certain transactions. More important transactions can move in front of those of lesser importance.

Resource Management Services

A resource manager provides for concurrence control and integrity for a single data resource (e.g., a database or a file system). Integrity is guaranteed by ensuring that an update is completed correctly and entirely or not at all. Resource management services use locking, commit, and rollback services and are integrated with transaction management services.

Transaction Management Services

Transaction management services coordinate transactions across one or more resource managers either on a single platform or on multiple platforms within the network. Transaction management services ensure that all resources for a transaction are updated or, in the case of an update failure on any one resource, all updates are rolled back.

Transaction Partitioning Services

Transaction partitioning services provide architectural support for mapping single logical or business transactions into the required multiple physical transactions. For example, in a package or legacy environment, the single logical transaction of changing a customer address may require the partitioning and coordination of several physical transactions to multiple application systems or databases. Transaction partitioning services provide the application with a simple, single-transaction view.

GUIDELINES FOR DETERMINING A DTP ARCHITECTURE

Determining a distributed transaction processing architecture involves several major considerations:

- When to use a TP monitor
- How to choose the product best suited for the needs of the organization
- How to create the DTP components for the particular client/server or netcentric environment

The necessary steps for making this determination are as follows.

Step 1: Understand the Basics of DTP

A thorough understanding of the concepts involved in distributed transaction processing is a prerequisite for determining whether a TP monitor is necessary for the client/server or netcentric solution the organization is considering deploying. This chapter provided a high-level discussion of these concepts in the previous section.

Step 2: Determine the System Requirements

Systems developers must perform a thorough analysis of system needs before deciding on a TP monitor. The following system requirements may affect the need for a TP monitor:

- Number of concurrent users
- Distributed locations of users and servers
- Need for heterogeneous platform support or platform independence
- High transaction volumes
- Potential future growth of the system (scalability)
- Nature (type) of applications

Another "need" concerns the imaging or document management integration. When integrating in either of these technologies, a transaction control mechanism for ensuring both relational database management system (RDBMS) commit and file system write, or image store write, is often necessary.

In many imaging and document management systems, the DBMS cannot support this integration alone. This points to the need for a TP monitor that can provide ACID properties for data stores other than DBMS (e.g., file systems). Any of these requirements either indicates the need for a TP monitor or points to significant benefits that could be achieved with one.

Step 3: Determine Whether a TP monitor Is Needed

A TP monitor is not necessary for all distributed environments. When the system requirements have been identified, developers must complete an evaluation to determine the need for a TP monitor.

Step 4: Create a Product Features Matrix

If the need for a TP monitor is established, developers must choose the most appropriate TP monitor for the system. (See the section "Choosing Among Monitors" for a list of questions and a matrix with which to compare the features and usability of the different TP monitors an organization might consider.)

Step 5: Map System Requirements to Product Features

Systems developers should compare the product matrix and the needs of the system to find the best TP monitor for the project. Functional requirements as well as other business needs (e.g., skill base within the organization) should be mapped to the features provided by each TP monitor.

Step 6: Determine Target Product and Architecture

The next step is to design and develop the TP monitor and the rest of the execution architecture. Extra effort should be made to ensure that all layers and components of the architecture will work together and that they will meet the application, system, and organization requirements.

Step 7: Confirm the Architecture by Performing a Benchmark

Developers should conduct a benchmark of the technical architecture to confirm the assumptions made in defining the architecture. The benchmark ensures that various parts of the architecture work together and provides the functions and features required by the system. This benchmark also allows developers to install, configure, learn, and test the selected TP monitor.

STEPS TO DETERMINE WHETHER A TP MONITOR IS NEEDED

Although a TP monitor may be a crucial link in systems projects, a monitor is not necessary or even desirable in every situation. Systems developers must complete a careful evaluation to determine the need for a TP monitor. In this evaluation, developers must consider several questions.

Step 1. How Many Users Access the System Concurrently?

Because TP monitors can be used to manage the system resource requirements of large communities of users, the organization should evaluate the use of a TP monitor in large client/server and netcentric environments — where there are perhaps hundreds or thousands of users.

Different sources give different answers as to the number of concurrent users that necessitates the use of a TP monitor. The monitor vendors themselves give low values; the database vendors give high values. The middle ground seems to be somewhere greater than 250 to 400 concurrent users. This is by no means definitive, however, and an organization should consider this question in conjunction with each of the other questions before making the choice.

Step 2. Does the System Require High Throughput?

Because TP monitors provide load balancing capability and because they may effectively reduce the number of connections that must be made to databases (depending on DBMS product architecture), they will help conserve the resources of the data servers and, as a result, can increase the overall throughput of the system. Systems with high throughput requirements should consider using a TP monitor. As a guideline, systems requiring greater than 50 to 100 transactions per second throughput are good candidates for a TP monitor.

Step 3. Does the System Require High Availability?

Because of their fault tolerance, TP monitors make a valuable addition to systems that require high availability. The automatic restart/recovery feature helps a system recognize when components have failed and attempts to restart them. Also, because of the location transparency capabilities, if an entire node in a system goes down, clients may be able to reach the service they need on another node providing the same service.

Step 4. Is the System Distributed Across Multiple Nodes?

TP monitors provide common administrative facilities to manage groups of distributed servers. These facilities allow a system to be managed from one central location with a common set of commands for each platform within a distributed environment.

Step 5. Will the System Be Scaled in the Future?

TP monitors offer multiple scalability options. TP monitors can run on platforms ranging from workstations to mainframes in a client/server or netcentric environment. This feature can be used to grow client/server and netcentric applications as the organization and business volumes grow.

Monitors also scale by allowing new machines to be added dynamically to the system. Adding additional nodes in the production cycle is one TP monitor strength, although some monitors are better at doing this than others. If the organization anticipates that system volumes will increase during the system's lifetime, scalability provides an excellent reason for selecting and using a TP monitor.

Step 6. Do the On-Line Applications Need the Support of Interoperability between Autonomous, Heterogeneous Processors?

Some TP monitors are available across multiple platforms and maintain interoperability (e.g., communication and data translation) between those platforms. For this reason, systems projects that intend to support a heterogeneous hardware environment should consider using a TP monitor.

Step 7. Is the System Mission Critical?

TP monitors offer additional capability: two-phase commit, recovery/rollback, naming services, security services, guaranteed processing, and audit trail logging. Therefore, the more mission-critical the system, the more likely it is that the organization should opt for a TP monitor.

Step 8. Does the System Need to Integrate with or Access Legacy Systems?

TP monitors can access databases and services running in traditional mainframe systems environments. TP monitors frequently include mainframe networking capability and maintain transaction rollback during mainframe accesses. If access to the legacy system is read only, the messaging capabilities of the platforms are probably sufficient. If access is update, however, the messaging and two-phase commit capabilities of the TP monitor would be more dependable and reliable. In general, each TP monitor vendor offering provides varying levels of support for mainframe-based systems. The selection process should identify the legacy integration/access requirements and evaluate each vendor offering appropriately.

Step 9. Does the System Access Nonrelational Data?

Some TP monitors provide a method of accessing nonrelational data, such as VSAM files or flat files, independently of where the file physically resides. If these data sources require write access, a TP monitor would provide more dependable messaging and two-phase commit capabilities than the platform messaging capabilities alone.

Step 10. Do the On-Line Applications Access and Update more than One Database or more than One Type of Database?

A real strength of TP monitors is their ability to ensure a global two-phase commit over multiple, heterogeneous databases. A system that has this quality is a candidate for a TP monitor. Many client/server and netcentric database products (e.g., database access gateways) also provide this capability.

Step 11. Is the System not a Transaction Processing System?

Although TP monitors provide global two-phase commit transaction processing capability, systems that do not need this feature can also benefit by using TP monitors. For example, the load-balancing feature helps increase system performance. Also, the administrative facilities can help simplify system management.

CHOOSING AMONG MONITORS

When an organization decides to use a TP monitor in its client/server environment, the following criteria may be useful to differentiate among TP monitor product offerings.

Is the Organization Interested in Stable Technologies or in Emerging Technologies?

Many of the TP monitor products are new to the marketplace; others have been available for years. Systems developers should assess the organization's requirements regarding the stability of both the TP monitor product and the TP monitor vendor.

Is the Organization Installing a New System, or Is It Rehosting or Downsizing an Existing Mainframe System?

The UniKix, VIS/TP, and CICS/6000 monitors were developed specifically with rehosting of IBM mainframe applications in mind. Other TP monitors are best suited to fresh installations. Developers following this path must be sure to assess carefully the costs and benefits of their TP monitor selection.

Does the Organization Have Existing Personnel with Mainframe–CICS Experience?

CICS/6000 has a programming interface similar to mainframe CICS. The learning curve for mainframe–CICS programmers to use CICS/6000 is minimal. The learning curve for these same personnel to program using such other TP monitors as Tuxedo and Encina may be substantial. On the other hand, because CICS/6000's administrative facilities are not similar to mainframe CICS, administrative personnel face a steep learning curve: They need to learn UNIX, DCE, and Encina, the layers on which CICS/6000 is built.

Does the Organization Plan to use Windows NT Server?

TP monitor support for Windows NT is currently limited to BEA's Tuxedo, IBM's Encina, and Microsoft Transaction Server. As NT gains market share and proves to be a scalable, robust server platform, other vendors should make progress toward supporting the NT platform.

What Platforms and Operating Systems Do the Servers Run On?

Some TP monitors are capable of running on a wider variety of platforms/operating systems than others. Organizations should be sure that their TP monitor supports the current and planned platform technologies in their client/server and netcentric environments.

Does the System Require Mainframe Connectivity?

The leading TP monitors offer varying levels of mainframe connectivity, including 3270, APPC, VTXXX, and Transmission Control Protocol/Internet Protocol (TCP/IP). If mainframe application and data connectivity are required, the organization must ensure that their TP monitor supports the specific protocols.

Does the System Need to Integrate with Internet/Intranet Technologies?

The leading TP monitors provide varying degrees of Internet/Intranet integration. Some products, such as Microsoft Transaction Server, allow custom business services to be reused by traditional client/server applications, browser-based HTML applications, and Java/ActiveX applets. Some vendors are simply enabling their communications layer for the Internet by providing support for Internet security technologies, such as Proxy Servers and Firewalls. Other vendors, such as Sun's NetDynamics, are starting fresh, providing a new integrated Web-based DTP architecture.

Does the Organization Want Object Transaction Processing?

Recently, vendors of transaction monitors have started to evolve their products and create a new category of system software termed Object Transaction Monitors (OTMs). This new middleware has been formed by combining technology for creating systems from components, e.g., Microsoft's Component Object Model (COM) and the Object Management Group's (OMG) Common Object Request Broker Architecture (CORBA), with TP monitor technology. The result is the emergence of powerful infrastructure using components that provide developers with the ability to create high performance, reliable, and scalable application servers with the robustness that has always been the hallmark of high-end transaction processing environments.

Does the Organization Have the Skills to Develop and Manage a DTP System?

Microsoft is clearly positioning MTS as a black box product that allows average Visual Basic developers to create DTP systems without having to

Exhibit 3. DTP Product Features Matrix

TP Monitor	Description
Runtime features	
Synchronous service calls	Service calls from a client to the server that wait for the response
Asynchronous service call	Service calls from a client to the server that can continue processing without the response
Conversational service calls	Multistep service calls where context is maintained by the server for each step and all steps are within the same transaction
Embedded service calls:	
Embedded synchronous calls	Synchronous service calls contained within a service
Embedded asynchronous calls	Asynchronous service calls contained within a service
Service forwarding (pipelining)	Service call within a service, where the called service responds directly to the client
Global transactions (two-phase)	Transactions that can span multiple databases on multiple machines
Nested transactions	Subtransactions within transactions; these can be committed or rolled back independently of the main transaction
Cross-platform data translation	Automatic translation of messages between platforms, independent of the data representation on each machine
Reliable queuing	Service that allows transactions to be reliably saved for later processing
Mainframe connectivity:	
From server to mainframe	Ability to invoke mainframe applications from a server transaction
From mainframe to server	Ability to invoke server transactions from a mainframe application
Data-dependent routing	Ability to route a request to a particular service based on the content of the message being sent
Unsolicited client notification	Messages sent without client request
Multithreaded transaction processing	Ability to start another task concurrently using threads within an operating environment
Configuration features	
Load balancing	Ability to spread the transaction load evenly among all available servers
Dynamic load balancing	Automatic startup of multiple copies of a server when the load on a given server increases
Prioritized service calls	Service calls that can be assigned a priority weighting and then be processed in priority order
Multiple instances of monitor per machine (regions)	Ability to invoke multiple instances of the monitor on one machine, similar to CICS regions on a mainframe
Audit trail/event logging	Ability to record the events of all users for security and debugging purposes
PC connectivity	PC-based client messaging with the TP monitor
Automatic recovery/restart	Ability to recognize when services are down, and automatically attempt to restart them
Distributed TP networks	Networks of TP applications in a LAN/WAN environment
Kerberos security	Standard security approach developed at MIT used for authentication services
Other DTP Features	
Software distribution facilities	Utilities that facilitate distribution of application and/or system software in a distributed environment

worry too much about the intricacies of such things as load balancing, threading, and transactions. This is clearly different from Tuxedo and Encina, which are still very much technically oriented products that require a significant degree of skill to develop with and to operate.

Exhibit 3 lists and briefly describes runtime features and configuration features for TP monitors. When evaluating one or more TP monitors, an organization should determine which of these features are required by, or could benefit, its client/server and netcentric applications.

The features described can be used to evaluate and differentiate among the TP monitor products an organization chooses to consider. It is important to remember that the vendors are constantly adding to and modifying the features of their products. Each product should be carefully reviewed at the time the organization is selecting a DTP monitor.

CONCLUSION

This chapter has provided an overview of transaction processing in a client/server and netcentric environment. As more and more organizations become skilled and comfortable in this environment, the technologies and approaches discussed here will continue to become more prevalent in client/server and netcentric computing solutions.

Chapter 8
Environment Services

Client/server and netcentric applications run in an extremely complex environment. This book has described a number of these complexities already: challenges related to managing the user interface, communicating to other programs, or accessing information and data. Additional application and system level services that do not deal directly with user interface, communications, or information access are grouped together within the execution architecture in "Environment Services."

ENVIRONMENT SERVICES FRAMEWORK

Exhibit 1 shows the components of Environment Services, and each component is described below.

Runtime Services

Runtime services convert noncompiled computer languages into machine code during the execution of a program. Two subservices comprise Runtime Services: language interpreter and virtual machine.

Language Interpreter Services. Language Interpreter Services decompose a fourth generation and/or a scripting languages into machine code (executable code) at runtime.

Virtual Machine Services. Typically, a Virtual Machine (VM) is implemented in software on top of an operating system and is used to run applications. The VM provides a layer of abstraction between the applications and the underlying operating system and is often used to support operating system independence.

System Services

System Services are services that applications can use to perform system-level functions. These services include System Security Services, Profile Management Services, Task and Memory Management Services, and Environment Verification Services.

- System Security Services allow applications to interact with the operating system's native security mechanism. The basic services include

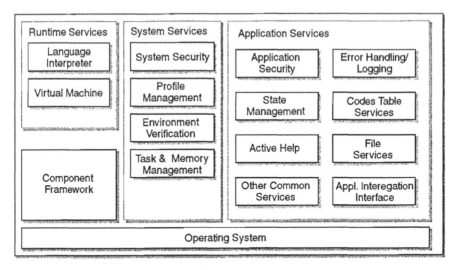

Exhibit 1. Components of Environment Services.

the ability to login, logoff, authenticate to the operating system, and enforce access control to system resources and executables.

- Profile Management Services are used to access and update local or remote system, user, or application profiles. User profiles, for example, can be used to store a variety of information, from the user's language and color preferences to basic job function information. This information may be used by other services, as well.
- Task and Memory Management Services allow applications and/or other events to control individual computer tasks or processes, and manage memory. They provide services for scheduling, starting, stopping, and restarting both client and server tasks (e.g., software agents). Memory management, the allocating and freeing of system resources, is one of the more error prone development activities when using 3GL development tools. Creating architecture services for memory-handling functions can reduce the frequency of these errors, which are difficult to debug. In theory, Java removes the problem of memory management by providing a "garbage collector." However, its implementation is not very efficient in current implementations of Java. Future releases of the Java VM promise a background-running garbage collector with significantly increased performance.
- Environment Verification Services ensure functionality by monitoring, identifying, and validating environment integrity prior to and during program execution (e.g., free disk space, monitor resolution, and correct version). These services are invoked when an application begins processing or when a component is called. Applications can use these

services to verify that the correct versions of required Execution Architecture components and other application components are available. In client/server applications, it may be necessary to implement Environment Verification Services to ensure that the client and server applications are of a compatible release level.

ActiveX framework provides services for automatic installation and upgrade of ActiveX controls. Internet Explorer, Microsoft's Web browser is integrated with Windows OS, so ActiveX controls can be automatically installed and automatically upgraded on the user's machine without the developer adding any additional code.

Application Services

Application Services are miscellaneous services that applications can use for common functions. These functions can apply to one application or they can be used across applications. They include Application Security Services, Error Handling/Logging Services, State Management Services, Help Services, and Other Common Services.

Application Security Services. In addition to system level security such as logging into the network, there are also security services associated with specific applications. These include

- *User Access Services:* a set of common functions that limit application access to specific users within a company or external customers.
- *Data Access Services:* a set of common functions that limit access to specific data within an application to specific users or user types (e.g., secretary, manager).
- *Function Access Services:* a set of common functions that limit access to specific functions within an application to specific users or user types (e.g., secretary, manager).

In the netcentric environment, application security becomes a more critical component primarily because there are more types of users (e.g., employees and customers) and additional types of transactions (e.g., eCommerce and Help Desks). In traditional client/server environments, most users are employees of the company. In netcentric environments, there are typically also external users (e.g., vendors and registered users) and the general public. Usually, different types of users have different application security requirements limiting what data they can see and what functions they can execute. Also, new types of transactions, such as verifying credit when doing eCommerce transactions, also require additional application security services.

Error Handling/Logging Services

Error Handling Services support the handling of fatal and nonfatal hardware and software errors for an application. An error handling architecture takes care of presenting the user with an understandable explanation of what has happened and coordinating with other services to ensure that transactions and data are restored to a consistent state.

Logging Services support the logging of informational, error, and warning messages. Logging Services record application and user activities in enough detail to satisfy any audit trail requirements or to assist the systems support team in recreating the sequence of events that led to an error.

Error Handling. Primarily there are three types of errors: system, architecture, and application.

- *System errors* occur when the application is being executed and some kind of serious system-level incompatibility is encountered, as a result of which the application cannot proceed with its normal execution. These errors can result from such things as memory/resource depletion, database access problems, network problems, or printer-related problems.
- *Architecture errors* are those that occur during the normal execution of the application. They are generated in architecture functions that are built by a project architecture team to isolate the developers from complex coding, to streamline the development effort by reusing common services. These architecture functions perform services such as database calls and state management.
- *Application errors* are also those that occur during the normal execution of the application. They are generally related to business logic errors such as invalid date, invalid price, and so forth.

Typically, an application is written using a combination of various programming languages (e.g., Visual Basic and C). Therefore, a common error handling routine should be written in a language that can be called from any other language used in the application.

Logging. Logging must also be done, however, to mitigate problems, centralize logs, and create a standard, usable log format. Third-party logs should be mapped into the central format before any analysis is attempted.

In a netcentric environment, errors are rarely logged on the client machine (although an exception may be for an intranet type application).

Logging can add a great deal of stress to a Web server and logs can quickly grow very large. Consequently, one should not plan to log all errors, but instead only those deemed necessary for processing exceptions.

State Management Services

State Management Services enable information to be passed or shared among windows and Web pages and/or across programs. For example, suppose that several fields in an application need to be passed from one window to another. In pseudo-conversational mainframe 3270 style applications, passing data from one screen to another screen was done using Context Management Services, which provided the ability to store information on a host computer (here, the term Context Management refers to storing state information on the server, not the client). Client/server architectures simplified or eliminated the need for Context Management (storing state information on the server) and created a need to store state information on the client. Typically, in traditional client/server systems, this type of state management (i.e., data sharing) is done on the client machine using hidden fields, global variables, messages, files, or local databases.

The popularity of the Internet's HTTP protocol has revived the potential need for implementing some form of Context Management Services (storing state information on the server). The HTTP protocol is a stateless protocol. Every connection is negotiated from scratch, not just at the page level but for every element on the page. The server does not maintain a session connection with the client nor save any information between client exchanges (i.e., Web page submits or requests). Each HTTP exchange is a completely independent event. Therefore, information entered into one HTML form must be saved by the associated server application somewhere where it can be accessed by subsequent programs in a conversation.

Advances in netcentric technologies now offer additional options for implementing state management on both the client and server machines.

Codes Table Services

Codes Table Services enable applications to utilize externally stored parameters and validation rules. For example, an application may be designed to retrieve the tax rate for the State of Illinois. When the user enters "Illinois" on the screen, the application first validates the user's entry by checking for its existence on the "State Tax Table" and then retrieves the tax rate for Illinois. Note that codes tables provide an additional degree of flexibility. If the tax rates changes, the data simply need to be updated; no application logic needs to be modified.

The following are some frequently asked questions with regard to Codes Table Services:

- *Is there a need for the codes table functionality?* Most applications need a code/decode facility. For example, an application may need to store codes (e.g., error severity codes) in a table instead of in the executable itself. In some cases, where there is a small amount of information that needs to be stored in the codes table, the profile file can be used instead of the codes table. However, in cases where the codes table needs to be used quite extensively, storing the code/decode information in the profile file will slow down the performance of the application because of the overhead of accessing flat files.

- *What basic services should an architecture provide in terms of managing/using codes/decodes functionality?* In cases where the application requires extensive use of codes tables, the architecture's Code/Decode component should provide the application developers with a set of APIs that can be used to create code/decode tables. This component should also provide the option of caching all or parts of the codes table in the application machine's memory for easier and faster access.

- *Where should Code/Decode information be stored and maintained?* Code/decode information can be stored at any layer of an n-tier architecture — client, application server, or database. The decision will need to be based upon codes table size and number, information update frequency, and write access to the client machine or device.

Active Help Services

Active Help Services enable an application to provide assistance to a user for a specific task or set of tasks. Context-sensitive help is most commonly used in applications today; however, this can imply more active support than just the F1 key. Typically, today's systems must be architected to include Help that is aware of the user's environment, process, and context; in this sense, it can be called "active." Active Help Services may include components such as Wizards (which walk users through a new process), stored or real-time multimedia support, and on-demand computer-based training.

Application Integration Interface Services

An Application Integration Interface provides a method or gateway for passing context and control of information to an external application. The Application Integration Interface specifies how information will be passed and defines the interface by which other applications can expect to receive information. External applications in this context could include anything from Integrated Performance Support systems to ERP systems such as SAP or Peoplesoft to external custom applications that have been previously developed.

Where possible, Application Integration Interfaces should make use of the Component Model defined by the project to broker information (i.e., OLE/COM interfaces) as opposed to custom building data sharing modules.

Other Common Services

This is a catch-all category for additional reusable routines useful across a set of applications (e.g., Date Routines, Time Zone Conversions, and Field Validation Routines).

Component Framework Services

Component Framework Services provide an infrastructure for building components so that they can communicate within an application and across applications, on the same machine or on multiple machines across a network, to work together. COM/DCOM and CORBA are the two leading component industry standards. These standards define how components should be built and how they should communicate. See Chapter 6 for more information on these standards.

Object Request Broker (ORB) services, based on COM/DCOM and CORBA, focus on how components communicate. Component Framework Services, also based on CORBA and COM/DCOM, focus on how components should be built. Currently, two of the most dominant Component Frameworks include Active X/OLE and JavaBeans.

- *ActiveX/OLE.* ActiveX and Object Linking and Embedding (OLE) are implementations of COM/DCOM. ActiveX is a collection of facilities forming a framework for components to work together and interact. ActiveX divides the world into two kinds of components: controls and containers. Controls are relatively independent components that present well-defined interfaces or methods that containers and other components can call. Containers implement the part of the ActiveX protocol that allows for them to host and interact with components, forming a kind of back plane into which controls can be plugged. ActiveX is a scaled-down version of OLE for the Internet. OLE provides a framework to build applications from component modules and defines the way in which applications interact using data transfer, drag-and-drop, and scripting. OLE is a set of common services that allow components to collaborate intelligently. In creating ActiveX from OLE 2.0, Microsoft enhanced the framework to address some of the special needs of Web-style computing. Microsoft's Web browser, Internet Explorer, is an ActiveX container. Therefore, any ActiveX control can be downloaded to, and plugged into, the browser. This allows for executable components to be interleaved with HTML content and downloaded as needed by the Web browser.
- *JavaBeans.* JavaBeans is Sun Microsystems' proposed framework for building Java components and containers. The intent is to develop an API standard that will allow components developed in Java (or beans), to be embedded in competing container frameworks including ActiveX or OpenDoc. The JavaBeans API will make it easier to create reusable components in the Java language.

Other component frameworks include

- *OpenDoc.* CI Labs, formed in 1993, created the OpenDoc architecture to provide a cross-platform alternative component framework, independent of Microsoft's OLE. The OpenDoc architecture is constructed from various technologies supplied by its founding members: IBM, Apple, and Word Perfect. The technologies include Bento (Apple's object storage model), Open Scripting Architecture (OSA — Apple's scripting architecture), and SOM/DSOM (IBM's System Object Model/Distributed SOM). IBM's SOM architecture provides analogous services to that of Microsoft's DCOM architecture.

  OpenDoc provides an open compound document infrastructure based on CORBA. It uses CORBA as its object model for intercomponent communications. OpenDoc architecture provides services analogous to those provided by OLE, and OpenDoc components can also interoperate with OLE components. The OpenDoc equivalent of an object is termed a "part." Each type of part has its own editor, and the OpenDoc architecture has responsibility for handling the communications between the distinct parts.

  Supporters claim that OpenDoc provides a simpler, more technically elegant solution for creating and manipulating components than does OLE. The drawback is that OpenDoc is not yet commercially proven, like OLE. Ironically, one of the more popular uses of OpenDoc tools is for creating and implementing OLE clients and servers. Because OpenDoc provides a more manageable set of APIs than OLE, it may be that OpenDoc gains initial acceptance as an enabler of OLE applications before becoming recognized as a complete component software solution itself.

- *ONE.* Open Network Environment (ONE) is an object-oriented software framework from Netscape Communications for use with Internet clients and servers. It enables the integrating of Web clients and servers with other enterprise resources and data. By supporting CORBA, ONE-enabled systems will be able to link with object software from a wide array of vendors, including IBM, Sun Microsystems, Digital Equipment, and Hewlett-Packard. Netscape is positioning ONE as an alternative to Microsoft's Distributed Common Object Model (DCOM). ONE also complies with Sun Microsystems' Java technology.

Operating System Services

Operating System Services are the underlying services — such as multitasking, paging, and memory allocation — that are typically provided by today's modern operating systems. Where necessary, an additional layer of APIs may be provided to gain either operating system independence or a higher level of abstraction for application programmers.

Chapter 9
Base Services

Base Services provide support for delivering applications to a wide variety of users over the Internet, intranet, and extranet. Base Services can be divided into the following areas: Web Server Services, Push/Pull Services, Batch Services, Report Services, and Workflow Services (Exhibit 1).

WEB SERVER SERVICES

Web Server Services enable organizations to manage and publish information and deploy netcentric applications over the Internet and intranet environments. These services support the following:

- Managing documents in most formats such as HTML, Microsoft Word, etc.
- Handling of client requests for HTML pages. A Web browser initiates an HTTP request to the Web server either specifying the HTML document to send back to the browser or the server program (e.g., CGI, ASP) to execute. If the server program is specified, the Web server executes the program that generally returns a formatted HTML page to the Web Server. The Web server then passes this HTML page just as it would any standard HTML document back to the Web browser.
- Processing scripts such as Common Gateway Interface (CGI), Active Server Pages (ASP). Server side scripting enables programs or commands to be executed on the server machine providing access to resources stored both inside and outside of the Web server environment. For example, server side scripts can be used to process requests for additional information, such as data from an RDBMS.
- Caching Web pages. The first time a user requests a Web page, the Web server retrieves that page from the network and stores it temporarily in a cache (memory on the Web server). When another page or the same page is requested, the Web server first checks to see if the page is available in the cache. If the page is available, the Web server retrieves it from the cache, otherwise it retrieves it from the network. Clearly, the Web server can retrieve the page from the cache more quickly than retrieving the page again from its location out on the network. The Web server typically provides an option to verify whether the page has been updated since the time it was placed in the cache and if it has to get the latest update.

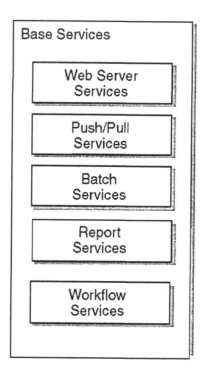

Exhibit 1. Base Services.

PUSH/PULL SERVICES

Push/Pull Services allow for interest in a particular piece of information to be registered; any changes or new information can then be communicated to the subscriber list. Traditional Internet users "surf" the Web by actively moving from one Web page to another, manually searching for content they want and "pulling" it back to the desktop via a graphical browser. However, in the push model, on which subscription servers are based on, content providers can broadcast their information directly to individual users' desktops. The technology uses the Internet's strengths as a two-way conduit by allowing people to specify the type of content they want to receive. Content providers then seek to package the requested information for automatic distribution to the user's PC.

Depending upon requirements, synchronous or asynchronous push/pull services may be required. Synchronous push/pull services provide a mechanism for applications to be notified in real time if a subscribed item changes (e.g., a stock ticker). Asynchronous push/pull services do not require that a session-like connection be present between the subscriber and the information. Internet ListServers are a simple example. Subscribers use e-mail to register an interest in a topic and are notified via e-mail when changes occur or relevant information is available. Asynchronous push/pull services can be useful for proactively updating customers on changes in order status or delivering information on new products or services in which they have expressed an interest.

WORKFLOW SERVICES

Workflow services control and coordinate the tasks that must be completed to process a business event. For example, at one major financial institution, prior to an employee promotion, employees must complete an essay explaining reasons for the promotion. This essay and the personnel file must be routed to numerous individuals who must review the material and approve it. Workflow services coordinate the collection and routing of this information.

Workflow enables tasks within a business process to be passed among the appropriate participants, in the correct sequence, and facilitates their completion within set times and budgets. Task definition includes the actions required as well as work folders containing forms, documents, images, and transactions. It uses business process rules, routing information, role definitions, and queues. Workflow functionality is crucial for the customer service and engineering applications to automate the business value chains and monitor and control the sequence of work electronically.

The business processes can be of a repetitive nature, automatically routing and controlling the review of a work plan through the approval stages. These are called "production workflows." Conversely it can be an ad hoc process. For example, for a utility company, a workflow can generate and deliver to am available meter reader a work order for a special meter reading. In production workflows the processes are predefined, whereas ad hoc workflows are created only for a specific, nonrecurring situation. Often it is difficult to determine how much ad hoc functionality needs to be provided. An overly strict production workflow may not support necessary special cases that must be handled in an ad hoc fashion.

Workflow provides a mechanism to define, monitor, and control the sequence of work electronically. These services are typically provided by the server as they often coordinate activities among multiple users on multiple computers.

The following are some of the architectural and integration issues that must be addressed in workflow services.

Process Integration

The workflow system must achieve a seamless integration of multiple processes. The workflow system must control the business process. For example, it should be able to open a word processor with the relevant data coming from a previous business process.

Infrastructure Integration from PC to Mainframe

The ability to interface with the host-based hardware, system software, and database management systems is critical. This is essential because the workflow system is located between the client-based and host-based processes, that is, it can initiate client-based as well as host-based applications.

LAN and WAN Connectivity

Connectivity must include all sites for the supported processes, enabling a large number and variety of users to use the workflow system, and thus to execute the business process.

Integration of Peripherals

The workflow system should support many different types of printers, modems, fax machines, scanners, and pagers. This is especially important because of the diversity of the users that will be involved, from field crew to managers, each with their own needs and preferences.

Integration with Workflow-Participating Applications

The key to the efficiency of the workflow system is its capability to integrate with office automation, imaging, electronic mail, and legacy applications.

Workflow Services can be further divided into the following components.

Role Management Services

These provide for the assignment of tasks to roles which can then be mapped to individuals. A role defines responsibilities which are required in completing a business process. A business worker must be able to route documents and folders to a role, independent of the specific person, or process filling that role. For example, a request is routed to a supervisor role or to Purchasing, rather than to "Mary" or "Tom." If objects are routed to Mary, and if Mary then leaves the company or is reassigned, a new recipient under a new condition would have to be added to an old event. Roles are also important when a number of different people have the authority to do the same work, such as claims adjusters. In this case, the request can simply be assigned to the next available person. Role Management Services provide this additional level of directory indirection.

Route Management Services

These enable the routing of tasks to the next role, which can be done in the following ways:

- Serial: the tasks are sequentially performed.
- Parallel: the work is divided among different players.
- Conditional: routing is based upon certain conditions.
- Ad hoc: work which is not part of a predefined process.

Workflow routing services route work to the appropriate workflow queues. When an application completes its processing of a task, it uses these services to route the work-in-progress to the next required task or tasks and, in some cases, to notify interested parties of the resulting work queue changes.

The automatic movement of information and control from one workflow step to another requires work profiles that describe the task relationships for completing various business processes. Users can be given access to these work profiles. Such access can be solely informational — to allow the user to understand the relationship between tasks or identify which tasks need to be completed for a particular work flow; access can also be navigational — to allow the user to move between tasks.

Route Management Services also support the routing and delivery of necessary information (e.g., documents, data, forms, applications, etc.) to the next step in the work flow as needed.

Rule Management Services

A business process workflow is typically comprised of many different roles and routes. Decisions must be made as to what to route to which role and when. Rule Management Services support the routing of workflow activities by providing the intelligence necessary to determine which routes are appropriate given the state of a given process and knowledge of the organization's workflow processing rules. Rule Management Services are typically implemented through easily maintainable tables or rule bases that define the possible flows for a business event.

Queue Management Services

These services provide access to the workflow queues that are used to schedule work. To perform workload analysis or to create "to do lists" for users, an application may query these queues based on various criteria (a business event, status, assigned user, etc.). In addition, manipulation services are provided to allow queue entries to be modified.

Workflow services allow users and management to monitor and access workflow queue information and to invoke applications directly.

SOME CONSIDERATIONS FOR WORKFLOW SERVICES:

Is There a Need for Reporting and Management Facilities?

Typically, workflow applications are created to provide better general management control and better management of change. Proactive system action, audit trails, and system administration features like work queue reporting are important administration tools. Some of the areas for monitoring for improvement are employee productivity, process performance, and forecasting/scheduling. Where any form of customer service is involved, features such as status reports on individual cases can sharpen customer response times, while performance monitoring of groups and individuals can help quality improvement and efficiency exercises. Note that reports and reporting does not necessarily mean paper reports that are distributed in a traditional manner; it can also mean electronic messages or even triggers based on specific events.

Are Cooperative Applications Present?

Workflow management is frequently required in cooperative applications for the following reasons:

- The users are generally professionals.
- The flow of work in the organization is frequently highly variable.
- The application units of work (legal case, sales order) are processed for long periods of elapsed time.
- Work often moves from one processing site to another.

As data and application logic are split, better control is needed to track processing/data status across location.

Will Business Processes be Reengineered?

Workflow is a logical complement to business process reengineering. The trend today is toward using workflow software to reengineer new business processes on a workgroup or project basis.

Is the Business Process Well Defined?

If rules or conditions can be identified that define the business process, with few exception conditions, workflow tools can then automate areas such as information routing, task processing, and work-in-process reporting.

Are Fixed Delays or Deadlines Involved?

Workflow has been used to regulate delays and deadlines such as those associated with government regulations, contractual obligations, accounting periods, customer service, and sales lead follow-up. Typical workflow goals are shorter time to market and quicker response times.

Are Many People Involved in the Business Process?

Workflow coordinates cross-functional, cross-departmental work activities and promotes accountability. It also enables dynamic redistribution and reprioritization of work.

Is There a Need for Work Scheduling?

Workflow management can be extended to automate work scheduling. A system may be able to do as good a job, or better, in scheduling a user's work. Reasons include a very large amount of work to be assigned to a large pool, a complex method of assigning priorities, and an extremely dynamic environment. Another advantage to work scheduling is that the system can initiate some needed activity automatically for the user in anticipation of the next task.

BATCH SERVICES

Batch processing is often overlooked in netcentric or advanced client/server computing. It is important to remember that, even with today's new technologies, architectures, techniques, and applications, many organizations have — and probably will continue to have — requirements for traditional batch processing. This processing is typically associated with the handling of a batch of many business transactions that have been accumulated over a period of time (an hour, day, week, month, or year).

Batch processing is used to perform large-scale repetitive processing where no user involvement is required as well as reporting. Areas for design attention include scheduling, recovery/restart, use of job streams, and high availability (e.g., 24 hour running). In addition, close attention must be paid to performance because batch systems usually must be processed within strict batch windows.

The design of batch architectures is often complicated considerably by the fact that batch jobs must be able to run concurrently with on-line systems. The general globalization of companies requires that on-line systems be available on a close to 24x7 hours basis, eliminating the traditional batch windows. Concurrent batch and on-line processing poses serious challenges to data integrity, throughput, and performance.

Batch application programs can include business processing such payroll or billing and can also include report generation. This is an often overlooked area in client/server architectures. Traditional client/server solutions and netcentric solutions often require batch processing; unlike the mainframe, however, the typical platforms and development environments used often do not have built-in batch or reporting architecture facilities.

Batch processing should be used in preference to on-line modules when

- The same process, or set of processes, must be applied to many data entities in a repetitive and predictable fashion.
- There is either no manual element to the process or the manual element can be completely separated from a batch element.
- The volume of information to be presented to a user is too great to be processed on-line or it can be better printed in batch.

Common steps for batch processing, in the order typically used, are

1. *Extract*: A program that reads a set of records from a database or input file, selects records based on predefined rules, and writes the records to an output file.
2. *Update*: A program that reads an input file and makes changes to a database driven by the data found in each input record.
3. *Format*: A program that reads an input file, restructures data from this record according to a standard format, and produces an output file for printing or transmission to another program or system.

However, between these common steps may be one or more of the following utility steps:

1. *Sort*: A Program that reads an input file and produces an output file where records have been resequenced according to a sort key field in the records. Sorts are usually performed by standard system utilities.
2. *Split*: A program that reads a single input file and writes each record to one of several output files based on a field value.
3. *Merge*: A program that reads records from multiple input files and produces one output file with combined data from the input files.

Batch Services are comprised of the following subservices

Driver Services

These services provide the control structure and framework for batch programs. They are also referred to as Batch Scheduling Services. Driver Services are typically supported by commercially available schedulers. They manage the flow of processing within and between modules and utilities (e.g., extracts, sorts, etc.) and manage interdependencies of applications and resources. They also provide integration with check pointing facilities and context management. More advanced services support parallel batch streaming and control the coordination between concurrent on-line and batch execution. Such services must handle process dependencies and process prioritization.

Restart/Recovery Services

These services are used to automatically recover and restart batch programs if they should fail during execution. The services support the restoration of context information and the repositioning of application programs and data sets to the point prior to the failure. This saves time in data recovery and program execution. Without these services, long running batch programs may need to be completely rerun when they fail; this could jeopardize completion of the batch run within the defined batch window. These services are typically supported by commercially available schedulers.

Batch Balancing Services

These services support the tracking of run-to-run balances and totals for the batch system. These services can reduce the effort associated with manually checking system control reports.

Report Services

Project reporting tools are used to summarize and communicate information, using either printed paper or on-line report. They should include reports against standard techniques (e.g., GANTT, PERT, and CPM) and ad hoc reporting. Report services should handle configurable distribution, printing, and archiving. Such services are facilities for supporting the distribution of reports. They assist in the splitting of reports into defined sections and the electronic routing of these report sections to specific targets, including user screens, e-mail, printers, faxes, electronic archives, and other device types. Report services should also support standard report layout features, such as breakpoints, summarizations, and font/color control.

COMPONENTS OF A BATCH ARCHITECTURE

Exhibit 2 and the text that follows provide an overview of batch architecture.

Driver Program

The driver program is the controlling entity in the batch architecture. This program can control one or more batch applications or control other driver programs. Multiple scripts are usually called in succession to form a job flow (analogous to CL on the AS/400, JCL on mainframes, DCL on VAX,

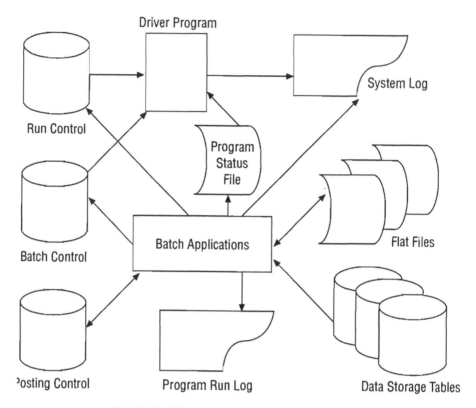

Exhibit 2. Client/Server Batch Architecture.

and so forth). This program is usually executed asynchronously, and thus an interactive session during execution is not required.

Subprograms invoked within this driver program can be executed in the background as well. This technique allows a single shell script to control multiple subprograms at once. The driver program will remain resident until all previously invoked subordinate programs have completed. Then status files are interrogated to ensure successful execution of subordinate programs. Appropriate completion messages are written to the System Log and the batch processing is concluded.

System Log

The system log is used to hold all error, warning, and status messages associated with the execution of the batch processing system. The system log becomes a history of all batch activity. This log can be built using the services described under Application Services.

Flat Files

Flat files are data files, usually containing ASCII or binary data in the form of fixed or variable length records. In ASCII form, they can serve as a means for information exchange between the operating environment, batch applications, and other operating components. They may be used as input and/or output to 3GL, 4GL, or UNIX driver programs.

Data Storage Tables

Data storage tables are relational database tables defined in one of several DBMS environments (Informix, Sybase, Oracle, DB2, and so forth). These tables can interact with 3GL programs using the DBMS embedded SQL language or with 4GL languages that are designed to support the DBMS. Data storage tables typically contain that information (data) that is processed by the batch applications.

Batch Applications

Batch applications are coded programs designed to operate in a batch mode. The most common programming languages used in a client/server environment are C and COBOL. Specially designed fourth generation languages (4GLs), such as Accell, may also be used. When 4GLs are used for batch applications, development times tend to decrease and execution times tend to increase.

Special techniques must be used to ensure data integrity, manage restart processing, and provide execution statistics. Like driver programs coded to run in batch mode, these programs are designed to run in the background — with no interactive processing or user screens required. After the program is executed with the proper input arguments, it will process continuously until successful completion or until a problem is encountered. Status information and run totals are reported in the form of a flat file, called Program Run Logs.

Batch application run times may vary from several minutes to several hours, depending on I/O requirements and complexity of the application. In general, file system I/O takes significantly less time than DBMS I/O due to DBMS overhead. It is important to ensure that you plan for your batch processing requirements (CPU, time, disk, and so forth) when you are planning and configuring your client/server environment.

Program Run Log

This log is a flat file that contains various statistics related to a single execution of a batch program. Statistics may include start and stop times and/or dates, number of records input/output, "hash" totals used to verify data integrity, or error information in case of abnormal program termination.

Program Status File

This file is usually a single byte file containing a 0 or 1, which is used to indicate the successful completion of a batch program. This file may be interrogated by driver programs that execute more than one subprogram to control restart processing and to ensure successful completion of batch applications. Only programs that have completed unsuccessfully for the most recent execution (as indicated by the existence of a 0 or 1 in this file) will be reinvoked by the driver programs.

Batch Control

This is a table used to control restart processing and run-time parameters for batch applications. The most significant reason for the existence of this table is to allow for efficient restart processing when a program normally takes several hours to complete execution.

The table is created containing a minimum of two fields: a character field and a numeric field. The character field will contain the names of the batch programs designed to use this table. The numeric field will indicate the number of records processed by a batch program at various points during its execution.

As the batch program executes, the record corresponding to this program in the table is periodically updated to indicate the number of records processed. If the batch program encounters an unexpected error, or a hardware failure occurs, the numeric field in the database table should still contain the count of records successfully processed before the failure occurred.

When the error is corrected, or the hardware recovers, the batch program is reexecuted (usually by reexecuting the driver programs). The application program's first activity upon restart is to interrogate the batch control table by reading its record count contained in the numeric field. If this value is non-zero, the program will start processing from the data element or record following the last element or record successfully processed before the error or failure occurred. After successful completion, the record count in the batch control table is reset to 0 so that the next execution will begin with the first input data element.

In addition to the record count, it normally is a good idea to also store in the batch control table a relatively unique value associated with each input data element. This will allow a data integrity check if restart processing is required and help ensure that no input data elements have been altered or lost.

It is important to note that most DBMS environments allow "transaction logging." This means that during execution, database data inserted or altered by the batch program can be made permanently to the database, or buffered and committed, after several input data elements are processed. Otherwise, disk I/O would be required after each input data element is processed. Transaction logging will allow a batch application to restart processing, after an abnormal termination, at the last successful commit.

The batch control updates are only required when data is committed to the database because the last commit will be undone, or "rolled back," in the case of program or hardware failure. Input data processed since the last commit will be reprocessed if restart is required. If transaction logging is not available, the batch control table requires an update after each input data element is successfully processed.

Because a batch program must always interrogate the batch control table upon execution to determine which data element to begin processing, "tunable" parameters can reside in the batch control table. These parameters can change characteristics about a batch program each time the program executes. Typical parameters might include

- Number of input data elements to process before committing database inserts, changes, or deletes.
- A value to indicate when to write a status message to the Program Run Log. The message usually includes the number of records processed as well as a time stamp. This can be a useful technique to track performance and progress of a batch program which requires several hours to complete.

Posting Control

This is a table used to contain totals of numeric fields on large database tables. As batch modules alter database data, the corresponding totals on this table are also adjusted to reflect adds, changes, and deletes to those numeric fields.

This table serves as a reference to ensure that

- Totals across tables are always equal, or "foot."
- A given database table contains the correct total(s) across all records, and no data have been lost.

Run Control

This is a table used to indicate the status and file size of flat files. Because most operating systems only support basic update locking, this table is used to ensure that a batch program does not attempt to alter a flat file that is being read or altered by another batch program. In addition, the file size is used to ensure that files passed between programs retain their data integrity. For example, consider a flat file that is output by one batch program and then serves as input to another batch program at some later time. To ensure that the data integrity of the file is preserved, the program to read the file as input should check to ensure that the batch program creating the file is finished writing output and that the file size has not been altered since file creation.

In order to accomplish this, the run control table is first updated by the program creating the file to indicate when output is being written and then to indicate the resultant file size produced.

The program to read the file then interrogates the Run Control Table upon start-up. If the "in-use" flag indicates that output is still being written to the file, the program will shut down and indicate a "retry later" error message in the Program Run Log. If the in-use flag indicates that output has been completed, the program to read the file then will check the file size to ensure data integrity has been preserved since flat file creation.

The program first performs an operating system call to determine the current physical size of the file. If this size does not match the file size in the Run Control Table, as indicated by the program that created the file, a "file size" error is written to the Program Run Log, and again the module shuts down. Otherwise, processing continues normally.

OTHER ISSUES TO CONSIDER FOR BATCH PROCESSING

The following is a discussion of factors to consider when defining and implementing batch architecture and applications.

- To minimize I/O requirements, perform as many operations as possible in internal memory. This ability is most flexible when coding in "C."
- Be wary with regard to data integrity. Make sure all batch programs and driver programs contain adequate controls to preserve data integrity, even in the event of hardware failures. Perform as many "sanity" checks as required to ensure that data makes sense. (For example, making sure that a data field that normally ranges from $1 to $5 does not suddenly read $1,000,000.) A database table, containing field name and common minimum/maximum values, might be used for this purpose to allow for changes over time to these "sanity" check values.
- If data aggregation, or summarization, is required for reporting purposes, increment stored totals as often as possible when data is being initially processed, or "posted," to the database. This practice will minimize the need to reprocess the data at a later time to obtain aggregate totals.
- Build common routines, or linked functions, to perform common processing across all batch programs. This might include database I/O, error processing, or restart/recovery routines.
- In batch programs, try to retain as much memory as the environment will allow for the duration of the program's execution. Perform memory

allocation at module start-up, and do not release memory until program completion. This will minimize the need to perform time-consuming reallocation of internal memory many times throughout the execution of the batch program.

- Make sure to plan and test the processing time and resource requirements for all batch applications.

Batch Process Types

Design and construction of application, report, and interface batch processes can start with work unit partitioning. The business events defined during the system design phase will be split into client, server, and batch processes. Definition of the work units will include defining the operations to be contained within a work unit. A separate batch work unit will be defined for each batch program in the application.

Batch procedure diagrams can be used to describe the design from which the code for a batch process will be built. These structure charts will be built using the Functional Specifications defined in the system design phase as input. Additionally, batch process models can be created for the batch process types defined. These design models will be used by the designer as the starting point in design; programming shells defined for each batch process will be used by the programmer as the starting point for programming. The following is an overview of a sample batch design.

Sample Batch Design

Database-Driven Program Model. This model is used for database update and database extract programs that are driven by rows or values retrieved from the database. This model will open a database cursor as input, then update the database, create error files, or create temporary files, depending on the requirements of the program. Different subprograms are used depending on whether the database driven programs require checkpointing, and depending on whether they require the ability to custom define when their checkpointing procedures are called.

File-Driven Program Model. This model is used for batch programs that are driven by records or values retrieved from a file. This model will read a file as input, verify the input, then update the database, create temporary files, or create error files, depending on the requirements of the program. Subprograms are used depending on whether file driven programs require checkpointing or not.

Format Report Program Model. This model is used for programs that must format data output for standard reports. This model will take an input file (originally created by an extract program) and format the data as required for the output product. The report will be written to an output file. The Format Report Program will create headers and footers, format the data rows, and define report control totals.

Called Module Model. This model is used for procedures that are called from a batch program. Different subprograms are used for called modules that select a single row from the database, that select a list of rows from the database, and that update the database.

Basic Program Model. This model is used for programs that do not fall into the other categories.

Design models for each batch process type are defined to support application design and programming.

Batch Process Structure

The structure of batch process models and programming shells should be general enough to accommodate the different types of processing that are expected in most organizations. Batch processes should contain both shell and application components. Batch shell components should be developed as procedural copybooks separate from the application code. The shell components required by each batch process type should be included in the models previously described.

Batch Process Content

The following is a sample set of batch application standards. These are presented as an example only. You should define the standards that are appropriate for your organization, architecture, and applications.

- All batch programs are written in COBOL. Batch program design models and programming shells are used, as described, to simplify and standardize development and to enhance programmer productivity. These shells also improve the maintainability of programs.
- All I/O routines appear in separate paragraphs within the program. These paragraphs are located at the end of the program (that is, in A6xxx, A7xxx and A8xxx paragraphs) or in separate called modules. I/O routines are isolated from the main code of the program to prevent changes in the underlying data format and storage mechanism from rippling through the program. Further, I/O routines are commonly reused in multiple places through the main program, e.g., priming reads and "end of" loops. Placing code that is frequently used in the same area of the program helps reduce paging.
- All batch programs that interact with the database are SQL standard compliant. Changes in the SQL DBMS with which the program interacts

cause only implementation or tuning changes to the program. The programs do not require a complete rewrite.

- Each batch program has an SQL communications area (SQLCA). When an SQL statement is processed, a return code is placed in the SQL-STATE field of the program's SQLCA. This SQLSTATE is examined after each executable SQL statement to determine whether the SQL call was successful.
- DECLARE CURSOR statements are placed in the PROCEDURE DIVISION in the same paragraph as the associated OPEN CURSOR statements. Only one OPEN or CLOSE statement is defined per cursor.
- Each batch program is reviewed by the relevant database expert to ensure that physical I/O's to the database are minimized. In particular, the following four common flaws are watched for:

  1. Reading data for every transaction when the data could be read once and kept in working storage
  2. Rereading data for a transaction where the data was read earlier in the same transaction
  3. Causing unnecessary table or index scans
  4. Not specifying key values in the WHERE clause of an SQL statement

REPORT SERVICES

Report Services are facilities for simplifying the construction and delivery of reports or generated correspondence. These services help to define reports and to electronically route reports to allow for on-line review, printing, and/or archiving. Report Services also support the merging of application data with pre-defined templates to create letters or other printed correspondence. Report Services include

- Driver Services
- Report Definition Services
- Report Built Services
- Report Distribution Services

Driver Services

These services provide the control structure and framework for the reporting system.

Report Definition Services

These services receive and identify the report request, perform required validation routines, and format the outputted report(s). After the request is validated, the report build function is initiated.

Report Build Services

These services are responsible for collecting, processing, formatting, and writing report information (e.g., data, graphics, and text).

Report Distribution Services

These services are responsible for printing, or otherwise distributing, the reports to users.

FUNCTIONS AND FEATURES OF A REPORT ARCHITECTURE

The report architecture within Environment Services supports the generation and delivery of reports. Applications request report services by sending a message to the reporting framework.

The following types of reports are supported by the reporting application framework:

- *Scheduled*: Scheduled reports are generated based upon a time and/or date requirement. These reports typically contain statistical information and are generated periodically (invoices and bills, for example).
- *On demand*: Some reports will be requested by users with specific parameters. The scheduling of these reports, the formatting, and/or the data requirements are not known before the request is made, so these factors must be handled at request time.
- *Event driven*: This report type includes reports whose generation is triggered based on a business or system event. An example here would be a printed trade slip.

REPORTING APPLICATION FRAMEWORK

Exhibit 3 shows the major components of the reporting application framework.

Report Initiation

The report initiation function is the interface for reporting applications into the report architecture. The client initiates a report request to the report architecture by sending a message to the report initiation function. The responsibility of report initiation is to receive, identify, and validate the request and then trigger the report build process. The main components of reporting initiation are the following.

- *Receive, identify, and validate a report request.* The identification function determines general information about the request, such as report type, requester, quantity to be printed, and requested time. Based on the report type, a table of reports is examined in order to gather additional

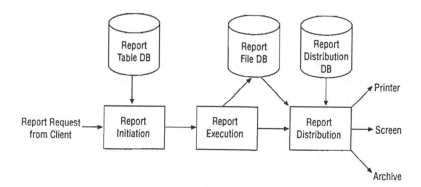

Exhibit 3. Reporting Application Framework.

report-specific information and perform required validation routines for the report request.

After the report identification and validation functions have been successfully completed, the reporting process can continue. If any errors are identified, the report initiation function will return an error message to the requester application.

- *Initiate report execution.* The initiate report execution function processes the report profile and specific distribution requirements and determines the report to be created. It then passes control to the report execution process.

Report Execution

Report execution is the core of the reporting application framework. The main components of report execution include

- *Format the report.* This function is responsible for formatting the layout of the outputted report, including standard headers, column headings, row headings, and other static report information.
- *Collect the information.* This function is responsible for collecting the information (for example, data, text, image, and graphics) that is required for the report. This function would utilize the Information Access Services component of the client/server architecture.
- *Format the information.* This function is responsible for formatting the collected information into the appropriate display format based upon the report type and the report distribution requirements.
- *Output the report.* This function initiates the report distribution function to distribute the created report to the specified devices (printers, disks, and so forth) and individuals.

The process of collecting, processing, formatting, and outputting report data can be accomplished in several different ways. For example, one method is to create a program in C for each report format. Here, many aspects of report printing — such as page size, headings, footings, and printer control values — would have to be programmed in function calls to facilitate the report programming process. Information access to files or the database would be through Information Access Services.

Another option is to use a third-party report tool, such as the SQR (Structured Query Report Writer) from SQL Solutions. SQR is a robust report generator designed to be used with SQL-based relational databases. SQR insulates the developer from programming in a third-generation language by providing a higher-level programming language. SQL queries (Information Access) are placed directly into the SQR program.

Report Distribution

The final requirement of the reporting application framework is the report distribution function. Once the report has been generated, it must be distributed to the specified targets (devices and/or users). The report distribution function will locate completed report files and route them to the appropriate devices within the client/server network.

Typically, a report distribution database is used to specify the destinations for each report supported by the report architecture. The report distribution database specifies where, when, how, and to whom to distribute the produced report. Specific destinations can include printer(s), user(s), user groups, archives (permanent storage), and/or specific display devices such as workstations and terminals.

Several additional options exist for distributing reports, including timed reporting, multiple copy distribution, and report archiving. Also, a user interface function can be built to open and browse report files.

EVALUATION CRITERIA

There are two primary approaches to implementing a reporting architecture: custom and package. Evaluating custom and package solutions involves both functional and technical criteria. The following is a discussion of various functional and technical criteria that should be considered during the planning for a report architecture. Note that not all of the criteria may be required by any particular organization.

Functional Criteria

1. *Report Repository*: The report architecture should work with, and support maintenance of, a report repository on the platforms within

the client/server architecture. The report repository contains the detailed definitions of the reports.

2. *Workgroup Report Support:* The report architecture should work with and support distribution of reports generated on the workgroup server.

3. *On-Demand Reports:* The report architecture must support distribution of reports requested by users on demand. Typically, these reports will not have a set schedule or frequency for distribution. The report architecture must support distribution of these reports without the requirement of manual or user intervention (subsequent to initial set up and conversion).

4. *Scheduled Reports:* The report architecture must support distribution of regularly scheduled reports. Typically, these reports will have a set schedule and frequency for distribution. The report distribution package must support distribution of these reports without the requirement of manual or user intervention (subsequent to set up and conversion).

5. *On-line Preview:* The report architecture should allow preview of reports on-line from a user's intelligent workstation prior to actual distribution. Ideally, the report architecture itself would provide support for on-line preview of reports through software located on the intelligent workstation.

6. *Graphical User Interface:* The architecture should provide users with a graphical user interface.

7. *Bilingual Support:* For companies where two or more languages are used, the report architecture must provide a multinational user interface. (Note that large report runs targeted for multiple users may require the ability to change languages during the report.)

8. *Basic Preview Functions:* The report architecture should support basic preview functions. These include:
   Scrolling up and down
   Scrolling left and right
   Advancing to end or beginning of report without scrolling through intermediate pages

9. *Advanced Preview Functions:* In addition to the basic preview functions listed previously, certain advanced preview functions may also be necessary:
   Page indexing (allows users to jump to specific report pages)
   Section indexing (allows users to jump to specific report sections)
   Search capabilities (allows users to search report for occurrence of a specific data stream)

10. *Report Level Security:* Reports may occasionally contain sensitive information. It is therefore important that access to certain reports

be restricted to authorized users. The report architecture should provide a mechanism for implementing report level security. This security must be in place on all platforms with the client/server architecture. At the workgroup level, the security may consist of downloading sensitive report files to a secure directory and having the LAN administrator release the report as appropriate.

11. *Section, Page, and Field Level Security*: Defining security at the report section, page, or field level would provide greater flexibility in determining and implementing report security. This is a desirable, though not mandatory, requirement of the report architecture.

12. *Background Processing*: The report architecture should support the processing of reports in the background while the application works in the foreground during on-line hours. In other words, processing of reports should not negatively affect on-line response times, or tie up the user's workstation.

13. *Automatic Report Addressing*: The report architecture should provide a "humanly intelligible" address for all distributed reports. The address may be used by a print site operator, LAN administrator, or other personnel to manually sort printed output (if required). This criterion can be satisfied by automatic creation of banner pages or other means.

14. *Delivery Costing*: To provide sufficient information to users to avoid accidentally downloading or printing very large reports during peak usage hours, a distribution costing function can be useful. This function would warn users of reports that would overload the network or a printer. This costing function might provide recipients with a rough estimate of the amount of time that distribution might take. Finally, during the on-line day, the delivery costing mechanism might disallow transmission of reports that exceed a predetermined cost.

15. *Multiple Destinations*: The report architecture should support distribution of a single report to single or multiple destinations.

16. *Destination Rationalization*: For some systems, it is possible that multiple copies of a report will be sent to the same site — to several different users, for example. In these cases, it is highly desirable to have the report architecture recognize these situations whenever possible and distribute the specified report only once.

17. *Automatic Printing*: The report architecture should provide automatic print capabilities. Once a report has been distributed for printing (either through a "push" distribution scheduling mechanism or through a "pull" user request), no further user or operations personnel involvement should be necessary to print the report at the specified location.

18. *Multiple Print Destinations*: The report architecture should support distribution of reports for printing at centralized, remote, or local print sites without user or operations personnel intervention.

19. *Variable Printer Types*: Printing on multiple types of printers, including line, impact, and laser printers, should be supported. This should not require user intervention, that is, the user should not have to specify the type of target printer. Ideally, the report architecture would default this information from the user's profile or the default printer defined in the local operating system. This criterion requires that the report architecture support several print mechanisms, such as postscript drivers and host/mainframe protocols (e.g., Advanced Function Printing, or AFP).

20. *Variable Printer Destinations*: The report architecture should default the destination printer for a specific report (from the user's profile or operating system parameters). Additionally, the architecture should allow the user to change the printer specified. Validation of the print destination also should be included.

21. *Special Forms Printing*: The report architecture should support distribution of "regular" reports and special forms reports.

22. *Font Support*: Some reports may be printed on laser printers and/or may support electronic forms text (i.e., including the forms text in the report dataset as opposed to printing the report dataset on a preprinted form). The architecture should allow multiple fonts to be specified.

23. *Report Archival*: The report architecture should provide and/or facilitate archival or disposition of report datasets. Ideally, the architecture would permit definition of retention periods and disposition requirements.

24. *Report Download*: The report architecture should allow distribution of the information contained in a report dataset to a user's intelligent workstation. The information should be in a form that can be imported to a local word processing software, decision support software package, or other appropriate application.

25. *Application Transparency*: It is desirable for the report architecture to appear to the users as if it were part of the overall application. This does not necessarily mean that the architecture must integrate seamlessly with the application; a message interface between the systems might be acceptable.

26. *Selective Printing*: It would be desirable for the report architecture to provide users with the ability to print only selected pages or sections of the report. This should reduce paper usage, while still allowing users to obtain a hard copy of the information as required.

27. *Print Job Restart*: It would be desirable if the report architecture allowed a print job to be restarted from the point of failure rather than having to reprint the entire report. This of particular concern for very large reports.

Technical Criteria

The following is a list of technical criteria that should be considered during the planning for a report architecture:

1. *Platform Compatibility*: The report architecture must be compatible with the platform architecture. It also should be compatible with local area networks and standalone workstation technology specified in the platform architecture.
2. *Wide Area Network (WAN) Compatibility*: Most systems will include support for WAN communication, so the report architecture should be compatible with this environment.
3. *Technology Standards*: The report architecture should be compliant with existing formal and de facto standards (e.g., SQL Database Language, COBOL Programming Language, and C Programming Language).
4. *External User Directory*: The report architecture should make use of an external user directory of preferences and locations.
5. *Data Compression in Report Repository*: To reduce the storage requirements for the report repository, it is also desirable for the report architecture to support data compression in the repository.
6. *Code Page Compatibility*: Code page compatibility must be considered when translating characters to ASCII.

Exhibit 4 summarizes the functional and technical criteria just discussed, and provides a framework with which to evaluate particular reporting packages.

CUSTOM REPORTING APPROACHES

If a commerciallyavailable reporting product cannot meet your report requirements, you may have to consider a custom approach. Exhibit 5 is an example of how a custom report architecture relates to a workstation platform technical architecture.

This custom report process is responsible for processing all messages requesting generation, manipulation, or distribution of reports. The following services are provided:

- Report generation
- Report deletion
- Report printing
- Report status maintenance

Report generation is supported by an additional report writer process that contains all application-defined report writer modules. These modules contain the logic to produce each of the report types that may be requested. The report process receives generation requests and ensures

Exhibit 4. Functional and Technical Criteria			
Criteria	**Vendor A**	**Vendor B**	**Vendor C**
Functional criteria			
1. Mainframe Report Repository			
2. Workgroup Report Support			
3. On Demand Reports			
4. Scheduled Reports			
5. Online Preview			
6. Page-by-page Preview			
7. Graphical User Interface			
8. Bilingual Support			
9. Basic Preview Functions			
Scrolling up and down			
Scrolling left and right			
Advancing to beginning or end of report			
10. Advanced Preview Functions			
Page Indexing			
Section Indexing			
Search Capbilities			
11. Report Level Security			
12. Section, Page, Field Level Security			
13. Background Distribution			
14. Automatic Report Addressing			
15. Delivery Costing			
16. Multiple Destinations			
17. Destination Rationalization			
18. Automatic Printing			
19. Multiple Print Destinations			
Centralized Mainframe Sites			
Remote Print Sites			
Workgroup Print Sites			
20. Variable Printer Types			
21. Variable Printer Destinations			
22. Special Forms Printing			
23. Font Support			
24. Report Archival			
25. Report Download			
26. Architecture Compatibility			
27. Application Transparency			
28. Selective Printing			
29. Print Job Restart			
Technical criteria			
1. Enterprise/Departmental Platform Compatibility			
2. Wide Area Network Compatibility			
3. Workgroup Compatibility			
4. Technology Standards			
5. External User Directory			
6. Data Compression During Transmission			
7. Data Compression In Report Repository			
8. Code Page Compatibility			

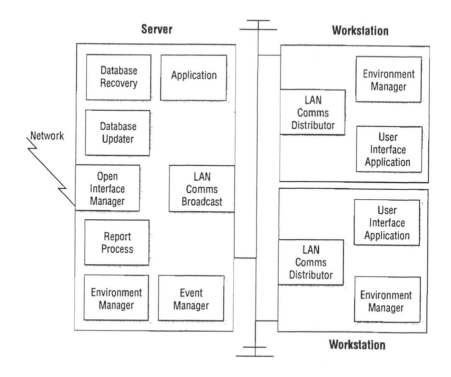

Exhibit 5. Custom Report Architecture.

that they are forwarded to the report writer process at the current or specified time. All report requests are processed in an asynchronous manner (e.g., service requesters do not wait for completion of report processing).

Exhibit 6 describes the relationships between the major components of the report process and the report writer process.

Design Approach

For the report process in a client/server system, a set of APIs is provided for use within application programs and within the application report writer modules. Each API requests a specific report service (generation, printing, or deletion), which is performed by a report manager module.

The report process maintains an internal database table, a report status table, containing information about each report that has been requested for generation, including

- Requester ID
- Report name

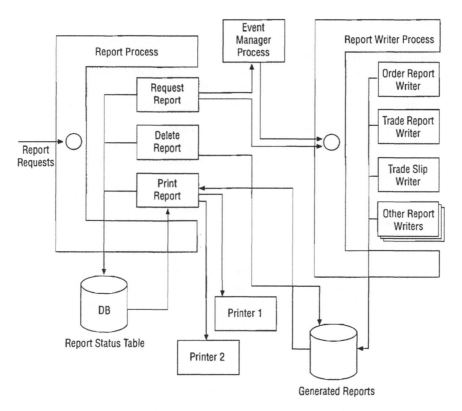

Exhibit 6. Report Processing.

- Date/time requested
- Status (requested, in process, complete, or error)
- Report-specific parameters

The requester ID, report name, and date/time are used to uniquely identify the report. These values are passed to APIs, which request report status, print, or delete a previously generated report.

All application-defined report writer modules invoke an API to update the report status table with a status of "completed" after a report has been produced or with "error" if the report cannot be generated. An API is also provided to print the report after the generation if specified in the original request.

Processed report records are removed from the table only after the output reports have been archived. Implementation and frequency of this table cleanup is to be determined in systems management design.

Report Process Flows

Report processing is messagedriven. Each defined API sends a unique message to the report process. The report process reads the messages from a queue and invokes the appropriate modules to handle each request. Subsequent process flows differ based upon the requested service. In the case of a report generation request, the process flow proceeds as follows:

- A record is added to the report status table.
- A message is sent to the report writer process for immediate generation or to the event manager for generation at a specified time (report scheduling).
- The appropriate application report writer module generates the report, prints it if specified in the original API request, and updates the status in the report status table.

A request to print a report proceeds as follows:

- The report status is retrieved from the report status table.
- The output file is located on disk and sent to the specified or default printer or the request is sent to the event manager for report scheduling.

Report deletion proceeds as follows:

- The report record is removed from the report status table.
- The report file is removed from disk.

Status information requests are performed directly from the API using Information Access Services APIs. No interaction with the report process is necessary, which results in improved performance.

Modules

Exhibit 7 shows the module hierarchy for the custom report process. The diagram shows the relationships between modules, not their associated processing flows. It should be used to identify the calling module and the called modules for the process. The report process is supported by the Architecture Manager library.

The functions designed to support this process are

- Generate Report
- Get Report Status
- Control Reports
- Request Report
- Delete Report
- Print Report

Generate Report. This module is called to request report generation and printing (optional). Input data blocks specify the following:

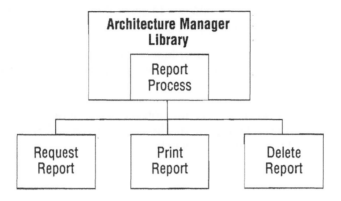

Exhibit 7. Process Module Hierarchy.

- Report name
- Report parameters
- Report generation time (default is immediately)
- Printer name

The report name must be one of the defined application report types. Valid report parameters vary depending on the report type. Reports may be requested for generation immediately or at a designated future time. All reports are written to a reserved area on disk; however, specification of a printer causes the output to be printed as well as stored on the file system.

Get Report Status. The Get Report Status function retrieves status information about all reports that have been previously requested for generation by the calling process. Returned is a list containing the requested data as well as the number of reports found.

Control Reports. The Control Reports function is responsible for performing various operations on reports. The following services are provided:

- Delete a report request and any associated output
- Print a previously generated report
- Update report status

In all cases, the report name is passed through an input data block. For the print service, a printer name is passed. For status update, the new status code is passed.

Request Report. The Request Report function is responsible for processing report request messages written to the report process queue. It creates a new entry in the report status table with a status of "requested" and initiates the report writer process for immediate generation or sends a message to the event manager for future report generation.

Delete Report. The Delete Report function is responsible for removing a report from the Report Status list and deleting the generated output file (if any).

Print Report. The Print Report function sends a generated report output file to a specified or default printer. The report name and requesting process ID is passed to identify the report.

Chapter 10
Development Architecture

FOUR COMPONENTS OF SUCCESSFUL DEVELOPMENT

As with all types of systems development, successful execution and control of a netcentric project require certain basics to be defined and in place — a methodology, organization, tools, and a process (Exhibit 1).

Methodology

A methodology defines what needs to be done. It specifies the key steps to be performed, the inputs to the steps, and the output deliverables of the steps. It frequently specifies a project organization; it also determines the tools used to support the methodology and organization and provides a framework in which to define detailed processes to support the steps of the methodology. Methodology is a critical component in defining how a project will work and how tools can be used to improve productivity, quality, and execution.

Organization

Organization refers not only to the way a project is organized but also to the types of roles and skills required and the training provided to enable project personnel to be effective. Although the methodology drives organization and the desired skills, the actual skills and the actual roles influence decisions made about the development environment.

Tools

Tools allow parts or all of the development process to be automated and aid in the creation of deliverables to provide leverage in performing a particular activity. This leverage can be in the form of improved productivity, improved quality, and improved satisfaction with the job. The emphasis is on facilitating the work being performed by the project personnel to make them more effective.

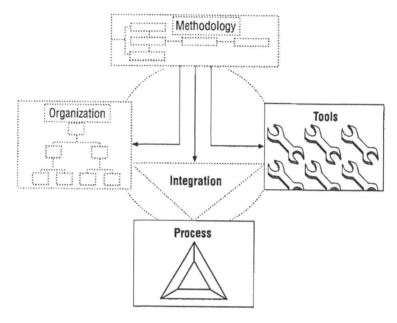

Exhibit 1. Components of Successful Development.

Process

Process is a specification for how to perform a particular activity. Although the methodology defines high-level tasks and their input/outputs, many activities within a project must be customized for the culture, environment, and project.

For example, the process for handling bug reports or change requests typically varies from project to project based on the culture of the organization, the philosophy of project management, and the priorities of the project. Some projects track these formally with weekly reports and meetings; other projects may keep a loose-leaf binder with handwritten notes of problems and suggestions. A process documents how these activities should be performed for a specific project. Each process is supported by procedures, standards, and tools. Depending on the process and project, the relative emphasis on and formality of these three differs.

- Procedures specify *how* to perform the task so that the result is in accordance with expectations. Procedures may specify which techniques and tools to use and may offer guidelines.
- Standards specify *what* the result should look like.
- Tools support the tasks of the process. In addition to automated software tools, there are many useful, simple tools such as templates and spreadsheets with precoded formulas and macros.

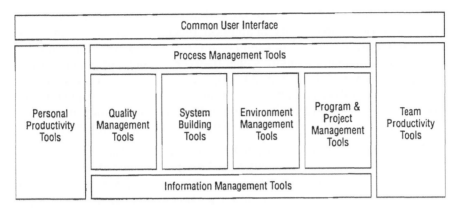

Exhibit 2. Development Architecture Framework.

Integrating the methodology, organization, tools, and process is critical. The tools must be chosen to support a specific organization as it works on specific tasks which form well-defined processes. If one of these is out of sync with the others, the results typically include lost time, lower developer productivity, inconsistent results, ineffective or inefficient communications, and general project management headaches.

Equally important is starting with the methodology in mind, because methodology drives the organization and process and thus the tools that are appropriate. Based on a netcentric methodology, the rest of this section describes a development environment that has been successful in supporting this methodology on projects.

For the purposes of this discussion, the development environment covers portions of the tools and process components and elaborates on standards, tools, and procedures useful in netcentric development. Organization is discussed further in the sections that deal with planning and managing netcentric projects.

DEVELOPMENT ARCHITECTURE MODEL

A development architecture is a combination of development tools, methods, standards, and procedures that define a development environment. An architecture framework such as the one depicted in Exhibit 2, which places tools into related groups, helps organize the many types of tools, standards, and procedures that may be used on a netcentric development project.

As demonstrated throughout this discussion, many of the tools and functions described by this model apply to traditional development as well as to client/server and netcentric development. As such, the focus of this chapter is on highlighting those areas that are different for client/server and netcentric environments. In addition, this model represents the set of tools that a project may find useful or important. It is based on what has been successful in implementing client/server and netcentric applications using large teams (more than 20 people), in tight time frames (6 to 12 months comfortably, 2 to 6 months on the aggressive side), using high levels of automation to maximize productivity and consistency. It does not represent the complete set of tools that every project must have in place.

This model is comprehensive and is useful as a "checklist" when establishing the development environment; based on the specifics of a project, only some portions of the model will be appropriate and necessary and should be implemented. Rarely can every capability this model describes be implemented for a first project (though frequently some developers iterate toward more complete implementations of the model). Finally, for readability, "tools" means "tools, standards, and procedures" unless otherwise indicated.

At a high level, Exhibit 2 represents the various types of tools required in systems development and management along with common capabilities to integrate these tools. The vertical boxes represent the common development tools and the horizontal boxes represent the capabilities to integrate the tools, to coordinate the definitions being created and maintained by the tools, and to provide a common launching place or look and feel for the various tools.

- A common user interface for all the tools, particularly a common launching place for the tools, helps provide a consistent, simpler and more integrated environment for developers.
- Process management tools provide structure and control over the development process.
- Repository is the communications backbone of the development environment, making it easy to share and manage information between different processes.
- Personal productivity tools are used for miscellaneous single-user activities commonly encountered on a project: writing memos, preparing presentations, and performing simple what-if analyses. These tools are typically oriented toward individuals rather than teams (i.e., no collaboration is required).
- Quality management tools ensure an agreed-on level of quality in the system being developed and provide information and process for improving the quality over time.
- System development tools are the heart of the development environment. These are the tools used by the majority of the development team to capture the system requirements, the functional design, the detailed design decisions, and the detailed coding and testing and to manage the resulting components.

- Environment management tools are used to treat the development environment as a production environment (with its users being developers). These tools support monitoring performance, providing help desk support, managing and distributing changes to the development environment, administering the environment, and monitoring and planning development environment capacity.
- Program and project management tools aid in the planning and scheduling of a project along with the tracking and reporting of its progress against the plan.
- Project communication tools facilitate communications across the project team. These include individual communications, such as electronic mail (e-mail) as well as tools to facilitate communication across a large number or personnel (e.g., groupware and publishing capabilities).

Common User Interface

The system development tools should be accessible from a single facility and should be coordinated for the user (developer, manager, and tester). The common user interface provides a graphical user interface (GUI) that allows users to access the development environment tools easily and consistently. The system should be simple to learn and intuitive to use and should assist the developer in navigating through the development environment. The following are recommended capabilities of the common interface.

- *Interactive and graphical interface.* Client/server and netcentric tools are predominantly graphical in nature, typically making use of the Windows operating system. Graphical tools are essential — developers of netcentric systems are constantly multitasking, and windowing systems are the only practical way for a developer to manage and coordinate their work activities. However, many of the utilities required to efficiently build a system are driven from the command line (e.g., build utilities); the development environment should provide a GUI interface to these tools to speed development and reduce errors.
- *Shield system-level details.* The developers should concentrate on the purpose of their applications, not the syntax, location, or integration of the tools or data they are using. Developers should only need to pick the service by selecting it from a menu or an equivalent action. They should not be required to have knowledge of, for example, file names, working directories, and configuration files. Automating simple details such as naming files and manipulating directories goes a long way to ensuring standardization and maintaining the control and integrity of the development environment.

- *Support multiple, concurrent activities.* Developers should not be restricted to a single development task. They should be able to execute multiple tools and facilities simultaneously. Netcentric development may require developers to be working simultaneously with client-side HTML documents running in a Windows browser, middle tier components on a Unix platform and backend database tables on an MVS mainframe. Developers can become very adept at executing these activities when their environment provides them with convenient, simultaneous access to the various computing platforms involved.
- *Completely integrated.* To the extent possible, developers should never be forced to leave the interface to use a service. The interface provides the services, control, and support for a highly productive environment. For example, many manual steps can be involved in creating code on a desktop, moving it to a Unix server for source control and finally building the application. Integrating these steps, which occur across machines, makes life simpler for developers, many of whom will not have a depth of experience with all of the platforms involved.
- *Security.* The interface should provide access to files, code, and tools, for example, based on privileges defined for each user of the environment. This is especially true on larger projects that may have formal controls for the review and sign-off of deliverables. In a netcentric environment, the number of "moving parts" that make up the final solution need careful management — applying security and procedures that prevent inadvertent change — can save many hours of debugging problems that have nothing to do with either the application or the technology.
- *Standards.* The interface should support the execution architecture standard user interface (Windows, Presentation Manager, and Motif).
- *Help.* The system should provide interactive, context-sensitive help to the users. Architecture teams should be encouraged to deliver their API documentation, standards documentation, and procedures in an on-line help format. Today's developers are very accustomed to searching and browsing for answers at the point of need; paper documentation is rarely used.

Today's client/server development environments are more mature and sophisticated, with many of the leading tools (e.g., Visual Basic or Visual Age) providing capabilities that makes it reasonably simple for the development architect to provide some basic integration (e.g., with source code management).

Process Management

This category provides structure and control over the development process as a whole (e.g., the methodology, procedures, and supporting processes).

As such, it provides for deeper integration than just graphical or desktop integration. It integrates existing and future tools, both package and custom, provides intertool communications where appropriate, and integrates tools with the repository.

The process management implementation may vary greatly in complexity. At the simple end is a menu system that presents a single user with the recommended development tasks and can launch the tool appropriate for the selected task. At the high end is a custom, complete work flow implementation that integrates the efforts of different development groups and enforces the project methodology (e.g., it supports the correct sequencing of tasks including reviews and sign-offs).

This latter type of support is provided in some computer-aided software engineering tools but is still fairly uncommon among the mainstream point tools. A once common implementation was software "backplanes" or workbenches that provided a common integration point for the development tools. Examples include SunSoft's ToolTalk, Softbench from Hewlett-Packard (HP), and FUSE (Friendly Unified Software Engineering) from Digital Equipment Corp (now Compaq).

When selecting or implementing process management support, some of the considerations are as follows:

- *Customizability.* This is the ability to tailor the tools to support a specific methodology and process for the organization or project.
- *Platform support.* Because the flow of work across the development process may span multiple developer platforms (Windows, UNIX), it is important to choose an implementation that supports the key platforms — both current and planned.
- *Work flow sophistication.* A more advanced implementation allows status information about a task or deliverable to be stored and routing decisions to be based on this information. For example, a design spec could be routed to a reviewer once its status is changed to "complete." After a successful review, its status could be changed to "final" and then marked as frozen in the configuration management system. Finally, sophisticated integration would allow context information (user ID, deliverable being manipulated) to be passed into the selected tool.

Repository

The development repository is the communication backbone of the development environment, making it easy to share information between people working on different processes. It stores design, construction, and maintenance information such as window layouts, processing specifications, code fragments, and references to source code files. By storing this information in a development repository, several benefits can be realized.

Pervasiveness. Repositories succeed when they are pervasive in the development environment. The use of the repository needs to be made an integral part of the designers' and developers' daily activities. Ideally, the repository should be a tool that assists the team, but even simple repositories, such as a well-managed set of shared directories on a network server, can provide significant benefit. The key to success is ensuring that the repository is at the heart of the development processes, remaining intact and populated with current information.

Consistency. By providing a common "template" for the content and format of design information, developers are more likely to create consistent specifications. In addition, by providing a "pool" of common definitions (especially for such low-level objects as data elements, table/record definitions, windows, and reports), a repository can facilitate consistent use and interpretation and, in some cases, reuse.

For example, by providing a common place for element definitions, and including such display information as literals and field size, windows and reports are more likely to integrate with the database definition and more likely to display or interact with the end user in a consistent manner (field validation, the literal to the left of the field, and the length of the field). Without this information in a repository, it would be up to individual developers to seek out the "common" information and apply it appropriately while they define their windows and reports.

Consistent capture and organization of information makes it much easier for more automation (e.g., code generators) to be provided in the future.

Dependency Management and Impact Analysis. Client/server and netcentric systems are typically built with a large number of pieces, many of which are shared. For example, many windows may communicate to a smaller set of business components, which then interact with a large set of database tables. When managing the construction and maintenance of such systems, it is absolutely essential to understand the interdependencies between components and the impact of changes made to any of these components.

Dependency management allows a development team to create the "bill of materials" for the system. This is crucial in the construction phase of the project — budgets and schedules can easily be blown if a large construct team starts to build a system whose interdependencies are not understood. Understanding the interdependencies between the pieces of the system allows the construction of these pieces to be scheduled in an efficient manner, ensuring that each piece can be coded and tested. As more and more of the system is built, understanding the dependencies allows the support team to effectively perform regular builds of the systems — dependencies tell the team the order in which the pieces of the system need to be assembled.

By maintaining relationship information such as window to element, impact analysis can be performed more accurately and easily. Changes are constantly occurring during a project as a result of requirements changes or clarifications and design considerations. Being able to accurately and quickly assess the impact of a change is critical to ensure that appropriate decisions are being made (i.e., that the cost benefit of a change is being considered properly) and that the change is being implemented correctly and completely.

For example, if the system under construction (or in maintenance) had to convert from five-digit ZIP code to nine-digit ZIP code, the repository information could be used to identify which tables, windows, reports, and common structures used ZIP code and were thus affected. Although the details of the change cannot necessarily be assessed without looking at each individual item affected, an order of magnitude of the change could quickly be determined to arrange for the appropriate prioritization and any necessary resources for making the change.

Traceability. Utilizing the relationship information just discussed, it is possible to link from high-level requirements down through low-level code modules and table definitions. With this information, it becomes practical to trace requirements through to their implementation to ensure that all requirements have been satisfied by logic and data and all requirements (or an agreed-on sufficient set) have been tested. This information can provide a level of comfort on the completeness and quality of the resulting design and implementation.

Reuse. A repository cannot force reuse to occur, but it is a building block on which to start a program of reuse. Because information about low-level (elements) and high-level (functions, subsystems) entities is stored in the repository, it is a logical place to begin looking for reusable building blocks. This reuse commonly happens within a team on a project but can also happen across teams within a project and eventually across projects.

Although a development repository is, in theory, useful for any size project, in practice it is most effective on medium- to large-scale projects (i.e., more than 10 developers or designers). This is because a repository requires a discipline and structure on the part of the development team, a level of tool integration (e.g., database management system definitions, GUI painting tool, source code management, and programming tools), and usually a level of support that may not be cost-effective on small projects (where communications and coordination can still be effective across the team).

Personal Productivity Tools

Personal productivity tools are used for miscellaneous, single-user activities commonly encountered on a project (e.g., writing memos, preparing presentations, and performing simple what-if analyses).

These tools are typically oriented toward individuals rather than teams (i.e., no collaboration is required) and consist of the following:

- *Spreadsheet.* Developers should have the ability to access and create spreadsheet data that is used in each phase of the development process. Spreadsheet analysis may be used to analyze reports from the repository, to view test data/results, to perform what-if analyses for impact analysis or estimating, and to assist in modeling such system aspects as performance. Examples include Lotus 1-2-3 and Microsoft Excel.
- *Graphics.* These tools are most commonly used to prepare presentations and supporting graphics for documentation. These may be standalone tools but are much more useful when they can be integrated directly with the repository or at least the spreadsheet package to allow graphical presentation of information (such as productivity information and quality statistics). Examples include Microsoft Powerpoint, Lotus Freelance, and CorelDRAW.
- *Word processor.* A word processing tool should provide basic forms and utilities that can be used (e.g., a form letter or memo template) by developers to document project information. Examples include Ami-Pro, Word, and WordPerfect.

Quality Management Tools

Quality management tools are used to ensure that an agreed-on level of quality in the system is reached. They are also used to provide information and process for improving the quality over time.

Although it is easy to agree that a focus on quality must be maintained in all development work, time pressures can weaken the commitment to quality in some cases. To counter this, putting good procedures and tools in place helps reduce this conflict, by making it easier to "do the right thing." Quality management tools provide the plan, the measurement, and the feedback for improvement to meet the quality objectives of a project.

Quality Function Deployment. Quality function deployment is basically the quality plan for the project or the organization. It is the basis for quality management. This plan should specify or reference the following:

- *Quality objectives that are important for a project.* These should be expressed in measurable terms whenever possible. For example, quality objectives may be expressed in terms of reliability (in defects per function point), usability (user training or overall productivity), efficiency (use of systems resources), and maintainability (cost/time to correct problems and provide added functions).
- *Defined input and output (I/O) criteria for each development phase.* This is typically integrated with the development methodology and defines sufficiency criteria for moving from one phase of the project to the next. These criteria are important to ensure that all necessary documentation for a phase has been created and is of the expected quality before beginning a phase. This helps reduce rework due to miscommunications or misunderstandings.
- *Identification and definition of the types of test, verification, and validation activities to be carried out.* This includes a description of the activities, what they apply to (e.g., validate a functional specification), and when they should occur (e.g., before beginning technical design).
- *Specific responsibilities for quality activities.* For instance, who is responsible for reviews and tests of the various development components, who has responsibility for configuration management and change control, and who has responsibility for defect control and corrective action? For smaller projects, this responsibility may be spread across the individual developers or teams; on larger projects, responsibility may be assigned to a specific quality team that interacts with the individual development teams.

Quality function deployment tools are used to reveal, document, and prioritize the requirements for the systems under development. Based on these requirements, it is possible to define meaningful goals for product quality along different dimensions (e.g., maintainability, complexity, and performance).

The value of a business system can be measured by business case metrics — demonstrating the benefit of a change brought to the business process. In turn, the business case metrics are supported by product metrics (or quality attributes), such as capability, reliability, usability, efficiency, maintainability, and portability. These characteristics, which have a great deal of influence on architectural design decisions, must be tied directly to the business value they are to enable.

Finally, process metrics support the product metrics by measuring whether the process is likely to result in a system that satisfies the product quality requirements. These metrics typically include productivity and defects.

Measurement and Metrics. Metrics are an important part of quality because they provide operational definitions of quality attributes. An operational definition, according to W. Edwards Deming, is one that is expressed as a method for sampling, testing, and determining whether a work product meets a given criterion.

With operational definitions, different stakeholders can agree that a product objectively meets a requirement or that a process has been improved by a measurable amount; without operational definitions, stakeholders can only have subjective opinions that may or may not agree.

To fine-tune the development process, it is necessary to be able to measure the important quality attributes. These measurements are still evolving as software engineering matures, but sample metrics could include the following:

- Average number of defects per design packet at the moment construction starts
- Average number of defects per program at the time of its first migration to product test
- System availability and causes of downtime
- Time needed for a new user to learn to use a function of the system
- User error rate per function
- Maintainability in terms of time to fix a defect or to add new functions

To facilitate capture of this kind of information, it is important that the tools used to perform a function provide support for capture of quality statistics. For example, the source code management tool set could allow information to be specified about reasons for a change and the stage the component had reached (e.g., initial construction, product test, and production). This information could be placed in a quality statistics part of the repository for later reporting.

Quality Process Control. Process control pertains to methodology, work flow, and tools usage. It ensures that quality gets built into the end product from the beginning. Standards and procedures pertaining to quality assurance of the process describe how to use simple tools, such as templates and checklists, and document the mandatory outputs from each work process. Other procedures cover common tasks such as design reviews and code reviews.

Continuous Improvement. These are the tools for capturing feedback on the quality process and taking action to improve it. Such a tool can be as simple as a suggestion mailbox (paper or electronic) or a more proactive approach in which statistical information on productivity and cost of quality is taken into consideration for making improvement suggestions. Once changes are made, the statistics being tracked must reflect the version of the process to which they correspond so that an accurate assessment of the change can be made (improvement, no change, or degradation).

Systems Development Tools

Systems development tools are the heart of the development environment. These are the tools used by the majority of the development team to capture the system requirements, the functional design, the detailed design decisions, and the detailed coding and testing and to manage the resulting (frequently large number) components. Because there are a large number of tools in this category, it is efficient to group them as follows:

- Analysis and design tools
- Reverse engineering tools
- Construction tools
- Testing tools
- Configuration management tools

Analysis and Design Tools. Analysis and design tools are used to capture the requirements for the system being developed, to analyze and prioritize them, and to transform them into a functional definition and then into a detailed technical definition suitable for construction. In other words, analysis tools help specify "what" a system needs to do, and design tools help specify "how" a system will implement the "what."

A number of the analysis and design tools are typically part of an I-CASE (integrated computer-aided software engineering) package such as FOUNDA-TION, Paradigm Plus, and Software through Pictures. Exceptions to this will be noted in the appropriate discussion. Regardless of whether I-CASE is used, when tools are being integrated across the various analysis and design categories, it is important to take into account the compatibility of the tools and their ability to integrate. For example, can the window painter access element definitions used in the data modeling and database design tools?

There are several types of analysis and design tools.

- *Data Modeling*. These tools provide the capability to graphically depict the logical data requirements for the system. Typically, a tool for data modeling supports diagramming entities, relationships, and attributes of the business being modeled on an entity-relationship diagram (ERD). The key difference from a traditional data modeling tool is the ability to capture information necessary for making data distribution decisions (e.g., ownership of data and frequency of access/manipulation by location). The increasing use of components in the construction of client/server and netcentric systems requires that the data modeling and object/component modeling tools be integrated — you have to know which components use which data elements and how they map.

10-13

- *Process Modeling.* These tools provide the capability to depict (prefer-ably graphically) the business functions and processes being sup-ported by a system, including, for example, tools that support documenting process decomposition, data flow, and process depen-dency information.

  As with the data modeling tools, the main difference in these tools for netcentric is the ability to capture the information necessary to make process placement decisions — for instance, where the process needs to occur (on a mobile personal computer or at a stationary workstation), the type and volume of data it requires to perform the function, and the type of function (user interaction, reporting, or batch processing).

- *Event Modeling.* These tools provide the capability to depict the busi-ness events and associated responses of the system. A variety of tools and techniques can be used for event modeling, including word pro-cessors to develop simple textual lists of events and diagramming tools to show events and responses. These tools inherently are closely tied to the process modeling tools because events result in a response generally described by a process.

- *Database Design.* These tools provide the capability to capture the database design for the system. They enable the developer to illus-trate, for example, the tables and file structures that will be physically implemented from the logical data requirements. The tools also cap-ture the definition of data elements, indexing decisions, foreign keys and referential integrity rules.

  Many I-CASE products integrate data modeling, database design, and database construction. Such tools typically generate the first-cut database design from the data model and generate the database defi-nition from the database design.

  As with the data modeling tools, the key difference in database design tools for client/server and netcentric is the ability to capture data distribution decisions and to provide support for creating sche-mas for multiple database products. For example, the standalone lap-top database management system (DBMS) may be different from the work group and enterprise DBMS choices (such as SQL-Anywhere on the laptop and DB2 at the enterprise).

- *Application Logic Design.* These tools provide the capability to depict the logic of the application, including application structure, module descriptions, and distribution of function across netcentric nodes.

  A variety of tools and techniques can be used for application logic design, including structure charts, procedure diagrams (module action diagrams), and graphics packages to illustrate distribution of function across client and server.

- *Presentation Design and Prototyping.* These tools provide the capability to depict the presentation layer of the application, including screens, windows, reports, and dialog flow. Tools in this category include window painters, report painters, and dialog flow diagrammers.

   Window painters let the developer design the windows for the application using common GUI window controls and application variables. The behavior associated with the window can either be captured directly in the window painter tool or using a deliverable known as a CAR (control, action, response) diagram. Frequently specified as a matrix or structure chart, the CAR diagram captures the response to an action taken on a particular control — for example, what to do when the user exits a field or clicks a button.

   Report painters let the developer design the report layout interactively, placing literals and application data on the layout without specifying implementation details such as page breaks. Typical window, screen, and report painters also generate the associated application code or a structure in which remaining code can be placed during construction. In addition, many window painters provide the capability to rapidly prototype the user interface.

   Prototyping allows developers to follow a more iterative functional design approach, which is important when dealing with developers and users that may be new to the GUIs typical of client/server and net-centric systems. In addition, given the responsive nature of a GUI, prototyping becomes an effective way of clearly communicating how the system appears to the user.

   Prototyping does not eliminate the need for detailed narrative specifications, but it does improve the users' and other developers' understanding of the system design. The essential feature for prototyping is enabling developers to rapidly build and modify screens and windows. Beyond this basic requirement, some tools may support the specification and prototyping of the dialog flow (e.g., linking windows), simple data interaction such as validation, or more complex data interaction such as the ability to insert, save, and transfer data between screens.

   Examples of window painting and prototyping tools include Sybase's PowerBuilder, Microsoft's Visual Basic, SQLWindows from Centura Software Corp., and Visual Edge's UIM/X. Examples of report painters include Sybase's SQR and Crystal Reports by Seagate.

Communication Design. After the fundamental communication paradigms have been chosen (message passing, remote procedure call, and structured query language-based), each exchange must be specified in detail to take into account the detailed design of the sending and receiving modules (clients, services, subroutines, and functions) and to lay the basis for more refined performance modeling. Multiple tier client/server and net-centric systems can only be built efficiently if the interfaces between the tiers are precisely specified. Communication Design tools allow designers to specify the contents of an exchange and define the "contract" of the exchange in terms of the processing to be performed, the expected precon-ditions, and the handling of error or unexpected conditions. They can also provide a generation capability for the code or common structures required in construction to send and receive the message.

Performance Modeling. The performance of a system, especially in a cli-ent/server or netcentric architecture, needs to be analyzed as early as pos-sible in the development process. Performance modeling tools support the analysis of the system performance. A simple spreadsheet may be suitable in some well-known and understood environments, but dedicated perfor-mance or simulation modeling tools should be considered on any project with high transaction volumes or complex multitier architectures involving several platforms.

In netcentric systems, the performance of the network is critical. How-ever, it is impossible to guarantee the performance of an application once it has passed by the ISP (Internet Service Provider). Therefore, the perfor-mance modeling tool must be able to model the performance to the ISP as well as provide the ability to do "what-if" scenarios for the network design and security implications. For example, given a certain application design, what if the protocol was changed ? What if the data or processing site was changed ? If the firewall was placed here, what are the security implications?

Object and Component Modeling. Tools with specific support for creating object and component models can be used to automate the component design process as well as create and document the component model. Some of these tools are also capable of generating code.

Reverse Engineering Tools

Reverse engineering is a set of techniques to assist in reusing existing sys-tem components — either directly (e.g., code/modules) or indirectly (e.g., design rules or algorithms and record layouts). The activity is well-known on many projects in that it is sometimes be necessary to look at certain pieces of code to understand how they work.

Most of the time, this work is done manually. One person sits down and studies thick listings to understand data layouts and processing rules. The person gradually builds a higher-level understanding of how the compo-nents work and interact — effectively reverse engineering the system into a conceptual model.

The process can be time consuming and is notoriously difficult to estimate. Tools to support the effort exist and have been used successfully to streamline the process. Although these tools cannot completely automate the analysis process, they can reduce the amount of manual effort needed and significantly lessen the amount of non-value-added automatic activities such as "find all the places in a program that affect the value of a given variable." These tools generally fall into four categories.

System Structure Analysis. These tools are used by a developer to identify requirements for a new system from the capability and design of a legacy system. They enable the developer to interactively and graphically navigate through the legacy system, analyzing such system characteristics as system structure, module flow, flow of control within a module, calling patterns, complexity, and data and variable usage.

The tools can also provide cross-reference listings or graphical representations of control or data flows. These tools are most effective when they are used to find and understand the business rules implemented by a system (that may no longer be documented) to provide comparable features in a new system. Examples for the multivendor system environment include VIA Insight, VIA Renaissance, and Compuware PATHVU.

Extraction. An extraction tool, in conjunction with a repository population tool, provides the developer the capability to reuse selected portions of a legacy system. The extraction tool can typically read and extract information from source code, screens, reports, and the database.

The most common information extracted from a legacy system is the data: record or table structure, indexes, and data element definitions. Although it is difficult to extract functions and processes from source code, source code containing complex algorithms is another candidate for extraction. Examples of this type of tool include Adpac's PMSS and Viasoft's Alliance.

Repository Population. The repository population tools are used to load the information from the extraction and structure analysis tools into the development repository. These tools convert the information from the legacy system into the syntax of the repository of the development tools.

Restructuring. Restructuring tools are not analysis tools like the previous categories of reverse engineering tools but rather design and construction tools. They enable the developer to rebuild a legacy system rather than replace it. Examples of this type of process include restructuring spaghetti code into structured code, replacing GOTOs with a PERFORM construct, streamlining the module calling structure, and identifying and eliminating dead code. These are most often encountered on projects that are rehosting one or more applications to a netcentric environment and want to upgrade the existing code to make it more maintainable and extend its useful life.

Examples of such a product for COBOL programs is Compuware's PATHVU, Compuware's RETROFIT, Knowledgeware's Inspector, Knowledgeware's Recoder, and IBM's SF.

Construction Tools

Construction tools are used to program, or build, the application: client and server source code, windows or screens, reports, and database.

Sophisticated tools to support the rapid creation of client/server systems are readily available. These visual programming tools (e.g., Power-Builder and Visual Basic) simplify the creation of 2-tier client/server systems by providing tools and languages geared towards user interface development while also providing graphical controls that link directly to relational data sources.

Building on these successful 2-tier client/server tools, several vendors have advanced their products to support multitier development. Tools such as Microsoft's Visual C++ provide sophisticated end to end development environments complete with debugging across multiple tiers. However, these tools are often aimed at a specific vendor's platform or technology. The netcentric developer's construction tool set typically contains a set of point tools that support the creation of user interfaces using markup languages such as HTML, DHTML, and XML that contain embedded scripts for controlling Java applets that interact over the network with business logic constructed from reusable components.

There are five categories of construction tools. Except for some specific utilities, it is unlikely that these tools will be purchased separately. All of the major tool vendors package these tools into an Integrated Development Environment (IDE), many of which provide links to Configuration Management tools.

Publishing and Page Markup. Netcentric systems using browsers for the user interface require tools that support the creation of documents in HTML, DHTML, and XML. These tools allow developers to create the individual pages that are displayed in the browser along with the links that allow the end user to navigate between pages. Tools such as Microsoft's Front Page are able to manage large complex webs of HTML documents, providing visual analysis of broken links and page hierarchies.

These tools also support the creation of scripts (e.g., VBScript and JavaScript) within the HTML. Script languages allow the developer to code behavior into the page to support basic validation and capture of data.

Source Code Editor. A source code editor is used to enter and edit source code for the application. Typically, editors are provided by an IDE, but many IDEs allow editors to be replaced by popular and more powerful editors such as Brief. Most editors provide source highlighting and integration with on-line help systems. Within the IDE, the editor is coupled to the compiler to provide incremental syntax checking, rapid compilation, and the ability to run and test the application without having to leave the editing environment (e.g., C++ development environments from Borland, Microsoft, and IBM).

Generation. These are automated tools that generate some component of the application: source code, common structures, windows, reports, and the database definition. They convert the application design into some form of source code.Some common types of generators include the following:

- *Procedural code generator.* Also known as source code generators, these typically take a pseudocode specification of a module and generate a module in the appropriate programming language. Alternatively, the procedural code may be specified in the repository using the target programming language (this eliminates an additional language that would have to be learned by a developer). This approach is common in I-CASE products that allow logic to be generated for multiple platforms (such as FOUNDATION and IEF).
- *Shell generation.* When it is not feasible or desirable to specify detailed code within the repository, a shell of a module can be generated with markers for where module specific code should be entered by a programmer. These markers are frequently encountered in window painting tools that can generate the modules required to implement the window with all the housekeeping code already in place. Visual C++ from Microsoft is an example of a tool that offers such a capability — it generates the shell code for windows painted in the environment and allows the programmer to add the business logic at specified drop points.
- *Data design language (DDL) and data manipulation language (DML) generator.* Based on the data and access definitions specified in the repository, these would generate the schema definition for the appropriate DBMS and the structured query language (SQL) and support code for performing the database I/O. DDL generators are frequently included in some of the I-CASE offerings discussed earlier. DML generators are either custom developed for a project or may be built on top of general-purpose query tools (such as Q&E or report writers). In the latter case, the query tool is used to build the query and the resulting SQL is copied into the appropriate module.

These types of tools are useful in an integrated development environment as they reuse design information, thereby eliminating errors caused by transcription or redefinition as well as providing additional incentives for keeping the design documentation up-to-date.

Compiler/Linker/Interpreter/Debugger. These tools are invariably part of an IDE — it is rare today to be able purchase a standalone compiler (the exceptions are midrange and mainframe platforms, although products such as IBM's Visual Age are also becoming popular on these platforms).

A compiler/linker converts source code to executable code and packages it into a runtime module. 3GLs such as C, C++, and COBOL are all compiled languages. An interpreter executes the source code directly (or indirectly through a pseudocompiled intermediate representation). Java and Visual Basic are the best known interpreted languages, although the latest versions can also be compiled.

A source code debugger (sometimes known as a symbolic debugger) is used to step through a program or module at the source code level (as opposed to the machine code level). Although commonly used for debugging programs, source code debuggers are also effective in supporting component testing because variables can be changed to cause logic to be executed that might otherwise be difficult to simulate using external data (e.g., time sensitive logic or logic for handling I/O hardware failures). Debuggers are typically included in an IDE.

Construction Utilities. Construction utilities are an assortment of tools that facilitate the construction process. The construction tools provided as part of an IDE are normally adequate for use by individual developers. Developers responsible for the overall build of a large system will require standalone tools, particularly for managing and building all of the source code.

These types of tools include the following:

- *MAKE utility.* The MAKE utility uses information (contained in a makefile) about the dependencies between modules of the system to automate compilation and linking of an application. By examining timestamps and dependencies the MAKE utility streamlines the build process because only those components dependent on the change are recompiled/linked.

    The makefile can either be hand coded or it can be generated based on information in a repository. Generation of the makefile tends to eliminate troublesome mistakes, assuming that the repository administrator has done a good job of maintaining the integrity of the repository. MAKE utilities are available either standalone (such as NMAKE from Microsoft or MAKE from Opus) or built into an integrated workbench environment (e.g., the "project" concept in Microsoft Visual C++ or Visual Basic).

- *Portability checker.* This is a utility that checks compliance with basic portability standards, particularly with programming standards that ensure portability across platforms (ANSI C or POSIX). These utilities are typically used only on the C and C++ programming languages because these are the dominant languages available on numerous platforms and operating systems. Portability checking is sometimes built in to the compiler and can be turned on with a switch or flag specified at compile time or can be performed by separate tools (e.g., the lint utility available under UNIX).

- *Application shells.* Application shells depicting basic application functions for common module types can be used as a starting point (a shell) for design and programming. These shells can be used in detailed design and programming phases of the development life cycle to enable designers and programmers to focus more on the essential business logic and spend less time worrying about structural aspects that can be solved once for everyone (e.g., a structure for dealing with the paging of large lists and an approach for handling data passing between modeless windows). Furthermore, shells are a good mechanism for enforcing standards as they typically embody them and thus the programmers get the standards for free. Because shells are usually project specific, their initial creation is done manually (rather than being generated).

- *Profilers.* These analyzers can provide the information and metrics needed to monitor and improve code quality and maintainability and make suggestions on how to package the code into modules and libraries for performance optimization.

Testing Tools

Testing is the process of validating that the gathering and transformation of information have been completed correctly and to the expected quality level. Testing is usually considered the process that makes sure there are no bugs in the code. However, in a broader sense, testing is about making sure that the system does what it is expected to do (i.e., meets the requirements specifications) at an acceptable quality level (e.g., acceptable numbers of defects per function point, or defects per module).

The Testing chapter of this book contains a detailed discussion of testing tools.

Stubs and Drivers. Stubs and drivers are used to test components of the application or architecture before a complete set of components is available. These are generally custom coded as part of the component testing effort:

- Stubs emulate subroutines or external functions in a minimal fashion, that is, they basically return with some sample data and the various return code values (e.g., successful and failed). They are useful for testing a module when the modules it calls are not yet ready or available for testing.
- Harnesses and drivers call up a module and emulate the context in which the module will be called in the production environment.

Configuration Management Tools

Configuration management is a broad area that often means different things to different people. In this book the term means the "management of components in an environment to ensure they collectively satisfy given requirements."

"Configuration" designates a set of components in a given environment satisfying certain requirements. The management ensures that consistency is maintained over time, even with changes to the components.

The components are typically hardware, system software, and application components (such as source code, executable modules, load libraries, database DDL, and scripts or job control language) together with their documentation. The development environment also includes test data, test scripts, and other components that must be aligned with a given version of the configuration.

Version control and compatibility of components are key considerations when managing these components. Version control applies to all types of components, not just application components. In case incompatibilities are discovered, it must always be possible to "roll back" to a previous consistent state, that is, to revert to an earlier version of one of more components. To do this, it is necessary to know which versions are compatible. It must be possible to define releases of a configuration — a list of version numbers, one for each component, which together form a consistent configuration.

The environments can be many, and they can have complex relationships. On a large project they may include the following:

- *Design and construction.* This is the most commonly encountered environment, one in which the basic definition, build, and test activities of a project occur.
- *Assembly and product test.* This is where the different system level tests occur (assembly test, product test, and performance test). Depending on the organization and the scale of the project, there may be different environments for each of the different system-level tests.

- *Production test.* This is typically the final staging area before a release is turned over to production and the operations group.
- *System software acceptance.* This is where new versions of system software (the operating system, the DBMS, and middleware) would be installed and tested before rolling out to the rest of the project.
- *Architecture build and test.* This is where the architecture is developed and maintained. Fixes and enhancements are made here and tested prior to being released to the development teams for their use.
- *Production.* This is the current version of the "live" software.

Migration of consistent configurations from one environment to another is a central part of managing the environments. Examples of migration include the following:

- Migration from design and construction to product test
- Distribution of software from the architecture team to the designers and programmers on the development project
- Migration from test to production

The key to successful migration is the knowledge of what constitutes each environment. Given the number of components commonly encountered on client/server and netcentric development projects, and given that these components may be spread out geographically and over different platforms, the use of tools to aid in tracking these components becomes more important than in traditional environments.

Based on the previous discussion, configuration management for the development environment is divided into version control and migration control.

Version Control. Version control tools control access to source code and other development components as they are developed and tested. They typically allow releases to be defined and multiple "snapshots" (i.e., the versions of all the components in the release) to be taken and maintained to facilitate rolling back to earlier releases if necessary. Examples of version control tools include Intersolv's PVCS and the UNIX Source Code Control System (SCCS).

Migration Control. Migration control tools control multiple versions of source code, data, and other items as they are moved across the environments previously discussed. The source code migration control tools manage multiple versions of source code to ensure that changes are applied in the proper environment and that thoroughly tested modules are subsequently migrated to the next environment.

Data migration control tools manage multiple versions of the database and its data to ensure that accurate data and structure are maintained in the environment and that versions of application code and database are deployed consistently. Types of data that would be migrated include base codes data or other reference data (e.g., a state code table or valid order code table) and converted business data.

Other migration control tools manage other types of system objects to ensure that a complete version of all components reside in the production environment (e.g., architecture support files, test definitions, and scripts).

Environment Management Tools

The immediate result of thinking of a development environment as a production environment (for producing a system) is making sure that environment management is planned, organized, executed, and supported to ensure a predictable and productive environment.

Adopting a structured approach to environment management, applying the same principles to development as to production, has several advantages:

- It provides high-quality support for developers.
- It can provide significant experience with the operations management tools in an environment that is generally smaller and carries lower risk than the full production environment.
- It facilitates the tuning of the production support approach before production roll-out. The approach is refined from experiences using it to support the development team.

In some respects, the development environment is simpler than the production environment. For example, the development environment is generally smaller in terms of the numbers of hardware components, locations, and users.

In other respects, however, the development environment is more complex. For example, the amount of change in this environment is generally higher than the amount of change in the production environment. In fact, the environment can be so fluid that extreme care must be taken to maintain control.

The greatest need for technical support is generally during detailed design and programming. It is, however, necessary to start building the technical support team and processes (e.g., the help desk for applications developers) before detailed design.

This chapter discusses the components of environment management briefly. In Section III of the book, "Management of Distributed Operations" describes how netcentric production environments can be managed.

Because the development environment is a form of production environment, that section details each of the following components.

- *Service management.* These are the tools for defining and managing an agreed-on level of service, including service-level agreements, information gathering to check against the service-level agreements, and help desk support for the developer community.
- *System management.* These are the tools for managing the development environment. They provide support for managing security, starting up and shutting down the environment, and performing backups.
- *Managing change.* These are the tools for making, tracking, and distributing changes to the development environment. The most common type of change is upgrading of software (system, architecture, or application), but changes to hardware configurations and network configurations must also be supported.
- *Service planning.* These are the tools for supporting a capacity planning function for the development environment. The environment needs to be monitored and sufficient lead time allowed to support required capacity changes for shared disk space, server size (e.g., central processing unit size, memory, and number of users), network, and workstations (either the number of workstations or the configuration of the workstations).

Program and Project Management Tools

Experience has shown that effective planning and progress tracking are necessary for the success of most netcentric projects. Given the more complex nature of netcentric systems development and the new types of skills required, good project planning and management are even more critical for a successful outcome.

Although the basics of project management do not change, the estimating factors, the skills required, the learning curve, the level of contingency, and the "management instinct" (i.e., the gut feel developed from lessons learned over multiple projects) are different and must be taken into account by project management. Many of these changes are discussed in more detail in the chapter on "Project Management" in Section III.

Program and project management tools include the following:

- *Plan.* These tools are tightly linked with the development methodology. They help in estimating the development effort, defining the project tasks and activities, and identifying the type and quantity of resources required (subject matter experts, architects, and designers).
- *Schedule.* When estimates and resource requirements have been determined, these tools assist in scheduling the work, identifying dependencies and critical paths, and balancing (level loading) the

work across the resources. On an ongoing basis, the scheduling tools also provide administration features that allow tasks to be assigned and reassigned as the project evolves.

- *Track.* These tools provide a mechanism for members of the development team to report time against the project plan. This is typically done on a weekly or biweekly basis.
- *Report.* These tools provide reporting capabilities to reflect the status of the project against the plan. In the simplest form, the reporting consists of budget and schedule information, such as time spent by member, budget variance, schedule variance, estimates to complete, and planned vs. actual results. More advanced tools can provide information on productivity and efficiency.

Most project planning and management tools available today provide some capability for each of the above. Examples of these tools include Microsoft Project and ABT Project Manager's Workbench.

Project Communication Tools

When a project team grows beyond 10 to 20 people, communication among project members may deteriorate unless a conscious effort is made to ensure that ideas, decisions, and results are shared in a timely fashion. The problem is more acute if development is distributed across sites. The consequences of communication breakdown can be serious: duplication of work, rework, budget overruns, and declining motivation among project members. On large projects it is therefore crucial to plan how communication will be facilitated throughout the project, and to communicate the decisions to the project team.

The local area network generally provides the basic infrastructure for sharing information. If development is distributed, a wide area network should be in place to connect the different locations.

But networks by themselves are no guarantee that people actually will exchange the kinds of information they should be sharing in a timely manner. At the very least, higher-level tools are needed.

The repository is one such higher-level communication vehicle, but the repositories that are commercially available are generally not sufficiently flexible. For example, most repositories are useful for documenting specific design decisions but not quite as useful for documenting design guidelines and basic design philosophies. They are also not very useful for communicating every kind of information to the project (such as planned server downtime or the scheduled release of a new version of the architecture).

There are several categories of project communication tools.

Mail. An e-mail system (e.g., cc:Mail, Lotus Notes, or Microsoft Exchange) is valuable for sharing such dynamic information as design documents, meeting schedules, project events, and resource availability. Because these mail tools allow mail to be stored, forwarded, sorted, and filtered dynamically, they improve the quality of communication; they also speed up the flow of information.

E-mail and voice mail are also effective in facilitating communications in environments where people may be difficult to reach at their desks (e.g., if they spend time in meetings or working with their teams). Rather than play telephone tag or leave notes, which can get lost, e-mail and voice mail allow communications to happen asynchronously, reliably, and easily.

Groupware. Groupware (increasingly called teamware) is a category of tool that allows groups of people to share information easily. These tools typically provide a forum for people with a common interest to share information and ask questions of one another. Depending on the environment, these forums may be called newsgroups, bulletin boards, or databases. What they have in common is the ability to post questions and comments and to search through the existing discussion to see whether the information required is already present. Like e-mail, the posting and reading of information takes on the look of a mail letter. Unlike e-mail, however, the "letters" are openly available to everyone with access to the bulletin board and are saved for an extended period of time.

These databases are similar to the traditional bulletin boards already encountered in offices, except that the type of information is now more specific and the volume of information is much greater than could ever be handled by a traditional, manual bulletin board. Examples of such products include Lotus Notes and Microsoft Exchange.

Publishing. Large computer systems are among the most complex deliverables produced by humankind. Although repositories go a long way toward organizing the information to make it accessible, there is also a need to publish information on the design and the implementation of the system. Publishing is necessary for the following:

- Information that needs to be communicated externally.
- Users who wish to review the system design but who do not know how to navigate the repository.
- Information that simply cannot effectively be understood when viewed on-line. Because of old habits and small screens it may still be useful to spread paper documentation across a desk when assimilating complex information.
- Legal or contractual obligations that may require the production and archiving of hard copy documentation.

Publishing tools allow individuals to print anything from single deliverables or specs all the way through the complete set of documentation for the system. Because documentation may be spread over several hardware platforms, and because it may reside in different libraries in different formats and may have to be printed using different tools, it is important to ensure that any chosen publishing tools can interoperate or integrate to allow aspects such as common headers and footers and consecutive page numbering to be handled without overly intensive manual involvement. Examples of publishing tools include Aldus PageMaker, Microsoft Publisher, and Corel Ventura.

CONCLUSION

An effective development architecture, implemented correctly and managed as a production environment, can make a complex project manageable and successful. It is important to make sure that the tools support the development process and that there are corresponding standards and procedures when necessary.

The rapid change in netcentric tools and technologies make it even more important than before to create a development architecture that is flexible enough to be able to incorporate new or changed tools while still providing the integration necessary to make developers productive and to ensure that processes are followed.

The development architecture as described here represents a useful guide. However, developers do not need to implement the whole model on every project. Rather, the model is something to aim for during iterations. There will always be enhancements and maintenance for systems, and these should be tied to iterative evolution of the development architecture.

Chapter 11
A Framework for Testing Netcentric Applications

Testing is an often-overlooked and underestimated facet of systems development. In a client/server environment, testing can make up 50 to 80% of a development effort. The age of netcentric computing adds significant complexities to systems development. Netcentric applications integrate customers and suppliers, cross multiple technologies, and involve multiple user groups, each with varying expectations, requirements, and level of knowledge. Therefore, the importance of testing rises significantly. This chapter provides a detailed look at a structured approach to testing using a model well-suited to managing the risks of the convergence environment.

The structured approach to testing advocated in this chapter has been successfully applied to save organizations time and money while increasing software quality and delivery reliability. The savings are realized through the implementation of what is termed the "V-Model" of testing, metrics, and automation to dramatically improve the productivity and effectiveness of the software delivery processes. The V-Model framework for testing has been successfully applied to custom development, package installation, and maintenance in traditional development environments as well as in iterative, rapid development, and object-oriented environments.

WHY CREATE NEW TESTING FRAMEWORKS?

Testing costs organizations significant amounts of time, effort, and money. In many cases, the value derived from traditional testing procedures does not match the effort expended. For typical systems projects, 50 to 80% of the development budget goes into testing-related activities, including test execution, impact analysis, and error resolution. If organizations can gain a mere 10% reduction in the overall testing effort, this would translate into significant annual savings for the average IS department. New testing approaches must also increase the value of the testing process. Typical traditional testing approaches cover only 40% of application code, leaving an average of 3.79 defects per thousand lines of code (KLOC) and as many as 5 defects per KLOC.

There is cause for concern, then, that testing approaches that are ineffective in the current computing environment will only worsen as the computing environment becomes more complex. The risk to the average company today is significant. Customer expectations are escalating; the average business person is now familiar with computer technology and is less tolerant of imperfect solutions. In addition. the definition of a "user community" has expanded to include customers and suppliers, meaning that these users cannot be trained by IS departments to make up for poorly tested solutions. Finally, netcentric computing brings a company's customers into direct contact with corporate systems, so one can no longer count on a customer service representative to cover for shortfalls.

Testing approaches were left behind in the client/server revolution. Design, development, code, and architecture were all significantly changed by the client/server revolution, but testing was not. Consequently, for many organizations today, testing looks very much like it did 20 years ago, although the applications are very different. In addition, software testing for many companies has not kept pace with the technology revolution; automation in the testing process has been vastly underused. Tools to automate test planning, test preparation, and execution are now available in the marketplace, as are tools for test data management and configuration management. These are all highly integrated, labor-intensive tasks that can benefit from the use of tools not only to increase speed and productivity but also to reduce the occurrence of human error.

However, in spite of the availability of more mature tools in the marketplace, the use of automation in the testing processes remains limited, partly because the tools available have only recently matured to the point where it makes sense to invest in them. Many organizations are either unaware that tools exist to automate testing activities, or they looked at testing tools years ago when the tools market was immature and do not realize the advances made since. Another common reason for a lack of testing automation is that IS departments begin considering the automation requirements of the testing process too late in the project, when there is not enough time to evaluate, select, and implement tools.

Traditional testing processes do not address the complexities of client/server computing, much less those of netcentric. Multilayered architectures, graphical user interfaces (GUIs), user-driven or decision-support systems, and the need to interface heterogeneous systems and architectures all present new risks and challenges for information technologists. A proliferation of users and user types in netcentric applications all provide and demand information from an enterprise system. Further, netcentric often means not knowing what the exact target execution architecture will be. This situation presents complex design challenges as well as security and error-avoidance requirements. All of these complexities must be recognized, designed for, and built into a set of applications. Then, just as important, they must be tested to ensure that they perform as expected.

As the industry becomes more comfortable with client/server development, and as the demands of netcentric become more evident, IS departments' attention increasingly turns to testing. Recent recognition of testing as an important facet of successful systems delivery can be seen in the significant increase in the number of seminars and conferences dedicated to testing and software quality. Likewise, there has been a trend toward increased emphasis on testing indicated by the identification of dedicated testing or software quality managers or entire departments within large IS organizations.

All of the complexities mentioned — increased complexity, higher level of effort spent on testing, increased risk, and minimal revision in testing approach — lead to the clear need to "reinvent testing." New testing frameworks and approaches are part of the current movement toward quality in systems development. These new frameworks make use of concepts introduced in manufacturing, such as quality management (QM) and just in time (JIT), which are then modified to apply to software development. Applying these manufacturing concepts to systems development requires IS development managers to adopt new or modified models of the development process and project organization. The key components of the V-Model testing approach presented in this chapter are

- Well-defined development processes, each with suppliers and customers, in which an overall quality product is achieved only when quality is delivered at every point in the chain.
- Structured, repeatable testing.
- Definition of metrics to be used for continuous process improvement.
- Use of automation to improve speed and reduce errors.
- New management approaches to organization and communication.

By applying a V-Model testing approach, many organizations have realized improved quality, reliability, efficiency, and delivery time. They have also achieved better risk management and cost avoidance. For example, an internal software development organization within Accenture was able to achieve an 80% reduction in the software defects delivered to customers while improving testing productivity and delivery speed. Another example is a large drugstore chain in the U.S., which realized a 100% improvement in testing productivity while achieving nearly fivefold improvements in software quality.

THE V-MODEL FOR NETCENTRIC TESTING

The V-Model of testing provides a structured testing framework through-out the netcentric systems development process; it emphasizes quality from the initial requirements stage through the final testing stage. All solution components, including application programs, conversion programs, and technical architecture programs, are required to proceed through the V-Model development process.

The V-Model charts a path from verification and validation to testing. After each process in the development life cycle has been defined, each major deliverable in the development process must be verified and validated, and then the implementation of each specification must be tested.

Verification is a process of checking that, as a deliverable is created at a stage of development, it is complete and correct and properly derived from the inputs of that stage. In addition, verification checks that the process to derive the deliverable was followed and that the output conforms to the standards set in the project's quality plan. For example, one form of verification is desk checking or inspection of a design specification to ensure that the process was followed, the standards were met, and the deliverable is complete.

Validation checks that the deliverables satisfy requirements specified in the previous stage or in an earlier stage and that the business case continues to be met. In other words, the work product contributes to the intended benefits and does not have undesired side effects. Given the top-down nature of systems specification, validation is critical to ensuring that the decisions made at each successive level of specification continue on track to meet the initial business needs.

Proper validation techniques can ensure that a system actually meets business needs and does not result in unintended consequences that may undermine the business value of the system. For example, at one large organization, developers of a call center system implemented the ability for customer service representatives to view the company's recent print ads at their terminals. However, the overriding business case for the system development project was to improve the speed of the reservation agents. There was no overriding business need for the reservation agents to view print ads, and a great deal of time was spent designing functionality that, if implemented, would have actually slowed the reservation process rather than speed it up.

Testing is designed to ensure that the specification is properly implemented and integrated. Ideally, testing activities are not in place to ensure that the solution was properly specified; that activity is done via verification and validation. Rather, testing activities associated with each level of

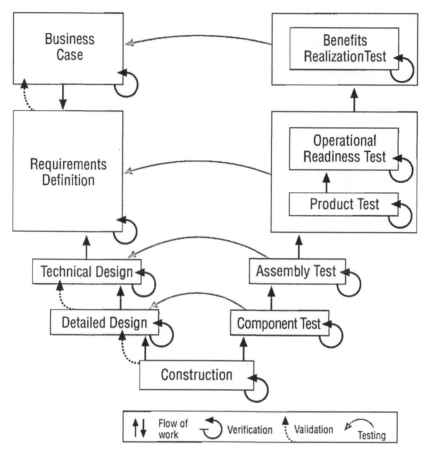

Exhibit 1. V-Model of Verification, Validation, and Testing.

the specification ensure that the specifications are properly translated into the final solution.

The V-Model of testing is depicted in Exhibit 1. This figure shows the work flow in the development process, with a series of design activities and systems specifications on the left side (i.e., top-down), and a series of corresponding testing activities on the right side (i.e., bottom-up).

In concept, the core process stages of requirements analysis, design, and construction consist of creating a series of increasingly detailed specifications. The exhibit specifies the systems from the top down, making decisions and adding detail at each stage. Work flows between stages in the V-Model when a work packet or deliverable has met the exit criteria, that is, all the verification and validation requirements for that stage. Testing is designed to ensure that the components of the application are properly constructed, put together correctly, and that they deliver the functional, technical, and quality requirements.

The specification stages are

- Business case
- Requirements definition
- Technical design
- Detailed design

The test stages are

- Component test
- Assembly test
- Product test
- Operational readiness test
- Benefits realization test

Component Test

Testing at the component level refers to the typical testing that a programmer does to verify that a component behaves as expected. All components are subject to a component test, including application programs, conversion programs, and input/output modules.

The component test verifies that the component specification (detail design) has been properly implemented. When testing components in isolation, upfront planning is required along with the development of generic stub and driver logic that can be used throughout the component testing process.

In a netcentric or client/server environment, the flexible nature of the graphical front end provides numerous navigation paths to perform the same business function. The component tester is responsible for testing each of these paths completely. Therefore, the number of test conditions and test cycles identified is much greater for client/server applications than in traditional systems.

Assembly Test

The objective of assembly testing is to test the interaction of related components to ensure that the components function properly after integration. During assembly testing, application designers verify that data is passed correctly between modules and, as required, that messages are passed correctly between a client and a server.

This is essentially a technical test; functional testing is limited to verifying that the flow through the assembled components supports the defined transactions.

Typically, the application designers create the test plan. This plan ensures that all interfaces within the application are exercised. These interfaces could include one program calling another (such as a browser program requesting data from a net server), data being passed from one program to another, signals or flags being passed from one to another, or transaction files moving between components.

The first problems with configuration management usually arise during assembly testing. Client/server and netcentric systems invariably have more discrete pieces that need to be fitted together. It is important to institute a sound configuration management discipline for tracking which versions of which components are required for each assembly test, and to control the movement of components (such as source code) through the test stages.

Product Test

Product testing focuses on the entire application to ensure that the system has met all functional and quality requirements. Product testing may occur at multiple levels. For example, the first level tests assemblies within an application. The next level tests applications within a system, and a final level tests systems within a solution.

The product test focuses on the actual function of the solution as it supports the user requirements: the various cycles of transactions, the resolution of suspense items, and the work flow within organizational units and across these units. The specification against which the product test is run includes all functional and quality requirements. The testing is organized by business function.

The product test determines whether the system is ready to be moved to operational readiness testing and subsequently into rollout. At this stage, the business worker becomes heavily involved in the testing process.

Using a "Model Office." A "model office" may be assembled so that users can exercise all dimensions of the new system in a realistic setting. This involvement of users is to ensure that the system meets functional expectations. It is the last opportunity for the project team to resolve logic and interface problems in a controlled environment before the system is moved from the development team to those responsible for release management and rollout.

The product test conditions are defined to emphasize testing of the system's business functions rather than testing every processing condition, as this has already been done in component and assembly test. Users, assisted by the development personnel, usually define product test cycles.

Performance Testing. The team should do an overall performance evaluation for the application at this time. The development team measures and verifies response time of the product stipulated by the users in the service-level agreement (SLA) during the system design phase. The SLA provides the criteria for success of the performance test. Testing should be conducted for both production load levels and high volume stress levels.

Both client performance testing and server performance testing should be conducted. Client performance testing measures the end-to-end response time of one of more client/server or netcentric transactions. End-to-end response time includes the time when a user initiates a server process using the application interface until the return value is displayed in the GUI interface. Typically, in a netcentric application a significant part of that time is spent in the intranet or internet. During a client performance test, the tester can monitor the behavior and performance of the applications in a simulated environment, synchronize transactions, and collect results for off-line analysis.

Server performance testing focuses on testing the performance of the database or net server under production load to assess whether the server performs according to requirements and provides acceptable response times for transactions.

Operational Readiness Test

The objective of operational readiness testing is to ensure that the application can be correctly deployed, and that those responsible for systems operations are prepared for rolling out and supporting the applications and associated data in both a normal mode and an emergency mode (e.g., to repair a fault discovered in production). Operational readiness testing also tests for SLA compliance.

The increasing focus on distributed solutions has caused a dramatic increase in the need for operational readiness testing. Distributed client/server and netcentric systems typically consist of a relatively large number of discrete components that need to be installed on a number of client and server machines, potentially across a wide geographic area. This is a new and very different problem from rolling out an application on a single centralized mainframe.

In addition, systems sometimes must be installed and operated by personnel at local sites who may have limited knowledge of complex application systems. In these cases, in particular, it is essential that the system be tested as an installable whole prior to being rolled out to the user community.

Operational readiness testing has four aspects:

1. *Rollout test.* Ensures that the rollout procedures and programs can install the application in the production environment.
2. *Operations test.* Ensures that all operational procedures and components are in place and acceptable, and that the personnel responsible for supporting production can operate the production system.
3. *Service-level test.* Ensures that when the application is rolled out, it provides the level of service to the users as specified in the service level agreement.
4. *Rollout verification.* Ensures that the application has been correctly rolled out at each site. This test, defined by the work cell or team performing operational readiness testing, should be executed during each site installation by the work cell or team in charge of the actual rollout of the application.

Operational readiness testing assumes a completely stable application and architecture in order for it to be successful. Therefore, it relies heavily on the previous testing stages.

Operational readiness testing is the point in the development process when all the applications development, architecture development, and preparation tasks come together. Operational readiness testing brings all these areas together by testing that the application and architecture can be installed and operated to meet the defined SLAs.

Benefits Realization Test

The benefits realization test ensures that the business case for the system will be met. The emphasis here is on measuring the benefits of the new system, such as increased productivity, decreased service times, or lower error rates. If the business case is not testable, the benefits realization test becomes more of a buyer sign-off.

Ideally, benefits realization testing occurs prior to complete deployment of the system and utilizes the same environment that was used for the service-level testing component of the operational readiness test. Tools are put in place to collect data to verify the business case, such as "count customer calls." A team of people is still needed to monitor the reports from the tools and to prove that the business case is going to be achieved. The size of the team depends on the number of users and the degree to which tools can collect and report the data.

An underlying concept of the V-Model is that the boxes in the exhibit represent distinct development and testing stages. It is essential that the stages of the V-Model, and the processes to complete each stage, are well defined, structured, and standardized. Defined, standard processes are repeatable and measurable. Processes that are not repeatable or measurable therefore do not easily lend themselves to improvement. Testers cannot collect meaningful data about ad hoc processes because there is no clear understanding of what the steps and outcomes are meant to be. Developers cannot learn from their experiences if they take a completely different approach each time they set out to develop software. Also, there is significant margin for error in undefined processes. Too often, the designers' expectations of what that process is to produce differ from the expectations of the construction and testing teams. This leads to gaps and overlaps between the processes. At best, these gaps are inefficient; at worst, they create errors.

ENTRY AND EXIT CRITERIA

Of special importance is the verification and validation performed at hand-off points between work cells or teams or from the project team to the users. Each inspection, performed at hand-off points or other important checkpoints during the development process, must satisfy a set of specific entry and exit criteria. As processes are defined, it must be clearly stated what each process is responsible for, and where it begins and ends. Entry and exit criteria are a mechanism for articulating what is required from previous processes to support a given stage (i.e., entry criteria) and what is required of a given process to determine completeness (i.e., exit criteria). Entry and exit criteria are defined for each stage to ensure quality deliverables from one stage to the next. If a deliverable fails to meet these set criteria, it is demoted to the previous stage or to the stage determined to have caused the nonconformity.

One stage's exit criteria are largely the next stage's entry criteria. Some exit criteria, however, may satisfy the entry criteria of a stage other than the one next in line. There are three types of entry and exit criteria in testing:

1. Those that must be met in one test stage in order to proceed with the next test stage.
2. Those that must be met in the specification stage to facilitate test preparation.
3. Those that are required for repetition of the current stage, in maintenance or enhancement activities.

All three types of entry and exit criteria should be defined and communicated as part of the standard process definition. Entry criteria may also be inspected throughout the development process, as opposed to right before the test stage requiring the criteria to be met is about to start. Inspection helps to build quality into the process and thus the solution,

Exhibit 2. Sample Exit Criteria

Stage	Sample exit criteria
All Stages	Deliverables must conform to standards
Requirements	Requirements specification must be reviewed with user
	Test cases must be generated
Design	Design must be traceable to the requirements specification through cross-reference
Construction	Code must be analyzed for adherence to standards and complexity guidelines; analysis results must fall within defined thresholds
	Code must be traceable to the design through cross-references
Component test	Component test data must be traceable to the design through cross-reference
	There can be no abends in component test results
	Component test results must be repeatable
Assembly test	All paths within the application flow must be executed
	Assembly test results must be repeatable
Product test	The product test model must be traceable to the requirements specification (both functional requirements and quality attributes) through cross-references
	Product test results must conform to predicted results
	Product test results must be repeatable

rather than retrofitting the solution to work correctly, and inspection saves the cost of rework, which only gets more expensive as the life cycle progresses. Although inspections cost time and effort on the front end, experience shows that the cost of formalized inspections is more than gained back in future stages of the life cycle.

There are three key success factors with regards to inspection of entry and exit criteria. The developer should:

1. Ensure that the entry and exit criteria are understood.
2. Validate and verify content as well as format.
3. Conduct inspections throughout the process.

Developers should not wait until the end of the stage to start inspecting deliverables. People are less willing to go back and rework something from a previous stage if the next stage is well underway. This reduces any rework in the next stage or in the related test stage and ensures that nonconformity to the entry and exit criteria can be communicated to the rest of the work cell or team to prevent replicating nonconformity throughout the remaining deliverables for that stage. Sample key exit criteria for each stage are shown in Exhibit 2.

VERIFICATION AND VALIDATION

Verification and validation are a means to test specifications and other deliverables. Approaches to verification and validation include walk-through or peer reviews, formal inspections, and prototypes. Other approaches are paper system testing, desk checks, and stakeholder reviews.

Verification

Verification is most commonly accomplished through an inspection. Inspections involve a number of reviewers, each with specific responsibilities for verifying aspects of the specification package, such as functional completeness, adherence to standards, and correct use of the technical architecture. According to Tom Gilb, software quality expert and author of *Software Inspection*, inspection, done before an application is finished, can remove 95% of all defects before the first tests.

Validation

Validation is most commonly accomplished through management checkpoints or stakeholder reviews. Two effective techniques of validation are repository validation and the completion and review of traceability matrices.

Repository validation can be used when a design repository is used (such as development workbenches, CASE tools, or even very strict naming conventions), and cross-checks can be executed against the repository to ensure integrity of dependencies between deliverables. Such a cross-check is designed to confirm that each deliverable is derived from a higher-order deliverable and that each higher-order deliverable breaks down into one or more implementation level deliverable.

A traceability matrix is a technique used in defense contracting. A matrix of all requirements is developed, cross-referenced to the designs, code, tests and deployment deliverables that implement the requirement.

With either repository validation or a traceability matrix, what is accomplished is a cross-check that all business-case criteria are directly linked to one or more specifications and that at each level of specification there is a direct link back up to a business case criteria. The objective of validation in this way is the direct relation of the specifications to the requirements and business case items that they implement, facilitating the identification of missing requirements and specifications not contributing to the business case.

How validation is performed depends on the nature of the requirement in the specification document. Certain requirements can be traced directly from the specification to the implementation. They bear the same name, and there is a one-to-one correspondence between the requirement and some component in the implementation. For example, a business objective to support a new operational process may be directly tied to portions of the application under development.

In other cases, the specification concerns a quality factor or an emerging property of the implementation. Therefore, a direct comparison is not possible. In this case, validation can be done by analyzing a model of the implementation. For example, the work flow can be analyzed to ensure that headcount does not increase and that cost is reduced. It can also be done by creating and testing a prototype or by a peer or expert review, as in validating the design for maintainability criteria.

STRUCTURED, LAYERED TESTING

The V-Model specifies that testing in one stage must be completed before the solution moves on to the next stage of testing. Before moving major deliverables to the next stage, testers must determine that the exit criteria defined for that stage are met. A part of the exit criteria for each stage is that the test has been successfully executed. This ensures that the test objectives, or primary focus of the test, are accomplished before moving on to the next stage. This layered approach to testing is vital to successful implementation of the V-Model. Done properly, testers can now avoid the frustrations of spending hours, if not days, in the product test stage pouring over an issue, only to realize that the problem could have been identified during assembly test.

Additionally, when the objectives of one test stage are met, there is no need to repeat the same testing at the next higher stage. This is a key concept of the V-Model, but one that proves difficult to accept and use in practice. Better-defined testing stages and objectives allow developers to understand and verify the testing done at one level so it does not need to be repeated at the next higher level. Additionally, definition of the testing stages allows developers to understand and communicate the objectives of each testing stage to identify potential gaps in the testing approach. In other words, when properly followed, the V-Model minimizes gaps and overlaps between the testing stages while ensuring quality of delivery.

Even so, two stages of testing may be executed together, using the same scripts, but both sets of test conditions must be identified and tested (i.e., both sets of objectives must be met). While each stage of testing is distinct, it is sometimes possible to test multiple stages with very similar scripts. In such cases, it may make sense to combine the scripts into one set; however, all test conditions for each stage must be identified and tested in the resulting combined scripts. For example, a thorough assembly test cannot make up for inadequate component testing because the objectives of each test stage are different. They are looking for different problems.

MAKING THE MODEL WORK

The objectives of the V-Model testing approach for today's client/server and netcentric applications are simple. They include

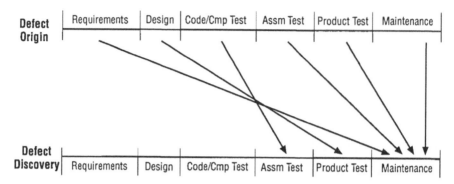

Exhibit 3. Stage Containment: Current.

- Stage containment of defects
- Effective testing
- Efficient testing
- Risk management

Stage Containment of Defects

Stage containment is a mechanism designed to ensure that as many problems as possible are detected during the system development stage in which they occur and are not passed along to the next stage. It is a means to build quality into the system. The goal of containment is to decrease both the cost of fixing problems and the number of residual problems in the finished system.

Traditionally, most of the problems in the system are caused very early in the development process but are not captured and corrected until very late, that is, during testing or production (Exhibit 3).

By the time the cycle is in testing or production, the IS department has not only lost the faith of its users but also has potentially assumed a business risk of poorly performing software, downtime, or excessive costs to correct defects. Industry studies show that defects are more costly to correct (by orders of magnitude) in the product testing or production stages than if they had they been contained to the stage in which they were caused. Fixing problems found at the point of introduction is generally accepted to be one-fourth to one-twentieth the cost of fixing them at the test stage, with the cost skyrocketing once the system has been deployed. Defective software is often deployed globally throughout an organization, only to be redeployed months later because of quality problems, necessitating a full repeat of the packaging, roll-out, distribution, installation and training effort for hundreds of sites.

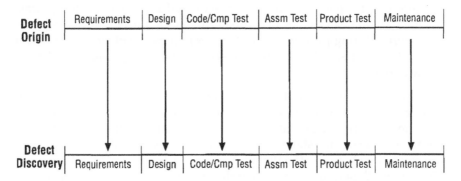

Exhibit 4: Coupling of Stage Containment and Process Improvement.

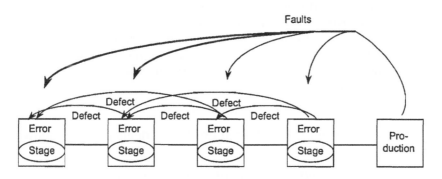

Exhibit 5: Stage Containment: Desired.

Stage containment, for early detection of problems, coupled with process improvement to prevent problems, saves tremendous amounts of time and effort (Exhibit 4).

Stage containment is achieved through the development processes as follows. Any aspect of a deliverable that does not meet its exit criteria (i.e., that does not conform to specifications and standards) is an error. If an error is handed off to the next stage, it becomes a defect. A defect that is passed along to the end customer is a fault.

Stage containment aims to minimize the number of defects and faults being passed along from one stage to the next by finding and fixing errors in the stage in which they were committed. If a team finds a problem that was caused by some error in a previous stage, this problem is classified as a defect or a fault and is passed back to be fixed by the team that created the defect (see Exhibit 5). The process of determining the stage that was the origin of the defect is called "root cause analysis."

Thus, design specification errors discovered and fixed in a design walk-through would be examples of errors. Problems in the coding of a program discovered during product testing are examples of defects. Problems in production that should have been discovered during product test or earlier are faults.

Generally, the longer a defect remains undiscovered, the more difficult and expensive it becomes to correct. Because each stage relies on the decisions made during the creation of the specification in the previous stage, detecting an error in a stage after it was made may invalidate some or all of the work done between the time the error was created and the time it was discovered. Experience has shown that as the verification and validation procedures improve, stage containment of defects also improves, saving both time and money.

Stage containment can be accomplished only by strict adherence to entry and exit criteria. Testers can measure stage containment by measuring the ratio of errors to faults. This essentially measures what percentage of the problems are being caught and fixed, as opposed to being passed along to the customer. Stage containment for any given stage is defined in the following equation:

$$\text{Errors}/(\text{errors} + \text{defects})$$

Stage containment for a released product is defined in the following equation:

$$(\text{Errors} + \text{defects})/(\text{errors} + \text{defects} + \text{faults})$$

A level of 100% stage containment means that all errors are discovered and corrected before the software is promoted to the next stage. Although 100% stage containment may be unrealistic or even undesirable (given the effort that would be required to achieve it), stage containment levels of 95 to 98% have been consistently achieved by organizations applying the V-Model concepts.

Effective Testing

Effective testing improves the quality of the solutions delivered to the customer and, ultimately, the success of the business change. The V-Model testing approach improves the effectiveness of testing by providing a means to set the proper scope of testing activities based on risk to the business. In a test strategy, the exact testing stages are defined, with the scope and objectives of each stage clearly documented. In determining the scope of each testing stage, consideration must be given to what can and will be tested, as well as what cannot or will not be tested. Then the risk of the untested areas of the application can be identified, documented, and managed. This approach to defining the scope of testing to be performed, combined with an approach to trace the tests back to the components of the scope, allows staff to focus testing efforts on the critical aspects of the solution, improving the coverage of testing, as well as the quality of results.

One of the most commonly asked questions about testing applications is, "How does the staff determine when they have tested enough?" The techniques discussed in this chapter help to identify what needs to be tested (i.e., the risks), to plan a test for each identified risk, and to ensure coverage of those high-risk areas of the solution. The ideal method is to trace the actual test results to the test conditions they were derived to test and to the requirements and risks that gave rise to those test conditions. Testing is complete when all planned tests have successfully been executed. Structured testing is therefore not only repeatable but also more effective.

Efficient Testing

The V-Model testing approach is efficient. The approach to determining testing conditions and designing test scripts allows for increased testing density and more test conditions covered by fewer scripts. The standardized approach to test planning provides for repeatable processes and repeatable tests. Tests can be reused within a release for regression of fixes and across releases as enhancements are made, ensuring a consistent level of testing with a minimum level of effort. The traceability provided by the structured testing approach provides an efficient means to perform complete impact analysis of changes and reuse of the test model.

One organization experienced the inefficiencies of unstructured testing over and over again. The test team developed and maintained a huge test bed, with thousands of scripts contained in binders lined up across the back of the development room. Unfortunately, they had no idea what the test bed tested. For all they knew, it tested the same activity a thousand times. Every time they had an application change or fix, they had to add a new piece to the test model because they had no way of determining the impact on the test bed nor could they find a piece of the test model that would test the change.

Another organization learned similar lessons. Several developers spent a considerable amount of time writing test scenarios, only to scrap their test plans and start over every time the project underwent a scope change, which happened 3 times in 18 months. Because they did not tie their test model to their specifications, they could not perform an impact analysis on the affected test components to determine where or how to update the test to reflect the scope changes.

Another common testing inefficiency is redundant testing. In the past, product tests have included testing the business functions and have itemized and executed test conditions at the component and assembly levels.

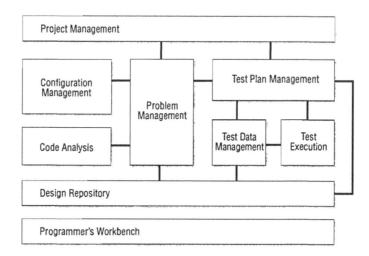

Exhibit 6. Integrated Testing Environment (ITE).

If properly educated on the V-Model, the test cell or team should feel comfortable testing the appropriate levels of conditions in the appropriate test stage. In addition, formal inspections ensure that adequate testing has occurred at each level.

Another example of redundant testing is "monkey" testing. Some analysts believe that planned test models for either this test stage or the next test stage do not catch all errors and continue to examine the system. If problems are found during these efforts, the problems may be difficult or impossible to recreate in order to fix. The lesson here is that, if a risk area exists within the system, it should be covered in the structured test. If it needs to be tested, it should be put it in the test plans.

The User of Automation. Finally, automation can be introduced to the repeatable testing processes to improve productivity and reduce human error. As testing environments become increasingly complex, automation has been successfully implemented to alleviate labor-intensive tasks, such as test data generation and test script execution. Automation also helps to increase the control over the testing environments by managing the configurations of test data, test models, and the applications being tested. Exhibit 6 is a schematic of an integrated testing environment, outlining the environment components required to support the V-Model testing process.

When planning for automation of the testing process, consideration must be given to the investment for the tools, the learning curve that will result, and the impact on the process vs. the anticipated benefits. Different factors have a varying degree of influence on the decision to automate testing and should be reviewed in light of the characteristics of the development approach, of the application, of the testing team, and of the testing tools themselves. For example, the cost to automate the scripting process for a new application is likely to be warranted if enhancements to the application are anticipated requiring regression testing or if the critical nature of the application requires a highquality level. Where automation has been implemented, along with repeatable testing processes, companies have achieved up to an 80% reduction in the effort required to fully regression test a complex suite of applications.

Automation facilitates the reuse of existing test models. Reuse can occur by reuse of a test model to test future enhancements, regression tests of the same application, or across applications (e.g., an order-entry product test designed for system A may be useful in testing the order entry for business application B).

The decision to automate, however, affects the way tests are designed and planned, so these are decisions to be made early in the development life cycle. For example, automated results comparison requires the creation of expected results in an electronic format recognized by the tool. Exhibit 7 shows where in the development life cycle testing tools apply.

MANAGING RISK THROUGH METRICS

Measurement is a crucial tool for managing progress and quality. A metric is a combination of measurements that tell something about a process or product. Without effective metrics, IS managers have no way of truly knowing their productivity levels. However, with well-defined development and testing processes and a few consistently applied metrics, software development becomes predictable, which in turn allows for more reliable delivery.

Metrics also support process improvement — indeed, often drive it — by identifying areas that may require attention and by determining if corrective actions were successful. It is not worthwhile to measure any activity if some actions for improvement will not result. It is not only a waste of time to collect metrics that are not used for decision making or action, but it may also be detrimental to team morale because managers will have eliminated the excuse of not knowing a problem exists.

The Need for Balanced Metrics

Metrics should be used to track some significant goal or objective. If the achievement is at variance with the goal, some change must be made to increase the chances of meeting the goal, for example, improving the standard process and exit criteria. Goals are continually examined, and as improvements are made, stricter goals can be set. Tying metrics to organizational goals is important because the mere act of measuring a process

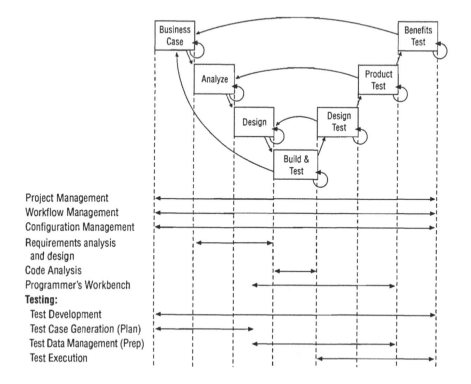

Exhibit 7: Automating the V-Model.

causes a behavior change. For example, if a manager were to visibly measure the time of day each person on the team arrives at work, the staff would all begin to arrive on time. They might be arriving at work without having finished breakfast, but they would have begun to arrive on time, nonetheless.

However, if the manager's goal were to improve productivity during the morning hours rather than to have everyone arrive by 8:30 A.M., that same manager may have caused a behavior change at odds with his or her goal. What if, for example, the new policy resulted in everyone needing a longer midmorning break? Measurement causes behavior change, and this highlights the need for a balanced set of metrics. The manager in the example would want to measure not only the time of arrival but also whether people have had breakfast.

A more realistic example would be a manager who measured only the speed of the developers. With this metric, developers would soon become very fast at completing coding work units. However, the chances are great

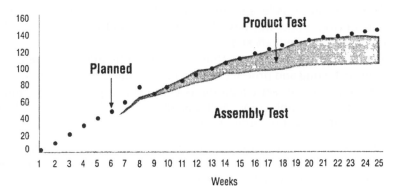

Exhibit 8. Defects Detected Over Time.

that the *quality* of these work units would deteriorate. The answer in this case would be to measure both speed of development and product quality.

Finally, as with all metrics, it is important to understand that these metrics should not be used to measure individual performance. The purpose is to measure the *process*. The assumptions are that people are following the process and that a quality process results in a quality solution. Therefore, if there is a problem, the process should be updated or training should be conducted. If metrics are perceived as measuring individuals rather than process, the behavior changes can be drastic and not only invalidate the metrics, but also potentially worsen the process.

Applied metrics during the testing process provide the capability to

- Improve management, productivity, and quality by providing both data points and trend information required to manage with facts
- Focus on the problem, not the symptom
- Facilitate predictability
- Facilitate continuous improvement

If an organization can collect only a small set of metrics, strong consideration should be given to closely tracking defect rates and collecting a testing variation of the stage containment metric. Tracking defect rates means collecting information on incoming error and defect levels. Simple trend analysis can then provide information to support or question the management assumptions made about planning the tests, staffing levels for defect correction, and determination of readiness for production. Exhibit 8 depicts the defects detected over time by the assembly and product test stages, mapped against the planned incoming rate for defects. With the graph, management easily can see if the defect levels are expected. If defect levels are higher than planned, investigation can be done to determine if

- The application is less stable than anticipated, indicating that the entry criteria may not have been met and that the code should be demoted to a previous stage.
- The tests are more robust than planned, indicating that the investment in testing and product quality may be more than required.
- The sequence of test execution is exercising a particularly difficult section of the application, and it is anticipated that the defect levels will recede as testing progresses.

In any case, the information on the graph derived from measurement allows management to manage by facts, rather than going on blind faith that staff can somehow make up the time.

A second set of measurements, the testing variation of the stage containment metrics defined earlier in the chapter, can be defined as tracking all problems found during the testing stages, with recognition of where they should have been found. This metric provides information on the quality levels of each testing process by quantifying what percentage of the problems are being captured at each testing stage, as opposed to being passed along to a subsequent stage.

This information can be used to identify the holes in the testing process, which continuous improvement techniques can address, and to make management decisions for the remainder of the project. For example, if the testing stage containment metrics indicate that a significant level of defects being found in the product test should have been found by the assembly test process, management can analyze the assembly testing process to plug the hole so these problems do not continue to slip through. Management could also analyze the actual problems to address the specification or construction process that caused them in the first place or to use the information to determine the level of regression testing to be completed by the product test stage.

If metrics indicate that the deliverables from the assembly testing process of work cell A are at a 95 to 100% stage containment level, decisions can be made to relax the regression testing requirements for that work cell's deliverables, or it may be feasible to accept code from that cell in the middle of a cycle execution, because data indicates that it is relatively safe. However, if metrics indicate that the deliverables from work cell B have a much lower level of stage containment, the decision may be made to require full regression testing of all code completed by cell B, and to only migrate code from that cell before the start of a new product test cycle.

NEW MANAGEMENT CHALLENGES

Managing the test process is a continuous task, beginning with completion of the test strategy and continuing until the release is in production. Testing is where all work cells or teams and the user communities come together to ensure the solution works as specified. Testing is also characterized by numerous complex issues and risks, such as requests for changes and aggressive schedules. Occasionally, there may be budget overruns. Morale of testing teams must be monitored. Effective management of these factors is critical to ensure delivery of a quality solution within the expected time frame and budget constraints. New management challenges include facilitating communication, managing resources, and monitoring scope and schedule to increase the overall effectiveness of the test process.

Coordination and Communication

The testing process requires more communication and coordination among work cells or teams than any other process. The activities of the architecture, development, training, user, and technical support work cells or teams are closely interdependent, and communication and coordination are critical to success. For example, requirements for testing the solution's ability to perform in a production setting often necessitate large, complex, and expensive environments. In spite of this fact, management may still tell the technical support team on Friday that a full test system for product test is needed on Monday. Effective coordination of activities and schedules would have management tell them at the beginning of the project, determine responsibilities, and ensure all activities are on the appropriate work schedules. This planning also allows for optimizing the use of these environments, sharing test configurations to minimize both acquisition and setup costs.

Changes should not be accepted, approved, and implemented by architecture and development cells or teams without communication to the test cell. At peak development times, proper communication may break down, even if unintentionally. Additional client requests or changes get communicated to development and implemented so quickly that communication to testing is overlooked. To minimize these types of changes, managers should ensure that the test cell is required to sign off on changes as an indication that they have been notified of the change request.

Scope Control

Testing stages are a breeding ground for "scope creep." Many of the defects identified in testing stages are really enhancement requests, leading to additional effort and missed deadlines. There are both planned and unplanned changes in scope during testing. Unplanned scope changes resulting from process problems can be mitigated with process improvements including validation and verification, education on V-Model approach, and a formalized issue control process.

In contrast to scope changes caused by process problems, scope changes may also result from changing user or technical requirements because of external business conditions, forces, or regulations. The traceability embedded in the test model allows management to determine the effort required to react to these changes, information that should be considered when deciding whether to address the requested changes.

THE IMPACT OF THE V-MODEL TESTING APPROACH ON DEVELOPMENT

The V-Model approach to testing requires developers to consider testing challenges from the start of the development effort. This allows them to design and build the system to be testable, including the introduction of probes and diagnostics to facilitate error detection, handshaking between applications to ensure configuration management integrity, and even having the application take the date from a table rather than the system to ease month- and year-end testing.

Additionally, testing exit criteria from requirements analysis and design, and early planning of test conditions may increase the effort on the left side of the "V," with anticipated payback in quality and productivity during the test execution stages, maintenance, and future release projects.

Although this may result in a better product, all of these have impact on the activities completed before what is traditionally considered the testing stages. World-class testing requires an update of the entire development approach.

THE IMPACT OF THE V-MODEL TESTING APPROACH ON THE ORGANIZATION

The increasing need for professional testers of IT systems demands people with the skills to develop complex systems, which are not necessarily the skills required to *test* complex systems. Many organizations are establishing testing directors and even entire testing or software quality organizations. Experience has proven the effectiveness of a dedicated testing function. Dedicated testing teams provide for testing experts — people who know the difference between assembly and product test conditions. Also, a dedicated testing team provides for ownership of the test model, ensuring that the test model is maintained and reused. Finally, a dedicated test team means developers can schedule the development of the test concurrent with the development of the solution, thus compressing the delivery time frame.

Given a dedicated test team, the test manager should be at a peer level with the development manager, if not higher. This gives the manager the authority to enforce entry criteria, and creates the proper professional relationship to ensure a balance between schedule and quality.

CONCLUSION

The V-Model approach to software development and testing positions an organization to face the challenges of client/server and netcentric development through improved quality, improved productivity, and improved predictability. Defined processes, verification that those processes are followed, and the use of metrics as a monitoring and process improvement vehicle allow executive management and IS directors to be sure the issues of developing and testing applications in the age of convergence are addressed.

Experience with the V-Model of testing shows that

- Software development stage containment can be better.
- Better testing and stage containment saves time and money.
- Better testing and stage containment supports continuous process improvement.
- Continuous process improvement saves time and money and improves software quality and reliability.

Viewed as opportunity, the V-Model approach to testing positions an organization to move into advanced technology and business challenges.

Chapter 12
Operations Architecture

OVERVIEW: DEFINITION OF OPERATIONS ARCHITECTURE

Although the visibility of information technology within a business is typically driven by the Execution and Development Architectures, the Operations Architecture plays a crucial but often underestimated role in the successful delivery of computing service to end users.

An *operations* architecture describes the tools and support services required to keep a production system up and running well. It differs from an execution architecture and development architecture in that its primary users are systems administrators and production support personnel. In addition, it differs from the operations *infrastructure* in that the operations infrastructure represents operations processes and organization as well as the technologies and tools.

This chapter will describe several categories of Operations Architecture tools. It will also discuss netcentric computing's impact on operations architecture tools and technologies.

When considering operations, addressing the operations tools alone would be misleading. To be successful, the operations tools must integrate closely with an effective organizational structure as well as a set of operations processes driven by the requirements of the user community. Although this chapter focuses only on the operations architecture and tools, a framework called MODE, or Management of Distributed Environments, addresses the process and organization as well as the technology facets of operations. MODE is described in detail in Section III of this book.

EVOLUTION OF THE OPERATIONS ARCHITECTURE

In the mainframe environment, operations tasks are performed by those in the data center who constantly watch, monitor, and react to problems with the host or network.

Keeping a mission-critical client/server application system available and under control, while providing a high level of service to the end user, is more complex and difficult than in a mainframe environment. Unfortunately, not all organizations are aware of this complexity as they should be.

When client/server computing first emerged, organizations expected the cost and complexity of operations to be reduced because of reduced administration and because of common operating systems on workstations and servers. Time has shown that client/server environments tend instead to add rather than reduce complexity, therefore increasing operations costs.

More recently, netcentric computing has emerged as the next technology generation that will coexist with host and client/server environments. Again, while the initial hype around netcentric suggested that it would significantly simplify operations, experience is beginning to indicate that netcentric only adds an additional level of complexity through additional processes, tools, and support services, thus creating an environment even more potentially difficult and expensive to manage. The operations architecture now needs not only to keep an organization's internal production systems up and running but also to maintain production systems that extend to business partners and customers.

The complexity and cost of operations architecture keeps increasing, which suggests a strong need for a structured and disciplined approach to implementation of tools and technologies to support eased operations.

OPERATIONS ARCHITECTURE TOOLS

When implementing an operations architecture, an organization must select among the wide variety of tool categories. Tool categories cover the spectrum of functions provided by the operations organizations, from software distribution to Help Desk. Although the industry has slowly progressed toward the vision of a single, consolidated multifunction operations product, usually a suite of products must be purchased and therefore integration work must be performed.

The most common categories of operations tools support such things as

- Software distribution
- Configuration and asset management
- Fault management and recovery management
- Capacity planning
- Performance management
- License management
- Remote management
- Event management
- Monitoring and tuning
- Security

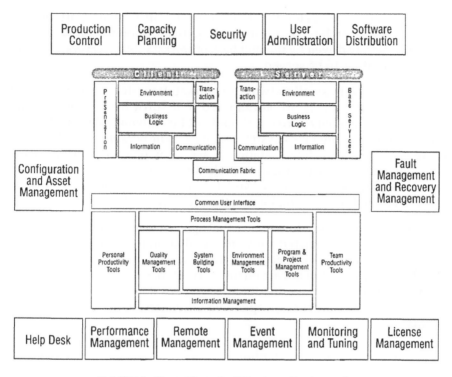

Production Control	Capacity Planning	Security	User Administration	Software Distribution

Exhibit 1. Operations Architecture Framework.

- User administration
- Production control
- Help desk

These tools must provide visibility and control over the events of a distributed environment. In essence, they can be viewed as support and control mechanisms for both the execution and development architectures. This relationship is shown in Exhibit 1, where the major categories of operations tools are depicted as supporting the development and netcentric execution architectures.

An overview of each of these tool categories, as well as some implementation considerations for each, are provided through the remainder of this section.

SOFTWARE DISTRIBUTION

Software distribution is the automated delivery to, and installation of, applications and systems software on servers and end user devices (e.g., workstations, kiosks, etc.). This can be for an organization's internal computing environment, as well as for its extended one, i.e., its business partners and customers. The architectural support required to support software distribution is largely driven by the numbers of workstations, servers, and geographic locations to be served.

For a relatively small network of workstations in a single physical location — where it is not anticipated that software changes will be frequent — a manual approach should not be automatically ruled out. A manual approach involves systems management personnel loading software upgrades on each workstation or server by physically visiting each machine. This approach does not scale well, however, when either large numbers of workstations or servers in a single environment need to be updated or multiple geographic locations are involved.

When it is unrealistic to use a manual approach, an organization should consider adding automated software distribution tools to the operations architecture. Many products from leading vendors such as Microsoft, Tivoli, and Hewlett-Packard are on the market today that include or specialize in automated software distribution. Systems developers must look for several important features, depending on the specific support requirements.

Creating a Software "Distribution"

The server component of a software distribution solution enables administrators to build distribution packages and to control distribution. A distribution is a package of related software files, data, and installation scripts that form an installable unit.

Few significant application installations, systems software installations, or even upgrades can be achieved simply by sending a single file. Configuration files (e.g., config.sys) and system files (e.g., autoexec.bat and .login) as well as multiple software files for a particular application or systems software component, often require changes.

In addition, it is usually desirable to upgrade multiple applications or combinations of systems software and applications in a single distribution rather than performing multiple independent software distributions. Bundling software upgrades together also reduces the amount of release testing required.

A distribution is created by selecting the files and scripts, often through a point-and-click interface. The components are then combined into a single file for transmission. Some software distribution tools provide compression capabilities to reduce the physical size of the distribution. This is particularly important in a wide area network (WAN) environment where line speeds are an issue.

Scheduling a Distribution: Push vs. Pull

There are multiple approaches to scheduling software distributions. Some solutions use a rigid scheduling mechanism that requires all target machines to be powered on at a specified time when the software distribution is to occur. This mechanism could be characterized as a "push" strategy, where the server machine pushes the software to the client machines at a specified time.

The push strategy may be possible in some smaller situations, but in large organizations it is difficult to ensure that users will leave their machines on, particularly if it is common practice to turn them off at the end of the day.

A more flexible approach is the "pull" strategy, where the workstations check for software updates and pull the software from the designated server or servers at log-in time. Thus, when the user signs on either in the morning or at some point during the day, any pending updates are downloaded to the client machine. When combined with a forced log-off capability, which most networks support, this can effectively mimic the push strategy without the attending problem of some machines being powered off.

Neither the push nor pull scheduling approach is sufficient when large numbers of target workstations are involved. For example, a sales office automation system developed several years ago and used by 1,400 salespeople distributed across scores of locations encountered a problem with these strategies on its first major software upgrade. The sales office used the pull strategy because it was not feasible to have all workstations, locations, and dial-up users connected and powered up at the same time. The distribution was scheduled to be available when the users logged in on Monday morning. This was a substantial functional upgrade to the system, so the software distribution was several megabytes in size.

The problem was that 1,400 machines could not simultaneously download one copy of software off of a server. As a result, most users were unable to retrieve the new software or use the system for several days. The problem was eventually solved by "staging."

Software Distribution Staging

Faced with the problem of scale, two alternatives can be considered. One is simply to acquire more servers with more copies of the software to be distributed. Of course, this is an expensive solution, particularly when these machines are not needed for any other purpose.

An alternative solution that may be better involves the concept of staging. Software distribution staging works by sending a new version of the software in advance of the cut-over date. In effect, the client machines have two versions of the application physically resident simultaneously, but only one is in use.

The existing software is used until the present cut-over date is reached. At that time, the client portion of the software distribution architecture automatically completes the installation and redirects the user to the new version. Using this approach, it is possible to selectively download the software update to subsets of machines well in advance of the cut-over date, thus eliminating the bottleneck.

An enhancement of staging is the ability to cut over to the new version on the receipt of a small command file rather than a preset date. This gives operations more flexibility to alter the cut-over date due to unanticipated events. For example, many adopters fail to anticipate the requirements of having multiple copies of applications stored simultaneously when determining the size of the workstation hard disks required for the users.

Remote Installation

Most software distribution solutions include a client portion as well as a server that resides on the target machine. The client software is responsible for installation of the software distribution onto the target machine's hard disk.

The first step is the unbundling (and uncompressing) of the distribution into the component files, data sets, and scripts (although the better products will first check to see that the required disk space is in fact available). Next, any preinstallation scripts are executed. These scripts may do such various tasks as checking for required components or adding or modifying lines in the target machine configuration or systems files that will be required by the new software (e.g., changing the number of buffers or adding a line to install a necessary driver at startup time). The directories in which the software is to reside are checked or created, and then the actual software files are moved into the proper location on the hard disk. At this point a postinstallation script may be invoked that could include rebooting the machine so that the changes to the system and configuration files can take effect.

Cascaded Distribution

In large networks, where tens or even hundreds of servers support individual groups of workstations, a "cascaded" approach may be required. A cascaded software distribution approach allows for a central administrator to schedule the distribution of software updates to designated servers within the network environment. These servers, in turn, distribute the software updates to their associated client workstations.

This approach allows the simple push and pull strategies to be used for larger numbers of workstations without requiring staging. It also better utilizes the servers and communications links in these larger environments. Most products that support a cascaded approach also support staging concepts as well, thus providing much flexibility in how software is to be distributed.

Relationship to Configuration Management

Many of the available software distribution packages offer integrated asset and configuration management capabilities (described in the next section) as well. Although not specifically required for software distribution, these functions are naturally related, and integrating these capabilities simplifies the operations architecture.

A useful feature is the ability to check to see whether all the system and application files required by a software distribution, but expected to be already resident on the target machines, are in fact there. For example, when sending a Visual Basic application, this feature checks the target machine to see that the user has not moved or deleted a required file such as VBRUN001.DLL.

A full-function software distribution system needs many of the same capabilities as a configuration management or asset inventory tool. The trend toward combining these functions within the products market will certainly continue.

Error Handling Reporting

When dealing with larger networks of workstations, errors inevitably occur in the software distribution process. There may be insufficient disk space or a required component may be missing. Capability is required both to report errors and to take appropriate actions.

Error reporting normally takes the form of a distribution log file that records success, failure, or errors encountered. In some cases a more active form of error reporting is required, where e-mail messages may be automatically generated and sent to either the administrator or, in some cases, the affected user. If a fatal error is detected, the software distribution system should be capable of reversing any changes made to that point and restoring the user's machine to its previous state.

Platform Constraints

The choice of software distribution tools is somewhat limited by the types of workstations, servers, operating systems, and networking software in use. Some products are UNIX based and support only UNIX clients or at least require UNIX servers. Others work well with Windows workstations.

In environments where intermittently connected dial-up users need to be provided with software distributions, the existence and unreliability of dial-up connections adds more complexity to the software distribution task.

CONFIGURATION AND ASSET MANAGEMENT

To manage a netcentric environment successfully, one must have a solid understanding of what is where, and one must maintain rigor in the change control procedures that govern modifications to the environment. Configuration and asset management information that may need to be tracked includes such details as product licensing information, warranty information, vendor names, logical and physical device information (such as total capacity and current utilization), product configuration tracking, software and data version levels, network configuration parameters, physical location, and perhaps accounting information.

For relatively small netcentric environments — under 100 workstations, for example — it may be reasonable to use a manual approach. A manual approach keeps track of information in a personal computer database or in a collection of spreadsheets. For larger environments the manual approach has proven time and again to be inadequate, and automated tools are required for collecting asset and configuration information and for periodically auditing the environment.

In larger netcentric environments, it is often necessary to have an underlying configuration and asset management database or repository. This database becomes a key information source for those managing, maintaining, and adding to the environment. However, it is only useful if the database is current, reliable, and perceived to be that way. Otherwise, configuration and asset management databases quickly fall into disuse.

Automated Tools

Automatic asset and configuration collection capability is included in many vendor solutions, including OpenView from Hewlett-Packard (HP) and POLYCENTER Systems Census from Digital Equipment Corp. These products can interrogate the network, discover network and computing devices, and collect related information. In addition, these products can perform the needed periodic auditing to detect changes to the environment over time, for example, when a user moves a machine or installs a network game.

Another important and related feature is the ability to restore a machine to a known or initial configuration for problem resolution. The configuration and asset management architecture component both provides facilities for determining the correct initial state for a given machine or network device and initiates any software distribution or configuration changes needed to bring the device back within compliance.

For more dynamic environments, where machine and network configurations are changing frequently, it is even more important to have an active configuration and asset management system. The capability to automatically change configurations of a large number of machines and network components or even to roll back to previous configuration settings for any particular device becomes increasingly important.

Many products that can form the core of asset and configuration management are bundled with additional related functions for fault and performance management. HP's OpenView is just one example of an integrated suite of operations architecture products that can greatly simplify piecing together an integrated architecture.

Multivendor Problem

When sourcing asset and configuration management products from the marketplace, it is important to consider that they are quite particular in the types of networks and devices they can support. For example, the field of suitable asset and configuration management products becomes quite limited when the netcentric components are not in the "mainstream" — such as the Pick operating system or Wang servers — although management standards such as the Simple Network Management Protocol (SNMP) have increased the coverage of many solutions.

Second, products that specialize in serving smaller market segments, such as Macintosh clients or lesser known network protocols, sometimes do not support as wide a variety of client machines, operating systems, mainframes, and network protocols.

Finally, integrating multiple management platforms is complex, costly, and in many cases impractical.

In sum, if the hardware, systems software, and networking that make up the environment are out of the business computing mainstream, it is more difficult to find adequate configuration management solutions from the marketplace. This leaves developers with the daunting challenge of custom development of configuration and asset management capabilities.

Impact Analysis

A well-functioning configuration and asset management component becomes a vital information source for conducting impact analysis for any requested changes to the environment. The frequency with which unexpected negative side effects are caused by relatively minor configuration changes to the netcentric environment has been an embarrassing and frustrating surprise for many adopters of the technology.

Much of the source of these problems relates to the high number of execution architecture components and complex interdependencies between them. Another problem is the reality that most netcentric networks involve numerous independent vendors. Changing even the release level of one systems software component may have a ripple effect and may require updates to, or newer versions of, additional software components or applications.

To support this type of impact analysis, dependency information must be maintained. For example, version X of the Oracle database management system requires version Y or greater of the HP-UX operating system and version Z of yet another vendor's Transmission Control Protocol/Internet Protocol product.

It is not uncommon for a user organization to wish to return to a previous operating system release to acquire an application package that does not yet support the latest operating system version. Without an effective configuration and asset management system that maintains relationship information, it is purely guesswork if in fact the proposed version change will break any required dependencies. Unfortunately, this is how many organizations approach this problem in the netcentric world today — typically with unsatisfactory results.

Appropriate Degree of Standardization

One of the keys to effective configuration and asset management is enforcing the appropriate degree of standardization across environments. For large netcentric networks, where thousands of workstations are involved, it is not feasible to effectively manage the environment if each machine has its own unique configuration and combination of software products. On the other hand, it is not typically appropriate to give thousands of users the exact same configuration if the users perform different functions within the organization.

For example, users in such diverse areas as sales, product development, and human resources are likely to require different computing capabilities. The goal is to strike the correct balance between standardization, which simplifies the required operations architecture and tasks, and accommodation to each business area's unique computing needs.

FAULT MANAGEMENT AND RECOVERY MANAGEMENT

Failure control is important in a netcentric environment. The presence of heterogeneous equipment, however, makes it difficult to determine the origins of a fault. Multiple messages may be generated within the system from a single fault, making it difficult to separate the fault's cause from its effects.

The fault management services of an operations architecture assist in the diagnosis and correction of system faults. Faults may include network-, server-, workstation-, or even application-level faults. Fault diagnosis may require services for isolation, viewing of host, server, and workstation error logs; and determining the software and data versions and configurations of affected machines.

Managing Networks

Fault management services also encompass network management and diagnostic tools for monitoring and reporting on network traffic and failures. Additional diagnostic tools such as protocol analyzers are required in some cases to determine the true source of the problem.

A wide variety of tools and products for fault management is available on the marketplace. When selecting a tool or vendor, it is important to take into consideration the breadth of netcentric networking components to be managed to ensure that the fault management products selected have the necessary breadth of vendor coverage.

Another factor to consider in this selection is the choice between integrated operations environments (typified by HP's OpenView or CA-Unicenter TNG), and point solutions that provide only one function. Although most integrated tool sets today do not adequately address the full breadth of fault management and diagnostic requirements, they can reduce the number of vendors and the complexity of integrating these point solutions.

Once again, multivendor environments increase the complexity and difficulty of providing fault management services. It may be difficult or even impossible to find products that cover the scope of capability required as well as the various hardware and systems software components needing to be managed. In larger netcentric installations, some level of centralized fault management is usually employed to leverage specialized skills.

Recovery capabilities are also included in failure control. Recovery capabilities span the range from those required to bring up a device after it has failed to those required in the event of a major disaster. With critical business applications being rolled out on distributed technologies, the recovery of these systems must be easy, quick, and efficient. Loss of the system for even a short period can result in significant financial losses to the business.

A wide variety of architectural services may be required for fault recovery. These range from strictly network-oriented components (for restoring links or reconfiguring components) to more systems-level components (for restarting processes on machines or restoring databases). More involved tasks, such as the distribution of software fixes to workstations or servers, may require the ability to remotely reboot and reinitialize machines, printers, or other network components.

CAPACITY PLANNING

Capacity planning tools focus on components of an environment such as the network, physical space, and processing power to understand the need to change the capacity of those components based on organizational changes. The tools typically focus on components that are considered to be heavily sensitive to changes in computing resource usage. The tools may use historical management data combined with estimates for growth or changes to configuration to simulate the ability of different system configurations to meet capacity needs.

Capacity Planning tools can sometimes be integrated into a larger integration platform, or they can be standalone applications.

PERFORMANCE MANAGEMENT

Performance management is more difficult because of the lack of tools to assist with performance in heterogeneous environments. Performance is no longer confined to the network or to the central processing unit. Performance needs to be viewed in an end-to-end manner, accounting for all the factors that affect the system's performance relative to a user request.

The creation of a customer order, for instance, may involve multiple server accesses for data and information to be exchanged between the workstation and the host. The performance relative to the entire business event needs to be considered, not simply the performance of a single component involved. To make performance management even more difficult, not all devices provide performance information. It may be necessary to develop surrounding processes that monitor the performance of devices to calculate and provide end-to-end performance information.

LICENSE MANAGEMENT

Since the advent of computer networks that allow applications software to be shipped around the network as required, the issue of license management has become increasingly important. Applications software vendors have been experimenting with various licensing strategies, including unrestricted site licenses, fixed concurrent user licenses, and floating licenses that actually enforce the restriction on concurrent users.

Independent of these actions by software vendors, large organizations have been struggling to keep a handle on exactly what software products they own and how many copies they own. They have also been working to ensure that they are in compliance with software licensing agreements while not paying for more copies of software than they truly need.

In netcentric environments, license management is challenged by other issues such as the unpredictability of number of copies required, and the management of licenses distributed to anonymous users on the Internet.

The market for license management solutions is immature at this time. The problem is difficult to solve in the absence of standards to which applications software vendors can adhere. From an operations perspective, however, the risk is that major applications software vendors will thrust their own license management solutions upon their customers, leaving the operations organization no choice but to support multiple and noninte-grated license management solutions. The problem becomes even more complex as vendors move to more of a usage-based charge, requiring that billing information be extracted from the license management component of the operations architecture.

In addition to guaranteeing compliance with software licensing agreements, license management provides valuable information about which people and how many people are actually using a given software product. If, in fact, usage statistics indicate that the organization has overpurchased, it may be possible to realize some savings by reducing software licensing agreements.

REMOTE MANAGEMENT

As distributed environments allow users more flexibility in terms of where they work, the ability of a centralized support group to effectively manage remote users is challenged. Visibility to a user's system configuration is only possible by physically sitting at the workstation and diagnosing problems or by accomplishing the same remotely.

Remote Management tools allow support personnel to "control" a user's desktop over a network so that they do not need to be physically present at a workstation to diagnose problems. Once control of the desktop is established, screen updates for the controlled desktop are displayed at both locations. The support person is then effectively sitting at the workstation he/she controls and can do necessary diagnostics.

In addition to problem diagnosis, remote management tools can provide visual explanations to user questions. For example, if a user has a question about a certain application feature, the support person may remotely control the user's desktop and then walk through the solution while actions are displayed on the user's screen.

Remote Management tools are also useful in organizations where 24x7 support is required. Rather than requiring support personnel to be physically present for all events, they may be able to dial in through remote management tools from home and accomplish the same tasks. The ability to perform these tasks remotely can have positive effects on overall support costs through a reduction in the amount of time needed to resolve problems.

Remote Management products may come bundled with an integration platform such as HP OpenView or Tivoli TME, or they may be purchased as third-party software packages.

EVENT MANAGEMENT

In addition to hardware devices, applications and systems software also generates events. Common event-handling mechanisms are required to provide information to management in a simple, consistent format and to forward on important events for management purposes.

In most environments, events should follow an open format rather than a proprietary one as managed devices are rarely all from a single vendor. Filtering capabilities may also be needed at remote locations to prevent the streaming of events to central/master management consoles.

MONITORING AND TUNING

The number of devices and the geographic disparity of devices in a netcentric environment increase the effort required to monitor the system. The number of events generated in the system rises due to the increased complexity. Devices such as client machines, network components, and servers generate events on startup or failure to periodically report device status.

SECURITY

The security concerns of netcentric environments have been widely publicized. Although requirements for netcentric security architectures are constantly evolving as new security breaches are discovered, there are many tools categories that can help provide reasonable levels of security.

It is a common misperception, however, that security technologies in and of themselves provide the necessary protection from intrusion. It is equally important to have in place the people and processes to detect and react to security events. Without these components, the generation of security information by technologies can only go so far in protecting the assets of an organization.

Because of the priority and complexity of the security subject, a separate chapter in this book has been devoted to the subject. Refer to Chapter 28 for a detailed discussion of the people, process, and technology aspects of security.

USER ADMINISTRATION

The netcentric environment introduces many new challenges to the task of user administration. The majority of these stem once again from the dramatically increased number of system components. Adding a user to the system may require adding a user to the network, one or more server operating systems, one or more database systems (so that the user can access data), an e-mail system, and an existing host-based system.

In some cases, the addition of a user has required entries to be added to upward of 15 individual system components. Even determining all the subsystems to which a user must be added can be a frustrating and often unfortunately iterative task with the user.

Deleting a user from the system is even more difficult. Unless careful records are kept, it can be very difficult to determine to which machines, databases, and applications the user had been added originally so that this information can be deleted. From an administration standpoint this may seem to be only a headache, but from a security standpoint it represents a substantial risk.

Problems related to adding or deleting users from a system are exacerbated by the number of user types and the dissimilarity of their configurations. For example, in a financial services organization, mortgage officers, commercial lending officers, and risk management users all have access to different combinations of systems and servers. If one wants to alter or delete access for one particular user, it may be necessary to know something about that person's role in the organization in order to determine which components that user was added to. The problem becomes completely unmanageable as individual users within a department or work group themselves have unique access privileges.

In larger netcentric environments with many components and combinations of user capabilities, user administration becomes a significantly more resource-intensive task than in the centralized mainframe environment. In the mainframe world, it was possible to acquire tools such as RACF that could interface with the various systems software components to add, change, or delete user attributes. It was possible to develop these products largely because of the homogeneous and consistent nature of the mainframe environment. (Typically, all the systems software were sourced from one vendor, such as IBM or Digital Equipment Corp.)

In the more heterogeneous netcentric environment, few tools can manage user administration across a broad variety of products. For example, adding a user to the Sybase database product is different from the Informix product or Oracle product, and few user administration solutions cover all the combinations of even a typical netcentric environment. The result is often that operations must train personnel in how to do user administration for the various systems software products within the environment and must develop custom utilities and tools that are unique to the shop for automating user administration tasks.

Most user administration products on the market today focus on the operating system aspect of the problem (adding user access to the server, setting file permissions, and group associations). Although these solutions are certainly helpful, they do not cover many of the more difficult user administration challenges such as database access, e-mail, and networking software. Each of these products often comes with its own administration tools which may simplify the individual administration tasks but do little to help with providing an integrated user administration approach.

An alternative approach to user administration is to implement a Single Sign-On (SSO) application. These applications are meant to eliminate the need for users to remember user names and passwords to all of their business applications. The first time they log in, users enters a user name and password into the SSO application, which then automatically logs into applications through a scripting process. An additional advantage to this approach is that through implementing SSO, a database that maps users to the applications they access is created. This significantly simplifies user administration, and can increase security as well. A key drawback to SSO applications is failover. If a SSO server fails, users cannot access applications as they do not remember passwords to all their applications.

PRODUCTION CONTROL

In distributed environments, processes may be taking place across the entire system on multiple platforms in either a parallel or a serial fashion. Batch dependencies may be required across platforms, and multiple time zones may be involved.

In addition, many non-mainframe-based products do not provide production scheduling capabilities included with the platform. For these reasons, scheduling processes across a distributed environment can be quite complex, requiring significant management effort to ensure that the processes run smoothly. Many other day-to-day activities become more difficult in a distributed environment, including print management, file transfer and control, mass storage management, backup and restore, archiving, and system startup and shutdown.

Backup and Restore/Archiving

Backup and restoration processes become more complex in a distributed environment as business-critical information becomes distributed across the system. Backup strategies must coordinate the information across the system and must determine where the backup copy or copies of information will reside.

As with centralized computing environments, restoration processes are directly dependent on how backup was performed. A single restore process no longer suffices. Depending on a particular fault, restoration services may only need to be performed for a portion of the system, while the rest of the system stays up and running.

Some technical expertise may be required on site to perform backups/restores (e.g., on/from server tape drives). In this case, backups and restores may need to take place during the business day, potentially affecting the processing that takes place at the distributed sites. If coordination of the distributed and centralized backup/restore strategies requires participation from someone at the remote locations, scheduling of these tasks becomes more difficult and complex, particularly across time zones.

The issues surrounding archiving are quite similar to those surrounding backup. Distributed architectures also place limitations on the amount of information that may be archived on a remote system as a result of the space limitations on servers and workstations.

Additional problems are created with archiving in a distributed environment because users have no incentives to perform housekeeping tasks on their devices. Depending on the users' ability to store information on their machines or on the local server, these machines may become cluttered with seldom-used files. Lack of space may affect other processes that need to take place on these devices, such as software and data distribution.

HELP DESK

As netcentric computing puts the operations Help Desk closer to the "end user" in terms of visibility and influence, the Help Desk will need to become integrated with the business processes being supported through netcentric. Unless the operations Help Desk is well integrated with the business process, there is risk that the user may be given information that is incorrect, forwarded to the wrong department, or otherwise mishandled. It is also important that the information collected by the Help Desk about a user be properly shared with other stakeholders in the business process.

The role of Help Desk tools is changing as well. The latest generation of Help Desk tools turn Web browsers into interactive clients of the help desk with the power to enter, query, and modify Help Desk requests. End users directly perform many of the services without assistance from the Help Desk staff.

Another key consideration of the Help Desk function in netcentric computing is that users must more effectively support themselves. In Internet environments, it is usually prohibitively expensive for a service provider to provide interactive Help Desk support to all interested Internet users. This is due to potential volumes of support requests as well as the diversity of technical environments that could be encountered. Consequently, it is often more reasonable to provide Internet users access to the tools required to support themselves. This can be accomplished through means such as a download site where patches, drivers, and self-help support materials are available.

Netcentric Help Desk organizations may also need to consider new metrics for measuring the performance of support personnel that consider interactions via e-mail or video. An example might be "number of e-mails answered per hour." In addition, existing metrics may need to be refined to fairly reflect netcentric characteristics.

The hours of Help Desk coverage may be affected by netcentric. To implement global 24x7 support, some service providers are deploying phased 8-hour "follow-the-sun" support windows that are based in different areas of the globe. The windows hand off support tickets among each other at the beginning and end of each phase so that all tickets are being addressed at all times. This is an effective way to ensure that there is no downtime for tickets; however, special attention should be paid to maintaining consistency of service across multiple regions when tickets are handed off.

In netcentric, there may be additional complexities of Help Desk operations introduced by global interactions. For example, multiple languages may need to be supported by Help Desks. Although this introduces people and process issues to Help Desk operations, from a tools perspective there may be a need for documentation to be published in multiple languages, and for the ability to switch easily between those versions.

OPERATIONS ARCHITECTURE INTEGRATION ISSUES

The operations architecture typically consists of different operations tools that focus on different functions, such as Help Desk or Fault Management. Each tool introduces a predetermined set of operations services such as core management logic and event generation. Although product selection decisions are often based on the functions that a product provides, true integration of these tools into a cohesive operations architecture requires a service-based view rather than a functional view. In other words, operations architecture integration across functions is eased when different operations tools share core management logic, management data repositories, etc.

It is therefore important to consider the services provided by operations architecture tools when selecting operations tools.

These services are

• Core management logic
• Integration platform
• Event/data generation
• Event processing
• Repositories

Core Management Logic

Core Management Logic applies business roles to management data. Core Management Logic is typically specific to the function being served by an operations tool. For example, core management logic of a backup/restore application would initiate a backup process based on the time of day information it receives from a system clock. Core management logic receives data from event/data generation, event processing, and repositories services and then sends data for presentation or to repositories services. In addition, core management logic often polls the event/data generators for information.

Examples of Management Applications include a Help Desk package that automates the trouble ticketing process, a network management application such as HP OpenView, or a backup/restore utility that is used to create backups of server databases on a periodic basis.

Integration Platform

The integration platform provides a common platform for operations tools. At the lowest level this means deciding on common standards, interfaces, message formats, and file logging forms to be used with all the management tools. Although the Integration Platform can be homegrown, these applications are growing extremely complex, suggesting the use of one of many available third-party integration platforms.

There are two types of third party platforms available. The first group are framework-type products such as HP OpenView, CA-Unicenter TNG, and Tivoli Management Environment. These products are modular. Each module within the suite can be run separately; however, they all conform to a common framework that allows for greater compatibility, integration, and better performance.

The second type of integration platform is point-solution oriented. Products such as Boole and Babbage implement this approach, which typically results in best-of-breed solutions for various management solutions, but a larger amount of integration work between tools is required.

Event/Data Generation

Event/data generation interacts with all the managed components in the execution and development environments to produce the required management information. The output of event/data generation services is actual raw management data that can then be processed and acted upon.

Event Processing

Event processing manipulates the raw data obtained by event/data generation services into a form on which operations personnel can take action. This service may perform several functions such as

- *Event filtering.* When management events are generated, event filtering mechanisms constantly compare predetermined event thresholds to current management events to determine the need for a management alert. If the threshold is exceeded, the event filtering function takes a specific action based on predetermined rules.
- *Alert generation.* When an event filter has noted the need for an alert, the alert generation function creates the proper notification. This may take one of several forms: a page, an e-mail, a display change (icon changes color to red), etc.
- *Event correlation.* Event correlation functions use logic to tie different events together with the intention of understanding potentials causes of problems. For example, nightly processing utilization shortages may be tied by event correlation functions back to a nightly batch job.
- *Event collection and logging.* It may be determined that historical analysis of management events is important. If so, the collection and logging of management events into repositories is important so that reporting and correlation activities can be performed at a future time.
- *Automated trouble ticket generation.* For certain events, it may be desirable for trouble tickets to be generated automatically in an organization's help desk system so that action can be taken.

Repositories

Repositories contain all the management data generated or used during the management process. These data include historical data, capacity data, performance data, problem knowledge bases, asset databases, solution sets, and management information bases (MIBs).

MANAGING THE PHYSICAL ENVIRONMENT

The operations architecture can also include a set of tools and configurations used to ensure that the physical environment is manageable and protected against unplanned outages. The following are examples of systems that may serve this purpose.

- *Uninterruptible Power Supply (UPS).* To protect against loss of computing resources due to power outages, it is common for separate power units to be used as backup for critical computing resources. They may be implemented to support the power needs of an entire data center such as with an independent generator or may be implemented to support a single machine through battery-based UPS. Typically, UPS systems are designed to provide enough power for users and administrators to do the backups necessary to prevent catastrophic loss of information.

- *Raised floor.* To ease organization and provide spaces for systems components such as wiring and heating/cooling/power systems, it is common in data centers to implement raised floor environments.

- *Wiring/cabling.* The wiring and cabling of an operations architecture may be of many types. 10-BaseT (Unshielded Twisted Pair) and Fiber Optic cable are typically used for LAN and backbone links. Wiring systems are typically housed in wiring closets and/or under the raised floor to encourage an organized environment.

  Distribution panels for wiring to users' desktops may be used. Rather than having the cable from each desktop plug directly into a networking hub (which can cause difficulties in managing moves, adds, and changes) the distribution panel provides an intermediate connection between desktops and network hubs.

- *Fire suppression and climate control systems.* It is common in data centers or computer rooms to implement systems that protect computing resources from damage due to fire or other catastrophic events. Halon or other chemical systems may be implemented.

- *Disaster recovery.* If applicable, organizations may employ entirely redundant physical facilities to support disaster contingencies. In these cases, all of the above physical environment management services would be duplicated at the backup site.

MANAGING HARDWARE

In addition, there are hardware tools directly used in managing a distributed environment. These components are devoted to systems management functions. Examples of products that manage hardware include the following:

- *Management Servers.* These are servers that house management software. These may be a Tivoli Event Management Server, or a CA-Unicenter TNG server.
- *Management Consoles.* The operations center or computer room may have several consoles in a central location that serve as the nerve center for management information. On these consoles, management information for virtually all components of the environment can be accessed and action can be taken. System Administrators are typically the only users of management consoles.
- *Probes and sniffers.* These hardware devices provide diagnostic information by making physical measurements of electrical activity on wiring. These signals are then interpreted at a very low level (i.e., each data packet is dissected), which produces data that can be used to diagnose problems. Probes and sniffers can be extremely expensive, sometimes costing upward of $10,000 to $20,000.

CONCLUSION

The operations architecture consists of a set of tools that allows administrators to effectively manage a distributed environment. Although progress has been made in creating management frameworks that span the entire spectrum of management services, typical organizations must integrate different tools together to create a cohesive management picture. This integration effort is further complicated by the coexistence of host, client/server, and netcentric technologies.

Although this chapter has focused on operations tools, organization and processes are equally crucial success factors to managing a netcentric or client/server environment. As this chapter has shown, there are a multitude of considerations related to implementing and running a successful operations architecture; thus a structured, comprehensive framework that addresses the technology as well as people and process aspects is needed. Such a framework is introduced in the chapter in Section III that discusses the Management of Distributed Environments (MODE). Readers should understand the perspectives of both these chapters to ensure they have a comprehensive view of the operations architecture.

Chapter 13

Transition Frameworks for Netcentric Environments

Chapter 2 introduced the idea of the "astounding solution." In the absence of sustainable competitive advantage, organizations today must deliver an astounding solution — a new way to conduct business and a new way to reach and serve customers better — and then quickly get rid of all the bureaucracy used for that solution to develop a new astounding solution. Netcentric computing becomes the technology infrastructure that gives organizations the resilience and ability to change quickly to meet this need for rapid solution delivery.

At the heart of this new environment for delivering solutions is a sobering fact: today's cutting-edge business and technology solutions almost immediately become a "legacy." Most information technology professionals look with displeasure on an organization's legacy computing, but, from a business point of view, one must remember that those systems house much of the critical knowledge of the enterprise. They also represent a large investment. If the organization can build on that legacy and transition it to a new environment, the organization can leverage it and get further returns. More important, by ensuring that today's systems can transition to tomorrow's environments, the organization can be more confident that its knowledge capital can continue to grow.

The challenge in taking yesterday's systems into tomorrow is that they are characterized by outdated technology, antiquated technical architecture, and unreliable documentation. Many systems are inflexible and costly to maintain. Unable to justify the cost of maintaining these environments, many businesses are using this as an opportunity to move the business to more technology-enabled netcentric solutions.

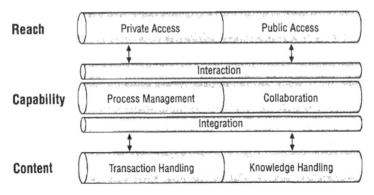

Exhibit 1. Netcentric Application Framework.

The Netcentric Application Framework, discussed in Chapter 1 (see Exhibit 1), acknowledges that enterprises must be able to tap into the wealth of information and knowledge that exists in today's legacy environments. The Integration layer in the application framework provides for access to all the transactional and analytical information and knowledge that has been collected over the years. Up to this time, nearly all information technology (IT) investments and business solutions relying on IT have been focused on transaction and data/knowledge handling. However, in the netcentric environment, computing solutions seek to obliterate organizational boundaries and provide stakeholders with more flexible, timely, and customized access to a greater array of goods and services. To do so, they must use the IT investments made to date. This transition support provides the reach into the legacy environment to continue to realize return on those investments. As today's solutions become tomorrow's legacies, transition support becomes embedded in the solution, making future transitions easier to implement.

Unless organizations can leverage the legacy environments through transition support, new netcentric solutions will necessarily involve reinventing old work. Therefore, although the netcentric solution from a technological point of view would be leading edge, it would lag behind older technological solutions in terms of the knowledge base represented within the solution. It might take decades to build up their respective knowledge bases to the levels of their predecessors.

This chapter takes a look at some ways of providing transition support through what is called "transition architectures." These architectures enable different transition approaches to optimize the business benefits of the legacy environment, while providing a clean path to the new netcentric solution. Although the transition approach should be driven by the overall business strategy, the transition is a system-by-system decision-making process; one approach will not typically suffice for all of an organization's systems. The transition architectures implemented are dependent on the organization's unique situation, the business objectives driving the transition, the status of the legacy systems, and the expected final technology environment.

WHAT IS A TRANSITION ARCHITECTURE?

A transition architecture is made up of tools, techniques, procedures, and standards that enable the integration or interfacing between existing and target solutions through a transition period. This definition implies several things. First, target solutions have been identified. The netcentric framework offers a way of identifying the types of business solutions that will likely be built in the future. Target solutions allow an enterprise to converge on its stakeholders (e.g., customers, suppliers, and regulators), removing the boundaries that once existed between it and its stakeholders. Netcentric solutions also eliminate the boundaries between enterprises, making entire value chains tighter and closer to the stakeholders. These make possible "astounding solutions" of the future, not the traditional transaction and data management solutions that IT has provided to date. Organizations need to refocus their IT investments on building netcentric solutions in order to compete in a more competitive world.

Second, the legacy environment needs to be well understood. This is often not the case. Thirty years of development and patches mean that many systems are complicated, undocumented, and impossible to maintain, often because their original developers are no longer with the organization. This situation presents a challenge that needs to be addressed by the transition architecture.

Therefore, transition architectures integrate parts of the overall technology architecture rather than stand-alone technical architectures. They are components of the development, execution, and operations architectures of the new netcentric solutions. These architectures, therefore, must to be viewed as part of the new solution rather than simply maintenance patches on the legacy.

An important factor to consider is that the transition period will likely last many years. That is, moves to netcentric solutions need to be deliberate and well-planned. This means that legacy environments, including processing logic and information, are in place for some time, while the new solutions need to use the legacy's assets. Therefore, the transition architecture must be robust enough to be working throughout the transition period.

BENEFITS OF THE TRANSITION ARCHITECTURE

Transition architectures can provide substantial benefits to enterprises seeking to move to new technology environments while making the most of the investment in legacy systems. A transition architecture can enable an enterprise to

- Map the current technology environment to an organization's targeted position using well-defined, business-focused releases that are measurable and manageable.
- Assist in enabling an enterprise for technological change; the people and process aspects of the change must be also addressed through other means.
- Maximize the value of legacy systems and ensure that future systems efficiently interact or integrate with them.
- Leverage existing skills, processes, and technologies to implement change.
- Have better implementation options, because of the set of standards, procedures and reusable components.
- Make better-informed decisions about how to transition to netcentric solutions, which can translate into higher-quality systems and new solutions.

A TRANSITION FRAMEWORK

The transition architecture must encompass all issues associated with moving to new technology and netcentric solutions. The architecture must account for all the legacy system components that could be valuable to the new solution as well as methods to execute, develop, and operate the transition of the components. Just as it is useful to have a framework to assist in identifying new solutions, it is useful to have a framework for the transition strategy. This framework acts as a completeness check: it helps ensure that the transition strategy has accounted for all the issues.

Three key components make up the framework for a transition architecture: transition approach, system components, and technical architecture environments (Exhibit 2).

Transition Approach

The transition approach defines the ways in which an enterprise can move from its legacy environment to the netcentric computing paradigm. The transition architecture may have to provide support for one or more of the approaches, especially if the legacy's components can be of high value in the future. The chosen approach, or approaches, is entirely dependent on the organization's vision of the future. Without this vision, it is impossible to pick a rational transition approach.

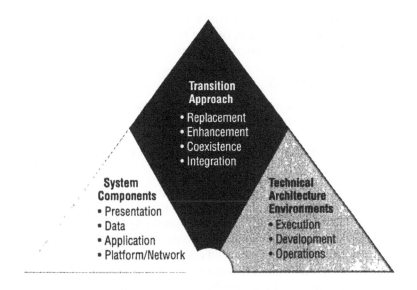

Exhibit 2. Transition Framework.

System Components

The system components are the pieces of the legacy solution that could be leveraged by the new solutions. They include the presentation component of an application (commonly referred to as the user interface), the data, the application code itself, and the hardware platform and network on which the application runs. These components represent the primary investments made by IT over the last 30 years and are therefore pieces that may be of value to the new solution. Organizations must have a thorough understanding of the relative merits of these legacy components in order to have a rational transition approach and architecture.

Technical Architecture Environments

The transition framework also shows that three environments must be addressed in any transition strategy:

1. *Execution*, or how the architecture will run in production
2. *Development*, which defines how to build the transition from legacy to new
3. *Operations*, or what needs to be done to properly operate the transition architecture

All three environments must be considered when designing and building a transition architecture. The consequences of not striking some balance could be a transition architecture that is designed to execute elegantly but cannot be reasonably developed or one that can easily be developed and executes well but is difficult to operate and maintain.

A TRANSITION STRATEGY

Based upon the transition framework just discussed, the development of a transition architecture can be divided into three main steps.

Step 1: Determine the Transition Approach that best Fits the Business's Strategy

In determining the appropriate transition approach, an enterprise must understand its legacy environment and the direction it needs to reach its vision — its business strategy, objectives, and imperatives. The direction the enterprise needs to go can be used to determine the business value of a solution, that is, an asset that could contribute to the business direction has a higher value than one that cannot. Understanding the legacy environment essentially means knowing what valuable assets of the legacy solution can have a role in the new solution environment. An analysis of these components must determine the relative functional quality (i.e., how well the legacy solution provides for supporting the business processes they were designed for) and the relative technology quality (i.e., how well-positioned is the technology environment of the legacy solution relative to the new technology environment).

Step 2: Analyze and Prioritize the System Components Necessary for the Transition from each of the Three Architectural Perspectives: Execution, Development, and Operations

Next, the transition steps must be identified to implement the chosen approach. Based on the chosen transition approach, these steps define what needs to be done to build the transition architecture, what changes must occur in business and IT processes, and what people and organizational changes are necessary. The steps are then prioritized so that a rational plan can be established to move to the new technology environment.

Step 3: Build the Transition Architecture to Assist in the Legacy Integration with the New Solutions

Finally, as the organization and the business processes are changing, the transition architecture supporting the chosen approach is built. This architecture then allows the enterprise to focus forward toward its technology. Therefore, first, the approach is chosen, and the necessary steps are identified and prioritized, and a plan laid out. Once this is done, building the transition architecture to support the organization's move to a new business and technology environment needs to be given the same attention and stature as any comparable application development effort. The actual construction of the transition architecture should be handled as any other IT development effort.

The remainder of this chapter focuses on the transition approaches, presenting a way to determine which approach to use and giving some examples of real scenarios where each approach was employed.

TRANSITION APPROACHES

"Cheshire-Puss," she began, rather timidly, as she did not at all know whether it would like the name: however, it only grinned a little wider. "Come, it's pleased so far," thought Alice, and she went on. "Would you tell me, please, which way I ought to go from here?"

"That depends a good deal on where you want to get to," said the Cat.

"I don't much care where ..." said Alice.

"Then it doesn't matter which way you go," said the Cat.

"... so long as I get somewhere," Alice added as an explanation.

"Oh, you're sure to do that," said the Cat, "if you only walk long enough."

From Lewis Carroll's *Alice's Adventures in Wonderland*

As enterprises create their annual budget or map out their 3-year plans, they often employ an implementation strategy just to be making progress without clearly defining the purpose of the implementation. It is common to hear tactical statements ("We will develop intranet capabilities") that are not linked to business value to be derived from the tactic. These statements define a path but not the destination. As Cheshire Cat tells Alice, the road you take only matters if you know where you are going.

As shown in Exhibit 3, all enterprises are engaged in some initiatives which, if left unaltered, will lead them to what could be called their "current future state."

Often, this end state is one of chance — simply a point reached, as Cheshire Cat states, after walking long enough. Where an enterprise desires to be is what can called, by contrast, the "desired future state." Unfortunately, this is often not articulated in any actionable way. If it were, there would likely be a vision gap between where the organization is going to end up in its wanderings compared to where it really wants to be.

To reach the desired future state, an organization should build on where it is today. Therefore, the transition approach that should be taken is based on a solid understanding of where the organization is today with respect to its IT assets and where it wants to go based on solution visions, or "application

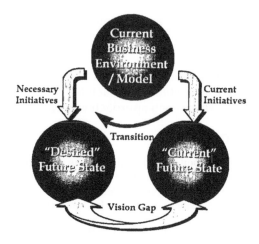

Exhibit 3. An Enterprise's "Current Future State."

blueprints," identified through the netcentric framework. An application blueprint is an articulation of a future solution that describes

- The business functions
- The manner in which technology (e.g., hardware, software, information and knowledge, and other equipment) might enable the functions and be used by the functions
- The effects of the new solution (e.g., changes in skills needed, organization structure, rewards, and incentives) on the people

These application blueprints help define the future business value and provide a benchmark against which all current IT assets may be compared.

The matrix in Exhibit 4 pulls together this information to assist an enterprise in determining what transition approach to follow. The selection of an approach during the transition strategy development is a system-by-system decision; one approach typically does not suffice for all of an organization's systems. By positioning each legacy solution in a quadrant according to a relative scoring of (1) its future business value and (2) its technology capability, one can get an idea of the appropriate transition approach that can best move the organization to the new solution and technology environment.

Future Business Value

This is a determination of how well a legacy solution can contribute to the application blueprints which specify the desired future state. This determination can be based on the components of the legacy solution, such as the integrity of its information or particular functional services or routines in

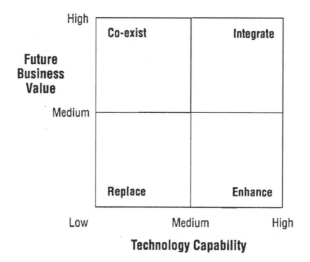

Client

Exhibit 4. Selecting a Transition Approach.

the legacy solution, and does not have to be based on the legacy solution as a whole. In other words, IS managers should determine whether pieces of the legacy system can be broken out and contribute to the future business value.

Technology Capability

The technology capability of a legacy solution is based on the ability of its technology components and architecture to support the new business environment as defined by the application blueprints. This assessment must evaluate user interfaces and interaction, system documentation, stability, ease of maintenance, information accessibility and integrity, extensibility or flexibility to interact with other netcentric solutions, and the ability to add new technology to extend the solutions' reach.

Using this matrix, one arrives at four different types of transition approaches:

- Replacement (low business value, low technology capability)
- Enhancement (low business value, high technology capability)
- Coexistence (low technology capability, high business value)
- Integration (high technology capability, high business value)

REPLACEMENT

A system with low future business value and technology capabilities requires a significant investment to maintain and transition, which makes replacement a likely option in this case. Major functional and technical enhancements are required to ensure that the system can reliably share data or functions, or both, with other systems. Also, a system's lack of stability, extensibility, and openness indicate that functional enhancements would be difficult and would likely act to further destabilize the system.

Is anything from the legacy solution salvageable? This is a key question to ask prior to undertaking a replacement approach. Generally, the years of data and knowledge that are stored within the legacy's databases is of some value. There are at least to ways to maintain the value of this data:

1. Convert the data to be usable and store it within the new solutions environment
2. Use the data in parallel with the new system to compare results and assist in testing the accuracy of the new solution.

The replacement option is often favored by organizations looking for cost savings from a standard technology architecture. Organizations may also seek to use the new solution as a catalyst for other changes, such as alterations in the business processes affected by the new solution. Because this approach carries high costs and risks, significant business benefits must be identified before it is applied. If the benefits to the business are minimal, changing technology for the sake of technology alone should be avoided. Such a transitional approach may be appropriate when the application is adequate by itself but is unable to operate with other system environments. Moving to a new platform, language, or database management system (DBMS) may also make future application changes easier to implement given better tools and skills. Exhibit 5 shows the implications of a replacement strategy for the other aspects of the transition framework: system components and technical architecture.

A development architecture will ensure an accurate and comprehensive understanding of the system components that will be replaced. The requirements for additional execution and operations architecture components are dictated by the target platform. The execution and operations impacts are much greater when the target environment is new to the enterprise. This is often the case when rehosting mainframe applications to a new (e.g., UNIX) platform.

An example of an appropriate replacement approach is upsizing. The enterprise may benefit from making a single-user application available to the whole department. An example of this approach might be a PC-based dBASE-IV application that had been developed for single use but was

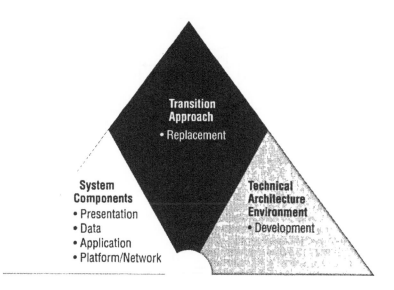

Exhibit 5. Implications of a Replacement Transition Approach.

migrated to Sybase on UNIX when others decided they wanted access to the application.

Another replacement example involved a large government agency that completely replaced an old, outdated and inflexible benefits system. A development tool was built to allow the agency to compare payments coming out of the new system with the most recent payments made by the old. This enabled the agency to quickly identify any significant differences and make manual payments if needed. This approach was needed due to the large number of payments that were processed and the importance and visibility of the system. The execution architecture components developed assisted in testing the validity of the replacement system (Exhibit 6) during the 6-month transition period.

ENHANCEMENT

A system with low future business value but good technology capabilities is a strong candidate for an enhancement architecture approach. Such a system is typically stable, it has been architected well, and its data integrity is acceptable. The system is often reasonably well documented and provides a sound technical basis for the future. Functional enhancements may be the easiest way to address the future business needs specified in the application blueprints. This may be a good short-term approach while a better and possibly more strategic functional solution is being implemented. In this case,

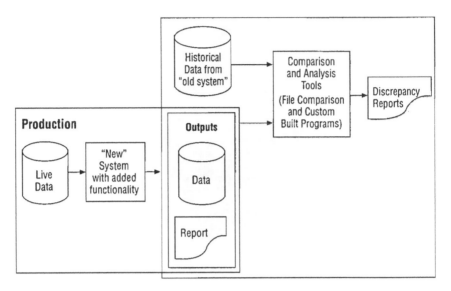

Exhibit 6. Replacement Example.

however, care should be taken to ensure that appropriate analysis is done beforehand to confirm the validity of such an approach (i.e., confirming requirements, functional fit, and its technological ability to support vision).

With the enhancement approach, the existing application's functionality is enhanced through a new release. A fine line separates traditional maintenance and an enhancement-transition approach. Maintenance is an activity that is performed to keep the legacy running to support the way business is currently conducted. Enhancement, on the other hand, is an improvement process to allow the legacy to support the new business, as represented in the application blueprints.

Enhancing the existing application is often beneficial because it can offer a fast and cost-effective way to address the business issues identified. Such an approach is most appropriate when existing applications are well structured and relatively easy to maintain. In addition, this approach is best used when the organization's business requirements do not dictate the need for a new technology environment. Exhibit 7 shows the implications of an enhancement strategy for the other aspects of the transition framework: system components and technical architecture.

A good development architecture will ensure appropriate implementation of the application's new release, allowing a thorough understanding of the existing systems in preparation for the enhancement. Impact on the operations and execution environment is typically minimal because the

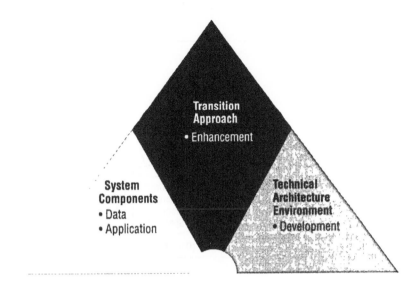

Exhibit 7. Implications of an Enhancement Transition Approach.

technical environment (hardware, network, system software, and DBMS) remains unchanged as a result of the enhancement.

An illustration of the enhancement approach can be taken from a consumer products company that sought to restructure the numbering approach used to identify its products. The company had determined that its future business was going to take it into more and different products. The application blueprints had specified the need to be able to offer these new products in very short time frames. The old product codes were inflexible and caused difficulty in introducing new products. The company restructured by consolidating product codes and including additional product information to identify each product uniquely. Because the client faced no need to move to a new technology environment, it developed an enhancement architecture that analyzed existing applications for change impacts. Again, the architecture consisted of a methodology and supporting development architecture components, such as code-scanning tools. These tools were instrumental in performing the high-volume scanning and decomposition. They also provided several reports to aid the analysts at all stages of the project (Exhibit 8).

COEXISTENCE

If the legacy solution has high future business value but low technology capability, coexistence is an appropriate transition approach. Future value can be

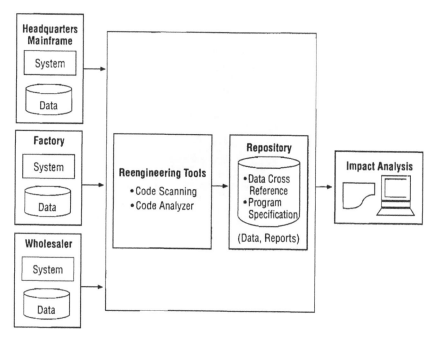

Exhibit 8. Enhancement Example.

defined in many ways. Databases in the legacy may contain information that will be needed in the future. Certain application functions may embody business process knowledge that could not easily be recreated or replaced.

In spite of the value in this legacy solution, however, some technology used by the solution might limit its ability to actually deliver this value in the new business environment. For example, a new application blueprint for a manufacturer envisions that customers will have direct access to the work in process, thus allowing them to better plan for receiving the finished product. The manufacturer's mainframe solution might contain all the information in which the customers would be interested, but the mainframe technology would limit its ability to provide direct access to the customers. In this case, a coexistence approach might provide for newer, distributed presentation technology to put on the front end of the work-in-process database, permitting the legacy to coexist in the new business environment. Exhibit 9 shows the implications of an enhancement strategy for the other aspects of the transition framework: system components and technical architecture.

The execution architecture for coexistence challenges the current notions regarding the legacy solution's presentation, data, application, and

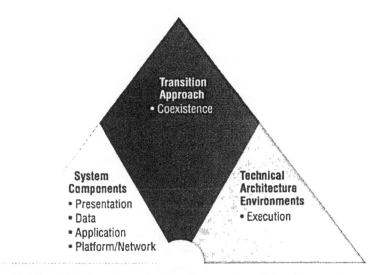

Exhibit 9. Implications of a Coexistence Transition Approach.

platform/network components. New technology is integrated with old in order to take advantage of new capabilities while leveraging assets from the legacy such as data or application functions. With convergence, the execution architecture's platform and network are often taxed heavily as new capabilities are driven closer to the customers, who now have access to data and application functions they never did before.

An example of the coexistence strategy involved a major credit-card processor that wanted to provide better customer service by opening a direct channel to all its customers: member banks, merchants, and end consumers. The member banks had IT departments and technology-support organizations, but few merchants and no end consumers had such support. Because of the large and varied customer base, the solution needed to give the customers an intuitive user interface that was easily distributed to all customers. The credit-card processor had a large investment in its old mainframe CICS/DB2 solution; in addition, the information in the database had maintained its integrity over the years and had performed well. Because the credit-card processor was eager to leapfrog its competition and get a solution out quickly, the organization created a coexistence architecture that used Internet technologies.

The greatest challenge in implementing this architecture was to integrate a set of technologies that had been used as an information publishing medium with pieces of the legacy transaction-processing application. The key to this coexistence architecture was a set of Java applets on a Web server that was able to communicate with CICS on the mainframe. A messaging middleware product was used on the mainframe to receive messages from and send messages to the Java applets on the Web server and perform the actual communication with CICS.

The Internet technologies provide a rich user interface, and minimize most of the age-old issues of application configuration management and software/hardware compatibility in a highly distributed environment. They also provide relatively easy and consistent access to the application, regardless of whether the customer is a sophisticated IT shop, such as member banks, or an individual end consumer. The solution is also fairly secure and virus-resistant for the customers (Exhibit 10).

INTEGRATION

In those environments in which the future business value and technology capability is high for a legacy solution, and the legacy must work with other systems in the new environment, some form of integration is often desirable. This allows the enterprise to continue to realize a return on its investments over the years in the legacy and leverage the knowledge that has gone into its creation. There are two ways of integrating legacy with new solutions: data integration and application integration.

Integrating the legacy solution into the new solution environment is potentially the easiest transition approach. It is also potentially the most difficult. IT departments have been using a form of the data-integration approach for years, as file extracts were created from a source system, transferred to the target system either electronically or mechanically by tapes or disks, and then loaded into the target's database. This is a fairly straightforward transition approach that leverages the legacy's data by using it for purposes other than that for which it may have been originally intended. On the other end of the spectrum, however, there are now emerging requester or broker techniques using object-oriented (OO) or componentware technology. These complex architectures assist in the isolation of functions, services, or data within the legacy and the creation of application programming interfaces (APIs) with which to access them. New solutions can then utilize the functions, services, or data from the legacy by using the APIs.

Data Integration Approach

A data integration architecture approach is recommended when a system has basic data integrity. This type of system often effectively addresses the organization's business requirements and does not require immediate functional enhancements. Systems of this nature often excel in capturing and recording transactional data but do a poor job of providing analytical

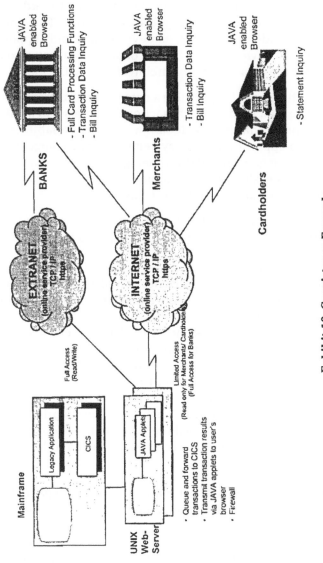

Exhibit 10. Coexistence Example.

or decision support from this database. Even though the system's technology capabilities may not be sufficient to enable its functions to be used by other systems, it may permit data to be exchanged in a reliable manner.

Data integration is the most flexible of all transition approaches because it enables the organization to move at the desired speed toward its vision, with the enterprise's objectives and goals as its driver. This approach, however, generates additional costs, as development and support skills are required for two environments. The IT organization may also need a support group for the data integration architecture itself.

Many organizations are also pursuing a data integration transition strategy to consolidate data from their transactional systems into a data warehouse for enhanced analysis or decision support capabilities. Data integration is also appropriate when systems covering a large functional area of a business (e.g., financials) are being consolidated into an integrated system. This scale of transition may take place over a few years requiring systems of similar function to coexist.

There are two basic types of data integration, asynchronous store-and-forward architecture and near real-time asynchronous architecture.

Asynchronous Store-and-Forward Architecture. This is probably the most straightforward of all transition approaches; it is also what IT departments have chosen for years. This is the "create extract file, transfer file, load file" scenario for sharing data from one system to another. Generally executed in batches of data, it is reacting to some particular time schedule. The asynchronous store and forward architecture is easy to develop and relatively easy to maintain. Maintenance is only needed when a file or database structure changes on either end, which causes the extract file format to change. The architecture is also relatively easy to operate; if the file does not transfer properly, one simply tries again. This is a very appropriate transition approach when the new systems need the legacy data but do not need it in real-time, or when the integration architecture needs to be developed quickly.

Near Real-Time Asynchronous Architecture. The second type of data integration is a much more complex architecture that requires more sophisticated automation and capabilities. Here, the transfer of information is usually triggered by a wider variety of events, such as a change in state of the legacy data or a business process event. These events trigger the architecture to extract a small piece of legacy information and send it to the target environment for processing. At the heart of this architecture is a guaranteed message and data delivery system that ensures that once information is put in the architecture, it will eventually get delivered.

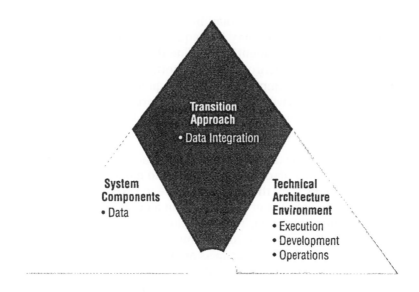

Exhibit 11. Implications of a Data Integration Transition Approach.

As information updates occur that need to be replicated to other platforms or databases, the updates are first performed and committed to the local database, and then the replication architecture guarantees that the replicated target databases will eventually be made consistent through a guaranteed message delivery system. Several middleware or messaging products offer much of this capability. This is a concept called "eventual consistency," which says that the data in both systems will eventually be consistent. This architecture delivers the data immediately, but the two systems are not synchronized in real time. This architecture is explained in an example later.

Another approach for sharing data between two or more systems in real-time requires extremely complex two-phase commit processing and is not generally acceptable as a transition approach for data integration. Two-phase commit protocols exist in leading database products but generally only work between databases from the same vendor. Unfortunately, when transitioning from legacy systems to new technologies, the environment is usually heterogeneous from both a platform and database product perspective. Exhibit 11 shows the implications of a data integration strategy for the other aspects of the transition framework: system components and technical architecture.

To achieve the required integrity, the synchronization among data must be defined as part of the business requirements and service levels. In some cases, overnight batch updates may be sufficient, while in other cases immediate synchronization may be required. Each business function should be analyzed independently to define the synchronization requirements. To enable data synchronization in both execution and operations environments, interface components will be required. For example, application data access modules will facilitate the transparent sharing of data across applications. Some of these components may have to be custom developed because off-the-shelf products do not always satisfy all requirements.

One illustration of the data integration approach is the case of an electronics component manufacturer that wanted to move all of its enterprise or corporate systems from the IBM mainframe to UNIX servers. This decision was not made lightly, but was based on a compelling business case that is beyond this discussion. The transition to completely eliminate the manufacturer's reliance on the mainframe was determined to be a 5- to 10-year program, and the first business area to move was to be inventory management. To complicate this first step, the corporation had up to 10 different inventory management systems, plus numerous other manufacturing and planning systems that needed inventory information.

A data integration transition approach was chosen that would introduce the new UNIX server computing environment to house the integrated inventory information. Thus, for the transition period, the corporation would have a three-tiered architecture for inventory management and information:

1. The mainframe systems for enterprise computing functions such as inventory planning.
2. The lower tier transaction systems, for manufacturing and warehousing.
3. The new, midtier platform that all systems would eventually run on.

The data integration challenge was to be able to integrate all the inventory information on the midtier platform so that each application requiring this information could be moved to the new platform in a rational manner while still receiving the inventory information it needed from all the other systems. Eventually, the mainframe would not be needed for any inventory functions, and those functions could be turned off. Any new applications requiring inventory information would be built for the new processing environment.

A key design goal of the transition architecture was to minimize disruptions to the existing applications to eliminate digging into legacy code that was poorly documented and not well-understood. A data integration architecture was designed to capture all transactions that modified inventory information and replicate the results to the midtier platform.

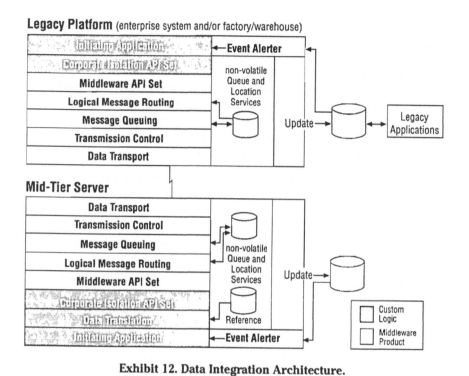

Exhibit 12. Data Integration Architecture.

Exhibit 12 depicts the data integration architecture designed for this company.

The architecture created a federated database of inventory information composed of physical databases at the enterprise, factory and warehouse, and midtier or server levels. This federated database would function as one logical inventory database, with all inventory-related transactions being integrated on the new server platform. A guaranteed database synchronization component that sits on top of a guaranteed message delivery system makes the federated database possible. This component ensures that updates performed on the enterprise DB2 or the factory and warehouse systems are reflected in the midtier server component and vice versa. Thus, applications can trust all physical DBMSs to provide accurate, identical inventory information.

Inventory information from the manufacturing systems and the warehouses are transferred across the replication manager component, the information backbone, of the architecture. The replication manager ensures the delivery of data from the individual sites to the central, midtier server component. Also key to this architecture is the reference data, which provide the mapping between the multiple systems' data structures and perform syntax (e.g., the size of data fields) as well as semantic translation (i.e., the meaning of the data such as what a *sale* or *customer* actually mean between the two systems). Finally, the architecture had to be able to handle concurrent updates; updates to the same information could arrive at nearly the same time from either platform. Because of the low probability of this occurring, the simple approach was to have the architecture report to a single database when a concurrent update had occurred and require manual intervention to resolve the conflict.

This transition architecture was developed to enable an enterprise-wide view of inventory information through asynchronous, reliable information delivery across heterogeneous platforms and to create a transition step toward the enterprises' goal of moving off the mainframe. The business benefit of this architecture is that it allowed the organization to more quickly and more accurately confirm product delivery schedules with its customers. It also ensured the data integrity, provided high availability of the data and efficient and timely delivery of the information. Also, because the architecture was not intrusive to the legacy systems, no modifications were needed to the legacy environments. They are able to operate oblivious to the new data integration architecture. This is a good example of a transition architecture that needed to be very robust because of the expected long transition period. The legacy factory and warehouse systems will be around for a long time; they will not be replaced anytime soon.

Application Integration Approach

A system that has both high future business value and technology capabilities is a good candidate for an application integration approach. Generally, such a system has been enhanced throughout years of maintenance and includes complex business functionality. It is built on a solid architecture that allows for extension and flexion. The system is often reliable enough to allow the development of dependencies between it and the new systems; functions of this legacy system may be used by the new systems.

This approach positions legacy systems as direct participants in the new system architectures. Instead of simply exchanging key information, an application integration architecture adapts legacy systems to interact with new systems. It makes selected legacy system functions and data accessible to newly developed systems and other legacy systems; legacy components can act as service providers to new components and vice versa. This is a reuse strategy.

An application integration approach enables the organization to add value to existing legacy functions by combining them with new systems

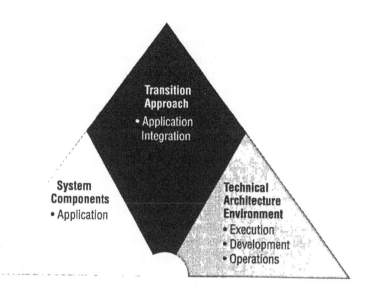

Exhibit 13. Implications of an Application Integration Transition Approach.

components such as PC-based applications and networks to form more powerful solutions.

The application integration approach works best when legacy systems are well modularized. It typically takes several years to move legacy systems into new environments; often, the knowledge capital contained in these systems reflects an accumulation of efforts of many individuals. Rebuilding this type of expertise in a new system is almost impossible within a reasonable time frame. An application integration approach removes the need to rebuild this expertise. An application integration (reuse) approach eliminates the need to create multiple instances of the same functionality that can grow apart over time.

Exhibit 13 shows the implications of an application integration strategy for the other aspects of the transition framework: system components and technical architecture.

Application integration architecture components are largely required within the execution architecture to allow communication among all applications. They enable an application to communicate with legacy applications. The solution should be comprised of packaged and custom components whose processing is independent of the participating applications. It supports a many-to-many interface structure.

An example of the application integration approach comes from a large overnight shipping company that was building a new client/server customer service system to include a feature enabling the quotation of shipping rates for customers. The mainframe billing application already contained the business rules for calculating the cost of a shipment and for writing the invoice. Fortunately, the relevant logic was already separated from the CICS screen presentation logic to allow invoices to be produced either in batch or on-line modes.

Using middleware messaging technology, the new customer service system supplied the package shipment information to the rating engine, and the rating engine returned the cost for the shipment. Customer service representatives are now able to quote rates to customers using the new computing environment and front end, but through the same back-end engine that will ultimately print their bills, thus satisfying the user requirements and virtually eliminating the potential for conflicting quoted and billed amounts.

This example highlights a service request broker (SRB) transition architecture. An SRB is a generic concept driven out of emerging transition and application integration technologies such as object request broker (ORB), wrappering, and componentware. These complex architectures assist in the isolation of functions, services, or data within the legacy solution and provide for the creation of application programming interfaces (APIs) with which to access them. New solutions can then use the functions, services, or data from the legacy by using the APIs.

CONCLUSION

Transition architectures will become increasingly important over the next decade of computing solutions. They are critical as companies leverage their existing knowledge base, embedded in their legacy systems, and also as they position their current solutions for change as those become legacies themselves. Just as important, however, is the manner in which transition architectures will support interorganizational work. Alliances will only be successful when companies can optimally share data and information stored in a wide variety of systems. Transition support applications will help companies operate in a seamless way.

Chapter 14
Platform Architecture

The netcentric platform architecture provides a way to identify and select the major technology platform components of a netcentric system. The platform architecture creates the foundation on which the execution architecture, development architecture, operations architecture, and — most important — the business application are implemented and deployed. This chapter will focus on explaining the potential types of platform roles in a netcentric environment, and the common selection criteria by which to choose a specific platform. Because of the speed of change in this field, specific vendors and technologies are not discussed.

A netcentric application has a wide potential scope. It is designed, in most cases, to meet the needs of employees, business partners, suppliers, and direct consumers. Because of these different user groups, it is helpful to break the platform decision into primary and secondary considerations. The primary considerations address how one determines the types of platforms required and their roles. The secondary considerations for each required platform are then applied to determine the actual products to select and implement.

PRIMARY CONSIDERATIONS

Three considerations are paramount when selecting platform technologies:

1. The capabilities and roles of various platform components, given the specific business application needs.
2. The user access requirements, which determine the clients to support.
3. The processing role of the servers, which means determining the split of routing, transaction management, application processing, and data among the potential server processing tiers.

Consideration 1: Capabilities and Roles of Platform Components

The netcentric environment can be a complex mixture of differing platform roles. Exhibit 1 illustrates the major platform components and their roles within a netcentric environment. The exhibit shows a typical netcentric environment addressing core company locations, links with key business

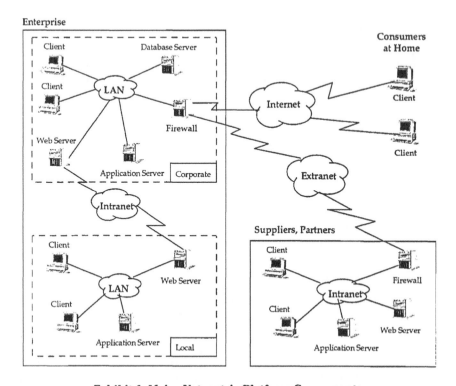

Exhibit 1. Major Netcentric Platform Components.

partners, as well as with external users or consumers. In determining the scope of a netcentric environment it is vital to work from an understanding of the application requirements in order to understand the platforms required.

The following discusses key types and roles of the platform components.

Clients. In client/server solutions a "client" primarily meant a desktop or a mobile desktop. In netcentric environments, the term "client" is much broader; it implies a wide array of access platforms that meet the needs of a variety of users (Exhibit 2).

Illustrative types of clients are

- *Telephone.* In the netcentric world the telephone remains a key access device, perhaps the most ubiquitous. Through a phone's touch-tone capabilities or through voice recognition technologies, users get access to such things as call center agents and voice response applications.

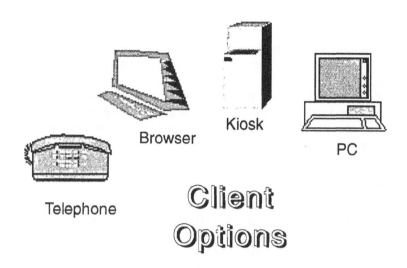

Telephone   Browser   Kiosk   PC

Client Options

Exhibit 2. Client Options.

- *Desktops.* Desktops are usually based on the Wintel platform. Desktops can support local programs or they can use browser technology to access Internet applications. A variation of the desktop is the Windows terminal environments that support the running of applications from a shared server.
- *Browser.* Browsers are now the traditional Internet platform. They allow an organization to provide a browser-based application that can be supported by any user's platform that can handle the specific browser capabilities required by the application.
- *Kiosks.* Usually multimedia oriented, kiosks are standalone information systems that can provide connectivity allowing users to call or video conference for direct interaction with a support agent or sales advisor. They also support browser access to the Internet to run transactional applications.
- *Others.* There a multitude of other emerging devices in the marketplace that are trying to meet more specific needs. Some examples are
  Set-top boxes, which the cable industry is introducing in an attempt to make the TV the processing device of choice.
  Smart appliances, cars, and other devices, which use specific embedded operating system networking technology to broaden their service capabilities to consumers.

Intranet/Internet/Extranet Infrastructure. The communications infrastructure of an enterprise consists of three general areas to address: intranet, Internet, and extranet.

- Intranet refers to the communications capabilities for supporting communication within (intra) the enterprise.
- The Internet refers to the communications capabilities outside of the enterprise.
- An Extranet is a specific type of Internet capability typically targeted to support a specific business or trade group. Extranets typically have tighter access, uptime and security capabilities than general internet networks.

Networking infrastructure is discussed in detail in chapters in both Sections II and III.

Firewall. Access to the interconnected network is through a firewall or similar security access checkpoint. By their nature, netcentric applications are about extending the reach of computing — not only across the enterprise but also outside the enterprise. This means that the infrastructure must support the ability to secure itself properly. Firewalls should exist as a part of the specific corporate networking infrastructure. In planning any netcentric application, it is vital to consider the need for external security capability if it does not exist or for understanding the current policies around external access. The policies and capabilities of this part of the infrastructure can directly determine the ability or constraints around external user access. Establishing or understanding the security issues is a key part of finalizing a netcentric applications capabilities. Netcentric security is discussed in detail in Section IV.

Web Servers. Web servers are the "traffic cops" for Internet/intranet applications. The role of the Web server is to direct incoming requests to the targeted application server. Web servers typically do little application processing so that they remain efficient "traffic cops."

Application Servers. Application servers support the core processing needs of an application. Physically, these may represent one or more actual processing platforms. In some cases they may consist of existing, or legacy, applications that have been architected to be more accessible.

For larger-scale environments with multiple application servers, there is sometimes a need to introduce a transaction handling server that can run the middleware to maintain common session/state information for users as they access applications across multiple servers.

Database Servers. The DBMS server may physically be the same platform as an application server, or it may be a dedicated shared DBMS platform.

Consideration 2: User Access Requirements

To determine the user access capabilities required for a netcentric platform environment, the applications must be reviewed to determine the types of client platforms that need to be supported.

Internal Users with Mixed Application Requirements. Users within the enterprise will probably be accessing a mixture of browser-based and traditional packaged executables. Users with needs for both packaged executables and browser-based applications will probably run some variation of the Desktop PC with browser capability as their primary platform.

External Users. A number of platforms are to be considered here. The phone platform is attractive because of its pervasiveness. Some uses include using a phone platform to allow users to interact with systems through agents or automated voice response systems. However, agents are a high-cost method and many applications cannot justify such expense. Automated voice response applications help lower the cost but remain limited in how many services they can realistically offer using a touch tone interface. Advances in speech recognition are helping expand the capabilities but may not be ready for critical applications.

The most high-profile approach today to meet external user access needs is to target the browser platform. This requires an understanding of the heterogeneity of the target audience and the implications of audience characteristics on the application's capabilities. Most applications will need to determine a common subset of browser capabilities to support and support a number of additional features (such as allowing the users to "turn off" graphics if they are negatively affecting download times).

Internal/External Users from a Common Location. Some applications will have requirements more suited toward providing user access from a common, centralized location. These types of applications may be best met through the use of kiosk platforms. These platforms have internal uses, such as an employee benefits application, which can be accessed throgh a kiosk in an employee cafeteria. External uses include a bank sales/service application, located on kiosks in major shopping areas, which allows customers to apply for loans or transact other business. Although many of these applications will be browser based, they may have unique platform requirements that kiosks can best meet: such as secure durable packaging, secure and limited access for repair work, and remote diagnostics.

Consideration 3: Server Processing Role

In selecting servers, the processing role and number of distinct processing tiers of the servers must be derived from the requirements across the applications. This means determining the overall split of routing, transaction management, application processing, and data among the potential server processing tiers.

- *Routing.* The overall traffic and its routing complexity, especially peaks, will determine the Web server platform strategy.

- *Transaction management.* The transaction management tier could retain context information so that the user can seamlessly access distinct application areas without having to reenter information during a single visit or session. Environments that have few applications may not need this type of processing tier. The need for this tier is determined by the underlying execution architecture and the needs of the applications that use it.
- *Application/DBMS tier (s).* The platform strategy for the application processing tier and its companion DBMS tier is also determined by the overall execution architecture and the applications that use it. A more homogenous application mix supporting access to a common DBMS will have a different platform requirement than one supporting highly heterogeneous applications accessing a mixture of new and existing legacy DBMSs.

SECONDARY CONSIDERATIONS

Five additional considerations can be used to further narrow the list of platform candidates

1. Capacity
2. Growth/scalability
3. Price/performance
4. Vendor viability
5. High availability or fault tolerance

Capacity

Depending on the specific role of the platform the capacity must be considered across the Web, application, and DBMS servers. Each must be looked at specifically in terms of the demands that that tier will handle. In the case of the Web server this involves a consideration of the overall traffic to be handled. In the case of the application or DBMS server, more traditional application sizing techniques apply.

Capacity may constrain the field of hardware vendors and products that can be seriously considered for deploying the system. In all cases, capacity must be thought of in an end-to-end manner, including the capacity of existing legacy systems to handle the additional traffic. Many companies view their legacy systems as having high capacity until they experience sudden increased demand from transactions generated by external users.

Growth/Scalability

In some cases a system starts out small and then grows over the course of a few years. This growth may be in terms of transaction volumes, function, or number of users. In such cases, preference should be given to a hardware product line that is easily scalable in small and less expensive increments.

There are different types of scalability. An organization may wish to add additional client platform roles and processing tiers as their business strategy evolves. This can be referred to as access scalability. Scalability can also refers to the disks and network of the system.

Price/Performance

Much attention is now focused on the total cost of ownership, or TCO. Price/performance of any platform should be viewed in terms of the overall business benefits of the application or system. The aggressive cost structures of various vendors may make a component appear very impressive from a cost-per-MIP standpoint. However, the true cost should be viewed on a cost-per-seat or cost-per-user basis. Cost per seat or cost per user is determined by totaling all the necessary computing and communications hardware and software costs, the operational people costs, and then dividing by the number of users. The business benefits can then be compared against the system or application cost.

Vendor Viability

If the system is going to be mission critical for the organization, and is expected to have a lifetime of 5 or 10 years or more, it is probably not a good idea to buy unproven hardware, even if it is inexpensive. For critical systems, an enterprise cannot afford to be tied to hardware from a small company that may be out of business in a few years.

High Availability or Fault Tolerance

Fault tolerance is not important to all systems, but some systems may have difficult requirements in terms of high availability. Airline reservations systems or emergency response systems may require no downtime at all, for example. The need for high availability substantially limits the number of viable hardware providers and drives the use of redundancy in configurations.

In netcentric computing there is often a tendency to declare that everything must be available "24x7," because the system supports the external user — especially the customer. Using this reasoning, companies start to make all "Web" hardware fault tolerant; however, they may neglect to address the basic availability of the core legacy systems that are being opened up for external access.

In many cases there are ways to introduce high availability to a Web site and yet still allow a user to understand that an application may not be available at a specific time. The key is to have a consistent and stable Web platform and common site available to inform the externals user what is available and not available at any specific time. Some within the industry now refer to this as providing a "consistent Web dial tone" to the customer.

CONCLUSION

This chapter has discussed the important considerations for choosing a platform architecture. The primary criteria outlined how to think of the complex netcentric platform environment as a series of roles and their capabilities. The secondary criteria applied some key considerations for deciding which platform should be selected for a role.

Section III
Designing and Implementing Netcentric Solutions

Chapter 15
A Framework for Netcentric Implementation

As organizations move to client/server computing, and then to the more complex dimension of netcentric computing, they do not always carefully think through issues associated with successful implementation. Because of the distributed environment, client/server and netcentric applications are more complex and difficult to implement than traditional applications.

Successful delivery of netcentric solutions depends on the following key areas:

- Project organization
- Technology architecture decisions and implementation
- Application design and implementation
- Network design and delivery
- Site preparation and installation
- Systems management
- Change management

These areas interact with each other in a flow of work, depicted in Exhibit 1.

NETCENTRIC PLANNING CHART

These workflows can then be fleshed out into a comprehensive planning chart for netcentric development projects (Exhibit 2). This planning chart has been used successfully on hundreds of such projects around the world. Each box in the planning chart represents a work segment to be done to address one or more netcentric implementation issues.

The arrows and lines suggest a sequence as well as an interdependency of the efforts. The completion of a segment usually means that a major work deliverable has been completed.

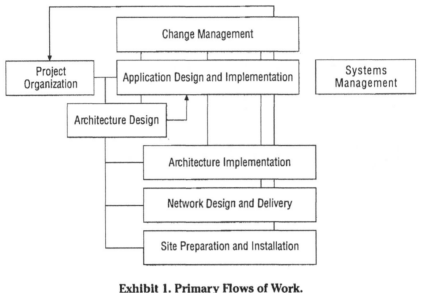

Exhibit 1. Primary Flows of Work.

The diagram is complex because a complex set of interrelated problems must be addressed. At the same time, the exhibit is still at a conceptual level because it does not show all the interrelationships or the actual work tasks to be done.

This chapter provides an overview of each of the major development streams within the overall planning chart. Subsequent chapters within Section III of this book go into more detail on each of the streams.

PROJECT ORGANIZATION: ROLE OF KEY MANAGERS

Defining organizational structures can be a high-risk undertaking. Such structures often imply a change in who is in charge, a change in goals, and changes in how work is to be done. Put another way, organizational structures strike right where people live. As such, organizational charts tend to be the source of a great deal of concern and, on occasion, angst. However, the fact remains that to undertake the development of a netcentric or advanced client/server system, organization must be a key concern.

Exhibit 3 depicts a generic organizational chart. It is high level, but it provides a starting point for a netcentric or client/server development effort. Many other factors have to be compared against this sample before an organization can come up with its own usable model. These factors include the skills of personnel involved, their desires, their past histories, and their expectations.

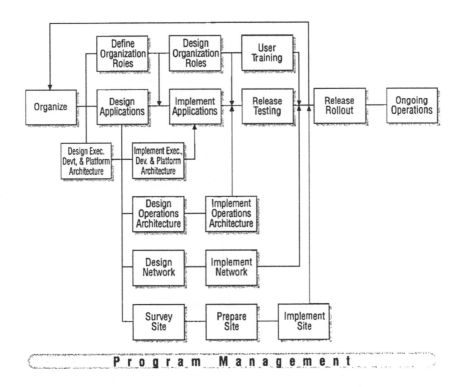

Exhibit 2. Netcentric Implementation Planning Chart.

The size of the project must also be taken into consideration. The organizational structure discussed here is applicable to projects of roughly 150 to 200 people or fewer. For larger, more complex engagements, additional roles come into play — roles such as an overall architecture strategy function or an enterprise architect — which are concerned with coordinating the functional, technical, and business aspects of the system. These roles are outside the scope of this book, although Accenture has additional methodologies for these larger projects.

Strategy Manager

The structure shows a single overall leader for the project — here, the "strategy manager." There is a great deal of value in having a single individual responsible for, and with authority over, the project as a whole. Such individuals, when they welcome the responsibility, seem to bring to the effort a commitment and concern that is lost when the project is divided among multiple leaders, each with a mix of concerns, constituencies, and objectives.

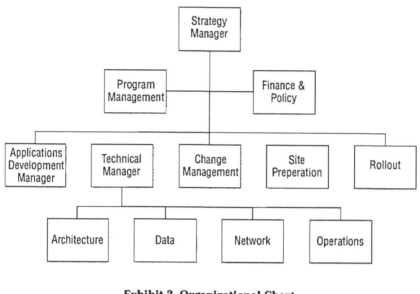

Exhibit 3. Organizational Chart.

Program Management

The program management role appears as an adjunct to the strategy manager. The role of this group is to monitor all the projects that are being pursued to deliver a netcentric or advanced client/server application. This monitoring function involves more than just tracking overall status. It also includes evaluation of the quality of the deliverables as well as their cost-effectiveness.

Even when program management itself does not have the direct responsibility for quality review and approval, this function is responsible for ensuring that these reviews occur and that they are done by qualified people.

Also, if one or more strands of the work start to run late or encounter difficulties, it is program management's responsibility to note the issue, evaluate its impact, and pull together strategies to deal with the situation.

Finance and Policy

The organizational chart also shows the finance and policy group reporting to the strategy manager. This group tracks overall spending on projects and verifies expenditures as time passes. A development project often places new demands on organizations, and new policies to deal with these demands have to be devised.

For example, a netcentric engagement may be inherently distributed and require that people be on the road for extended periods of time. The company may have limited policies on reimbursement of expenses and handling of costs that need to be expanded for the project. This expansion would fall to the finance and policy group.

The next level of the chart shows organizations more focused on the actual building and delivery of the applications.

Applications Development Manager

Often, a netcentric development project addresses several business applications such as multiple lines of business and related claims. Each of these applications may have its own project manager. These project managers then report to the applications development manager.

The applications development manager has the overall responsibility to deliver the applications in accordance with time, budget, and quality standards. As such, this manager can make decisions about redeploying resources between applications and also provide a single voice to the business users and to the rest of the project teams about the applications development process.

An interesting question here is whether large application projects should have direct access to the strategy manager or report through an applications development manager. The first issue here concerns span of control.

Even with the relatively simple reporting structure shown in Exhibit 3, the strategy manager has five direct reports, as well as the program management and finance and policy groups. This is often near the limit of effectiveness of the strategy manager. Second, experience suggests that the applications often have a natural set of related concerns that are best resolved by bringing them together under one individual who makes the decisions necessary to get the job done. A common example of such a concern is the need to move resources between different application teams. Each team manager may have difficulty giving up the resources, but the applications development manager can take the broader view of what is best for the suite of applications as a whole, and can make the hard decisions on moving resources.

Technical Manager

The technical manager is responsible for delivering the technical components of the application. As noted, larger projects will most likely have a function or role concerned with overall architecture strategy. On projects of the size discussed here, the technical or technology manager will handle overall architecture questions, working between groups and within his or her own group. A number of key technological areas report to this manager

- *Architecture.* The architecture function is responsible for the delivery of key architecture components, including the development and execution architectures.
- *Data.* Netcentric projects often involve difficult decisions about the design and allocation of data across multiple nodes and between multiple applications. Often these decisions must be made at the conceptual, logical, and physical levels. There also may be difficult data administration and security demands. Responsibility for addressing these issues falls under the data area.
- *Network.* The logical and physical networks play a dominant role in netcentric development. There should be a group devoted to the design and implementation of these networks, and it should report to the technical manager.
- *Operations.* The operations group has responsibility for implementing the operations architecture. Often, the operations group is also responsible for operating the system in the first few iterations as the system rolls out. Experience shows that an operations group, knowing that it will have to operate what it implements, tends to produce better answers. As suggested elsewhere the operations architecture is very dependent on the definition of Service-Level Agreements (SLAs) and Operational Level Agreements (OLAs). Also, this group has extensive interaction with the Architecture group described previously.

Some interactions among these groups should be noted. Both the data group and the network group, for example, can be used to illustrate some worthwhile points. First, although these groups report to the technical manager, their work lies in working with the applications. As a result, most of their time should be spent moving among the applications where they are responsible for the data design and network design for the applications. This responsibility includes ensuring the quality of the design, its timely delivery, and the design's ability to meet current demands and evolve for the future. Further, much of the evaluation of the individuals' contribution to the effort should be made by the application team managers with whom they work.

The groups report to the technical manager primarily because much of what they decide has a significant impact on the overall technical approach. Changes are best addressed through the technical manager.

Second, because the groups report to the technical manager, they have a person who can resolve conflicting technical issues. For example, if the data design group comes up with a database design that must pump large volumes of information through the network, causing unanticipated impacts on network performance, it may be left to the technical manager to resolve the conflict.

Change Management

Change management is responsible for moving the user community through the change process. In this role, change management must interact a great deal with the applications group. However, change management must be viewed by the business community as a conduit to make sure that concerns and issues are being heard, and that changes are made based on the trial, evaluation, and ongoing use of the systems.

In some cases the change management group has reported through an entirely different line, often the user community structure. The risk with that reporting structure is that the change management group may become a defender of the status quo rather than an active advocate for change.

Site Preparation

The site preparation group is responsible for preparing the site for a release of the applications. In this role the group addresses the management of the upgrade of each site and the installation of hardware, applications, and procedures in preparation for taking the site live in the rollout process.

Rollout

The rollout group has responsibility for ensuring that the systems function successfully as each site comes on line, which often means managing conversion of data, completion of go-live checklists, and completion of any miscellaneous tasks that are still outstanding. With early sites this group may be physically present as the site goes live. However, as experience builds, this group can increasingly work from a remote site and still deliver successful installations.

This management structure is a basis from which a project can develop a structure appropriate for its own unique circumstances and needs. The process of defining such a structure can be time consuming and difficult because of the many concerns that organizational change bring about. However, it is fair to say that without an appropriate organizational structure the question of success in implementation will be left too much to chance.

The remainder of this chapter walks through each of the development streams (reproduced in Exhibit 4). More detail on most of these streams is found in the remaining chapters of Section III.

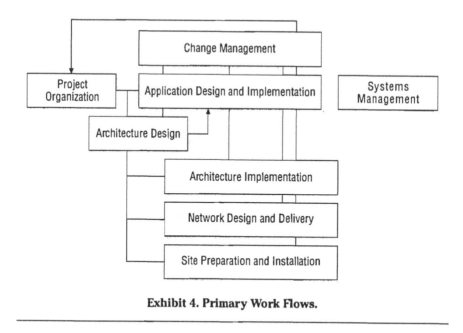

Exhibit 4. Primary Work Flows.

CHANGE MANAGEMENT

The cost and difficulty of netcentric and client/server computing can be justified only if the organization is fundamentally changing its business processes. Business process reengineering reflects changes in the roles, responsibilities, and rules that define a business. New processes are essential for any organization attempting the implementation of netcentric computing.

To define the reengineered business process, the first thing needed is an understanding of the business, the information technology, and what the technology can do for the business. The organization must analyze the business process and each of its steps, asking why and how they contribute to the business. Only then can a reengineered process emerge.

The most difficult part of business process reengineering is getting the users to accept the new process. Business users must change their behaviors — change the manner in which they perform the process — or reengineering will fail. Successful reengineering and netcentric implementation require an extensive change management effort.

The first major segment of work is to define the new business organization. The next work segment is to design the specific work roles in terms of daily tasks and deliverables. Finally, training is defined that ensures that the business user can take on and fulfill the newly defined roles.

Where Does Change Management End and Systems Development Begin?

Change management includes ensuring user awareness and knowledge and conducting trials and evaluation of the reengineered work process. These tasks are some of the most challenging and creative jobs to be found in netcentric solution delivery today.

The real difficulty is defining where the responsibilities for change management end and where the role of the systems developers begins. There can be an overlap between what the change management personnel and the systems-building personnel address in their respective work.

In essence, both groups are making commitments on what the system will do. It is important that these work efforts be coordinated and managed. The key to avoiding the potential overlaps is to have the change management and systems people sit down and determine explicitly what each group will deliver separately, and what deliverables will result from joint efforts.

It is worthwhile to note that change management applies as well to the Information Systems (IS) person involved in a netcentric effort. The objective of IS change management is to complete the learning curve in the application of netcentric computing. Today, netcentric computing technology, although an evolution from client/server, is still new and different for many IS professionals. Thus, the change management effort may be significant and difficult. This effort tends to be overlooked or treated in an ad hoc fashion. This is unfortunate because netcentric technology can succeed only if systems personnel are well informed, trained, and experienced.

ARCHITECTURE DESIGN AND IMPLEMENTATION

Technical Architecture Development

The design architecture work segment refers to making the many decisions about hardware, systems software, and networking. The decisions made in the design architecture work segment of Exhibit 4 form the basis for building the infrastructure of tools, standards, and methodology (the implement architecture segment) that the systems builders need.

Included in the technical architecture are the following:

- Going-in positions on hardware platforms to be allocated by site.
- Associated decisions of operating systems, graphical user interfaces (GUIs), and network strategy.
- Decisions related to the database management system (DBMS) and development tools and languages.
- Positions on the intent to provide support for the developer and user. For example, will the design environment be highly integrated with the implementation environment? Will a repository strategy be used?

What testing facilities and capabilities are to be provided? What training and help facilities are to be provided?

- The implemented infrastructure that will be used to connect applications to the technologies. This infrastructure is usually packaged as a set of services and application programming interface (APIs) for use by applications developers.

The following are some additional architectural considerations:

- Two key considerations of netcentric architectures are scalability and openness. Architectures must be built to be able to quickly accommodate rapid changes in end user populations and data volumes. Additionally, architectures should take into account the type of access requirements that might be possible in the future (e.g., how to support hand-held devices or CTI).
- Architecture and performance go hand in hand. The best architecture is achieved by a smart architecture design. One of the key roles of an architect, whether that is a technical or systems architect, is to make tough decisions and manage the juggling act of systems development. For example, the level of quality of graphic images transmitted over the network will have dramatic effects on response time. If the network is of medium bandwidth, this will be a significant issue, because slow response times will be noticeable. In this case there is a tradeoff between quality, which is a usability issue, and network bandwidth utilization. The higher level of interaction, and the greater number of components in the system, the greater the juggling act.
- Good design is crucial for scalability. For example, components developed locally on a single machine may run properly during testing but perform miserably once distributed across machines. A good design will show which components will be distributed and how distributed components should communicate effectively.

Platform Architecture

One of the most common yet difficult questions organizations have when moving to netcentric computing centers on the platform architecture — the technology to select. Exhibit 5 provides a framework with which to evaluate the technology decisions.

This exhibit portrays at a high level the concept of a layered technical architecture. Fundamental technology decisions are needed to define a technology architecture and to address the following:

- Operating system
- System software, including DBMS, transaction monitor, and work flow
- Networking
- GUI

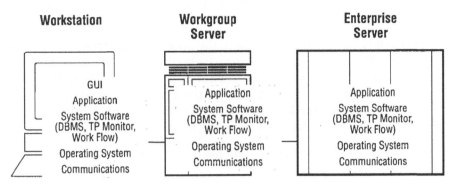

| **Workstation** | **Workgroup Server** | **Enterprise Server** |

Exhibit 5. A Framework for Evaluating Platform Technologies.

After these decisions have been made, the next step is a set of decisions on development tools and systems management approaches. These decisions in turn lead to a development architecture and an operations architecture.

These decisions are difficult to make because, in an open systems environment, there are often many options to consider. For example, there may be four to five hardware vendors, an equal number of networking vendors, two to three operating system strategies, four to five DBMS vendors, and two to three GUI vendors from which to choose.

The number of possible combinations of solutions could reach into the thousands. At a minimum, IS should focus on those components that affect the enterprise's ability to interoperate or share data across departments. If possible, IS should define, at the enterprise level, those components that allow departments to share information.

For example, mixed hardware such as RISC and CISC processors can present ongoing problems with sharing data because of basic dissimilarities in bit patterns. Different networks in different departments present ongoing problems when those departments want to share data. Different DBMSs present basic problems when there is a desire to access one department's information from another department. In each case, a means can be found to circumvent these problems, and systems integrators are widely involved in solving them. However, if IS sets basic guidelines on what constitutes a consistent technical architecture, it does not need to find or pay for workarounds.

Most enterprises, unfortunately, end up with incompatible technical architectures. Many factors contribute to that result, particularly legacy decisions. IS personnel contribute to the problem when they take too long to come to a decision about the technical architecture. When that happens, the end-user community often goes ahead without IS involvement. Therefore, the major reason to focus on interoperability as a criterion for technology decisions is to define a minimal subset of all the decisions so that they can be made more quickly and cohesively.

This ability to have options is both the good news and the bad news of netcentric. The good news is that many technologies are available. The bad news is that an organization has to choose from among them. It is also important to note that many IS organizations are not structured to make technology choices and decisions. They are accustomed to sole sourcing most, if not all, of their technology from a single vendor.

The following are important additional points about vendors in a netcentric environment:

- Developing applications with tools that are "bleeding edge" is difficult. Much of the environment changes quickly, there is little expertise to leverage and vendors are focused on bringing products to market and not on supporting and stabilizing existing products. In addition, all of the vendors for your project cannot be expected to be in synch with their product releases. Expect delays.
- Vendor management is important and difficult in rapidly changing netcentric product marketplace. It is important to understand a vendor's motivation as well as to spend the time to build a relationship. Many vendors are new and are not well organized to deal with the myriad of support issues that can arise. However, even well-established vendors may have difficulty with support. This is an interesting paradox. Choosing a very successful product or vendor may mean that its support is stretched. In either case, plan for higher levels of vendor management.
- Internet product development life cycles make "analysis paralysis" a real risk. Products are being developed and released by vendors at a tremendous rate. However, waiting around for the latest and greatest product to hit the market can spiral into a long analysis phase waiting for the best fit software. Be decisive.
- Allot time in the workplan to deal with vendor code problems. This is especially true when dealing with products that are new to the market place. Test early.

Operations Architecture

The design operations architecture and implement operations architecture work segments address the steps needed to put the systems management approach in place. It should be started early in the project life cycle — after the technical architecture decisions have been made and as the functional capabilities and requirements of the application are beginning to be defined. Project teams must be careful not to underestimate the work load.

Information on functional capabilities and requirements — as well as technical requirements such as performance, availability, and reliability — is needed to help determine service-level agreements. The service level agreement is key to defining and delivering the overall systems management architecture.

When the decisions on the overall systems management architecture have been made, implementation work begins. This is often a matter of purchasing individual tools and integrating them. Included in this effort is the definition of help desk features and the beginning of training and actual implementation of the help desk, along with other support components.

Delivery of Infrastructure

When making decisions on the technical architecture, IS must begin thinking in terms of what reusable components the enterprise must build to make the technical architecture usable by developers and business users. These enterprise-built reusable components are what is called infrastructure.

In a traditional IS shop, guidelines for designers and programmers are often referred to as the development standards. Equivalent guidelines are needed for netcentric computing. Indeed, the equivalent may be even more critical because often the designers and programmers do not have the experience in advanced client/server to fill in the gaps.

Some of these standards are addressed by the methodology decision, but many are not. For example, standards for the input/output design of applications using a GUI may be needed. Programming and design standards for workstation environments may be required. Time and effort can be saved if the execution architecture discussed throughout this book is used (Exhibit 6.)

Such an architecture must be established, defined, and explained to developers as a consistent framework for all developers to use. After this infrastructure is defined, developers must select or create tools to provide the components, as well as develop designer and programmer guidelines and training in how to use the infrastructure.

APPLICATION DESIGN AND IMPLEMENTATION

Five major activities are conducted in the design applications and implement applications work segments:

- User requirements
- Requirements analysis
- Applications design
- Technical design
- Development planning

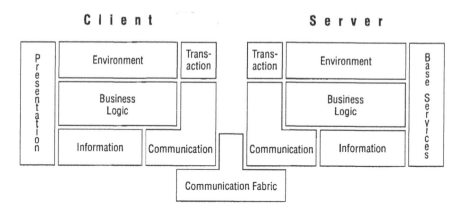

Exhibit 6. Netcentric Execution Architecture.

These are, of course, the traditional tasks — the actual work of building the system — found in any systems development. The fact that these are now just one part of a much larger effort points to the additional work required for a netcentric project.

In release testing, work is completed to ensure that all components come together as a complete, cohesive, and working system. By definition, netcentric systems run in the business environment, perhaps thousands of miles away from the systems developers. Furthermore, if an organization bases a new business process on the system, the business could then become critically dependent on the system. Releasing a system that is not completely tested would be damaging.

Tests are needed to ensure that

- The application works as a whole
- The infrastructure and technical architecture to be released are the ones on which applications have been running
- The installation procedures are usable by someone at the local site
- All the support mechanisms are in place to keep the applications running smoothly

Any emergency procedures or error recovery procedures should be tested to determine whether they are understandable and workable by people at the local site. End-to-end performance must be addressed at this time to ensure that the SLAs are met. In addition, operations and help desk procedures should be tested to ensure that they perform as expected.

A common way to test all the above is by creating a model office environment. This environment includes an office configured as it would be to run the new systems, a network connected to the model office, and a model operations area that reflects the configuration of hardware and systems software found at both the work group centers and the enterprise level.

Release testing can make a significant contribution to the ongoing reliability and usability of the system. At the same time, it is not a trivial effort — it lasts perhaps as much as 2 to 3 months.

NETWORK DELIVERY IN MULTIVENDOR ENVIRONMENTS

The network is the key to making netcentric computing happen. Netcentric represents the convergence of communications and computing, so there must be as much focus on the network side as on the computing side. The network design and network implementation work segments should begin once the functional capabilities of the application are known.

Netcentric computing demands a much tighter integration of network and systems design and building compared with traditional development. Careful attention should be paid to the evolving network design and how extensive an upgrade may be needed from current network capabilities.

The difficulty with network delivery is twofold. First, the typical information processing person is not strong in networking knowledge and design. For many years, the proprietary networks associated with traditional technology were largely the domain of the network specialist or the technology provider. The IS person simply provided the network specialist with requirements, and the specialist did what was required to meet the needs.

At the same time, the network specialist is confronted with a new set of terms and concepts for modern networking technology. In addition, the network has such a profound impact on the capabilities of the netcentric solution that network specialists must be brought into the design process much earlier. Often they are the ones to say yes or no to a functional requirement on the basis of the networking capabilities.

The actual delivery of the network usually requires greater lead time to assemble and integrate the required components. With earlier proprietary solutions, the network components usually arrived from the vendor with assurance that the vendor would integrate them after assembly.

In a netcentric environment, components from different vendors usually are being integrated to build and support the network, so effort will be required to ensure end-to-end consistency, performance, and fault management. There may also be a need to upgrade the overall network, which can greatly lengthen delivery time frames and costs. Even as the components are assembled and tested, it is common to encounter miscellaneous problems that take extended time to resolve. When the network goes into production, ongoing network problem solving may still be necessary to make the network stable.

SITE PREPARATION AND INSTALLATION

Site preparation and installation work refers to the following:

- The process of reviewing sites and determining what is required to prepare them for installation of the advanced client/server or netcentric technology
- The process of readying and installing the sites
- The process of testing an installed site to ensure that it works as expected
- The maintenance of an inventory of the site and its status for running an application until systems management can take over the effort

Some may argue that these efforts are not directly related to netcentric computing. In fact, however, most sites involved in the first-time application of netcentric or client/server technology for business solutions encounter significant and difficult problems at the site preparation stage. If hundreds of sites require upgrades, site installation and upgrade may be the single largest line item in the development budget and may require the longest lead time.

There are many issues in this process of establishing the sites. A first consideration is the state of the current distributed applications. If the enterprise has already installed client/server applications, decisions need to be made on using the installed base of technology for future applications. However, for first-time applications, issues need to be resolved regarding the site's suitability to run a netcentric application and to support advanced client/server technology. Site readiness issues include power, air conditioning, and possibly the installation of physical wiring.

Some potential problems may be a surprise. For example, at one manufacturing site, a stamping process created a heavy vibration that required additional protection for disk drives. Another site was next to a radio station, which created potentially damaging electromagnetic fields. Such issues as these need to be addressed before they become surprises.

These issues must be recognized and resolved before the purchase and installation of hardware and software. Moreover, revisiting sites to ensure that in the process of building the system, the initial survey/assessment stays up-to-date is an ongoing issue.

There are often issues of arrangements at local sites for local contractors such as carpenters, electricians, and air-conditioning specialists who may need to come to each site to make any necessary changes. Often, there need to be negotiations and ongoing contract management to find parties qualified to do this work. A building contractor may be retained to see the work that is to be done. When many sites are involved, a management challenge arises for which the organization might have little competence. The question of outsourcing vs. insourcing this type of work must be addressed with regard to site upgrades. These questions are addressed in more detail in the Site Preparation chapter.

SYSTEMS MANAGEMENT

Systems management addresses the ongoing operation of the netcentric application when it is in production. A central issue in establishing systems management for netcentric is the definition of service-level agreements.

These agreements are, effectively, commitments to meet certain levels of overall system performance, reliability, and recovery from problems. Until these agreements are defined, it is difficult to resolve questions on those parts of the systems management environment that specifically contribute to meeting and confirming conformance to service-level agreements. These components are the key deliverables from the systems management efforts.

The typical areas that must be addressed as a part of the systems management in a netcentric environment include, but are not limited to, the following:

- Configuration management, which involves managing components found in the application, architecture, and environment, and also managing the status and version of these components.
- Activation and execution of components of the netcentric application and architecture. This activity can include bringing up such on-line and batch components as the DBMS.
- Fault management, which is the determination of fault status, the assessment of reasons for failure, and the initiation of recovery from failure.
- Help desk facilities to answer inquiries from the user and system communities on problems, questions, and steps to recover from problems.
- Determination of performance, reliability, and, potentially, assessment relative to service management contracts.
- Vendor contract management and associated contacts and payments.

Although this list is not complete, it is representative of the range of issues to be addressed when starting with a service-level orientation. For netcentric solutions, many tools are currently available to the systems builder, but most cover a narrow range of demands. In comparison, traditional computing environments offer highly integrated solutions, often as part of the system software.

The cost of preparing solutions for systems management in a netcentric environment is high. Experience suggests that 10 to 40% of the development budget for initial netcentric solutions should be devoted to the delivery of the system management facilities.

At the low end of this range, a strong help desk facility can be built. On the high end, organizations can consider building some sophisticated automated support for ongoing operation and problem resolution in a systems management environment. The risk with regard to this investment is that these technologies are evolving very quickly and thus a custom tool assembled today may be rendered obsolete by commercial products in the future.

PROGRAM MANAGEMENT

A key concept in the netcentric development framework is the just-in-time delivery of components of the parallel work segments. Ideally, people like to do work in a sequential fashion; in today's business environment, this is not practical. Furthermore, it is essential to have results shared between the work segments as the work proceeds. As a result, many of the work segments shown in the netcentric implementation framework should be performed in parallel.

This just-in-time approach, in which several teams must be kept tied together and working as a whole, is a major challenge. To manage the overall effort, a program management strategy must be used that ensures that individual efforts are proceeding according to an overall plan and that the deliveries from each team meet expectations in terms of quality and timeliness.

Program management establishes an overall plan giving expected deliverables and due dates. This plan includes defining the levels of quality that are expected. It includes evaluating the work being done and providing an ongoing assessment of the status of work against plans. Also, if delays become evident, program management sets up contingencies to address delays.

AN ITERATIVE APPROACH TO NETCENTRIC

The return arrow at the top of the netcentric planning chart (see Exhibit 2) signifies that the adoption of netcentric computing requires an iterative approach. Applications have to be delivered to the users in a timely manner, but technology and business needs change rapidly. Iterations provide the opportunity to rethink architectures to determine whether previous decisions and approaches have aged or are no longer valid.

Iterations must be done quickly. According to one view, iterations should be done in six months or less; however, it is difficult to get all of these parallel efforts organized and drawn to a conclusion in six months. A more practical approach is a 12- to 18-month cycle for each iteration, considering the number of parallel work efforts involved.

Managing Parallel Efforts

The execution of a set of parallel efforts as described earlier is inherently a risky process. On occasion, in the rush to meet dates there is a tendency to begin the strands of work with little or no contingency. This is not a good starting position, given the risk inherent in netcentric implementation.

Thus, each strand should have built into its plan a contingency in schedule that will allow it to deal with the unexpected, while not delaying the overall effort. Contingency is not intended to hide mismanagement. Rather, it should be used on a rational basis to cope with the unexpected. Its use should be one of the watch points in the program management effort.

Netcentric computing provides the next level of technology that organizations need to solve the problems of business process reengineering. At the same time, it is a more complex and inherently more difficult technology than traditional computing to implement successfully. It is safe to say that business problems demand that IS address and contain these risks to advance the value of business computing.

Course of Action

For IS, the course of action depends on where the organization is in the application of netcentric technology. The following suggestions apply for organizations just beginning the application of netcentric technology:

1. Choose applications that would benefit from the distinct technology features of netcentric and client/server computing, such as the ability to put processing where it is needed and its inherent communications capability. Publicize that the application is a first delivery of processing capability in a netcentric environment. Ensure real and lasting commitment from the business community and management for the application.
2. Build a team with skills in advanced client/server technology. This can be done through the use of training for in-house personnel and by retaining outside expertise. Ensure that users with credibility in the business world are committed to the effort.
3. Organize an effort such that time and resources are dedicated as follows:

    An overall program plan is created to reflect the interdependencies and contingencies of each team's effort.

The change management team defines the reengineered business process and begins its work activities.

The technical team defines a technical architecture addressing the components of the execution, development, and operations architectures discussed throughout this book.

The design of an application to support the reengineered business process is begun and coordinated with the change management effort.

As business worker requirements for performance and reliability under the reengineered business process begin to appear, a systems management effort should be initiated to build the systems management capability that can determine whether these needs are being met over time.

A network design effort is started that brings on-line the network required to support the effort.

As required, the site evaluation, installation, and delivery effort should be planned so the sites are ready to run the application as it is implemented.

A program management effort can be instituted to ensure that all these strands of work deliver the components needed on a timely basis and at a sufficient level of quality to make for an acceptable application.

CONCLUSION

This chapter has described a set of complex issues, all of which must be addressed to successfully implement a netcentric application. The issues are interrelated.

For example, the change management process can have an impact on many other areas. Thus, not only must the various issues be addressed, but they must be addressed in an integrated fashion. The answers from one strand of the work have to be made available on a timely manner and at acceptable levels of quality for the other strands.

Timely and high-quality delivery does not happen by accident. The delivery must be planned and managed — a complex challenge best addressed through an activity of program management. Essentially, program management addresses the issue of managing multiple strands of parallel but interdependent work. It provides an ongoing assessment of the status, quality, and cost of the work. In terms of addressing all these issues in a timely fashion, the implementation of program management may be a key step in succeeding at netcentric.

Chapter 16

Design and Implementation of Client/Server and Netcentric Architectures

Chapter 15 introduced a framework for client/server and netcentric development. Four of the activities in this framework revolve around the architectures for the implementation and support of client/server applications. The design and implementation of the platform, development, execution, and operations architectures follow similar approaches. The main difference in approaches is the timing of the efforts because of different due dates for final results. Exhibit 1 highlights the development activities in the "architecture stream."

This chapter focuses on the activities and considerations involved in this architecture stream.

PHASES OF DEVELOPMENT

In many ways, the process for architecture development is similar to the process for applications development. Developers identify and collect the requirements for the architecture, create a design for the architecture, and then undertake implementation. Architecture implementation shares a number of issues with applications development. Implementation frequently involves a number of "make vs. buy" decisions, early piloting and prototyping are common, and designing for performance is important. The two phases described in the framework are "architecture design" and "architecture implementation."

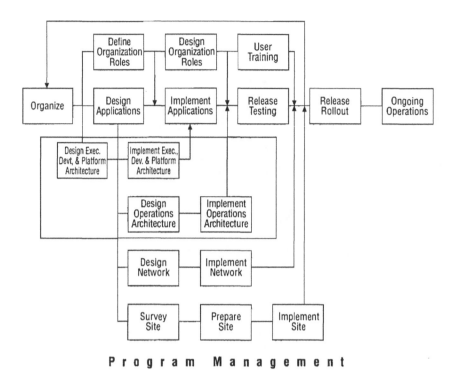

Exhibit 1. Architecture Stream of Client/Server and Netcentric Development.

Architecture Design

This first phase in architecture development is equivalent to the requirements gathering and initial design done for applications development. The first step of this phase, the conceptual design, identifies the broad application styles and describes the corresponding architecture requirements. The business requirements and the vision of how client/server or netcentric applications can help meet these requirements drive these application styles. In addition, developers preliminarily prioritize application styles and architecture capabilities to help sequence the remaining activities.

After they prioritize these application styles, the next step in this phase is to define the architecture at a detailed, logical level. Developers create a description of the types of services and features necessary to support the business applications and recommendations for purchase or development of the various components for the physical implementation.

The detailed execution, development, and operations architectures described throughout this volume are examples of logical architectures created in this phase. They describe general classes of capability with specific types of services or tools and they provide a structure for organizing and implementing these capabilities as well as for communicating them to the appropriate audiences.

Architecture Implementation

This is the actual implementation, along with the supporting documentation and procedures for the various pieces of the architecture. In most cases, these consist of purchased and/or custom-developed tools and services combined with any necessary procedures to support the development and operations process.

ARCHITECTURE DESIGN

There are two primary steps to architecture design:

- Conceptual architecture design
- Detailed architecture design

CONCEPTUAL ARCHITECTURE DESIGN

In the conceptual design phase, the goal is to collect the key architecture requirements, structure, and prioritize them and create or identify any constraints or assumptions that affect the architecture design and implementation. The output, the conceptual architecture, is typically a high-level deliverable that addresses the layers of a business solution and their interaction and is used in the next step of architecture design.

A typical time frame for the development of a conceptual architecture is up to 4 months (with a team of 5 to 10 people), depending on the formality of the process and documentation, the scope of the design, and level of innovation. This step utilizes experienced systems personnel along with representatives from the business community. It is important to ensure that sufficient time is allowed for this activity due to the impact on subsequent work. However, it is also important to avoid falling into "analysis paralysis" as a result of the lack of experience or the rate of change of the technology. Experienced technology and architecture personnel must be available.

At a high-level, the process for defining the conceptual architecture consists of the following three steps:

- Identifying architecture requirements
- Analyzing the requirements and make preliminary decisions
- Confirming suitability of the architecture decisions

Step 1: Identifying Architecture Requirements

The objective of this first task is to articulate the key requirements of the architecture based on the business solution needs.

There are four categories of architecture that provide some structure in analyzing the architecture requirements and facilitate focusing on the important decisions and issues. (For a more detailed discussion of the full enterprise information architecture on which this model is based, see Chapter 3, "Architecture Frameworks for Client/Server and Netcentric Computing.") These four architectural layers are:

- *Business solutions.* This category includes the key characteristics of the business solution and the corresponding requirements on the application. This typically encompasses such business decisions and requirements as providing support for field or mobile professionals, using work flow to automate process control, using knowledge-based software to enable less experienced personnel, or extending the system to the customer.
- *Application architecture.* This layer represents the components that provide the automation support for a business function or activity in the business process (but does not include the platform and cross-application architecture). This layer may include applications that interact directly with the user or batch-type functions that perform a function and/or generate a report.
- *Technical architecture.* Technical architecture is the layer of base software and extensions to system software on which the application is built. It consists of the development architecture, execution architecture, and operations architecture discussed throughout this book.
- *Platform.* Platform includes the core hardware (workstations, servers, and printers), systems software (e.g., operating system, database management system, and transaction processing monitors), and network components (the physical network).

As part of the conceptual architecture definition, each of these layers would be broken out into more detail to clearly define their scope and their relationship to the other layers. The emphasis, however, should be placed on the business solutions and application layers because these have the greatest impact on the design of the technical architecture and on the selection of the platform.

The goal is to identify the key requirements, assumptions, and constraints imposed by these two layers and to make sure that the architecture requirements are tied to specific business and user requirements. The result is a set of "guiding principles" for the architecture design and implementation, which is key in making feature prioritization and product selection decisions.

The business solutions layer is where the following decisions are documented:

- How work flows to achieve a specific outcome
- The types of processing involved
- External dependencies (such as customers and suppliers)
- The organization of the involved work groups and departments (distributed or centrally located)
- The types of business personnel involved in performing the work

These define key characteristics of applications, which in turn define the requirements of the architecture and platform. The most important considerations revolve around decisions that affect:

- The style of processing
- The class of user service
- The degree of distribution of data and processing
- Dealing with existing architectures.

Style of Processing. Client/server and the rapid evolution of technology have made new styles of processing possible, each of which may have different architectural demands. Some of the more common application characteristics (or styles) include the following:

- *On-line transaction processing.* This is the most common application style. It is characterized by simple, routine business events that translate into a single transaction, completed within seconds or minutes after arriving from the user interface. An example of on-line transaction processing is order entry. The basic architecture requirements are typically graphical user interface (GUI) interaction, support for local and remote data access, access to enterprise processing and data, and high-performance control of transactions that may span multiple platforms. The emergence of netcentric widens the implementation choices of this style.
- *Batch processing.* This style is characterized by the lack of a user interface and the need to recover from failures in a timely manner. (Rerunning a complete batch of 1 million items is not very desirable.) Processing usually occurs on groups (or batches) of records/transactions according to a schedule, usually by day. The outputs are typically updated databases, as well as printed reports and documents.
- *Team processing (or work flow management).* These applications support the interaction of teams of personnel to perform business events that are complex and can translate into several transactions which may be processed at different times. The business event involves multiple individuals and may have a long life, typically days or months. Thus, the order in which the related transactions occur cannot be

determined in advance. The user is usually a knowledge worker who has latitude to make routine decisions and who may need a supervisor to review and authorize exceptional cases. An example of team processing is insurance claims processing. These types of applications typically require an architecture to support GUI interaction, work flow, document management (which may include support for image, voice, and video), and perhaps rule-based processing for advising on business rules and decisions.

- *Management and control reporting.* Management and control reporting provides the information that middle management needs to monitor and direct the organization (e.g., general ledger reports, investment performance reports, and case management work flow analysis).

- *Decision support.* This supports unstructured and unpredictable information retrieval by infrequent computer users. Decision support typically integrates information from multiple operational systems and allows users to view it in many different ways.

- *Mobile operation.* Many traditional applications are delivered to a fixed location, usually on a desktop terminal or workstation. With the advent of lighter, portable computers and improved wireless communications, applications can now be delivered to users who are not consistently located in one place. For instance, it is now possible to provide computing support to sales forces and field workers. The typical architectural requirements are GUI interaction (in some cases with pen support), local or standalone operation, dial-in communications support, and support for store-and-forward type messaging (for transactions and electronic mail).

Many applications combine characteristics of several of the types discussed previously. For example, a financial system may have characteristics of transaction processing, batch processing, and work group support applications. Many transaction processing applications and all case processing applications have a strong office component. Thus, the architecture must address the particular mix of application styles that satisfies the user requirements.

Class of User Service. A class of user service defines both a work style and a way for a class of users to interact with a system. If there are several classes of users, there are likely to be multiple architectural traits.

For instance, a patient care system to be used by physicians, nurses, and administrative personnel has several levels of capability. Physicians are mainly interested in reading information; they are typically not interested in spending time being trained on a workstation. Thus, the user interface for physicians must be immediately intuitive and simple. Administrative personnel have more transaction processing to perform; they typically use the application several hours every day and so a training effort can be justified for them. Depending on the hospital's approach to nurses' duties, nurses have requirements somewhere between those of the physicians and administrative personnel. The architecture must thus support several classes of users.

Following are the most common traits that characterize the class of user service:

- Types of users (e.g., mobile vs. stationary, line vs. management)
- Response times required
- Types of inputs and outputs (e.g., forms, images, and queries)
- Scheduled system availability and recovery time (in the case of failures)
- Level of security
- Data integrity and timeliness of data synchronization
- Process and data volumes

As with the style of processing activity, an objective of identifying the classes of user service is to ensure important requirements are addressed and to avoid unnecessary architectural features. For instance, an organization should not provide multimedia capability unless the users need it or sophisticated on-the-fly recovery processes if 24-hour recovery is sufficient.

Degree of Distribution. Another key influence on the architecture is the degree of distribution of processing and data. Starting with the requirements of the business, decisions need to be made as to where data will reside and where processing logic will reside. For example, will customer data reside centrally or be distributed to the local organizations serving a group of customers? Will transaction control occur on a client or server platform? Will reports be generated centrally or on work group servers?

These decisions (especially data distribution) can have significant impact on the architecture. For instance, an organization may choose remote data management instead of distributed logic. This decision affects the database decision and the need for a middleware package. Similarly, having to support synchronized, distributed data instead of a single copy results in a very different set of architecture requirements.

Dealing with Existing Architectures. In some cases, the organization implementing a system may have one or more existing processing environments that satisfy a need of the new architecture. In such cases, it is important to confirm whether these existing processing environments (and their associated architectural components) satisfy the requirements posed by the new styles of applications and classes of user service. There may be new classes of user service. For example, a traveling sales force must be supported in addition to stationary telephone sales clerks, or the telephone sales clerks require response times not currently supported by existing processing environments. If these new classes of service are present, developers must identify and document any additional requirements during the conceptual architecture phase.

Step 2: Analyzing Requirements

At this point, the developer has identified the key requirements for the architecture. They must now analyze these requirements to make initial decisions on the direction of the architecture and possible approaches for its design and implementation (make vs. buy, possible products, and so forth).

A common approach is to start with the deliverables that articulate the following:

- The various platforms (workstation, departmental server, and enterprise server)
- The types of processing and data they will host
- The interactions between these platforms

Working through each platform in turn, developers identify the key requirements and use them to identify options. On the workstation, for example, the requirement is for delivering a GUI application that integrates with a rules-based engine and can access departmental data and enterprise data.

Using in-house knowledge, outside experts, vendors, and information systems publications, developers identify options for satisfying these requirements. In some cases, many options exist, and the evaluation list may be initially pruned down by high-level criteria such as cost, vendor size, or vendor reputation to keep it manageable. In other cases, few or no products may be available. Thus, developers must consider a custom design and implementation.

In either case, the objective is to identify the options so that the design effort can be estimated and planned. Concurrently, developers should prioritize the architecture features because the effort, cost, and risk for a complete client/server architecture is likely to be too high to be palatable in a single "big bang" approach. The prioritization identifies the work that must be completed initially and then must be followed by iterations to implement the remaining functions (over one or more iterations).

Finally, although the business requirements should drive the architecture, it is important not to ignore the standards and direction of the information systems (IS) organization that play a part in such things as interoperability and maintainability. At this stage of the architecture development, it usually suffices to identify the IS principles and standards that should be taken into account during the architecture design. Examples of these principles and standards could include the following:

- The ability to operate over the standard organizational network (e.g., TCP/IP)
- Preferred database management system (DBMS) and access method (e.g., structured query language, or SQL)
- Choice of end-user workstation (PC running Windows 98 or Windows NT or an OS-neutral client running a browser and Java)
- Preferred development language (e.g., Visual Basic or COBOL) or mixture of languages (e.g., Java user interface with COBOL business and data access logic)

The intent is to provide some considerations that are not directly business related to help make the right decisions during the architecture design.

Step 3: Confirming Suitability

Once developers have collected and analyzed the architecture requirements, it is important to come back and confirm that the architecture direction supports the business and application requirements with an appropriate level of complexity and effort, that is, it is important that the architecture be neither "overboard" nor "underboard."

It is useful to look at the architecture from a broader perspective to ensure its suitability to the project and the enterprise. Experts can help analyze options and confirm choices. In addition, it is useful to review the analysis and choices with corporate IS, project management, users, and other stakeholders. In preparation for these reviews, it is important to understand the expectations and values of all the stakeholders and objectively assess how the conceptual architecture stacks up against these expectations. Some common questions in preparation for this process include the following:

- Are all the processing environments necessary, or is there a way to consolidate some of them (potentially reducing the number of distinct architecture components to be built and supported)?
- Is the degree of distribution warranted by the application's requirements, keeping in mind the costs and complexity associated with building and supporting distributed data and processes (e.g., issues of data integrity)?
- Does the architecture direction meet unique application requirements (user requirements, quality requirements)?
- Is the direction compatible with existing architectures in the organization and corporate standards?
- Will the direction allow for a proper fit with existing applications?
- Is the direction in step with market directions, and will it provide the required longevity?

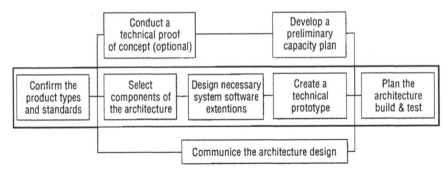

Exhibit 2. Detailed Architecture Design Process.

DETAILED ARCHITECTURE DESIGN

The focus of this step of the architecture design phase is the detailed architecture design. The objective is to design a technically feasible, affordable architecture that supports the application's requirements and is consistent with corporate standards and directions. Ideally, architecture development leads the applications development and rollout. However, project schedules do not always accommodate this. In such cases, where application work is occurring concurrently, this phase also identifies the boundary and interaction between the application and the architecture and articulates them so that application design can begin. The detailed architecture design process (see Exhibit 2) consists of the following activities, discussed in more detail throughout the remainder of this chapter:

- Confirm the product types and standards.
- Select components of the architecture.
- Conduct a technical proof of concept (optional).
- Develop a preliminary capacity plan.
- Design necessary system software extensions.
- Create a technical prototype.
- Plan the architecture build and test.
- Communicate the architecture design.

Confirm Product Options and Standards

The conceptual design for the architecture, created earlier in this phase, primarily addresses the following:

- The types of products (e.g., Windows-based workstation, mainframe server, relational DBMS, UNIX operating system)
- Any relevant standards to be used (e.g., SQL in the DBMS domain, TCP/IP for networking)
- Potential products that should be considered during the design

The first activity of detailed design confirms these going-in positions. For each processing environment, the direction established by the conceptual design is updated, based on several factors.

Architecture Direction. Confirmation of the conceptual architectures may have adjusted the processing environments, system topology, or degree of distribution. Adjust the hardware, system software, and network direction as required.

More Detailed Application Requirements. If applications development is occurring in parallel (as is common), preliminary results may be available from the user requirements or quality requirements-gathering activities. These results should be used to confirm and adjust the architecture direction as required. If the system cannot meet any application requirements, it is important to provide early feedback to the analysts with suggested standards that will conform to the architecture direction.

Technology. If a significant amount of time has passed since the completion of the conceptual design (perhaps 6 months or more), it is important to account for any market or technology changes (e.g., new vendors or alliances). All relevant areas need to be addressed, including

- Hardware for workstations and servers
- Operating system software
- User interface management software
- Data management software
- Network components and connectivity software
- Programming languages
- Tools (development and system operations)

Select Components of the Architecture

The objective of this activity is to evaluate and select products for the architecture. The selection process begins by establishing firm requirements and evaluation criteria. Requirements should cover the aspects of hardware, software, training and consulting support, and operations support. Evaluation criteria typically include the following:

- Economic criteria (including rollout costs)
- Technical criteria
- Business criteria (vendor stability, reputation, reliability)
- Ease of operation
- Previous experience with the vendor
- Availability of support for vendor's products

Section II of this book describes, in detail, considerations for each area of the technical architecture, and these should be utilized as input to this evaluation preparation process.

Depending on the component and volume, a request for proposal (RFP) may be appropriate to communicate requirements and evaluation criteria to prospective vendors. Initially, an RFP gives a vendor the data required to prepare a proposal. Later, it is a framework for checking the completeness of proposals. In today's client/server market, it is often unlikely that a single vendor can respond to a complete RFP. As such, it may be necessary to create separate RFPs for individual components of the architecture.

When an RFP is not necessary or appropriate, communicating the requirements and evaluation criteria to vendors is useful for letting them know of the organization's interest and soliciting their assistance in evaluating their product. The time required to select architecture components varies depending on how new or unfamiliar the components and vendors are, the amount of earlier selection work done, and the degree of innovation and complexity in the environment. If a proven environment is used, this activity requires relatively little time (perhaps 6 to 8 weeks). In a new or innovative environment, significant time (as much as 6 months) may be required to select and acquire the necessary components because more validation is required.

For projects that are going to use leading-edge and unproven hardware and system software, or when the company is integrating many products from different vendors, it is essential to conduct technical proof of concept tests. These ensure that the resulting architecture will perform as expected before finalizing all the decisions and negotiating final contracts. In addition, when performance is a key issue, it may be necessary to benchmark the winner or leading contenders from the evaluation process to confirm suitability and to provide capacity planning information.

For each product, the organization should finalize choices for specific product models, options, sizes, and releases based on the following:

- The unique requirements of the application
- The schedule for the project and the system rollout
- The results of any testing done to date (product testing or technical proof of concept)

Throughout this activity, it is important to manage the process carefully. Project managers should communicate effectively with vendors and upper management and document the whole process rigorously. This helps eliminate mixups and later challenges to their decisions (which can start this process all over).

Technical Proof of Concept

In today's fast-paced technical environments, it is always prudent to conduct a technical proof of concept. The newness and multitude of products and technologies being integrated and the many ways these products can be used (sometimes never intended or envisioned by the vendor) make it difficult for vendors to know whether their product will work with the various other products required to meet the functional requirements.

It is not uncommon with newer products or environments to end up with a product combination that has never been used before. In these situations, project managers should conduct more extensive proof of concept tests to ensure successful end-to-end connectivity and interaction of components.

Most of the time, this activity is performed prior to finalizing the selections. However, the resulting environment setup is usually maintained and used to allow new versions of products to be installed, integrated, and tested prior to being incorporated into the architecture being used by the rest of the project.

Finally, project management needs to monitor the scope of these proof of concept activities closely. It is easy to fall into the trap of perpetual evaluation. This results in an environment that is more of a "play/experiment" environment than one focused on assessing areas of critical risk from a product integration and compatibility standpoint. As such, it is important not to initiate any proof-of-concept activities without specific goals, objectives, a plan, and a schedule. Then it is important to track progress closely to ensure that goals are met on a timely basis.

System Software Extensions

The purpose of this activity is to identify any missing functions in the selected system software environment and to design or select additional software to provide these missing functions. An example of this might be security extensions to the selected GUI tool and desktop to allow applications and fields to be enabled/disabled based on user privileges.

This task may not be necessary if the selected system software provides the required capability or if an existing set of system software extensions (an existing technical architecture) can be used. This task generally becomes critical when working with new and unfamiliar hardware and system software or with system software that does not provide a full set of basic services.

Technical Prototyping

The purpose of prototyping the technical architecture components is to reduce uncertainty and to identify potential problems before the cost of rework is too great. This is especially important in an environment with new or unfamiliar hardware, system software, or architecture components. The prototyping should be detailed enough to reveal subtle problems and to ensure that requirements can be met using the selected products and approaches. In contrast with the proof of concept performed earlier to confirm the considered products' compatibility, the technical prototype is an evolving product used to test new ideas or risky areas of the architecture.

The benefits of performing a technical prototype include developing skills for the project team and risk (rework) reduction, both of which improve the team's ability to meet the implementation estimates.

Preliminary Capacity Planning

The capacity requirements estimated at this stage are used as input to make preliminary decisions on the specific sizes of hardware and network components. Project management revisits these decisions in the architecture implementation phase and during application construction.

The objective of this initial work on capacity planning is to help define any constraints within which the application must operate. The resulting constraints affect the later implementation of the architecture, the application, and the databases.

For example, in designing a user interface, it is helpful to know the workstation's available memory capacity and central processing unit (CPU) speed and the network load the system can support. If developers determine that the design will not work within these constraints, they must make a decision whether to change the constraints or change the design.

Although this initial capacity planning is necessarily broad, it is also generally shallow. Sometimes characterized as "back-of-the-envelope" capacity planning, it typically involves paper analysis or electronic spreadsheet models. In this respect, this effort is not intended to be extremely accurate. Rather, it is a means to determine an order of magnitude approximation and to confirm that there are no overwhelming problems. (Discovering the need for a hardware platform 10 times larger than anticipated would be an overwhelming problem.)

If developers use an electronic spreadsheet model, it is important they not get caught up in the implied accuracy of such a model. The model is addressing order of magnitude regardless of how many decimal places the spreadsheet can show.

Developers can take several steps during preliminary capacity planning:

- Describe the typical transaction and message profiles — the composition of the work carried out by the system in response to a transaction or message. Factor in the overhead required by the architecture, for example, to access configuration data or support processes that reside on a remote platform.

- Use the available information on business process volumes to estimate transaction arrival rates and network message rates. Extrapolate from the current system volumes where appropriate (e.g., if the new and the old systems are similar implementations). Factor in growth projections.
- Use volume information from the data design to estimate database sizes. This affects database server sizing and, potentially, the number of platforms required to handle the database size and transaction volume.
- Look at existing network traffic and utilization to assess the kind of capacity available if the network is not being replaced or upgraded.
- Take into account the impact on the GUI tool of large windows or large numbers of windows and what this does to response time and platform requirements. Also consider any graphics or media that will be required to be transferred over the network to the GUI platform (because these can add several thousand bytes to a message).
- Combine this information with prior experience, published data, or information from reference sites to estimate hardware and network size requirements.

It is important to use information coming from the technical prototype in estimating capacity and performance of the system because these numbers more closely reflect the final system (as opposed to a paper model based on other systems). It is also useful for developers to continue to refine the model as they acquire more knowledge about platforms, users, and applications.

The amount of time spent in capacity planning varies depending on a number of factors:

- The degree of experience with the selected hardware and system software
- The importance of performance to the success of the project
- The perceived likelihood that performance requirements can be met
- The sensitivity of the business case to capacity requirements

Finally, although the main focus of the capacity planning activity should be the production environment, it is important to consider the development environment and its operation too. In other words, developers must consider the development hardware, system software, and network components that are required by the builders of both the architecture and the application to ensure that the current plans are adequate. Providing insufficient capacity in the development environment can affect developer productivity, which in turn can affect the development effort and time frame negatively.

Communicating the Architecture Design

Applications development activities are generally occurring in parallel with the architecture development efforts. Thus, it is important to proactively communicate decisions and status information to personnel outside of the architecture team.

Executive or Management Summary. A high-level summary of the architecture design is recommended to communicate architecture capability to management personnel. It is important to ensure that management understands the importance of the architecture and its progress to date. This summary is also useful for providing an overview of the architecture to the applications development team.

Architecture Designs. Developers should provide design documentation similar to what would be provided for an application design. The primary users of this documentation are the personnel who build and test the architecture components. The level of detail required varies depending on the continuity of personnel between the architecture design and architecture implementation phases. In addition to documenting the components, it is important to document key design issues and the rationale for resolving these issues.

Proof-of-Concept, Technical Prototype, and Capacity Planning Results. The results of these activities should be documented, including the approach taken as well as the conclusions and findings.

Standards. The organization should document the information needed by application designers and developers. This should include the following:

- Functions provided by the technical architecture components
- Application program interfaces to the execution and operations architecture components
- Standard dialog flows to be supported
- Standard program types
- Program models and templates to be provided
- Standards on how to use system software components, including things to do as well as things not to do

Planning the Architecture Implementation Phase

After the technical architecture components have been designed and prototyped, it is important to reassess the approach and effort for building and testing these components. Project managers must prepare a plan that identifies the sequence for proceeding, keeping in mind the dependencies among architecture components and the schedule requirements of the applications developers.

Estimating the effort is generally done "bottom-up." In other words, project managers create estimates for the implementation of each component and roll them up into higher-level units.

For second-time implementations and those based around mature tools, the effort required for the architecture implementation phase is smaller. For first-time implementations or those using new tools, this effort may be substantial and may require additional architecture team skills and resources to meet schedule requirements.

It is important to include sufficient time and budget for architecture testing as well as development and delivery of training for the applications developers. Once project managers produce estimates, they create a schedule for the implementation based on these estimates and a realistic assessment of the available resources (and practical limits on team size).

When scheduling an implementation, especially a first-time implementation, it is essential to address key risk areas prior to the beginning of the application construction phase. The only exception occurs if the chosen platform and architecture have a proven record and experienced personnel have been assigned to the project. In addition, the project team needs to understand the scheduling risks and plan contingencies accordingly.

Considerations for Managing Architecture Risk

Throughout the architecture design and implementation phases, it is important to identify and assess the overall architectural risks. The most common risks involve the following:

- Using a new product or new approach.
- A lack of sufficient vendor support or skills in a product.
- Trying to integrate products from multiple vendors.
- Using products on a different or larger scale than they have been used before.

The project team must recognize these risks and address them throughout the architecture development. There are several ways to address the identified risks, and the various approaches may be used in combination.

Manage Innovation. As much as possible, the project team should use existing architectures or similar experiences to avoid the risks associated with innovation. Projects involving architectural innovation may be subject to high risk and need to have budget and schedule contingency to compensate for the risk. This is not to say that innovation should be avoided at all costs; rather, it must be managed and applied where it makes sense, not just where it might be "interesting." In addition, project managers need to assign higher-skilled resources to the team to help reduce the risk.

Reference Sites. The team should discuss risks with current users of a product. This may not be relevant if the project is scheduled to be the beta site for the product. However, other beta sites may exist that are further along.

Prototype. The team must develop a working example of the risk-related function or component to evaluate whether the product works as specified, the interfaces are stable and maintainable, and the new features are worth using for the application. The scope of prototyping clearly determines the resources required, but prototyping costs less than substantial redesign work later in the project.

Benchmarking. Benchmarking is an expensive option, usually used to evaluate hardware and system software performance under a unique work load. Benchmarking may be used to help choose between hardware and system software finalists when performance requirements are likely to push the capabilities of the current technology.

The project team may be able to have each vendor benchmark and demonstrate at the vendor's facilities a standard application developed for or by the project team. This procedure lowers the hardware resource costs of the project.

ARCHITECTURE IMPLEMENTATION

Considerations for architecture implementation are similar to those for application implementation: Products must be installed and tested; a collection of modules must be coded, tested, and documented; and training/support must be provided — although now for applications developers and operations personnel instead of end users.

Exhibit 3 highlights aspects of the architecture implementation process that are critical to client/server and netcentric implementations. The implementation of the architecture has the same objectives as do the application programs, and the management, review, and control techniques the application phase uses are also applicable to architecture implementation.

Because installing and testing software or coding and testing software is no different in the case of architecture, this section discusses the following considerations, specific to architecture implementation:

- *Testing the architecture.* The bulk of the complexity is in the end-to-end assembly testing and performance testing.

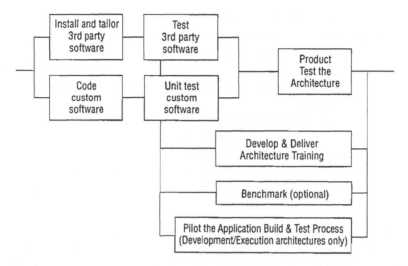

Exhibit 3. Highlights of the Architecture Implementation Process.

- *Developing and delivering architecture training.* This is important to ensure the successful and effective utilization of the architecture by the users of the architecture — the applications developers and systems operation personnel.
- *Benchmarking the architecture.* Benchmarking is an optional activity when performance of the system is critical and when performance estimating is either not accurate or shows marginal results.
- *Piloting the application build-and-test process.* This is mostly relevant for the development and execution architectures, and is an important step in "shaking down" the environment the first time through. (The operations architecture is piloted during the application operational readiness testing before rollout.)

Testing the Architecture

Testing the architecture involves the following activities:

- Testing the functions and features to ensure they are behaving as expected
- Assembly testing to ensure all components are working correctly together without unintended, negative side effects
- Performance or stress testing to ensure the architecture meets its performance criteria

Throughout all these testing stages, it is important to pay attention to the architecture's ability to meet its objectives, in particular:

- *Performance.* Even if the project team has performed a benchmark, it is important to track performance characteristics and to fix performance problems in a timely fashion.
- *Reliability.* As much as possible, the project team should test boundary conditions to ensure that the architecture components perform reliably and with integrity.
- *Usability.* The team should ensure that developers and operators can use the architecture components and that the components support the usability objectives of the application.
- *Flexibility.* The team must ensure that the architecture isolates the effects of changes; the team should test specific portability and interoperability requirements.

Testing the functions of the architecture is a process similar to performing a function test on an application subsystem. Architecture assembly testing is also similar to application assembly testing. In fact, both assembly testing and product testing follow the same basic process for architectures and applications alike. That process includes preparing a test plan, preparing test cycles, executing the test cycles, verifying the results, making changes, and retesting as necessary.

Differences begin to appear, however, because the architecture is used as a base for building applications. As such, architecture assembly testing should test the interaction among components of the technical architecture and between components of the technical architecture and the application.

The goal is not to test applications but to ensure that different components work properly once they are integrated. Several common test cycles are useful for staging the assembly test work of architectures.

Development Architecture. As appropriate, project managers should ensure that different tools developed or acquired (perhaps from different vendors) work properly once integrated. They must be sure that any new tools or procedures added to the development architecture are included in the test. The architecture should be easy to use; a designer or programmer should not have to go through many complicated steps to develop a deliverable, such as a module.

Execution Architecture. It is especially important to test the interaction of components that cross platforms. A good example is a test cycle that requires a workstation to request data from a server. All aspects of the execution architecture (in particular, the information access services and communication services) must work together to fulfill such a request.

Operations Architecture. This is an area in which the project is likely to be using new or custom-developed tools. In an innovative environment, the operations architecture may have to address issues that the system has not previously encountered. For example, a traditional mainframe shop may face a new set of issues when moving to client/server applications running on multiple platforms (in particular, configuration management, data integrity and control, and system administration).

Development and Execution Architectures. Components created or generated from the development architecture must function properly with the execution architecture. For example, a generated dialog should run successfully with the execution architecture. Project managers must also ensure that testing tools work properly with the execution architecture.

Development and Operations Architectures. The components of these two architectures may overlap and interact, in particular the configuration management components. Project managers must ensure that these areas work properly when integrated.

Execution and Operations Architectures. The project team must focus on performance and resource monitoring and tuning, batch services, and error handling. For example, the team must test that performance monitoring hooks included in the execution architecture can properly feed the performance reporting components of the operations architecture.

Development, Execution, and Operations Architectures. Project managers must include test cycles that touch all areas of technical architecture, such as data management. They should use the development architecture to define and populate the test databases and to create data manipulation statements (e.g., SQL). They should use the execution architecture to process the data manipulation request, perhaps crossing platform boundaries. They should use the operations architecture to synchronize multiple copies of data and to test backup/recovery scenarios for the databases.

Entire Technical Architecture and a Piece of the New Application. Project managers should test the application program interfaces (APIs) between the new application and the technical architecture components. Although these tests could include stub programs, ideally they use actual application code being developed as part of a pilot development effort.

Entire Technical Architecture with Existing Systems. Testing must confirm that new or revised software does not have an unacceptable impact on the performance of existing systems. It is also important to verify that the architectures being developed are compatible with other non-application-related software typically found on a user's workstation, such as word processors, spreadsheets, and electronic mail.

Because the architecture is being developed and tested before applications development, a representative piece of the application may not be available in time for such testing or the piloting process described later. If this is likely to be the case, it is important to allow additional budget for building this test/pilot application to ensure that the budget and resources are available.

Develop and Deliver Architecture Training

Successful delivery of an application requires that users of an architecture understand and utilize the architecture effectively. The applications developers, including designers, programmers, and testers, are the primary users of the development and execution architectures. As such, their training should focus on how these architectures are used to design, construct, and test an application.

Training should address the relevant standards to be followed, appropriate shells and templates available, a description of the services offered by the execution architecture and how they should be used, and the capabilities of the testing tools (such as script capture and playback and test data version management). It is especially useful to have sample design specs and programs to help developers understand what an application looks like using the architecture. Developers can then be walked through the creation process to understand how the tools are used.

Operations personnel, the target users of the operations architecture, require training on the procedures and tools available to them. It is generally useful to structure these around common scenarios that they will encounter on a day-to-day basis (e.g., performing backups, shipping out new versions of software, or adding new users). This helps operations personnel understand the various components of the architecture and their capabilities.

Performance Benchmarking

The purpose of performance benchmarking is to verify that system components can perform adequately with expected volumes of activity and data. This is especially important in an innovative environment where the performance characteristics of new products may be unknown or where existing products are going to be subjected to a new type of work load. On the flip side, there is less need to conduct a performance benchmark if the performance characteristics are predictable (e.g., if an existing technical architecture is being used or the type of work load to be processed is similar to existing applications).

Although some benchmark tests may also have been conducted during the hardware and system software selection process, the prior tests were intended to confirm a selection or to help in selecting from multiple alternatives. If earlier tests were conducted, it makes sense to evaluate whether additional benchmark tests are required.

Benchmark tests usually concentrate on areas of innovation or areas identified as problems by performance analysis. Project managers should conduct benchmarks when the project requires a higher degree of confidence than performance analysis provides.

The activities involved in performing a benchmark test are similar to those involved in assembly testing. There are several special considerations for performance benchmarks.

Scope. The benchmarking team should focus on the areas of greatest performance risk and uncertainty. The performance model can help indicate which transactions and processes to benchmark. Team members should document the requirements, goals, and objectives for the benchmark and verify these with the applications development teams, project management, and the operations team. It is important to ensure that there is a clear understanding and agreement as to what the performance goals are and that they are expressed in measurable terms. Only with that understanding can the benchmarking team know if and when those goals are achieved.

For example, a goal of "three seconds end-to-end response" is concrete and measurable, but "acceptable response time" is subjective and open to misunderstandings. If developers have defined service-level agreements for the application, they should be used as a starting point for the benchmarking goals.

Approach. It is usually not necessary to create a great deal of application code. In general, the runtime required by the application's accesses to the database and interprogram communication is likely to make up the vast majority of the runtime for the final application.

It may be possible to use application stub programs or to reuse code being created as part of the application pilot. Alternatively, if the user–interface code is being benchmarked, it is necessary to have actual or test windows that represent the situations under review (e.g., windows with 50 or more entry fields). In this case, however, data and network access may not be necessary. If end-to-end performance in worst-case scenarios must be tested, the actual application or equivalent code must be utilized.

Resources. The benchmarking team must ensure that adequate hardware is available (e.g., sufficient secondary storage for production-size data volumes). Also, the team must ensure that the right software is in place to permit executing tests (such as network simulators and scripting tools) and to monitor and measure performance of hardware, system software, network, technical architecture, and application components. Finally, project managers must assign a sufficient number of personnel to the benchmark to ensure it is performed adequately and that it is practical to act on these recommendations.

Benchmark testing typically requires a standalone environment to ensure isolation from other system activity. This could require configuring additional components, using existing components during off-hours, or a combination of both.

Test Cycles. The test cycles may vary in their specificity. Some test cycles are designed to test a particular architecture component, such as the communication link from a workstation to a server. Other cycles involve observing how the system responds when a high-volume transaction work load is pumped through it.

Repeatability. As with any testing, benchmark tests should be repeatable. This means that it should be possible to rerun a test cycle and get the same results. More important, it means that it should be possible to change the configuration of some component, rerun a test cycle, and accurately measure the impact of the change.

Repeatability should be designed into the test cycles. Also, while conducting the benchmark tests, it is important to control changes to the benchmark configuration to ensure repeatability. After the benchmark has been defined and the tests run, team members should compare the benchmark results to the performance requirements of the area being tested. They should identify, test, and recommend alternatives to alleviate potential performance problems or to reduce the need for additional resources. These alternatives might include the following:

- Changing the application design (e.g., changing the program-packaging model, changing the placement of data or processes, or changing the time periods when components run)
- Changing the database design
- Changing the technical architecture design
- Changing the hardware, system software, or network configuration

Team members should discuss final conclusions with project management and other affected parties, such as applications developers, database administrators, performance analysts, capacity planning group in corporate IS, and IS operations. The team should publish a benchmark report that documents the approach, results, and recommendations from the benchmark effort.

Finally, based on the benchmark results, project managers should review and confirm previous selections of products and vendors and finalize product options and sizes. Although most selections of hardware and system software vendors and products were made in the architecture design phase, some of these selections may have been deferred to this point, when everyone concerned understands the proposed environment. These changes should now be identified. There should be compelling reasons for changes made at this point because any changes are likely to result in significant rework to the architecture and applications.

Pilot the Application Build and Test

The purpose of this task is to let a group of applications developers use the architecture components, tools, and standards to develop a piece of the new application. This pilot is a beta test for the execution architecture, the development architecture, and the associated development process. If there are any problems, they can be identified and resolved early enough so that their impact is minimized. Successful completion of this activity results in a stable and thoroughly tested architecture and development process.

The pilot is different from a prototype. A prototype is usually thrown away, but the pilot is intended to be the first real application area to be developed. It may have to be significantly refined before it is completed, but it is not intended to be discarded.

Six steps are involved in piloting the application build-and-test process.

Step 1: Select a Pilot Application. The selected application area should be a representative sample of the rest of the system. In particular, it should represent the types of components that account for the majority of the development time during the installation phase. If possible, the pilot should also include new hardware or software components that the project team has little or no experience in using.

The capability of the pilot should be as simple as possible while still exercising the complete architecture and the development process. A pilot application with complex capability may cause too much time to be spent resolving functional issues. This slows down the pilot and diverts attention from the primary purpose (testing the development process and the architecture). On the other hand, a single window or dialog probably is not representative enough.

Step 2: Plan the Pilot. Most of the pilot time should be spent on detailed design and programming tasks. Ideally, the pilot can also test out the product test tools and process, but that is a secondary objective.

Depending on the previous experience of the team and the maturity of the environment, the estimating used for the pilot can range from one and a half times the estimates for standard development to 10 or more times the standard estimates. The target should be a small team (two to five developers) working for 4 to 6 weeks to ensure a thorough "shakedown" from the pilot.

Step 3: Staff the Pilot. The team selected to develop the pilot application should possess a blend of business, technical, communication, and interpersonal skills. Their technical skills should be stronger than the average applications developer because the pilot group has to interact frequently with the architecture team. This also allows for faster diagnosis and resolution of architecture problems. Because the developers who work on the pilot are likely to play lead roles during the installation phase, good communication and interpersonal skills are essential.

Step 4: Develop the Pilot Application. It is important to capture the necessary metrics as the pilot application is being developed. Some metrics assist with planning the application implementation work. These include, for example, metrics on productivity rates for developing different types of application components (e.g., windows vs. data access modules vs. server programs). Other metrics assist with measuring the effectiveness of the architecture (e.g., the number of problems identified or the time required to resolve problems).

An effective process should be in place for identifying and managing issues. Developers need a mechanism for recording problems they encounter and managers need a way to authorize problem resolution and assign priorities. The attitude going into the pilot should be one of openness and desire to improve (by both the pilot team and the architecture team supporting the effort). The end result should be an environment that the architects are proud of and an environment that is productive and desired by the applications developer community.

Step 5: Manage the Pilot. Estimating a pilot is difficult, and the results are often not close to the estimates. As a result, the pilot usually becomes an exercise in scope management and prioritization. It will more than likely be necessary for management to revisit the scope of the pilot periodically because the pilot is a learning opportunity for both management and the developers. Similarly, as lessons are learned, it may be necessary to adjust plans to ensure that the pilot is meeting as many of the planned objectives as possible. Finally, it is important to finish a pilot to ensure that the team has exercised the process and tools from end to end.

Step 6: Act on the Results of the Pilot. To maximize the benefits of the pilot, the development team should document and communicate the results. Also, they should communicate issues and status continually. At the conclusion of the pilot, the development team should summarize its experiences, interpret metrics, and make recommendations for the application construction phase. The pilot affects the following areas the most:

- *Standards.* The applications development process is largely documented in standards. The team should update them to reflect the results of the pilot.
- *Development and execution architectures.* The team should update components of the development and execution architectures as required. In particular, the pilot may identify the need for additional development tools or new common routines and services to be included in the architecture. The team should update any accompanying project standards when necessary to reflect changes made to the architecture.
- *Application construction planning.* The results of the pilot should be a key input to the application construction estimating and scheduling activities. The pilot provides productivity metrics and helps management understand and plan for dependencies among components.
- *Training material.* Training for applications developers should be updated to reflect any changes made to the standards and architecture and should share lessons learned in applying the architecture and development process.

The Importance of Continuous Communication

Throughout the architecture implementation process, and especially as experience with the development and execution architectures grows from testing and piloting, it is important to communicate the capabilities and limitations of the architecture to the development team. Guidelines and standards that are part of the development environment should be updated to provide consistent communications.

Implementation Staffing Considerations

Because the architecture is evolving during the pilot application build activity, this activity typically requires applications developers with better than average technical skills. This activity also requires significant architecture team support to ensure effective understanding by the application build team and to provide timely turnaround on problem reports.

Because of the broad coverage of performance benchmarking, this activity requires deep skills in the chosen hardware, system software, network, and application segments being benchmarked. To supplement available skills with the necessary deep, specific skills, the support team may require vendor personnel or contractors. As with the piloting effort, extensive architecture team support is required to ensure that problems are resolved and that any necessary performance enhancements are made to the architecture on a timely basis.

Although sufficiently skilled personnel are important to the success of the implementation activities, there are also opportunities to leverage the existing skills and begin developing additional skilled resources. For instance, during application piloting or benchmark testing, activities such as performing initial tests and rerunning tests do not require the full-time attention of the more experienced team members. Whenever possible, it is prudent to assign personnel to these activities who can take maximum advantage of the learning opportunity and who will be effective at transferring their knowledge to others during the applications development activities.

Other Architecture Development Considerations

Throughout the architecture development process, the enterprise should consider a number of general factors. These include the following:

- Role of the architect
- The effect of innovation and complexity
- The compelling need to stay ahead (of the applications development team)
- Communicating the architecture
- Ongoing architecture support

The remainder of this chapter discusses these key factors and how they affect the planning and execution of the architecture development activities.

Role of the Architect

Based on experience, an architect is crucial to the success of architecture development and to the entire project. The architect primarily leads the architecture development effort but typically gets involved in various aspects of the applications development effort to ensure that the architecture is appropriate, that it is being utilized properly, and that the overall structure and performance of the applications are within the project quality expectations. An effective architect demonstrates the following attributes:

- An ability to integrate information from multiple domains and perspectives into an overall system-level view. Domain knowledge should include
- The business organization and its business processes
- The system's functional requirements
- The selected or comparable hardware and system software

- The selected or comparable development tools and the development process
- The systems operational requirements and expectations

Experience. An architect should have extensive systems development experience (both applications development and architecture development). Experience with client/server and netcentric architecture development is also crucial. The following characteristics are especially important:

- *An ability to develop abstractions or models creatively.* A good architect should be able to create models that capture the essence of complex problems in a simplified way. This allows broader, more complex systems to be undertaken effectively.
- *Outstanding communication skills.* In addition to creating a feasible vision of how the system will work, the architect must be able to communicate this vision effectively to others.

On most successful projects, one person fills the role of architect. In part, this is because it is often difficult to find more than one person with the proper qualifications. However, it is generally desirable to have only one or two people leading the effort because it reduces the time required to formulate a vision and minimizes the chances of conflicting visions. When a project is too big or complex for one architect to lead effectively, it is possible to supplement the chief architect with a team of one or more specialized architects who possess in-depth knowledge of a single domain (e.g., a technical architect, user interface architect, or application architect). Also, the architect and the project manager roles usually require different skills and therefore are usually different people.

Effect of Innovation and Complexity

Projects involving architecture innovation or extensive customization may be subject to high risk because of new and unfamiliar hardware/software, unstable software, or the challenge of being the first to integrate a set of products from multiple vendors. Using one or more of the following techniques, the enterprise should take these risks into account when planning architecture development:

- Allow more lead time for hardware and system software selection. It may take significant time to identify vendors, solicit bids, visit reference sites, and test products working together.
- Allow more time for custom architecture development, because there may be gaps in the coverage of the selected products. This time may be as long as, or even exceed, the time required to develop the application itself. Also, allow for time to update and review the business case. The business case should reflect the costs of development and ongoing maintenance of the custom architecture.

- Allow more time for all forms of testing:
  Proof of concept testing
  Technical prototyping
  Benchmarking
  Assembly testing
  Stress testing.
- Acquire outside expertise as required and maintain close relationships with vendors.
- Allow adequate time for skills development by project team members.
- Allow for time and resources to revise corporate standards. This step also requires commitment from any corporatewide groups to participate in the development and evolution of these standards.

Because architecture innovation often implies building or extending system software, it is important to keep in mind some of the differentiating characteristics of system software development:

- The users of the development and execution architectures are programmers and analysts. They are technically sophisticated and have high expectations and needs.
- The architecture is usually generalized, so it can be used on future applications. Generalized software is much more complex to design, code, test, and support than software that is designed for a specific application.
- Architecture development is often done in a lower-level language than that required for normal applications.

The Compelling Need to Stay Ahead

As discussed earlier, the basic steps required to develop architecture components are similar to those required for developing applications: requirements gathering and analysis, design (high-level and detailed), programming, testing, roll-out, and support. However, because the architecture is an application to be used by system developers, it is critical that development of architecture components precede development of the application by one or more life-cycle phases. This allows applications development to continue with clear guidelines on how to proceed and minimizes disruption and rework.

Architecture development and applications development can be thought of as related but separate activities that are staggered and occurring in parallel (see Exhibit 4). Architecture development may be an entirely separate project if multiple application projects need to be executed concurrently while the architecture is being developed.

Architecture

Analyze	Design	Build	Test	Roll-out	Support

Application

Analyze	Design	Build	Test	Roll-out	Support

Exhibit 4. Relationship of Architecture and Applications Development Activities.

Communicating the Architecture

Because architectures are frequently abstract, and given that new concepts are likely to be communicated, documentation and training are particularly challenging and important. Some of the more successful techniques are

- Creating a sample application that demonstrates the capabilities of the architecture and how to use it. This approach is very effective because it shows the target applications developers what the end result will look like and how it is built on and around the architecture.
- Transferring resources from the architecture development team to the application team (or placing applications developers temporarily on the architecture team and then returning them to applications development). This is especially effective in larger project environments because it helps ensure a consistent interpretation and use of the architecture capabilities and limitations. Because of the relationships established by the time previously spent on the architecture team, this approach also has the benefit of providing very concrete and direct feedback to the architecture team on the strengths and weaknesses of the architecture.

Ongoing Architecture Support

When the architecture is implemented, a team needs to be put into place to handle fixes, enhancements, and Help Desk types of support. In many ways, this is similar to putting an application into production and having a support team, but the audience in this case is applications developers instead of business users. The main point here is to plan for this function to ensure that sufficient budget and staff are available to provide it. It is important to take into account any iterations necessary to expand the architecture's capability based on the original plan or to take into account features that slipped in the current release. If new and evolving technologies have been used, it is also important to plan for investigation, testing, and incorporation of new releases of products into the architecture.

The architecture support team must also deal with many configuration management issues as more and more application teams begin to use the architectures — because they typically work on different cycles and are likely to need capabilities in a different priority sequence. One team's critical feature may be something another team will not need for another 12 to 18 months.

Chapter 17
Overview of Data and Process Distribution

DISTRIBUTING CORPORATE PROCESSING

Netcentric computing has led many businesses to reevaluate their entire corporate processing strategy. With the existing systems of these businesses, processing may be centralized at corporate headquarters. However, that strategy may be inappropriate for the organization's future needs.

Larger organizations making the transition to netcentric often face the additional challenge of distributing their corporate processing. When the decision to distribute has been made, a difficult question arises. What should be done with the business application processing and data? Should data be located at one central site, at local sites, or in some combination of central and local sites based on usage?

This chapter highlights the benefits and issues associated with distributed systems. A high-level, step-by-step process is provided for making decisions about the data and application placement.

The concepts introduced in this chapter are, in many cases, very technical in nature. However, application designers should at least be familiar with these terms and techniques to work effectively with the architecture team in defining a data and process distribution strategy.

APPLICATION AND DATA DISTRIBUTION

The following definition of netcentric computing was introduced in the Introduction. *Netcentric is an emerging architecture style and an evolutionary stage of client/server computing that :*

- *Expands the reach of computing both within and outside the enterprise*
- *Enables sharing of data and content between individuals and applications*
- *Uses applications that provide capabilities to publish, interact, or transact*
- *Uses Internet technologies to connect employees, customers, and business partners*

Because netcentric computing is an evolution of client/server, this definition implies, of course, that at least two computers are involved: one a client and the other a server. Even this level of complexity, only two computers, means that one has to decide whether data should be on the client or the server. Processing and data allocation then becomes exponentially more complicated with large netcentric systems, where thousands of workstations and hundreds of servers are spread out across a global network.

Processing and data allocation questions lead to the need for distributed data management. This section begins by defining the concepts and approaches to managing and implementing distributed applications and data in a netcentric environment. It also provides some insights on how to approach the application and data placement decision process in a netcentric environment.

The terms "centralized" and "distributed" also apply individually to data and processing (e.g., centralized data with distributed process). With centralized data, all data physically resides in one place and data access is managed by one database management system (DBMS). Centralized processing means that all processing occurs on a single machine. Data that are distributed physically reside on a number of machines, potentially at a number of locations. Distributed processing indicates that processing required for a single business transaction will involve services on multiple machines at one or more physical locations.

There is a spectrum of possibilities and variations of distribution between fully centralized and distributed. Exhibit 1 shows an example of some trade-offs that should be considered, in the areas of flexibility vs. complexity, when moving along the distribution continuum.

In the past, best practices have conceptually been broken into two separate sets: one for data and another for processing. As both technologies have changed and converged, the need to consider both areas together has become more important. Because of this tight coupling, the two subjects merge together and will be cross-referenced throughout this chapter.

Exhibits 2 through 5 show examples of various architectures, ranging from centralized, through distributed data and distributed processing, to a fully distributed (both data and processing distributed) architecture. These are not the only four solutions possible in the distribution spectrum. There are many other possible combinations. These four are intended to illustrate the range of distributed and centralized architectures. Although the clients are assumed to be dumb, they could represent intelligent terminals, PC workstations, network computers, or any other end-user machine.

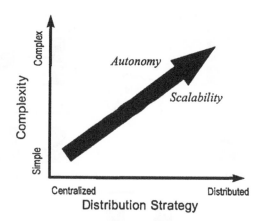

Exhibit 1. Distribution Trade-off Considerations.

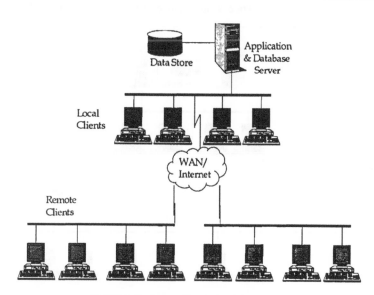

Exhibit 2. Centralized Architecture.

Exhibit 2 shows a centralized architecture, that is, one where the processing and data are both located on a central server. Client operation is limited to accessing the application on the server, although an intelligent client platform may perform other tasks for other applications, but not within the architecture of a specific business capability. If some functionality were moved to the clients, this could be considered an architecture with distributed processing and centralized data.

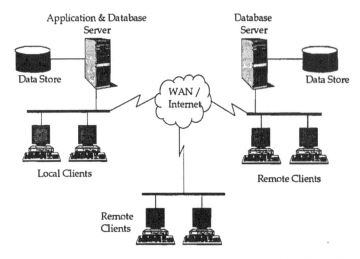

Exhibit 3. Centralized Processing Architecture with Distributed Data.

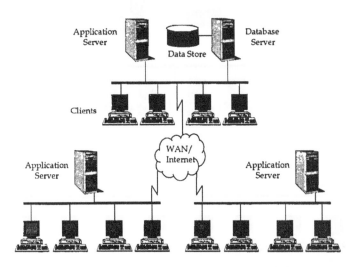

Exhibit 4. Distributed Processing Architecture with Central Data.

Exhibit 3 shows an architecture that has the data distributed, although the application is still centralized on a single server. Again, the clients are considered dumb for this architecture; however, the effects of the network must be taken into account in performance analysis, as does the application access to the remote data server. If some of the processing were moved to the client system, this could then be viewed as a fully distributed system: both data and process distributed.

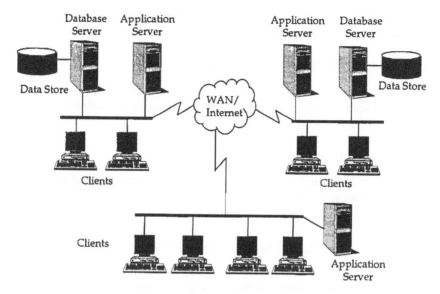

Exhibit 5. Distributed Data and Processing Architecture.

Exhibit 4 shows an architecture that has distributed the server processing but keeps the application data in a single data store. This is a typical architecture for a distributed organization, one that needs the performance advantages of localized processing but which has too much data to distribute efficiently.

Exhibit 5 shows an architecture in which both the data and processing are distributed. The flexibility of this architecture is high; at the same time, however, the complexities of synchronizing data stores and network access limitations may prove limiting.

DEFINITION OF DISTRIBUTED DATA

For the purposes of this book, distributed data are defined as "data that are physically located separate from the application processing or that are spread among two or more server computers, which then must be kept coordinated." Distributed data can be spread over multiple sites or multiple machines in whatever manner best supports the business application processing requirements.

In our discussions of distributed data we will use terms specific to relational databases, for example, "rows" instead of "records." This does not mean to imply that these strategies are only relevant to relational databases. Most of these strategies can be applied to data stored in any format.

For consistency, and because of the increasing popularity of relational databases, the terms used are primarily relational.

WHEN TO CONSIDER DISTRIBUTED DATA

Distributed data and distributed processing may be worth considering if business process to be supported has one or more of the following characteristics.

Geographically Distributed

The business functions are spread over several sites, making it inconvenient or impractical to support some (or all) of the processing requirements from a central site.

Local Decision Making and Independence Is Important

The organizational structure is distributed and the business has several local sites with the authority to make local decisions as to how to process their data. Where centralized processing is used, individual locations are more or less stuck with the level of investment and support decided on by the central site. Where locations have more autonomy to make investment decisions (such as organizations employing "profit center" management), distributed processing allows for each location to choose whatever level of information systems investment they feel is appropriate. A sales organization could decide to invest in a multidimensional database without the approval, or even awareness, of the centralized IS function.

Special Price/Performance Issues Are Present

The response time at the local site becomes unacceptable or the cost of adequate communications bandwidth is excessive due to the transfer of significant amounts of data between the central and local sites.

POTENTIAL BENEFITS OF DISTRIBUTED SYSTEMS

Using distributed data or systems has the following potential benefits.

Better Reflection of an Organization's Structure

An organization's structure is often logically distributed (divisions, departments, projects) as well as physically distributed (plants, factories, warehouses, and branch offices). Distribution of data allows the organization unit that uses the data to make the IS decisions and to control the resources. This can lead to better IS-related decision making and resource allocation.

Local Autonomy

Distributing a system allows individual groups within an organization to exercise control over their own data, while still being able to access data at remote locations when necessary. This makes them less dependent on a remote data processing center, which by definition cannot be as deeply involved in purely local issues.

Increased Availability

A distributed system can offer greater resilience than a centralized system in that it can continue to function (though at a reduced level) even if an individual site or communication link fails. To gain these availability benefits, care must be taken when designing the strategy to deemphasize the dependence on real-time access to data stored at other locations. Also, with the support of replicated data, availability is improved in that a replicated data entity remains available so long as at least one copy of that entity is available.

Increased Efficiency

Response times and communications costs are likely to be reduced, because data in a distributed system can be stored closest to its point of use, enabling most data accesses to be local.

CHALLENGES OF DISTRIBUTED SYSTEMS

Distribution may address many requirements, but there is typically a substantial cost also associated with a distributed solution. This cost is not only in terms of expense, but in terms of technology risk (e.g., control, systems management, complexity, and performance). The role of the architect is to achieve balance between business requirements, systems management, costs, performance, and reliability. Some of the issues that architects should consider in developing distributed architectures include the following:

Systems Management Challenges

Management of distributed environments implies that there are more parts in more locations that need to be tracked, maintained, repaired, and upgraded. As a result, more skilled technical resources may be required and possibly in a greater number of locations. In addition, there is rarely an integrated, high caliber, single-vendor solution for all system management requirements with a distributed architecture.

Increased Operations Skills and Resources

In a distributed environment, data and services may be located on several platforms and/or at several sites. With this increase in complexity of the environment comes a requirement for a corresponding increase in the skills and resources to support a distributed architecture.

Increase Development Skills and Resources

With the distribution of the various components, the ability to develop and thoroughly test the system usually requires significantly more hardware and additional performance and testing skills. This can significantly impact the size and skill sets required of the development and test teams.

Higher System Complexity/Fragility

Distributed systems have more components in more places, making them more difficult to test thoroughly. Adding components means that there are more pieces that can break, rendering a distributed system more fragile. This added complexity and fragility increases the risk of the project and can threaten its success.

Increased Communications Complexity

In these systems, messages containing data, processing requests, acknowledgments of previous requests, etc. are passed continuously between various remote sites. As processing is distributed, this complexity of communications must be taken into consideration.

Although there may be less reliance on the network for the end-user portion of a distributed application, the architectural infrastructure is often more complex, requiring a correspondingly experienced set of network management resource and skills.

Harder Update Control

There are several areas that result in more complicated data update procedures.

Data Redundancy

If data exist in more than one location, they must be kept synchronized, and the system must ensure that there are no update conflicts.

Integrity across Data Stores

Logical units of work (LUW) may need to be coordinated across distributed data stores. If there is a failure at any point during the transaction, the system must maintain the data integrity and roll back the portion of the transaction that has already completed.

Disaster Recovery

With data resident in many places, the ability to create a complete, check-pointed data backup for the entire business capability may be significantly more difficult than with the data in a single, central place.

These issues increase complexity for scalability and recovery from a failure.

Location Transparency

Location transparency is an architectural goal, whereby, in the ideal distributed environment, the end user or application programmer should have access to all data and processes without having to know where that specific data or process is physically located. This feature can place a substantial burden on the architect at design time but often simplifies application design. Additionally, movement of data locations is now independent of source code changes.

From the data perspective, this means the architecture must efficiently locate the data and transport it to the application upon request, without excessive processing delays. From the processing perspective, the architecture must handle location transparency so that the client can call a server without knowing its physical location. This allows servers to be physically moved throughout the system without having to modify the client.

If is often the case that full location transparency cannot be provided. In this situation, the application architect needs to be somewhat aware of where data is stored, how it is segmented, etc. This makes the design, coding, and testing of the application more difficult, which must be taken into consideration.

Greater End-User Support Complexity

Location transparency complicates end-user support. A single application problem may originate from any number of remote sites that are transparent to the user, making the problem more difficult to identify and resolve.

Network Dependency

Some distribution approaches are very network dependent. In these environments, the network plays an increased role in the reliability of the system. This increased reliability usually requires expensive duplication of network resources to provide an acceptable amount of system availability for the users.

Security

Managing and transferring data between sites increases security concerns, in terms of prevention of unauthorized access by both internal and external parties.

Change Management

Although not a technical area, there is an inherent risk in distributing a system in a manner that too closely maps to some organizational structure. Changes in the organizational structure could impact the system architecture design. The ability to migrate the architecture as the organization changes needs to be considered when distributing data and processing.

WHICH IS RIGHT, DISTRIBUTED OR CENTRALIZED?

Many organizations today are too quick to settle on a distributed, replicated data solution. Just because the technology exists and the organization *can* distribute data does not mean it *should* distribute data. Much of the motivation for distributed data begins with dissatisfaction with the cost or performance of communications lines that link locations. In a world with infinite wide area communications speeds and no costs, few organizations would take on the issues of distributing their data.

With the ever-decreasing price of wide area communications, organizations have recently begin to shift back toward centralized data storage. They are providing remote locations with adequate communications bandwidth and reliability in order to access and update centralized data from remote locations.

The motivation for this trend toward recentralization has been the realization that it is difficult to manage, control, and handle recovery for data that is distributed across many locations. Where is retail customer information? Where is financial information? Where is sales information? As organizations try to make more and more information available to decision makers, hiding the complexities of data location from these users is turning out to be exceedingly difficult.

A small retail store chain with 20 stores spread across the southeastern United States recently faced this decision. Each store had its own data and processing resources locally. When a major new systems initiative was undertaken, it was assumed that the stores' computing systems would be expanded and data would be replicated between the stores and headquarters. Individual store management did not want to give up housing their systems and data locally because they didn't want to be dependent on traditionally unreliable communications links, and they wanted "control" over their data.

The problem, however, was the investment in upgrading all of these systems and putting in sufficient communications bandwidth to support the substantial data replication load. Also, hiring and training additional computer support personnel at the stores to deal with all this new complexity would have cost far more than holding and managing all of the data at one central location.

By centralizing the data, only one set of systems support personnel was needed, and they could give 24-hour, high-quality support at a fraction of the cost. Second, by not maintaining multiple copies (up to 20 in this case) of some information, the total systems investment in database licenses and disk storage was substantially reduced.

To preserve the autonomy the store managers had before, 20 servers (one for each store) were actually housed in 1 location, managed by one operations staff. Each store still had its own server and much of its own data, but the server itself was not physically located in the store. Some of the savings were then used to upgrade the communications infrastructure, adding capacity and redundancy to deliver response times and availability actually better than when the stores managed their machines locally.

MAKING THE DISTRIBUTION DECISIONS: DISTRIBUTION DRIVERS

Distribution Drivers

On all systems delivery projects, technical architects will be confronted with data and processing distribution decisions, which often represent a vital part of their role as architects. Unfortunately, these are usually not decisions with "cookbook" answers. With many factors impacting the overall distribution strategy, designing a distributed architecture frequently involves trade-offs, working within business and technical constraints and anticipating future requirements.

This chapter covers the various drivers that are inputs to the decision process for a distributed system architecture. It will guide architects through the processes of

- Determining the organization's business drivers
- Identifying the relevant technical drivers
- Understanding the impact of drivers on the distribution strategy
- Recognizing the costs and benefits of various distributed solutions

Distribution Drivers and the Key Inputs

For architects to make many of the fundamental distribution decisions, they must first collect, analyze, and understand the business and technical environment in which they are working. These can include such things as the organization's business requirements and priorities, the current technical

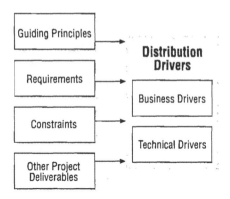

Exhibit 6. Distribution Drivers and Key Inputs.

environment (including technical constraints), and both business and technical guiding principles and technical requirements. These factors, which influence the distributed architecture, are "Distribution Drivers."

There are two main types of distribution drivers: business and technical. Understanding the organization's business and technical drivers is crucial to developing a viable and sound distribution strategy. To determine whether drivers are applicable to a specific organization's environment, architects must have an understanding of the organization's requirements and guiding principles. This section is intended to help architects drill down into the information to understand fully what is required to assist in formulating the distribution strategy in later stages, leveraging the guiding principles, requirements, constraints, and other deliverables produced by the project team as shown in Exhibit 6.

There are often overlaps among guiding principles, requirements, and constraints, and it is useful to recognize their cascading nature.

Guiding principles are high level and typically enterprise- or division-wide. They represent statements of direction, ideals, or strategic intent.

Requirements are medium level, focused on the project or function, often developed during analysis, and represent the mode specific detailed goals.

Constraints are low level, often detailed points. They usually represent cost or technology barriers and are very difficult to influence or change.

These overlaps and dependencies will be highlighted, but it might be difficult, and superfluous, to draw hard lines between the different areas. Architects must understand the factors to consider and their importance, in order to be able to agree on their priority. They should not, however, spend unnecessary time debating into which category they fall.

Guiding Principles

Guiding principles are statements of direction as formulated and agreed to by key stakeholders regarding key areas of the enterprise or application, including information technology (IT). They are "stakes in the ground" representing basic philosophies and strategies of the company. Guiding principles are particularly useful in setting direction on important decision points and helping make difficult or controversial decisions. Guiding principles differ from requirements in that they are tied more to a particular client and their current situation. They may include

- Political/geographical/regional/organizational characteristics
- Organization emphasis on the amount of data or access time
- Strategic direction of project — performance, cost reduction, administration overhead, accuracy, speed to market, or older technology
- Strategic direction of technology (e.g., use of client/server)
- Strategic direction of business (e.g., improve customer service)

Often, the guiding principles are broken into two areas: business guiding principles, which focus more on the business aspect of the project, and technical guiding principles, which focus on just the technology strategy and statements of direction. The business and technical guiding principles are especially valuable to the process of identifying the distribution drivers.

Due to the need to limit scope, it is unlikely that all project areas will be completely covered by the guiding principles. The focus of guiding principles is usually those areas for which there are ambiguities, known disagreements, or indecision. That said, architects must be aware that there are often areas left open for interpretation, some that may result in requirements, others in constraints.

Requirements

Requirements are the primary success measurement for the project. They must be met either completely or with agreed to modification in order for the project to deliver its value. Requirements exist for both the business and the technology sides. The business requirements are the primary driver for the business integration design.

Constraints

The other key input is constraints. Constraints are often determined from the current business and technical environments compared with what is considered reasonable for the organization's future environment. Constraints are what "is" and what "needs to be." Some examples include the

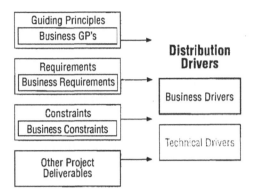

Exhibit 7. Inputs to Identify Business Drivers.

number of users, users' locations, and current network infrastructure vs. future network infrastructure. For example, the organization may not want to change their network. This is a constraint, and the architect's solution must work within the capabilities of the current network infrastructure.

Business Drivers

The objective of this section is to help architects recognize the business drivers that are also distribution drivers in an organization's environment, by discussing factors for consideration and identifying possible project deliverables that should have been developed in earlier stages of the overall methodology. The output from this process should be a complete understanding of the business requirements, constraints, and guiding principles and their potential impact on the distribution strategy (Exhibit 7).

To determine whether business drivers are applicable to a specific organizations's environment, architects must have an understanding of the company's business requirements and the business guiding principles. This section is intended to help architects drill down into the information to understand fully the business drivers to help formulate the distribution strategy in later stages.

The inputs to help identify the business drivers are

- Guiding principles
- Business requirements
- Business constraints
- Other project deliverables

To help differentiate between guiding principles and requirements, examples are

- Guiding principles

  Time to market of new products is top priority.

  Systems should last 10 years.

  Business strategy is to increase barriers to entry.

  Centralization of IT organization, including support organization.

- Business requirements

  Application must support users located in the United States, Europe, and Asia.

  User numbers and profiles (could also be a constraint).

  Business expects annual growth of 25% for the next 3 years.

  External interfaces to credit card companies.

Additionally, business constraints may include

- User numbers and profiles.
- Financial trading applications with 100% data integrity and no latency permissible (e.g., the data accessed must never be even a second out of date).
- Existing operations center must be utilized and may not be moved.
- Budget and schedule agreements.

Following are some of the common business drivers that often influence distributed solutions. This is not intended to be a complete list, as there are many factors that influence the decisions. Business drivers are additional considerations for potential distribution drivers are discussed in detail in the following sections.

Geographical Distribution. The business functions are spread over several different sites, making it impractical to support some (or all) of the processing requirements from a central site.

Local Autonomy. The local sites must be able to operate independently from the central organization.

Performance. Performance improvement goals, as measured by response time and/or batch throughput, often drives the technology solution

Scalability. Business growth has caused the volume of data to expand, the volume of processing to increase, or has resulted in the expansion to new sites.

Mobility. The business functions require workers to have access to corporate information even when they are unable to connect to the corporate network.

Geographical Distribution

Geographical distribution is a driver in environments where the business functions are spread over several different sites, making it impractical to support some (or all) of the processing requirements from a central site. In addition to the guiding principles and the business requirements, applicable project deliverables include

Current IT assessment:

- Inventory of user profiles
- User profiles by location matrix

The resources will provide information on where current users and/or systems are located. While this may change with the new system, it is important information to have, as unexpected answers may cause architects to raise various issues earlier rather than later.

A useful process is to identify and understand the user profiles that are supported by the application systems project(s) and the organization location(s) where they reside. These profiles can continue to be used throughout the project life cycle.

The other valuable activity is to create an inventory of existing and potential processing sites and data storage locations. A site may support one or more organization locations. In creating the inventory, consider both geographic distribution (e.g., multiple data centers) and known processing platform distribution (e.g., mainframes, file servers, database servers, and workstations). The Current Network Infrastructure may provide useful information. Processing sites with unique characteristics should be identified individually; for example, order processing centers that also include distribution functions should be identified individually.

At this point, consideration should also be given to the organization's philosophy on system operations; for example, many organizations have a heavy bias toward consolidating their data centers into as few centers as possible to reduce costs and leverage resources.

Next, it is important to map user profiles to one or more sites. This mapping is based on the organization location(s) that are supported by the site and the user profiles supported by those organization locations, for example, a human resources department that exists only at the central site or order entry users that exist at sales centers and are supported by a local site. In these examples, some of the users must be documented at a specific level (human resource department) and others at a more generic level (all sales centers). Where a user group crosses potential data storage locations should also be reported. For example, if a division has individual users in multiple geographic locations, each is considered a separate local site.

This information will be useful when it is determined that data is owned by divisions. Since the division users are at multiple sites, some data replication or remote processing is required.

Local Autonomy

Local autonomy is the ability for local sites to operate independently from the central organization, which results in increased availability. This may be required for business-critical applications like a store that needs to have its systems up to sell goods and services. Other examples of local autonomy include global operations subjected to regulations governing where data must reside. Again, guiding principles and business requirements are key inputs. In addition, the following documents may be relevant:

- Current operational level agreements
- Current IT assessment

These documents may reveal relevant information on the required availability of current systems. The current location of data and systems may again raise some issues for consideration earlier in the process.

Performance

Performance, specifically response time, is often ambiguous, primarily because what is considered acceptable to some may very well be unacceptable to others. Response times may be a result of the transfer of data between the central and local sites or the complexity or size of calculations that are required.

To understand the expectations on performance, referring again to the guiding principles is a good starting point. Business requirements also may articulate the response times for some systems or functions. These are inputs for the Service Level Agreements (SLAs), which are critical for the system to meet organization and user expectations. In addition, the current systems SLAs may also provide valuable information at the function level for the current applications. If an SLA does not exist for an application, it is crucial to create one to properly manage requirements and expectations. Additionally, batch, synchronization, and background performance are just as important as on-line and all require SLAs.

Understanding how the data is used is crucial when discussing response time and may present architects with some constraints that they must work within. The classification criterion presented here include: frequency of update and access, currency, and security.

Frequency of Update. If multiple data copies are maintained, user requirements will determine how often the data is refreshed and updated.

Exhibit 8. Basic Measurement Classification

Criterion	Measurement classification
Required currency of data	Real time
	Near real time (few second or minutes delay)
	Periodic (nightly, weekly, etc.)
Frequency of update	Dynamic: frequently updated
	Static: infrequently updated, sometimes called reference data
	Transaction: finite life span and/or distinct status through which it moves
Frequency of use/reference	Infrequent
	Frequent

Currency. User requirements for the freshness of data will determine if real time or close-to-real time data currency is necessary.

Typically, data entities are classified according to some measurement for each criterion. The measurement for each criterion should be specifically defined for the enterprise based on its relative importance and impact on the business. For example, for data currency, the enterprise must establish the measurement for the period in minutes, hours, or even days.

Distribution strategies can be established for the enterprise using these measurement classes as inputs. These factors affect the data placement decisions and also drive the choice of processing strategy.

The criteria in Exhibit 8, and a basic measurement classification for each criterion, should be considered and defined for the enterprise.

Scalability

Scalability is the ability to upgrade and expand the software, hardware, and network infrastructure to meet changing business needs. Business growth can significantly impact systems in three ways: increasing the amount of data, increasing the volume of processing, and adding additional locations for end-users. These factors may also impact the technology drivers. While business growth is sometimes difficult to predict and varies by economic and market factors, architects need to be aware of its potential impacts. Guiding principles and business requirements often include organizations' growth estimates, but it is a role of the system architects to understand its repercussion on the system.

Scalability is not free and has to be planned for like everything else. Project deliverables that may be valuable when evaluating this business driver include

- Current and expected data volume matrix
- Current and expected transaction volume matrix

- Current technology infrastructure
- Current IT assessment
- User profiles by location matrix

The data volumes enable architects to understand the amount of data being processed on any given day, extrapolate out and determine the expected data volumes based on varying growth percentages. The transaction volumes matrix enables the same forecasting on the number of transactions that occur every day, both on-line transaction processing and batch processing. Growth projections should be based on the organization's business plan. This is to prevent optimistic projections, which can result in excessive expenses, as well as pessimistic projections, which may jeopardize future expansion.

Mobility

Mobility is necessary when the business functions require people — for example, a sales force — to have access to corporate information even when they are unable to connect to the corporate network. This information may be found in the guiding principles and the business requirements and may be discussed when factors of geographical distribution come under consideration. Project deliverables that may provide insight include

- Current IT assessment
- Inventory of user groups
- User profiles by location matrix

If mobility is determined to be a driver, understanding the data usage of mobile users will be a valuable input as well (e.g., frequency of updates or currency requirements).

Additional Considerations

In addition to the distribution drivers, there are additional factors that cannot be ignored when proposing a distributed solution. These factors include

- Cost or time to develop
- Cost or time to operate/maintain
- Complexity
- Skills required to develop/support
- Flexibility
- Existing infrastructures
- Existing standards and approaches

These factors are significant enough to prohibit satisfying the other drivers. They must be included in the process and the issues and possible risks associated with them need to be resolved. Architects need to be aware of

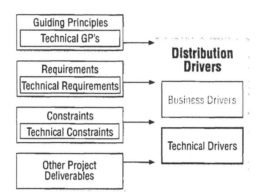

Exhibit 9. Inputs to Identify Technical Drivers.

them, plan for their impact, and actively manage them because, while they are not considered primary distribution drivers, they could become drivers. For example, if the system must be delivered in a 6-month time frame to enable the organization's time-to-market for a new product, the time to develop obviously becomes a driver with significant impact on the technology decisions that are made (i.e., installing a TP monitor may no longer be an option).

Also required may be change management skills. For instance, when introducing a distributed client/server environment into a traditional organization, whose systems may have always been mainframe-based or centralized client/server is a significant impact to the current IT organization. The existing skills, processes and infrastructure may all have to change as the organization comes up to speed on the different technology and the new issues associated with it. This impacts not only the existing systems management framework but also the development and support staff (or outsourcing organization).

Technical Drivers

Along with business drivers, a number of technical considerations must be taken into account to address how data and processing will be distributed. Some are purely technical drivers, others become technical drivers as a result of business drivers.

Analogous to Exhibit 7, showing the Business Drivers and Key Inputs, there is a similar set of key inputs to identify and understand the technical drivers (see Exhibit 9).

To fully understand technical drivers and their potential impact, architects must leverage the following information:

- Technical guiding principles
- Technical requirements
- Technical constraints
- Other project deliverables

Technical guiding principles are technology statements of direction while technical requirements define the detailed needs of the system. Examples of technical guiding principles include

- Organization prefers to buy packaged solutions and customize rather than build customized solutions
- Limit number of vendors
- Get off the mainframe
- Deploy open solutions
- Organization finds emerging technologies unacceptable

Examples of technical requirements include

- International languages support (presentation and data)
- Specific transaction processing volumes (e.g., 900 transactions/second)
- Specific response time (e.g., new accounts must appear at all locations within 5 minutes)
- Volume of data is expected to grow 10% annually

Requirements often result from technical constraints that the system must run within. Examples of technical constraints include

- Need to use a particular vendor
- Current network infrastructure must be used without any additional network investments
- Must utilize existing hardware

The following list is not exhaustive, but shows examples of technical drivers that often result in distributed architectures. These technical drivers will be addressed in the following sections. Additionally, there are further technical factors for consideration which may also drive distributed solutions.

- Communication capabilities — The current network infrastructure may not meet the requirements of the new system (e.g., availability or performance).
- Complexity of processing — Calculations are either extremely data intensive or processor intensive.
- Transaction volumes — The current or projected transaction volumes are extremely high.

- Resource availability/reliability — The capabilities of the current platform may jeopardize the ability to meet the system availability and reliability requirements.
- Number of users — The number of users of a particular process or application is extremely high.

Communications Capabilities

The capacity and availability of the communications infrastructure becomes increasingly important for situations where processing is to be split across platforms. The frequency of exchanges between processes and the speed, reliability and availability of communications will have an impact on the performance of an application and must be considered when choosing a processing strategy.

To determine whether the communications capabilities are a driver in a specific environment, the current network infrastructure should be analyzed for speed, performance, reliability, and current bottlenecks. In addition to performing an assessment of the current IT infrastructure, assuming upgrades are planned for the new system, the capacity plan (the planned IT infrastructure) needs to be analyzed.

The guiding principles and the technical requirements are key inputs into this process to understand the organization's willingness to invest in the technology infrastructure. Additionally, the Current IT Assessment and Data and Transaction Volume Matrices contain information needed to determine whether the current or planned network infrastructure can handle the projected network traffic. Technical requirements and the current and proposed SLAs should also provide information on the required response time that the communications infrastructure must meet.

Transaction Volumes

Understanding the impact of a large volume of transactions is crucial to distribution decisions from the network perspective, as well as the server perspective. If the transaction volume exceeds the capacity of the server, then the decision to scale the solution upwards or consider distribution will need to be made. Fully understanding transaction volumes requires a thorough analysis of the transactions (different types of transactions, consumption of resources by each transaction type, etc.).

The technology requirements may contain the projected transaction volumes. Additionally, the transaction volume matrix may have already been created for the projected transaction volumes, or may exist for the current system.

Complexity of Processing

Processing may be complex in two ways: First, the amount of data that is being processed must be accessible to the processing location. Second, the complexity of the application processing may take up significant processor resources. For example, insurance applications and financial trading analysis applications are known for the complexity of their computations and for the amount of data that is processed. At this stage of analysis, it may be useful to leverage delivery vehicles to understand the proposed styles of processing that the organization is requiring.

The Current IT Assessment may provide vital information in regards to both, as well as understanding the organization's business processes and industry. Additionally, the Business Requirements may highlight some of this complexity.

Resource Availability

The capabilities of a platform must be considered to ensure that it can deliver the required availability and be recovered reliably in the event of a failure. This often involves managing the expectations of the users and understanding the availability requirements.

The technical requirements and guiding principles, in addition to availability guidelines, should highlight whether it is a mission-critical system. To understand the organizations expectations, the Operational Level and Service Level Agreements for the current system and the operational requirements for the new system should be reviewed as well. The Operations Level Agreements and the Service Level Agreements for the new system are defined as part of the MODE framework and are critical to managing the organization's expectations of the new system.

Number of Users and Resource Usage

The number of users of a particular process and the usage of system resources by that process may influence the choice of platform or the strategy for distributing a process across platforms.

For instance, the input validation portion of a processing intensive application may well run better on the user's workstation than on a highly leveraged, high-powered, shared processor, server. However, if the workstations will need to be upgraded as the application changes, this consideration will need to be balanced against the cost of upgrade and support in the long term.

Additionally, the number of users will impact the projected transaction volumes. To understand the current activity, key inputs include

- Current IT assessment
- User profiles
- User profiles by location matrix

Additional Considerations

As with the business drivers, there are factors in addition to the technical drivers that we cannot ignore when proposing a distributed solution. Specific organization guiding principles, requirements and constraints may make these factors technical drivers as well.

Frequency of Change to Application Code. If an application is subject to frequent changes or updates, the number and location of target platforms become a consideration in terms of the overhead required to roll-out updates and ensure that the system is configured correctly.

Systems Management and Operations. Systems Management complexity increases as a result of more components and data in more locations that need to be tracked, maintained, repaired and upgraded. As a result, more skilled technical resources may be required, and possibly in a greater number of locations. In turn, this may increase operating costs. Additionally, the systems are more fragile and the cause of problems is more difficult to track down. This added complexity and fragility increases the risk of the project and can threaten its success.

Platform-Specific Capabilities. Some applications may require the capabilities of a particular platform. Examples include GUI capabilities, imaging capabilities, high-MIPS capabilities, an attached high-speed printer, or other special environment (e.g., a secured check printer). In addition, there may be a requirement for development tools that are only available on selected platforms.

Packaged Software Constraints. The appropriate use of packaged software to meet specific business functionality may necessitate the distribution of data to a specific processing platform.

Platform Interoperability. The extent to which multiple platforms can work together (inter-operate) must be considered when defining the process topology. In addition, any restrictions must be taken into account: only certain data types are supported in translation and/or only certain protocols are supported.

Interface Constraints. For distributed data design, special emphasis should be placed on identification of the data that is being passed and the ownership of the data (originating user group or receiving user group). To do this, it is crucial to identify the internal, e.g., to other systems, and external, e.g., Electronic Data Interchange (EDI), interfaces required between the proposed and existing application systems as well as the form that it takes, e.g., on-line vs. batch.

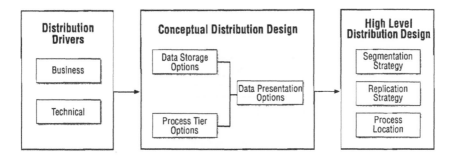

Exhibit 10. Conceptual Distribution Design Activities.

Security. The need to incorporate system software that requires a valid user ID and password to access the data and that will deny access to unauthorized users must be taken into consideration. This is of particular importance in a netcentric or public accessible application, where the perception of insecurity is a high profile issue.

MAKING THE DISTRIBUTION DECISIONS: THE DECISION PROCESS

Conceptual Distribution Design

This chapter describes the design processes involved in creating a conceptual distribution strategy as one of the activities required for the BIM task "Define Business Architecture Blueprint." The overall flow for the conceptual distribution design stage is shown in Exhibit 10.

When creating the conceptual distribution design, it is important to look at the distribution of the data from the viewpoint of both the data architect and the application architect. In addition, the process distribution strategy must be considered at the conceptual level, to decide upon which tiering options should be used, if any, to distribute the application processes both within and between platforms.

Exhibit 10 gives an overview of the activities that will be addressed during the conceptual design of the distribution strategy. As with all design activities, these should not be construed as discrete tasks unrelated to each other but rather as steps in an *iterative* process.

At any time, the architect should be focusing on one or two of the main areas of the process, but will still need to understand and consider all the other areas involved to make the appropriate tradeoff decisions. The use of well defined scenarios, that can be validated against the proposed architectures, is one, widely-recognized way of performing this task, either on paper, whiteboards, or via some simple prototype or benchmark activity.

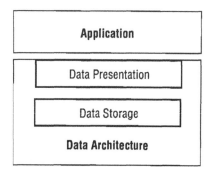

Exhibit 11. Data Architecture.

Consideration of the data storage and presentation options needs to be addressed with some knowledge of the proposed segmentation and replication strategy, as will linkages between the style and number of the process tiers and data storage location. Indeed, all activities are quite closely coupled, such that a change in any one of them can affect the assumptions on which another is based.

Data Storage Options

The data architecture can be treated as two distinct layers: one for the data storage side and one for the data presentation (to the application), as shown in Exhibit 11. This section will focus on the initial decisions required as to how and where the data storage should reside.

The data presentation mechanism is a combination of the data access mechanism that will be adopted and the application architecture middleware layers that may be used.

The data storage strategy governs where the data will be physically located within the enterprise, and the nature of any copies of physical data that will be used. The data presentation strategy governs the appearance of the data to the application(s) that make use of it.

As with all architectural decisions, it may be possible to create an architecture that will perform well, but not be affordable. Throughout the evaluation and recommendation process, the cost of distributing or not distributing should be carefully weighed against the benefits. However, it is recommended that the initial distribution strategy look at the identified drivers first and then cost out the alternatives as a solution becomes firmer.

Choosing a Data Storage Option

The data storage options can be classified into five identified styles.

Central Data Storage. Data is stored on a single machine. Because this option does not require either segmentation or replication, it is usually the preferred option and starting point in most architecture designs.

Distribution by Instance. Data stores are accessed through more than one DBMS engine, although they are located in the same geographical location.

Distribution by Location (sometimes also by instance within a location). Data are accessed from more than one geographical location, with data storage accessed through one or more DBMS engines. In most cases, the fact that multiple locations are involved is of more impact than the fact that more than one server is used.

Location vs. User Site. Distributing the data by location does not necessarily mean putting the data servers at the user site. It may be appropriate to identify regional or local distribution points to avoid having too many instances of the data. Although distributing to regional centers may alleviate some of the network performance problems, it may not be as effective as taking the data distribution down to the user site, where high-speed LAN access is available.

Mobile. The mobile data user is a special case, where data access is required to an amount of the main data storage, although there is no network available to provide access to a remote server. This is often the case for both the "occasionally connected" user and the small footprint system.

The discussion in this subsection is aimed at analyzing data distribution strictly from a database perspective. From an application perspective, the fact that that the data resides in several different places should be transparent, depending on your middleware solution, because, by providing data access services, you can eliminate some of the concern described about data distribution.

Exhibit 12 summarizes the characteristics for the different data storage types, together with the main drivers that force a particular storage option. These are discussed in more detail in the following sections.

There may be occasions when an architecture will be used that implements more than one of these data storage option. However, for analysis purposes, it is assumed that the same basic data storage mechanism is used throughout the system, and the strategy for distribution will have to take into account the complexity levels required for each option.

Data Storage Option Decision Tree

The starting point for the process should be the assumption that a central data store should be considered, unless there are drivers that might force

Exhibit 12. Data Storage Architecture Styles

Architecture characteristics	Data storage option			
	Centralized	Distributed by instance	Distributed by location	Mobile
No. of DBMS engines	One	Multiple	Multiple	Multiple
No. of data servers	One	One or more	Multiple	Multiple
No. of physical locations	One	One	Multiple	Multiple
Ratio–users/data store	N:1	X:1 where X<N	Y:1 where Y<X	1:1
Main drivers toward this data storage style	Simplicity; this is the preferred solution for most systems	Need additional performance or high availability/reliability	Local autonomy or network bandwidth requirements exceed capacity	Disconnected users

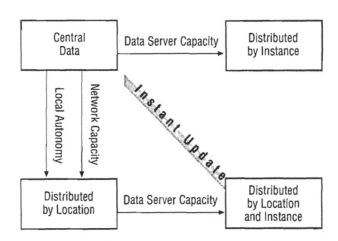

Exhibit 13. Main Data Storage Decision Drivers.

the direction towards a distributed architecture. The central data store provides the simplest solution to build and maintain, albeit not always providing the best performance.

Exhibit 13 shows the main drivers in the data storage option decision. However, additional business and technical drivers, including costs, will shape the final decision, in some cases even outweighing the technical decision tree.

The main decision drivers are discussed in more detail below, followed by some of the secondary drivers that would come from the distribution drivers identified for the particular project or system. It should be noted that as technology advances, the impact or importance of these drivers may change as the cost of networks, hardware, disk space etc. come down, but it is likely that the current trend of extending the system to fill the available resources will keep this change at a relatively slow pace.

Network Capacity

The first consideration is whether the network appears capable of handling the messaging load required for the application to be implemented with a central data storage architecture. This involves looking at the current and proposed network infrastructures and determining the transaction message sizes, volume, and characteristics and loading estimates from other network users.

Initially this limitation may appear to support the central data storage architecture, but other factors such as the location of the application processing and the type of data access and middleware used must also be addressed. The architecture choice here should be constantly reevaluated during the decision process for confirmation. If the result is in doubt, then further investigation should be performed. As always, the ability to throw additional expenditure into upgrading the network infrastructure is an option that should be investigated with the other scenarios.

If operating a central data store architecture with high volume access requirements over the network proves not to be feasible, and the organization is not willing to invest in upgrading of the network infrastructure, it may become necessary to distribute some or all data entities.

Local Autonomy

One of the drivers that may be identified for the organization is a desire to have some degree of local autonomy at outlying sites. This involves locating appropriate data at more than one site and is often practiced to ensure that the whole business function is not overly dependent on a single point of failure or bottleneck, be it network or the central store.

If the organization determines that the level of network resiliency offers is an acceptable risk, then the question of local autonomy becomes more focused on the business case for distributing to more than one location. This is often another tradeoff between the cost of lost business due to down time vs. the cost of providing a high availability, networking solution. This expectation for this requirement should also be established early in the analysis.

Data Server Capacity

Although this may be considered the prime driver, the location of the data storage is not determined by capacity. The implementation of the hardware support, however, is a major factor in ensuring adequate performance.

Whether the data resides at one or at multiple geographical locations, the data server may not have the capacity to handle the transaction volume with a single machine. This may be due to various limitations including: number of simultaneous database connections, disk I/O, or memory constraints.

One solution is to split the data server load between several machines, here called *distribution by instance*. Analysis of the data server transaction loading and performance requirements will reveal whether this appears to be a risk to the architecture.

Instant Updates

When considering the data storage architecture, it is important to note the requirements for latency on shared data. A strong driver *against* distributing data would be the need for a local update to be immediately available to all users. Because the distribution strategy is formed in an iterative manner, this would probably be caught later. However, it is useful to consider this scenario when selecting the storage architecture.

Certain data transactions must be instantly available to all users of the data, both electronic and human. Examples of this type of data would be financial transactions or airline seat allocations.

Two options exist for handling the type of transactions that require instant update for shared data. The first is the central shared data store, which means that an entity exists in only one place. The second would be the use of distributed data AND a two-phase commit mechanism. (Note that the use of a two-phase commit mechanism is strongly discouraged due to the limitations in performance and reliability, especially in high volume environments.)

Secondary Driver Considerations

In addition to the main decision drivers that always need to be addressed, there are a number of less urgent, but equally important, secondary drivers that should be considered.

These are drivers over which the architect may have some latitude, in terms of influencing the organization to accept one tradeoff or another. To show the complexity of the decisions involved, some of these additional drivers have been identified in Exhibit 14.

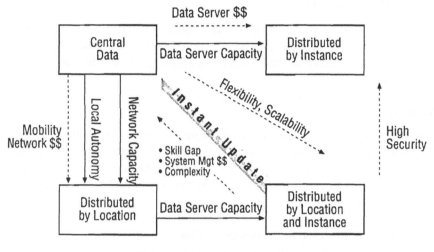

Exhibit 14. Main and Secondary Data Storage Drivers.

The secondary drivers and enablers are more subjective and fluid than the primary drivers, in that the organization's viewpoint can heavily influence their selection and identification.

Data Server Cost

The decreasing cost of hardware components is an enabler that can encourage a choice of distribution of data storage to multiple machines.

Flexibility and Scalability

A central data store does not necessarily offer great flexibility and can leave little room for scalability as the system changes and/or grows.

High Security

The ability to control security on a single data store is significantly simpler than performing the same task in a distributed environment. Often, there can be difficulty finding a suitably secure physical location at all proposed locations. Similarly, the need to establish high logical security over the network may add significantly to the overhead of the system.

Skill Gap

It is important to recognize that the move from a central architecture to a more distributed one, brings with it a need for much deeper skills in development and operations areas.

System Management Cost

Most experts agree that the cost of managing a distributed environment can be significantly higher than a centralized one. A well-chosen architecture can mitigate this cost and/or provide additional benefits that outweigh the costs.

Mobility

For truly mobile users who wish to work independently from the main system, there must be some amount of data present on their own systems. This may be a selected subset of the data, belonging to that user, or just a read-only cache of replicated data. A central-only solution cannot provide mobile support.

Complexity of Development and Operation

The more platforms and network components that are involved will lead to a significant increase in development effort and capital expenditure to provide a realistic, yet safe, test environment. Similarly, more errors may be created due to differences in operational techniques and requirements.

Speed of Development

Under some circumstances, the centralized solution can offer the fastest development path for a simple application. All resources are in one place, with only one database administration location required.

Network Cost

The network can provide a bottleneck to the ability to implement a central data storage solution with high volume access requirements. If the organization is not willing to invest in upgrading of the network infrastructure, then it may become necessary to distribute some or all data entities.

Central Data Storage

The most basic data storage style is a single, central data store, in which all data required by an application is kept in a single database with access to the database through a single data manager on a single host (Exhibit 15).

A central data store can be characterized by

- A single data manager instance
- A single host accessing the database directly
- A single physical location for all data
- Multiple users sharing this one data store

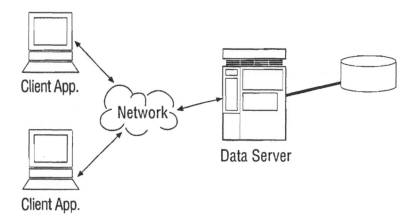

Exhibit 15. Central Data Storage.

Advantages

The advantage of the central data store is relative simplicity: It is simple to implement, maintain, operate and to find data. This make it ideal for the really large data storage applications, such as data warehouses, where replication would be very costly.

Since all data is located in one database and serviced by one data manager, it is possible to perform more complex data manipulation, such as retrieving data in a join across tables (relationally). This in turn can lead to a more streamlined operation, since the data manager has the ability to perform any data access or manipulation without as much reliance on additional architecture services.

The single store also means that all data administration, backup, maintenance, etc. can be performed on one machine. Additionally, since all data is located in a single location, there is no need for any data routing components to find the required data.

Limitations

There are several limitations, however, that may preclude the use of this data storage style. Because all data are serviced by one machine, the processing capability, number of active users/threads, or communications throughput might create performance bottlenecks.

Equally important is the consideration of possible single points of failure. If the machine is not reachable by the user, due to processor, power or network failure, then all serviced business capabilities are no longer available to the company, nor the associated data. This may be unacceptable in a mission critical application.

The reliance on a single data store architecture also precludes the ability to perform *preventative* maintenance on a 24×7×365 application. Without this maintenance, the system is more likely to go down under the heaviest load, which is likely to be at the most critical time of day. The availability requirements for the system need to be determined and then specified in the appropriate SLA or OLA to ensure that time is allotted for administrative activities.

In addition, this data storage style will become more inflexible as the data grows. If changes arise and the data needs to be distributed, it may be difficult to migrate from the central style to a distributed style. Once storage is full, the ability to add-on disk packs or segment data, or even to perform backups, may be curtailed. A high-water warning point should be established for the system to allow some spare capacity for upgrading the architecture or extending the application functionality.

In cases where these constraints cannot be overcome or tolerated, it may be necessary to consider some form of distributed data storage, as described in the subsequent sections.

Distribution by Instance

Once the data becomes too much for a single system to manage, it becomes necessary to split the database between two or more data servers. As a result, the database will now be managed by multiple database managers and the data will be segmented among multiple machines. In most cases, several hosts will be responsible for providing access to the stored data. In this data distribution style, data servers would be located in the same room or building and connected by some type of high speed network.

A data store that is distributed by instance is characterized by

- A single physical location for all data storage devices
- More than one server accessing the database directly
- One data manager instance for each access host
- Many users sharing one data store

Distributing data across multiple data servers brings with it the requirement for some form of segmentation strategy. Since all the data is no longer managed by the same data server, the decision must be made as to what data should reside together and what data can be separately located. The segmentation strategy is covered in detail in the next chapter.

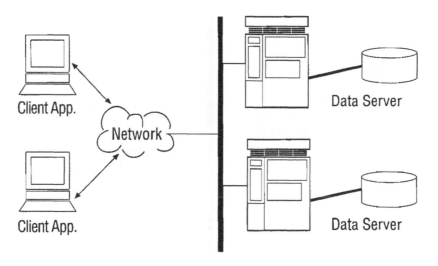

Exhibit 16. Data Distribution by Instance: Data Storage with Exclusive Data Server.

With the distribution by instance storage style, there are two primary implementation options: exclusive disk storage and shared disk storage. Each of these options will be discussed further.

The most common style is where the data storage devices are each associated with separate data servers, as shown in Exhibit 16. This greatly improves data access throughput, as there is now potentially twice the amount of CPU power, I/O bandwidth, and network throughput available for the data architecture.

Another variation is to have the data on one storage device, yet accessed by more than one data server, as shown in Exhibit 17. This could yield a high availability architecture but requires both specialized hardware and software to support it. It is possible to keep a system operational near 24X7 by configuring the data servers such that, should the one server fail or be taken out for maintenance, the other server can take over.

Advantages

Although locating the data on multiple data stores within a single location creates additional costs in areas such as backups or version control, this architecture is scaleable as the organization grows, providing that the data partitioning and data access routing software is configured with scalability in mind.

In many "by-instance" architectures, data partitioning will be done on a horizontal segmentation basis — putting different sets of rows on different

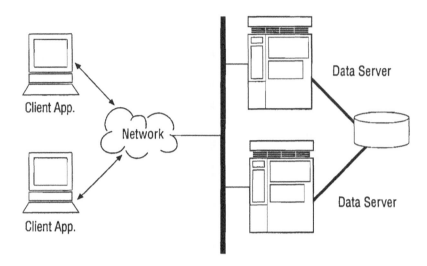

Exhibit 17. Data Distribution by Instance: Shared Data Storage Devices.

---

machines. This allows the dedication of a machine to a particular user group, region or division, which may be useful when scheduling a maintenance or batch window on machines whose users have different habits (time zones, etc.). In certain cases, vertical partitioning by table or by column, or a hybrid of the two styles, may be more appropriate.

Limitations

One limitation of having physically distinct data stores is that updates cannot be easily made across the segments. Things such as two-phase commit, distributed locking and timeouts can also be introduced, particularly if vertical segmentation is used. Because of these issues, a doubling of the number of processors may not give an overall doubling of performance, since the data is now in more than one place. In addition, any views or joins which span data on more than one data server will need to have data transferred across the LAN between the data servers. This should be taken into account when performing the partitioning and LAN capacity analyses.

Another limitation of breaking up the data storage is that any referential integrity mechanisms within a data manager will have to communicate with the data manager that services the other data stores involved in the integrity event. This can be achieved by the application and/or using triggers, thus becoming a custom solution. For the sake of quality, and ease of development, it is best to try to use the built-in referential integrity features of the RDBMS package, where possible. If this cannot be done, great care

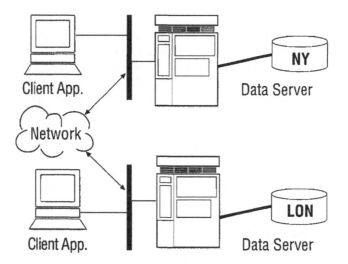

Exhibit 18. Data Distribution by Location.

must be taken in identifying and specifying the appropriate integrity action scenarios, to ensure that data coherency does not become corrupted.

From the network access point of view of a remote user, distributing data by instance at a central site is no different than keeping it in a central store. In such a situation, the network capacity might still not be sufficient to service this distribution style. Depending upon the location of the data users and the amount of data that needs to travel between their machine and the data architecture machines, it may still become necessary to move some of the data closer to the user site to reduce the bottleneck caused by the network.

Distribution by Location

When most people think about data distribution, they generally come up with a mental image of data distributed by location: that is, a data store per user processing location stored at the remote location. The prime drivers for this style are network capacity and autonomy.

Data storage that is "Distributed by Location" is characterized by

- Multiple data manager instances
- Multiple data servers accessing the databases directly
- Several physical locations for all data
- Many users sharing one or more data stores (but usually not all users)

An example of an architecture where data has been distributed by location is shown in Exhibit 18.

Advantages

As already mentioned, the network can be a serious bottleneck. If the data traffic is expected to be significantly higher between the user and the data store than between data stores, then it is worth considering relocation of the data store closer to the user location. This would give the user access at LAN speeds instead of WAN speeds. However, with the rapidly changing cost of network bandwidth and service, it may still be cheaper to look for more bandwidth than to implement a distributed solution.

The other main driver is the desire for local autonomy. Providing local availability may be required to protect from network downtime. Other factors — perception of poor service from the corporate IT group, for instance — might play a part. If the data are located in more than one place, the chances of a single failure causing the entire business capability to be lost will be reduced greatly.

Whatever the reason for wanting local autonomy, the end result is that some, or all, of the data must be located away from the data center. Once again, it will be necessary to perform an analysis of the data usage and transaction design to work out the optimum location(s) for each part of the data and which partitioning and/or replication strategies should be employed.

Limitations

One of the downsides of distributing data by location is the number of issues related to operations and management that *will* arise. Central backup is not likely to be possible and various additional safeguards need to be put in place to protect against loss of enterprise data integrity. Other issues such as security, database administration, physical infrastructure and required employee skills will also be more complex.

In addition, some data will be common and needed across the different locations. Replication and partitioning strategies are needed to keep those data stores synchronized. These strategies are often complex, having trade-offs between factors such as replication latency, frequency of update, relationships between segments, master/slave replication schemes, selective vs. full replication, etc. The accompanying increase in effort required to implement and administer a distributed system using such techniques should not be understated or underscoped.

Locating data in multiple places can also lead to a significant increase in the complexity of some of the otherwise simple subsystems. For example, if cross-location reporting is required, data access to multiple stores may be required. If some entities or occurrences need to move from one location to another, a complete audit of the associated relations will need to be performed to ensure that the referential integrity is maintained.

Mobile Data

Mobile users present a completely different set of issues for the architect. Most client/server products make an assumption that the user will have a continuous connection to the database. With a mobile user, that is not the case.

At a basic level, the user will require some, or all, of their working data to be portable. The characteristics of a fully centralized data store are therefore required on their own system. At the same time, this is really a distributed data store — assuming that there is more than one mobile user in the corporation — because each user will have a copy of the data.

This distribution style has all the complexity of the other styles and will be implemented in different manners, depending upon the type, size and sharing requirements of the data concerned. Mobile data systems will require at least one of the partitioning/replication options described in the next chapter, if not all of them.

PROCESS TIER OPTIONS

This section addresses the decisions related to the degree of distribution and style of separation of the modular software pieces that make up the overall system.

Several key areas should be addressed when evaluating the options for process tiers, including

- The amount of processing that should be located on the client
- The number of logical software layers that will be built
- The number of different physical hardware tiers that will be involved in servicing a transaction
- The communications mechanisms between the layers

There is a large amount of inconsistency over the use of the terminology used in this area. Therefore, before describing the options and decision processes, an overview of the basic relevant material will be presented, then the decision process will be presented in more detail, based on the terms described.

The decisions relevant to process tier options are mainly related to systems that are being built in a relatively green-field environment, in a traditional client server manner. For other evolving technologies, these decisions still play a part in the overall architecture, although in the case of publicly accessible applications, they may well be shaped more by the existing infrastructure that will be used (e.g., the Internet/intranet for net-centric systems).

Exhibit 19. Logical Software Layers

Logical SW Layer	Implements
Presentation	Presentation services
	Presentation logic
Business logic	Application logic
	Business rules
Data storage	Data access
	Data manipulation

The common view of the execution architecture of an application consists of three logical software layers, which each implement specific areas of functionality, as shown in Exhibit 19.

The three layers are:

- *Presentation.* Responsible for the presentation and collection of information from points external to the system (also known as the user interface).
- *Business logic.* Responsible for the executing the business (application) rules.
- *Data storage.* Responsible for holding and retrieving the information about the business.

What Is a "Tier"?

In the client/server world, the term "tier" is commonly used to describe a number of similar, yet distinct, notions related to an n-tier architecture. All are valid concepts, but not all are equally relevant to the distribution strategy. In all these variations, there are two important concepts:

- *Physical — Hardware Tiers.* These refer to the number of different machine types on which the software runs to complete the business function. This is the "how many tiers?" question.
- *Logical — Software Layers (three tiers).* This concept refers to how the three logical layers (Presentation, business logic and data storage) are separated.

Together, these components can describe a number of tiering styles that can be implemented.

Example Scenario

Throughout this section the concepts will be illustrated by an example of a simple hotel reservation system. The scenario to be addressed is the flow of data during the creation of a reservation request (Exhibit 20).

The agent uses the presentation layer (user interface, or UI) to enter details about guests and their stay. The Business logic performs checks on

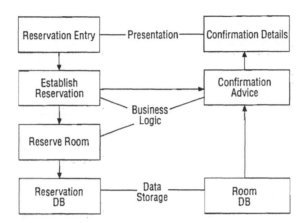

Exhibit 20. Example System.

the availability and pricing of the space and if the result is agreeable, creates a reservation record for the guest in the data storage layer. The presentation layer then provides the confirmation number information for the agent to give to the guest.

Although there can be deviation, applications are generally said to fall into one of three categories: One-tier, two-tier, and three-tier. The defining characteristic for each is the existence of well-defined interfaces between the tiers.

ONE-TIER SYSTEMS

One-tier applications are those where all three application layers work directly with each other. Most mainframe systems built using traditional languages, such as COBOL, fall into this category.

In the one-tier system, all three layers are located on the same box and are not separated by interfaces (Exhibit 21), communicating directly between modules. This is very quick to put together, because it can be built and extended as required, without having to define interfaces. However, this approach is not recommended, because the impact of change on such a system may affect multiple, closely coupled areas, that is, there will be more to test and the system may not be scaleable or distributable if the future need arises.

Two-Tier Systems

Two-tier systems are those that have only one boundary between the layers. Because there are three layers, it is possible to have two types of two

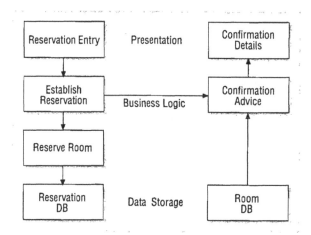

Exhibit 21. One-Tier Application.

tier systems. They are generically referred to as Fat- and Thin- client systems.

The existence of the interface between two of the software layers is what categorizes these systems as being two tier. The implementation may call for both pieces to be placed on the same machine or, more often, to separate them on different platforms to take advantage of the extra processing power or make them shared resources.

Thin-Client/Fat Server

A Thin-Client/Fat-Server system is one where the business logic layer and the data storage layer are kept together (Exhibit 22). This means that the only tier boundary is between the presentation layer and the business logic layer.

With the more widespread availability of stored procedures in databases today, this option is becoming more popular, especially with middleware packages that provide shared, distributed services.

Fat-Client/Thin Server

A Fat-client/Thin-Server two-tier system has both the presentation layer and business logic layer together (Exhibit 23). This means the only tier boundary is between the business logic layer and the data storage layer.

Most early client/server systems followed this model, using a programming language or 4GL to develop a presentation layer that both implemented business rules and used generic or external interfaces to access the databases.

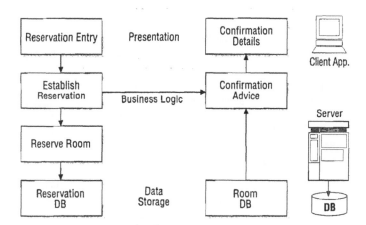

Exhibit 22. Thin-Client/Fat-Server Two-Tier System.

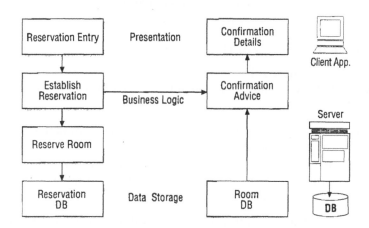

Exhibit 23. Fat-Client/Thin-Server Two-Tier System.

Three-Tier Systems

Three-tier systems are those that have two tier boundaries. Each logical software layer is separated from the others by well-defined interfaces.

Commonly, these types of system are implemented on separate machines, but the three tier style does not preclude implementation on any form of physical configuration — one, two or three physical hardware tiers. Exhibit 24 shows a typical implementation of the system using a separate platform for each software layer.

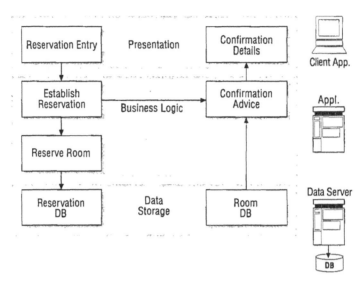

Exhibit 24. Three-Tier System.

Deciding on the Number of Tiers/Layers

This section discusses the decision as to how many logical layers and physical tiers to use. There is no definitive style that will meet all application needs:

- From the point of view of maintainability, the most modular design will be the easiest to maintain and enhance.
- On the other hand, every additional interface or level of indirection will negatively affect the performance of the processing as well as increasing the initial development cost.

Historically, the starting point for this decision depended upon a designer's background. A mainframe expert would start at the one-tier application and look for reasons to move to more tiers. On the other hand, a client/server person might decide to start with three platforms and move down or up only if required.

The most common starting point for traditional distributed architectures today is to start with the assumption of two logical layers and two physical tiers. This can be seen in design of major "out of the box" solutions, such as PowerBuilder™, Visual Basic™, and other data-oriented products. The trend in the netcentric world is more oriented toward starting with a three physical/three logical tier system because this often offers two tiers over which the architect has control and a public client that is not owned by the application owner.

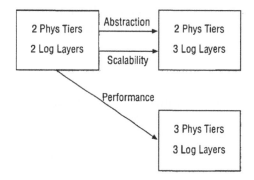

Exhibit 25. Tier/Layer Decision Process.

The decision process is affected by three major drivers, as shown in Exhibit 25:

- Abstraction
- Performance
- Scalability

Abstraction

Maintainability is best served by separating the modules with well-defined interfaces. This will allow developers to work on selected modules, without worrying about changes in the other layers. Thus using three logical layers is an architectural decision that affects the development and ongoing maintenance of a system, but does not affect the operation as much.

Abstraction also offers the benefit of implementation transparency.

When a client requests service X, it is not required that the client know how service X has been implemented. It may be coded in C, COBOL, or even assembler. Such independence allows for both development and maintenance flexibility now and in the future. When a service needs to be replaced, the client does not have to be aware of this maintenance process.

Performance

In a high-volume transaction processing environment, optimization of resources is critical. While one- and two-tier architectures requires trade-offs to be made between optimal configuration of database and application resources, the three physical hardware tier model actually facilitates an optimized environment. Application servers can be tuned and configured to provide high CPU cycles for processing application logic, while database servers will be tuned to provide large cache buffers for the fulfillment of data requests. With the application and database functions resident on their own physical devices, each can be optimally tuned for the work they are designed to perform.

Scalability

Implementation of a system with only two physical tiers generally counteracts one goal of scalability: that a platform can be *right sized* independently of the other platforms in the system. By loosely coupling the systems through known interfaces, the right-sizing can be performed with minimal impact on operations.

In the three physical tier model, client applications no longer connect directly to database servers. Instead, only application servers connect to the database servers. This can effectively reduce the number of connections that must be managed by the database. Therefore, valuable resources are freed up and, as a result, the throughput of the system is increased. The provision of a transaction manager effectively serializes data requests for the database, thus off-loading a great deal of the "non-data-serving" functions the database manager must provide, such as flow control. The benefit using a transaction manager is an increased, and usually more predictable, throughput, because the database essentially becomes scaleable based on throughput of data requests rather than on connected users.

DATA PRESENTATION OPTIONS

The goal of the data presentation decision is to determine how the data should look to the requester, irrespective of the actual data storage option chosen. The ideal solution is to make the data look as much like a simple data store as possible, so that neither the user nor the application need be aware of the physical location or the low level segmentation of the data. However, this is not always practical or feasible, and, as in other areas, there are a number of tradeoffs to be considered.

In this section, the factors influencing the choice of data presentation option are evaluated, and recommendations are made for ensuring that the data locations and segmentation options support the requirements, while maintaining system flexibility.

CHOOSING A DATA PRESENTATION OPTION

There are three major classifications of data presentation options available to modify a client application's perspective of the data stores. The applicability of each data presentation style depends upon the data storage option that has been chosen, as shown in Exhibit 26. The styles are

Exhibit 26. Application of Data Presentation to Data Storage Characteristics

	Data presentation style		
	Centralized appearance	**Segment aware**	**Location aware**
Description	All data for an application appears to be on a single data server	Application can get to any data source, but must be aware of multiple sources	Application can get to any store, but must be aware of the data location and mechanism for retrieval
Data storage options	Centralized or a distributed DBMS	Distributed by location or instance with data routing and distributed transaction services	Distributed by location or instance with no architecture services

Exhibit 27. Effect of Distribution Services on Data Presentation

	Data storage option			
Distribution service style used	**Central data store**	**Distributed by instance**	**Distributed by location**	**Distributed by instance and location**
Distributed DBMS		Centralized appearance	Centralized appearance	Centralized appearance
Data-dependent routing/ORB		Segment aware	Segment aware	Segment aware
Replication		Segment aware	Centralized appearance	Segment aware
No distribution services	Centralized appearance	Segment aware	Location aware	Location aware

- *Centralized appearance.* This allows the application to treat the data as if it were in a central data store.
- *Segment aware.* This allows the data to be accessed without knowledge of the location but with knowledge of how the data has been partitioned.
- *Location aware.* This requires the application to have some knowledge of both the structure of the data partitioning and the location of each data store.

The key distribution service styles are considered in Exhibit 27 in terms of their effect on the type of data presentation that results from applying them to a particular data storage option.

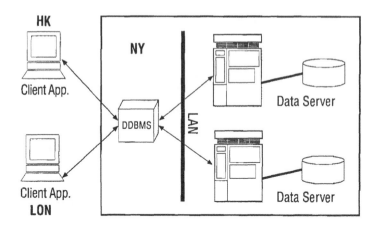

Exhibit 28. Centralizing Data that are "Distributed by Instance" via DDBMS.

Centralized Appearance

For ease of application implementation, the desired option would be to be able to provide an architecture with centralized data presentation appearance. This option describes a data distribution system that enables an application to treat the data access as if it is centrally stored. This means that the application need not be coded with any knowledge of either the true location of the data or the segmentation structure of that data.

This can be achieved in several ways, depending upon the data storage option that has been chosen and the type of distribution services that are employed.

Central Data Store. The central data storage option will always give the appearance of being central. If analysis suggests that additional distribution services are required solely for data presentation reasons, the analysis should be revisited for confirmation, as the presentation is already optimal.

Distribution by Instance. If the data stores are located on separate data servers, but co-located physically, the best approach for making the data appear to be central is a distributed database management system (DDBMS) (Exhibit 28). A DDBMS will typically deal with issues such as coordinating multiple, heterogeneous, data manager products and operating systems, enabling cross-node joins, providing a two-phase commit (2PC) mechanism, and allowing data updates to be performed across multiple data stores. Usually, the DDBMS will be implemented as a packaged solution, although a low throughput DDBMS could be constructed for non-mission-critical operations using a custom integration approach.

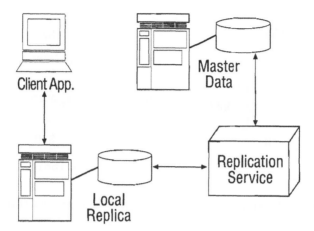

Exhibit 29. Centralizing Data that are "Distributed by Location" via Replication.

At the current state of technology, DDBMS performance is only acceptable on smaller scale systems, since the overhead associated with the distributed two-phase commit and integrity functions make it impractical for larger or highly distributed systems. High transaction volumes, heterogeneous DBMS, and network capacity will normally limit the situations in which a DDBMS is a usable solution.

Distribution by Location. The main solution here would be to implement a replication scheme that will meet the latency and network load limitations that have been set.

Replication

This form of distribution service will put a copy of the relevant data at each location. To the application, the data appear to be in one place, but is in fact distributed, with some form of replication services working behind the scenes to ensure that all the copies of the data are in a coherent and consistent state (Exhibit 29).

Depending upon the form of replication that is chosen, the overhead may be tolerable, but the latency requirements may not met. It is critical to consider whether or not the overhead required to give sufficiently small latency is acceptable, before pursuing a replication strategy like this.

If replication is chosen, it will need to be implemented using a bidirectional replication scheme, as the data may need to be updated across distributed segments. This cannot be done if data update is limited to the local replica.

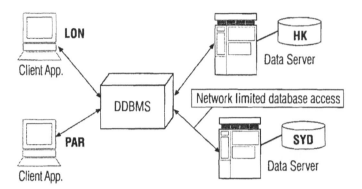

Exhibit 30. Centralizing Location Distributed Data via a DDBMS.

The most serious limitation of a bidirectional replication architecture is the strong possibility of simultaneous, yet contradictory updates being made at different locations. There is currently no known automated solution to this problem.

Bidirectional Replication should be limited to situations where all three conditions below are satisfied:

- The probability of conflicting updates is low.
- Temporary loss of integrity due to those conflicts can be accepted by both the system and the business.
- Conflicts can be manageably resolved by manual intervention.

This effectively restricts the choice of bidirectional replication to situations where the data integrity may be considered low to start with.

DDBMS

It is *technically* possible to implement an architecture that provides central appearance using a DDBMS (Exhibit 30). With the current state of DDBMS and network technology, however, it is typically much too network and processor intensive to be a viable solution for high volume/performance systems.

Segment Aware

The segment aware data presentation style requires that the application be aware of which entities are located in which segments, but not where those segments are located. Thus, a segment-aware application need be only slightly more knowledgeable about the data distribution than one that uses a centralized appearance architecture. Although the application need not be aware of the actual platform location of the data store(s), it must be aware of the fact that the data are not all in one central store, so that data queries and updates will not be attempted across segments.

This segment knowledge will be required by the application developers to prevent them from trying to perform impossible actions, such as a single update to data that is distributed across database segments. The amount of additional information and logic required in the application is usually relatively small, but still critical, and can sometimes be implemented within the DBMS itself. This is especially true where there are plans to scale the solution by adding additional segmentation. In that case, the distribution service becomes a key component in hiding the location of the individual data stores. Segmentation options refer to either horizontal or vertical partitioning of the data across data stores.

Horizontal-partitioned data require that the application either be aware that all rows for a table may be in separate data stores (for cross segment queries) or that the information to which it has access is limited to a subset of data relevant to that application. Thus, a corporate wide query will need to be made against the master data using a different query set.

For vertically segmented data, the application needs to know that a logical record may be stored in more than one place, and so access to the entire record will take more than one request.

As with the centralized appearance, different data storage options can be made to offer a segment aware presentation style to an application by the use of replication or other distribution services.

Data Dependent Routing (DDR). It would be helpful if the application was given some assistance in finding the correct data to access. To that end, several middleware products offer forms of data-dependent routing that allow an application to request data with an additional parameter set that is sent to the DDR manager (Exhibit 31). This parameter is used as a lookup key by the DDR mechanism to ensure that the data request is directed to the correct data manager.

One drawback is that the application can only access data for one DDR key at a time, unless it happens to be aware of exactly how the segmentation has been performed. This leads to a trade-off between the innate awareness of the application vs. the scalability of the data segmentation. In most cases, a directory service is provided as part of the distribution services that will allow the application to become aware of the locations and issue requests accordingly.

The new generation of distributed component systems often make use of an Object Request Broker (ORB) architecture. The ORBs will basically behave in a similar manner to the data dependent routing option, since they are usually implemented with some sort of directory-based distribution service support.

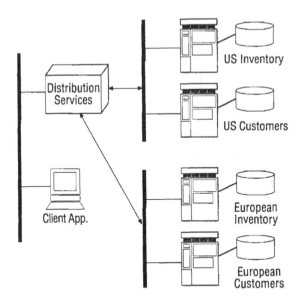

US Inventory

US Customers

European Inventory

European Customers

Distribution Services

Client App.

Exhibit 31. Hiding Data Storage Locations by Using Data-Dependent Routing.

Replication. The options for both data storage distribution by instance or by location and instance are similar, with only the implementation being different. As before, a bidirection replication service would be used to allow this data presentation option to be implemented. Whether the replication is full or partial will depend upon the data needs of the application users and other factors such as system and network overhead and management complexity.

With the replication option, the application still needs to be aware of the segmentation scheme in some detail and is vulnerable to a change in segmentation that might block data access until the application is updated.

Minimal Distribution Services. If the data stores option chosen is distribution by instance at a single location, then the natural appearance of the data will require only a segment aware application. It is still recommended that distribution services be considered to provide future proofing of the application architecture.

Location Aware

The lowest level of data presentation, and also the least desirable, is for the application to have to be aware of both the segmentation of the data and the location and type of each segment. Without any form of data presentation services, the application needs to understand both where data resides and how it is segmented. This will lead to difficulties in maintainability and operations such as disaster recovery and will seriously impact the potential for a scaleable, extensible solution, that is, if the data moves, the application must be changed.

Unidirectional Replication. When a simple replication service is in place, the application may still be required to direct updates to a different data store from the one that it uses for data access. This can be acceptable for relatively static data, but is often enhanced by the addition of application functionality to ensure that a transaction has been effected completely by accessing the master data after each update. The choice of replication timing and/or triggers may be critical to the success of this option.

No Distribution Services. At the lowest level, the application is required to perform the distribution functions programmatically with no distribution services.

CONCLUSION

This chapter has provided an overview of the basic concepts of data and processing distribution as well as the basics of formulating a strategy for the allocation itself. The next chapter describes the mechanics involved in finalizing the distribution strategy.

Chapter 18
Finalizing the Distribution Strategy

This chapter covers the guidelines and high level tasks required to finalize the distribution strategy (Exhibit 1). In most cases, it will be necessary to perform the high level analyses to form the appropriate replication and segmentation strategies. Once the decision to distribute the data has been made, the question turns to how it should be done. In addition, the final portion of the high level design will look at additional techniques that may be required to provide better performance and/or availability of an architecture or application by locating the processing in multiple places.

SEGMENTATION VS. REPLICATION

Segmentation is often confused with replication. Although they often are closely linked, they are distinct techniques for distribution, which need to be considered together with any availability or performance enhancing techniques.

- *Data segmentation.* This entails partitioning a set of data into fragments that will be located on different data servers.
- *Data replication.* This involves copying sets of data from one location to another while still providing some level of synchronization between the data at each location.

Neither one is required by the other, but they are often used together to fulfill the business requirement. As a result, segmentation and replication requirements will also have direct impact on the design of the applications or application architecture. As seen in Exhibit 2, both replication and segmentation strategies can be implemented independently. However, it is not uncommon for them to be considered together, especially when data have been segmented by user site for replication at that site.

DATA SEGMENTATION STRATEGY

Segmentation is the process of breaking the data entities into multiple pieces (sometimes called partitioning or fragmentation). This can be done

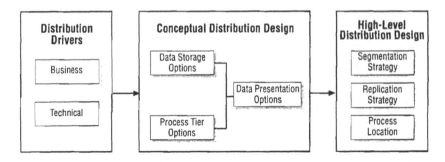

Exhibit 1. High-Level Distribution Design Activities.

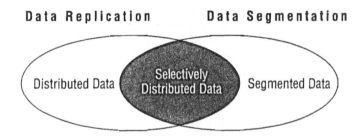

Exhibit 2. Replication and Segmentation Interactions.

either by row or by entity (column/table). In some cases, this might be done both ways. The basic segmentation styles are

- *Horizontal segmentation.* Some rows of the table are physically stored in one data store, while other rows are physically stored in a different store.
- *Vertical segmentation.* Some entities of the table are physically stored at one location, while other entities of the same table are physically stored at another location. For example, the set of order data entities may be physically distinct from the set of product information entities.

Within this chapter, the database segmentation referred to is for a relational database management system (DBMS), although the techniques can be applied to other types of DBMS.

Before looking at segmentation, it is crucial that a Logical Data Model (LDM) for the system is available. Understanding the basics of data modeling is critical to deciding upon an appropriate data segmentation strategy. The LDM will present a view of what data attributes each entity has and how the entities are related to one another.

Why Segment?

Before discussing why to choose a strategy, we should discuss the reasons why data needs to be segmented. As mentioned in the data storage analysis in the last chapter, the main technical driver towards segmenting is the data server capacity. Either the server does not have the capability of handling the amount of data involved, or it cannot handle the transaction volume against that data.

Additionally, there are the distribution factors. If data *are* being distributed to multiple sites, we may not want every site to have every piece of data. Different user groups need different information from the data. Take, for example, a parts database. The accounting department probably does not care about the specification for a part, and the mechanic does not care who delivered the part, but the warehouse may need both pieces of information. Within the distribution side of segmentation, it is often less complex to only send the part of the database that is needed to a remote site, to save bandwidth usage.

Thus, segmentation and distribution are not synonymous, any more than segmentation and replication were.

CHOOSING A SEGMENTATION STRATEGY

A segmentation strategy will rarely be a simple case of "We will segment horizontally, period." Segmentation will need to be considered both at the enterprise level for the different sites or data servers as well as at the logical level for the various sets of data entities.

- *Evaluate the physical need to segment.* It may be that there will be no strong need to segment at all. If the data storage option selected includes distribution by instance, then some form of segmentation will be required. If data are to be distributed by location, there is a chance that replication of data may be required to make sure that all users have the same information.
- *Evaluate data entity grouping.* Before pursuing the segmentation analysis, it is important to understand the data entity groups concerned and the interactions between the various entities in these groups. Start by identifying the five main data entities on which the capability relies, and then investigate their relationships with each other and other entities
- *Consider implementation without any segmentation.* This would be the full-replica model. If data are required to be made available for a high-availability solution (i.e., to provide local autonomy), allowing the complete data set to be located at each site allows implementation without any segmentation being performed.

- *Evaluate Horizontal Segmentation Strategies.* When data storage is distributed by instance, there is an opportunity for investigating horizontal segmentation of the data across multiple, collocated data servers. Because the data are centrally located, the driver here is the power of the data server. If there is no plan for distributing by location, then the choice of segmentation key can be made according to any reasonable grouping that is available for the degree of partitioning required.

  For distribution that is caused by network limitations or desired autonomy, the data will be distributed by location. Consequently, the segmentation analysis needs to take into account who the major ("power") users groups for the data are. The data analysis for each entity group should then look at whether all the users need equal access to all data or whether it can be restricted at the high level to a limited set of user groups for segments of data at sites closer to these users.

- *Evaluate candidate entities for vertical segmentation.* Considering vertical segmentation generally implies looking for groups of entities that have similar access patterns, or share closely linked references, such as subject-based entity sets. As a result, all data entities related primarily to the ordering functionality may be resident on one data server, while all entities concerned with the customer characteristics may be candidates for a different server. Use of call pattern analyses and transaction volumes will aid in this determination.

  Data segmentation is an iterative rather than a one-time process. Care should be taken to try various scenarios on the proposed segmented PDM to ensure that the performance will not be unduly affected by some massive queries that try to access every segment. The segmentation strategy can be supplemented by a replication strategy, although, in general, segmentation is easier than replication but often provides a lower level of performance. In general, the segmentation strategy is very dependant upon the particular types of access that are required.

Horizontal Segmentation

Horizontal segmentation is often used within a corporation to cover the situations where the access to every record in a table is not required. It is often the case that local/regional users will only be required to work on data pertaining to their locality.

Additionally, when data is distributed by instance, one common choice for deciding on how to split up the data is based on a horizontal segmentation strategy. An example might be a large corporation who wishes to keep personnel data in one central data store but is forced to segment due to the size of data involved. The split might be keyed on the personnel number,

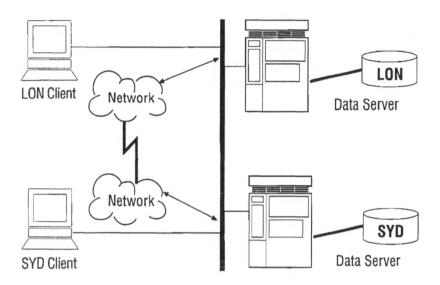

Exhibit 3. Horizontal Data Segmentation.

office location, alphabetic last name, or division, depending upon the breakdown of people for that company.

A location-distributed example might be a global company that has offices in London, New York, and Sydney. The HR function at each site is performed by local personnel. If the London office does not have a great need to access the Sydney office data, it makes sense for the Sydney office to keep its data in Sydney and the London office to keep its in London (Exhibit 3). At each office (data site), the application may see the partial employee data for that office as if it were the entire data for the application.

Determining Segmentation by User Group

When looking at horizontal segmentation as a partitioning strategy, one question to ask is whether the majority of the data access will be coming from the same location as the data. A good rule of thumb is to ensure that at least 80% of the data access volume is being generated at the local data site. Otherwise, it is probably better to position the data at a more central location.

The largest drawback of performing segmentation of data in a horizontal manner is the difficulty of performing simple cross-segment activities because the data are located in different databases.

As long as the data access is only required by local users, the problem remains hidden. However, once someone tries to implement a corporate-wide activity on these distributed segments as a whole, the application performance will decrease sharply — possibly affecting all other users of that data while the activity completes because the entire data for the remote data sites would need to be reconstructed at the local site before the query could be performed. There are a number of ways to get around this in terms of data presentation and replication, which will be covered.

Another major problem is the transfer of data between segments. How do you handle an employee who is transferring from London to Sydney? Perhaps London needs the information for two months after the transfer to handle close-out on vacation balances, yet Sydney needs it two months before the transfer to handle visas, payroll set-up, etc. Common entity life events need to be included in the analysis scenarios that are used designing the final segmentation strategy.

With horizontal segmentation, rows are grouped according to a defining key. This requires that the records be identified uniquely across the entire data store, and that they be located and grouped together according to the characteristics of part of this record key.

Examples of horizontal segmentation schemes could be by

- First letter of last name
- Telephone number area code
- Employee office code
- Birth year
- Account branch code
- Account manager (mobile sales force data)
- Site (inventory for one location only, etc.)

Performing segmentation in a horizontal manner effectively requires that all the subordinate tables for the master segmentation key and all frequently accessed reference data be located at the same site. For example, it is not always a good idea to locate employee personnel data at the local site but keep department information elsewhere, unless the employee/department relation is rarely used.

Choosing the correct key is crucial to the success of the segmentation. The decision should reflect the ownership of the data. The following are some guidelines for choosing an appropriate identifier:

- *The identifier should be fairly static.* An identifier such as a last name may appear to be a relatively static candidate, but might be still be unsuitable if the mechanism for handling such life events as marriage and divorce is not in place.
- *The identifier should be meaningful to the location of the data.* U.S. Social Security numbers (SSNs) are issued based in part on the location issuing the number. Using a SSN as a segmentation key for location-based information, however, may not be a useful choice because

the SSN digits denote the place of issue, not the current place of residence/business. Thus, although the segments will be sized according to birth location, the data relevant to that location might end up being stored on a different data server.

- *The identifier should be unique at all sites.* The U.S. 10-digit phone number does not present uniqueness for international segmentation, as there could be duplication of the identifier at several sites in the Asia, Europe, or other continents that use a local 10-digit phone numbering system.

In addition, for distribution by instance, the key should provide the best data spread in terms of physical placement and volume of transaction. For distribution by location, the key should match the business organization's distribution approach.

In effect, these are similar to the rules of database design, and they also reflect some of the common sense that needs to be applied to distributed data design.

When performed correctly, horizontal segmentation will reflect a natural way to partition data that is in line with the way the application structures its transactions. With all of the keys being unique, this form of data segmentation is able to support the use of referential integrity because all of the records for the key will be located at one data site.

Vertical Segmentation

The most common form of vertical segmentation is storing related entity groups on different data servers. These segments are often viewed as "subject databases" because they are located together based on the type of data contained, not the master identifier.

Examples of subject databases (vertical segmentation) might be

- Order data separate from customer and product data
- Corporate financial accounts separate from customer accounts
- User access kept separately from user information for security reasons.
- Specialty data type content separate from the description/index, e.g., digital asset information (images, sounds, etc.) kept separately from their catalog descriptions

If the vertical segmentation is designed along the same lines as the various, related subject matter, then adding new subject databases is *relatively* straightforward, requiring only an additional segment.

Performing vertical segmentation presents architects with a trade-off in the opposite direction to horizontal segmentation; where one strategy appears strong, the other may be weak and vice versa. For instance, transactions that are interested in a limited amount of detail on all records within an entity can easily be accommodated in a vertically segmented system. On the other hand, those that are concerned with all information about a record may have to access more than one data store.

Implementation of a vertically segmented data store may lead to a more complex strategy for maintaining referential integrity because the data for a single record is now distributed around the corporation. Basically, vertical segmentation is good for breaking up a large database into smaller subject areas; whereas horizontal segmentation is better when the data model is consistent for the various applications and locations, but the data content varies.

In general, vertical segmentation is of most use for either reference data, which is read only, or relatively static data, as well as data that is not as frequently accessed as the main entity information, for example, not every transaction needs to access a photo of the account holder. Vertically segmented data are also useful where the applications do not cross segment boundaries often, i.e., a separate application may service the checking account from the one that deals with CD account transactions. Other situations where vertical segmentation may be considered include those where security is a high priority issue, semirelated data are used in very different ways, or when related data have different storage/retrieval mechanisms.

Segmentation Issues

It is not uncommon to come across implementations where the data has been segmented — both horizontally and vertically. This cannot produce the strengths of both types if the same entity is involved in both types of segmentation, but does present architects with a system that has the limitations of both. Such a system may have complex referential integrity and offer poor performance with either record intensive or entity intensive queries. However, if the system is mostly read only, this scheme may prove valuable. Once the decision to investigate segmentation has been made, several key issues need to be addressed:

- *Segment size.* It is important to determine the number and size of segments in the system for capacity planning, performance testing and other design considerations.
- *Scalability of data size.* Architects should look at areas like the work involved in resizing the segments in a different grouping. For example, if segmentation is performed on the basis of last names, and data space on one server is not sufficient to handle all the Smiths, then it will become necessary to investigate segmenting at an even lower level than last name.

- *Scalability of transaction volume.* Information on the transaction volume expected should have been analyzed while performing the earlier conceptual design steps. These numbers and the growth projections for a horizontally segmented entity need to be analyzed and validated before continuing the segmentation strategy design, in case certain segments have an unnaturally large transaction volume. For the vertical model, this is less of a danger, since additional data stores could be added to support new data entities.
- *Cross-segment intensive transaction handling.* For horizontal partitions, cross-segment intensive transactions are those transactions that attempt to access many records in a table — regardless of site. The normal candidates for creating such transactions are batch processes or global updates. For vertical segmentation, the cross-segment intensive transactions are those that need access to *all* the information about a record, wherever it is stored. Overall, the operational impact of performing segmentation should be studied closely.

DATA REPLICATION STRATEGY

This section looks at the design of the replication strategy, including why replication is used and the various forms of replication available.

The previous section covered the segmentation strategy and among other things the limitation of segmenting the data, in terms of retrieval and update across segments. One way to get around some of the limitations of segmented data is to create synchronized, working copies of the data at the local site. This technique is called replication.

Replication allows multiple copies of a complete data entity to be stored at different sites and, depending upon the chosen strategy, can provide local retrieval or update capabilities. There are several reasons replication is used:

- *Increased local performance.* By providing a local replica, data access is faster than remote network access. Thus, it is not uncommon for data that is used often, yet changes rarely, to be replicated down to the client level.
- *Mobile user support.* In some cases, such as for mobile users, data must be replicated to their mobile systems. The user will attach to the network and either manually, or automatically, up- and download the changed data from their system. Upon disconnecting, the user should still have enough data available to perform their daily workload.
- *Reliability.* Replication also contributes a component for providing local autonomy as part of the distribution strategy. With a local replica, it is possible for the application to continue to support the local users, even if some or all of the nonlocal data is not accessible. Thus,

replication is a strong component to many failover or high availability environments. The downside is that system integrity is deferred until the replication jobs can be run.

- *Reduced network costs.* The cost of improving a network to get high speed access may be significantly greater than adding local data and a replication strategy to keep the data current. If the data replication is not required on an urgent basis, then the replication can take place outside of the normal business hours, allowing the users to get the benefits of both local data performance and autonomy and still have accurate data to work with. The cost of performing the synchronization outside hours is that there will be significant system latency.

There are also very good reasons to avoid replication:

- *Replication is complex.* The very fact that replication is attempting to synchronize multiple data stores, can lead to more effort being put into the replication effort than is put into the main applications. Replication requires that the consequences of lost communications between nodes be accounted for in the design decisions. In addition to the execution costs of replication, system maintenance is also complicated, requiring a deeper skill set from the operations staff.
- *Replication can be risky.* If some form of bidirectional (peer-peer) replication is used, there is always going to be a chance that the replicas will get out of synchronization. There is no known way to undo the damage due to business decisions that have been taken from such contradictory data.
- *Replication can affect performance adversely.* If the wrong replication strategy is chosen, the replication of data may take up more bandwidth on the network than the normal network traffic.

Choosing a Replication Strategy

This section will discuss the two basic styles of replication and the strategies that can be implemented using these styles. In addition, the advantages and disadvantages of the approaches will be discussed. The two basic replication styles are:

- *Unidirectional* — Updates for an entity are sent from master databases to slave databases but not the other way around.
- *Bidirectional* — Updates are sent from multiple replicas for the same entity. Establishing a single master database that owns each entity makes bidirectional replication significantly more manageable. A bidirectional replication scheme with multiple owners is not something to be undertaken lightly.

In addition, the implementation of the different replication strategies can differ by such factors as

- *Latency* — This is the amount of time that a replica is allowed to be out of synchronization with the master data.
- *Write-ability of replicas* — The ability to write to a replica as opposed to just read-only access.
- *Initiator of synchronization* — The choice of update initiator. Primary pushes data to the replica vs. replica requests updates from the primary.
- *Full or partial updates* — Replication of all data to every replica vs. limiting replication selectively to data known to be required locally, i.e., just data that has changed.
- *Replication trigger mechanism* — Replication between data stores could be initiated by several means: batch jobs, periodic updates, just-in-time, or manual.

The main trade-off comes in terms of improving the speed of access to the data vs. maintaining the multiple copies with the same data in them.

In addition to the high level styles and characteristics of a replication strategy, there are some equally important, lower level considerations in the implementation of the strategy that will affect the latency, network traffic, etc. Among the mechanisms available to effect the data copying exchange are such enabling technologies as snapshots, transactional replication and trigger-based replication.

Typically, no one custom develops replication tools anymore. The sheer complexity of replication implies that architects should be looking to major software vendors (generally via database vendors) for tools to address replication if required.

Unidirectional Replication

One of the easiest compromises between no replication and full replication is to limit replication to a single direction. This means that the "local" replica is effectively read only data and any updates must be transmitted to the master copy (often at the central site). This form of replication is most often used for data that requires significantly less update access than read access and so is particularly useful for relatively static data or providing a warm standby data store for disaster recovery. Styles of unidirectional replication include

- *User initiated extraction.* The users data store takes responsibility for requesting and/or extracting updated data from the master copy. This is a pull technology, that is often used for read-only data. The strategy relies on human intervention and so may not be suitable for mission-critical systems/large user groups/large data sets.
- *Data snapshot.* A snapshot is a copy of data that is frozen and sent to the replica data managers at a prearranged time. Generally there is a

batch process involved, and between the transmission of each snapshot, there is the probability that the replicas will be left in a state of incoherence. The snapshot mechanism can be built-in with some DBMSs.

Two variants of this technique exist, allowing either the complete data store contents or differential update of all the changes from the last known checkpoint to be sent- the latter saving bandwidth and processing power.

• *Publish/subscribe.* This form of replication allows the master database (at a "central" location) to broadcast updates to the replicas. In its simplest form, this would be performed by storing transaction updates until a pre-arranged threshold was met. At this point the updates are published for the replicas. The replicas in turn, subscribe to the publication and look out for relevant broadcasts. This technique can be useful when selective replication is being performed, as a replica may only wish to know about some of the updates. This technique can also be used for bidirectional replication.

With any periodic update mechanism, the lower the setting of the update period threshold, the smaller the latency (out of synchronization period) becomes.

Taking this to its logical conclusion would be a threshold of a single transaction. This is the algorithm used to provide a "real-time" update capability, with the transaction being updated on the replicas as soon as it clears the master. The disadvantage of this update method comes in the amount of network and CPU resources required to support the updates, and the fact that the replication effectively requires the implementation of a synchronous or transactional update system.

Under certain circumstances, the publish/subscribe method can be extended into a hierarchical topology by designating a subscriber to perform the role of publisher for a lower tier of data stores

Bidirectional Replication

Under certain circumstances, the ability to update at more than one site becomes a requirement. This calls for a more complex, dedicated data manager capability to perform bidirectional replication. Bidirectional replication is used in strategies known as peer-to-peer, fast, or symmetric replication.

Whenever a change is made on any of the data stores, the information is transmitted almost immediately to all the peers in the network. The system can be implemented using either a central mediator or directly between peer systems.

The main advantage to this form of replication is improved local performance, with the local replica providing a fully functional copy of the data that can be accessed and updated locally.

The main cost of implementing this style of replication is the additional task of dealing with the inevitable replication conflicts that will come from simultaneous updates of the same records. This can be exacerbated by the network being out of commission, since the updates will accrue without being propagated.

Note that conflict resolution is not an insignificant issue, but a major consideration in the decision to use bidirectional replication. The architect should be wary of choosing a bidirectional replication scheme without thoroughly investigating and addressing the issues that will come from that decision. The penalty for not addressing these issues can be very high, when crucial business decisions are made from inconsistent data.

Another trade off is the requirement for additional network and processor resources to handle both the normal updates and the conflict resolution; a cost that grows exponentially with the system.

Selective Replication

A variant in the architects tool kit of replication choices is selective or partial replication, which gives the ability to combine the tactics of segmentation and replication. In this variant, only a subset of data is replicated, often with different subsets being chosen for each replica. This is often the most complex of all the options to architect, without risking other areas such as scalability at a later date.

One scenario where employment of this option is applicable would be a mobile sales force automation application.

1. Typically, such an application would only contain the data relevant to that day's sales calls (*horizontal segmentation*).
2. The sales manager may require specific data pertinent to executing a sales, but may not need other customer data, which is stored in a master database (*vertical segmentation*).
3. Last, the sales force should have access only to copies of the data to mitigate the risks created by a catastrophic event, such as losing the only copy of data if a laptop is stolen (*replication*).

Replication Scenarios

This section will address a number of the typical replication scenarios that are used.

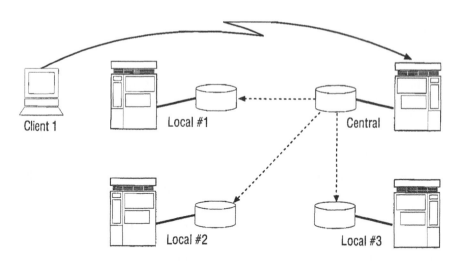

Exhibit 4. Single Updatable Master with Remote Logon Capability.

Single Updatable Master. In this scenario, there is a single master copy of the data at a central/coordinating (Master) site with multiple replicas distributed across the network to individual local sites. Because there is only a single master, the update scheme will use unidirectional replication. The master database may be updated in several ways.

Central Update. Any updates made to the master data are made only at the central location and then distributed out to the various local databases. This approach is generally used for data that apply to the entire organization, data that by its nature are maintained by a single user group. One example would be the part numbers of all the products in a company's product line.

Remote Logon. The users of the local databases can make changes to the master data owned by their location via remote logon to the central master site (Exhibit 4), albeit with latency issues. This approach would require security controls to regulate the access by local sites to the coordinating/central site and to the data. The changes made by the local site are then reflected in the next distribution of data to the users' local database via the selected replication mechanism. This approach allows local update of central data, while still maintaining a centralized master database.

Remote Batch. The local users make changes that are batched locally, then sent to the coordinating/central location for processing (Exhibit 5). Once again, the changes are reflected in the next update of their local database.

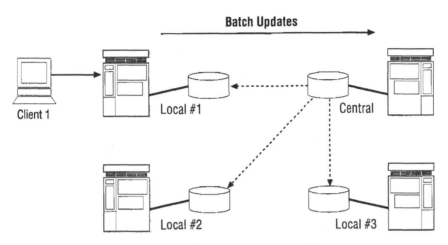

Exhibit 5. Single Updatable Master with Remote Batch Update.

This approach also requires adequate security controls to ensure that the local site is updating only their own data. This is fundamentally the same approach as remote logon but allows the actual update processing at the master location to be scheduled at convenient times. If this approach is extended to allow multiple sites the ability to update the same data, the central site must have processing in place to resolve update conflicts and notify the local sites if their transaction has been rejected.

Local Checkout. This scenario allows the local site to dynamically acquire ownership of any master data and modify it. The data is transmitted from the master database (checked out) to the local machine, updated, and then returned after the update. While the master data is checked out, others are restricted to read-only use.

This approach is most effective when many users require the ability to update the same data, but there is no clear owner of the data, and data integrity must be guaranteed. Implementation of this approach may require building a custom locking system, if one is not already supported by the DBMS. This strategy would require the data to be transferred upon request from the central site to a local site.

The single updatable master scenario maintains the most centralized control of the data and therefore is more suited for data that needs tighter security. This scenario is also the least complex to implement.

Local Update: Single Owner. In this scenario, updates are made locally by the one local site that owns the data. Each local database contains the data required for local operations and can update data that is locally owned. This

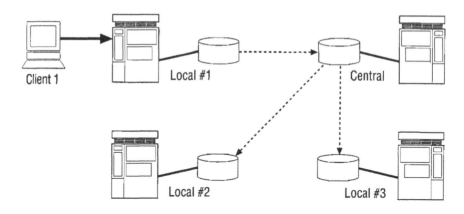

Exhibit 6. Local Update with Coordinator Site.

scenario applies when the data are segmented and reside at only one local site and at the central site or when data reside at more than one site and a control mechanism is in place to restrict update authorization to a single site.

There is still only one owner for each data instance or row in the system, but the changes are made locally first and then either shipped to a central/coordinating site for distribution or distributed directly to other local sites. There are two possible update scenarios that could be used to distribute the changes from the local database to the other remote databases:

Local Update with Coordinator Site. The local site transfers all of the data changes to the central/coordinating site. The coordinating/central site then propagates the changes to other local sites (Exhibit 6). The coordinator maintains the information needed to distribute the changes to the local databases. Because the distribution of data to other sites is performed by a single coordinating location, this is probably the easiest way to distribute changes to other local databases.

Local Update with No Mediator. This strategy places the burden of distribution on the local machine, because each local site distributes its changes to the other local sites on the system (Exhibit 7). Thus, each local site must then be responsible for routing the data to the other sites.

If the central site is retained in this scenario and is not responsible for distribution to other sites, it may be required for several other reasons. First, as an backup copy of the data. This can be quite useful if data becomes corrupted or lost at the local sites. Second, as a source of data for management reports. If the report needs to span multiple sites, it is easier to use the central site for data than to go to each local site one-by-one.

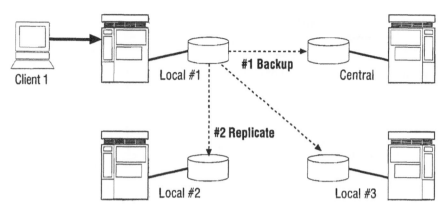

Exhibit 7. Local Update with No Mediator.

Third, as a "hot backup." If communication is lost between the local sites, it may still be possible to get the information from the central site.

Local Update: Multiple Owners. This scenario allows multiple sites the ability to update the *same local data*. This scenario either removes the ownership from the data or allows multiple owners of the same data.

Because there are multiple owners, this will need to be implemented using bidirectional replication. Therefore, this scenario is very complex to implement as it allows multiple sites the authority to update the same row. With this scenario, update conflicts are inevitable. Because of these conflicts, a means must be found to mediate between conflicting update requests and determining which update should be performed and which should be rejected.

Two major ways of implementing this type of update scenario are

- Use of a central site mediator
- Peer-to-peer database updates

Central Site Mediator — A central/coordinating site, with a master database, acts as a mediator for a group of semiautonomous databases (Exhibit 8). This scenario allows the local sites to update their local data and then send the update to the coordinator. The coordinating site must then be able to mediate conflicting updates to the master database from local sites.

This conflict resolution mechanism also requires the addition of error processing. The rejection of the update by the master site must be communicated to the remote site that initiated the update, typically in the workflow process. If that update was made to the local database, that update will be lost when the new master is distributed to the local database.

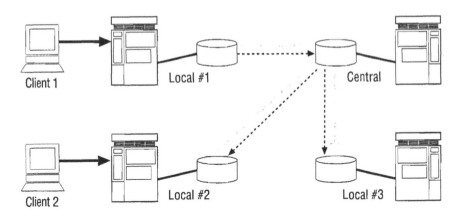

Exhibit 8. Bidirectional Replication with Central Mediator.

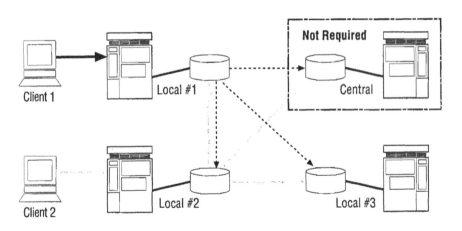

Exhibit 9. Bidirectional Replication Using Peer–Peer Coordination.

Error processing procedures, like those needed for the above example, add to the complexity of a central site mediator scenario. In addition, the complexity increases in magnitude when multiple transactions, affecting multiple rows, in multiple tables, that comprise a single logical unit of work (LUW) are added to the application.

Peer-to-Peer Database — In this scenario, all databases in the system are equal, there is no single site controlling the update process (Exhibit 9). Changes made to data on one database are transmitted to all databases containing duplicates of that data. This feature is one that many relational database vendors are attempting to integrate into their Distributed Database Management Systems (DDBMS).

Note that a central coordinator site is not required in this scenario, but it may be retained for the same sort of archiving and coordination activities described for local updates with no mediator.

PROCESS LOCATION OPTIONS

This section covers some of the additional considerations that may need to be addressed in the area of application process distribution. These areas, described in detail below, include

- Database communications style
- Context management
- Synchronous and asynchronous processing
- Resilience
- Load balancing

Distributing the processing almost always means that the processes must communicate, which implies some form of middleware or distribution services, which, in turn, implies complexity.

Some of the reasons that processing might be distributed include

- Desire to off-load processing to another machine (often cheaper), freeing the (expensive) one for other processing.
- Improving data server throughput with a flow controlling server.
- Providing common interfaces to legacy systems (and data) on a centrally maintained server process. Sharing legacy system interfaces means that processes are distributed and can therefore be reused rather than replaced or rebuilt.
- Provide system scalability.
- Provide for systemwide resilience and/or autonomy.
- Provide the features and flexibility of middleware, where 3+ tiers are not otherwise required.

Database Communications Style

There are two models that are concerned with the interface between the Business Logic and the Data Storage layers. This interface is also involved in the three-tier world, typically between the application server and the data server.

The two models — *Distributed Function* and *Remote Data Management* — differ significantly in terms of the communication style over the interface. There are two fundamental approaches to implementing this interface in most situations, both are used regularly.

Data-Moving Interface. The *Remote Data Management* model uses what is known as a data-moving interface. The Business Logic layer talks locally to the Data Management layer on the client side, using, in most cases, an embedded SQL (E-SQL) language and some form of local database runtime library.

The effect of this is that the data requests are passed to the data server, which retrieves the bulk data and moves it down to the client for processing. This means that the complete data set may be sent down to the client, and the client will process this data set and extract/update the required fields. Even for a small result set, the amount of data that is sent to the client can be large.

Message Passing Interface. The *Distributed Function* model uses a technique known as stored procedures (SP). These are essentially precompiled queries that are located on the data server, waiting to be triggered with the appropriate parameters. Communication is in the form of small, preformatted messages and appropriate responses.

The client does not need to see all of the data, as it is preprocessed on the data server, within the SP. Thus the amount of network traffic is reduced as little unused data is sent over the interface between the data server and the client.

Choosing a style is, once again, a question of trade-offs in a number of areas:

- *Network traffic.* Using Stored Procedures can significantly reduce the amount of network traffic, especially for small result sets.
- *Server performance.* Using Stored Procedures means that an amount of the processing is now taking place on the data server. This will have a more significant impact as the data server is scaled upwards, until the load is too large to handle.
- *Configuration management.* Often overlooked during the architecture phases, the issues involved with implementing matching software versions on two systems can be horrendous, particularly with a rapid release schedule. Significant development and production procedures should be implemented to ensure that when a stored procedure is called, it is the correct version, not one from the last release.
- *Software licensing.* Although less important lately, due to more flexible licensing agreements, the issues involved with licensing can drive a decision towards placing all specialized software as close to the data server (on the least number of machines) as possible.
- *Performance.* Network traffic aside, the implementation of stored procedures means that the data transfer across the Business Logic/Data Storage layer interface will take place on a single machine, at Internal Bus speeds, rather than network speeds. This can be very advantageous to performance, if the load can be handled by the data server.

Context Management

Context management is concerned with the control of the end-to-end transaction session.

Stateful Session Servers. Some systems require that the server take responsibility for maintaining the session state, such that clients can disconnect, temporarily, and return at a later date to pick up where they were.

A stateful system is usually implemented using in-built architectural capabilities of a middleware package. This will allow the client to make a request of the middleware and have that package act as the flow controller and director for the resources and services required by the session. This relieves the client of some of the load and knowledge about the system topology, making the transaction appear to happen in a transparent manner.

If the state-carrying server dies, then the transaction must be abandoned, in whatever state of completion it might be, and resubmitted when a new server can be found. The outcome of the initial transaction depends upon the recovery mechanisms that have been implemented by the system designers.

Stateless Servers. Other systems are designed such that the client is responsible for tracking the session flow and letting the server know where they were when communication was last dropped. A stateless system relies upon overhead in the client application to track what is happening with the session. This results in a more complex application, with the client either updating its own state or receiving and storing updates from the server.

If the server is lost, the client has the state information locally, and can continue the transaction/session with another server. This means that the overall system will be more robust, as the client can transparently make use of resilient and load-balancing features of the architecture.

Synchronous vs. Asynchronous Processing

Although not a direct feature of distributed systems, the distinction between processing modes is important to understand, especially when choosing or designing distribution services and middleware.

With a synchronous processing service, the application makes a request and then stops all processing on that thread, until the response returns. This style is also known as a blocking service.

On the other hand, an asynchronous service will allow the requester to make a request, disconnect, and then come back later to look for the response, thereby continuing to work, while the transaction Is handled elsewhere. The client will carry the state of the transaction or some piece of reference information that can be used to ask for the status of the request. This style is also known as a nonblocking service.

Each style has its own use, and the decision as to which is appropriate should be gathered from the business requirements for each business capability.

Resilience

Although left to the end of the this section, the issue of resilience is one that requires a lot of understanding for each system. Resilience has been partially addressed on the data side, by the use of segmentation and/or replication techniques to provide some, albeit limited, capability at a local site that is cut off from the data center.

The process side is somewhat simpler, in that the existence of two or more copies of a process is not a problem in the same way that two copies of a data entity are. The main issue is making sure that a copy of the process that offers a particular service can be found.

This is where the choice of context management style comes into play. By choosing a scheme whereby the client retains the information needed to continue to perform a transaction, resilience can be made easier.

Load Balancing

Like resiliency, load balancing is another related facet in the distribution strategy. Whereas resiliency involves the duplication of processes on more than one box, with in a tier, load balancing involves segmenting the services that make up an application onto more than one box. This allows the entire system to be sized at the enterprise level.

It is not uncommon for different platforms on an office automation network to provide different services. There may be boxes dedicated to supporting the files for different organizations, another set dedicated to supporting printers on each floor, and yet another for modem support, external access, etc. This is a form of load balancing at the macro level; the number of servers for each function can be adjusted to support the load on that function.

In a similar manner, an enterprise architecture may well want to perform the same sort of segmentation at the custom service level. For instance, only one or two boxes may need to run some of the batch functions, however, there may be a need for a large number of report services or other lookup services. Complex transaction processing may require the dedication of transaction processing servers on multiple machines, in order to ensure that the response time can be kept constant and within agree levels.

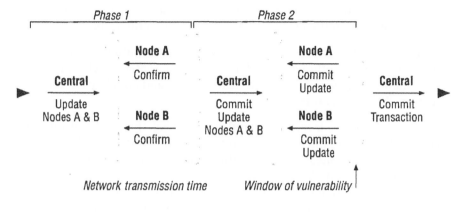

Exhibit 10. Two-Phase Commit (2PC).

Two-Phase Commit

Two-phase commit (2PC) is a key component of a true DDBMS. It is the integrity mechanism that attempts to ensure that a transaction is protected and either completed or undone across all sites This integrity mechanism is divided into a PREPARE phase and a COMMIT phase. The work done by the DBMS during these two phases may differ depending on the DBMS. A common approach is described below (Exhibit 10).

- *Prepare.* The PREPARE phase queries all the remote sites to verify that they are ready to commit. The PREPARE phase initiates the clean-up tasks of the memory management facilities at each site. If a participating site (not the coordinating site) is unable to receive the PREPARE message (and any subsequent rollback), it periodically checks for unreleased locks (or checks when communication and processing is restored) and queries the coordinator about the status of the transaction. The coordinator responds that the transaction was rolled back since all sites could not participate and the participating site also rolls back, releasing all locks.
- *Commit.* The COMMIT phase tells each participating local site to write a commit log record. If the commit is successful at all of the remote sites involved in the transaction, and the originating site receives a successful acknowledgment from each of the remote sites, the transaction at the originating site is committed.

This 2PC implementation does leave a small margin of vulnerability. If the remote site commits, but the initiating site does not receive acknowledgment of the commit, the initiating site does not know whether to commit or roll back. As a result, the initiating site will try to hold on to the locks indefinitely, waiting for the acknowledgment. The probability of this occurring increases with the number of sites involved in the transaction.

2PC is the best way to ensure that two separate databases remain synchronized. If some other approach is used to guarantee synchronization, it must incorporate similar synchronization logic and could mean building a custom 2PC architecture.

However, the 2PC is more honored in the breach than in the observance. The strategy is complicated, time consuming, and costly. It relies on complex synchronous messaging over the network. Communications failures can have a substantial impact on the usability of this system. In addition, the common approach requires participation and success from all sites involved in the transaction. If one site cannot complete the transaction, the entire transaction fails.

Until the technical issues are resolved, or if the potential problems are not an issue, 2PC is best used for retrieval and update scenarios where only one site is being updated although multiple sites may be queried.

In many cases over the years, if the integrity constraints of distributed data were so demanding as to necessitate 2PC, it was worthwhile to reopen the question of the validity of the use of distributed data. Often the absolute need for 2PC indicates that the data under consideration is not suitable for distribution due to some underlying functional issues.

BUILDING DATA DISTRIBUTION SOFTWARE

When it is not possible to use a distributed database product, it may be necessary for the architecture team to build a custom data distribution approach. The following two approaches, application driven and data driven, have been developed successfully in support of large client/server systems. However, a note of caution is necessary, as implementing the data distribution schemes often proves to be the single most difficult part of such projects.

Application Driven

In the application driven strategy, the data is modified by an application; the application then transfers the updates out to the remote databases as required. One way to apply the application driven strategy is for the application to be responsible for both modifying and distributing the data. Or, the application can modify the data and then send a message to another program, which is responsible for distribution of the data. In both cases, the application must "know" that the updated data should be distributed to other locations. For example, some code, no matter how small, must be executed after data have been changed. In the first case, the application must also know how to route the data to other locations.

At the initiating or sending site, each application is designed to perform two main functions. First, the application must perform all the processing required to update the database with the new data. Second, the application must decide if the updated data should be distributed to other remote sites, then distribute the updated data or trigger their distribution.

At the receiving site, applications are performing the normal processing for that site, as well as waiting for messages from other sites containing updates to their database. As these messages are received, they are processed by applications and the updates are made to the database.

This application-driven strategy provides for one of the quickest distributions of data as the completion of activity at one site triggers the transfer of the data to other sites.

The application driven strategy works best when

- The routing of the data is static
- Data are always routed to a remote location
- No further processing is required after the initial update

For example, modification of product description information that is always distributed to the same sales offices would be a suitable fit for the application driven strategy.

If the installation is such that the update to the data will require further processing, and that processing may be local or remote, this strategy may encounter some complications. For example, consider an organization with sales locations and warehouse locations. Some of the sales offices and warehouses are physically located at the same place. If an application (called "take_order") was creating a sales order, it would have to know which local offices were sales or sales/warehouse operations in order to determine if and where the order should be distributed.

If an order required distribution, the application would then send that order to the appropriate warehouse where it would be received by another application program (called "fill_order"). Fill_order would finish processing the order, creating a pick list and reserving inventory. If an order can be filled locally, the message is sent internally to the local version of fill_order, which then creates the pick list and reserves inventory.

In this example, the loss of a message anywhere in the process is a serious problem to either of the applications. The take_order application is relying on a message to trigger further processing by fill_order. A means must be found to guarantee the delivery and processing of messages in all situations or there is the risk of incomplete processing. To prevent incomplete processing, programs can be developed to continue processing even after message failure. However, these error correction programs can add considerably to the complexity of the installation.

To reduce the complexity of the applications, the routing of messages between application programs can be incorporated into common distribution modules. For example, a send_message system module can be created to handle the actual routing of the message to the remote site. The application program would call the send_message module, passing it a list of parameters, and allow it to perform the actual routing of the message across the network. The application programmer would be insulated from the detailed steps required to route the message to the remote site, greatly simplifying the application.

The application driven transfer strategy is very flexible and can be appropriate for many retrieval and update scenarios. It can generally be adapted to the requirements of most installations. The approach was used, for example, by a large government system for processing and sharing benefits information throughout hundreds of sites.

The major weakness of the application driven transfer strategy is that some form of record locking must be used in conjunction with this strategy to prevent update conflicts. For that reason, an application driven transfer strategy is usually combined with the Central Site Mediator scenario to handle record locking. An additional drawback is that application programs must be much more aware of which data is held in which locations. Without proper forethought about the structure of applications with regard to data location, this strategy can produce a maintenance nightmare as data locations are moved, split, and combined.

Data Driven

The data driven strategy requires the initial application to process the data, and then set a status flag within the data to signal the completion of a processing step.

With a data driven strategy, one application does not call the next when complete, but rather marks the status in the data. Because of that, an event-based or time-based mechanism is needed to continue the flow of processing. This can be done in several ways:

- A scheduler initiates application processing every (n) minutes.
- An application program "wakes up" and checks for new transactions it should process every (n) minutes.
- A scheduler monitors a log file of modifications to the database and initiates processing when detecting record changes.

- A database trigger is fired whenever a record is updated that checks to see based on the new status if an additional application program should now be run. For example, order status has been changed to "shipped," therefore run billing program.
- A user chooses an option on a menu to process all new transactions with a particular status.

In the data driven strategy, the status of the data drives its processing. Consider what would happen with the addition of multiple sites. A separate group of modules would need to be created to distribute data to other sites. These modules are also triggered by the status of data. If the status changes to an appropriate value, the distribution module will transfer that data to another location. Take the same example given previously in the application driven strategy. If the order status is set to FILL by the take_order program this can trigger two separate responses:

- If the sales and warehouse are at the same location, the FILL status is discovered by the fill_order program when it automatically checks the database. The fill_order program then creates the pick list and reserves the inventory.
- If the sales and warehouse are at different locations, the FILL status is discovered in the database by the sending distribution modules when they are awakened by the scheduler. The sending distribution modules transfer the order to a warehouse where the receiving distribution modules insert it into the local database. At some point, the fill_order program is awakened by the scheduler and it discovers the FILL status of the order by checking the database. The fill_order program then creates the pick list and reserves the inventory.

The datadriven strategy does not require that the decision of whether to fill the order locally or remotely be made by the take_order program. In fact, the take_order program does not even know of the existence of the fill_order program and does not communicate with it. Each of these programs performs independently of the other. The decision of whether or not to fill the order locally or remotely is made by the presence or absence of the distribution modules. If you have combined functions into the same office, you simply do not install some of the data distribution modules.

In this strategy, the fill_order application is no longer triggered by the arrival of a message, but is initiated by the scheduler. If the scheduler or application fails, the processing will be delayed. Because the application recovery processing is built into the system, it will automatically complete when the problem is corrected.

At the initiating or sending site, applications perform their processing based on the data entered by the user or based on the status of key fields in the data. When the applications have completed their processing, they set the correct status value in one of the status fields and quit processing. A separate set of system data distribution modules is responsible for transferring the updates to the remote site, based on the status of the data. If local processing is completed, based on the status of the data, the data will be extracted and transferred to a remote site by the distribution modules.

At the remote or receiving site, the data distribution modules wait for incoming data from other sites. When new data arrive, the distribution modules insert that data into the database. The receiving site application modules are then able to process this new data the next time they are started, by the scheduler, database trigger, or by some user action.

The easiest way to design a database for this strategy is to make the database definition for all sites *identical*. This allows all the application modules to be placed anywhere in the system and be assured they will always be able to access the data using the same database calls.

If the database definition is different at each location, different database calls will need to be incorporated into the same application depending on where it is located. This can quickly complicate the efforts needed to track system configuration as well as the distribution of later system updates and fixes. Despite the common database definition, there is no need for the database to be completely populated. Each location maintains only the data it requires for its local functions.

The data driven approach provides excellent de-coupling between individual application programs. Rather than applications *calling* each other, and thus knowing where each other are, applications communicate with each other solely by updating status fields within database records.

The data driven strategy is suitable for update scenarios. Like the application driven strategy, it may require additional enhancements if update conflicts are possible, and the DBMS does not provide appropriate locking mechanisms. This approach was used, for example, in a global sales and order processing system to enable countries and locations to operate more or less independently and without an undue reliance on communications availability.

Whatever decisions regarding frequency of updating and the quantity of information to be moved, chances are that the decisions will be modified over time as business requirements and other conditions change. This is even more pronounced in a distributed environment than in a non-distributed environment. Distributed environments by their nature are dynamic: the location of data may change, the refresh requirements may change, or the business functions may move from one site to another. It is critical to incorporate flexibility into the implementation of a data refresh strategy so it can easily change with the business.

PROCESSING DISTRIBUTION

Client/server and netcentric computing allow for an application to be divided across two or more computers — typically an end user workstation or PC, and a multiuser server machine. In contrast to traditional centralized mainframe application design, client/server supports dividing a single application across multiple machines. How the application logic is to be divided between client and server is dictated by the nature of the application, the data needed by the application, and the specific benefits of client/server that the project is trying to realize. The following are some of the potential benefits of dividing processing in a client/server architecture.

Dedicated Processing Power

In the traditional mainframe configuration, hundreds or even thousands of users share a single mainframe computer. To run mainframes economically, a shop likes to keep processors utilized over 70%. This means that the mainframe is busy at least 70% of the time when a user strikes a key requesting processing; the user must wait in line to be served.

The model suggests that the *computer* is the important resource and that people should wait in line to use it. Client/server reverses this view by providing each user with a dedicated machine, as well as access to additional shared machines. The desktop computer now has processing power ready and waiting for the user to take some action.

Consider one example of the impact of dedicated, inexpensive processing power. One organization recently implemented a client/server system that replaced an existing mainframe system. The original system supported 800 users with a single 100 MIPS mainframe computer. The new client/server system supported 500 users with *12,000* MIPS of processing power for half the price. The result altered the way the organization thought about the system, and about the importance of efficiently using people time rather than computer time. It opened the organization's eyes about new uses of cheap and always available processing power.

Price/Performance Increase

The price of computer cycles on desktop PCs continues to be dramatically less than computer cycles on multiuser mainframe computers. Depending on the configuration, this price differential can be as much as two orders of magnitude. It was this price/performance gap that provided the first spark for moving at least some of the application processing workload off of the mainframe and onto the "cheap" PC.

Enhanced Usability

One direct benefit of the increased availability of cheap dedicated processing power is the ability to devote large amounts of processing resources to produce a better interface for the end user. The most common first step toward ease of use is to provide the user with a GUI. A graphical interface demands large amounts of processing capacity (as anyone can attest who has tried to run Microsoft Windows on a 286 PC). In addition, the processing must be dedicated; making a user wait after clicking on a pull-down menu does *not* increase usability.

Availability

Availability is an issue in a traditional mainframe environment where all application processing occurs on a centralized mainframe machine. If the machine becomes unavailable for any reason (such as for maintenance, backups, or system failure), all hundreds or thousands of users who depend upon it will be without any computing access. With client/server, even if the server or servers become unavailable, users still have access to their own workstations.

We should note one important caveat about increased availability: you must carefully think through what *data* as well as processing resources the user needs access to in order to continue work. In most client/server configurations, overall availability is not improved by having workstations because all of the applications require data (such as inventory statistics) that are stored only on a shared server. If the server goes down, every user is out of luck, just as in the mainframe scenario.

PROCESSING DISTRIBUTION APPROACHES

Of the five styles of client/server processing (see Chapter 2 for a discussion of the Gartner Group's five styles), the three most often implemented are

1. Remote data management
2. Distributed logic
3. Remote presentation

Remote Data Management

In the remote data management approach, the entire application runs on the client workstation, sending SQL or SQL-like messages to the server, which functions as a shared database machine.

In practice, the server also ends up running the application "batch" load as well. The introduction of client/server computing almost always leads to moving significant portions of application processing out — off the central mainframe and onto the client workstation. The great majority of client/server applications being developed today fit this category. In fact, most popular development tools, such as PowerBuilder and Visual Basic, are largely geared toward building this style of client/server application.

The remote data management distribution approach is excellent for database-centric style applications such as data maintenance or reporting because it off-loads application processing from the server platform and is an easy development model to implement.

Distributed Logic

In the distributed logic style the application is split in half, with part running on the workstation and part on the server platform. This configuration allows for the placement of application code on the machine (client or server) that is best suited to the task.

This flexibility can be useful if a particular application routine is very processing intensive (such as rules-based or linear optimization) and can be executed on a high-powered server computer instead of the user's desktop PC. In practice, with each increasingly powerful generation of desktop machines, there has been a decrease in the percentage of application situations that can benefit from moving processing to the server (which is *shared* by many users).

A second benefit of the placement flexibility is the opportunity to reduce network traffic. In the remote data management style, data-intensive application routines that need to scan large volumes of data (but don't need to display that data) can waste network resources because all of the data must be transferred from the server to the workstation in order to perform any required calculations or processing. With distributed logic, the routine that scans the data can be placed on the server with the database sending only the result back. This eliminates the need to send large volumes of data across the network. This savings can be particularly valuable when the client and server are separated by a relatively expensive WAN communications link.

The flexibility of distributed logic does not come without a cost, however. Developing distributed logic style applications is typically more complex and difficult. The chief culprit is the bit of code that allows a client program and a server program to interact. Remember that in remote data management, the client-based application talks to the server-based database via SQL and the communications infrastructure is typically supplied by the database.

Remote Presentation

A third client/server style, used less often than the previous two, is to perform all application processing and data manipulation on the server, reserving the workstation for only presentation and user interaction. This has proven to be the least popular client/server form because it fails to utilize fully the low cost processing capability of the desktop workstation.

Instead it places almost all of the processing load on the shared server machine.

The X Windowing System popular on UNIX-based machines supports implementing client/server applications that fit this model. With the X Windowing System, the entire application and database can be located on a server in the network. The application can "display itself" on the client workstation by sending protocol messages (such as "create window" or "show menu") to the X Windowing System's workstation component. That component then renders the application display messages.

Mix and Match

In reality, few applications of any real size fit nicely into just one of these client/server processing distribution scenarios. Some parts of the application may be well suited to the remote data management approach, while others may require the power and flexibility of distributed logic. A powerful feature of client/server computing is that it supports the mixing and matching of various process and data distribution strategies across applications or even within them. There are those who believe, with almost religious conviction, that *all* client/server applications should be implemented with one or another of these approaches. In fact, all three styles are valid. The trick is to know when to use which.

How to Choose

The ultimate choice of a processing distribution strategy can be hotly contested. Our experience has shown that a philosophy of "keeping it simple" offers the best chances of successfully delivering a system.

The simplest approach (not surprising, given its frequent usage), is the remote data management style. Here, the application resides on the workstation and the database resides on the server; all messaging is handled by the DBMS product. Start with this as a going in position for all applications within the system you are developing. Only after it is proved that this approach will not work for a particular function should an organization even consider implementing a more sophisticated approach. Even if it turns out that the development team must implement some function using a message-based, distributed logic messaging architecture, the team should still implement each individual function with the simplest processing distribution approach feasible. Above all, avoid the temptation to over engineer.

Chapter 19
Netcentric Integration with Existing Systems

Over the last 4 decades computers have penetrated to the very fabric of our businesses, society, and culture. This would not have been possible were it not for the ability to integrate these machines and devices together to share information and knowledge.

Netcentric computing, as defined in this book, is built on client/server technologies but expands its capabilities to provide far greater reach as well as much richer content. Companies today are experiencing the new capabilities of netcentric. Many have installed a Web server and have created an electronic presence on the Internet. They are broadcasting company and product information targeting a specific audience and enhancing their brand image. They are soliciting customers and employees for feedback on products, services, and policies. All of these netcentric information systems can and do deliver value to the enterprise. However, here's the rub: these new systems at this point still reside only on the periphery of the systems that run the enterprise.

Today, the heart and soul of the operations of most large companies still reside with the legacy information systems on mainframes and in client/server solutions. Wholesale replacement of these systems is an unrealistic expectation for most companies. The cost, length of time, business downtime, and in some cases lack of knowledge of the legacy systems prohibit complete replacement of these systems. Even the need to ward off a potentially catastrophic issue such as the "Year 2000 problem" faced by many companies cannot offset the challenges of replacing legacy systems.

The larger point is that legacy systems contain immense value, in the form of historical data, processes, and knowledge. These systems form the core of the enterprises' information technology, and they may hold the key to new "astounding solutions" — one that can enable enterprises to collaborate with business partners, directly transact with end consumers and suppliers, tie virtual enterprises together, and form new markets. For these solutions to have their full power, netcentric systems must be able to infiltrate the entire enterprise or industry. They must be able to get into the core systems of the enterprise to the key customer, product, sales, marketing, and financial information and processing.

Legacy systems usually represent a large investment. Further, they also contain a very rich store of business processes and data. Continuing to leverage existing processes and data without having to duplicate them is critical.

Can netcentric solutions form the new core systems of an enterprise? Absolutely yes … in time. Until that time, however, companies must have a way to take these new technologies that are currently on the periphery and integrate them with the core operational information systems. This is the netcentric integration challenge.

A HISTORICAL PERSPECTIVE

In the first generation of integration — that is, 10 to 30 years ago — an important era was reached when it became apparent that computers could do more than process large batches of accounting transactions. On-line processing then emerged, and it suddenly became advantageous to tie multiple information systems together. These first interfaces were crude but classic. Extracts of information were taken from the source system, made into a file on tape, physically moved to and then copied on to the other machine, and then finally loaded into the system. Later, this type of interface evolved a bit as electronic file transfer protocols were developed and as physical machines were able to be connected together by wires. However, the basic concept remained the same. This was the dominant type of "integration" for many years; in fact, even in today's interconnected world it still has its relevance.

The second generation of integration saw two techniques emerge. One technique was typified by the creation of a custom, integration database that was positioned as the common denominator between multiple systems. Databases called the "Client File" or "Product Information File" sprang up in businesses as information was collected that was common to multiple information systems. The operational, transaction systems still performed their duties on their own databases, but updates were regularly synchronized with the common database through a bidirectional update process. This way, multiple systems could share the information common to them. The challenge presented by this type of integration was in determining the interval between synchronization and in building the procedures to perform the synchronization reliably. Many checks were created, often manual ones, to validate that the correct and necessary information was transmitted and stored.

The second generation also saw the advent of personal computers (PCs). PCs brought graphical user interfaces (GUIs) and distributed computing to the information systems world. These two significant capabilities gave rise to a new method of integrating information systems commonly called "screen scraping." At first, screen scraping appeared to be simply a way to leverage a legacy mainframe system and extend its usefulness to users by putting a GUI front end on it. In addition, however, screen scraping techniques also made multiple information systems available to end users through a single, common interface and allowed information and transactions to pass between information systems. This was a form of integration through the front end of an application.

A screen-scraping language, such as IBM's 3270-based Extended High Level Language Application Program Interface (EHLLAPI), provided a facility for intercepting a formatted screen, interpreting the fields of information, and redisplaying them in the appropriate window fields of the new GUI. This technique worked well for mapping a screen from one legacy application to a screen from another, thus allowing information to move between the two.

The current generation of integration is focused particularly on transparently tying systems together and making available in a more timely manner their information and processing to the network of systems. In addition, as enterprises become more virtual and as they create partnerships with other enterprises, they must be able to provide integration across, not just within, enterprise boundaries. The remainder of this chapter presents implementation options and challenges for netcentric integration — how to integrate the new netcentric solutions with the core systems that are running enterprises today.

Three key questions drive the integration discussion:

1. What are common techniques for integrating netcentric solutions with core business systems, such as Enterprise Resource Planning (ERP) systems and legacy systems?
2. What technologies are available to help an organization achieve netcentric integration with core business systems, extending their existing World Wide Web (WWW) presence?
3. What future trends in netcentric integration are emerging?

Each of these questions is discussed in turn in this chapter.

NETCENTRIC INTEGRATION TECHNIQUES

Achieving data or application integration entails more than a middleware product selection. The ways in which products are combined to provide a solution are varied; however, several techniques in developing integration architectures are becoming common.

DATA INTEGRATION

Example

One data integration approach is illustrated in the case of an electronics component manufacturer that wanted to move all of its enterprise systems from an IBM mainframe to UNIX servers. This decision was not made lightly, but was based on a compelling business case that is beyond this discussion. The system transition was determined to be a 5- to 10-year program, and the first business area to move was to be inventory management. To complicate this first step, the corporation had up to 10 different inventory management systems, plus numerous other manufacturing and planning systems that needed inventory information.

A data integration transition approach was chosen that would introduce the new UNIX server computing environment to house the integrated inventory information. Thus, for the transition period, the corporation would have a three-tiered architecture for inventory management and information:

- The mainframe systems for enterprise computing functions such as inventory planning
- The lower-tier transaction systems, for manufacturing and warehousing
- The new, midtier platform on which all systems would eventually run

The data integration challenge was to be able to integrate all the inventory information on the midtier platform so that each application requiring this information could be moved to the new platform in a rational manner while still receiving the inventory information it needed from all the other systems. Eventually, the mainframe would not be needed for any inventory functions, and those functions could be turned off. Any new applications requiring inventory information would be built for the new processing environment.

A key design goal of the integration architecture was to minimize disruptions to the existing applications to eliminate digging into legacy code that was poorly documented and not well understood. A data integration architecture was designed to capture all transactions that modified inventory information and to replicate the results to the midtier platform.

Exhibit 1 depicts the organization's data integration architecture.

The architecture creates a federated database of inventory information comprised of physical databases at the enterprise, factory and warehouse, and midtier or server levels. This federated database functions as one logical inventory database, with all inventory-related transactions being integrated on the new server platform. A guaranteed database synchronization

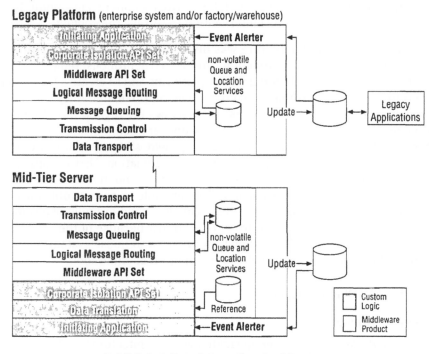

Exhibit 1. A Data Integration Architecture.

component that sits on top of a guaranteed message delivery system makes the federated database possible. This component ensures that updates performed on the enterprise DB2 or the factory and warehouse systems are reflected in the midtier server component and vice versa. Thus, applications can trust all physical DBMSs to provide accurate, identical inventory information.

Inventory information from the manufacturing systems and the warehouses are transferred across the replication manager component, the information backbone, of the architecture. The replication manager ensures the delivery of data from the individual sites to the central, midtier server component. Also key to this architecture is the reference data, which provides the mapping between the multiple systems' data structures and performs syntax (e.g., the size of data fields) as well as semantic translation (i.e., the meaning of the data such as what a *sale* or *customer* actually means between the two systems). Finally, the architecture had to be able to handle concurrent updates; updates to the same information could arrive at nearly the same time from either platform. Because of the low probability of this occurring, the simple approach was to have the architecture report to a single database when a concurrent update had occurred and require manual intervention to resolve the conflict.

This integration architecture was developed to enable an enterprise-wide view of inventory information through asynchronous, reliable information delivery across heterogeneous platforms and to create a transition step toward the enterprises' goal of moving off the mainframe. The business benefit of this architecture is that it allows the organization to more quickly and accurately confirm product delivery schedules with its customers. It also ensures the data integrity, provides high availability of the data, and efficient and timely delivery of the information. Also, because the architecture is not intrusive to the legacy systems, no modifications were needed to the legacy environments. They are able to operate oblivious to the new data integration architecture. This is a good example of a transition architecture that needed to be very robust because of the expected long transition period. The legacy factory and warehouse systems will be around for a long time; they will not be replaced anytime soon.

APPLICATION INTEGRATION

Message Brokers

Message Brokers are an emerging middleware architecture trend that have the potential to improve enterprisewide integration strategies. The concept is to use an intelligent third party — a "broker" — to pass messages among multiple disparate information sources and interested consumers. A message broker architecture provides an approach for integrating heterogeneous applications by facilitating program-to-program communications.

Message Brokers are unique in that they are not "off-the-shelf" products; they represent an architectural concept and a way of using middleware and custom components. More than simply message transports or message delivery infrastructures, Message Brokers implement many value-added features in integrating applications. Exhibit 2 provides a framework describing the functions that can be implemented in Message Broker solutions.

Specifically, the following capabilities are commonly implemented within each functional category in the Message Broker framework:

- *Message transfer*: provides the foundation for moving information. Basic functionality includes asynchronous messaging, synchronous messaging, and bulk data transfer.
- *Routing*: directs information to the intended destination. Basic functionality includes destination routing, message sequence preservation, multicast (send once, receive by many), publish and subscribe, and workflow.

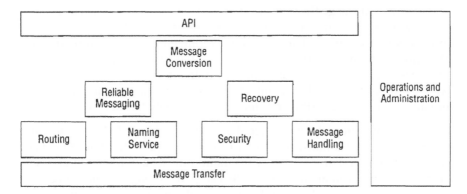

Exhibit 2. Major Message Broker Functions.

- *Naming Service*: provides the capability for locating resources and obtaining required information about those resources. Functionality offers directory services and location transparency.
- *Security*: provides required identification/authentication, access control, and encryption.
- *Message Handling*: enables additional message treatment. Functionality includes prioritization, scheduled messages, compression, application triggering, load balancing, and communications status check.
- *Reliable Messaging*: enables highly-available, fault tolerant message delivery including notification and transaction management.
- *Recovery*: provides the ability to recognize an error; the mechanism automatically reprocesses message(s) and transactions or notifies the appropriate administrators. Basic functionality includes event logging, messaging logging, and monitoring.
- *Message Conversion*: provides the ability to transform a message or data for the appropriate platform, application, or database. Functionality ranges from simple character conversion (e.g., ASCII to EBCDIC) to more extensive data element mapping.
- *API*: provides the primary interface to access the message broker. It typically includes a custom wrapper application programming interface.
- *Operations and Administration*: enables pervasive monitoring of core message broker functions and provides for effective management/maintenance of the message broker infrastructure. Functionality could include monitoring of errors, throughput, security, and queue sizes; adding new applications; and maintaining routing information, naming services, and message handling policies.

The use of Message Brokers is illustrated in the case of a global electronics products company that turned toward Message Brokers to achieve application integration. This company employed a strategy of distributed IT control, which, over the years, had resulted in a highly diverse suite of business applications among its divisions. Integration had been achieved, where required, through a mainframe system common to all parts of the organization. The resulting architecture was largely batch oriented.

With the advent of diverse netcentric technologies and ERP applications throughout the company, the integration techniques that had been used were beginning to fail. The use of the mainframe as a common interface to all systems required an inefficient extra step in moving information across the organization, and the batch cycles that these interfaces depended upon resulted in unacceptable delays in information delivery. For example, delays inherent in the order fulfillment process often resulted in products arriving in warehouses before tracking information and shipping instructions. Further, many interfaces were still implemented as manual processes due to the difficulty in developing automated solutions within the existing infrastructure.

The primary goals of implementing a Message Broker architecture were to enable:

- Real-time data integration to optimize the business process flow
- A flexible architecture to enable system modification according to business requirements
- Smooth data flow to integrate independent systems, simplify data transfer, and promote reuse

The Message Broker solution that was designed achieved these goals through five main architecture components.

1. *Message queuing infrastructure*. A message queuing middleware product was selected as the underlying message transport mechanism. This point-to-point messaging product offers the primary advantages of simplified mainframe integration, multiplatform and multiprotocol support, and strong guaranteed messaging/recoverability.

2. *Routing engine*. The point-to-point architecture of the message transport product was abstracted to support global messaging through the construction of a routing engine. Routing engines ran on regional hub servers that concentrated traffic from application servers within a given region and were responsible for resolving logical destination addresses (which were easier for the application developer to use) to physical queue names via an external naming service. Message delivery authorization was also implemented at the routing engine.

3. *API layer.* A custom set of APIs providing common access to the architecture served several functions:

   Simplified developer use of message sending/message building functions

   Addition of multiple, value-added functions such as message sequencing, message prioritization, notification, and character conversion

   Layer of abstraction, allowing the addition or enhancement of other products to the architecture or replacement of products without affecting application code

4. *Application adapters.* Business applications made use of custom, noninvasive extensions to interface with the Message Broker. Rather than modifying application code to send/receive messages natively, adapters enable the combination of specific application access methods (e.g., SAP IDOCs, Oracle Interface Tables, and mainframe screen scraping), business logic to process transactions and transform data, and the Message Broker API within a single interface process.

5. *Recovery architecture components.* Recovery functionality was supported both by a common event logging mechanism for all components in the architecture and a message log, enabling the "replay" of entire messages through the Message Broker.

The Message Broker solution that was implemented fully supported a transition strategy, allowing a gradual migration away from mainframe-based interfaces to near-real-time message delivery. By adopting an application integration approach, this company was able to maintain its investment in legacy systems while simultaneously pursuing the implementation of flexible netcentric systems. Rather than building "silo" functionality, integration through a Message Broker enabled the key strengths of each generation of systems to be exploited.

COMPONENT INTEGRATION

While a Message Broker approach is appropriate for larger-scale integration, another popular integration technique is one using component/object wrappers. As organizations implement netcentric solutions, component technology is difficult to avoid. Much of Microsoft's Active Server Framework and Transaction Server are constructed using Component Object Model (COM). Additionally, Internet Application Server technology such as Sun's NetDynamics and SAP's Business Application Programming Interface (BAPI) is rapidly advancing using technologies such as Common Object Request Broker Architecture (CORBA). Components are a fundamental building block in netcentric computing.

The following definitions summarize two different views on components.

Business Components. Business Components represent concepts within the business domain. They encapsulate the information and behavior associated with those concepts. Examples include Customer, Product, Order, Inventory, Pricing, Credit Check, Billing, and Fraud Analysis. This perspective is most appropriate during solution planning, analysis, and design.

Physical Components. From an application viewpoint, physical components are building blocks used in the assembly of applications. They encapsulate data and operations, and they fulfill distinct services through well-defined interfaces. Partitioned Business Components fall into this category; they are application building blocks that fulfill distinct business services. This perspective is most appropriate during design, detailed design, and construction. From a more technical viewpoint, physical components are units of code — things such as user interface controls and distributed objects. An example of a user interface control is an ActiveX control. An example of a distributed object is a JavaBean. This perspective is most appropriate during construction, packaging, and deployment of a business capability.

Legacy systems pose a unique situation to developers of component-based solutions. Commonly hosted on mainframes, legacy systems do not conform nicely to the component model of communication. They rarely have standard APIs for existing processes or data, and they are asynchronous in nature. How can a component-based architecture integrate with a legacy system?

Solutions need to be developed that allow organizations to take advantage of integrating new systems with business processes and applications in the existing legacy system. Newly developed components on Internet Application Servers need to be able to communicate with existing business systems; at the same time they must be consistent with the organization's current communications architecture.

Many mechanisms for communicating with legacy systems have been proposed and developed. Two common approaches for integrating netcentric solutions with legacy systems include screen scraping and message-based solutions(e.g., messaging queuing). Screen scraping takes information from things such as Web pages and applets and converts it (usually a wrapper using HLLAPI) to a format for the legacy system interface screen (e.g., 3270). The message-based solution communicates with the legacy system using asynchronous messaging queues.

Message Queuing

Message queues are a type of middleware service, similar in functionality to a pull type event service. In a message queue, components put and pull messages to and from a buffer. One of the key advantages of a message queue approach is that the message sender and receiver do not need to know anything about each other: when each is available, how many there are, or even if the other exists.

Using message queues for communication is applicable for distributed solutions needing to leverage existing business systems. In particular, this solution is useful when

- Investment in existing legacy systems is significant. In this case, an organization is unwilling or unable to forego the existing system to develop a complete replacement system. Solutions need to leverage the business processes from the existing legacy system into the new application.
- Developing new functionality in the existing legacy system is deemed impractical or not strategic. Solutions want to add new functionality (new processes) without investing in the old legacy system.
- Solutions want to isolate the intricacies of a legacy system from the new application.
- Solutions want to partition the existing legacy system functionality.

There are several benefits to the message queuing approach:

- *Encapsulation.* It provides a separation of concerns between new system and legacy system. By providing a wrapper to the legacy system, one can minimize the amount of extra development to ensure the legacy system is leveraged.
- *Migration.* It allows for slower migration of functionality from the mainframe to components. By continuing to use the functionality of the existing legacy system, the immediate need to build the same functionality in a pure component-based solution is lessened.

There are some possible disadvantages to message queuing, as well:

- *Coupling.* Changes in the legacy system may require changes in the legacy wrapper component or host-based application.
- *Communication complexity.* Asynchronous communication is typical with message queues. The need for synchronous communication between wrapper components and the legacy system may add additional complexity.
- *Architecture complexity.* Wrapper components require that adapters be built for the legacy systems. This adds complexity over a pure component-based solution.

Exhibit 3 shows how a Legacy Component might be integrated into a component-based model. A key advantage using this modular approach is improved flexibility and adaptability across application and business systems.

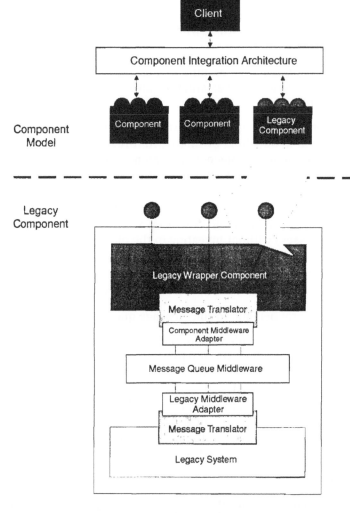

Exhibit 3. Legacy System Components.

Component Model. The upper part of the figure shows the Component Model, which shows the main units of a component-based solution:

- The *Client* is the application resident on the user machine responsible for user interface presentation, local business objects, and communication using client resident proxies.
- The *Component Integration Architecture* is the component that allows clients to communicate and remotely invoke functions on the server components. Typically, this is based on some middleware specified standard (e.g., CORBA or MTS).

- The *Component* in this figure represents the server components. These are the business domain components and the process components. They are invoked by the Client via client proxies.

Legacy Component. The Legacy Component in this model is seen as identical to any other component. However, internally it performs a very specialized function. The lower part of the figure expands the Legacy Component. The expansion shows the individual elements, which comprise the Legacy Component. These elements are

- The *Legacy Wrapper Component* is responsible for presenting the same functionality provided by the legacy system to the rest of the component-based solution. Other components of the new component-based solution will interact and communicate with this component. Although this component wraps the existing legacy system, it should behave as any other component in the newer solution.
- The *Message Queue Middleware* is the part of the architecture that sends and receives messages between the server and host machines.
- The *Message Translator* is responsible for translating messages received into the appropriate API for the Legacy System. Additionally, the Host-Based Application translates any return data from the legacy system back into a message to be sent to the wrapper server component.
- The *Component Middleware Adapter* is custom component of the Message Translator responsible for the translation from the Legacy Wrapper Component to the particular implementation of the Message Queue.
- The *Legacy Middleware Adapter* is the custom component of the Message Translator responsible for the translation from the particular implementation of the Message Queue to the Legacy System.
- The *Legacy System* is the existing system that needs to interact with the newer component-based solution. Changes to the Legacy System in order to accommodate the new component-based solution should be minimized.

The application on the host is responsible for translating messages between the message queue and the Legacy System. For example, the application must know how to format calls to CICS appropriately as well as interpret results and reformat them in a way appropriate for the Legacy Wrapper server component.

The degree to which the wrapper components are specialized to partition the functionality of the existing legacy system can vary. They include

- Pure Legacy Wrapper Component
- Hybrid Component

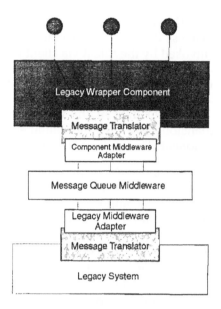

Exhibit 4. Legacy Wrapper Components.

Pure Legacy Wrapper Component. This component simply adapts the legacy system to the new component-based solution. No new business processes are added. The interface methods on the Legacy Wrapper Component "pass through" to the message translator, as shown in Exhibit 4.

Hybrid Component. Another type of Legacy Wrapper Component is the Hybrid component. It is a mix of legacy system adapter and some new business processes built in a single component. Some of the interfaces of the wrapper component pass through to the message translator, while other interfaces communicate with objects, which may in turn call the legacy system. This is shown in Exhibit 5.

There are potentially more variations, including use of an Event Service to allow the mainframe to initiate work from the wrapper components.

NETCENTRIC INTEGRATION TECHNOLOGIES AND MIDDLEWARE

Application and data integration can be achieved using a packaged, custom, or hybrid approach with many technologies available in the marketplace today. Whatever the approach, middleware seems to be at the core of many of these enabling technologies.

Middleware is the set of software services, either custom developed or vendor provided, that enables elements of distributed business applications

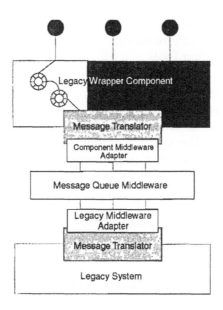

Exhibit 5. Hybrid Component.

to interoperate. These elements share function, content, and communications across heterogeneous computing environments. Middleware allows for reconciliation of differences and incompatibilities in underlying communications protocols, system architectures, operating systems, databases, and other application services.

Another way of stating it is that middleware is the "glue" that binds business applications to technical infrastructure through programming interfaces. It enables distributed communications in heterogeneous environments, bridges differences and incompatibilities, and provides architecture services.

As defined, middleware is a term that implies both breadth and depth — a fact that is reflected in the highly fragmented and complex middleware marketplace. The breadth of middleware products comes from the great *number* of services they provide, including transaction management, data access, directory/name services, and error/event handling. The depth of middleware products is a result of the different *levels* of services provided, from high-level distributed object communication to low-level remote procedure calls or communications protocol messaging.

TYPES OF MIDDLEWARE

To achieve the netcentric integration that enables integration architectures, several specific types of middleware are commonly employed. These include

- Core Messaging Products
- Netcentric Enabled Middleware
- Data Transformation Tools

Core Messaging Products

Historically, the products that have been central to the middleware market are those that provide messaging services, usually between distributed or heterogeneous applications. These products grew out of the need to simplify the work of an application programmer by providing standard services to guarantee delivery of business transactions among applications.

Today, the most common classes of message middleware services are

- Message Oriented Middleware (MOM)
- Transaction Processing Monitors (TPMs)
- Object Request Brokers (ORBs)

Message-Oriented Middleware. This refers to the process of distributing data and control through the exchange of records known as messages. Programs or processes communicate either asynchronously (connectionless) or synchronously (connection oriented). There are three communication models supported:

- Message passing
- Message queuing
- Publish and subscribe

Transaction Processing Monitors (TPMs). These provide synchronous messaging and queuing along with other transaction management services designed to support the efficient processing of high volumes of transactions. Core services include load balancing, rollback/commit, and recovery. TPMs also act as a database connection concentrator because programs and processes connect to the TP Monitor and not the DBMS directly. In general, these products are providing many of the same functions as the IBM CICS transaction monitor for mainframe environments but have since been adapted to provide similar services in client/server and netcentric environments.

Object Request Broker (ORB). This is the middleware that establishes the client/server relationships among objects. A client application uses the ORB to transparently invoke a method (or function) on a server object, which can be on the same machine or across a network. The ORB intercepts the call and is responsible for finding an object that can satisfy the request, passing it the parameters, invoking its method, and returning the results. The client application is completely isolated from the location, programming language, and operating system of the server object. This feature

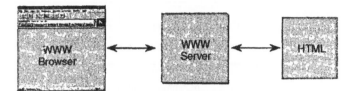

Exhibit 6. Static Web or Static HyperText Markup Language (HTML).

allows the ORB to provide interoperability between applications on different machines and operating systems. Some associate an ORB with the CORBA standard; however, the term can be broadly applied to include not only CORBA but also Distributed Component Object Model (DCOM) and Java's Remote Method Invocation (RMI).

The trend in the middleware market today is toward significant convergence in functionality and services between middleware products and even between categories. An example of this is the convergence of TPM and ORB solutions to form Object Transaction Monitors (OTMs).

Netcentric Enabled Middleware

To date, the Web and netcentric computing have primarily focused on making static information available to a wide audience including customers and business partners. Exhibit 6 illustrates the basic architecture components of a static Web environment.

Next-generation netcentric computing will go beyond providing static Web information. It will be vital to provide netcentric integration with core business systems to ensure on-demand personalized information. Using netcentric technologies, enterprises can offer such things as 7x24 automated order processing capabilities for customers, access to inventory level information for key suppliers, or simple customer billing/account inquiries. A key architectural element facilitating integration between the WWW and core business systems is a second type of middleware, called Netcentric Enabled Middleware (Exhibit 7).

Netcentric Enabled Middleware is a set of reusable business object components that can supply the basis for Internet-, intranet-, and extranet-ready commercial application systems. Its purpose is to transform the static nature of the Web, accelerate Internet application development, and enable cross-network compatibility and interoperability among an organization's employees, customers, and business partners. Additionally, Netcentric Enabled Middleware provides for greater reach of computing and for the delivery of rich content both within and outside the enterprise. Examples of products that provide this capability include Sun Java/Java

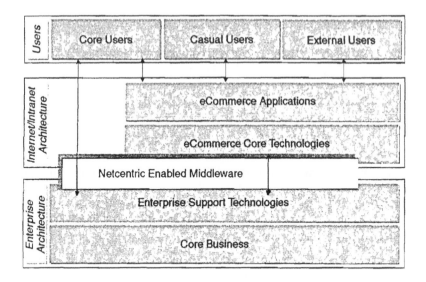

Exhibit 7. Netcentric Enabled Middleware.

Beans, Microsoft Active X/Component Object Model Platform, and Sun Java Remote Method Invocation & NetDynamics Enterprise Network Application Platform.

Netcentric Enabled Middleware products attempt to

- Provide services to integrate netcentric solutions with the core operational systems of the business
- Provide a set of cross-industry business objects to support business-critical applications
- Provide the underlying foundation services supporting communications, transactions, runtime administration and configuration, and security
- Automate the use of complex infrastructure services to support robust, portable, multitiered, scalable, dynamic, and secure Internet-enabled applications

In general, there are four approaches utilized by most Netcentric Enabled Middleware:

1. Dynamic Web
2. Two-tiered
3. Three-tiered HyperText Transport Protocol (HTTP)
4. Three-tiered non-HTTP

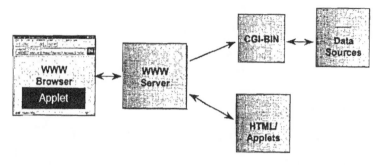

Exhibit 8. Dynamic Web.

Dynamic Web Approach

One of the most common approaches used today to generate dynamic Web content is through Common Gateway Interface (CGI). CGI is a standard mechanism for extending Web server functionality by executing programs or scripts on the server in response to browser requests. A common use of CGI is in forms processing, where the browser sends the form data to a CGI script on the server, and the script integrates the data with a database and sends back an HTML page containing the results.

In general, CGI is fairly straightforward to implement. CGI components are incorporated within Web servers and use a familiar function/procedure-calling paradigm to call a program external to the Web Server (e.g., get_date_and_time). However, CGI is not very flexible. When the call is made, the program must be in the expected location and provided with the expected inputs. Error handling using CGI can be especially challenging. Additionally, the program called by the CGI must return the result set to the user through HyperText Markup Language (HTML).

Exhibit 8 shows an example of CGI-based middleware.

Other forms of dynamic Web include Microsoft's Internet Server Application Programming Interface (ISAPI) and Netscape's Netscape Server Application Programming Interface (NSAPI). Virtually all Web servers on the market support CGI, while NSAPI and ISAPI are vendor-specific modifications of the CGI architecture. NSAPI code has to be packaged in dynamically loadable modules such as Windows DLLs or UNIX-shared libraries and needs to have a predefined C-style programming interface. These modules will be loaded and executed within the same process as the Web server. ISAPI is similar, with a more object-oriented interface, and is limited to Windows-based platforms.

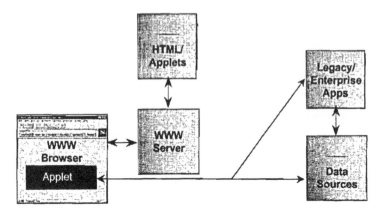

Exhibit 9. Two-Tiered Approach.

Two-Tiered Approach

Two-tiered integration enables client applets to directly call or access server (i.e., core business system) applications and databases (Exhibit 9). Some major challenges with the two-tiered applet approach include security, fat clients, and manageability. Downloading applets that have access to core business systems has risks and in the wrong hands might present a security issue. In some cases, these applets can become quite large with business processing logic and create bottlenecks when downloading. Additionally, managing applets that frequently change when distributed to hundreds even thousands of client platforms can be challenging and again creates additional processing overhead and network bottlenecks. Examples of two-tiered netcentric middleware include Microsoft's Active/X Data Objects (ADO) using Open Database Connectivity (ODBC) or Sun's Java Database Connectivity (JDBC).

Three-Tiered HTTP-Based Approach

Three-tiered HTTP-based architectures extend a basic Web server through integration with the middle-tier application server. Exhibit 10 illustrates this type of netcentric integration architecture. Three-tiered HTTP middleware uses HTTP as a common communications transport protocol and enables integrated access between the Web server and existing business systems using the application server. Examples include Microsoft's Active Server Framework and Sun's NetDynamics. There are several challenges with this approach, which include the following:

- *Session management.* By design, Web servers do not easily perform session or state management. Development teams can use mechanisms such as cookies or application servers to maintain context

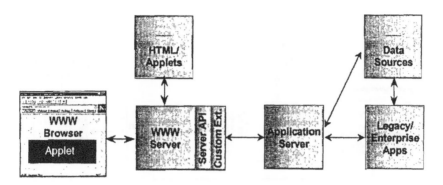

Exhibit 10. Three-Tiered HTTP-Based Approach.

within or between transactions. However, those approaches often present challenges as well (e.g., what if the browser has cookies turned off?).

- *Web server performance.* The Web server needs to perform additional processing such as executing business logic, passing calls to application servers, and maintaining communications with both the application server as well as browsers.
- *High connection/communication overhead.* The Web server is the focal point for all interactions and therefore needs to manage all of the communications.

Three-Tiered Non-HTTP-Based

The primary difference between three-tiered non-HTTP-based and three-tiered HTTP-based middleware is that the Web server is not the focal point in all communications. For example, initial setup of the configuration (i.e., downloading the applet) may be carried out by browser–Web server interactions, but future communcations can be from the applet directly to the application server, thus bypassing the Web server altogether. Exhibit 11 illustrates three-tiered non-HTTP-based middleware.

Three-tiered non-HTTP-based middleware may present a potential communications challenge with firewalls because some firewalls may filter out non-HTTP protocols. One way around this issue might be to use HTTP Tunneling. In general, while this integration architecture may work with firewalls, it may be more appropriate in intranet and some extranet environments.

A typical configuration for three-tiered non-HTTP-based middleware might be Microsoft's Internet Information Server (IIS) with Active Server Framework and Microsoft Transaction Server (MTS) as the application

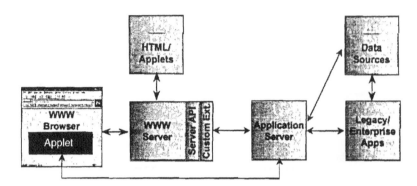

Exhibit 11. Thre-Tiered Non-HTTP-Based Approach.

server. Another configuration might use Netscape's (formerly Kiva) or Oracle's Application Server platform.

Data Transformation Tools

A third type of middleware is Data Transformation Tools. These middleware products are becoming an increasingly important class of tools as organizations build and maintain interfaces among numerous distributed systems. As the name implies, the core function of these tools is to provide a mechanism for application programmers to easily manipulate data from a source system, transforming it into an "expected" data format to be used by a target system.

For example, consider the elementary case in which customer name data from System A is stored as two separate fields: "Last Name" and "First Name." Rather than writing custom code, a Data Transformation tool could be used to combine these fields into a single "Customer Name" format, expected by System B. The power of these tools becomes apparent when constructing and maintaining multiple, highly complex interfaces that transfer information across an organization.

Data Transformation tools typically provide

- A graphical development environment that allows developers simplified control over data type definitions and data transformation rules (e.g., "drag and drop" field combination)
- Distinct run-time environments that can be integrated with custom code, responsible for executing transformation logic
- Generic "rules-based" engines that allow not only data transformation, but also more complex business logic to be built into interfaces
- Predefined interfaces (data types and transformation rules) to common systems/formats, such as EDI or SAP

Selecting Middleware

As previously noted, the middleware market is highly complex, offering many complementary and sometimes overlapping solutions to integration issues. Selecting a middleware direction can be difficult, given the often conflicting requirements from different constituencies of an organization. Typically, a middleware direction is established at one of three possible stages in the development life cycle.

1. *Define business architecture.* At this stage, one comes to an understanding of an organization's vision, including guiding principles, preferences, and the business capability definitions. In this stage, most of the business drivers are identified which may indirectly help the middleware selection.
2. *Capability analysis.* Here, key high-level requirement areas are identified, such as service level requirements. At this stage, major requirements should be known that will directly influence the middleware selection.
3. *Capability release design.* Tasks here focus on designing the releases of the services required to deliver the business capabilities. From a technology perspective, this means identifying what, how, when, and where key technology infrastructure services will be released.

The middleware selection considerations that must be addressed by an architect vary in style and focus according to the development stage described above. For example, when defining the business architecture, architects are primarily focused on the definition and implementation of a coherent strategic direction for an organization. One of the primary considerations faced by the business architect is the alignment with an organization's tolerance for emerging technologies, including middleware technologies.

From a technology perspective, organizations tend to fall into two categories: early adopters or those that take a more conservative, "wait-and-see" approach. In either case, it is important to understand the level of maturity in middleware technology an organization desires to use. Middleware technologies exist throughout the spectrum of maturity. For example, host-based TP monitor middleware products such as IBM's Customer Information and Control System (CICS) have been around for more than 2 decades. At the other extreme, less mature distributed component architectures have only been available for a few years. Other middleware products fall somewhere in between. Without a solid business case or competitive advantage, it may not make sense for more conservative organizations to implement object request broker or component-based middleware. At the same time, pioneering organizations may be prototyping emerging middleware technologies such as message broker or object transaction monitor. Thus, an organization's tolerance for new technology is a key decision factor in defining a appropriate business architecture that employs middleware.

Capability analysis considerations, in contrast, tend to be more focused on providing an appropriate middleware architecture given the constraints of a specific business problem. Today, one of the more common problems addressed at this stage is the implementation approach for architectures requiring support of a large number of application-to-application interfaces. Many organizations today face this problem as they realize the value of moving from a "silo-based" application infrastructure to one in which information is shared across their applications.

These organizations have an option to implement single point-to-point interfaces between each of these applications or to implement a common interface/integration architecture. File transfer and message-oriented middleware are the most common forms of middleware used for point-to-point interfaces:

- File transfer for nightly and near real-time (1 hour and greater) interfaces. These interfaces are often controlled by scheduling tools and adapt well to older legacy batch systems.
- Message-oriented middleware for near real-time (from just a few minutes or greater) interfaces. These interfaces are usually either event driven or use a periodic polling mechanism. When a message arrives, processing is either triggered by the event or will begin at the next poll.

Both file transfer and message-oriented middleware are acceptable as point-to-point solutions. However, as the number of interfaces grows, the architecture can become overly complex to manage. In addition, incremental interface development can be significant to add a new interface between two applications. The industry trend toward a common interface/integration architecture using message broker middleware seems a better solution. Advantages of this approach include long-term flexibility, lower life cycle maintenance costs, and improved manageability. However, this implementation can be time consuming and costly due to a lack of integrated vendor products.

Another typical selection decision faced during capability analysis regards the mission-critical nature of the architecture being implemented. Mission-critical architectures should first consider using proven and mature products such as TP monitors, database access, or message-oriented middleware. Only if an organization is willing to take on higher risk or if there is a substantial competitive advantage should an organization consider other middleware options.

TP monitor middleware offers robust functionality: two-phase commit, recovery/rollback, naming services, security services, and audit trail logging. Therefore, the more mission-critical the architecture, the more likely it is that a TP monitor should be used. Although database access and message-oriented middleware do not offer quite the degree of functionality as TP monitor middleware, both offer robust functionality in other areas. Message-oriented middleware offers proven asynchronous message passing and queuing functionality: guaranteed message delivery, basic restart/recovery, and integrated security services. Database access middleware offers robust functionality focused primarily around the database management system (DBMS). In general, the DBMS handles the two-phase commit, recovery/rollback, audit trail logging, and security services.

One key aspect of a mission-critical system is high availability. Architectures that recover from failures with minimal or no user/business impact are considered near fault tolerant. An architecture needs to address high availability and fault tolerance at multiple levels: computing platform and physical network, DBMS, and middleware. It is up to the architect to determine the appropriate mix of configurations to meet the availability service level requirements.

From a middleware perspective, most TP monitors provide near fault-tolerance and high availability architectures. The automatic restart/recovery feature helps a system recognize when components have failed and attempts to restart them. (This is an example of near fault-tolerance.) Also, because of the location transparency feature of service calling, if an entire TP monitor node within the architecture fails, clients may be able to reach the service they need on another TP monitor node providing the same service. (This is an example of high availability.)

Typically, home-grown, in-house middleware applications can be tailor-made to meet specific needs, but it often takes months or even years to develop, depending on the complexity and required functionality. Organizations using custom-built software are finding that their systems become more complex and unmanageable as products and markets change. Consequently, they are looking to commercial products to provide lower-cost, more flexible solutions to replace existing custom programs. On the other hand, available packaged middleware software often falls short of required functionality.

Given the rapidly changing nature of the present middleware market and the increasing functionality being built into middleware products, the trend in this area is clearly toward a "buy before build" mentality in middleware component selection. When precisely fitted packages are not available, often a balance between packaged and custom is appropriate. In some cases today, a hybrid packaged middleware solution (e.g., MOM and

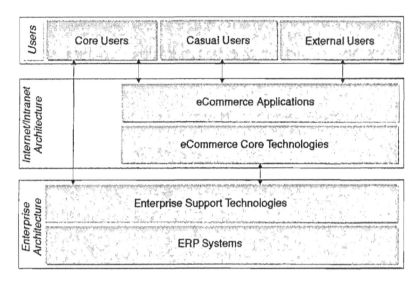

Exhibit 12. Extending the Reach of ERP Systems.

DBAM) can meet many of the organization's middleware requirements with minimal customization.

FUTURE TRENDS

The remaining part of this chapter briefly describes two key emerging trends from an integration perspective.

Packaged Integration Architectures

In general, achieving data or application integration requires an intensive effort and a significant amount of custom development. To achieve the level of functionality desired, those seeking to integrate systems must select multiple middleware packages and determine the most effective way of using them in concert. A recent trend attempts to extend the reach and limit the complexity of integration by prepackaging integration solutions between packaged applications. This trend is particularly common for Enterprise Resource Planning (ERP) systems getting core business information to customers, business partners, and employees (Exhibit 12). A number of recent start-up companies provide preconstructed interfaces to leading ERP systems, built over several popular message transport middleware products.

The advantage to implementing such as solution is a decrease in time and effort to implement the complexities of middleware products. This allows an organization to focus its resources on solving business problems rather than technical problems.

Cross-Organization Integration

Data and application integration techniques are still relatively new. Therefore, organizations are focusing much of their efforts on internal integration among legacy, client/server, and netcentric systems. In the increasingly global environment, companies are finding new ways to deliver value to customers by implementing business processes in conjunction with other organizations rather than in competition with them. Simple technologies such as EDI (which is analogous to the classic, first-generation integration techniques used to support mainframes years ago) now enable basic sharing of transactional information.

In time, these cross-company interfaces will be replaced with the same application and data integration technologies currently being implemented *within* organizations. Additionally, newer standards offering even greater sharing of information and functionality and superceding those of the past are just around the corner. One example is XML (eXtensible Markup Language). XML is currently being hyped to have the potential of extending and personalizing content on the web. Many experts predict XML will

- Make the exchange of data and content easier
- Allow a user to control or personalize the presentation, user interface, and content being used to access the information
- Standardize data interfaces across organizations

The result will be a much richer, flexible, and real-time information-sharing infrastructure, one better able to support customer needs.

Chapter 20
Interface Design

The design of netcentric applications requires major changes to the traditional approaches of application design in several areas, including the graphical user interface (GUI).

GUI presents significant new design challenges. Users are demanding easy-to-learn and easy-to-use software. The GUI gives the applications designer the capability to deliver on this demand, but achieving ease of use is more easily said than done.

This chapter begins with an overview of usability concepts and then discusses techniques to make these concepts a reality in application design. The remainder of the chapter outlines a process for designing GUIs to deliver on the goal of usability.

DESIGNING FOR USABILITY

Usability and user-centered design have become essential features of today's application design environment. Netcentric computing has opened up information technology to almost every person in the workplace. However, this egalitarian and democratic characteristic of computing also puts demands on the design of applications. They must be usable by a wide spectrum of people from different cultural and educational backgrounds and with differing levels of patience for the intricacies of information technology.

Today's computer "users" do not define themselves in terms of the computer; they demand that the computer systems define themselves in terms of human capabilities. They demand that systems and applications support workers in the manner in which they actually conduct their activities in business.

Today's technologies continue to move us away from rigid interfaces that provide only limited access to segmented information. It is becoming more feasible to provide flexible interfaces with seamless, shared, and even mobile computing access to information that crosses traditional boundaries within organizations.

Usability Drivers

The attention being paid today to principles of advanced computing usability is driven by several phenomena:

- *Disappointing preliminary results.* There is a growing sense on the part of users that information technology and the new intuitive interfaces developed to date have not fulfilled their promise to increase organizational productivity and effectiveness. Many new applications still require traditional approaches to training. Classes must be designed and conducted, resulting in direct costs due to lost personnel productivity.
- *Companies are "hiring the customer."* Organizations today are finding new ways to bring customers into processes, allowing them to perform tasks that workers previously did. Solutions based on such things as kiosks, voice response units, and the Internet proliferate. However, as the novelty of these approaches begins to wear off, customers are rebelling against poorly designed systems. If an organization is to be successful at implementing customer-operated applications, the systems must be designed for maximum intuitiveness and expedience and must require little or no support from a company's service representatives.
- *Shrink-wrapped software packages are "raising the bar" for usability.* Because of successful software in the PC marketplace, users have high expectations for how their business systems should work. Software such as Quicken™ has set a standard to which business applications are being compared.
- *Functionality is exceeding people's ability to use it.* In today's environment, technology can overwhelm users if applied in the wrong way, actually hindering and not enabling their work. For example, in one system, technologists determined that users needed to view images, such as an image of a bill. After implementation, however, the organization discovered that retrieving the image took too much time and effort by the users. What the users wanted was not the image, but a more understandable data representation of the transactions and balances. A key usability concept is spending time with the users, understanding what they need, and then designing a process that matches those needs.

Usability and System Acceptability

Usability is one aspect of the overall *acceptability* of systems. There are at least four interrelated dimensions of system acceptability:

- Social acceptability
- Practical acceptability
- Usefulness
- Usability

Although the industry at times seems to stress the usability of systems above everything else, it is just as important to address practical acceptability, social acceptability, and usefulness to determine what the users need. In some cases users have been unable to use systems efficiently, and designers made the mistake of addressing the problem only in terms of usability. Their conclusion: the metaphor and the icons must be wrong. Bring in some graphic designers; try new metaphors; make new toolbars. However, these did not work either because the entire design had flawed social or practical assumptions.

Social Acceptability. Social acceptability may be a particular problem for customer systems such as automated teller machines. The customers may resent being forced to do work that the company previously did for them. They may also resent the fact that there may be a charge attached to a service that used to be provided for free.

Social acceptability problems may arise in new customer service environments that, for reasons of efficiency, redirect customers away from their local store or branch to a new call center or a corporate Web page. For example, a local branch or store manager may have waived charges for certain important customers. However, when that customer is rerouted, no such relationship exists. In this case, the impersonality of Internet banking or a call center may actually start driving customers away.

Social acceptability problems also arise when organizations do not take the time to understand their customers. Some companies have introduced 24-hour access voice response systems, only to discover real resistance after implementation. Their customers are hanging up on the voice response system, or pressing "0" for an operator, or even traveling to a local branch to speak with a representative in person. Designers may fail to recognize a variety of factors: perhaps some customers want more personal interaction or look upon these calls as partly social experiences, not just business ones, or perhaps customers are seeking more complex information that cannot be handled efficiently by the voice response system.

Practical Acceptability. Problems with practical acceptability can surface through flawed practical assumptions. Flawed practical assumptions are usually related to underestimating the cost impacts of a particular technology or architecture. Take, for example, the decision to use multimedia or imaging as key components of a new system. This decision implies that it will be practical to do so — that the benefits will justify the necessary and potentially costly new network requirements. However, what if the benefits cannot justify it? Sometimes designers will attempt a scaled-down version of the original concept, but this version may end up being unusable simply because it is too slow over the kind of limited network capability that could be set up. The system makes the customer wait too long for a response.

The impact of practical acceptability must be assessed early in the planning phase for a new system, especially one demanding major infrastructure or operational upgrades.

Usefulness and Usability. Finally, a system must be both useful and usable. "Useful" relates to the utility or actual use of the system or application. If a system or application does not prove useful to a user, it does not matter how usable it is. The user will have no reason for the application.

Usable relates to how the system or application is used or operated. If a system or application is difficult to use, acceptance of the system or application becomes an issue for the user, and the productivity goals will not be achieved. Usability has five major dimensions. A usable system is

1. Easy to learn
2. Efficient to use
3. Easy to remember
4. Prone to fewer errors
5. Subjectively pleasing

Each of these dimensions can be measured quantitatively by task timings, error rates, and user satisfaction ratings.

USABILITY BUILDING BLOCKS

A number of things must come together to create highly usable software (see Exhibit 1).

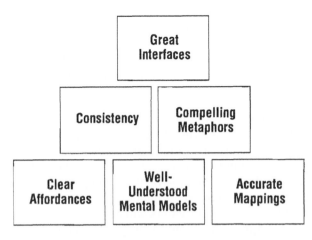

Exhibit 1. Usability Building Blocks.

Clear Affordances

The first building block of usability is clear "affordances." Affordances are the capabilities and functionalities of the system — what the system lets the user do. One way to understand affordances is to look at a chair: from its appearance, its behavior when you touch it, and from your general experience of living, you can easily figure out what it can do for you — what it "affords you." The chair's affordances are visible and unmistakable.

With systems, a button on a window is not an affordance in itself; the button *affords* pushing and the button label describes what will happen when the button is pressed. Affordances are made visible through metaphors that take advantage of the other building blocks.

Well-Understood Mental Models

How do users think of the task? What picture(s) would they draw to describe the different objects and their relationships to each other? For example, a user of personal finance software already knows and understands the concept of a checkbook or check register, so Quicken uses that model in its software.

Compelling Metaphors

Metaphors make affordances visible to the user. Applications can have powerful affordances that are not clear to the user. DOS, for example, has powerful functionality and affordances, but they are hidden behind the C:\ prompt.

Interface metaphors are usually representations of real-world objects — such as notebooks, trash cans, or buttons — that take advantage of a user's prior knowledge. When users see a button on an interface, they can press on it with a mouse click and have a high degree of confidence that something will happen. If the button is also well labeled, users will also have some confidence about what behavior the button will invoke.

There are many possible mental models from which to choose during design; good metaphors map clearly to the proper mental model of the user. If the user's mental model is well understood, developing appropriate metaphors is simplified.

Accurate Mappings

Designers should seek direct mappings — clear links — between the user's mental model and the system's affordances. The more direct the mapping, the more usable the system is. Users can find features quickly because their mental model is synchronized with the interface. The internal workings of the software may be entirely different from the interface's model. What is important is that the user is never reminded of this difference.

Consistency

The mappings of a user model to system affordances must not only be accurate but consistent as well. Consistency reinforces both the mappings and the user's mental model. Consistency also shields the user from the mechanics of the system.

For example, applications should be consistent about when a user needs to single click or double click during any list selection function. Although the PC software world has some strong examples to follow, it may not offer designers the examples they need. In many cases, designers have struggled to make "File — open, close, print, exit" and "Edit" meaningful for their business applications. What works for the document publishing world may not work for every business. Maybe "Customer — retrieve, search for" is more appropriate. Designers should be consistent but use judgment as well.

These usability building blocks lead to powerful interfaces that are fun and engaging, are invisible (i.e., the user is thinking only of the task, not the mechanics of operating the interface), improve performance of the user, and increase the value delivered to the organization.

USABILITY AND THE DESIGN PROCESS

Advanced usability ultimately is a function of *process*, not tools. Tools such as style guides and GUI development software (discussed later) provide some low-level consistency: windows, for example, are laid out consistently and have the same font sizes and color schemes. However, tools cannot help design interfaces with accurate mappings to a user's mental model of a task. These mappings require human experience and knowledge. A tool can provide a methodology but cannot substitute for direct experience.

In addition, usability is not a science. Unlike conventional system performance, an interface's intuitiveness and learnability cannot be easily predicted with a model or algorithm. It must be tested with real users.

As with performance, usability can and should be measured. Usability objectives, along with other goals related to such things as performance, response time, and business objectives should be set at the beginning of the development effort. They can be set by examining benchmarks from the current process and systems, if similar ones exist, and competitors' approaches in the same or a similar industry.

Attention to usability concepts moves designers further along toward the ultimate goal of meeting the users' business needs. The challenge of today's technology advancements is not just technical integration but also functional integration. The functionality bar is being raised by the ability to process and access more and varying types of information, but usability is the key to fitting into or redesigning the user's work environment.

GUI APPLICATION DESIGN

A GUI can be more intuitive for users, but it forces designers to think of presenting functionality in a new and different way. User interface designers should be aware of a set of basic guidelines as well as a documentation technique for capturing and communicating GUI application designs.

DESIGNING THE GUI FOR USABILITY

GUIs are a driving force behind netcentric technology because they are a major factor in delivering systems that are intuitive, efficient, and easy to learn and use. However, these benefits are not gained automatically simply by throwing a graphical front end onto a system. An inexperienced GUI designer can actually create a graphical interface that is *more* difficult to learn and use. GUI design gives designers much more freedom, but freedom can easily become anarchy and chaos. The flexibility and multitude of design options that the GUI affords heightens the importance of a more methodical approach to interface design.

This chapter focuses on the tasks related to designing the GUI segment of a netcentric application. The planning chart in Exhibit 2 outlines the activities relevant to graphical user interface design within the design application task.

Task Analysis

Task analysis defines the activities that users perform or need to perform. If a development project is automating existing tasks, task analysis can be performed through observation. However, the goal often stressed with netcentric development projects is not simply to automate existing processes but to use the technology as an accompaniment to a business process reengineering initiative. In that case, task analysis becomes a matter of reinventing processes and user roles.

The goal of task analysis is to identify the steps within the performance of a task or process as well as the typical and possible orderings in which those steps can occur. In contrast to conventional functional analysis, task analysis is much more user centered. Whereas functional analysis highlights the need for certain data to be maintained in a system, task analysis describes how users would like to maintain that data. Often, users complain that, to complete what they consider to be one task, they must navigate through several windows and software modules. Task analysis helps organize functionality according to user needs, thus increasing usability and productivity.

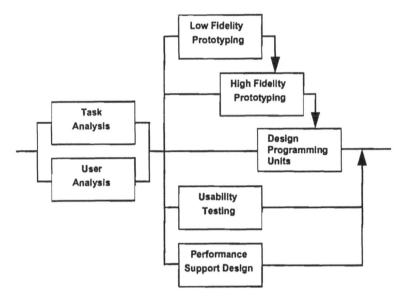

Exhibit 2. Process for GUI Design.

User Analysis

User analysis defines the types of users who will be using the application. When creating any human–computer interface, it is important to understand the "customers" of the system. A system that is appropriate for clerical workers may not be appropriate for executives. The two most relevant dimensions of user characteristics are their understanding of the task (how much they know about the task to be performed) and their experience level with computer systems.

When designing an interface for users with a low understanding of how the task is to be done, the user interface must be much more supportive of the performance of the business process or task, leading users step by step if necessary. Designers must consider how much on-line help and reference material to make available and how to make that help available within the context of performing a task (e.g., context-sensitive help or on-line reference materials). In addition, designers must consider the fact that users will need much more support the first few times they use an application. If users will be using the application every day, their need for help may be minimal after they have become proficient, and so the help facilities should not slow their task performance.

The emergence of the Internet has led to situations where applications are built that a user may use only once — for example, a customer purchasing insurance on-line. Obviously, you can't send the customer to a training course on how to use the application. The need to design such "one use" applications further underscores the requirement to build extremely intuitive, zero training, applications that walk the user through the business process.

Users who already have experience in a graphical windowing environment can be expected to understand common user interface metaphors such as file folders and the desktop. For these users, it is best to try to keep the user interface consistent with GUI applications with which they are already familiar. If, on the other hand, the users are not familiar with computer systems and GUIs, it is worthwhile to look for yet more intuitive metaphors that users can understand without training.

Careful study of the user types can also help in selecting appropriate interface metaphors to which users can relate. For example, if the user population is doctors, a flip chart metaphor that closely resembles the information organization of their current manual system may ease user learning and acceptance.

GUI Design Prototyping

Prototyping is an essential component of the process for designing graphical user interfaces. Prototyping gives designers the chance to test various design concepts on real users. User interface designers often think they know what the user will like or dislike, but their track record of accurate predictions has not always been good. Without the appropriate use of prototyping, these wrong assumptions turn up in the final product. When users then object to some aspect of the interface design, they are often told it is too late and too expensive to make a change. The goal of user interface prototyping is to catch design problems in design when correcting them is usually easier and less expensive.

There are two types of prototyping: low-fidelity and high-fidelity.

Low-Fidelity Prototyping. A common mistake in user interface prototyping is to invest too much time and money constructing a running prototype of an interface before showing it to the users. The problem with that approach is that few people then want to spend money revising the prototype based on user feedback. Typically, the entire prototyping budget is spent simply creating it. After so much time, effort, and investment of emotional capital, user interface designers are not often receptive to criticisms other than the minor tweaks they expected. If the entire interface metaphor is inappropriate, for example, requiring a total reconstruction of the prototype, it may be too late.

Why not make sure that the basic user interface approach — that is, desktop metaphor vs. notebook vs. flip chart — is basically on track before making virtually *any* investment? The key to verifying the basic approach is "low fidelity" prototyping. Using computer tools that require programming or scripting look good but require too much investment at this early design stage. An alternative approach that has proven successful is to construct simple, hand-drawn mock-ups of windows on paper. To give the user some sense of navigating through the system, another person plays the role of the "computer" — perhaps placing another paper window on the desk in front of the user as though the mouse click caused the window to appear.

This may not seem at first like a very professional way to go about systems design. However, it can be highly effective in producing a more usable design at a minimum cost. Because it is fast and simple to draw windows on paper and sticky notes, GUI designers can create numerous alternative user interface styles and let the user select the one that is most appealing and effective.

The message is in the medium. Simple low-fidelity pencil-and-paper prototypes also send a message to the user reviewing the mock up. Because the interface is not computerized or polished, the reviewers of the design are less likely to be intimidated. A pencil and paper prototype implicitly tells users that they should be free to speak their minds about the design. User interface designers are more likely to listen to feedback from users during low-fidelity prototyping. Because designers have not invested a great deal of time in the design, they feel less ownership of the prototype. Thus, they listen to criticisms and changes rather than simply defend the design, or only think about how they can do quick fixes. This leads to more iterations of the user interface design before the financial and emotional lock-in occurs on a given design.

Given the low cost of this approach, the scope of the prototypes can be extensive, perhaps covering the entire functional scope of the system to be developed.

High-Fidelity Prototyping. After the basic user interface design has been defined and refined through low-fidelity prototyping, designers can build a more realistic computer-based "high fidelity" prototype. The goal of a high fidelity prototype is to present the user with the true look and feel being proposed for the system. Designers should make the high-fidelity prototype as realistic as possible, including providing a sense of what job performance using the system will be like. Designers should also simulate delays where time consuming queries or processing are to occur. This gives users more information about performance of the system that will help refine the design. For example, in the low-fidelity prototype a particular operation may have been instantaneous. In the high-fidelity version the same operation may take sixty seconds. Seeing this, users may suggest that the order of certain operations be switched so they can use that wait time productively.

A high-fidelity prototype can also be a valuable tool for the systems development team. Ideally, the high-fidelity prototype is implemented using the intended tools and technical environment for the end system. Constructing the prototype gives implementers an opportunity to see how easy or difficult it is going to be to code and deliver various aspects of the user interface. The prototype also provide a chance to test some of the technical implementation details on a small scale before committing the project to any unproved technical concepts. Developer feedback should also be included in the refinements to the user interface design to reduce costs, risk, and implementation complexity.

High-fidelity prototype development is not an inexpensive process. In order to keep the costs of a high-fidelity prototype under control, designers should choose a narrow scope. Implementing one or two functions of the overall system may well be sufficient.

Performance Support Design

There is more to usability than just the design of the GUI. Performance support design activities focus on additional services and support needed to increase user productivity in performing the business task. Areas of opportunity for design improvement can many times be found in items that support the application, including on-line training or reference materials.

On-line training can be used to supplement or possibly even replace instructor-led training. The goal of on-line training is to speed users through any learning curve the system may require. On-line training has the added benefit that it can be delivered at the place and time of need. As a result of logistical difficulties, an enterprise often conducts instructor-led training too far in advance of when the users actually receive the system or begin using it. This time lag reduces training retention and in some cases forces the need for retraining. Furthermore, after the instructor has gone home, the users are often left to their own devices if they have a question or problem later about how to use the system.

Developing on-line tutorials has become an increasingly popular way to provide task-specific training on demand. This enables users to learn on the job rather than as a separate "training event" off the job.

On-line reference services, which are increasingly being delivered over a corporate intranet, can improve user task performance by presenting job-relevant information from several sources: an organization's internal knowledge base, public databases, and vendor-supplied databases. On-line reference material may include policy and procedure manuals that specify how certain situations are to be handled, internal product descriptions and details, or external information sources that can improve the quality of user decision making. The challenge for designers is to understand what information would enhance the performance of the user and then to make it available on-line and easily accessible.

Usability Testing

Usability testing ensures that the overall usability of the application is maximized. The most productive usability testing is focused toward the achievement of some quantifiable usability goals or targets that are tied to the business case for the system. A usability goal for one application might be that new users achieve 90% proficiency within 1 week. For another application, the goal might be that users enter one order per minute with less than a 0.1% error rate.

The idea of such goals is to move usability designers beyond soft and vague goals such as user "satisfaction" with the system, which is a subjective and unquantifiable concept. Designers must focus on more specific goals that translate into business benefits. Without such goals, interface designers often stray toward merely creating "pretty" user interfaces. Although users may like to look at them, the mere aesthetics may come at the expense of systems development dollars and end user productivity.

Usability testing requires a more stringent process compared to conventional user testing. Key differences include the following:

- *Test earlier.* Low-fidelity interface testing should begin early in the design of the system, before coding (even of the high fidelity prototype) has even begun. The purpose of testing early is to learn more about how users perform tasks so that the interface can be improved and optimized, as opposed to merely confirming that the interface provides at least some way to accomplish the task.
- *Involve more users.* Usability testing sessions should involve enough users to ensure that the views of the test subjects accurately reflect the views of the entire user population. This requirements becomes much more difficult if the users of the system are consumers rather than the company's employees. In such cases, focus groups or limited deployment pilots may be useful.
- *Test more often.* Usability testing must be conducted throughout the development process, beginning with focus groups and ending with formal scripted testing of the software.

ACHIEVING CONSISTENCY IN GUI DESIGNS

Consistency is often touted as the "holy grail" of user interface design. Consistency is certainly a valid goal, considering the amount of time and money spent on training users to use new software programs. An application designed to present a consistent user interface has great advantages. When the users learn how to use a subset of the software or have learned a similar application, they can expect to learn new functions quickly because menu options and controls will behave similarly to windows they have already learned.

Consistency becomes even more powerful if it can be achieved not just within a single application but across a number of user applications. If new applications are designed to present the same or similar operations (e.g., File/Save) in the same way, users do not need to relearn how to perform these basic operations. Cross-application consistency substantially reduces the learning curve for new applications and gives users the confidence to accept and explore new applications and new features.

Designers should consider what other software their users already use or will be using as part of the system under development. The user may already be familiar with a suite of third-party software such as word processors and spreadsheet programs. Such product suites (e.g., Microsoft Office™ and Lotus SmartSuite™) are designed to provide consistency across common operations. If users are familiar with a such a suite, it is a good idea to adhere to these conventions and the underlying "style guide" on which they are based.

A style guide is a set of very basic rules for defining the look and feel of computer applications. A number of style guides have been developed over the past few years, from vendors such as IBM (CUA), Microsoft, and Apple. Each guide has converged or standardized an approach to most user interface issues. Thus, a user familiar with applications based on one style guide could learn applications based on the others with little or no formal training. The degree of difference is not unlike the amount of difference between driving a Ford and driving a Chrysler: the brakes are always in the same place, although things such as wiper controls may be in one of several different spots.

Models-Based Design

Style guides provide a base for ensuring that windows have a consistent look. However, they tend to focus on lower-level aspects such as what a button should look like or where standard menu choices should be. They do not generally provide a designer with much guidance on how to consistently implement support for tasks commonly performed by users (such as

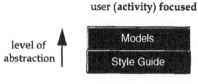

Exhibit 3. GUI Models.

adding an item to a list). Exhibit 3 depicts models useful in supplementing style guides to help designers implement functions consistently.

A model is an example of how a window or section of a window should look and behave for performing a particular user operation, such as maintaining a list of items. The concept of models-based design is founded on the idea of creating a set of models that encompasses the majority of common abstract user activities. User activities include such low-level tasks as the following:

- Selecting an item from a hierarchy
- Maintaining a list of items, such as adding, changing, or deleting items from a list
- Entering tabular data, such as inputting a table of parameters
- Simple parameter entry, such as entering hard-copy printing parameters

These activities also include more complicated higher-level abstractions. Higher-level user interface abstractions include groupings of controls or widgets that allow users to perform more complex tasks than simply pushing a button. Examples include collections of controls for free-form spreadsheets or multicolumn list manipulation.

Models-based design aims to increase interapplication consistency and developer productivity. Models-based design is different from a style guide in that it has a top-down instead of a bottom-up focus. A style guide typically encourages consistency by specifying a set of rules and constraints governing how an individual widget will look, where it will be placed, and how it will function when activated.

Unless some control is placed on design consistency, two designers can too easily implement different combinations of widgets for performing the same abstract user activity. For example, to allow a user to add items to a list box, designer "A" may use a pull-down menu; designer "B" may decide, arbitrarily, to use a button beneath the list box. As long as the button is labeled and placed in accordance with the style guide, both approaches would be consistent with the style guide, yet inconsistent from the user's perspective.

As this example shows, the potential problem with style guides is that they address the problem of consistency from the bottom up — how the individual widgets should look, act, and be placed. In contrast, models focus on how widgets are combined to enable users to accomplish common activities, such as adding an item to a list of items.

Across applications, users should be presented with the same user interface (combination and arrangement of widgets) for performing the same user activity. Style guides alone encourage consistency only at lower levels — for example, how buttons are shaped or where menu options are to be found. Models are therefore useful to encourage consistency at higher, more user-oriented levels of abstraction.

However, models do not eliminate the need for a style guide; instead, they are an addition or enhancement to the style guide. The models themselves must be created to be consistent with the underlying style guide rules and constraints.

The total number of models for a given set of applications depends on the variety of distinct abstract user activities. At organizations that have pursued this approach, the number of standard models has ranged from as few as three to as many as 50, but a number between 10 and 15 is most common.

Contents of a Model

A model encompasses both the look and the behavior of the interface. It is not enough to create applications that just look similar visually; they must behave similarly and give the user the same feel. To encourage this level of consistency, a model includes the following:

- A picture or diagram of the appearance of the window or group of widgets
- A high-level description of the abstract activity the model addresses — for example, maintaining a hierarchical list
- A behavior diagram or similar document that clearly states how both the user interface and the application respond to the set of possible user actions
- A data model that shows the relationship of the data entities or attributes included in the model (optional)
- A window flow diagram for models that involve multiple windows and/or a sequence of windows (optional)
- Shell code or reusable routines that are appropriate for this type of model (optional)
- A guide/discussion for determining where the model should and should not be used

Benefits of Models-Based Design

Models-based design has three major benefits:

- *Consistency.* A models-based approach can result in greater user interface consistency across applications and across designers when compared with the typical style guide technique of laying down rules and regulations.
- *Increased productivity.* Models-based design encourages reuse. When a designer begins to design a window, the first step is to review the available approved models and select the one most appropriate to the user task. If no model fits, the designer asks the project member responsible for the user interface design for an exemption or consultation on the development of a new model. Productivity can further be increased by providing "starter packs" for each model, which may include reusable code routines or templates customized to the model.
- *Better leveraging of user interface expertise.* For projects with more than just a few application designers, it is helpful to designate one team member as the lead user interface designer. The lead user interface designer is responsible for the definition, design, and approval of the set of models to be used for the project. If subsequent designers use approved models, there is less need for additional review from the lead user interface designer. This frees the time of the user interface designer to focus on the few windows and user activities for which no standard models have been defined and for which creativity and expertise are required.

The process outlined here, coupled with the right skills, leads to the design of user interfaces that are not just pretty to look at but are affordable to implement, easier to learn, and, most important, increase user efficiency in performing business tasks.

BASIC GUIDELINES FOR GUI DESIGN

The following set of sample rules helps the GUI designer deliver better end products.

Rule 1: Break the 3270 Habit

If designers have spent time designing traditional, mainframe terminal screens, this may at first impede their ability to design effective GUIs. GUIs are not an extension of the 3270 paradigm but a new paradigm entirely.

Exhibit 4 is an actual first attempt by a developer of traditional 3270s to design a GUI. The designer has merely substituted entry fields, buttons, and a radio button control for standard 3270 screen elements and PF keys. This kind of result is not unusual; new GUI designers often have a difficult

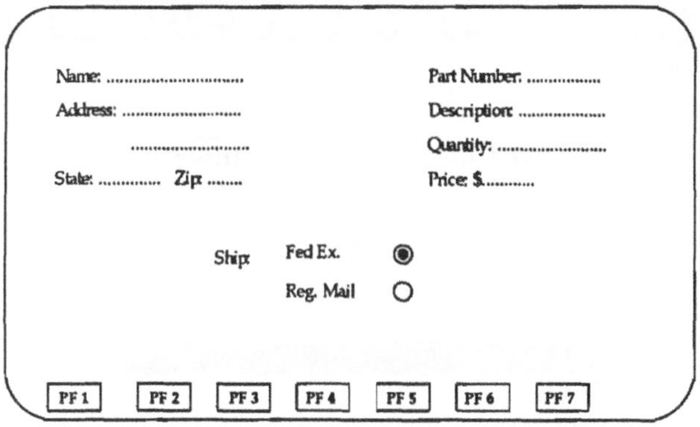

Exhibit 4. The 3270 Paradigm Can Impede Good GUI Design.

---

time leaving their tried and true 3270 screen layout principles behind. When graphical interfaces first came along, interface designers often took their 3270 screens and mapped them almost one for one to the GUI: screens became windows, PF keys became push buttons, and maybe they added a radio button or two to get really fancy. On the second design iteration they would often say, "Oh how silly, instead of PF1 and PF2 down here at the bottom of the screen, we can use the words that the buttons stand for like Page Up and Page Down."

A fairly large mental shift is involved in truly exploiting the power of the GUI. It may be helpful to immerse new designers in a GUI environment, allowing them to see and use as many examples of good GUIs as possible. This experience will help designers see how to exploit the capabilities of a GUI as well as see a variety of implementations.

Rule 2: Avoid "Pop-up Mania"

One of the first reactions of some people who are new to GUI design is to fall prey to "pop-up mania": they fall in love with the idea of having many windows pop up. Only later do they realize what a chore it is for users to have to close all those windows once they have popped up. This phenomenon is common in GUI design. Something that is a wonderful idea on day 1 may be annoying on day 7.

User review of early designs may actually not help this phenomenon. Users who are not accustomed to a GUI can easily be seduced by flashy things. Users often encourage designers to use GUI features that may not ultimately be helpful to them when they have been using an application for many weeks.

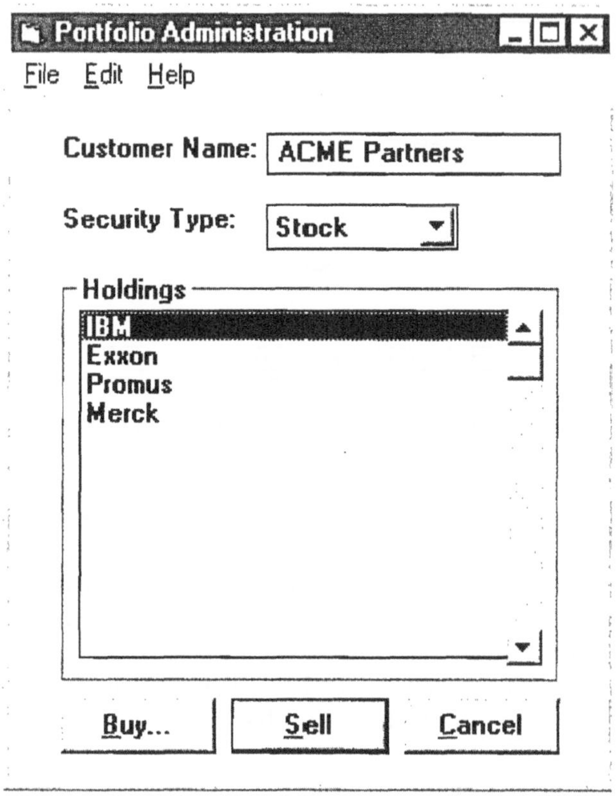

Exhibit 5. One Window Makes All Necessary Information Available.

Suppose in an application a dialog box pops up and prompts the user to enter a customer name and security type. The user can then request a list of holdings by clicking on a button. Another window pops up with a list of stocks. The user can then choose to buy or sell holdings.

What's the problem with this design? When performing portfolio administration, the user is always going to choose this dialog to buy or sell something. Therefore, there is no need to use two windows. The best thing to do in this case is to avoid all the pop-up windows and create one larger window with all of the information immediately accessible (Exhibit 5).

An initial design tendency for many developers is to use too many small windows. A better design is to consolidate this functionality into a larger window. This window allows the user to select the customer name, the security type, the holding, and whether or not to buy or sell, all with one window.

Does this mean it is always better to present more information on a single screen? Not at all, for the designer then may make the screen slightly more complex for the first-time user to understand. Designers must find a balance between ease of learning on the one hand and ease of use or long-term productivity on the other hand. One rule of thumb (acknowledging the inherent limits of "rules of thumb") is that, if the user is going to need a particular list or control at least 50% of the time, the designer should use a bigger window, making available all the necessary information all of the time. This rule must be tempered by certain constraints, however: screen size, user skill level, and how frequently the user visits the window in question.

Rule 3: Avoid Excessive and Gratuitous Graphics

First time Web page designers often fall victim to creating pages with bulky, slow-to-load graphics and "eye candy" animations more suitable to Saturday morning television than facilitating a user completing a business task. Surprisingly, the projects' executives and sponsors often encourage these designs in an attempt to make the Web site look "cool" and in style. Unfortunately, user reaction is often less than enthusiastic when their patience is tested as they wait for graphics to download — graphics that really do not help them achieve what they are trying to do.

Rule 4: Know What Controls Your Windowing System Supports

Many popular windowing systems do not support all the kinds of controls that an enterprise would expect or need in order to build a business-oriented system. Most windowing systems were originally designed to support the development of personal productivity software applications such as spreadsheets and word processors. These types of applications do not require certain kinds of controls that are essential to developing business-oriented applications.

One common example is the multicolumn list box. Most business applications use multiple column lists somewhere — for reports, if for nothing else. However, few windowing systems provide such a control or widget for the programmer. Designers may have to go through extra effort to develop some of these special business controls. In this case, the architecture team may have to create architecture extensions to make these business functions easier to deliver.

An alternative strategy is to understand the set of controls that are natively supported by the windowing system and development tools and then constrain the user interface design to use only supported controls. This approach often leads to a system that is far easier to implement and may get the job done just as well.

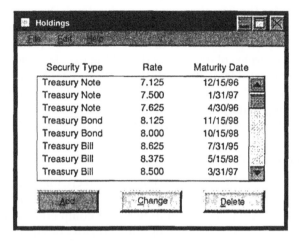

a. Buttons That Cannot Be Selected Are Disabled

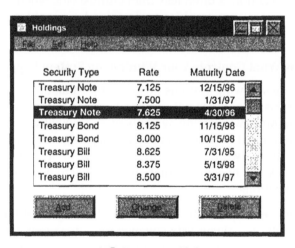

b. Buttons are enabled

Exhibit 6. Object Action Design.

Rule 5. Obtain User Feedback and Guidance

The user interface should give the users guidance about what actions should be taken and then feedback about the actions they do take, that is, users need to understand both what has happened as well as what is now possible or what should happen next.

Exhibit 6 (a) is a multicolumn list box in which no row has yet been selected. The Delete button is disabled (indicated to the user by the word "Delete" being grayed out). It does not make sense to have the Delete button enabled if nothing has been selected. This is a good example of one style of interaction called "object action." The idea is that users need to select an object before they can perform an action.

Consider what would need to happen if the Delete button were enabled and nothing were selected. Designers would have to design a message box reading "Please select a row" to anticipate users clicking on the delete button prematurely. This message box can be avoided simply by disabling the button. When the user clicks on a row, the buttons become enabled.

Why even show the button if it cannot be used? It is always better to show users everything potentially available to them in the window. It would be confusing to use the interface if buttons were constantly appearing and disappearing from the window.

Exhibit 6 (b) shows how the user interface changes to reflect the user's action. In addition to highlighting the selected row, the "Delete" and "Change" buttons are now enabled (not gray), indicating that these operations are now available. Enabling the buttons when the user selects a row tells the users that new actions are now available based upon what they have just done.

Rule 6. Use Color Appropriately

After being constrained by black and white interfaces for so long, designers often get carried away with color and may make the first-time design error of splashing gratuitous color all over their window designs. As a general guideline, designers should use color only where it conveys meaning. On first impression, users are often dazzled by lots of pretty colors all over the computer display. However, like so many other glitzy interface gimmicks, the bright colors become distracting and irritating for users in the long run. Color should be used to draw the user's attention to some important item on the screen. If color is overused for decoration it becomes ineffective for that purpose, thus limiting its ultimate effectiveness.

Designers should keep a few things in mind when using colors:

- Color blindness affects a number of people. On several occasions, when user interfaces relied on color exclusively to convey key information, the interfaces had to be redesigned once it was discovered that one or more key users were color blind.

- Colors may have different associations and connotations in different countries. For instance, mailboxes are blue in the United States, red in the United Kingdom, and yellow in Greece. The Japanese language does not have a clear distinction between the colors green and blue. Culture may also attach different meanings to specific colors. For example, in Japan white is sometimes associated with death.
- Humans cannot see color in their peripheral vision very well. Try it. People lose track of colors when they turn away from an object, especially in low light conditions. This implies that, on a large screen, the user may not notice that the color of an icon in the corner of the screen has changed from gray to blue.

Rule 7. Avoid Making the User Wait

Users should not have to wait, doing nothing, while certain processing functions are occurring. Designers should take advantage of the multi-tasking features of the operating system that they are building upon. If the user can be doing something else on the workstation while a relatively lengthy process is operating, the designer should make that happen. An application can allow this by releasing control to the operating system or by creating an asynchronous task that can be run on the server rather than tying up the workstation.

Rule 8. Design for Performance as Well as Usability

Designers of GUI applications must often make trade-offs in their designs — choices that may sacrifice a degree of usability in order to improve system performance. Large windows that are rich with information and controls can lead to high user productivity. In some cases, however, the response time penalty of creating and populating the large window may lead the designer to carve the functionality into multiple smaller windows, ensuring more rapid response times.

Another performance vs. usability choice centers around collecting data in advance of the user opening the window that needs it. Building windows and reading databases in anticipation that the user may need the information can provide users with more immediate response, greater usability, and higher productivity. The performance trade off is in the excess systems load associated with collecting data that the user may never request.

Rule 9. Design for "Implementability"

Evaluate the user interface for implementability, not just user friendliness. What does that mean? There is a great deal of value in having cognitive scientists telling us what a great user interface would look like because it is important to understand these concepts in order to come up with more innovative solutions. However, once designers know what the "ideally usable" design is, they must analyze it for implementability. Can the design be coded cost effectively? Will performance be adequate?

Various windowing systems and operating systems impose limitations and constraints on the visual appearance of applications. If the interface is too difficult to implement, design iterations may be required until a happy medium can be found.

DOCUMENTING A GUI DESIGN

Appearance

When documenting the design of a GUI, it is necessary to capture both the *appearance* and the *behavior* of the interface, as well as the application business logic. The appearance of the user interface is simply the basic layout of controls within a window.

Many tools are currently available for painting windows. Window painting tools range from simple prototyping tools to more advanced computer-aided software engineering (CASE) environments that can be used to carry the design documentation forward into construction. As discussed previously, another "low-tech" approach is to document the user interface design through hand-drawn windows on paper or sticky notes.

Behavior

The behavior of the user interface is more challenging to document. The behavior is what happens at run time in response to user actions. The interface behavior of an application includes the answers to questions such as

- What happens when I click on this button?
- What if I double click on a row in this listbox?
- What happens if I drag this icon onto this other icon?
- What if I choose this menu option?

There can be a fine line between *interface* behavior and *application* behavior. Interface behavior is really only what is happening from a visual standpoint: a dialog popping up, rows being inserted in a list box, a button being enabled, rows within a list box being sorted. Application behavior encompasses more of the traditional data processing activities such as database reads, calculations, and business functions. When documenting the interface behavior it is important to keep the distinction between the two in mind. Later, this chapter introduces a simple method for documenting user interface behavior with a CAR (control, action, response) diagram.

Finally, the application behavior or logic design should be documented using any conventional programming design method, such as flow charts

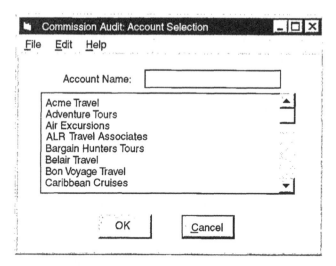

Exhibit 7. Example Appearance Documentation.

---

or pseudocode. The point here is that the application logic can be specified in a way independent of the type of user interface being used. Alternatively, the CAR diagramming approach can be used to document both interface and application behavior.

The Role of Prototyping

Why document a graphical user interface design? Why not just create a prototype and give that to the developers? A prototype, by its nature, expresses both the appearance of the windows as well as the behavior of the controls. Undeniably, a prototype is a key tool in the design of a user interface. The prototype can be used as an iterative design vehicle for gathering user input and feedback on the evolving design. Although a necessary aspect of design, a prototype is not in itself sufficient for capturing the design of a system to the degree necessary for coding to begin.

Typically, a prototype is not developed for the entire system, but rather for some key portions. In addition, a prototype may not cover, nor explicitly show, many of the conditional kinds of processing that occur. For example, "If the list box row clicked on is a Treasury Bill, open the Treasury Bill maintenance dialog box."

Behavior Diagramming

Exhibit 7 is an account selection window. The window allows the user to select an account for auditing ticket commissions from a list of existing account names. The users can type in an account name and press Enter or

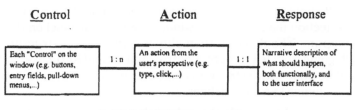

Exhibit 8. CAR Diagramming.

select an account directly from the list box. They can also cancel and close the dialog box by clicking on the Cancel button. The description of documentation techniques in the following pages will refer back to this simple window.

"CAR" DIAGRAMMING

A CAR diagram (Control, Action, Response) documents the behavior of the window by detailing the application's response to each user action on each control of the window. The CAR diagramming technique is a simple approach that has proven very useful on numerous client/server and net-centric development projects (Exhibit 8).

Control

A control is anything that a user can activate, click on, or drag to do something in an application window. Examples of typical controls include the following:

- List boxes, which display a scrollable list of choices
- Entry fields, which allow for entry of data via the keyboard
- Push buttons, which the user can click on to select an action

Action

For each control, one or more actions that can be performed. For example, with a list box, the user can single-click or double-click on an item. Each of these actions can invoke a different application response.

Response

The response is a common, non-computer-language description of what should happen in the application when this control is activated. A CAR diagram is meant to be readable by people other than computer programmers; its language is simpler, for example, "Fill the portfolio list box" or "Pop-up the account dialog box window." The response definitions serve as an initial description of the application code that eventually must be written for each control.

Exhibit 9 shows what a CAR diagram might look like for the example account selection dialog box. The window name is the label on the far left of the diagram. The diagram then shows a three-level structure chart approach going from left to right: Control, Action, and Response. Note that this could be done with a structure chart editor, as shown, or just as easily with four columns in a spreadsheet.

Exhibit 10 provides a walk-through of the CAR diagram. This diagramming technique is independent of any particular window system.

The benefit of using common, noncomputer language to describe the interface behavior, besides windowing system independence, is that after the CAR diagram is created it can be used for many purposes:

- The CAR diagram can be used as a high-level systems specification from which detailed designs can be created.
- The testing team can use the CAR diagrams to develop many of the test conditions and scripts that will be used later in the testing phase.
- Because the CAR diagram is readable by nontechnical people, the diagram can be given to those responsible for developing user procedures. User procedures and help manuals can then be developed concurrently with the actual software.
- Users can gain an understanding of how the system operates by examining both the screen prints and CAR diagrams.

DETAILED DESIGN SPECIFICATIONS

The CAR diagram is useful for capturing and communicating the application design at a high level. However, more detailed design specifications may be required before the application can be coded by programmers. Documenting the next level of design can be accomplished by adding a piece of information to the CAR diagram and creating an additional design document called a "Callback Diagram" (Exhibit 11).

The CAR diagram in Exhibit 12 is the same as in Exhibit 11, but in a spreadsheet format. One additional column has been added, entitled "Procedure." (Thus, some call this a "CARP" diagram.) This new column captures the design name for the callback procedure that is to be invoked.

The callback procedure is the piece of application logic executed when the user performs the specified action on the control. The reason for adding the procedure name is to provide a link to a callback diagram which can further describes the required application logic.

The procedure "OpenAccount" (shown in bold in Exhibit 11) appears twice on the callback diagram. This indicates that the same application routine is to be reused and that the user interface provides the user more

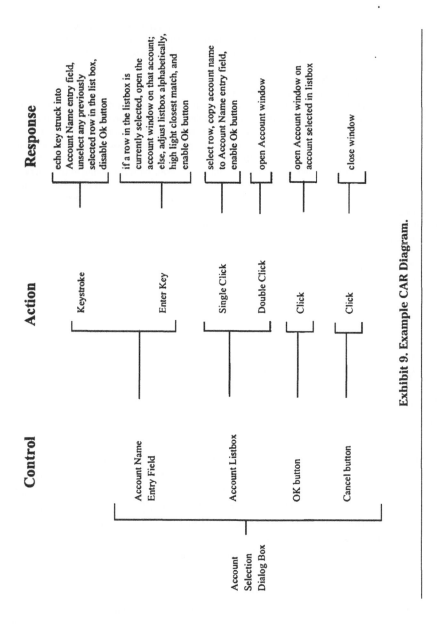

Exhibit 9. Example CAR Diagram.

Exhibit 10. Walk-Through of the CAR Diagram.

Control 1:	Account Name Entry Field
Action 1:	The action is to "type a letter"
Response:	When a key is struck, the response is to echo the value in the Account Name entry field, and disable the OK button. (The OK is disabled, because the user is keying in letters; therefore an account is not currently selected to be opened.)
Control 1:	Account Name Entry Field
Action 2:	The action is to "hit the enter key"
Response:	When the ENTER key is pressed, the response is dependent upon whether or not an account name is currently selected in the listbox. If an account row is selected, pressing the ENTER key results in the Account window (not shown) being lauched with the selected account's information. If an account row is not yet selected, the ENTER key causes the listbox to be adjusted such that the top entry is in aplhabetic order with the string in the entry field. If the user typed "P ENTER," the first name in the list box might adjust to be "Parker Travel" and the row would be selected (highlighted).
Control 2:	Account Listbox
Action 1:	A single click of the left mouse button
Response 1:	Copy the selected name to the Account Name entry field
Action 2:	A double click of the left mouse button
Response 2:	Open the selected Account
Control 3:	OK Button
Action:	A single click of the left mouse button
Response:	Open the Account window for the account currently selected in the listbox. (Note that this behaves the same as hitting ENTER in the customer name entry field.)
Control 4:	Cancel Button
Action:	A single click of the left mouse button
Response:	The window closes and the system returens to its prior state

than one way to invoke this function. An effective user interface often gives the user multiple ways of performing the same function (e.g., keyboard equivalents for pull-down menus).

The callback diagram can specify the design of a callback procedure to a much more detailed level. Whether this additional level of design detail is necessary depends largely on the skills and experience of the programmers who will be coding the system, and the complexity of the function. The callback diagram may be considered superfluous for all but the most complex callbacks on projects where the programmers are already experienced with developing graphical netcentric programs.

CONCLUSION

The design challenges of GUI applications are substantial but manageable with an appropriate design approach. This chapter presented an outline of a design approach and process as well as a few of the key tips and guidelines for producing excellent GUIs.

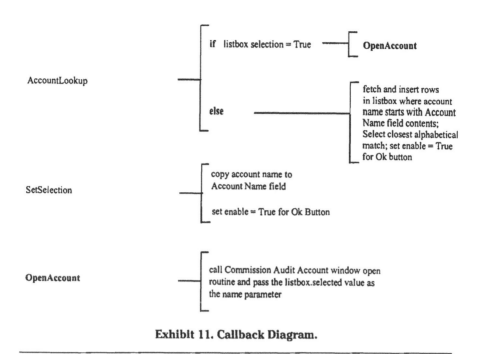

AccountLookup
- if listbox selection = True ——— OpenAccount
- else ——— fetch and insert rows in listbox where account name starts with Account Name field contents; Select closest alphabetical match; set enable = True for Ok button

SetSelection
- copy account name to Account Name field
- set enable = True for Ok Button

OpenAccount
- call Commission Audit Account window open routine and pass the listbox.selected value as the name parameter

Exhibit 11. Callback Diagram.

Exhibit 12. Callback Diagram — Spreadsheet Format

Control	Action	Response	Procedure(s)
Account name Entry field	Keystoke	Echo key struck into Account Name entry field, unselect any previously selected row in the list box, disable OK button	DeSelectListbox( )
Account name Entry field	Enter	If a row in the listbox is currently selected, open the account window on that account, or else, adjust listbox alphabetically, highlight closest match, and enable OK button	AccountLookup( )
Account listbox	Single click	Copy account name to Account Name entry field	SetSelection( )
	Double Click	Open account window	OpenAccount( )
OK button	Click	Open account window on account selected in listbox	OpenAccount( )
Cancel button	Click	Close window	ExitWindow( )

Chapter 21
System Controls

Perhaps no discussion is more likely to empty a room of technicians quickly than one on system controls. At the same time, in the netcentric environments in which systems are being delivered today, the need for controls has become increasingly important. Netcentric computing presents many concerns with regard to an effective running system. Inherent in such an environment is many distributed computers being operated in hostile environments by users who are not experienced.

For such people, problem solution and recovery often means turning the machine on and off. Data are transmitted across unreliable networks and may consist of messages for which no transaction management exists. In such an environment there may be no clear ownership of problems. Resolution of loss of data and corrupted data may often be addressed by simply doing the transaction over again. Given these types of issues the potential for loss of data and data integrity is very high. Indeed, it is safe to assume that the probability of loss would be 100%.

To some degree, the netcentric environment, with its dependence on unreliable networks and untrained users with machines in hostile environments, represents a return to the "wild west" environment of the early 1960s, which gave rise to many of the control techniques we use even today.

If an assumption of problems is 100% the need for controls on a netcentric system is 100%. Controls must be built in as a part of the system if one is to succeed in the reliable ongoing operation of such netcentric systems.

Having said this, one can find many netcentric systems going into production either with no controls or with only a few controls patched on as an afterthought. In such a case, experience suggests that often the systems seem to be working acceptably. Then, as time passes, what appear to be minor disruptions or odd events are found, in reality, to be indicative of major data losses or serious integrity problems. There have been cases, in such situations, where the worst of all possible cases arise. The new system has appeared to be working well enough that the old system is retired. Then it is determined that the new system has significant system integrity and data loss issues. At this point there may no way back to the old system. Further fixing the new system may mean that it continues to compound existing errors as repairs are made. Clearly such a situation creates many problems with regard to ongoing user confidence in the system. The image that comes to mind in such a situation is of an individual standing on two logs in the middle of a fast moving river. It is only a question of time until the individual falls into the river.

THE NATURE OF SYSTEMS CONTROLS

Having posed the problem as described above, it is worthwhile to spend some time on what is meant by systems controls. Controls can cover a wide range of topics. They can include validation controls, which ensure that the data a system accepts meets defined requirements with regard to values and interrelationships. Controls can also include security controls. These types of controls ensure that individuals accessing the system and data have the right to do so. In addition, such security can identify personnel or agents that try to access systems or information to which they are not entitled. These topics of validation and security are dealt with in Chapter 28 of this book and will not be addressed in this chapter.

This chapter will address what is called "Integrity Processing Controls." These are the systems controls that verify the integrity and processing of a system. Such controls ensure that the data that should have been received was, in fact, delivered. Such controls also ensure that the processing done against the data was completed and reflects the impact of the data. Further, the controls discussed in this chapter will address the question of problem resolution when they determine that data has been lost.

A FRAMEWORK FOR DEFINING CONTROLS

The case for controls in a netcentric environment is quite strong. However, the fact is that controls can present a "slippery slope" of endless possible risks and controls to meet the risk. Controls can become an endless task of trying to make sure that nothing goes wrong. This is not desirable. Controls are — as the name suggests — a means to *control* business risk. As such, the controls should be thought of as an investment to remove risk, that is, with controls, one evaluates the cost of the control against the potential loss combined with the probability of that loss. If the investment exceeds the potential loss represented by the risk, the further investment in that control is not advisable. Although that may seem abstract, it can be reflected in a framework for defining risks.

The framework is no more than a means to explicitly define risk, its impact, and the means to control the risk.

WHAT IS "RISK"?

What is a "risk"? A risk is the possibility that a system or procedure may fail to meet the control objective established for it. A risk has two components: a cause and a consequence.

- The cause is any original instrument or agent that makes a risk happen. Some frequent causes of risks are people, equipment failures, and natural forces.
- The consequence is the effect on an organization when a risk actually occurs. In information processing, the most common business consequences are losses of assets or information, disruption of normal operations, and legal sanctions. Consequences are often interrelated. For instance, the consequences of a fire that destroys a bank's data processing center would be a loss of assets, disruption of service to customers, and possible legal action by depositors.

CONTROLS

The process of controls design and implementation begins with an inventory of the risks that the systems faces, what practical events could cause the risk to become a reality, and the impact of the risk being realized. This initial step can be accomplished by a simple spreadsheet inventory of risks, causes, and consequences. The value of the effort is to establish a baseline of expected risks. The baseline has value in terms of identifying risks that could become a reality and for which there is clear value in managing the risk. It is also to make the point that any risk for which controls may be built are to pass through the process of analysis which verifies the risk and justifies the cost required to manage the risk. Often the dialog associated with the process of building the spreadsheet is of great value in getting an understanding of what the real risks are to a system. If nothing else, it can alert systems builders to the reality of risk inherent in building a new system. An example of such a starting spreadsheet is found in Exhibit 1.

For each of these risk/causes a means to control the risks must be defined. In doing so, one wants controls that are complete, effective, and timely.

A *complete* control is one that selects, tests, and acts. In other words, the control must detail:

- What will be controlled (e.g., terminal assets)
- How it will be verified or validated (records in a transaction file or the amount of sales in a sales database)
- What will occur when an invalid or unacceptable condition is obtained (report a transaction file out of balance)

An *effective* control successfully reduces the risk for which it was designed. It also must not hinder the business activities it is designed to control. For example, stopping all transactions when one file is out of balance may limit the impact but may also stop the business. A *timely* control is one that detects problems on a timely basis and reports them in time to avoid or minimize the

Risk	Cause	Consequence
The system will have more than 5000 sites from which daily transactions file are to be collected. The data could be loss causing lost of the days activity at the site.	A site may fail to close off the transaction file at end of day and thus make the file unavailable	The file would not be transmitted to the central site and the days events would not be reflected in overnight processing
	A transmission of a file may be loss in transmission	The file would not be available for processing. Given the number of sites this could be overlooked
	A file transmission may lose some component of the file due to a temporary network outage	Some individual records would be loss and not reflected in process
	A site may have an empty file due to no activity in a day	There could be an indication that a site was not received when in fact, there was nothing to send
	A site may fail to start with an empty transaction file due to failure to run end of day processing to close off the days file	The site could resend the prior days transmissions along with today's transmission. The prior days transmissions could be processed twice

Exhibit 1. Initial Spreadsheet Inventory.

consequences of a problem. For example, identifying an out of balance file and reporting it when identified to a control may be timely. Similarly, reporting invalid transactions at the time they are validated and allowing immediate correction is superior to forwarding documents for centralized processing and correcting errors in the next processing cycle.

It should be noted that the framework of Risk/Cause/Control is being applied here to the specifics of Integrity Processing Controls. However, the framework is clearly applicable to a wider set of control issues.

TYPES OF CONTROLS

When Integrity Processing Controls are to be defined, they can be thought of as including the following types of controls:

- *Processing controls* ensure that all data entered and accepted are successfully processed with all exceptions identified, reported, and resolved. Processing controls include

    Controls that ensure all transactions are processed

    Controls that ensure accurate updating of files

    Controls that perform data edits and validations either during data entry or processing

    Controls that detect duplicate processing

    Controls that ensure each processing step is performed and in the proper order

- *Database controls* help ensure that the database and other files used for processing are valid, current, and that proper relationships exist between the data.
- *Output controls* ensure that printed output is distributed correctly and on time to the authorized users.
- *Other controls* include data that are required for audit trails, data transmission, and system interfaces. Such controls could be placed in more than one category. Other controls include validate and error reports and other control reports that provide an audit trail.

DEFINING INTEGRITY PROCESSING CONTROLS

With this base of understanding of definitions and terms, the subject now moves to techniques to define Integrity Processing Controls. In one sense, many of these techniques are not new and were known in the time of sequential batch systems. The rest were defined with the advent of database technology. However, one can find systems implemented in the last 15 years that have few if any of these controls. It appears that many of the control techniques have been forgotten by systems developers in the last 15 years.

As suggested, one set of these controls was devised for the consideration of sequential file and another for database. These types of processing can be described as follows:

- *Sequential.* Transactions are staged for processing against a master file and sorted into a desired sequence for processing against the master file. Each transaction file record is read and processed against the appropriate master file record by the update program. Processing is prescheduled, often for the end of a reporting cycle.
- *Direct.* Processing sequence is based on the order in which transactions arrive (instead of the master file) and may be done each time a transaction is originated ("real-time processing"). Only the master file records that the transactions affect are read and processed.

In addition, netcentric processing requires us to think of sequential files that are a hybrid of the sequential files. For these files, transactions are staged at some site to be transmitted and processed at some other sites. The transactions are processed in either a sequential or direct manner based on the needs of the receiving system.

SEQUENTIAL FILE PROCESSING

Controls over sequential file processing ensure that the files created by the processing system properly reflect all of the data entered. They also ensure that the correct files are used in processing and that all data created in one program are read and processed in subsequent programs. This will need to occur across sites in netcentric environment.

Three types of sequential file processing controls are discussed here:

- Run-to-run controls
- File balancing
- Generation data sets

Run-to-Run Controls

Run-to-run controls control data flow between programs or systems and between sites. Run-to-run controls ensure the accuracy and completeness of the information that a program or site receives for processing. They also ensure that accurate and complete information is passed on to subsequent programs.

Run-to-run controls are designed to detect errors as soon as possible and to determine the program or site in which the errors occurred. Common sources of detected errors include program or network problems, operator errors, or site outages.

In a run-to-run control, a program accumulates a record count as records are written to the output file. A control record containing the total record count is written as the last block on the file or to a separate control file. When additional control is necessary to detect loss or destruction of records within the logic of a program or a string of programs, control totals, such as a total of quantities or dollar amounts (not a record count), should be accumulated and verified in subsequent programs.

A subsequent program accumulates a count of the records as they are read. Then, after the last record is read, it compares the accumulated total of counts and amounts to the control record created by the previous program, either from the sequential file or from the control file.

If an error is detected during processing, processing may continue or may be terminated at the end of the program where the error was detected. Typically, the application processing will continue until the end of the job, and the error will be resolved later.

Control reporting may be on an audit trail or exception basis.

- For audit trail reporting, each program reports the number of records written, number of records read, and contents of the control record. This provides an audit trail or reports that may be traced if necessary.
- An exception report is produced when the accumulated count differs from the control record amount. If exception reporting is implemented, information must be provided in the exception report to help trace the error.

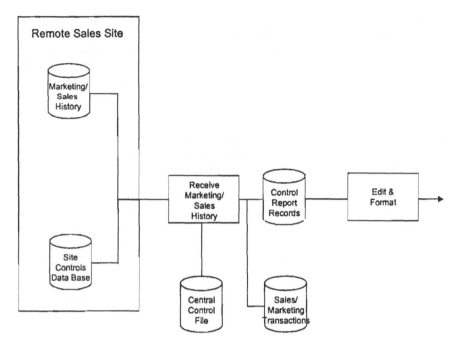

Exhibit 2. Marketing and Sales History System Example.

The following example deals with a marketing and sales history system. The processing is illustrated in Exhibit 2.

As shown, history data are accumulated from remote processing. The data is posted to a transaction file, which is used by marketing for other reporting purposes. At the same time, the history data are reformatted into report records, and these are passed to edit and format report processing. As records are posted, the site control database is updated.

The receive programs contain instructions for accumulating record counts and dollar amounts for items written to the marketing/sales control file. At the end of each processing cycle, each program writes a control record with the accumulated totals to the central controls file.

The Receive Marketing/Sales History program performs a similar accumulation, and, when processing of the marketing/sales history file is complete, the program shares the accumulation to the control record.

An identical process is performed for the report records file, which is passed between the Receive Marketing/Sales History and the Edit and Format programs. Exception reporting is used for run-to-run controls.

If control totals only are used, the system will recognize the loss of records that contain control total data. For example, assume the marketing and sales history file contains customer header records followed by individual order records. The order records contain the dollar totals. In this case, a record count should be used to detect lost header records.

File Balancing

File balancing is a second type of sequential file processing controls. File balancing ensures that errors in the master file update processing are detected and that the files accurately reflect all data entered.

In file balancing, when records are added or deleted to a master file, they are accumulated separately and added to or subtracted from the total read to compare to the total written or processed. Each record is counted as it is read from the master file. As records are added to the new master file, they are added to the total count; as records are deleted, they are subtracted from the count.

Finally, the total is compared with the actual number of records written to the new master file. If the numbers are unequal, an error condition has occurred. This may be a read/write error, a program error, or a system error.

In the following example, after the sales/marketing transactions are accepted, they are then used to maintain the master marketing sales file (Exhibit 3).

The file balancing technique is used in the update program that is part of the Maintain Marketing/Sales History program. The information stored on the current period marketing/sales history file is merged with the marketing/sales history master file from the prior period to give the new marketing/sales history master file.

During the update program, a count is kept of the number of records read from the prior period master file. The master file contains one record for each of the customers. A count is also kept of the number of new customers to be added this period. Any records to be deleted are also counted. This resulting number is compared with the actual number of records on the new marketing/sales history master file. If the two numbers are not equal, an error report is produced.

Generation Data Sets

A third type of sequential file control is creating and storing generation data sets. Generation data sets are a common backup procedure for sequential files. The use of this control is shown in Exhibit 4.

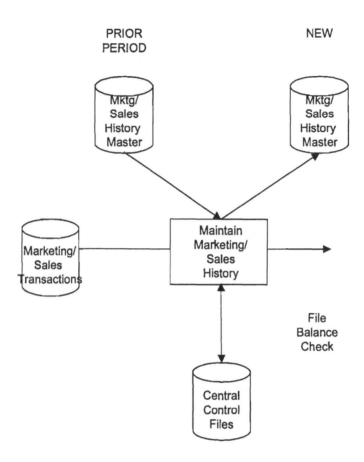

PRIOR
PERIOD

NEW

Exhibit 3. Maintaining the Master Marketing/Sales File.

During processing, labeled "Day 1," new transactions are applied to the current transaction file to create a new transaction file. During the next update period, Day 2, transactions are applied to a new transaction file to create a new master file. The old/new transition is typically accomplished by end-of-day processing, which marks the old transaction file as prior, and initiates a new transaction file.

Most sequential file processing systems maintain three generations of files: the "grandfather," "father," and "son." The previous transaction file provides the initial backup should it be lost in transmission to another site. Unless unique circumstances require it, more generations of files usually are not needed. There is value in sending a verification to a control site that all required files have been initiated.

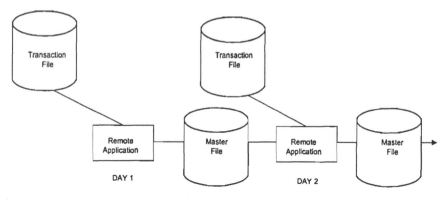

Exhibit 4. Using Generation Data Sets.

To ensure that the transaction file can be recreated is necessary, the backup files must be protected.

DIRECT ACCESS PROCESSING

Direct access processing involves real-time access to the database or master file. This requires an extension to the Integrity Processing Controls.

Database environments have unique risks related to lost data. In a database environment, because updates occur in place, old versions of the data are destroyed. There is little or no data redundancy, which makes recreating lost data difficult. It is typically addressed in a DBMS through the use of a log file or through mirroring.

Two types of controls over such databases are discussed here:

- Posting controls
- Recovery/restart controls

Database Posting Controls

To ensure the completeness, accuracy, and integrity of a database during application processing, database processing controls are required. Two common posting controls are

- System logs
- Database balancing

System Logs. Changes posted to the database over a specific period of time can be recorded on a system log. If the database should become corrupted, the database can be reconciled to the log. The system log is the most comprehensive means of maintaining an audit trail of database activity.

A system log can be kept on tape files or any mass storage device. A typical log keeps:

- A copy of each database record updated by a transaction, both before and after the record is changed
- The identity of the program that made the change to the database
- The date and time the change was made
- The identity of the database and record being modified

Database Balancing. Database balancing verifies that all authorized, valid transactions that were accepted for processing are posted to the database. To balance the database, the database totals from the last sequential processing and the transactions that have been posted to the database totals from current sequential processing are reconciled. Some of the amounts reconciled are created when the data are originally entered, that is, transaction counts and totals of important quantity fields.

Other reconciling numbers must be developed by accumulating counts of specific record types and totals of fields on the database during periodic processing when the entire database is read sequentially from beginning to end.

Procedures and schedules for balancing the data and handling balancing exceptions must be developed. If at any time during processing, database balancing is no completed or if the balancing process is unable to reconcile a file, systems and database administration personnel must be informed.

The following is an example of database balancing in a sales system. In the system, orders are entered throughout the week, both on-line and off-line. Each creates a new record on the open order database. The input controls provide a count and total dollar value of all orders entered each day.

The billing system maintains the database for orders shipped. At the end of each day, the shipments for that day are processed against the database. When an order is shipped, the open orders database record is copied to a receivables database, and the open order record is then deleted. A count and total order dollars shipped is maintained by the billing application.

At the end of the day's processing, the open order database is read sequentially. The records are counted and the dollar values are accumulated. The database is balanced as shown here:

No. of orders		Dollar value
Yesterday	536	$12,822
Orders Entered	2,387	68,926
Orders Shipped	(2,477)	(63,201)
Today		
Calculated	446	$18,547
Actual on database	446	$18,547

If the controls group finds a difference between the calculated totals and the totals actually accumulated, the database is out of balance. In this case, the controls group should follow the procedures defined for the system to report the discrepancy for investigation and correction.

Although this database balancing example is fairly simple, some databases have multiple record types to be balanced and many different kinds of updates. Large databases may be so long that there is not enough time to read them sequentially every day. The approach to balancing the databases would still be similar to our example, however.

Summary totals can be used to assure both efficient database file balancing and faster access to data for on-line processing. Summary totals are totals of data carried on a number of detail records on a file. Summary totals frequently are carried on summary or header records.

A typical use of summary totals is on a controls table. Consider an inventory database that has control table describing each part number (Exhibit 5).

As shown, beneath the control segment there may be a number of location segments, each showing the quantity on hand for each inventory location or bin. There may also be some on-order segments showing quantity on order for individual purchase orders, and other segments containing back-order quantities for individual customer orders. This location record would be found at each local site.

Because the total quantities on hand, on-order, and back-ordered are needed often for inquiries or other processing requirements, processing will be faster if these totals are maintained in the control segment rather than through some form of SQL real-time rollup. Without these totals, it would be necessary to read all of the lower-level segments and add the quantities. The system will adjust the totals each time any lower-level segments are changed.

The use of summary total procedure simplifies balancing the database because only the control segment need to be read. If there is no enough time to sequentially pass the entire database for balancing each night, the ability to balance only root segments will improve control over the database.

In controls processing, controls from the local site can be balanced to the central site Location Balance. An out of balance here indicates that there is a discrepancy between local and remote.

For larger databases, it may not be feasible to read all control segments during the time when the on-line system is not in use. In this case, summary totals could be maintained for the database as well. In the inventory example,

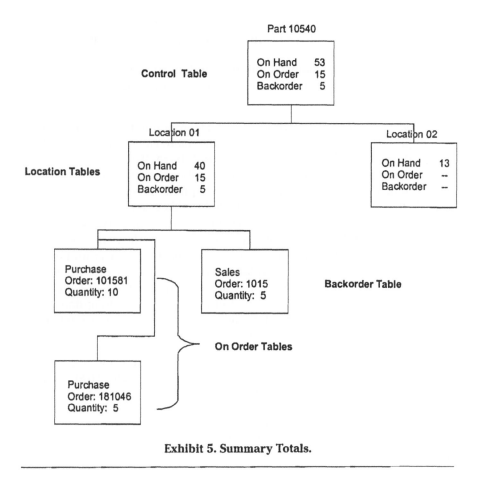

Exhibit 5. Summary Totals.

a control segment could be established and maintained for each unique part number prefix or item type.

If the users of a system frequently need summary totals in reports or on display screens, creating a Totals database may be helpful. This serves a dual purpose of allowing more effective retrieval of only the data necessary for totals and providing an independent source of control information to assist with the balancing of data in case the files become corrupt.

Recovery/Restart Controls

Recovery/restart controls are another type of control used in direct access processing. Recovery/restart is the restoration of a database. Recovery/restart controls are important because data in the database may become inaccurate, incomplete, or unreadable due to hardware or software failure. For example, an error in a new or recently modified application program may post updates incorrectly, a system software error might erase some database records, or a disk drive malfunction may make the disk unusable.

Recovery. There are many techniques for database recovery, yet they all accomplish the same objective: returning the database to an acceptable state.

- *Transaction log.* One method, called a transaction log, requires saving copies of all transactions applied to the database over a period of time and periodically copying the total database. If recovery/restart is needed, the most recent copy of the database is obtained and all transactions not posted to that copy are applied. Generation transaction file discussed previously may be used in this case.
- *System log.* Another recovery/restart method uses the system log described under database posting controls. As indicated, this log contains a copy of each database record just before it is updated (a "before" image), after it is updated (an "after" image), or both. Generally speaking, the before images are used to back out or cancel the effect of incorrect updates. The after images are used to update a previous backup copy of the database if the current copy is destroyed. This is usually faster than reprocessing all transactions.

Whichever method is used, once recovery is complete and the applications are available again, the system must be restarted. Before transactions can again be entered, the system must identify the last transaction processed so that the user knows where to resume data entry. For example, if the error occurred during the entry of a transaction, it might be necessary to reenter the entire transaction, it might be necessary to reenter the entire transaction, or only the portion beginning at the last screen.

OTHER CONTROLS: BATCH BALANCING

Batch balancing is a technique to maintain controls within a file. As such it extends control to a subset of the file and may make it more feasible to identify sources of out of balance conditions. This technique has been in use in accounting systems since before the computer age. However, netcentric applications have made it more important due to the risky nature of moving data from distributed computers over unreliable networks. With the correct approach, batching can allow controls to be applied by user or workstation and within sets of transactions from such a source.

To perform batch balancing, input transactions are collected into small, manageable groups called batches. Control totals for each batch are then traced through the processing using logs and reports. The logs are prepared by the sending system. The logs and reports are compared to see if the totals on the logs balance with those on the computer-prepared reports. If they do not balance, it is an indication that at least one of the batches is in error.

To simplify this discussion, we have divided the batch balancing process into two segments split by the computer's validation program: before validation and after validation. We will show how the transactions, manual operations, and the computer interrelate to control transaction processing.

Three key documents are used to control transaction entry:

- Batch header form
- Batch control log
- Batch validate and error report

Before Validation

Before data are transcribed and entered, the data entry clerks or the control group, whoever has the designated responsibility, creates batches and manually prepares two control documents.

The orders should be batched as soon as possible after creation. The longer the time before they are counted and controlled the greater the risk of undetected loss of a document.

Control documents prepared before validation are the batch header forms and the batch control log.

Batch Header Form. The batch header form is intended to control a batch (or group) of input documents. In the example shown in Exhibit 6, each batch consists of up to 25 orders. One batch header is prepared for each batch, as shown in the exhibit.

In this example, a batch number is assigned by the clerk who batches the input documents. Batch numbers are usually assigned consecutively. They provide a means of identifying and accounting for batches. The batch date is the date the batch was created. This date helps determine when a specific batch should be entered into the system. Control totals include the number of orders and total dollar order amount.

Batch Control Log. The batch control log is used before and after validation to manually reconcile any differences between control totals on the batch header documents and the system-calculated totals after validation.

Before validation the control information on the batch header is entered into a batch control log to provide a record of all the batches submitted. This is shown in Exhibit 7.

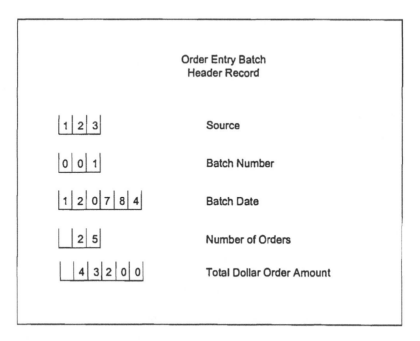

Exhibit 6. Batch Header Form.

During Validation

The system validates this input data to ensure it is accurate and complete. The system checks to see that the customer number is valid, that credit limits are not exceeded, and that the order information is valid. If the system detects an error during validation, the transaction is rejected. Accepted transactions proceed for further processing.

When the system finishes validating a batch, it calculates control totals. These computer-prepared control totals are the sum for each of the batches entered.

After validation, the system prepares a Batch Validate and Error Report. It has two purposes:

1. To identify validation errors found
2. To report manual and system control totals and balancing errors for each batch processed.

A sample Batch Validate and Error Report is shown in Exhibit 8.

Part A of the report identifies orders that contain errors. In the example, only one error was found in Batch 001. An error code is printed on the right

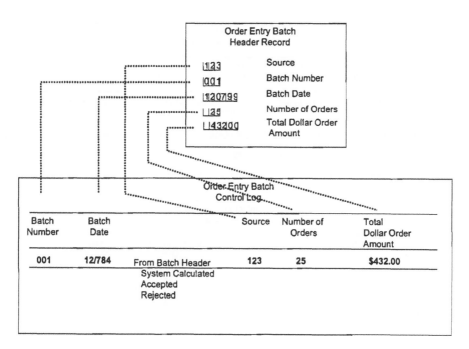

Exhibit 7. Batch Control Log.

	Order Entry Batch Header Record	
	1123	Source
	001	Batch Number
	120799	Batch Date
	25	Number of Orders
	43200	Total Dollar Order Amount

Order Entry Batch Control Log

Batch Number	Batch Date		Source	Number of Orders	Total Dollar Order Amount
001	12/784	From Batch Header	123	25	$432.00
		System Calculated			
		Accepted			
		Rejected			

Order Entry Batch Validate and Error Report

	Batch No.	Code No.	Customer No.	Customer Name	Item No.	Item Description	Qty.	Price	Error Code
A	001	3465	03698	J. P. Jones	16C	Vegematic	3	$29.00	E-025

	Total for Batch 001	Source	Entered	Calculated	Difference	Accepted	Rejected
B	Number of Orders	123	25	25	0	24	1
	Total Dollar Amount	123	432,00	432.00	0	403.00	29.00

Exhibit 8. Sample Batch Validate and Error Report.

side of the report to provide further information on the error found. Here the item number is in error and the error code E-025 refers the user to a manual that describes in further detail the item number error.

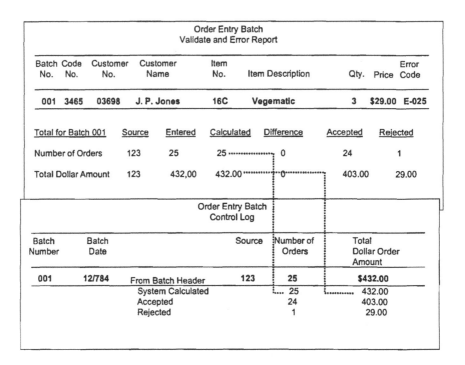

Exhibit 9. Transferring to the Batch Control Log.

Part B of the report shows the control totals for the entire batch.

- The numbers in the *entered* column are from the batch header form.
- The *calculated* numbers are system calculated.
- Any difference between the entered and the calculated numbers would appear in the *difference* column. The number of orders and the dollar amounts accepted and rejected are listed on the right. The rejected items are listed in Part A.

As shown in Exhibit 9, information from the Batch Validate and Error Report is transferred to the Batch Control Log. The calculated totals for the batch and the transactions accepted and rejected are recorded in the appropriate place on the Batch Control Log.

At this point, three checks are made:

1. A difference between a batch header total and the system-calculated total indicates an error in one set of totals. The difference must be reconciled.
2. Rejected items indicate an error in the input data. These must be corrected.

3. Any difference between the number of accepted and rejected transactions for each batch must be reconciled. This assures that all transactions have been entered.

Off-Line Data Entry Error Handling

Error handling controls include the procedures and methods used to ensure that transactions rejected during data entry are corrected and reentered in a timely manner. Many on-line, error-handling procedures and methods apply to the off-line environment as well. Some additional aspects concern the topics of detection and correction.

Detection. In an on-line data entry system, only one transaction is processed at a time. If an error is detected, the operator receives a message on the screen and the error can often be corrected immediately.

In an off-line system, a large number of transactions are validated in one processing cycle. Detection cannot be followed immediately by correction. When errors are detected in a batch system, the system must ensure the erroneous transactions are not processed further and the user is informed of the errors.

Correction. There are many reasons why transactions may fail validation checks. Clerical errors, data entry errors, or system errors are the most common reasons. The key is that some group is given clear responsibility to clear the error.

TRANSMISSION OF BATCHES

After the local site has completed entry of batches, they are then moved to another site for processing. When this occurs the Batch Log file is moved with the batches. At the receiving site the file level balancing, discussed above, is completed. Then, as the batches are processed, they are balanced back against the Batch Log file. If out of balances have occurred the batches may provide a closer level of detail to determine which transactions were lost by batch. Over time this more granular information can be of value in determining sources or circumstances where data is lost. Such identification of repeated patterns of loss may indicate systems issues that need to be addressed.

Inherent in this strategy will be a need to reinitiate the Batch Control logs and the assignment of batch numbers each day. The Batch Logs are typically initiated in end-of-day processing at the remote site. The use of batch numbers can be greatly simplified if the batch number is some combination of site, source, and then sequentially-assigned numbers.

CONTROL GROUPS

This discussion has addressed some techniques for addressing Integrity Controls in a netcentric environment. In addition to techniques and processes there is a need to consider people. Experience suggests that a curious thing happens with transaction failures between sites. People at the site where the failed transactions are created believe that they were OK when they left; and the people at the site where they fail believe that it is the sending site's problem. As a consequence, sometimes nothing gets done to address the underlying problem. There have been cases where the problem was so extreme that remote sites went for weeks with all transactions failing, but no one telling them of the problem.

The solution in this case are people in a Controls Group. This is essentially a group whose goal is to resolve any controls problem that may arise anywhere in the system. This group starts with an understanding that "there are no bad controls, just bad processes, systems, data, and luck." This may seem obvious, but it makes the point that this group must often look past an out-of-balance control to source causes and understand what has gone wrong at the site or system in the network. This is a group that can never say, "It's not my problem." It is also a group that must think very clearly when a control problem arises to determine what is the impact of a balance problem. In many cases it is no more that just the need to re-enter the transaction. Sometimes an out-of-balance problem may indicate off-setting multimillion dollar problems. It is up to the controls group to ensure that important problems do not become uncontrolled problems.

Of all the techniques and approaches discussed in this chapter, experience suggests that the Controls Group may be key to ensuring that the controls that are implemented are used to ensure the system maintains the integrity that it must have to meet user expectations.

Chapter 22

Network Infrastructure Options for Netcentric Implementation

Chapter 6, Communications Architectures, dealt with an architectural framework for networking in a netcentric environment. This chapter focuses on the specific physical networking technologies to be considered during implementation.

To be positioned for netcentric solutions, an organization's communications infrastructure must provide support for

- Client/Server computing
- Rich data types including multimedia
- User mobility
- Reach to the customer and to other business partners that is secure and extended

CLIENT/SERVER COMPUTING

Over the last several years, transaction and data management applications have continued to move off the mainframe to client/server architectures, becoming increasingly distributed and moving closer to the customer. These new architectures challenge the legacy network infrastructure in a number of ways, including the demand for more bandwidth and the need for multiple protocols to coexist.

Client/server computing requires faster networks (i.e., more bandwidth) for a number of reasons:

- There is much more dialog between clients and servers than among machines in traditional host-to-terminal architectures.

- The distributed processes and distributed data inherent within client/server computing can result in large messages and data sets passed over the network.
- Security checking between the client and server can slow transaction time and increase traffic.
- Resources and services (i.e., servers) are becoming increasingly more distributed across the network environment and in turn are creating an increase in the amount of network traffic required to locate and access those resources and services.
- Networks are becoming less centralized, less hierarchical, and more dynamic, which results in increased traffic to manage the routing of information not only to new networks but also around failed network links.
- Backup and recovery can cause large bursts of data to hit the network.

Most new client/server systems are developed to be run over a network using the TCP/IP protocol (the protocol that forms the common transport basis for the Internet). Many of today's legacy systems, on the other hand, were developed using IBM's host-based SNA protocol. These protocols are fundamentally different and a fair amount of work goes into getting them to cohabitate on the same network. These integration challenges are one of the fundamental reasons netcentric implementations are converging to more open, standards-based communications such as TCP/IP.

RICH DATA TYPES

Significant changes are occurring in applications as they evolve to support the knowledge workers — someone who interprets and applies information to create and provide value-adding solutions, and to make informed recommendations. The types of content delivered in applications for knowledge workers are broadening beyond data, text, and graphics to include audio, image, and video. In addition, interpretation applications, such as on-line analytical processing (OLAP), allow for visualization of data and information.

These changes present some interesting challenges to the network. Moving rich data types across the enterprise requires a tremendous amount of bandwidth — beyond the capacity of the typical local area networks (LANs) and wide area networks (WANs). For example, traditional text and voice connections usually require bandwidth from 20 to 70 Kbps, or a 28.8 modem up to ISDN, or a fractional T1 (e.g., 64 Kbits/sec). For static digital media, the peak communication rate is determined by the minimum acceptable delay for transmission of a page or segment of content. By contrast, a color photograph that is transmitted in 0.25 seconds requires a transmission rate equivalent to 22 Mbps, which is faster than most LANs can provide. It is generally accepted that 0.25 seconds is an effective instantaneous response rate for browsing. Even with full JPEG compression, a worldwide image compression standard, the color photograph would still require 4 Mbps. (JPEG stands for "Joint Photographic Experts Group," a group of experts sanctioned by the International Standards Organization.)

Multimedia, or document management applications, would quickly overload the bandwidth of a typical Token Ring or Ethernet LAN as the number of users grows. The limitations of the typical WAN for an organization are even greater.

Bandwidth is not the only limitation when dealing with rich data types. Most of today's computer networks are optimized for small-packet, asynchronous data communications. Real-time media, such as full-motion video and audio, require isochronous (i.e., time- and delay-sensitive) Transport Services. Real-time media are highly sensitive to variations in latency, while small variations are of no consequence to data traffic. Attempting to transmit real-time media over a network that is optimized for data traffic will result in unacceptable video and/or audio quality.

USER MOBILITY

Client/server and netcentric applications have the potential to greatly enhance the capabilities of the end user. Typically, the end users who have benefited under client/server computing were confined to the physical boundaries of the enterprise. In the netcentric environment, applications are moving outside the physical boundaries of the enterprise and into the hands of new classes of end users: the field sales or service representative, the road-warrior executive, the business partner, and the customer.

The trend now is to add mobility as a standard application design feature, that is, to make information available wherever and whenever a business user or customer requests it. Adding mobility presents a number of design challenges across all aspects of the systems architecture. From a communications perspective, the greatest challenges arise when an organization enters the domain of wireless data — a domain that enables real-time, untethered access to business applications and information.

The allure of wireless data networking can be great. The field service worker is enabled with real-time access to customer histories, in-house experts, and work-order management. The customer sales representative has real-time access to account information, credit histories, price lists, inventory status, and order entry. The truck driver can send and receive real-time shipment and route status, and the executive can send and receive e-mail and access groupware applications during the course of a day that includes time in the train, taxi, airplane, and client location.

Although the benefits of using wireless data can be high, there are significant network challenges to consider. Wireless networks are low capacity, low throughput, and intermittently available; this can cause great frustration among the users of wireless networks. While there are a number of wireless data service offerings from which to choose, the coverage of each service offering can be an issue as well as the integration available between service offerings. Many of the wireless mobile components are not standardized or prepackaged. Specialized messaging capabilities need to exist between mobile and stationary components.

EXTENDED REACH TO THE CUSTOMER AND BUSINESS PARTNERS

In the netcentric computing era, public access applications address the needs of the public, specifically consumers. Similarly, as business partners need to work more and more closely together and be linked electronically, more applications are being developed to allow for collaboration among business partners. Both public access and business partnering applications narrow the gap between an organization, its products or services, the various suppliers with which the organization works, and the consumer. Effective applications will give customers and business partners what they want, when they want it.

There are a number of ways to reach the end consumer. One approach is through the use of kiosk systems located in buildings accessible to the public or target user groups. Another method is to integrate with home devices, such as allowing the consumer to access the system through a touch-tone telephone or a modem-equipped PC. Most users today who are connected via a home PC use the public switched telephone network at speeds of 14.4 to 56.6 Kbps. This works well for small amounts of data, but performance slows to a crawl under the stress of more detailed images and graphics.

One access technology that is getting a lot of attention these days is the cable modem. The Gartner Group has forecast that, by the year 2002, 10% of U.S. households will access the Internet from home using cable modem technology; 65% will use an analog modem. Today, the cable network is, for the most part, a one-way network. The potential of a two-way interactive cable network is vast, although a number of technical and financial issues must still be overcome.

Netcentric computing also can extend an organization's network to support business-to-business applications, with which the enterprise establishes and maintains its links with other organizations, such as suppliers, distributors, alliance partners, and the government. These applications lead toward the true virtual organization, where enterprise boundaries are no longer rigid.

For netcentric applications that enable business-to-business transactions and collaboration, technologies will need to support large volumes of data and to be scaleable and highly secure. Connections will need to be fluid, and application/network interface standards will need to be less rigid and inflexible than the EDI standards of today.

COMMUNICATIONS TECHNOLOGY ENABLERS

To address the communications needs just discussed, many advancements are occurring in the following communication areas, which will help enterprises address the challenges of netcentric:

- LAN backbone options
- Public network offerings for private and virtual private WANs
- Connectivity to the customer and business partner — Internet and extranet
- Wireless support for the mobile user

The remainder of this chapter is devoted to a discussion of these four areas, which form the basis for the communications fabric of the future.

LAN BACKBONE ARCHITECTURES

One of the key building blocks of most enterprise networks is the LAN. This section examines three areas of advancement in LAN technology: high-speed access methods, switching architectures, and ATM (Asynchronous Transfer Mode) technology.

High-Speed Access Methods

Traditional LANs are shared media networks, which carry the traffic of multiple users over the same media. As a result, network access methods are required to regulate the usage of the shared media. Network access methods (i.e., Ethernet, Token-Ring, and FDDI) are therefore responsible for determining the key network characteristics, including bandwidth, latency, and throughput. The access methods with the largest installed base are Ethernet (10 Mbps) and Token-Ring (4 Mbps or 16 Mbps). Both of these standards are well documented, and products are available from a wide variety of vendors.

Recognizing the need for increased bandwidth, vendors have pushed to develop high-speed access methods (i.e., 100 Mbps and beyond). Exhibit 1 outlines the relative bandwidths from current and emerging LAN technologies.

The four most notable high-speed LAN technologies, both today and in the near future, are

- Fiber Distributed Data Interface (FDDI)
- Fast Ethernet
- Gigabit Ethernet
- ATM

Exhibit 1. Relative Bandwidth by LAN Technology

Bandwidth	Technology
2–8 Mbps	Shared Ethernet
3–4 Mbps	4 Mbps Token Ring
8–10 Mbps	Switched Ethernet
12–16 Mbps	16 Mbps Token Ring
20–80 Mbps	Shared Fast Ethernet
80–100 Mbps	FDDI
80–100 Mbps	Switched Fast Ethernet
100–140 Mbps	OC-3c ATM
200–800 Mbps	Shared Gigabit Ethernet
400–600 Mbps	OC-12c ATM
800–1000 Mbps	Switched Gigabit Ethernet
1600–2400 Mbps	OC-48c ATM

Irrespective of the particular technology, the goal of the networking vendors is simple: develop new, cost-effective options to allow organizations the capability to upgrade their networks.

FDDI. FDDI is the most mature of the high-speed access methods, with a wide variety of products currently available and commonly implemented. Although FDDI has several beneficial characteristics, it is primarily touted for its 100 Mbps bandwidth capacity. In addition to the substantial increase in bandwidth, other noted capabilities of FDDI include its deterministic access and — when implemented in a dual redundant ring configuration — its inherent fault tolerance.

Unlike Ethernet, FDDI is a deterministic access method. That is, like Token Ring, FDDI networks regulate the access of all users on the network, ensuring that no two users are simultaneously trying to transmit. Thus, FDDI networks are able to achieve higher degrees of efficiency than traditional Ethernet networks because they do not experience the collisions and thus the performance degradation found in shared Ethernet networks.

Additionally, FDDI has the ability to recover automatically from link failures when it is configured in a dual redundant ring. Referred to as a "self-healing ring," an FDDI network has the capability to bypass the failed link and still maintain the integrity of the ring. Because of this feature, FDDI is an attractive networking topology for environments requiring high degrees of fault tolerance and reliability.

FDDI continues to play a key role in many organization's LAN backbone environments and in specialized circumstances. However, it does not seem to be advancing at the pace of other technologies. Ethernet, for example, has seen a number of advances, from increasing bandwidth options to high-speed switching technologies.

Fast Ethernet. In response to the need for more network bandwidth, a substantial number of internetworking hardware vendors formed the Fast Ethernet Alliance. The purpose of this alliance was to develop a high-speed networking topology leveraging existing Ethernet technology. This goal was achieved by using portions of the Ethernet standards, and combining them with the physical signaling standards used by FDDI. In July 1995, the Institute of Electrical and Electronics Engineers (IEEE) approved the 100-Mbps standard developed by the alliance members.

A recently approved standard, IEEE 802.3u (commonly referred to as 100Base-T), creates a new shared media networking technology: 100 Mbps Ethernet. Essentially, 100Base-T is the same technology as 10Base-T operating at 10 times the speed. As a result, network managers find 100Base-T to be a relatively easy technology to understand and implement. Additionally, Fast Ethernet is supported on most existing cabling, and vendors have products with prices significantly lower that other alternatives such as FDDI or ATM.

Gigabit Ethernet. In 1997, the Gigabit Ethernet Alliance finalized another evolutionary Ethernet standard for 1000Base-T Ethernet. In 1998, the IEEE approved the Gigabit Ethernet standard as IEEE 802.3z.

Although this technology provides for substantially increased bandwidth, many of the limitations of current Ethernet technologies, such as collisions, still remain. Additionally, like 100Base-T, Gigabit Ethernet by itself still lacks any deterministic access method and proven priority queuing capabilities. As a result, Gigabit Ethernet alone is not suited to support large quantities of delay-sensitive data, such as voice or video. Due to its increased speed, Gigabit Ethernet has some distance limitations, cabling requirements, and repeater configurations which are more stringent than 10Base-T and 100Base-T. Gigabit Ethernet is designed to run primarily over fiber. The IEEE 802.3ab standard for Gigabit Ethernet over twisted pair copper cabling is targeted to be finalized in 1999.

From a positioning perspective, Fast Ethernet and Gigabit Ethernet are viewed primarily as workgroup and backbone technologies for use with servers and high-bandwidth users. In many cases, Ethernet switching will be viewed as a competing solution (see the next section for a discussion of Ethernet switching). However, many vendors are positioning Gigabit Ethernet as a complementary technology to Ethernet switching.

ATM. Although ATM is certainly a viable high-speed LAN access technology, it is difficult to justify the cost of the required upgrade necessary to deploy ATM down to the workstation. Instead, most organizations choose to go with the more widely accepted and less expensive Ethernet to the workstation. In some organizations which have a preference for IBM, Token

Exhibit 2. Ethernet Switching Technology

Layer	Function	Switching
4	Transport	Layer 4 Switching
3	Network	IP Switching, Tag Switching, Layer 3 Switching
2	Data Link	Frame Switching, Cell Switching, or Layer 2 Switching
1	Physical	Port Switching or Layer 1 Switching

Ring might be the LAN technology of choice. Additionally, ATM can emulate LAN technologies such as Ethernet and Token Ring. Keep in mind that this adds an additional layer of complexity to the LAN architecture. In general, ATM is commonly implemented in LANs under circumstances:

- Where high quality multimedia (voice, video, image) is required
- When a high level of reliability is important

In addition to the LAN environment, ATM is applicable in other physical network architectures such as wide area networks. ATM is discussed in more detail at the end of this section and within other sections in this chapter.

Switching Architectures

In the context of data networks, "switching" is usually meant to imply that dedicated hardware rather than software is forwarding data packets on to a destination. However, as switching technologies continue to evolve, this distinction is becoming blurred.

Migrating toward higher-speed access methods requires organizations to upgrade both the network hardware and the network interface cards located at the workstations. To allow enterprises to improve their LAN network performance without having to upgrade all of the network interface cards, vendors began to develop switching capabilities in network hardware. Linked with the OSI model as shown in Exhibit 2, switching technology exists at multiple levels.

Layer 1 Switching. Port level switches are devices that contain multiple network backplanes (i.e., network segments). Port level switches are essentially electronic patch panels. These switches allow the network administrator to patch cables to different segments on backplanes and hubs via electronics and software rather than physically repatching the cable.

Layer 2 Switching. With frame switching, shared media access methods (i.e., Ethernet and Token-ring) are still used. In a shared media environment, the total aggregate bandwidth of the network is shared among all of the connected network nodes. However, with frame switching, the total aggregate bandwidth is theoretically determined by the number of switch ports, although the backplane or switching fabric is rarely designed to that total.

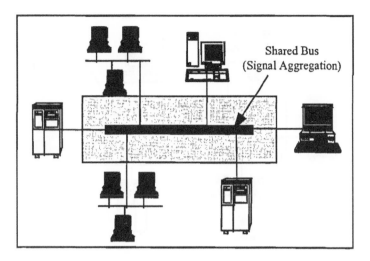

Exhibit 3. Shared Media LAN Segment.

Frame switching essentially changes the concept of shared media networks. With frame switching technology, users or LAN segments using traditional shared media access methods are connected into a switch matrix. In traditional shared media networks, these users and LAN segments would be connected to a backplane having the same bandwidth as each of the access ports, which would aggregate the signals (Exhibit 3).

This aggregation, or sharing of the media, limited the total bandwidth of the network and led to network congestion and network collisions. However, in a frame switch environment, the traffic is not combined. Rather, the switching matrix creates multiple simultaneous connections through the matrix, connecting only the appropriate switch ports together (Exhibit 4).

As a result of the switched nature of these networks, users are able to realize greater throughput and total aggregate bandwidth than would be possible using a traditional shared media LAN. For example, Ethernet LANs limit the total amount of traffic between network devices to no more than 10 Mbps. However, when multiple users are connected to an Ethernet switch, the total traffic between network ports can easily be 20 Mbps or more, depending on the traffic patterns on the network and the switch fabric capacity. Additionally, frame switching provides a fair amount of flexibility, allowing network managers to connect either individual users or groups of users (i.e., LAN segments) to dedicated switch ports.

Most vendors today are shipping frame switches for Ethernet (10/100/1000Base-T), Token-Ring, and FDDI. From a positioning perspective, frame switching enables network managers to quickly address performance

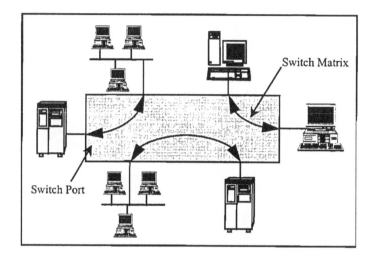

Exhibit 4. Switched Media LAN Segment.

issues in congested networks. Frame switches essentially replace the existing network hubs and use existing network interface cards and cabling. As
a result, the use of frame switching can represent an attractive alternative
for improving network efficiency.

Layer 3 Switching. Although frame switches enhance network performance at the data link layer, they do not directly address router performance issues. However, Layer 3 switches not only offload processing from
routers, but provide wire-speed routing for protocols like TCP/IP. There are
currently two distinct approaches to Layer 3 switching technology: packet-
by-packet technology and cut-through technology.

- *Packet-by-packet technology.* Packet-based Layer 3 switches work in a
  manner similar to traditional routers. These switches examine each
  individual packet before forwarding it on to its final destination; many
  switches support major routing protocols such as OSPF. The key performance gains over a traditional router are primarily due to the
  implementation of a hardware switching path instead of software-
  based switching. Basically, packet-by-packet technology in switches
  accelerates network performance through improved Layer 3 forwarding over traditional routers. As a result, packet-based Layer 3 switches
  have similar scalability attributes as a router-based network and can
  provide even greater throughput.
- *Cut-through technology.* Cut-through switches benefit from the advantages of both Layer 2 and Layer 3 switching and routing technologies.
  Cut-through switches examine the first few packets of a transmission

and, once a destination is determined, transmit all remaining data directly using Layer 2 (cut-through). These switches provide an increase in overall network speed by bypassing expensive router overhead; they also offer the same scalability attributes as bridged networks. Essentially, the increased performance comes from avoiding the examinations and rewrite of every packet being transmitted that would normally be performed by a traditional router.

Leading internetworking vendors have taken different approaches for Layer 3 switching solutions. These solutions are based either on packet-by-packet or cut-through technology. Cut through technology was initially conceived for ATM-based IP networks, while packet-by-packet began to emerge with high-speed Gigabit Ethernet switches. From a positioning perspective, Layer 3 switching is a key step in improving the performance and scalability of netcentric computing. However, there will be much standardization required before Layer 3 switching technology is available for large-scale networks.

Layer 4 Switching. Emerging Layer 4 switching can best be described as an application-aware internetworking technology. Layer 4 switching helps to enforce application-related policies and priorities on a network. For example, mission critical SAP traffic can be prioritized over standard Web browsing on the Internet. Layer 4 switching works by analyzing the transport-level information in a data packet (TCP socket information for Internet TCP/IP communications); based on the packet information and policies configured for the network, it makes a determination of the appropriate priority of the packet. Queuing technology is the primary mechanism behind Layer 4 switching.

One way to think of Layer 4 switching is the drive to gain back some of the control that was lost moving from host-based to client/server computing. There is still much to do in terms of getting Layer 4 switching technology to a level that can be implemented and managed in large-scale networks. When it achieves that level, Layer 4 switching will offer organizations the ability to more effectively manage scarce bandwidth, and better meet or exceed required application service levels.

ATM Technology

Many of the changes in LAN technology discussed thus far are evolutionary developments. By contrast, ATM is a revolutionary change. As discussed in the context of high speed access methods for LAN backbones, ATM is a technology with the promise of delivering video, voice, and data traffic over a single, high-speed, integrated network. The rush of both telecommunications providers and data networking companies to support ATM makes it poised to revolutionize industries, and to blur the distinction between local and wide area networking. ATM's unprecedented popularity stems from several things: its many technological advantages, its open definition, and its ability to solve problems that the industry has been dealing with for years.

By adopting existing standards for physical media transmission, ATM may finally make high-speed network links as common as LANs are today. By paying careful attention to the needs of all types of information (video, voice, and data), ATM designers have provided a single infrastructure capable of supporting multiple data types. ATM offers the promise of allowing enterprises to deploy video, voice, and data applications using a common technology both in the LAN as well as WAN.

However, ATM is still a relatively new technology — one that represents a significant departure from traditional networking. First, ATM is a connection-based technology. When devices wish to communicate over the network, virtual connections (i.e., paths between two nodes in an ATM network) are established. Given the nature of these virtual connections, ATM allows multiple users to share the network resources simultaneously. In addition, depending on the quality of service requested for a virtual link, ATM can guarantee end-to-end timing and a relatively low variation in network access time.

ATM is a new technology, yet traditional networks are still able to interoperate. ATM can host most older technologies, such as current network protocols, by emulating fixed capacity point-to-point links. In addition, ATM can reuse the physical links now in place, such as twisted pair cabling and fiber-optics in both the local and wide area environments.

ATM provides many advantages for networking. ATM transports information by setting up multiple virtual connections across a shared physical media. This allows multiple devices to use the network simultaneously but at a rate that is a subset of the total capacity of the link. An ATM network does not distinguish between local area and wide area networking because all network links are assumed to be relatively high capacity. Other characteristics unique to ATM are the ability to provide feedback to network devices about congestion and the ability to use physical connection rates from 155 Mbps and higher. All of these advantages allow ATM networks to reduce congestion and intelligently manage network traffic at high speeds. Additionally, through ATM Inverse Multiplexing (AIM), ATM is capable of running on speeds common in today's wide area networks such as T1/E1.

ATM is often touted as the solution to all networking problems, and numerous products continue to be rushed to market by the vendor community. Typically, these products can be classified into three distinct groups: workgroup solutions (i.e., small switches), premise solutions (i.e., large, local switches) and central office solutions (i.e., those used by carriers to provide public network services). From an enterprise networking perspective, the vendors developing premise solutions are the key players to watch.

LAN Summary

Whatever LAN technology an organization chooses to implement, each plays a key role in netcentric environments. From an the perspective of *expanding reach,* it is clear that multiple LAN technologies will need to be integrated. From the perspective of *rich content*, all technologies will need to increase their capabilities to support voice, video, image, and data traffic.

PUBLIC NETWORK OFFERINGS FOR WIDE AREA NETWORKS

In the past, many companies used dedicated or leased lines to provide data connectivity from their distributed locations back to corporate headquarters. These company-managed networks were typically constrained to a fixed bandwidth, and so were rather difficult to grow and evolve. On the positive side, however, a company had control over management of the network and could more easily establish and meet targeted service levels.

More companies are now relying on public network offerings to connect multiple locations. These network offerings provide more flexible bandwidth management, and move some of the network management burden from the purchaser of the service to the service provider. In fact, several key options are emerging that are coming closer to meeting the challenges of netcentric applications over the wide area. The service offerings discussed in this section are

- Frame Relay
- ATM
- Integrated Services Digital Network (ISDN)

Frame Relay

Frame relay is a packet switching technology that has been adopted especially for the needs of data communications. Rather than providing a user with a dedicated circuit (i.e., circuit switching), frame relay provides many users access to the same circuit, switching each user's individual packets of information over the same physical connection (i.e., packet switching). As a result, frame relay services provide much more efficient bandwidth usage than with circuit switching.

Most of the time, users have little or no data to send. However, when users do send information, they typically have a large number of packets which they send over a short period of time, which causes a burst in the network traffic. Because frame relay switches packets, not circuits, users may use anywhere from none of the available bandwidth to all of the available bandwidth. Thus, from a user's perspective, frame relay provides bandwidth on demand. As a result, frame relay services have become a very popular option for providing enterprisewide network connections.

Frame relay services provide network managers with more flexibility regarding bandwidth allocation. In frame relay networks, users subscribe to a committed information rate (CIR), such as 256 Kbps. This CIR represents the average loading of the particular link. If the amount of data that needs to be transmitted exceeds the CIR (i.e., 512 Kbps) during a particular interval, the network makes a best-effort attempt to deliver all the information while guaranteeing the delivery of at least the CIR. If for some reason the guarantee is not met, then the carrier typically extends a discount (contractually predefined) to the customer for the period.

Frame relay networks represent an evolution from X.25 networks. X.25 networks incorporated a significant amount of overhead relative to fixed packet sizes, extensive error correction, retransmission facilities, and fixed bandwidth links. Frame relay standards leverage the X.25 packet forwarding architectures while improving overall performance by eliminating some of the error correction and retransmission capabilities inherent in the network equipment.

Some X.25 components could be eliminated because today's physical networks are much more reliable than those in place when X.25 was initially developed. For example, most carrier networks are based today on more reliable fiber optics rather than copper wiring. With frame relay, error correction and retransmission is handled at the end nodes by higher-layer networking protocols, such as TCP/IP. Additionally, frame relay includes the ability to support varying packet sizes. This eliminates the inefficiencies associated with transmitting short bursty communications over the same network as larger file transfers.

From a market perspective, frame relay has demonstrated tremendous growth over the last several years. It has represented both a WAN option allowing companies to link distributed facilities, and a business-to-business option linking multiple companies in a common enterprise. Frame relay presents companies with a cost-effective LAN-to-LAN connectivity option, providing bandwidth availability in the range of 56 Kbps to 45 Mbps. Bandwidth in this range helps to address some of the wide area bandwidth issues of netcentric applications, although frame relay does not address the requirements of transmission delay-sensitive applications (e.g., multimedia). Frame relay has also proven to be an effective network option for supporting multiple protocols (i.e., the SNA and TCP/IP issue discussed earlier).

ATM

As a technology, ATM can be integrated into an enterprise internetwork in a number of ways. In the previous section on LAN architecture, much of the focus was on the integration of ATM into the end-user workstations and campus backbones. This section focuses on the development of ATM public service offerings by communications providers.

As mentioned previously, ATM holds the promise of unifying communications infrastructures to support all data types, including voice, video, and data. ATM is a connection-oriented service based on fixed sized cells (53 bytes). This use of fixed sized cells, and ATM's connection-oriented nature, allow it to provide predictable delays as well as quality-of-service features to support delay-sensitive information. In addition, ATM is extremely scaleable, supporting data speeds from DS-1 (1.544 Mbps) rates to in excess of OC-48 (2.4 Gbps) rates. However, end-user connectivity rates are still around OC-3 (155 Mbps).

The most prominent element of ATM service offerings is their quality of service capabilities. These features provide ATM service offerings the flexibility needed to support a wide range of applications. Specifically, ATM is capable of supporting constant bit rate (CBR), variable bit rate (VBR), available bit rate (ABR), and unspecified bit rate (UBR) traffic. CBR traffic is primarily associated with delay-sensitive material, such as voice and video. In these cases, ATM services guarantee applications a predictable delay for a prespecified data rate. VBR traffic is commonly associated with bursty, delay-sensitive traffic such as a compressed video stream that may need to send varying levels of content for each frame in the video. With ABR traffic, ATM guarantees a specific amount of throughput and then tries to provide as much additional bandwidth as possible without causing network congestion. Finally, ATM also provides UBR services, which allow users to use as much bandwidth as is currently available at any given time. However, with UBR services, users are not guaranteed any data rates and UBR traffic will always be discarded first if there is network congestion.

Although ATM encompasses many of the features provided by other service offerings, it is far more complex and expensive. Additionally, most organizations do not yet possess applications that require the sophisticated capabilities of ATM. Therefore, most organizations are still relying on frame relay services to support their data traffic and dedicated leased lines or ISDN to support their voice and video traffic. However, as ATM service offerings continue to become more pervasive, and as prices decline, ATM will become a very attractive service offering for many organizations.

ISDN

ISDN is a public network service offering, based on digital circuit switched technology, which provides the ability to integrate voice, video, and data. Due to the digital nature of the service, ISDN provides highly reliable transmissions. Additionally, ISDN is a scaleable service (up to 1.544 Mbps in the

U.S. and 2.048 Mbps in Europe) which is normally offered in either a basic rate interface (BRI) or primary rate interface (PRI) configuration. Commonly referred to as 2B+D, the Basic Rate Interface (BRI) provides 144 Kbps of throughput consisting of two bearer (B) data channels of 64 Kbps and one D control channel of 16Kbps. The Primary Rate Interface (PRI) is a DS-1 speed interface (1.544 Mbps in the U.S. or 2.048 Mbps in Europe) and is often referred to as 23B+D (30B+D in Europe).

ISDN services have been extremely popular in Europe and Australia. Recently, ISDN services in the Untied States have become more popular. Much of ISDN's recent success in the U.S. has been due to its ability to provide large amounts of bandwidth on demand as well as higher-speed Internet connectivity. Thus, ISDN has become an attractive service offering to provide dial-up, remote access. Additionally, ISDN capabilities have also been incorporated into networking equipment to provide dial-up, backup links to improve reliability. Finally, due to its switched nature, ISDN has also enjoyed significant success as a transport to support video conferencing.

CONNECTIVITY TO THE CUSTOMER AND BUSINESS PARTNER

In netcentric computing, particularly Internet-based solutions, public-access applications facilitate business-to-customer connectivity. Some of these applications may use kiosk-based delivery, but most companies today see access to the customers' homes as the final and most desirable frontier.

Some low-bandwidth examples of commerce to the home are already in existence. The most common example is home-based electronic commerce via the Internet. A typical setup would include a PC loaded with an Internet browser and a 28.8- or 56.6-Kbps modem. The home shopper connects to an Internet service provider via a standard dial-up line and accesses the desired Web site. There are definite constraints with this approach. Anyone who has accessed the Web on a regular basis knows the performance limitations even of a 56.6-Kbps modem.

Clearly, more bandwidth is needed to the home. Again, with the WWW as a benchmark, interactions with the user increasingly involve rich data types, which will make this problem worse under the current bandwidth constraints. The cable companies and the phone companies are racing to see who can deliver the most cost-effective solution — one that will support applications for which customers are willing to pay. The results, however, will probably not become apparent for some time.

The alternatives positioned by the phone companies are as follows. The phone companies began upgrading their network backbones to fiber in 1977. The trend was started to allow interexchange carriers to place huge volumes of calls on backbone trunks. Current commercial implementations of fiber trunks can carry 30,000 concurrent telephone conversations on a single strand of fiber.

The expanded capacity that fiber-optic cable provides over copper cable is undeniable. A problem for many of these communications companies, however, is the large amount of deployed copper cable; in many cases this needs to be amortized before it can be replaced with fiber. One source estimates that over 65 million tons of copper cable are deployed in the U.S. alone. Much of this copper is in the local loop to the home (or what is sometimes referred to as the "last mile") in the form of copper-based twisted-pair wiring.

The phone companies are attempting to provide broadband capabilities by making hardware and software enhancements to certain parts of their network but continuing to use the copper to the home. This allows them to ease into fiber technology and to spend less money in the near term — money that would not be offset by higher revenues. Under this approach, two alternatives being positioned are ISDN and Asymmetric Digital Subscriber Line (ADSL) technologies.

ISDN

ISDN was previously discussed in the section on public network offerings. The primary focus in that section was on enterprise and enterprise-to-enterprise communications. However, ISDN has made some inroads to the consumer marketplace as well. The service is typically available at a Basic Rate Interface, which supplies approximately 128 Kbps to users.

ISDN can be used to integrate voice, video, and data, which makes it ideal for delivery of netcentric applications to users. ISDN take-up in the marketplace has been slowed by lack of widespread availability, incompatible standards, high installation and monthly costs, and difficulty in installation. Most phone companies have not addressed the primary needs of the consumer marketplace, which include a reasonably priced service that is simple to install. In the meantime, other options are becoming available that just may hit the mark.

ADSL

Asymmetric Digital Subscriber Line (ADSL) is a technology that allows broadband services to be carried over existing copper twisted-pair infrastructure along with traditional telephone service. There are several flavors of DSL technology, but ADSL promises to deliver the most bandwidth, coming in somewhere around 9 Mbps downstream and 640 Kbps upstream.

ADSL was first introduced in the late 1980s as a mechanism for sending video signals over residential telephone copper wiring. ADSL may be implemented as an enhancement to current telephone company service offerings such as basic rate ISDN and POTS (Plain Old Telephone Service). Some cable companies may also have an interest in ADSL technology as a way of providing telephone services on twisted pair copper loop that they overlay on top of the coaxial cable in their networks. ADSL allows a greater degree of interactivity than current cable services and provides more functionality than traditional phone service.

ADSL may be viewed as an interim solution to an all-fiber network or as a component of a partial-fiber network. Projections for the completion of fully-fiber networks which promise switched digital video services range from 10 to 20 years into the future. The major factor affecting the take-up of ADSL is the cost of implementation, including the cost of ADSL modems that have to be placed on both ends of the twisted-pair wiring.

Cable Modems

The cable company alternative, one offered primarily in North America, is the cable modem. Many of the cable companies are in the process of upgrading their network to a hybrid solution involving fiber in the backbone and coax cable to the home (i.e., hybrid fiber/coax, or HFC). Many implementers of HFC networks will look into using cable modems to enable subscribers to tap into high-speed data transmissions.

Cable modems can be used to connect PCs to HFC networks, using an Ethernet card to connect the PC to the cable modem. This will allow the PCs access to interactive games, interactive shopping, the Internet, and other on-line services.

Cable modem technology will be used by cable companies and others as a way to offer services to compete with such technologies as ISDN. Cable modem standards are still evolving, and only a handful of pilot neighborhoods are underway as the technology matures. Therefore, early cable modem systems will be proprietary, and implementers will buy the modems from vendors and lease them to subscribers. However, in the next couple of years, look for standards to emerge and large cable companies and cable modem vendors to support those standards.

Cable modems offer speeds that are orders of magnitude higher than traditional telephone modems used for dial-up data access: 10 to 27 Mbps to the home and 1 to 10 Mbps from the home. The modems make use of the existing coaxial cable infrastructure to provide high-speed data access with a moderate level of interactivity. Implementers have been drawn to cable modem technology because it can be technically easy to implement as well as cost-effective, as compared with ADSL. In general, the coaxial cable used by cable companies has significantly better electrical properties for sending content at high bandwidths than twisted-pair cabling used by the telephone companies. Cable modems have also become popular, because of the increasing demand for faster information access. From the subscriber's perspective, cable modems are an attractive alternative to modems over twisted-pair wiring, ISDN, and ADSL because of low costs (no large up-front costs or usage costs), easy installation, and high speeds.

On the negative side, cable modem technology is subject to limitations on the amount of bandwidth to the home possible over coaxial cable. There are several interference issues that must be resolved to expand the bandwidth available for upstream data access. This is due in part to the fact that cable modems share bandwidth in both directions with other services such as HAM radios and television broadcasts.

WIRELESS SUPPORT FOR THE MOBILE USER

Mobile applications include the virtual desktop, one- and two-way messaging, long-distance file uploads, and ubiquitous e-mail and Internet. These applications are allowing workers — and, eventually, customers — connectivity to anyone, anywhere, at anytime. In recent years, wireless communication has experienced rapid advances in technology; these have made it a growing presence in the communications market. However, wireless technologies continue to be in a state of flux, and clear winners have yet to emerge. In fact, many observers have accepted the fact that there are multiple worldwide standards, and competing wireless technologies are expected to remain even in the distant future. This section addresses the following wireless technologies that will play a large role in empowering the mobile user:

- Circuit-switched cellular
- Personal communications services
- Cellular digital packet data
- Dedicated wireless data services
- Wireless LANs
- Satellite

Circuit-Switched Cellular (CSC)

CSC networks provide wireless connectivity to the public switched telephone network via a series of radio transceivers. The technology is circuit switched in that a user establishes a virtual connection with the destination at the beginning of the call and maintains the connection for the duration of the call. The technology is cellular because the transceivers provide coverage in adjacent circular regions, allowing users to roam between coverage areas and still maintain their connections.

A circuit-switched cellular data session is similar to a traditional landline modem session. However, several factors inherent to circuit-switched cellular require the use of a special cellular modem. Factors include increased signal distortion due to inherent noise of a wireless connection, and transmission interruptions due to channel switching and cell switching.

Current efforts in the cellular industry have, in part, focused on upgrading the existing analog cellular network to digital technologies. The major cellular carriers, however, have settled into three camps for the technology supporting their digital infrastructure. These include Code Division Multiple Access (CDMA), Time Division Multiple Access (TDMA), and Global System for Mobile communications GSM. Differences in implementations will continue to lead to equipment incompatibilities and limited roaming capabilities for users between different coverage areas. In addition, backward compatibility issues will require the use of dual-mode cellular phones.

The types of digital cellular methods include TDMA, CDMA, and GSM.

Time Division Multiple Access (TDMA). TDMA technology can route multiple calls simultaneously over a single channel. TDMA allocates time slots on a frequency, then assigns a user to each time slot. Through this technique, TDMA offers a capacity increase of three times the current analog cellular systems. Many successful field tests have been completed and dual mode (i.e., analog/digital) TDMA cellular phones have been released.

Code Division Multiple Access (CDMA). CDMA is a technique that uses spread-spectrum technology for digital transmissions. With CDMA, information is broadcast in encoded packets over a wide range of frequencies. Cellular phones using CDMA listen to the encoded transmissions and are able to interpret the codes and pick the properly addressed packets out of the air. By allowing the sharing of frequency by multiple encoded conversations, CDMA promises increased capacity of at least 10 times that of the current analog cellular systems.

Global System for Mobile Communications (GSM). GSM is the pan-European digital cellular standard based on the TDMA access method. The network offers many advanced digital features through its use of Signaling System Number 7 (SS7) and operates within the 900 MHz frequency band.

What does the future hold for Circuit-Switched Cellular? As cellular technology becomes more widespread and as costs decrease, the large rise in number of users that occurred during the late 1980s and early 1990s will continue. As more and more digital cellular is deployed in more areas and as data speeds and transmission reliability increase, the feasibility of circuit-switched cellular data as a mobile solution will increase. However, costs for circuit-switched networks will remain time based as opposed to the usage-based costs of other wireless data alternatives.

Personal Communications Services (PCS)

Personal Communication Services (PCS) are actually a combination of services and technologies with the intent of providing "anytime, anywhere" connectivity to information services. Although they initially supported voice communications only in limited areas, these networks will eventually support multiple information services on a widespread basis and will interoperate with a variety of other networks.

Central to PCS is the concept that communications address numbers (e.g., phone numbers and fax numbers) should be assigned directly to people rather than locations. This provides users with constant connectivity to required services regardless of their location. PCS networks will complement today's existing cellular networks by offering services that support higher call capacities and seamless roaming capabilities.

PCS networks rely heavily on microcell technology, a cellular concept that uses smaller coverage areas than conventional cellular. The smaller cell sizes of PCS offer two main advantages over existing cellular networks. The smaller cell size provides better in-building coverage because of closer proximity of mobile units to network access points, and smaller transmission range means mobile units require less power. This translates into smaller, lighter mobile units and longer battery life.

Smaller cell sizes require a larger number of base stations to be deployed to provide the same level of coverage as conventional cellular base stations. PCS rollout schedules have been impacted by limited location availability, local zoning restrictions, and public opposition to tower construction.

Although many of today's cellular networks use analog technology, PCS networks are envisioned to have an entirely digital infrastructure using one or more of the following digital communication techniques:

- Spread spectrum
- Code division multiple access (CDMA)
- Time division multiple access (TDMA)

These techniques help to reduce power requirements and to increase call volume capacity, as well as allowing the already-crowded radio spectrum to be shared by increasing numbers of wireless users.

Competitive pricing is helping PCS gain a stronger market presence in the wireless voice marketplace in the United States. Some PCS wireless data predictions are also quite optimistic over the next 3 to 5 years. For PCS wireless data to take off, a host of issues involving interoperability, roaming, and common air interfaces must be resolved.

In these early years of PCS, fragmentation and confusion in the wireless marketplace will continue as carriers jockey for position. Key differentiators during this period will be quality, equipment, ease of use, and the ability to meet consumer needs. Ultimately, all carriers will be providing high-quality, seamless wireless service through low-cost, small handsets. Distinctions between cellular and PCS will begin to fade. Consumers will sign up for a wireless service, not needing to distinguish between PCS, cellular, and others.

Cellular Digital Packet Data (CDPD)

CDPD is a method of moving data over an existing cellular communications network. The driving principle behind CDPD is that data traffic can be transmitted over the cellular network either through the empty spaces between voice calls or through a dedicated data channel. Standard cellular sites must be upgraded to accommodate CDPD and its high data transmission rate of 19,200 bps.

CDPD is based on the TCP/IP protocol and can integrate with TCP/IP-based applications. In addition, its TCP/IP origins make CDPD a "connectionless" protocol (as opposed to the connection-based nature of cellular voice). Rather than using a dedicated channel for transmission, each CDPD packet is self-contained and moves toward its destination independent of the movement of other packets. The movement of packets is controlled by intermediate nodes along the path. Costs for CDPD tend to be based on usage rather than on connection time. This way, a user can remain connected for extended periods of time and only pay for data transmitted and/or received.

A mobile user who wishes to send data using CDPD must subscribe to a cellular carrier that offers CDPD and has upgraded its cell sites for CDPD in the area. The CDPD upgrade hardware allows each site to

- Transmit CDPD packetized data over standard voice channels or dedicated data channels
- Monitor which voice channels are available for CDPD data
- Direct data to available voice channels
- Switch the channel if a voice call interrupts the CDPD transmission (this is called "channel hopping")
- Bill CDPD services per packet sent rather than the customary cellular billing per minute

Another component that must be used to send data via CDPD is a CDPD modem. In addition to supporting CDPD, some CDPD modems offer circuit-switched cellular data and basic phone line dial-in modem capabilities.

One major drawback to CDPD is the limited coverage available. In the United States, CDPD is scarce and spotty at best. Another issue with CDPD is that in areas of heavy voice traffic or high noise, a cell site must reserve a voice channel for dedicated data. In this case, all CDPD transmissions are directed to this dedicated channel, and voice channels are left untouched by data traffic. Without this data-dedicated channel, a cell site gives priority to voice transmissions over data packets. Consequently, CDPD cannot operate if all channels in a cell's capacity are being used for voice communication.

Another drawback to CDPD is its lack of store-and-forward functionality. In a network with store-and-forward service, messages addressed to an unconnected mobile unit are stored until the unit reconnects to the network, at which point the messages are received. In a CDPD network, messages sent while the mobile unit is disconnected cannot be received.

As a wireless data service, CDPD is positioned in direct competition with the dedicated wireless data providers, digital cellular data technologies and PCS. While CDPD is clearly growing today, it will most likely have a relatively short lifespan. CDPD was developed as a stop-gap solution, primarily to provide wireless Internet Protocol (IP) connectivity. However, an emerging data-oriented wireless technology on the horizon is Mobile-IP, which seems to be positioned to replace most of the CDPD infrastructure at least in the United States; it will be used in all new PCS systems as the de facto standard for data. CDPD's ability to succeed in the face of this competition lies in the willingness of multiple vendors and cellular carriers to endorse CDPD and commit to implementing it over their existing cellular networks.

Dedicated Wireless Data Services

Dedicated wireless data networks allow a user to communicate using public data services via packet-switched radio data bursts. These networks are connectionless and optimized strictly for transmitting data. Using a series of networked base stations, today's dedicated wireless networks provide data capabilities at speeds in the 9,600 to 28,800 bits per second range. These networks can be connected to an organization's wired network to provide access to internal information and data services. Like CDPD, these networks are connectionless, and billed based upon usage. In the future, the speeds and coverage of these networks will continue to grow as much as can be supported by the market for wireless data services.

Wireless LANs

Wireless LANs are emerging as options for near true "anytime, anywhere" computing in airports, hotels, universities, and offices. Wireless LAN technologies are providing flexible connectivity options with speeds continuing to approach those of conventional wired LANs. Most wireless LANs use spread-spectrum technology across frequencies that do not require any formal licenses (902–928 MHz or 2.4–2.5 GHz). Many of today's wireless LANs can also integrate with their wired counterparts to create a hybrid wired/wireless LAN solution.

Satellites

Different satellite systems are distinguished by the orbit or satellite constellation. Two widely used options include Geo-stationary Systems (GEOs) and Low-Earth Orbit System (LEOs). GEO satellites require only three or four satellites; however, they are complex, costly to build, and expensive to launch and maintain. This high expense is mostly due to the fact that GEO satellites have greater weight and must be put into higher orbit. LEO satellites are cheaper per satellite, but require many more integrated satellites to provide worldwide coverage. A number of new satellite options for wireless data will be appearing over the next 5 to 7 years. These options will provide an additional set of options for wireless data where true global coverage is a critical requirement.

CONCLUSION

Netcentric applications require a diverse assortment of powerful communications enablers. An organization's communications infrastructure, in addition to supporting client/server computing, must also support extended connectivity to customers and business partners, must deal with richer data types including multimedia, and must support the needs of a highly mobile user community. This chapter looked at four categories of communications enablers:

1. New developments in LAN backbone architectures help organizations meet their communication needs. High-speed access methods such as ATM, FDDI, Fast, and Gigabit Ethernet are providing increased bandwidth for users. New switching architectures, particularly Layer 3 (IP) switching and Layer 2 (frame) switching, now permit organizations to improve their LAN network performance without the need to upgrade all their network interface cards. ATM technology developments represent a potentially revolutionary change to traditional LAN networking.
2. In the area of public network offerings for WANs, new options are appearing: frame relay, ISDN, and ATM. They provide more flexible bandwidth management and move network management over to the service provider, rather than the service purchaser.

3. Connectivity to the customer is being accomplished in a number of ways. Telephone companies are using ISDN and ADSL to enhance parts of their network, while maintaining traditional copper connections to the home. Cable companies are offering cable modems to connect personal computers to HFC networks.
4. Mobile connectivity is supported through a number of wireless technologies: circuit-switched cellular, personal communication services, cellular digital packet data, dedicated wireless data services, wireless LANs, and satellite technology.

Chapter 23
Management of Distributed Operations

Distributed computing technologies and architectures, both client/server and netcentric, can provide a wealth of new capabilities and advantages for those enterprises that adopt them. Business processes are executed more quickly, integration with business partners is tighter, companies can sell their products directly to the consumer, and the ability of an individual to access the right information at the right time for the right use is greater. Today's information systems are increasingly mission critical. As such, the management of these systems requires careful consideration to provide the appropriate level of service to the organization at an affordable cost.

This chapter will introduce a framework that can be applied to structure and organize the complexities of operations in distributed environments. People, processes, and technologies must all be present for effective operations management. The framework in this chapter represents a view of the processes that are needed to manage this complex environment, but it does not describe in detail the tools and technologies that can be used to support these functions. The tools and technologies perspective, which supports the processes described in this chapter, is explored in detail in the Operations Architecture in Section II.

THE "MODE" FRAMEWORK

Management of a distributed environment is different and more complex than management of centralized computing technologies. As the power and flexibility of the system have changed and increased, so too has the effort required to manage the system.

MODE (Management of Distributed Environments) is a framework for managing the operations of both centralized and distributed systems. In its simplest form, MODE provides a mechanism for understanding what needs to be done and why management tasks need to be performed.

MODE was originally conceived to understand and organize the complexities of managing client/server environments. Since then, however, MODE has been extended and is recognized as an effective framework for managing host and netcentric environments as well. The technologies and tools are often different across these three generations of computing (host, client/server, and netcentric); however, the base functions required to manage them are mostly the same.

The MODE framework has been used to great advantage by a number of organizations during the implementation of both centralized and distributed systems. Often, the framework's greatest value is in forcing the deliberate consideration of all aspects of service and systems management early in the process, before problems arise. The MODE Framework can be used to

1. Help transform an IT organization's enterprise operations to be more effective and efficient and align with the business
2. Assist in preparing a client's IT operations area for the rollout of an organization's first significant or mission-critical distributed application or for an eCommerce application that is directly utilized by the customer
3. Assist application developers in designing the computing environments for operability, which enables the applications and the associated technology to be implemented with operations and maintenance activities in mind (as opposed to discovering this too late in the development process)

MODE: High-Level Diagram

Most frameworks for managing distributed environments address only portions of the overall management effort, not the entire management picture. The MODE framework represents one complete view of the centralized and distributed computing management picture. It was developed with the whole in mind, and is designed to be driven by the requirements of end users. Exhibit 1 is a high-level representation of the framework.

The framework focuses on four main areas:

• Service management
• Systems management
• Service planning
• Managing change

Service Management

Service management is the fundamental area within the framework. It involves forming relationships with users, developers/architects, and

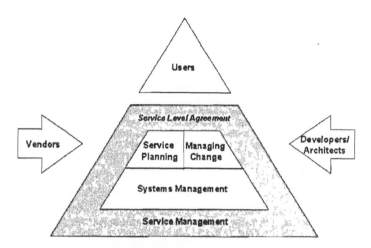

Exhibit 1. MODE Framework.

business partners, monitoring the services that are provided, and ensuring that the services are meeting standards as defined in service level agreements (SLAs).

The key to service management, and to the overall management of distributed systems, is the use of SLAs, which clearly articulate and document the level of service that users of the computing environment (internal users, business partners, consumers, etc.) expect to receive. SLAs should be used to drive out the requirements for the service organization and the operations architecture.

Service management is the direct interface to the users of the distributed system. Users are depicted at the top of the diagram; this represents the fact that a distributed system is managed to support the users of the system. Ultimately, the users of the system define the service offered to the customer base through SLAs. When the service management concept is implemented correctly, users have a single point of contact for all systems-related problems, suggestions, and planning. The service management function, in turn, navigates and coordinates the needed systems personnel and resources on behalf of the user.

Service management is also the direct interface to the developers/architects and business partners for the distributed system. Each of these groups has requirements for, and introduces changes to, the distributed environment. Service management controls the overall service to the users and handles the relationships with developers/architects and business partners.

In addition, many organizations rely heavily on strategic partners to provide key components of IT operations (e.g., desktop support and provisioning, WAN management, Help Desk, etc.). Establishing effective Operational Level Agreements (OLAs) with these partners and other internal groups that support the SLAs is another crucial component of Service Management. This has become even more important with the advent of netcentric computing and the many different components that are now involved in the business solution.

Systems Management

Systems management involves all functions required for the day-to-day operation of the systems (e.g., event monitoring, failure control, performance monitoring, and tape loading). Systems Management functions must maintain key interfaces with different management domains such as host, network, and servers. As such, Systems Management can provide detailed management views of the individual domains as well as a high-level, cross-domain management perspective.

Managing Change

Managing change includes all the functions necessary for effecting changes to the computing environment in a controlled and orderly way (e.g., software and data distribution and license management). As a result of the large number of interrelated hardware and software components in a distributed environment, assessing and controlling the side effects of system change are crucial to maintaining acceptable system availability.

Service Planning

Service planning includes all the functions related to tactical and strategic planning for effectively managing a computing environment. Service planning for a distributed environment requires an integrated approach. Effective planning for any one component such as network capacity cannot be done independently of an understanding of the whole system and how it will be managed. (For example, the chosen software distribution approach may impact the overall network bandwidth required.)

Systems management, service planning, and managing change are all represented at the same level in the framework to highlight the increased importance of service planning and managing change within a computing environment. Service planning is emphasized as a result of the degree of integrated planning necessary to meet service requirements. Managing change is emphasized to highlight the risks inherent in making systems changes and the importance of managing those changes.

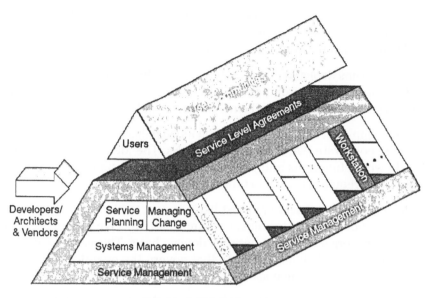

Exhibit 2. MODE Domains.

Effecting changes to the system, such as rolling out new releases of application software/data, is substantially more involved within a distributed environment. Previous centralized management frameworks did not give planning and managing change an equal representation to systems management, if they were represented at all.

Three-Dimensional View of MODE

Taking the two-dimensional framework and extending it to three dimensions introduces the concept of MODE domains, as represented in Exhibit 2.

MODE domains are represented as "slices"" of the framework. Sample domain slices include the following:

- Systemwide domain
- Host domain
- Network domain (LAN and WAN)
- Server domain
- Workstation domain
- Directory Domain

These domain slices indicate that each of the four areas is involved to some degree in managing a particular domain. For instance, some activities from service management, systems management, service planning, and managing change are performed on a systemwide basis. Within specific domains, however (e.g., network), the scope and level of activity associated with each of the components may change.

The domains depicted in the exhibit are merely samples of the domains that a distributed environment could have. Each organization needs to carefully review its distributed environment to determine its domains.

For example, a company could define its domains to be UNIX, Windows, intranet, corporate WANs, and remote LANs. The idea of domains helps decide which functions and activities — and, potentially, software and tools — are required to support their unique environment.

However, though users are most likely supported by the management capabilities of multiple domains, users must still receive support service from a single organization — not on a domain basis. This can be enforced through the establishment of SLAs that govern the overall relationship between users and the managers of the system.

As with the two-dimensional framework, developers/architects and business partners have access to the framework through service management only.

As can be seen from the diagram, while the domain being managed may vary, the shape of the framework remains consistent. This indicates that MODE functions remain consistent; they just apply to different technologies and environments. In this respect the MODE framework will continue to apply as future technology domains emerge.

MODE Areas and Their Functions

Each of the four MODE areas is further divided into multiple functions. A function is a set of related activities that needs to be performed. This section briefly introduces functions and then discusses them in greater detail.

It is important to note the multicompetency nature of MODE functions. Each function depicts more than simply technology — it includes the process and organizational aspects as well. The combination of the technology, process, and organizational components enable each of the MODE functions to be properly and successfully executed. In addition, functions do not translate directly into how a management organization should be structured. One individual or group within an organization may perform multiple functions. Similarly, the activities to perform a single function may be spread throughout the organization. Once again, the framework presents what needs to be accomplished without addressing who will perform the tasks or how they will be performed.

Each of the MODE functions, categorized by the four service areas, are described briefly below:

Service Management. Functions within service management are

- *SLA management.* Involves the creation, managing, reporting, and discussion of SLAs with users.
- *OLA management.* Involves the creation, managing, reporting, and discussion of operational-level agreements with internal groups, domain suppliers, and/or business partners.
- *Help Desk.* Provides end users with a single point of contact and controls the resolution of incidents and problems within the computing environment. In the netcentric computing environment, the help desk may support internal or external system users.
- *Quality management.* Ensures quality in the management of the computing environment through training, as well as through the design and execution of quality improvement plans.
- *Legal issues management.* Plans for and responds to legal events and scenarios involving distributed systems (e.g., security risks of the Internet).
- *Administration.* Handles the financial accounting and legal aspects of managing a computing environment.

Systems Management. The following are functions within systems management:

- *Production control.* Ensures that production activities are performed and controlled as required and as intended.
- *Monitoring.* Verifies that the system is continually functioning in accordance with whatever service levels are defined.
- *Failure control.* Involves the detection and correction of faults within the system, whether they are minor (a workstation is down) or major (a disaster has occurred).
- *Communications address management.* Involves the distribution and monitoring of communication addresses in a computing domain.
- *Directory management.* Involves the population and maintenance of directories that describe the contents and configuration of a distributed system.
- *Security management.* Ensures that the system is accessed only by authorized users, and that those users are restricted to authorized resources.

Service Planning. The following are functions within service planning:

- *Service management planning.* Defines the financial and training plans for the organization.
- *Systems management planning.* Determines the strategies for day-to-day operation of the system.

- *Managing change planning.* Develops the plans for releasing new sites, services, or updates to existing service.
- *MODE strategic planning.* Formulates the long-term strategy for managing the distributed environment, including people, tools, and processes. It also ensures that the management strategy is in line with the enterprise strategy.

Managing Change. Following are the functions within managing change:

- *Controlling.* Monitors change to make sure that change is delivered on time according to established plans, making adjustments to the plan when unforeseen issues or events arise (e.g., rollout management, change control, content management, and asset management).
- *Testing.* Ensures that changes to the computing environment in support of new applications and user requirements achieve the desired result and do not produce unwanted side effects.
- *Implementing.* Executes change within the distributed environment with tested components and techniques according to the appropriate plan(s). Implementing includes such things as initial installation, software and data distribution, and license management.

Key Functions

The MODE framework presents an ideal way to view what is required to manage distributed environments. In reality, because of constraints or the lack of requirements for the capability, subsets of this ideal framework are typically implemented. It is up to each organization to determine what the requirements are and how they can be achieved.

It is important to understand, however, that each of the functions should be carefully considered, and a conscious decision should be made as to how each function will be addressed. Functions can be implemented with varying degrees of sophistication and/or robustness, and these degrees are driven by factors specific to the organization such as budgets available, size of company, etc. Despite this, a conscious consideration of each function ensures that functions are scoped out of the work rather than simply forgotten. It also ensures that issues can be raised to both management and users about the impact of not including particular functions.

SERVICE MANAGEMENT

Focusing on the End User

The introduction of client/server and netcentric technologies further intensifies the demand that information systems (IS) organizations adopt a more service-oriented approach. As client/server-based applications are given to users higher in the organization, and for increasingly mission-critical purposes, meeting the needs of these users becomes vital to the organization.

More recently, netcentric computing has extended the computing capabilities of companies to the general public and to business partners. Although it is impossible to understand the specific needs of every user in a netcentric environment, the appropriate service levels must be established, because these users can be direct customers of an organization. As such, operations must maintain its focus on service and the end user in netcentric environments.

The discussion that follows describes in more detail the Service Management functions of the MODE framework. The key to the approach is the use of the SLA, which clearly articulates and documents the expectations of service receivers and providers.

SLA Management

A service-level agreement is an agreement between the users of the system and those managing it, which defines the level of service the users expect to receive. SLAs typically address such things as required response time, hours when the system is to be available, and the reliability of the system in terms of unscheduled service outages. They also provide a mechanism through which service managers and users can regularly communicate about the services delivered.

Other topics to be covered in the SLA include the following:

- Guidelines/assumptions on which the service level is based
- Chargeback costs, if necessary
- Descriptions of how service levels will be measured and reported on
- Definitions of roles and responsibilities for service provision and the management of service delivery

In a distributed environment, users of the system should only see the services being provided. They should not have to understand *how* service is provided to them because distributed environments are frequently built on a wide variety of complex components. SLAs make this distinction possible, providing the glue between the service seen by the user and the way in which the service is provided.

Conceptually, SLAs are not new. They have been used for a variety of contracting purposes, including the outsourcing of an entire business function to a third party (e.g., payroll), the outsourcing of a data center's operations, or the provision of internal IS support services for a particular business application (e.g., order processing).

The advent of distributed computing, however, increased the importance of using SLAs and affected the content of the agreement itself. In the client/server or distributed processing environment, many designs and configuration alternatives are available that affect a given system's response time, availability, development cost, and ongoing operational costs. An SLA clarifies the business objectives and constraints for an application system and forms the basis for both application design and system configuration choices.

In netcentric environments, additional challenges are experienced in the creation of effective SLAs. In an Internet solution, users are anonymous, thus making it impossible to truly define service level expectations directly with each user. Also, netcentric solutions often span components that are not under the control of the service provider (i.e., the Internet), thus introducing a degree of risk into any service level commitment. Finally, load prediction in netcentric architectures is less reliable; the population of users is global and, therefore, unaffected by typical 8x5 business hours usage patterns.

Ideally, SLAs are defined or enhanced during the functional requirements phase of any systems development activity. The architects and systems developers should have a good understanding of the service levels required by the user before designing and building the system. It is far easier to build the system to reflect service considerations vs. retrofitting service on top of a completed system.

In addition, the appropriate personnel should receive requirements in this phase to ensure that the proposed requirements are, in fact, manageable and affordable. Without such review, it can be quite easy to build unmanageable or excessively costly systems.

SLAs are difficult to define in a distributed environment, however, because of the complexities of the technologies and infrastructures. In a GUI environment, no longer can service be simply defined by average screen exchange response time. Instead, service may need to be defined around more granular measures, such as what the response time should be for the "commit order" button, or they may need to be alternatively defined for higher-level activities, such as the total system time it takes to complete a particular business event (e.g., the system processing/waiting time necessary to complete an entire order instead of the time to move from one screen to the next).

SLAs are also difficult to maintain in a distributed environment because the assumptions on which an SLA is based may change frequently. For example, if an SLA is based on a particular architecture that subsequently gets changed in some manner (e.g., software or hardware is updated), the SLA may need to change as well. Such changes require close monitoring and consideration to keep SLAs up-to-date and the overall SLA process working effectively.

Despite these many challenges, an organization must have an accurate way of measuring the service levels achieved. SLAs must not be defined without careful consideration given to how service is to be measured, recorded, and reported. The accurate measurement of an SLA (e.g., the time to create a new customer order) may require "hooks" into an application for isolating "system" time from "user think" time. It is important that this be discussed up front with the user communities to ensure that the information provided is sufficient enough for both sides to agree on the relative quality of service received. It is also important to maintain historical records of service to demonstrate to the users how service has improved (or degraded) over time. In cases where detailed service level measurement is impeded (e.g., the Internet) it is important that the zones of unpredictability be clearly defined and agreed upon with users.

Because of its importance and central role in the management of a distributed client/server environment, the Appendix of this chapter provides a sample SLA.

OLA Management

An OLA is an agreement between those responsible for the management of the system and the service providers (either internal or external) who are actually managing the system component(s) or domain(s).

OLAs are closely related to SLAs in the following way. An SLA cannot be formally set with users until it is clear that the required service levels can be met by one or a combination of service providers through one or more OLAs. To create a customer order, for instance, a user may need to access a database three times, use the WAN twice, and perform some processing on a centralized host. If an SLA is to be based on the time it takes to accomplish those activities, OLAs must be defined (or at least considered) for the level of service delivered from those managing the database, the network, and the host.

As Exhibit 3 illustrates, an SLA can be thought of as the sum of its underlying OLAs. For example, if the SLA dictates an end-to-end user response time of two seconds, the related OLAs will be used to allocate the overall two-second response time across the needed client, network, and server platforms.

Service providers cannot be viewed in isolation. They must work together to achieve their target goals. If the target goals are not achieved, however, the presence of formal agreements with service providers can be

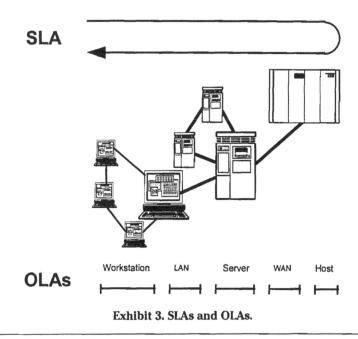

Exhibit 3. SLAs and OLAs.

an effective means of managing a provider's (either an internal provider or vendor) response to a poor service level.

As with SLAs, OLAs for a netcentric environment must consider the unpredictable nature of the Internet. In a client/server environment, the performance of all components in a solution could be reported on. However, a netcentric environment may not allow that luxury. As a result, organizations must acknowledge the areas they cannot control and implement strategies to meet needs in those areas. Examples of this may include strong OLAs with an Internet Service Provider (ISP) because they are the "gatekeeper" for an organization's Internet presence.

Often the greatest value of OLAs is their usefulness in cutting through the destructive finger pointing that can occur when an organization experiences service failure. (For example, long response times can lead to network personnel blaming the host or database personnel and vice versa.)

As with SLAs, OLAs must be redefined as the assumptions on which they have been based change. Because many third-party vendors have OLAs, it is important that the parameters of the OLAs be monitored to prevent vendors from pointing to changed parameters and declaring their contracts null.

The measurement of OLAs is as important as the measurement of SLAs. An OLA should not be agreed on until the organization clearly defines how it will be measured, recorded, and reported on. Historical metrics are also important with OLAs to provide the organization with some sense as to how well a particular service provider performs over time.

It is also important to establish the links between OLA terms and the conditions, terms, and penalties of contracts between an organization and its service providers. If there are discrepancies in the terms of these two documents, ambiguity may result and a course of action for events may be uncertain.

Help Desk

A Help Desk provides a single point of contact for users within the organization when trouble arises. The Help Desk sets the users' expectations for incident resolution and assists in managing those expectations during the resolution process. The Help Desk may also act as a first level of support for the organization. Users can get answers to simple questions immediately, resulting in a more effective use of high-level and specialized technical support resources. Today, a Help Desk may also be a point of contact for an organization's Internet customers, thus affecting public impressions of the organization as never before.

In playing these different roles, the Help Desk should be viewed as a problem manager having the authority to contact and prioritize IS and operations personnel and the ability to direct the users' work toward correcting the problem. This approach may raise questions about who has the authority for the direction of personnel. The issue must be resolved in favor of what best supports the business user in need of assistance as well as the entire organization.

The Help Desk may also be responsible for reducing the number of repetitive incidents within the environment by bringing to closure the process of determining, diagnosing, and correcting the underlying problem(s) causing the incident. Few things decrease user confidence and satisfaction as much as repetitive calls to the help desk to resolve the same incident. Although some problems may require significant rework and effort to fix (and hence longer time scales), notifying users of pending fixes and the provision of workarounds demonstrates an effort to assist the user and provide quality service. An effective and well-run Help Desk operation can go a long way toward redeeming an otherwise troubled application.

To help users in the ways outlined, a different level of expertise is required than what centralized systems previously needed. Typically, technical support personnel in a distributed environment require far broader and deeper technical knowledge. The interdependencies between the system software, applications, and hardware mean that technical support personnel must have a broader scope of knowledge.

In addition to core business applications, client/server environments typically provide the users with a broad set of office automation and data analysis tools ranging from word processors and spreadsheets to PC databases and ad hoc query tools. A decision must be made as to whether the Help Desk will provide assistance to users of these general tools as well. The depth to which an individual's knowledge extends varies, but individuals need to understand how they can work together to solve incidents that require varied technical expertise.

In addition to technical expertise, as Help Desks become a first point of contact for customers and/or business partners they will need to become more closely integrated with business processes of an organization. The Help Desk role is evolving even more as a result of netcentric computing and eCommerce. As Help Desk personnel work directly with the customer in these cases, the Help Desk function is in some cases integrating with the Call Center as a customer point of contact. This organizational relationship can help eliminate some barriers to the process and knowledge integration required for netcentric environments.

Help Desk tools have matured recently to more effectively meet the workflow-based nature of Help Desk activities. Most packaged Help Desk tools allow for customized interface and workflow definition, access via Web browsers, and event notification via multiple media types such as phone, pagers, email, and APIs to automate the event handling interface with systems management tools. In addition, most Help Desk tools accommodate integration with SLAs, thus proactively ensuring that user requests are addressed with the appropriate priority.

Quality Management

It is often easy to lose sight of how well an organization is or is not doing in managing its distributed environment. A good way to monitor this is to compare its success to the success of other similar organizations. This comparison helps an organization define where it stands within the industry and, potentially, how it can improve service quality.

Training is critical in ensuring the quality of service delivery. Well-trained support personnel are able to keep systems up and running more effectively, while providing higher-quality service to the users of the system. Users trained in how they can best utilize the services provided to them also improve the quality and perception of service delivered.

Administration

Billing and accounting may be required if chargeback schemes are put in place for users to pay for service usage. To accurately assess costs to users, charges should be allocated and assigned based on predetermined measures. This requires the careful measurement and accurate detailing of services used.

Although cost recovery applications are widely available in a host-based environment, systems that capture necessary statistics from many distributed platforms are either unavailable or rudimentary. Furthermore, tools to initially capture these statistics may be unavailable on many platforms, therefore requiring custom development.

Billing and accounting must also tie into the OLAs or any other arrangements with service providers. Such arrangements can be quite difficult to accomplish, because many situations require the reconciliation of bills sent to the organization by service providers against the operational levels actually measured. An organization must give careful consideration to how and when to reconcile these measurements as it defines the OLAs or other arrangements.

Administration also encompasses the legal aspect of managing a distributed environment through contract management. As SLAs and OLAs change, the formal contracts defining these agreements must also change. Contracts must be kept up-to-date at all times, preventing loopholes under which service users or service providers can make unwarranted claims.

SERVICE PLANNING

Service Management Planning

The two primary functions within service management planning are service costing and pricing and training planning. Each of these is directly related to how well a service can be delivered in the distributed environment. Each has direct impact on the quality of service delivered.

Service Costing and Pricing. Costs for service provision can be attributed to many things within the distributed environment including people, equipment, physical facilities, and development efforts.It is essential, first, to understand what the costs are so that strategies for managing those costs can be developed, implemented, and monitored. Users need to understand the cost implications of the service levels they request, and all costs should be tied back in some way to an SLA with the user community. If a cost cannot be tied back to an SLA, the organization must determine why it is incurring the cost and whether or not there is justification for the cost.

The cost to manage a system must be considered as the system is being developed. Design decisions can directly affect how the system will be managed and the relative costs for managing it. Helping users to understand what service levels will cost the organization helps manage user expectations throughout the systems development process.

Pricing is another way to manage user expectations. Pricing calculates the costs associated with providing a particular service and determines whether users should be charged for use of that service. Performing pricing activities helps an organization understand where the service costs truly lie and with whom. If a chargeback strategy is put into effect, users quickly understand the cost of the services requested and may be more reasonable in their service expectations.

Pricing in a distributed environment has proved difficult. In the host-based environment, simple chargeback schemes divided all system costs by the number of transactions and disk array storage device (DASD) space consumed. The distributed environment does not easily track and account for system usage. Because of the difficulty in accounting for system usage, many times the majority of systems charges are levied on a per-seat-per-month basis.

Training Planning. Training planning also affects how well service will be delivered within the distributed environment. The skill sets required by support personnel change with the introduction of distributed technologies. Support personnel are required to have greater breadth of knowledge. No longer can a single individual easily understand the network or the applications. The intertwined nature of a distributed environment forces individuals to understand, at least at a high level, how the system fits together.

In addition to having a wider variety of skills, support personnel need to have some specialized skills. As no single individual can fully understand the detail behind the entire system, teams of specialized support personnel will be required to work together to a greater extent in these environments. This group interaction may require new skill sets not frequently found in traditional support organizations.

Some training may be required for users who assist in the management of the distributed system. This is because local expertise may be required to help rectify faults as well as assist in day-to-day maintenance of the system (e.g., backing up a server to tape).

To determine a training plan, the organization must assess existing skills and define a forward-thinking training direction. The training plan is likely to emphasize newer technologies and different methods of training with the underlying goal of providing the appropriate level of service as required by the SLAs.

Systems Management Planning

To provide consistent day-to-day operational levels, systems management planning must be performed. The operational levels provided by the system should always be tied back to OLAs (and, ultimately, to SLAs) with the user communities. SLAs should be the driving force for how day-to-day operations are managed.

Several key areas are involved in systems management planning. Among the most important are

- Security planning
- Capacity modeling and planning
- Operations Architecture planning

Security Planning. With client/server and netcentric applications, security may no longer be handled through a single, centralized security application. Multiple levels of security access mechanisms can be used to protect applications, data, and networks. Whatever security approach is used must be understandable and manageable by those tasked with security administration and auditing.

Capacity Modeling and Planning. Capacity modeling and planning must coordinate the requirements across the system (networks, servers, workstations, central processing units). Once again, capacity is driven by the need to meet SLAs with the user communities and as part of the planning and modeling process.

Capacity planning in the client/server environment is made more difficult by the variety of system configurations. Unlike a host-based environment, no two client/server shops are the same. The variety of configurations has limited the availability of capacity planning tools and guidelines that can yield specific recommendations.

In addition, capacity planning in netcentric environments is made more difficult by the unpredictable nature of the Internet. Not only can capacity needs vary due to the global nature of the Internet, they may also vary significantly based on changes in content within the netcentric presence. It is important to note that netcentric capacity fluctuations affect server capacity as much as network bandwidth needs. Organizations may choose to identify contingency plans to accommodate unexpected demands on all affected components.

Most tools concentrate on modeling capacity for a particular component vs. the system as a whole. In addition, baseline metrics for these systems are difficult to obtain as historic metrics are not generally available within an organization for client/server systems.

Operations Architecture Planning. Operations Architecture planning refers to the process of identifying the tools that will manage the distributed environment. Strategic planning questions such as best-of-breed point solutions vs. Enterprise Management Frameworks will be discussed as part of this function. Operations Architecture planning also must identify the integration platform for management applications, thus providing the "single view" into the management of an organization's distributed environment. More detail on the Operations Architecture is provided in Section II of this book.

MANAGING CHANGE

One of the greatest differences between centralized and decentralized computing environments is the impact of change. Change in the distributed environment happens much more frequently and affects a greater number of devices and users, both internal and external. Changes must be adequately planned and controlled in a distributed environment to avoid creating faults and adversely impacting system availability.

Rollout Planning

Rollout planning handles the greatest period of change in distributed system's management: system rollout and installation. During rollout, every site and every user may be affected by the changes taking place. Rolling out new systems can be particularly challenging when both old and new architecture domains must exist concurrently until the rollout has been completed. The process can be complicated further if external users and business partners must be included in the plan.

Rollout planning includes the determination of everything from the high-level rollout schedule to the rollout activities that need to take place at each and every site. Successful rollout is likely to involve multiple groups within the organization as well as vendors external to the organization. Schedules and activities must be coordinated and agreed on by all the appropriate parties. Interdependencies within the schedule must be identified prior to rollout to highlight the importance of the schedule and the effort required from each group involved.

Release Planning

Release planning coordinates the release of updates (e.g., software, data, and procedures) to the distributed sites. An application, for instance, can no longer be delivered on successful completion of its system test independently but must be tested in the target environment.

Releasing a new application invariably introduces change into the environment, and client/server and netcentric environments are notorious for adverse side effects of even seemingly insignificant changes. Releases must therefore be planned carefully to ensure that a change does not negatively affect any other component of the system.

MODE Planning

It is important for an organization to have a high-level planning view of its operations organization. A MODE planning function can be used as a periodic assessment of an organization's effectiveness at providing operations services. SLAs can be validated, organizational structure may be assessed, and overall operations architecture strategy can be aligned with requirements. The role of MODE planning is to ensure that the overall service and systems management functions are up to the challenge of supporting future distributed applications.

SYSTEMS MANAGEMENT

Systems management involves all of the activities and procedures required to keep a distributed system up and running on a day-to-day basis. These tasks involve constantly monitoring and reacting to problems with the components of the distributed environment.

As netcentric computing has emerged, the initial hype suggested that the technology would significantly simplify operations. Experience is suggesting, however, that netcentric only adds an additional level of complexity through additional processes, tools, and support services, thus creating an environment even more difficult and expensive to manage. As complexity and costs of operations architectures continue to increase, there continues to be a strong need for a structured and disciplined approach to its processes, tools, and services.

When considering setting up a systems management capability to control this complex environment, it is vitally important that the effort start with, and be driven by, the definition of SLAs. These agreements represent specific commitments to the user community with regard to overall systems performance, reliability, and availability. These commitments form the primary requirements and justification for expenses associated with creating a systems management capability.

This section provides a sampling of the types of issues, decisions, and complexity drivers that make systems management functions so challenging in a distributed environment.

Geographic Distribution Impact

Pushing systems software, applications, and data out to client workstations and away from a central control point presents many challenges. These challenges are further compounded when multiple locations, cities, or even countries are added to the management puzzle.

Just as geographic distribution in client/server introduced complexities to operations processes, users in netcentric computing can be widely dispersed geographically. Rather than supporting entire distributed sites, though, netcentric operations groups may need to provide support on a single-user location basis. Complexity of operations due to this distribution is therefore increased.

Geographic distribution of servers can also introduce operations challenges. Although centralized location of servers may be desirable from a manageability standpoint, it may drive up WAN communications costs as all users at remote locations rely on WAN communication to access information. Performance shortfalls may also be experienced as WAN links tend to be slower and less reliable than local office LAN connections. Thus, another key decision for the IS organization is to determine optimal configurations of remote locations, balancing autonomy and capability with operational simplicity and a reliance on central control.

The most centralized approach would be to place only diskless or dataless workstations at remote locations. This minimizes the operational complexity associated with remote locations by reducing or eliminating the need for a software and data distribution architecture. However, the high WAN communications costs and/or the associated performance degradation may limit the attractiveness of this option. Many organizations, however, do use this model for supporting locations with only a few users where the costs of placing and administering server machines on site are not warranted.

Although placing servers at remote locations has clear benefits, these remote servers introduce a host of operational issues. For example, will a local support staff be needed to maintain these servers and associated LAN configurations, or can they be managed effectively from a central site? This is a key decision that has a substantial impact on the complexity of the operations architecture required.

Another complexity factor of remotely located servers is the tendency in netcentric for there to be multiple tiers of business logic on various servers. As such, operational troubleshooting may be more difficult as diagnosis must take place across multiple locations.

Multivendor Impact

In the traditional mainframe environment, most of the components — including hardware, systems software, and networking — were supplied by a limited number of vendors. For example, in the IBM mainframe environment, the hardware, operating system, on-line monitor, database management system (DBMS), even the networking hardware and software, were typically sourced from one vendor. In addition, if an organization used software from another vendor, all vendors tied closely to IBM standards, thus ensuring interoperability. By using a standardized environment from one vendor, it was relatively easy for the vendor to supply well-integrated management capabilities because they also supplied most, if not all, of the other system components.

In the client/server and netcentric worlds, no single dominant vendor supplies market-leading solutions for all the pieces of a solution. The market is much more fragmented: vendor A is the leader in workstations, vendor B in workstation operating systems, vendor C in servers, vendor D in database management software, and so on. Therefore, most organizations adopting this technology find themselves thrust into an unfamiliar, multivendor environment. They may buy workstations from one or more vendors and servers from yet another. Many cases today require the integration of technologies and products from 30 or more vendors.

It is usually possible, because of the many actual and de facto standards throughout the industry, to "plug and play" these multivendor solutions together. However, the operations architecture or systems management side of things may be the missing puzzle piece. Because of the vast numbers of combinations of different vendor products, it is difficult for vendors of systems management solutions to account for, and effectively support, more than a few vendor combinations. Products and standards are only recently coming on the market that attempt to simplify this multivendor problem.

Standards are ultimately the answer to the multivendor systems management problem, much as they have been the facilitating factor in enabling multivendor execution architectures. However, the evolution of standards is a slow process. In the interim, support organizations face the difficult challenge of assembling various vendor systems management components into an overall integrated operations architecture. To assist in that process, operations architectures such as the one described in this book can be used.

Complexity and the Role of the Workstation

Because the degree of centralization vs. decentralization greatly affects the operational complexity of the system, a key decision for the IS organization is to determine what the role of the client workstation will take. Experience has shown that simplified, centralized architectures such as host-based systems are less complex and expensive to operate than distributed client/server applications with complex and powerful desktop PCs. Operational complexity goes up exponentially as the client machines become more full-functioned and autonomous computing resources. At the same time, these factors must be balanced against the business needs of the application.

Netcentric computing introduces two client workstation variations that trade capability for operational simplicity. They are diskless workstations and thin client/server PCs.

Diskless Workstations. A diskless workstation, as the name implies, is a workstation without a hard disk. The workstation is complete in other aspects and has both a central processing unit and random access memory (RAM). Because the diskless workstation cannot store anything locally, it relies on a server or servers somewhere on the network (potentially in the existing glass house) from which to load the operating system and application from across the network directly into memory.

The diskless workstation simplifies many operational issues because, in a manner similar to the mainframe model, a single copy of the operating system, systems software, applications, and data can be maintained in a central controlled place and then downloaded at run time to workstations on the network. Because the workstations have no capability to permanently store information, there is no opportunity for multiple versions of systems software, applications, and data to permeate the network of workstations.

Network computers (NCs) are an example of diskless workstations. Introduced to reduce the ongoing support costs of distributed computing, network computers employ a "thin-client" model, usually centered around HTML and Java, with no local storage or expansion slots. These computers download and run applications and systems software from a centrally maintained server, thus simplifying administration of large networks. Although the devices themselves are cheaper than current PCs, the real opportunity for cost savings from network computers comes from lower network administration costs (data maintenance, user authentication, software upgrades, and so forth).

An obvious drawback of the diskless workstation alternative is that it becomes absolutely dependent on the availability of the network. These devices also generate a very high amount of network traffic. If the network or a segment should become unavailable, all diskless workstation users are affected immediately and completely. Because the workstation typically has limited RAM resources, it is constantly paging operating system and application frames across the network. If the network is down, the machines cannot resolve page faults and freeze up. This is typically followed by a spike in activity on the voice/telephone network, as users call to "express their concern" to operations. This degree of network dependence and bandwidth requirement is not tolerable for all applications.

Thin Client/Server PCs. Experience has shown that the complexities of full blown client/server applications — with flexible, powerful desktop environments, and distributed application logic — add up to skyrocketing operations costs. In response, alternatives have emerged that simulate the manageable centralized mainframe environment, but preserve the investment in desktop PCs and client/server software. So-called "thin client/server" products allow traditional client/server applications to behave like centralized mainframe applications by retaining and running client logic on the server. This allows software updates and other management tasks to be performed in one location. At the same time, the power of the PC environment is preserved at the desktop.

Although thin client/server products impose some centralization and manageability to client/server applications, they also introduce a reliance on the server for application availability. In addition, the server capacity required to support multiple simultaneous user sessions of a thin client/server application is quite large. As such, there are tradeoffs in ongoing cost savings vs. infrastructure investment when considering thin client/server.

Human Resources Impact

In the migration from host to client/server, significant changes swept the human resources aspects of computing operations. Significant amounts of retraining were needed, as well as new team structures and sourcing strategies. Now, with the introduction of netcentric, several other factors are challenging traditional organizational strategies. Organizations must address these concerns alongside the technology challenges of netcentric computing to succeed in the operations space.

- *Direct interaction with customers and business partners.* As netcentric operations organizations tend to have more direct contact with customers and business partners, IT strategy should reflect this crucial relationship. It should ensure that IT operations and business departments are organized in a way that ensures that netcentric users receive adequate service. For example, the organization may identify more direct reporting relationships between operations and business units.
- *Service levels.* In Internet environments, service levels are difficult to measure, due to user anonymity and lack of management services provided by the Internet. After determining target service levels, netcentric operations departments should assess the corresponding organizational impacts to ensure that targets can be met despite netcentric service level challenges.
- *Internet service providers (ISPs).* ISPs play a major role in the delivery of service in some netcentric environments. Because the ISP can affect service levels, an organization should be sure to establish comprehensive Operational Level Agreements (OLAs) with its ISP to manage service delivery.

- *Geographic locations.* Because of netcentric's global reach, organizational design must consider the need to support users of all types at all times of day. Organizations must clearly define the groups they plan to support, and then map out an appropriate organizational strategy. Organizations must also plan for interactions via multiple languages, and must be prepared to manage legal and cultural variations in the locations they service.
- *Role of user in support.* In netcentric environments, anonymous users may be required to more effectively support themselves. Organizational design should consider this possibility and align itself accordingly. One alternative to address this characteristic may be to shift resources to developing performance support materials within the netcentric capability, rather than direct support to the end user.
- *IT skills.* Given the global nature of some netcentric environments, IT departments may need to support users who speak multiple languages. Organizations must clearly define the groups and languages they plan to support, and then map out an appropriate organizational strategy.
- *Change readiness.* Netcentric may introduce a high rate of change in technology skills that must be maintained, and in business capabilities that must be provided. As a result, operations organizations must be prepared to undergo more frequent changes both in organizational structure, skill base, and team responsibilities in order to address rapidly changing needs. Netcentric operations organizations should define a strategy that will allow them to be nimble and to quickly retool to address changing requirements.

CONCLUSION

Despite the operations challenges brought on by netcentric computing, the technology, processes, and organizational components of an organization's IT operations are evolving to make the netcentric environment manageable. With adequate planning and resources, and with an upfront understanding of the issues and inherent risks in operations, the return on investment of netcentric technologies can be realized. In addition, the flexibility to accommodate the highly dynamic and evolving nature of netcentric environments is crucial to the successful management of the environment.

In the Appendix that follows, a sample SLA is presented, along with commentary (noted in italics). The SLA is based on a Revenue Accounting system developed for a major airline (called "UniversalAir" for our purposes here). The case has been altered somewhat to preserve anonymity.

Appendix:
Sample Service-Level
Agreement

SERVICE-LEVEL AGREEMENT

[Commentary: The title page defines the parties to the SLA. Once it is agreed to, the SLA is signed by the authorized representatives of both organizations. The "effective date" and "expiration date" define the period over which the SLA is in effect. Any reasonable time may be used. A shorter time frame provides both parties the opportunity to renegotiate terms and conditions as experience is gained with the system. A longer time frame reduces the administrative burden of negotiating agreements and enables more meaningful long-range service planning.]

between

Provider: UniversalAir Information Technology Organization (ITO)

_____   _/_/_

ITO Data Center

Receiver: UniversalAir Finance Organization (FO)

_____   _/_/_

VP-UAFO

For the provision of: Revenue Accounting (RA) application

Effective Date: 9/1/99   Expiration Date:9/1/01

BUSINESS OBJECTIVES AND SCOPE

[Commentary: This section provides a high-level summary of the business objectives the computer system is designed to address and the objectives of the SLA document itself. The scope of service to be provided should include a description of the scope of the application system functions covered as well as the nature of service and systems management tasks to be included. A detailed discussion of included scope is not necessary here because the remainder of the SLA defines the scope of service in much greater detail. Important exclusions from scope may also be listed here.]

The main objective of Revenue Accounting (RA) computer system is to support the processing of some 30,000 tickets per day, including such functions as revenue recognition, refunds, and interairline payables. The variety of product configurations and options required to satisfy our diverse end-user population has necessitated the development of an RA application incorporating advanced intelligent workstations and client/server computing. In addition, the geographic decentralization of our finance organization requires that application and data components be distributed among multiple locations.

The objectives of this document are to

- Define a framework for providing efficient high-quality Application Support services to the UniversalAir FO
- Provide a basis and justification for associated ITO hardware and systems software configuration expenditures

The SLA will achieve this objective by

- Outlining the formal interface between ITO and FO
- Describing the service items and service levels agreed between ITO and FO
- Outlining rules, procedures, and responsibilities for both ITO and FO
- Defining a reporting structure for reviewing the actual service levels achieved by ITO against specified targets
- Defining a process that allows changes and continuous improvements to service levels and the overall scope of service to be made in a controlled and structured manner

The scope of the SLA covers the RA computer application as defined in the RA project definition document. Services to be provided under this agreement include

- Provision and maintenance of all necessary computer and communications hardware equipment to FO, including intelligent workstations, application and database servers, local and wide area networks, and high- and low-speed printers.
- Provision and maintenance of all necessary systems software, including workstation and server operating systems, windowing systems, relational DBMSs, and communications middleware.
- Ensuring that all necessary components are operational and available during agreed to time schedules as put forth in this document.

Application maintenance is not within the scope of this agreement. The FO is responsible for the design, development, and testing of all maintenance changes and enhancements to the RA system. ITO is responsible for the rollout and installation of fully tested RA versions.

Changes to interfacing applications as a result of the implementation of RA or future RA releases are outside the scope of this agreement, although they must be formally communicated to ITO.

POLICIES

[Commentary: This section describes the policies by which the service provider conducts business. Policies are, in effect, applicable to all SLAs entered into by the service provider organization. This section may also include the service provider's standard procedures for handling and escalating incidents or processing requests for configuration changes or application version changes.]

The policies governing the provision of services under this agreement are as follows:

- Services will be delivered based on the service targets documented in this agreement.
- Actual level of service will be monitored, reported, and evaluated against the Service-Level Agreement.
- ITO is only responsible for requests that are logged through the Service Control Center.
- ITO Service Control Center will provide a single point of contact for users.

CHANGES TO THIS DOCUMENT

This SLA is jointly owned by the UniversalAir ITO and the UniversalAir Customer Care Organization. This document may not be altered without the consent of both parties. When agreed upon, changes to the document will be made by ITO.

Review Meetings

Review meetings shall take place the first Monday morning of every month. At least one representative from ITO and one representative from FO shall attend. The objectives of these meetings are to

- Resolve any outstanding issues and initiate any follow-up actions
- Update the SLA to reflect any changes in the environment

Each representative is responsible for communicating the outcome of these meetings to his or her respective group.

HARDWARE AND SOFTWARE SUMMARY

[Commentary: Optionally, some service provider organizations will specify the actual hardware and system resources to be used. Specifying the actual inventory of components to be used may clarify the scope of service and reduce misunderstandings.

Other service provider organizations prefer not to disclose specific components, thus allowing for flexibility in configuring the system to meet the customer's requirements at the least cost. In general, the language used in an SLA
should be meaningful to the business users rather than characterized by technology jargon and vendor specifics. This helps the user group to focus on actual
business requirements rather than dictating technology components.]

Client Workstations: 75

Compaq Pentium PCs

VGA Color

MS Mouse

12 Mb RAM

120 Mb internal SCSI

MS-DOS 6.0

MS-Windows for Workgroups 3.11

Servers: 3 (dedicated to RA)

HP 887

256 Mb RAM

6x1.2 Gb DASD

NT Server

Sybase System 10

Mainframe: 1 (shared with other departments)

IBM 3090-200

MVS

CICS

DB2

SERVICE TYPES

Scheduled Availability

[Commentary: The SLA must state the hours during which the users need to be
at the system. For some applications, this may simply be during the normal
working hours of 8:00 A.M. to 5:00 p.m., Monday through Friday. Other applications may be required to be on-line for a greater portion of the week. Some
applications may even be required 7 days a week, 24 hours per day (7 × 24).

Documenting the scheduled availability times allows the systems management organization to plan system downtime for tasks such as maintenance or system backups, during periods when the users do not need access to the application.

Special operational issues emerge as the scheduled availability approaches the 7 × 24 level. Many operating systems and DBMS products require some amount of downtime to effect maintenance changes, tuning changes, or upgrades to new release levels. The costs and constraints on suitable products for supporting a 7 × 24 schedule availability can be considerable. A 6 × 24 arrangement, or even an eight-hour/week scheduled maintenance window can significantly simplify these issues.

Another issue with high availability is how and when to process batch work loads and backup critical databases. Some operating system and DBMS combinations can accommodate concurrent on-line and batch processing (though often at degraded performance) or allow database backups to be made while the DBMS remains on-line while others cannot. These requirements and product constraints must be taken into consideration when determining the scheduled availability window.]

Service Description. Availability here is defined to mean that a user can access and execute any on-line application function from an available intelligent workstation. This definition therefore allows for the failure of the user's primary intelligent workstation providing a "hot" spare is available and accessible.

Availability must be measured on an individual user basis to calculate total RA availability. As a result of measuring difficulties with this approach, unscheduled outages will be approximated by measuring dropped connections to the ticket database on a per-user basis. Additional outage time will be tracked and tabulated via calls to the ITO Service Control Center help desk.

Provider Responsibilities. All RA on-line functions are required to be available during the following periods:

Monday–Saturday, 7:30 A.M. to 8:00 P.M.

Receiver Responsibilities. There may be a requirement for the service to support overtime requirements after 8:00 P.M. and during weekends under certain circumstances. An extension to the above hours can be accommodated, if required, provided sufficient notice is given to ITO.

Shared Responsibilities. Neither the provider nor the receiver shall remove a working client workstation or server from the network during the availability period outlined above.

Reliability

[Commentary: Reliability is the percentage of time the application is actually available during the scheduled time period. For example, if an application is scheduled to be available 40 hours per week, a 99.0% per week reliability requirement would mean that total unscheduled system outages cannot exceed 24 minutes in a given week. "Unscheduled system outages" includes downtime as a result of such things as hardware failure, disk failure, operating system failure, network failure, and workstation failure.

In a client/server configuration, it is very important to define in the SLA how reliability will be measured. In a centralized host environment, availability is typically the same for all users: If the host or some component of the host is down, no one has access to the system. These statistics are easily gathered through such facilities as IBM's SMF. The distributed environment complicates the calculation of availability due to the large number of processors and network links. One server failure may affect some, all, or no end users. The failure of a single workstation only affects one user.

The ideal way to track reliability is at the user's workstation. Few workstation operating systems, however, have facilities or tools for gathering and reporting these statistics. Some projects have remedied this shortcoming by building reliability statistics gathering into the application programs themselves.]

Service Description. Reliability is calculated as follows:

Total availability = (scheduled availability × # of scheduled users) – (unscheduled outage × # of affected users)/(scheduled availability × # of scheduled users) × 100

This formula takes into account that the loss of one client workstation or group of workstations is not as severe as an outage that affects all RA users. Therefore, it penalizes ITO in proportion to the degradation in customer service caused.

Reliability must be measured on an individual user basis to calculate total RA availability. Because of measuring difficulties with this approach, unscheduled outages will be approximated by measuring dropped connections to the ticket database on a per-user basis. Additional outage time will be tracked and tabulated via calls to the ITO Service Control Center help desk.

Provider Responsibilities. Because of the critical nature of the RA application, reliability must be at least 99.5% per month for the RA user group as a whole.

Receiver Responsibilities. The receiver must contact the ITO Service Control Center help desk as soon it is determined that he or she has lost access to the RA application.

Ticket Database Server Failure

Service Description. The Ticket Database Server is the server that maintains the local copy of the ticket information. A database server failure is considered to be one in which all RA users at a given distributed location are affected.

Provider Responsibilities. Because of the severity of this situation and the unfeasibility of a suitable contingency strategy, a single failure at this level may not exceed 5 minutes as measured from the time the failure is detected by the fault management system until service is restored.

User Workstation Failure

Service Description. A workstation has failed when a user cannot use any of the application capability from that device (e.g., RA or Office Automation applications).

Provider Responsibilities. If the Service Control Center help desk determines that the user's workstation is the point of failure, the user will be informed of the location of the nearest available workstation by the help desk and a replacement workstation will be installed and tested within one hour. If the user elects to use the nearest available workstation, the user must be able to resume work by logging in using the normal log-in procedure.

Receiver Responsibilities. It must be appreciated that the 99.5% per month availability/reliability figure can only be effected if all changes to the user environment occur with the consent of ITO. ITO cannot accept liability for user workstation downtime caused by factors outside its control (e.g., users installing personal software).

Performance

[Commentary: Most SLAs for the host-based environment typically measure performance in terms of "screen exchange" response time. A screen exchange is defined as the time from when the user hits "enter" or a PF key until the next screen is displayed on the terminal. Software is available that accurately measures a terminal's end-to-end response time, thus including both host processing time and network time. A consistent screen exchange response time could be expected even for queries that return "pages" of information, because the user would be sent the data one page at a time.

In the distributed environment, these metrics often do not apply and certainly are more difficult to record and report on. A well-designed graphical user interface (GUI) provides instant feedback to the user., and for many user operations this is feasible and expected. Some operations, however, require requests for services from one or more servers across the local or even wide area network. Given current technology, it is probably unreasonable to expect instantaneous response for these requests. Therefore, in the client/server environment, the response time for the user is highly variable and dependent on the nature of the user's task and where the required resources are located in the distributed environment.

There are several options for overcoming the difficulties of specifying performance targets in a distributed client/server environment, including

- *Set a high threshold.* State that the user will receive response time from the application in less than 10 seconds regardless of the operation. The threshold in this case must be set fairly high to accommodate user actions that may result in complex transactions that will be served by multiple and remote processing and data resources. This approach has the appeal of simplicity but may not work well with the application users because it does not clearly state how long it will take for them to complete a meaningful task (such as finding, updating, and saving an existing customer order).
- *Structure application to provide consistent response.* Many users of host-based systems find consistent response times reassuring (e.g., screen exchanges always take 2 seconds). It is possible to structure even a graphical client/server application to behave in this manner, but it will likely result in unnatural breakdowns of application processing (to fit everything into 2-second "chunks") and a less responsive user interface.
- *Lower-level detail in SLA.* Instead of stating that "all user actions will result in subsecond response time," identify meaningful user actions and provide a performance target for each. For example, the SLA may then state that returning product information given a valid product number will take less than 1 second, or returning all customers for a given ZIP (post) code will take less than 15 seconds. This approach, although more difficult to implement, has the benefit of providing more meaningful performance metrics to the end users, the applications developers, and the service/systems management organization. A useful simplification is to group user operations that consume similar computing resources into performance classes and assign performance targets for each class.
- *Higher-level SLA.* An opposite tack is to disregard individual user action response time and instead focus the SLA at the end-to-end business function being performed by the user. For example, an SLA can be constructed stating that a user will be able to enter a customer phone order in less than 2 minutes, as measured from the time the call is answered until the order confirmation number is returned. This approach simplifies tracking

response times, provides more flexibility to the applications developers and systems management personnel, and focuses on what really counts — the timely completion of the business function. However, in this approach the agreement must stipulate how much of the 2 minutes is to be allocated to the user for tasks such as entering information and how much is to be allocated for computer processing. In addition, many business functions are too variable in the amount of "user time" required to complete a transaction to use this approach.

- *Provide performance indication within the application's user interface.* Another variation is to provide indications to the user how long a response to expect for a given user action and tie the SLA to these. For example, a gray button may represent instantaneous response, a green button subsecond, and a red button an operation that will take the computer up to 10 seconds to complete. This approach, only applicable when a GUI is used, helps communicate to users and appropriately set their expectations about response time. The performance targets in the SLA can then be tied directly to the control type (or color). The application's user interface would have to be designed with this approach in mind.

Many of these approaches to specifying performance targets require the application program to be able to record and associate system responses with specific user actions. This requires applications or application architectures to be developed with the appropriate hooks or exits.]

Service Description. Response times are quoted as both an average and a maximum time within which 95% of transactions should occur. For RA, the on-line dialogs have been split into four classes:

- Retrieval of a specific item of information (e.g., a ticket or sales record).
- Retrieval of a list of items (e.g., tickets, pricing rules, or refunds).
- Saving a new or changed item of reference information (e.g., ticket or sales order).
- Saving a new or changed business transaction (e.g., a refund).

Provider Responsibilities. The required application response times for all users averaged over 1 day are

Log-in through RA main window	≤ 10 sec average
	≤ 15 sec 95%
Class 1 dialogs	≤ 2.5 sec average
Ticket given ticket no.	≤ 1.0 sec
Account given account no.	≤ 1.0 sec
Coupon given coupon no.	≤ 1.0 sec
	≤ 4.0 sec 95%

Class 2 dialogs	
(<200 items retrieved)	≤ 2.5 sec average
	≤ 5.0 sec 95%
Class 3 dialogs	≤ 1.5 sec average
	≤ 3.0 sec 95%
Class 4 dialogs	≤ 3 sec average
	≤ 5.0 sec 95%

Subsecond response will be expected for user actions and window manipulations that do not involve saving or requesting information (opening a blank audit window, switching between two windows).

A target service level is not provided for the RA ad hoc query window. Because of the flexibility of this dialog and the user's ability to submit requests that may return very large information sets, a performance target cannot be adequately determined at this time.

Output Handling

[Commentary: This section discusses any requirements and targets for the production of output, including such things as printing, microfiche, and removable magnetic or optical storage. The stringency of the users' output requirements will dictate the location, number, and type of output devices required.]

Service Description. Customer service representatives must have access to local letter quality (laser) printers for the printing of correspondence and simple reports.

Provider Responsibilities. Less than 1% of user print jobs can result in failure. In the event of a print failure, the user must be able to successfully initiate printing within 15 minutes.

Security Management

[Commentary: This section defines who is responsible for security administration tasks, how these services are requested, and the responsiveness of the service provider.

It is important to clarify the boundary in responsibility for security management. Typically, the service management organization is responsible only for ensuring that security policy is correctly executed. It is the responsibility of the user organization to ensure that requests for changes in security privileges are timely, necessary, and prudent (such as adding new users or changing authorization limits for users).

In addition, depending on configuration choices, the application and data security risks may be different from those of a centralized host-based system. For example, data placed on a local workstation hard drive is inherently less secure than data stored on a server or host in the "glass house" where physical security measures are used. It may be important in the SLA to categorize data and application resources depending on their sensitivity. For example, if a stock brokerage client's list is highly confidential, placing this data on the workstation where it could be physically removed is not appropriate. However, reference data like the "country codes table" is likely to require less security precaution and can therefore be placed accordingly within the distributed architecture.

Another security concern within the distributed environment is the LAN itself. LAN protocols such as TCP/IP and SPX are not high-security implementations and devices can be attached to the network to "read packets." Although it is not a concern to most organizations, some user organizations with highly proprietary or confidential data may require data encryption capabilities. As a result of the extra costs, processing, and network burdens that such security measures often require, the service provision organization needs to be aware of these requirements.]

Service Description. The RA application and all associated data assets will be protected in accordance with the UniversalAir corporate security policy with the following exceptions:

- User profile information may be stored on a local medium (PC hard drives).
- The RA codes table may be stored on a server not under physical security (such as a server in the office environment at remote locations).

In accordance with the UniversalAir security policy, access to all RA application functions and data assets will be controlled via unique user IDs and passwords.

The ITO security facilities must ensure that only authorized users may access secured resources in an allowable way.

Provider Responsibilities. The ITO Service Control Center will be responsible for all user security administration including adding and deleting user accounts, changing user privileges, and changing application and data security options.

Changes will be effected by the start of the next business day for requests received before 3:00 P.M. the day before.

Receiver Responsibilities. It is the responsibility of FO management to ensure that authorizations are properly documented and requested. It is imperative that FO management carefully scrutinize all requests for security access for FO employees to ensure that the requested privileges are necessary and prudent. Equally as important, FO management must notify ITO immediately if an employee's security access is to be revoked or changed.

To help control security management requests, only an FO department head or higher may request changes. All requests for security management services must be logged with the Help Desk in writing.

Schedule Execution

[Commentary: This section discusses any requirements and targets for the production of output including such things as printing, microfiche, and removable magnetic or optical storage. The stringency of the users' output requirements dictate the location, number, and type of output devices required.]

Service Description. Schedule execution refers to the scheduling and executing of the daily, weekly, and monthly batch runs for the RA application.

Provider Responsibilities. The scheduling of the various batch runs are as follows:

- All daily batch runs will be completed successfully by 8:00 A.M. of the following business day 95% of the time as measured per month (i.e., 1 exception/month).
- All weekly batch runs will be completed by 8:00 A.M. of the first business day of the following week 96% of the time as measured per year (i.e., 50 out of 52 weeks).
- All monthly batch runs will be completed by 8:00 A.M. of the third business day following the end of the month 90% of the time as measured per year (i.e., 11 out of 12 months).

Incident Management

[Commentary: This section describes how problems will be reported, classified, and prioritized. Service levels for responding to incidents are also included. The SLA may include a description of the problem management process and escalation procedures.]

Service Description. An incident is any unanticipated or unplanned event that deviates from standard activity or expectations. Incident management refers to the correction of incidents via calls to the ITO Service Control Center Help Desk.

Provider Responsibilities. All incidents are to be reported to the Service Control Center Help Desk where they will be assigned a severity. Each severity has a corresponding initial response time, update time, and target resolution time.

It is anticipated that all calls will be answered within one minute in 95% of cases. On receipt of an incident the help desk will assess its impact and assign a category accordingly:

- A:Entire RA system is down or batch schedule halted.
- B:Major breakdown of part of the system (>100 users affected).
- C:Significant impact on part of system (~ 40 users affected).
- D:Limited impact on part of system (~ 10 users affected).
- E:Single user affected.
- F:Minor complaints.
- G:Advice.
- Z:Problem can be cleared at time of logging.

Incidents will be prioritized based on these categories. The following are the target times for responses to the specified categories of incidents raised by users:

Incident category	Average	Maximum (90%)
Category A		
First feedback	5 min	10 min
Second feedback	20 min	30 min
Feedback frequency	30 min	1 h
Category B		
First feedback	20 min	30 min
Second feedback	1 h	2 h
Feedback frequency	30 min	1 h
Category C, D, E		
First feedback	30 min	45 min
Second feedback	1 h	2 h
Feedback frequency	1 h	2 h
Category F and G		
First feedback	4 h	8 h
Second feedback	1 day	2 days
Feedback frequency	1 day	2 days
Category Z	Not applicable	

The second feedback interval is measured from the time of the first feedback until the second contact has been made.

Receiver Responsibilities. The receiver should contact the ITO Service Control Center help desk as soon it is determined that an incident has occurred.

Contingency/Backup

[Commentary: In a distributed environment, it is important to clarify who will be responsible for backing up and restoring data at "remote" locations. Some organizations require users to perform backups; some staff remote locations with an operations person; still others perform systems management tasks remotely via network connections.

This specification of exactly how these tasks will be accomplished is not necessary within the SLA. The roles and responsibilities of both parties and the expectations of service, however, should be detailed.

It is also important in this section to define the level of the backup being taken. Backups, for instance, can be done on an "image" level or an application data level. Defining this level appropriately ensures that proper data is being backed up in the event of potential failure.]

Service Description. Two kinds of archiving will be performed on RA applications and data.

- Daily incremental backups
- Weekly full system archives, run each Friday

When it has been determined by the ITO Service Control Center help desk that a restoration of applications and data is necessary, restoration processes will be executed.

Provider Responsibilities. ITO is responsible for performing all backup and restoration operations without assistance from any RA personnel. Data stored at remote sites will be backed up or restored via telecommunications links.

The daily incremental backup tapes will be stored in the ITO data center's fireproof safe. The weekly tapes will be transported to and stored in ITO's off-site storage facility. Database logs are written to tape each evening and stored off site as well. These can be used in conjunction with the backup tapes to rebuild the database in the event of any loss.

Business Recovery

[Commentary: The business recovery strategy addresses how quickly service must be restored after a disaster such as flood or fire destroys a data center or user location. In a centralized environment, the definition of a disaster is relatively simple. In the distributed environment, the agreement may be more complex to account for the unlikelihood that all distributed computing resources would be effected by a single disaster.]

Service Description. Business recovery involves restoring the RA system for use in the event of a catastrophic loss of the ITO data center (e.g., flood, fire, or tornado). The recovery plans involve the data center facility itself, as well as the telecommunications links to this facility. Recovery of distributed sites (i.e., those not located physically with the data center) are excluded from the scope of this agreement.

Provider Responsibilities. In the unlikely event of a catastrophic loss of the ITO data center, it is imperative that the RA system be operational by 8:00 A.M.

on the first business day following such a disaster. All data must be restored and made current to within 24 hours of the disaster. It must be possible at least to manually reenter all orders taken on the actual day of the disaster.

In the unlikely event of a catastrophic loss of any one RA user building (any of the three primary RA user locations), the remaining RA locations must be able to handle orders by 8:00 A.M. on the first business day following such a disaster.

Receiver Responsibilities. It is the responsibility of each user location to formulate its own business recovery plans in the event of an on-site cata-strophic failure. These plans must include recovery schemes for all hard-ware and software up to and including the gateway at the user location.

Prior to their finalization, these plans must be agreed by ITO. Each user location will also be responsible for executing these plans as necessary.

Shared Responsibilities. Both the provider and receiver shall work together to achieve business recovery in the event it is necessary. The pro-vider and receiver shall each maintain a current contact list with the names and phone numbers of those individuals responsible for achieving busi-ness recovery.

Reporting Procedures

[Commentary: This section describes how the service provider will report actual service levels vs. plan to the end-user organization. Items to be covered include report frequency, contents, and distribution.]

Service Description. This section outlines the reporting procedures that are used by the ITO Service Management organization. Daily and weekly reports (contents listed below) are distributed to senior members of ITO and FO user management.

Provider Responsibilities. The following reports will be produced as stated and distributed by 8:00 A.M. on the first business day following the reporting period:

- Daily Report Contents:
  Planned service availability
  Actual service availability
  Time of failure
  Duration of failure
  User Groups affected by failure
  Reasons for failure (if available)
  Total downtime
  Categorized help desk incidents

Categorized help desk incidents closed
Categorized help desk incidents outstanding
Description of major incidents
• Weekly Report Contents:
Average service availability (rollup of daily figures)
Simple mean time between failure (MTBF)
Details of failures not discussed in daily reports for week
Performance response-time statistics
Output handling exceptions, including items missing postal dead-line, deviation of batch reconciliation, printer outages, tape diffi-culties, and reprocess requests
Problem management exceptions, including items not meeting feed-back criteria, planned vs. actual first feedback times, and planned vs. actual problem resolution times

Shared Responsibilities. Regular monthly meetings are held between des-ignated officers and supervisors and members of the ITO Service Manage-ment team.

Application Versions and Major Enhancements

[Commentary: In the distributed environment, rolling out new versions of appli-cations to a large number of workstations may be very complex and labor inten-sive, as well as destabilizing to the processing environment. For this reason, the service management organization may wish to limit the number of software releases that a user organization can request in a given period. The service man-agement organization also needs to discuss how quickly the major releases or emergency bug fixes will need to be distributed (e.g., in one evening or through a phased approach).]

Service Description. New application versions and enhancements shall be distributed to each of the user locations and updated according to agreed-on schedules.

Provider Responsibilities. ITO is responsible for the successful rollout of new RA application releases. Major releases will be phased out to all sites within a 1-month period. Bug fixes will be phased out to all of the sites within a 1-week period.

Receiver Responsibilities. Because of the costs and potential for service disruption this entails, FO will be restricted to no more than one major release and no more than three bug fix releases per 6-month period.

Shared Responsibilities. Both the Provider and Receiver shall work together to plan the rollout of new RA application releases. Major releases will be planned no later than 6 months in advance. Bug fixes will be planned on an as-needed basis.

Capacity Planning

[Commentary: Capacity planning in the distributed client/server environment is notoriously difficult. The most important inputs into any capacity plan are accurate and realistic business volume projections. It is unreasonable to expect an organization's information systems department to be able to generate the business volume projections. The user organizations serviced by the information systems department are best positioned to provide these projections. Some companies apply penalties to user departments that provide inaccurate estimates into this process. If such penalties are to be used, the SLA should specify the details.]

Service Description. Capacity Planning is performed to ensure that the users of the RA application have optimal use of the system. Capacity in this instance refers to the capacity of the network, servers, and local databases.

Provider Responsibilities. The ITO Capacity Planning team performs capacity planning on a quarterly basis, providing capacity projections for the following four quarters. These capacity projections are used to ensure that adequate processing and service resources to fulfill existing service level agreements are available. Because these estimates will be relied on in the making of significant expenditures, ITO expects a 90% confidence interval to be used and will track and report back FO's estimates vs. actuals. (A 90% confidence interval is a predicted low and high value within which the actual value will fall 90% of the time).

Any change in business conduct that may necessitate the installation of a new processing location or a substantial increase in the number of users (>50) at an existing location should be communicated to ITO as soon as it is known but absolutely no later than 6 months in advance.

Receiver Responsibilities. The primary input to the capacity planning process is an accurate projection of business volumes for the quarters being studied. It is the responsibility of FO management to provide accurate estimates of business volumes and end user head count projections on a quarterly basis.

Chapter 24
Testing Implementation

In the netcentric computing environment, it is more vital than ever to test throughout the life cycle of the development project. Testing cannot be done toward the end or as an afterthought to development. Testing must be carefully planned, designed, prepared, and executed. The requirements and the design are tested as well as the many layers of code. Testing requires quantifiable specifications, complex testing environments, architectures and tools, trained testers, and explicit exit criteria. Systems are designed to be testable; this ensures not only quality but also reliable delivery and maintainability. Testing is a complex activity that involves not only testing teams, but also users, technical support, development, training, documentation, roll-out, and program management teams.

This chapter builds on the V-Model testing concepts discussed in Chapter 11. As noted earlier, the V-Model is a testing framework that has been successfully applied to various types of business applications, using many different development approaches. Once the fundamentals of the V-Model are understood, the model can be adapted easily to a situation to identify risks as well as to identify an effective and efficient approach to mitigate those risks.

Successful delivery of a systems solution in the netcentric environment requires that the testing at each stage of the life cycle be well structured, clearly documented, and independently repeatable. Clearly, this is much easier when combined with integrated testing processes, tools, and techniques to achieve the goals of efficient, effective testing and on-time, quality delivery.

THE TEST STRATEGY

The first brick to lay in building a solid testing framework is the test strategy. The test strategy outlines a comprehensive testing approach for the entire solution. The test strategy is developed to determine and communicate precisely how the end product, complete with new hardware, software, work flows, and procedures, will be tested. When developing the test strategy, developers must be sure to apply the V-Model concepts not only to the applications under development but also to the technical and application architectures, the training and documentation, and the organization and work processes.

Traditional test strategies focused only on testing the application code and basically ignored the architecture, treating it as if it were developed through black magic. In today's world, the architecture components are too complex and too integral to the success of the solutions; thus, the same structure and rigor must be applied to developing architectures as to developing applications. Also, the comprehensive test strategy helps identify those forgotten, but important, components of the solution that nobody ever plans to test, such as the JCL, data conversion routines, and backup procedures.

DEFINING THE SCOPE OF TESTING

The test strategy defines the scope of testing: what will be tested and, just as important, what will not be tested. In the V-Model, applications are specified top down along the left side of the V, with each level of specification incorporating decisions and adding increased detail. Ideally, each level of decision would be tested, every added detail with an associated testing stage on the right side of the V. However, with the increasing complexity and unpredictability of netcentric application solutions, it is very often not possible, or at least not feasible, to test absolutely everything. Careful thought should be given to exactly what will be tested, what cannot or will not be tested, and how associated risks will be managed.

For example, in developing a financial services application to run in an Internet environment distributed at 200 remote sites with several hardware, network, and software configurations, it may be acceptable to test the application software only on the three most common configurations. The risks presented by deploying the application system to the untested configurations may be acceptable according to previous experience, or there may be plans put in place to monitor the first several weeks of operation on those platforms to identify problems. On the other hand, if the application system under development is critical to the operation of the enterprise, or if software errors would prove very costly, it may be necessary to test each and every configuration. Finally, experience in deploying the system may suggest additional or revised configurations.

Another example might be the introduction of a new set of application systems and business processes into an existing business environment. Decisions may be made to test only a subset of interfaces and to use a pilot environment or a set of representative users to test the work processes. The assumption here is that the risks presented by not testing all interfaces are acceptable or that the cost to test each interface was not justified by the problems that might arise if they were to not perform. The point is to identify and communicate exactly what will and will not be tested, preferably, based on the cost to test and risks to the business of not testing. Once complete, the definition of what is to be tested is often very useful in managing the expectations of the users and determining enhancements or expansions to scope.

The primary objective of the test strategy is to minimize gaps and overlaps in the testing of the end product. The test strategy should define what stages of testing will take place and what the scope and objectives of each testing stage are. Based on the development approach and the risks associated with the development project, testing stages will be defined to confirm proper implementation of each level of specification and each major risk area.

IDENTIFYING THE STAGES OF TESTING

The V-Model defines the main testing stages as component test, assembly test, product test, operational readiness test, and benefits realization test. A given project or set of projects may have more or fewer testing stages; the important thing is that the stages are identified and communicated early in the effort to ensure proper results.

Traditionally, if one were to ask the members of the typical IT organization what stages of testing were standard for solution delivery, the answers from the managers as well as the developers would most likely be inconsistent or vague. One cannot hope to achieve efficiency and effectiveness in testing processes if the people responsible for those processes do not have a consistent understanding of what the processes are. By outlining exactly what the testing stages are, where each one starts and stops, and who has responsibility for each, gaps and overlaps in testing activities can be eliminated.

Too often, redundant effort is spent in the later stages of testing, confirming things that were covered in an earlier stage. One of the most common causes of overruns in product testing stems from repeating the component testing of the application because there was not a concise understanding of exactly what was covered during the component test. Because a development team does not understand, and therefore cannot assume, what has already been tested in earlier stages, they find themselves retesting very basic conditions during product test.

Another factor here is that it is generally easier for a software developer to prepare and execute a component level test than to plan and execute a true product test. Product testing is largely a test of the requirements and business functions. It is much less tangible than testing if's and move's. Therefore, developers tend to focus on component testing at the expense of product testing. By articulating what each test is designed to accomplish — the scope and objective of each test stage, along with how conformance will be verified and validated — both the redundant testing and the omitted testing can be identified and addressed.

Another benefit of a comprehensive test strategy outlining the scope and objectives of each testing stage is that there is now a means to determine when testing is finished. One of the most common questions asked is, "How does one know testing is complete?" The answer here is that knowing when one is done depends on beginning with an established scope and approach to what will be tested and how. Only that initial agreement allows the team to know that the test, when successfully executed, has really achieved its objectives.

The test strategy should be completed as part of initial project plans. A common problem in systems development is setting in stone the project plans, budget, schedule, and due date and then telling the testing manager how many days are allocated for testing. This clearly compromises the testing, because it sets testing scope based on days available, rather than number of days required to deliver an acceptable level of quality and risk. The only way to avoid this common problem is to develop the test strategy early and to recognize that testing will often make up the majority of the effort, either by plan, by necessity, or in regret. To allow for the proper testing of the system and new business processes, it is crucial to consider the testing requirements up front, and to make decisions on the scope and investment for testing early, thereby allocating the proper resources in the project plans.

DEFINING TEST CYCLES

In addition to outlining the testing stages, the test strategy should include initial test cycle definitions. Preliminary definition of test cycles not only facilitates estimating the effort required to plan and execute the test, but also allows the development teams to sequence the delivery of components in alignment with the needs for test execution. The project delivery window can be shortened through tight coordination of the sequence of delivery from development to testing stages, allowing for the overlap of project activities. This is a big plus for projects facing an externally imposed due date such as a regulatory change. The test strategy allows the team to avoid the situation where the test teams plan to run the conversion programs first to build data for the product test, and conversion routines are the last thing the development team plans to deliver.

Definition of test cycles requires addressing the issue of overall test design. Test design considerations to be applied when outlining cycles

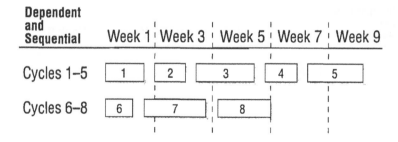

Exhibit 1. Dependent and Sequential Test Cycles.

include the balance between sequential and parallel cycle definition and the inclusion of test cycles to cover ancillary tests.

Sequential Test Cycles

Purely sequential or horizontal test cycles most closely reflect true business processing. However, sequential cycles tend to imply single-thread executions that can lengthen the elapsed time needed to complete. Also, the built-in data dependencies leaves a team at risk that a defect in early cycles can halt execution of the entire test. Data dependencies also make the test model more likely to incur significant rework if changes to the data model occur in early test cycles. A positive consideration for sequential test models is the ability to bundle all test conditions of a particular type into a single cycle, thus reducing the number of cycles to be regression tested when a particular area changes. For example, sequential test models typically have all data creation functionality (e.g., add customer and add account) grouped into the early cycles, therefore if the add process is changed, developers need only to regression test these early cycles (Exhibit 1).

Parallel Test Cycles

Parallel or vertical test cycles are designed by establishing a small amount of base data, followed by multiple, concurrent test cycles breaking off and testing groups of test conditions. Parallel test cycles reduce the risk that one error stops all test execution in its tracks. The parallel cycles exercise independent data; therefore, the inability to progress along one path will not necessarily halt others. However, there are some inevitable trade-offs:

- Parallel tests tend to be less representative of true business applications. Care must be taken to implement true product test level conditions as opposed to reassembly testing.

Independent and Parallel	Week 1	Week 3	Week 5	Week 7	Week 9
Cycles A	A				
Cycle B	B				
Cycle C	C				
Cycle D	D				

Exhibit 2. Independent and Parallel Test Cycles.

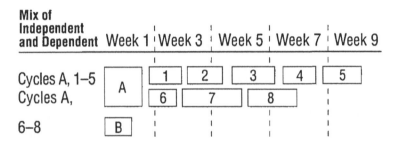

Mix of Independent and Dependent	Week 1	Week 3	Week 5	Week 7	Week 9
Cycles A, 1–5	A	1 2	3	4	5
Cycles A,		6 7	8		
6–8	B				

Exhibit 3. Mix of Independent and Dependent Test Cycles.

- Test conditions around a particular requirement tend to be spread across cycles, necessitating modification and reexecution of multiple cycles for a single requirements change (Exhibit 2).

The answer here is to strike a balance in cycle design. The cycles must be dependent and sequential enough to provide a flow of data and events through the application (because this supports the testing of true business processes) and also parallel enough so that there are multiple executors active at a time, reducing risk and elapsed time for execution (Exhibit 3).

Additionally, ancillary test cycles might be designed to cover groups of test conditions such as conversion routines, security, performance, or regression of a previous version. It is often advantageous to separate these tests into independent cycles due to the technical nature of the test conditions, thus requiring more complex test environments, tools (e.g., performance monitors), and personnel (Exhibit 4).

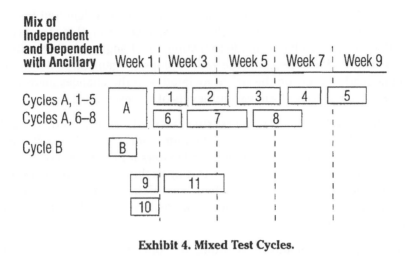

Exhibit 4. Mixed Test Cycles.

DEVELOPING THE TEST APPROACH FOR EACH STAGE

Building on the test strategy, the next step is to develop the test approach for each testing stage. The test approach is developed as part of the specification to be tested. For example, the product test approach is developed as part of the requirements specification, and the assembly test approach is developed as part of the technical design specification. This facilitates early identification of test requirements, thus providing the time to address action items.

Whereas the test strategy stated what will be tested, the test approach for each stage defines how things will be tested. The test approach further details the process, entry and exit criteria, and roles and responsibilities. The test approach also includes the work plan, schedule, and resource requirements for that test stage.

The concept of developing a test approach document is not new. However, historically the focus of the test approach was integration or system testing, and the approach was developed by and for the development team members responsible for testing. This chapter advocates developing a test approach for each test stage, and the reach of the activities defined in the approach includes team members from development, testing, technical support, users, training, and others.

REGRESSION TESTING

In addition to the test process itself (i.e., the "how"), the test approach should outline the steps to be taken to regression test changes, both fixes and scope changes, made when a solution component is demoted from a testing stage. Regression testing of changes can include anything from simply testing the actual change made to testing the change and all identified affected areas and fully retesting the entire solution. Again, these decisions should be made largely on the risk associated with the changes made and the effort required to perform various levels of regression testing.

Once the required level of regression testing is determined, several options exist for actually performing the regression tests. The most obvious approach is to have the developer and testers for the changed components perform the required regression testing as the changes are made and the component is migrated through the stages of the V-Model. This implies individually regression testing each change, which can become quite costly. Other options are

- Bundling changes and reexecuting appropriate tests (the tests are repeatable) when a threshold number of changes has occurred, for example, every 50 changes.
- Reexecuting the tests periodically, for example, every Friday afternoon, each work cell kicks off all regression test scripts to test changes made that week.

RESOURCE REQUIREMENTS

Included in the test approach are final resource requirements for the test stage. Testing netcentric applications suggests the need for many varied skills. Netcentric applications bring together many facets of business, and many technology components. Gone are the days when there was a single person in the technical support department who was capable of resolving any technical problem. Today, applications and the corresponding issues require a wide variety of skills to fully understand and support a solution. There may be unique requirements for business skills, organizational skills, and technical skills for the front-end, the legacy applications, the communications layers, and so forth. In addition, there are the pieces of applications developed on different platforms using different languages.

It is more than likely now that a team of technical and business experts is required to verify a system and to analyze and resolve problems. It is important to identify and schedule the proper levels of participation from all members of the team, especially developers.

When specifying the resources required for the testing effort, the level of external participation required should be defined. Applications involving major change to the business can be successful only if there is significant involvement of the user and customer communities.

PLANNING THE TEST

Test planning is made up primarily of the development of test conditions and expected results. The important difference in test planning in a netcentric environment as opposed to traditional test planning is the emphasis on when and how to derive test conditions.

When? The earlier, the better. Test conditions are now developed as part of the specification to be tested — on the left side of the V. The completion of the test conditions for the associated test stage should be an exit criteria for delivery of the specification. Identification of test conditions as part of the specification provides two major benefits:

1. Early test planning results in more quantifiable, testable specifications. As the requirements analyst is documenting the application requirements, the tester needs to be asking, "How am I going to test that?" In this way, a team gets better requirements. If the analyst cannot answer the question of how a requirement is to be tested, it is too vague, and thus there is a significant chance that the designer and developer will not understand how to implement the requirement. Thinking through how to test something eliminates many of the ambiguities and incorrect assumptions. The result is clear, understandable specifications.

2. The second benefit is that planning tests early allows test preparation to begin early and to happen concurrent with construction. Given the test conditions with the specification, the test team is able to begin test preparation concurrent with construction of the solution. Now, as the development activities begin to wind down, the team does not have to wait for resources from development teams to transition to the test team to start thinking about testing. The team is ready to start executing the test. This can save a considerable amount of elapsed time in the delivery of a solution, typically squeezing at least 2 to 3 months out of the delivery window.

Finally, for each test condition identified, the expected result should be identified. For example, a test condition for selection of an audio explanation from an entry screen would have the expected result that the correct audio clip plays and returns control to the entry screen. It is this definition of how the condition will be satisfied that forces the designers to quantify requirements and thus reduce ambiguities in the design or devise ways to make the system more testable. Definition of expected results also makes it possible to verify the test plans against the requirements to be tested.

How are test conditions derived? Directly from the specification. It is essential to tie test conditions to the specification they test. Tying test conditions to specifications provides the traceability discussed in Chapter 11. It also provides a means to determine and demonstrate what is and is not tested. Without a cross-reference from specification to test conditions, it is impossible to demonstrate that the test will cover all risk areas of the specification. Too often on projects, analysts sit down with a blank sheet of paper to begin documenting test conditions. The rationale for this is that the analyst is the expert, and thus best positioned to identify what and how to test. However, it is quite likely that the analyst will apply the same oversights/misconceptions to the test plan that existed during analysis.

An added risk is that it is almost certain that the analyst will be the only person who understands what is being tested and why, thus inhibiting the ability to effectively leverage the test plan for execution or reuse. In the case of drawing up test conditions from a blank sheet of paper, there is no means of identifying what each test condition, and ultimately test case, is designed to test. It is important for the test executors, and eventually those maintaining the test, to understand the objective of the test cases in order to effectively judge results and to identify the impact of changes. Likewise, if test conditions are not cross-referenced to specifications, there is no way to identify where in the test model specific requirements are tested. Therefore, we do not have the ability to judge test coverage or perform an impact analysis to effectively maintain the test model. Ideally, test conditions are generated from, and tied to, the specification they are designed to test (Exhibit 5).

Component test-level test conditions are drawn directly from the detail design specification. For example, each item on the Control-Action-Response (CAR) diagram or each video launch would have one or more associated test conditions designed to prove the item was properly implemented in the code.

Test conditions for the assembly test may be generated from application flow diagram detail or data access and window navigation specifications. Test cases can then be generated to exercise each primary or default path in the system dialogs and the passing of data from assembly to assembly to demonstrate correctness.

Likewise, each functional requirement and each quality requirement should have one or more associated product test conditions to demonstrate that the solution satisfies the requirement. Generating true product test-level test conditions may be difficult at first, particularly if previous testing experience focused on testing technical execution of code rather than systems functionality or business processes. One way of viewing product test is to take the perspective of the business user of the end solution. Assuming that the component test checked that the actual code works and the assembly test checked that the individual modules or components can pass control and data as designed, the product test can be viewed from a largely nontechnical perspective.

Specification	Objectives of Test Stage ←	Test Stage
Business Case	business benefits achieved	Benefits Realization Testing
Roll-out, Operations Procedures and SLA	availability reliability performance	Operational Readiness Testing
Application Requirements Specification	completion of business functions business results on screens & reports processing times	Product Testing
Application Architecture Design	screen navigation, module calls interface use context data handling	Assembly Testing
Automated Process Design	logic validation reads/writes displays error handling	Component Testing

Exhibit 5. Specification-Driven Testing.

Envision the users of an on-line banking application attempting to use the system via home telephone to transfer funds. The users know that they must provide a customer identification number and checking account number as well as the amount to be transferred. Most users neither know nor care how the system processes the data; they care only that the right transactions occur so the transfer can be completed. With this scenario, we can see that the individual component tests must check that the required data is obtained, that the customer identification number is verified, and so forth. The assembly test checks that the telephony equipment passes the right data to the system, which in turn accesses customer account information, sending data to activate the appropriate response message to the user. Product test then confirms that the funds transfer is reflected in the customer checking and savings accounts, and that the activity is recorded in the system which tracks the use of the on-line service for billing.

PREPARE THE TEST

For each test stage, after completion of the test approach and the test plan, we are ready for test preparation. From a process standpoint, the following activities occur during this stage:

1. Define test subcycles.
2. Define test scripts.
3. Link detail test conditions to test scripts.
4. Document test script details (expected results, input data, test script steps).
5. Confirm that all detail test conditions are tested.

The test design principles to be applied during preparation center around the desire for the test to be repeatable, modular, and expandable. It is desirable for tests to be repeatable to support audit and reuse. Generally, tests are repeatable if they are well structured and well documented. Modular tests can be executed piece by piece as need and resources dictate, thus improving productivity. Modular, well-structured, and documented tests are expandable, meaning that new or changed test conditions can be incorporated into existing test models easily. Expanding an existing test model allows for efficient testing of both new and existing risk areas.

Differences from traditional test preparation approaches arise from the increased level of structure and rigor applied to documenting tests, the high degree of reuse of scripts within and across tests, and the use of tools to automate execution and results verification.

A key consideration during test preparation is the level of detail to which input data and expected results should be defined. In general, time invested on definition of test data and detailed expected results is gained back in more efficient test execution and increased repeatability/reusability of tests.

From a regression testing standpoint, a "repeatable" test model is essential. It allows the engagement to allocate its usually scarce functional experts to other development tasks while not sacrificing the effectiveness of the regression test. Within the "Prepare Test" activity, the steps necessary to automate the test conditions are defined.

From a process standpoint, the following additional activities occur during the "Prepare Test" activity:

6. Define test subcycles.
7. Define test scripts.
8. Link detail test conditions to test scripts.
9. Document test script details (expected results, input data, test script steps).
10. Confirm that all detail test conditions are tested.

Test Data

Done properly, the use of common test data increases productivity. All too often, however, common test data is poorly designed and inadequately maintained and controlled, which renders it useless. Ideally, common test data is created and maintained to support the testers, thus eliminating the need for testers to design, develop, and maintain their own test data. Test data should be designed to be representative of the conditions to be tested, and should be dense, such that a minimum number of transactions can be executed to exercise all test conditions. Common mistakes to be avoided when creating test data include

- Inadequate control over master data to prevent corruption
- Inadequate documentation of test data to support users
- Inadequate resources committed to maintain data as requirements and data models change, resulting in obsolete data
- Unrealistic test data, which may confuse users and/or render false results

Another major data decision to be made is how the test model will use converted vs. created vs. system generated data. Converted data allows one to exercise the solution against real converted data, thus identifying problems with the data and/or conversion routines. This is important because many painful production problems are often due to data. However, converted data can be unwieldy and can often cause problems in the test that have nothing to do with the actual test conditions one is trying to test. Consider the ease with which a manageable subset of production data can be identified and sliced, while retaining data integrity across elements. Also, data conversion routines are typically developed very late in the project. Finally, be sure to address confidentiality issues with using production data for testing.

Created data means using the system to add the data needed to test — for example, using the customer entry application to add test customers. When using created data, start the test with essentially empty databases (with the exception of administration and reference data) and use the actual solution (system, processes, etc.) to create all of the test data needed by subsequent cycles. This approach ensures that the solution can create data and then process that data, Conversion routines — and thus converted data — would be tested separately.

The third option is to generate data using a utility. With this option, it is often difficult, if not impossible, to get the data integrity correct due to complex dependencies among data elements. However, this may be the only option if data not created by the system is needed for testing, but is not available — for example, data to be provided by an as-yet incomplete system or unsigned business partner.

In general, the best approach is usually to use a combination of two or three sources of data, designed to best address the risks being tested.

One final tactic to consider when scripting and designing test data is to develop scripts in the reverse order of execution: from the last cycle to the first. This way, one can identify all of the data needed for each cycle, and feed that information to the scripting of the previous cycles so that the data can be created and/or passed. This eliminates the common dilemma of attempting to script cycle five, and discovering that one needs two additional customer types which must now be created and passed along from the very first cycle, which then results in script changes for cycles one through four.

Expected Results

As with test data, the level at which one intends to document expected results must also be defined. Typically, expected results are very detailed: field by field for all effected databases, interfaces, and reports. Detailed expected results allows for detailed results verification, which supports maximum identification of discrepancies. Detailed expected results are also required to make the tests repeatable. Given the test script and expected results, someone other than the original test designer should be able to reexecute a test and verify results easily.

It may be difficult to predict expected results for some portions of the application, usually because of complex dependencies. In these cases, one must document input, output, and high-level expected results with a comprehensive, detailed, expert review of the actual results. Once the actual results have been reviewed and approved, these results can serve as detailed expected results for future executions.

An effective test preparation design technique is the use of multiple levels of scripts or test cases. This technique is often applied to product testing as a means to identify as many issues as early in the testing process as possible. Usually three levels of scripts are defined.

1. Level one is a set of high level scripts designed to execute all major system functionality. These scripts are designed to execute very quickly, covering the most basic processing. This allows one to identify any significant problem areas within the solution as early as possible. Because they are high level and cover all major functionality, the level one scripts are also an excellent foundation for regression tests and other testing, such as platform migration, training, and systems software upgrades. Typically, these scripts are developed by scripting the "story lines" to be executed and checking off the test conditions that are covered by the scripts. The level one scripts usually account for 25 to 30% of the product test conditions.

2. Level two scripts are the main body of the test. The level two scripts test the detailed test conditions. These are scripted more traditionally,

by grouping test conditions and writing scripts for each group until all test conditions are covered.

3. Level three scripts are sometimes used to cover independent and quirky test conditions, such as exception processing or hardware failure test conditions. These scripts are isolated from the level two scripts primarily because they require extensive set up or unique combination of data to test and would complicate the main test. By isolating the level three conditions into separate test scripts, one can execute them as time permits, often filling down time in the main execution.

ESTABLISHING THE TEST ENVIRONMENT

Most product tests lose at least the first 2 weeks of execution because of environment problems: missing common modules, incorrect configurations, communications malfunctions, incomplete data or source libraries, and so forth. Teams should bear in mind the need to start a few weeks earlier to establish and test the test environment.

This activity will most likely start early in the project, with the selection and implementation of tools and required hardware and software, followed by the establishment of the test configurations to be tested and the loading of test data. Several factors make establishing the test environment a critical line item on the project plans:

- *Complexity/expense.* Testing a complex solution will probably require creating a "model office" — an environment that simulates a production environment. These environments, particularly in netcentric computing, are extremely complex and often very expensive. Plan ahead to allow lead time for implementation of the environment and to take advantage of the potential of sharing environments with other teams (e.g., across testing stages or between testing and training).
- *Support.* To allow test execution to proceed smoothly, it is crucial to have proper technical support for the test environment. Environment support includes establishment and maintenance of test configurations, test data management, migration control, and problem solving. Migration of code and data for product testing can easily become a full time job. Repeatable tests imply backup data, and this in turn implies maintenance. If resources are not allocated to apply data structure changes to saved test data, the test model quickly becomes obsolete.
- *Control.* Strict control over the test environment — particularly the source code and data configurations — is essential to testing. Code and data changes must not be introduced directly into the test environment; instead they should be implemented in the development environment and pulled forward into the test environment. As the saying goes, "Test what you deliver, and deliver what you test." Improper

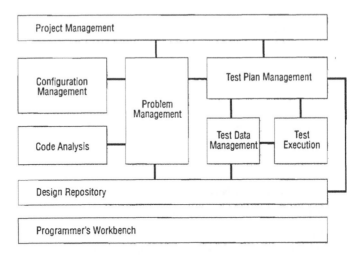

Exhibit 6. Integrated Testing Environment (ITE).

configuration management too often leads to incomplete solution configurations or inadvertent changes. Be sure to have environment control policies defined, complete with change approval processes and audit capability.

Test Automation

An automated test model is essential. The following are some of the benefits of test automation:

- Automated test cycles can be reexecuted over night (without testers present).
- An automated test model reduces the amount of time required by the tester to execute test cycles; thus, it frees the tester up to do other development activities.
- Subsequent tests of the application will be significantly easier for the tester to execute.
- An automated test model can reduce time to market for new releases of the application under test.
- An automated testing tool executes a test script the same way every time; it does not get tired and make mistakes.
- Automated test models can be used to test the effect of upgrades on the operating system, system software, or hardware on the application under test.

The diagram of the Integrated Testing Environment (ITE) (Exhibit 6) was introduced in Section II. The components of the ITE fall into two categories:

1. Components not specifically dedicated to the testing phase, used during most of the phases of a project development life cycle, including
   Project management
   Programmer's workbench
   Design repository
2. Components that are mainly needed during the testing phase of the project and after, including
   Test plan management
   Test execution
   Test data management
   Configuration management
   Problem management
   Code analysis

Project Management

Project management is not specific to the testing environment, because it obviously covers the entire project life cycle. It focuses on project planning, schedule, cost, and statistical reports. Project management tools are prevalent in the market. An example is Project Workbench for Windows (PWB) from ABT Corp., a Windows-based project planning and control system. Accenture offers its own proprietarytools, such as MANAGE/1.

Programmers Workbench

The Programmers Workbench represents the specific tools that support the coding and maintenance of the application software:

- Source code generator
- Source code debugger
- Source code comparator, which enables identification of changes between different versions of program
- Documentor, which enables recording of information about a program, data store or system, completely and systematically
- Auditor, which enables the verification of source code conformance to pre-established rules and standards

Programmers workbench tools are usually selected before the construction of the application and are not specific to the testing environment. It is important, however, that the test execution, test planning, and defect tracking system are integrated in the same environment so that the programmer can easily switch from one tool to another during the fixing activity.

Design Repository

The design repository represents the basis of the application development, providing impact analysis and application generation features. Typically, the design repository is used to centralize the application definition data. The design repository is mainly involved during the construction phase of the application. It is important to have good configuration management of design documentation within the repository. In this way, one makes sure that the test models are built upon the proper build levels of the solution design.

In a testing environment, the design repository is a safe mean of analyzing the impact of a problem on the whole application. Having two separated systems, one for problem management and one for application design, duplicates information and introduces errors. Therefore, integration among the design repository and the defect management, test planning, and configuration management components would significantly increase productivity and reduce the risk of errors.

Test Plan Management

Test plan management allows structured design and maintenance of test cases. During test planning, the business functions are broken down into test conditions. The test cycles, test data, and expected results are defined and prepared to be ready for execution. A test planning system helps the developer to find existing test cases, cycles, and scripts that may be appropriate for reuse. In addition, test planning helps keep track of test cycle execution scheduling and execution results.

All the test design data can be stored in a repository, which ideally would reference problem management information associated to a test cycle. Some of the functions that may be supported are

- Test model definition and repository support
- Test cycle definition
- Test schedule and test execution tracking
- Test condition generation
- Requirements management
- Test case generation

Test Execution

The test execution component of the integrated testing environment includes

- Scripting and playback tools, which automate the execution of tests by simulating the end user operations, and/or allowing reexecution in batch mode.

- Emulation tools for component and assembly test, mainly
  Stub modules
  Server back-end emulation
  Client emulator or injector to test servers
- Test results comparison tools (actual result data compared to expected results)
- Test coverage measurement comparison tools (during program execution, this provides comprehensive information about how many times each logic path within the program is executed in any number of runs)

SELECTING A TOOL FOR AUTOMATED REGRESSION TESTING

The marketplace has several vendors providing solutions to meet the demands in this area. There are several factors to consider when selecting an automated regression testing tool. The factors can be broken down into two major sections: Technical Considerations and Functional Considerations.

Technical Considerations

Technical considerations describe the characteristics of the project's technical environment that have an impact of the tool selection process. For example, if the client application runs on an OS/2 client, the testing tool market is quite limited. However, if the client application runs on Windows 95/98, the testing tool market is very good.

The specific technical considerations include the *client operating system*, *GUI application builder*, and *utilized emulation package*. The server operating system and relational database management system are also important technical considerations.

Before purchasing any testing tool, confirm that all of the functionality demonstrated by the vendor within their demonstration environments (e.g., PowerBuilder 5.0 on Windows 95 or Visual Basic 3.0 on Windows 95) works on all of the project specific technical environments (e.g., Power-Builder 4.0 on Windows/NT, Visual Basic 3.0 on Windows 95, etc.).

Functional Considerations

Test automation tools have many features and functions. A testing tool should be selected based upon how well these features meet the specific testing requirements. To determine these requirements, the test tool analyst must understand the full functional capabilities of these tools.

An automated testing tool basically performs the following functions: *test script development* and *test script execution.*

Test Script Development. There are three methods to develop an automated test script. The tester may either record a test script, program a test script, or automatically generate a test script. Typically, the technical architecture of the application under test will dictate which of these approaches will be used to develop the test automation. For example, with GUI applications, this decision will be based on the level of nonstandard GUI objects used by the application. If nonstandard, custom objects are used in the application, some level of test script programming will most likely be required.

Recording functionality has the following benefits:

- Most intuitive approach to developing an automated test script.
- Effective with application using standard object classes.
- For GUI-based applications, test synchronization is handled automatically (in most cases).
- Test result capture is very intuitive; the tester selects the objects to verify with point and click functionality.

Recording functionality has the following limitations at this time:

- The tester cannot record a test script until there is an executable for the application under test.
- A recorded test script is dependent upon the stability of the application under test.
- A recorded test script is dependent upon the degree the testing tool works with the GUI application builder.
- Recorded test scripts are typically harder to follow and maintain than programmed test scripts.
- For character-based applications, the tester must remember to insert synchronization points in the test script each time the screen changes in the planned test script.

Programming functionality has the following benefits:

- The tester can program a test script without the need for an executable of the application under test.
- A programmed test script is significantly more readable than a recorded test script.

Programming functionality has the following limitations at this time:

- A programmed test script is dependent upon the degree that the testing tool can be programmed to work with the GUI application builder.
- Programmed test scripts and test script functions must be designed, coded, and tested before they are executed in the actual development test stage. The design, code, and test specifications do not have to be as formal as in the typical development project. However, the effectiveness of these scripts during execution can be tied to the design, code, and test stages of the programmed test automation.

- Programming expected results is difficult with most automated testing tools. For most tools, the expectation is that expected results will be captured during the recording session. When the expected result is captured, other files are generated as part of the expected result structure. The expected result structure typically includes a file that defines the objects and the attributes of the objects that should be captured as part of the expected result. The second file in the structure is the captured expected results. For WinRunner and SQA Robot, to preprogram expected results, the tester must manually create the first file through a text editor. QA Partner is the only tool that allows the tester to program an expected result into a test script without having to develop any other constructs.

Automatic Script Generation has the following benefits:

- Relevant test scripts and test cases can be generated without tester intervention.
- The generated test scripts are useful to verify that future builds of the application do not adversely affect the GUI of the application.

Automatic Script Generation has the following limitations at this time:

- Automatic script generation can only be used to test the GUI of the application; it cannot be used to generate data-driven test cases (i.e., business function testing).
- Automatic script generation cannot be used to test cross-object validation, that is, it cannot create a test to check the affect that changing the contents of one object has on the attributes/status of another object.
- The test cases generated via the automatic script generation tool do not tie back to design requirements for the application. They are generated to test the application as coded rather than the application as designed.
- Automatic test script generation is very dependent upon the testing tool's ability to recognize and work with the object classes of the application under test. If an object class is supported by the tool, the tool will have functions to both act upon the object class and verify the contents and attributes of the object class. During test script generation, the tool will be able to work with these functions to develop specific test cases for the object. However, if an object class is not supported by the tool, the tool will not have these types of established functions. In this case, during test script generation, the tool will work with its "general object class" verification functions to develop test cases for these object classes. The "general object class" is used to classify nonstandard objects. The verification functions that work with this class are very generic. For more specific testing capabilities,

the tester must develop custom routines to verify the attributes of these nonstandard objects. These custom routines can be added to the test wizard and included in the automatic script generation.

Test Script Execution. The most prominent test script execution features include script execution control, batch test execution, test result verification, and reporting capabilities.

- *Script execution control.* Script execution control refers to the setting of all system parameters related to script execution. Examples of system parameters include playback speed, error recovery options, window/system timeouts, setting results directories.
- *Batch test execution.* Batch test execution allows the tester to execute a series of test scripts from a single test script in order to facilitate unattended test script execution and comprehensive test coverage.
- *Test result verification.* During the test preparation phase of a test stage, test conditions are allocated to test scripts. The test planner designs each respective test script to test these test conditions. During the test script design process, the test planner identifies and documents the system activities required to set up, test, and verify each of these test conditions. With test automation, all of these system activities are captured into the automated test script. The contents of the automated test script are further described in the "Components of the Automated Test Script" section of this document.

During the automated test execution process, the testing tool will automatically verify the current state of the system (i.e., actual results) against the expected state of the system (i.e., expected results) for each test case defined in the test script. Execution status will be reported through the reporting function of the toolset. As part of this script execution report, the status of each individual verification point (test case) will be reported. If a test case does not pass, the tool will capture the expected result, the actual result, and the difference between expected/actual results for the test case. If there is a difference between the actual and expected result for a test case and the expected result is correct, the tester adds a defect in the engagement's defect tracking tool. Alternatively, if there is a difference between the expected and actual results of a test case and the actual result is correct, the tester can replace the expected result for the test case with the actual result. This type of scenario occurs when a defect is reported against a particular test case and the incorrect result is captured by the testing tool as the test case's expected result. In this case, when the defect is fixed, the new test result will reflect the correct expected result for the test case.

- *Reporting Capabilities.* The stand-alone reporting capabilities of an automated testing tool are limited. These reports are designed solely to provide execution status for a test script or series of test scripts. Test management reporting functionality (i.e., test planning status, test execution status, defect lists, inventory of user requirements, inventory of test scripts, and inventory of test cases) is housed within the test management component of each respective toolset.

From the testing tool selection perspective, these capabilities have minimal impact on the overall selection decision. Test script execution functionality is fairly standard for the market-leading tools. The only real area of differentiation is in the reporting capabilities of the tools. For the most part, the reporting capabilities of an automated testing tool are limited. This functionality improves tremendously when the regression testing tool is used in conjunction with the vendor's test planning tool.

TEST DATA MANAGEMENT

Test data management can be seen as a link between test planning and test execution. During test planning, data are identified in terms of need; in test data management, the data are actually created and manipulated for test cycles preparation.

Test data management assists the developer in the creation of the test data and expected results in a medium such that it can be automatically used by test execution tools or loaded to the test environment. Test data management assists in switching between cycles, by refreshing the input data before running or rerunning a cycle. Test data management is composed of

- Test data manipulator (editing)
- Test data generator
- Extract and load facility
- Archive facility

Configuration Management

The main function of configuration management is to monitor and control the changes throughout the software development and maintenance process, including testing. It provides the following functionality:

- Version control of the software
- Version control of test model elements (test scripts and test data)
- Migration of sources from one development stage to the following one. (i.e., from coding to assembly test and from product test to production)
- Migration of test model elements

PROBLEM MANAGEMENT

Problem management logs issues and problems detected during the test process, to classify problems and to generate error reports. Problem management is essential for the capture of metrics information.

The major functions are

- SIR source and metrics information
- SIR resolution information
- Planning support for the SIR fixing and migration preparation
- Impact analysis capabilities, including
    Interface with the application design repository to get a precise impact analysis on a defect.
    Interface with the test plan management to keep track of the cycle where the problem occurred, the test condition and therefore the business function affected by the problem.

CODE ANALYSIS

Source Code Analysis tools contribute to software quality assurance for the project. The reports generated by these types of tools can be used by management to determine if the project's source code meets the entry criteria for their respective development or test stage. These reports can also be used to determine if the project's source code meets the exit criteria from the previous development stage.

Note that source code analysis tools measure the quality of the project's source code only; they do not measure whether or not the source code for a module matches the design for the module. This analysis must still be done manually through code reviews.

EXECUTING THE TEST

Test execution is the step to execute the scripts, verify results, document and resolve discrepancies, and regression test changes. Differences from traditional test execution arise from the complexity of the environments and configurations being tested and the use of automation.

Traditionally, test execution involved the repeated execution of cycle one (until clean), followed by the repeated execution of cycle two and so forth, until all cycles are complete. Using this approach, it is very difficult to assess progress during the execution stage. The time it took to achieve a clean run of cycle one may not be any indication of the issues which will be encountered in future cycles because they are testing different areas of the solution. Also, there is a risk that major issues are lurking in the later cycles, only to be discovered very late in the execution process.

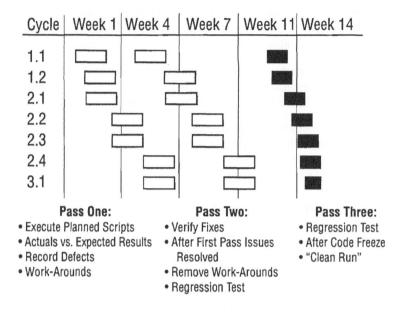

Cycle	Week 1	Week 4	Week 7	Week 11	Week 14
1.1	☐	☐		■	
1.2	☐	☐		■	
2.1	☐	☐		■	
2.2		☐	☐	■	
2.3		☐	☐	■	
2.4		☐	☐	■	
3.1		☐	☐	■	

Pass One:
- Execute Planned Scripts
- Actuals vs. Expected Results
- Record Defects
- Work-Arounds

Pass Two:
- Verify Fixes
- After First Pass Issues Resolved
- Remove Work-Arounds
- Regression Test

Pass Three:
- Regression Test
- After Code Freeze
- "Clean Run"

Exhibit 7. The Three-Pass Execution Plan.

More efficient test execution may be achieved through the technique of using multiple execution passes. In this approach, multiple passes of test cycle execution are planned. For example, the first pass would attempt to execute all cycles complete as possible, and identify all major defects. Data changes and detours may be used to complete a set of scripts, for example, a "best effort" execution pass. Then, after the defect fixes from the first pass are complete, the same scripts are executed a second time. In this pass, the purpose is to verify that the fixes were made correctly, to test that the fixes did not corrupt anything else, and to test those portions of the application that were not tested in the first pass due to defects or detours. Finally, a third and final execution pass is run to ensure all scripts execute successfully (Exhibit 7).

The three-pass approach to test execution allows one to identify problems with the solution as early as possible and helps give an indication of what the effort to complete the test will be. At the completion of the first pass, there is an understanding of the stability and quality of the application. The team can then make decisions for activities going forward.

For example, if the first pass uncovered a number of defects much larger than planned — defects that should have been uncovered by the component test — one might consider demoting portions of the application to be re-component-tested until the required level of stability is achieved. On the other hand, if the testing in the first pass reveals a number of defects aligned with the plans, the team can feel comfortable that the remainder of the schedule is reasonable.

For a typical product test, one should plan five execution passes. If the test is largely a regression test, or if the testing process is mature (e.g., high stage containment levels) then a three pass test may be planned.

Finally, during test execution, the goal should be to get ahead of schedule early to build schedule flexibility. No matter how well the test is planned and prepared, problems may arise. Then the team runs the risk of being at the end of the development project with no room to absorb delays.

NEW MANAGEMENT CHALLENGES

Sponsorship

Management must demonstrate a commitment to the application of the testing principles outlined in this chapter. The structure and rigor required to apply the V-Model testing approach require visible sponsorship from management for successful implementation.

Estimating

It is not safe to assume that the old estimating approaches for testing will still work. Most traditional approaches estimate testing activities as a percentage of development effort. When using the V-Model approach, consideration must be given to the early test planning, verification and validation activities, reusable test models, and automation. Testing effort is not necessarily correlated to development effort. A more appropriate estimating model takes into account:

- What will be tested in each stage
- The testing complexity of the units to be tested
- Whether an existing test model will be used

Determining what is to be tested in each stage is defined in the test strategy. Testing complexity of the units to be tested refers to the degree of difficulty involved in planning and executing a test; this is not necessarily the same as the complexity of the unit itself. An added piece of functionality may be very difficult to develop, but easy to test. On the other hand, a very simple code change may be a nightmare to test due to the dependencies required to execute the required test conditions. A current example of this is the application changes required to accommodate the year 2000. Very often, the actual code changes are isolated to a very small number of application units, but all calculation and printing applications must be tested as well as processing that spans the millennium change.

The use of an existing test model can significantly reduce the time required to plan and prepare a test. Time should be allocated to review and update the existing test model, but this will be significantly less than building the entire test from scratch. Also, tests and regression tests built on an existing (i.e., previously executed) test model usually encounter significantly fewer execution problems and therefore actually execute faster or in fewer execution passes.

Estimates for test stages therefore view the development and execution of the test model almost as a project unto itself. The estimates should look at the units to be tested, the process to complete the test, including the approach, plan, prepare and execute steps discussed earlier, and the assumptions for time required to complete each step. Estimates of work effort then need to take into account resource constraints and dependencies to be translated into the actual work plan, thus giving the schedule.

Problem Management

Effective problem management is essential to facilitate test execution and to manage scope and progress. Problems should be identified and as errors, defects or change requests, or rejected. Problems should then be resolved in accordance with defined procedures.

The first set of activities is problem identification, classification, and analysis. As each problem is identified through a review or test, it should be logged and classified as an error, defect or change request. It is essential to collect data on the numbers and types of problems for problem resolution and continuous process improvement.

Developers should monitor problem data throughout the test to identify opportunities for improvements. For example, there may be an inordinate amount of defects of a particular type which would lead to improvement in standards or training for the development teams.

Once the problem is documented and classified, it should be analyzed to determine the severity, priority, impact, and potential resolution. At this point the problem can then be approved, rejected, or deferred. The approval process should tightly control what changes are being made to the system. It is not necessarily optimal to fix all defects. Approved problems, and only approved problems, can then be addressed by the development teams responsible for fixes. Once the problem has been further analyzed and the fix has been designed, implemented, and regression tested, the problem is closed.

In addition to problem management procedures, it is important to identify escalation procedures: how will conflicts be resolved? Define who has the authority to approve design changes, change requests, migration of updates, and so forth. It is essential to have tight version control on the source code, data and test models, and this control becomes more restricted during the final stages of testing. Clearly identify what type of decisions should be escalated, and what the process is for doing so. For example, teams can document issues to management in weekly status reports or conduct daily issues meetings with management.

Quality Management

Management is responsible for tracking and monitoring metrics (e.g., stage containment and rework metrics) and ensuring that action is taken when the metrics data is at variance from plans.

Ideally, the original project plans established quality goals and the number of unresolved problems by type and severity that are allowed to be open at completion/conversion. These goals should then drive decisions made within the testing stage as to which defects are to be fixes rather than deferred and when testing can be considered complete.

It is recommended that a complete analysis of problem data is executed following each project to identify major process changes. This is often referred to as "post-mortem" analysis of the project, identifying both what went well and where there are opportunities for improvement. These sessions can be extremely successful if conducted in a timely and objective manner.

Organizational Challenges

The V-Model testing approach will likely result in new roles and responsibilities within the organization. Specific roles now exist for test designers (i.e., planning and preparation), test execution, and test management. In addition, testing related activities such as definition of test conditions and communication of changes may change the roles and responsibilities of analysts, architects, fixers, technical support, and users. It is important to review the testing objectives and the approach outlined for the organization and identify the roles and responsibilities each person has.

An example of a typical pyramid for testing organization would include

- An overall test director
- A test manager for each major testing effort
- Several (three to five) senior test architects for the test; one for each major piece of functionality being testing
- Several (three to six) test developers per senior test architect for test planning

For test execution, management should either add test executors to the test developer pool or have the application developers execute the test scripts as prepared, monitored by the senior test architects.

A general rule of thumb is that the test execution effort is roughly on par with the fix effort. For example, if there are nine test executors, there should be nine fixers for the duration of the test. Keep in mind that the test teams are the organization's test experts. Training on the V-Model approach will be required, as will training on the tools and the testing process.

THE NEXT LEVEL

Measure for Success

Effective metrics are essential to managing and improving the testing process. Applied metrics during the testing process provides the capability to improve management, productivity, and quality. Managers should

- *Manage with facts.* Metrics provide objective data upon which decisions can be made, actions taken, and goals achieved. When a team can know, for example, the average time it takes to fix a problem (Problem Fix Rate), they can track the number of problems found during inspection and can calculate the fix time savings realized. This helps reinforce the importance of completing timely and thorough inspections.
- *Focus on the problem, not the symptom.* Metrics lead to greater understanding of the underlying problem. For example, one company repeatedly experienced very high defect levels during the later testing stages, in spite of numerous adjustments to their development process. It was not until they began to measure and analyze their processes that they realized that the vast majority of the defects encountered were being caused by the fix process, not the development process. They were trying to solve the wrong problem.
- *Facilitate predictability.* If appropriate metrics are used and collected accurately and consistently, one can predict the quality and productivity of the remaining work, next stage, next release, and so forth. Process metrics and product quality metrics allow a team to reduce the number of unknowns in the development and testing process, thereby reducing the risk associated with successful completion.
- *Facilitate continuous improvement.* Throughout the process, one can review and analyze the metrics, identify discrepancies from plans, determine the reasons for the discrepancies, and improve the process or the estimating guidelines. This should be a continuous process. An organization can learn from previous mistakes and benefit by eliminating the recurrence of those difficulties. Improvement can occur from stage to stage, release to release, and project to project.

As discussed in Section II, metrics are most effective when used to manage a process, and they are only worthwhile if specific actions will be taken based on measurements in question. The metrics discussed here were developed to support the following three goals:

1. Improve management of the test process
2. Improve the quality of the test process
3. Further refine and improve the quality of the process and the product

Goal 1: Improve Management of the Test Process

To manage the entire test process more efficiently, organizations must start with a set of fundamental metrics: measurements of the process, which allow the team to understand and control that process.

These metrics are

- Test planning rate: hours per test condition
- Test preparation rate: hours per test cycle scripted
- Test execution rate: hours per test cycle executed
- Incoming problem rate: problems detected per hour of execution
- Problem fix rate: problems fixed per elapsed hour

These metrics provide a means for determining the earned testing progress and value, the amount of testing remaining, and when testing will be complete. In addition, they can justify the purchase of tools and the implementation of process improvements. Finally, these fundamental metrics also include actual productivity rates, which should be used to revise estimating guidelines. They will help management make decisions on scheduling issues, and help the estimation and scheduling for subsequent releases.

Goal 2: Improve the Quality of the Test Process

Another set of metrics allow greater understanding of a process and provide a basis for improvement of the process. The metrics associated with the second goal must provide information about the development and testing process at a level of detail to allow appropriate action to be taken. Specifically, these metrics are

- Stage containment by stage: errors or errors plus defects
- Defect repair effectiveness: percentage of defects fixed correctly the first time

Industry studies indicate that defect repair processes are successful only 50% of the time, and many repair efforts simply caused additional errors. This means that, every time a development team submits a defect for correction, there is as much chance of not fixing the defect or introducing another defect as there is of actually fixing the reported defect. This 50% failure rate is an often overlooked opportunity for process improvement.

When an organization discovers high defect rates in software, it often assumes that the problems were caused during the development process. Further investigation often reveals, however, that a significant portion of the defects are actually caused by the fix processes themselves. For example, upon analysis of the defects uncovered by the first pass of product test, one organization realized that although they had detected nearly 200 defects, over 150 of the problems were caused by the fix process. As problems were submitted for analysis and fix, they were often returned incomplete or the fixes caused other defects. Improvements to the fix process resulted in significant time and cost savings in the future development and testing stages.

Goal 3: Further Refine and Improve the Process and Product Quality

Finally, the last goal focuses on metrics that can be used to fine tune the process. They will help determine why problems are occurring by calling attention to error-prone or complex modules. These metrics are

- Inspection effectiveness: problems found per hour of inspection
- Problems per module: errors and defects and faults per module

In addition, several industry standard metrics exist to measure the complexity and, thus, the testability and maintainability of designs and code. These are

- Zage design metric:
  (Modules called × calls of module) + (data in × data out)
- McCabe Cyclomatic Complexity: Edges − nodes + 2

By identifying portions of the solution that are highly complex, these metrics can be used to support a decision to allocate additional resources or to redesign those areas. Either way, a risk area has been identified and addressed in the project plans.

Design for Testability

The V-Model concepts can be extrapolated to improve not only the testing of the solution but the design and the product itself, making the product more maintainable and thus more flexible. Several key drivers for testability include fault tolerance, controls, error handling, multiple operating modes, and self-testing applications.

- *Fault tolerance.* Developers design the systems such that errors can be recovered from, or at least logged without interrupting processing. For example, they should not allow the system to crash upon encountering corrupt data; instead, they should correct or log the data and move on. This not only makes it easier to test but allows the system to perform better in production. In addition, people certainly would prefer not getting a call in the middle of the night because the production run abended, but instead getting an error report first thing in the morning.

- *Controls.* Developers should put design counts and cross checks into the systems to identify problems and inconsistencies early. (See the chapter on controls in Section III.)

- *Error handling.* Developers should implement functionality for the systems to identify errors and, upon identification of an error, log all relevant data and attempt to correct the error, such as by searching for a similar error and its associated corrective action. At a minimum, they should open a problem record and notify the appropriate parties, perhaps by e-mail or paging.

- *Test vs. production mode.* Developers should design the system so it contains a test and production mode. In test mode, control data may be logged, dates may be taken from a file rather than from the processor (to enable aging or year-end process testing), generated fields may be altered, and so forth. All this facilitates testing.

- *Self-testing applications.* Developers should embed validation of entry criteria and/or test conditions into the system at the application or object level. This allows the application or object to verify inputs before attempting to process and to report inconsistencies in expected inputs vs. actual.

SUMMARY

Implementation of the V-Model approach to testing not only produces significant improvements in the typical testing process and results, but also positions an organization to continuously improve its testing capability. Repeated, measured processes can easily be analyzed to identify opportunities for improvement, thus initiating a never-ending cycle of plan-do-measure-improve.

The testing process detailed in this chapter has been used by Information Systems organizations over the last several years to achieve significant benefits. The V-Model framework is now being applied in a netcentric environment. Teams have realized as much as a 50% reduction in the effort required to test new applications, up to an 80% reduction in the effort required to regression test applications for changes and enhancements, and a 50% reduction in rework due to poor verification, validation, and testing in the first place. Organizations now use information gathered during the testing activities to analyze and improve the systems development processes, which, in turn, can lead to further improvements in productivity and quality.

Chapter 25
Site Preparation and Installation

Site preparation and installation may not be topics that spring immediately to mind as primary components of netcentric and client/server computing. However, the preparation and installation of the physical sites are, in fact, vital considerations in today's computing environments. For the sake of simplicity, this chapter will use the term "client/server," although the lessons are also applicable to netcentric implementations.

SITE PREPARATION: AN ISSUE NOT TO BE OVERLOOKED, OR UNDERESTIMATED

Consider, for example, one site that was implementing an insurance application. The client/server technology was to be installed in a single large campus that had already been extensively upgraded over time and had terminals spread throughout the campus. Going in, the organization's view was that the technology would only require some renetworking for the specifics of the network protocol; other than that, management believed no additional major effort was required.

During the initial installation of the applications, however, the organization realized that the desks for the business users were not set up for the use of workstations. If the base processor of the workstation was put on the desktop it took up too much room. Those people who put their processors beside their desks found that people were bumping into them. Eventually, new office furniture had to be purchased and the office layout had to be changed to accommodate the machines. This added time and expense to the project.

Perhaps more important, the business users were left with the impression that the systems people had not thought through all the issues of using the system and had not considered the users' needs, when an insensitivity to the user was precisely what the new system was supposed to be overcoming.

At another site, new applications were being developed as part of an enterprisewide reengineering effort. Part of this effort involved moving certain critical customer service activities to a newly built campus.

The developers used a program management effort to manage the overall implementation. It became apparent from the program management effort that the critical path was not applications development. Rather, it was the time needed to build the campus. The lead times for the system construction and for the site were off by several years. In this case, the organization decided to deliver the applications to the existing physical sites and then move to the new campus over time.

In a third case, an organization was preparing to roll out client/server applications to more than 500 sites. Some of the sites were buildings that were 50 to 100 years old, and that presented some real problems. For example, how does an organization run local area network (LAN) wiring when the walls are made of mud and stones? In this case, upgrading the sites for client/server technology was the single largest-cost line item and was often on the critical path for delivery of the applications.

Although none of these examples illustrates a technology issue, the problems all certainly result from the technology. Perhaps more important, these problems can threaten success as much as an unreliable workstation or a database management system with bugs. This chapter looks at some of the risks associated with client/server implementation and some strategies that can control those risks.

Breaking the Job Down into Three Parts

The previous examples are indicative of the problems an organization can encounter in the rollout of a client/server application. Often, computing and communications technologies are being introduced into an almost alien environment. Succeeding in such an environment requires planning and structured execution.

Systems management can break down the site preparation and installation effort into three parts:

1. Understanding what is at the sites now
2. Deciding what needs to be done to upgrade the sites for the installation of the technology and the applications
3. Implementing the required changes

If the appropriate technology is already in place and being used, additional effort is minimal. If, on the other hand, there is little or no technology, the site preparation and installation effort can be time-consuming and demanding.

A FRAMEWORK FOR SITE PREPARATION AND INSTALLATION

At the highest level, site preparation and installation consists of three major phases:

- *Site survey.* In the site survey phase, the project team evaluates the site for its readiness to accept and work with the client/server application. The team focuses the evaluation primarily on the readiness of the physical site rather than on the personnel. The change management effort should address personnel readiness, which is discussed in Chapter 17. Site survey addresses a wide range of concerns from office layout to electricity to air conditioning. From this evaluation comes a plan to make the required changes to the site.
- *Site preparation.* Site preparation is the physical process of preparing the site for the installation of client/server technology. In this phase it is not uncommon to see electricians and carpenters on site making required changes so that the site can be made ready for the implementation.
- *Site implementation.* In the site implementation phase, developers install the required software and deliver the procedures to the site so that it is ready to begin running the application. It is the final activity before going live with the applications in the rollout of the applications.

A set of common considerations apply across all phases of site preparation and installation. These considerations include the following

- Use of contractors
- Setting up contracts and plans
- Use of checklists

The expertise required to succeed at the three phases of site survey, preparation, and installation goes well beyond the training and experience of even the best information systems (IS) personnel. It would be rare to find an IS manager who is qualified to review the work of an electrician to determine whether it meets local building regulations and vendor power requirements.

Because of the unique knowledge demands here, it is common in doing site preparation to use contractors to do much or all of the work. However, who decides how much of the work goes to outside contractors and who manages the work these contractors perform so that it meets required levels of quality and timeliness? Different choices are appropriate in different circumstances, but the options must be thought through and resolved early on.

In general, the enterprise should be actively involved in the site survey and then should place more responsibility on outside contractors for site preparation activities. Project personnel may then assume more responsibility for the site implementation.

The discussion that follows presumes that outside contracting is a key component of the site preparation activity. Most designers are not experts in carpentry, architecture, building codes, air conditioning and electricity. Experience shows that most sites choose to use contractors for this work.

Contractors

Coordinating the work of contractors can be a major concern. If an organization is implementing client/server applications at hundreds or thousands of sites, such as occurs with food franchise operations, the sheer problem of managing all that effort may make a general contractor an important part of delivering a quality solution.

If there are multiple sites or sites spread out geographically, the multiple parallel efforts can be coordinated through a general contractor. The organization then has a single point of contact to coordinate, plan the work, evaluate status, react to problems, and ensure that adequate quality is delivered.

However, how does the organization ensure that the work being done by outside contractors meets expectations in terms of timeliness, quality, and cost?

Occasionally, organizations view these issues only as the contractor's problem. This is a dangerous point of view. Having someone to blame does not fix the problem. At one site an organization found that its fuses would blow any time more than eight workstations were turned on. The users did not see this as a contractor problem; it was a system problem.

Although the contractor may be ultimately responsible, the key to contractor success is oversight of the implementation process by the organization. The most effective procedure is to use contracts with contractors, agreeing beforehand on work to be done, work plans, time lines, checklists, and sign-offs.

Contracts and Plans

The workplans that the contractor submits must be integrated with the overall program plan to implement the systems. In some cases a rollout plan had to be revised based on the ability of various contractors to get the work done. A rollout driven by the speed and skill of carpenters is often not in accord with system objectives. The contractor must be a part of the overall program management team, reporting and coordinating on work done against plan.

Contracts are essential because they define what work is to be done and who is responsible. For example, if carpenters are moving around the site and drop a two-by-four on a customer's foot, the contract should have made it clear who is responsible. The contract should describe the typical things found in building contracts, such as steps in the escalation process. It should identify the basis for payments and the process for settling questions in payments.

The objective of the contract is not to provide an easy way to shift the blame to a contractor. The contract is to define what is expected of each party in terms of specific deliverables, dates, and quality. It is a mechanism to ensure that communication and understanding have been achieved.

If at some point in the difficult process of defining contracts, management finds itself thinking that it has slipped something past the contractor, all it has done is bring greater risk to the project. Such practices are inherently questionable.

So that the organization can track work status, some form of deliverable must be provided to note that the work was done and that it meets quality and cost expectations. In one instance, because the work to be done was to install wiring and air conditioning, the organization assumed that it would be apparent when the work had been done simply by looking at it.

That approach might work at a limited installation, but, as the number of sites and their distribution increases, the use of "look and see" proves increasingly impractical. Further, if things do not go well and litigation becomes a concern, problems must be documented. The ongoing collection of proof of milestones achieved can be a key aspect of maintaining control of an effort.

Checklists

The proof collected can follow several different formats. One format is the checklist. A checklist defines the steps to be completed and the results of the work for each stage of work at each site.

The contractor is expected to provide the checklists as proof of work steps completed and as a condition for payment. Typically, the checklist has sign-offs both for the contractor and for someone at the site who can verify that the work was done.

Also, if there are documents such as local building inspections to be completed, these are a part of the sign-off package. If the work has met specific quality requirements, such as power supply quality, the sign-off checklist may include an independent evaluation of the work.

The checklists themselves can vary in detail but must be detailed enough to give assurance that the work was done and that it meets expectations. For example, if partitions are to be installed, steps might include the following:

1. A date is set for review of the site to evaluate building impact and the needs to conform to any building code requirements.
2. The review is held and a contractor's report is submitted to describe the work to be done.
3. The work is agreed to and the date for the work to be done is agreed to with the local site and with program management.
4. The work is done and signed off by the local site and, perhaps, by a local civil engineer.

Checklists such as this can vary widely in scope and detail, but at the least they set forth the broad set of steps and provide a means to determine that agreed-to work has been done.

Finally, although the following discussion will treat the site preparation and installation phases as three discrete phases, in reality the phases usually overlap. Site surveys occur at some sites while site preparation and implementation are occurring at others. This overlap is usually unavoidable if the job is to get done on an acceptable time frame.

However, the parallel activities imply a significant additional work load to manage and coordinate the ongoing work. Particularly important is the need to ensure that if one phase is encountering problems that could be addressed by a prior phase, this is captured and used to improve the work being done.

Using the previous discussion as a broad framework, the next sections provide more detail on work to be done within each major phase.

SITE SURVEY

A big part of the first phase, site survey, is considering the impact that the implementation has on business users. The change management process should have been started well in advance of this activity. Ideally, business users should already be aware of, and knowledgeable about, the system and its impact on their work. (For some organizations, unfortunately, not enough advance preparation is done, and users may be simply unprepared or avoiding the changeover.)

The beginning of site survey may be the moment when the user has to come out of "denial" and face the fact that this change really is going to take place. As a result, the initial visits should be handled with some sensitivity to the local business users' concerns. By implication, these initial visits are likely to be more successful if done with participation of personnel from the project team.

The initial visit often involves a presentation of what the system is about and reminds users of what they have seen about the system up to now. Because the business user should have seen this information through the change management effort, much of the focus is on what the site implementation is about.

Generally, the point of these discussions is not to go over function or system concerns (although listening to concerns is always a good idea). The main point is to demonstrate that the systems development effort is proceeding and that, as a result, work needs to start at the local site to get it ready.

Also, the presentation should be honest about the fact that some of the site preparation work may occasionally be disruptive to the daily work of the business and its people. Obviously, the project management should explain that all efforts will be made to minimize disruption. However, the fact remains that a carpenter hammering a nail makes a lot of noise and people are going to hear it.

Ongoing communication to business users is vital to ensuring the success of implementation. In some cases organizations have actually tried to disguise development, thinking that would minimize disruption to the business user. At the site survey phase, that strategy always hits the rocks. As workers begin to move through the work space taking measurements, people who were not told about the new system often come to the conclusion that they were considered insignificant parts of the process. That perception makes the already difficult task of site implementation even more difficult.

Unions must also be carefully considered. Unless long-term and ongoing involvement with unions is coordinated, misunderstandings and problems can arise. If the unions are allowed to understand what the system is about and the reasons for going forward, they can be an organizing force to move the effort forward. Without their involvement, problems can arise at site preparation.

A consideration with unions is that they may have cooperative arrangements with other unions; if one goes out on strike others may follow. Given that many of the construction trades are unionized, cooperative actions can shut down the entire implementation effort. Once again, the key point is that relentless and open communication can address the concerns of people and unions. Moreover, such communication must begin well in advance of site preparation.

The Initial Site Visit

The goals of the initial site visit are (1) to understand what is already in place and (2) to define what needs to be done to ready the site for implementation. To this end, the project team should address several issues.

Overall Office Layout and Floor Plan. Usually, offices are selected and laid out to support the work of the current business process. Because client/server goes hand in hand with process reengineering, the office layout must be reconsidered in light of the new business process.

Office Furniture. Client/server introduces technology directly where the worker works. This means that designers should evaluate the type and style of work furniture to see whether it will work with the technology. Anyone who has used a workstation at a desk not designed for typing on a keyboard knows how uncomfortable it can become.

Also, designers should check for lighting in the office, not only electric illumination but also the natural lighting. A computer display in direct sunlight can be unreadable. It is better to anticipate that problem before the first day of conversion. In general, designers must realize that the organization's existing office furniture may or may not work with the new technology. The initial site visit is the time to begin considering this issue.

Hardware Placement. The placement of new hardware such as servers and printers needs to be thought through. This may mean looking at office layout to see where servers and printers might be placed. Work group printers can generate considerable noise and traffic and so should not be placed too close to peoples' desks. The servers may have specific electrical and air-conditioning requirements, so the office needs to be evaluated on that basis. Also, servers can be very expensive and may hold important information. Their physical security needs to be addressed.

Electrical Requirements. Contractors need to address the various questions relating to electrical infrastructure. One important question concerns the ability of the office power supply to meet demands of the application. For example, does the area have a history of brownouts in the warm months? The need for uninterrupted power supply should be considered.

If a good deal of new technology is being introduced, the designer may need to extend or increase the number of electrical outlets. Running a series of extension plugs from a common outlet may bring a visit from the fire inspector, if not the fire department.

If the new process requires a new office layout and this is going to be achieved with partitions, how will the electricity be delivered to the partitions? Many partitions allow one to run power wires through the partition but above the floor. Contractors should check that the local authorities do not view such wiring as a fire hazard. It may be worthwhile to determine whether they have preferred partitions.

Air Conditioning. Client/server technology can introduce a good deal of heat into the local office environment. In addition, as processors increase in speed they often run hotter to deliver higher clock speeds. Because of this, designers may have to consider more air conditioning to keep the site within acceptable temperature ranges — both for the people and for the hardware. Additional servers may require specific cooling to meet their needs, which may in turn require a separate room and separate air conditioning for the servers.

Air Quality. The air itself is also a consideration. In one case, an organization introduced client/server to a site that made a chemical that was a fine black dust called carbon black; another site was a fast-food restaurant where a good deal of flour dust hung in the air. Both of these situations created problems for the computer disk drives. Keeping the air clean may be an important consideration for some sites, especially those near manufacturing or mining sites, or in parts of the country that are naturally dusty. In any case, it is better to have asked the question than to be surprised.

Communications Technology. Here, designers must evaluate how well the site is prepared for supporting the demands of client/server communications, both LANs and wide area networks (WANs).

With regard to the LAN, the designer must decide what the site currently has and what must be done to upgrade the site to meet the new communication needs. If the site already has LAN technology, designers might assume that the current wiring can be used for the new initiative. This assumption can be incorrect at the physical level if the wrong type of wiring is in place. It may be incorrect at the technical level if the wrong type of software or network servers are used. It may also be wrong if a check on LAN reliability suggests that it will not meet the demands of the application. The main point here is that the designer should not assume that the installed LANs will meet the future needs.

The physical structure of the new site also poses some challenges for new LAN technology. Simply running the wire is a well-known problem, but there may be other concerns. In one case LANs were run near elevators that had large magnets, which caused intermittent interruptions. In another case, the LANs were run near an oven and the heating caused problems. Designers must evaluate the local office for its fitness for the LAN technology.

A previous example noted the case of the nineteenth-century building that was not well suited for LAN technology. The general environment of the office should be considered for activities that could affect the use of LAN technology. High-energy radio frequencies, for example, may cause problems for an inexpensive LAN installation.

Finally, the running of the physical wiring for the LANs may be affected by local building codes. In some situations the LAN technology may be viewed as open wiring and local regulations could alter how the LANs are built.

WAN technology presents it own concerns. For example, many requirements may be negotiated once for the project as a whole. Often, there is a need to negotiate by site for specific needs. Looking at the overall planning framework discussed in Chapter 15, site evaluation begins after the systems design effort has begun. One reason for this is that the organization should have some clear notion of what is required for WAN communication speeds and reliability. This information should be available to the site evaluation team. The site evaluation team will use it to assess what is in place and to begin discussions with the local telecommunications providers at the site concerning what is needed and when it will be needed.

Lead times for delivery of changing technology vary by region. Lead times can be very short in the United States but may be longer in other areas around the world. Also, requests for exceptional services, such as a dedicated international line or very high line speeds, can add significantly to delivery lead times. The site evaluation team should consider supplying redundant lines and should review with the local telecommunication provider any special considerations regarding availability. As a part of the discussion, the team should obtain commitments on dates for availability for testing.

When dealing with international telecommunications, legal counsel may be needed to provide guidance about the movement of information across borders or about interfacing different telecommunications providers. This should be done prior to site evaluation, and any appropriate documentation should be available for the site visits.

Site Security. A client/server implementation introduces thousands of dollars — if not hundreds of thousands of dollars — of computing equipment. Can the site be secured against physical theft? The machines provide access to the corporate data assets. Can the site be physically and logically secured to restrict access only to those entitled to it during business hours? At one site 50 workstations were installed on a Friday for a Monday application implementation. On Monday morning eight of the workstations had disappeared.

In high-security situations developers may even need to consider the risk of access to information on display screens. Do windows or open partitions risk letting the wrong people see information?

Current Hardware. The hardware currently at the site poses unique challenges. Sometimes information systems (IS) personnel are surprised to find a good deal of computing and network hardware installed at a site. In addition, they often underestimate the level of development found at the site. It is usually not a good idea to assume that whatever is installed at the site can simply be disregarded or thrown away. Often the local user may have invested a good deal of time and money in that hardware.

The hardware and software may also represent a commitment by the local office manager; that manager feels ownership of the installed systems. In this situation the site evaluation team needs to show real interest and concern for what is installed. Inevitably, business users are concerned that the new system will result in a loss of capabilities. The IS people must remember that although the new system may be better, the loss of the old system is still that — a loss — to the users.

Usually, the site survey is not the time to conclude what to do with the installed systems. It is the time to understand what is there and how it is being used. As the site survey team prepares the site installation plans, team members should conclude what is to be done with the installed systems.

General Environment of the Site. It is always worthwhile to stand inside the building and simply look out the window of the site, then walk around the exterior of the site, and then consider the following questions: If large trucks are rolling in and out of nearby buildings, can personnel feel vibrations that might affect the machines to be installed? Is there a manufacturing plant nearby emitting smoke into the air? Air pollution can affect reliability of the machines. Is the neighborhood at risk for theft or vandalism to the hardware investment? What will be the reaction of suppliers when they are asked to make deliveries to the site? If the site has a history of minor earthquakes, what tolerance does the site have for what level of quake?

When wrapping up the initial site visit, it is worthwhile to schedule a closing visit with the local site manager who is responsible for physical property. Discussing the results and next steps is part of the communication effort within change management.

Furthermore, developers may want to consider a brief presentation with site personnel to thank them for their help and to let them know about future visits. A brief discussion of major observations can give local site personnel a sense of involvement. For example, a statement that "clearly something must be done to improve air quality" suggests that the developer has been observant and intends to take action. At the same time, the organization must recognize that specific conclusions about what is to be done may be subject to change.

Site Assessment Report

When returning from such a visit, the developer should immediately prepare an assessment of what needs to be done at that site. The immediate assessment is a pragmatic suggestion. After several site visits, it is easy to forget which office already had open layouts and which did not. Developers should write down everything about the site that they may need any time in the future. Memories fade quickly, especially after many different site visits. From the assessment, designers can develop a site preparation plan giving time frames for when the work needs to be done at the site.

Site Feasibility. A first point to consider is the feasibility of the site. Any of the previous considerations can be a basis for deciding that the site is not viable and a new site must be found.

For example, the application may require an open office layout so that work and communications can flow from one person to another, with verbal communications occurring across the desk. If the local site is an older building with closed offices, tearing out the walls may not be practical from a cost or structural standpoint. In this case the effort may shift to finding a new site for the application. That in turn brings up serious change management considerations for the organization.

If the office is feasible, developers should prepare a detailed definition of the work to be done. What does the office layout look like? Where will servers be put? Are air-conditioning or air purification systems needed? What is needed from a power supply standpoint? What needs to be done to provide physical security?

Site-by-Site Reporting. These and related considerations need to be pulled together on a site-by-site basis, indicating what must be done at each site. In addition, based on application needs, developers need to set the date for final site readiness. From this date, developers can establish a site preparation plan to ensure that the work defined in the site assessment is done on a timely basis.

Tracking Costs and Time Tables. The site preparation plan, by site, should then be registered with the program management team. They, in turn, will begin to track the progress of the site preparation plan in terms of results, quality, cost, and timeliness.

The site assessment and site preparation plan are provided to contractors who will work during the site preparation phase. Prior to this plan, contractual negotiations must take place to make clear what is to be done, at what cost, and in what time frames. Progress through these steps depends on project specifics. If a general contractor is a part of this effort, he or she should be involved in developing the plan.

In some cases, the general contractor agrees to a contract that gives certain standard costs and time frames to upgrade a site. Given that the costs and time estimates were made prior to knowing the specifics of the work to be done, contractors may have misestimated the required effort. If there has been a significant underestimate, the general contractor should expect to hear about it. (The possibility of overestimating the effort exists, but it is unlikely anyone will hear about that.)

If the general contractor views a cost overrun, as many do, simply as a contractor problem, the general contractor may inadvertently be responsible for lowering the quality of the project, as the contractor is forced to cut costs. At another extreme, the general contractor may only succeed in bankrupting the contractor, which puts the entire project in jeopardy. The point is to listen to the contractor to understand concerns about misestimating the costs and try to work constructively to solve the problems.

If no such prior contract exists, the general contractor will work with contractors at each site going through the assessment and the site preparation plan as a basis to arrange work to be done. The contractors need specifics on what is needed and when. In most cases, they have participated in the initial assessment, so they can often provide a reasonable estimate of work to be done and the costs.

If no general contractor has been used, a site preparation team must perform a negotiation process on a site-by-site basis. This process can be time-consuming. Furthermore, success may be a matter of luck if the general contractor does not know the local contractors on a site-by-site basis.

In this approach it is essential that a complete plan be maintained on a site-by-site basis as to what things are to be done and when. As the site preparation proceeds for a large rollout — hundreds of sites, for example — it may be extremely time consuming to track results in terms of work done, its quality, its timeliness, and its cost. This is not a task to be left to two clerical people who view the job merely as sending out and receiving forms.

As the site preparation team puts together the site assessment and establishes the site preparation plan, it is worthwhile to share this information with local site managers. There are several reasons to do so:

1. So that site managers can see that progress was made based on their cooperation and assistance.
2. To communicate what is planned so that site managers can understand it and also share it with the local personnel.
3. So that site managers can review the plan to assess its impact and to approve the changes from the standpoint of reasonableness. The site preparation team should ask for some sort of written confirmation of the work.

The site preparation team should also share plans for the installed hardware and software with site managers. This can be a very sensitive issue and may take some care. Team members need to clearly communicate the plans; at the same time, they need to communicate a recognition of the good work done. In addition, they must communicate how the implementation of the new systems and the changes anticipated may affect users.

Keeping Plans and Documents Current. The site assessment, the site preparation plan, and all contracts for doing the work should come under strict configuration management as a part of program management. Changes to the plan should require approval by all concerned parties. At a minimum this includes the site preparation team and the contractors doing the changed work.

In addition, the site preparation team should keep assessment documents current. If something occurs at a local site, this should be reflected in the site assessment and, possibly, in the plan. In one case a site was disrupted due to a riot. The site assessment and implementation plan became moot at that point, as effort turned to the bigger task of selecting a new site.

Communicating Back. As the assessments and plans are pulled together, the information should be communicated back to the local office manager. In addition to its general value as a communication initiative, site preparation teams also want local office managers to be thinking about how the local office will work during the implementation phase.

For example, if installing LAN and WAN technology will disrupt phone service, the local office manager needs to begin to think about impact. The manager may reasonably expect some guidance from the site preparation team about what to worry about and how to address it.

Given the amount of work all these issues suggest, an organization might wonder if all offices or sites need to be evaluated. Generally, site management should be forced to prove that an office should *not* be evaluated. In some cases, such as franchise operations, it may well be that most sites correspond to a limited number of configurations. However, there may still be site-specific items that are difficult to be sure of without inspection. For example, proximity to a plant making carbon black is difficult to predict.

One of the values of the site visit is to bring home the idea that the system is going to happen and that people need to begin thinking about it. The visit gives the site personnel a chance to feel a part of the process rather than someone to whom the process is happening.

It also gives system developers the opportunity to see what people on the "other side" of the system are thinking. This can build goodwill that is valuable during the difficult conversion stage. In short, the value of a site visit is so great that skipping it should only occur after great consideration and careful thought.

SITE PREPARATION

The site preparation phase begins as contracts are completed based on the site preparation plan. Contractors are lined up and the sites begin upgrades for the applications.

In the site preparation phase, the work to upgrade every site is done. Three items are key to this effort:

- The site preparation plan, which defines what is to be done
- The site preparation contract, which defines who is do what, the levels of quality, and the costs
- The ongoing use of checklists, which assess that work has been done at expected levels of quality

Checklists and Schedules

The three items just noted assume that contractors will do the work. Thus, much of the effort is to ensure that work begins and ends on schedule. Toward that end, checklists are vital.

The dates when the checklists are to be completed and delivered are also key to managing the overall effort. They can ensure that the work to be done is completed as expected in a consistent manner across sites. Although such checklists tend to depend on site specifics, a few general points can be made about what should be included. These include the following.

First Contact by Project Team. Whenever work is to start on a major segment of work — such as redoing electrical supplies or installing new air conditioning — the site preparation team should make the first contact. This contact should occur ahead of when the work is to be done. Often the contact can be made over the phone to explain the work and when it is to start and to identify the contractors who will be doing the work. There are several reasons for this contact. The key reason is that the project team may be sensitive to the impact the project will have on the site when the contractor begins to move desks around. The initial project team contact can show this sensitivity and concern. Also, although the local office manager should be aware of what is going to happen, he or she may not have actually considered the impact of that work on the day-to-day operations of the business. The completion of this contact, and any results or follow-up, should be recorded as a first step in any checklist. This ensures that all ensuing work is done with the full knowledge of the people at the site.

Aggressive Communications. During this initial contact, the site preparation team can go over the changes to be made and suggest ways to get ready for the work. Personnel should be advised of the work that is to be done and how work will continue in the office. A briefing package for the local office manager may be helpful to explain the work to be done. Finally, even with the best configuration management, changes slip through and this is the opportunity to identify such changes. In one case, the local office manager went out and bought computers and LAN technology and got them running at the site over the weekends. He did so with the best intention — to decrease the effort to get the site ready. Unfortunately, much of the software was not compatible and additional work had to be done to change things at the site.

Setting Up the Checklists

The checklists typically are organized by major work segment and by contractor. Thus there may be a checklist of work to be done for the electrical work and another for the contractor. Most checklists adhere to the following broad outline:

- *Verify with the local site manager the work to be done and when it is to start.* Generally, a contractor should not turn up at a site without having been introduced by the project team.
- *Identify and itemize deliverables from work and the criteria by which the work is to be accepted.* Some construction work may require approval by local authorities such as building inspectors. It may also include criteria specific for the project. For example, a building inspector may approve the wiring done by a local contractor. However, the project team may mandate an additional review to ensure that the electrical supply is of adequate quality. Both these checks may be required for approval of the work.
- *Sign-off and verify the work.* The types of approvals noted previously need to be formally signed off by the appropriate authority. The local office manager needs to be involved in the process and sign-off on the work done is one way to do this. Contractors need to be sensitive and flexible with regard to the local office manager's sign-off. It is not reasonable to expect this person to sign off on things he or she knows little about. For example, the manager cannot be expected to sign off on whether the air conditioning has met the needs of the system. If the office layout was to be reworked, on the other hand, he or she can verify that work was done according to plan. This sign-off responsibility may get the manager thinking about how the office will work with the new layout. Also, the involvement in the sign-off provides the manager with the opportunity to voice any concerns or reservations. For example, if painting has been done as a part of the implementation but looks shabby, the local office manager should have the option to raise concerns and issues.

- *Identify additional work required.* One may complete a phase of contracted work and find that additional things remain to be done outside the original plan. Local building inspectors may mandate additional work in order to ensure compliance with local building codes. Installed air conditioning may not reach all parts of the building. These types of items need to be inventoried so that they may be subjected to the assessment/planning/contractual process. As a result, the checklist should identify additional work to be done. The site preparation team needs to focus on these items; "small" additional changes can cascade into an avalanche if they are not controlled early in the process.

As the checklists come back, the site preparation team should review each one carefully to ensure that scheduled work was completed. With good contractors and contracts this tends to be the case. However, in a large rollout an organization should be prepared for problems at some point. These inevitably entail contractor negotiations. Ideally, the negotiations are resolved with discussions. If not, the negotiations can move to some form of arbitration or litigation.

The information services industry on the whole has had remarkably little litigation, given the amount of commerce associated with it. As a result, many IS personnel have little or no experience with the sort of verbal legal sparring to which other industries are accustomed. To the uninitiated, threats of litigation are disconcerting. In fact, however, these kinds of threats are a part of this business and IS personnel need to come to grips with them as a part of the negotiations process.

An organization needs to remember to turn to legal counsel if it has no personnel qualified for these kinds of negotiations. If it appears that litigation is a possibility, a lawyer must become involved quickly. The organization must keep all available documentation and continue to document everything.

Another issue to consider as the preparation proceeds is continuous improvement. Site preparation work often proceeds in multiple parallel activities.

On occasion, as site preparation proceeds, team members may encounter problems that could have been avoided by an improved site evaluation activity. Work plans should include a periodic review of site implementation activities; this review communicates what the implementation problems are and whether changes to the site evaluation activity could improve results. Although this may appear to an obvious procedure, the different work groups on the respective phases are often so distributed and on the move so much that these exchanges fail to occur. Scheduling periodic meetings to share results as a part of the planned work can help.

As a part of knowing what is happening, plans should include quality assurance reviews at sites as the site implementation proceeds. These reviews use on-site visits to assess what did and did not work during site implementation.

Part of this assessment can include discussions with local site management and contractors about the work done: what went well and where rework or additional work is needed. The assessment should include tests that the work completed meets expected goals. For example, can all the hardware be turned on and does it appear to work? Are all items installed, and do the item numbers reflect what is found in the configuration management system?

In general, quality assurance reviews should be fairly intensive in the early site implementation efforts. They can then be performed on a selected basis as the implementation begins to proceed in a fairly procedural manner.

The site installation process by nature tends to disrupt and change local office activities. As a result, it is common to expect local office management to communicate what is happening as the installation proceeds. It is good for the site preparation team to be part of those communications.

To that end, team leaders should plan on periodic communications to describe how the site preparation activity is going. These communications can have many formats: a memo to local office management or part of a program newsletter. (One organization started a newsletter column called "In the Rollout Corner.")

The report should cover which offices have been evaluated and implemented. It should also touch on the experiences of site preparation: what worked well and what did not work well. For example, if the site upgrade involves improvement to the phone service, a comment from a local office manager on how helpful the new phone system is could be useful. If the new office air conditioning makes life more pleasant, even though the office is not yet on the system, it is worth noting that fact. Conversely, if there are problems such as work disruption, the report should communicate that fact, along with steps planned to address the problem.

As local office managers will be communicating the problems, the site implementation team should be proactive and provide leadership on the communications. Because the site implementation team is often disrupting work at the sites, this can be a source of interesting or amusing stories (e.g., "interesting things we found when drilling through the wall to run LAN cable"). Humor in these cases never hurts and can provide a more human dimension to the entire process.

SITE IMPLEMENTATION

As site preparation proceeds, those sites that have been prepared move into the site implementation phase. Site implementation consists of the tasks required to install the applications at the site and tests required to be run.

This phase of work is done more by project personnel than by personnel who have not been a part of the project, because developers are concerned at this point with the specifics of the application. It may be difficult to find contractors who have the required level of application knowledge to be successful.

There are many viewpoints about when to do site implementation vs. site preparation. In rollouts with relatively few sites, the work may be done at the same time, which minimizes disruption to the local office. This strategy may help to find problems in the survey/preparation process. It may also help avoid a last-minute rush to bring over a large set of sites as conversion nears.

On the other hand, the application may not be available and stable for early sites. Also, if the application is changed after a site has been through preparation, it may be necessary to disrupt the local users again. It certainly presents a more difficult configuration management problem.

As a general guideline, if there are a large number of sites (probably greater than 10), preparation must begin long before there is a stable application. In this case, to avoid disruption (as well as to avoid looking somewhat confused), scheduling preparation and implementation as distinct phases is often the answer.

With regard to the physical implementation of the application, the installation should be an automated process driven from the development site. This automation, particularly on a large rollout, may be essential. For example, if the rollout team finds as a part of release testing that many tables must be set or that code must be modified for each site, the team can halt the installation until the automated procedures are completed.

Automated procedures should be in place to install the software and to build local databases and reference files. If, as often happens, personnel, roles, and routes must be described for the application, a starter set of information should be provided so that local personnel can make modifications rather than starting from scratch. For example, if each employee must be identified in a table, the initial version of the table should be provided based on who is believed to work at the site. Then local site personnel should modify the table. Doing so can reduce the learning curve and also reduce errors, as long as accurate lists of personnel are kept.

Test Before "Going Live"

How far should site preparation proceed in getting the site ready for going live? This is a somewhat controversial subject, but experience suggests that the following discussion represents a workable approach.

One useful strategy is to have the site preparation team take the installation to the point where the applications are installed and ready to run for the users when the system goes live. The advantages include the following:

- At this point, users know the site preparation team and they will be comfortable having the site preparation team on the ground for the final installation.
- The site preparation team has been responsible for getting the site ready for running the applications. Thus, to some degree, team members can be expected to take ownership of the site and its readiness to go live.
- The experience of bringing the system up and testing it can provide valuable feedback on the site preparation approach that can improve downstream implementations.

If the site preparation team is to do the implementation, the following applies to them. When the site is installed, it needs to be tested. The objective here is usually not a full-blown test of all capability; that objective should have been met in release testing. Rather, this test is to ensure that all components of the application that are dependent on local site specifics are working as expected.

The test should also determine that all required applications are in place and complete. It should ensure that all physical components work, including workstations, servers, and LANs. It should test that the expected flow of work between personnel performs as expected and that all routes, roles, and personnel are properly described and work. Because client/server systems usually involve communications to other sites, the communications capability should also be tested. If the communication has restrictions or dependencies based on role or personnel, this should be tested. For example, if only a chief agent at a site can exchange information with a buyer, this should be tested now.

As a result of doing tests, information and data are often built up in files both local and remote. These files must be purged prior to conversion because after that they can cause problems. For example, in one case a site tested that authorized personnel could request printing of checks. Those requests were still in a print spool when the system came up live and began printing them. This test cleanup needs some careful thought because there are usually some subtleties that can cause problems.

The entire process of site installation testing and cleanup should be guided by checklists. In this case, the checklists verify that expected tests were done and that results were as predicted. The checklists should also verify that installation cleanup has been completed.

"Go Live" Checklists

When installation is complete, the site moves toward conversion. In this stage, the site is ready and tested. A final "go live" checklist should be completed that verifies that all needed hardware, software, procedures, and forms, for instance, are in place.

These checklists are completed at each site and rolled up to a supervisory level, such as local office to region management. These levels in turn complete their own checklists and verify that lower levels have done their checklists. Finally, at the program level, the intent is to have a relatively straightforward set of checklists that verify that all levels of checklists are completed and that one is ready to make the go-live decision.

There are several objectives for this process:

1. To verify that things are ready to go at all sites to be converted
2. To have the local manager participate in the process of deciding to go live
3. To ensure that program management has some basis on which to decide that all planned work has been accomplished and that the conversion can go forward

CONCLUSION

The preparation of sites for client/server computing tends to be an underestimated and understaffed effort. The work can be complex and demanding and can require considerable coordination and planning to execute successfully. Doing the work successfully can result in a set of sites successfully converted and can leave users with a strong sense that the development program knows what it is doing and how to do it.

Chapter 26
Project Management

Many, perhaps most, information system personnel view client/server and netcentric development only as a technical process. They see the process of systems development as making technical decisions about how things work and how tasks should be completed. Inherent in this technical view is the perspective that qualified technical employees who work hard can complete any systems job. This view is naive at best.

It has become increasingly clear that any systems job can frustrate even the best technicians working with the best of intentions. Balancing the time, cost, and personnel aspects is at the heart of management control of systems development. The key to successful management control of systems development lies in the often-observed management cycle of planning, executing, and evaluating the results of the work and revising the plan based on these results.

Although this management cycle is well defined, it is poorly executed more often than not. Most problems with systems development arise from a breakdown in this management cycle.

PLANNING THE WORK: THE USE OF METHODOLOGIES

Even in traditional systems design, many organizations fail to create a systematic plan. Reasons for this vary:

- The project is considered state of the art.
- The method to complete the work is undefined.
- There is no estimating basis to use.
- The deliverables are not defined.
- The scope is unknown.
- The expectations are not understood.

Another reason may be that developers feel they are so busy *doing* it that they cannot take the time to *plan* it. These reasons have never been valid — and much less so with today's complex development environments.

With some thought and understanding, information systems (IS) managers can customize and extend the various well-defined methodologies for almost any client/server or netcentric development effort. Such methodologies are

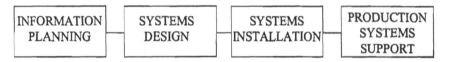

Exhibit 1. A Simple Example of a Systems Management Methodology.

available from various vendors and consultants, including Accenture (see Exhibit 1).

Regardless of the methodology to be used, netcentric system development still requires an organization to plan its systems, just as in traditional systems development. The organization must

- Design its systems
- Code and test its systems
- Support its systems

Although there is no generally agreed-on basis for estimating systems development projects, many useful bases for estimating projects are available. Often, a comprehensive project development methodology has an estimating basis.

The key for IS managers is to select one methodology and estimating basis based on previous experience. When estimates are created for a systems project, IS management typically comments that the project cannot possibly take that long. "The estimate has to be wrong — cut it in half." When a project is in progress, however, the most frequently heard comment is, "These estimates are impossible; we'll never make them."

EXECUTING THE PLAN

Many times, a great deal of effort goes into developing a plan that is then ignored. Several underlying reasons cause this problem.

First, IS management has many responsibilities and distractions to address every day. These activities tend to move focus away from developing and executing project plans.

Next, IS management may not know how to use a plan to manage a project. Many systems project managers seem to have trouble connecting the plan to their daily activities. For example, if a plan states that one employee is designing inputs and outputs from April 10 to April 28, the actual project should have a corresponding activity. However, in fact, many systems project managers have trouble committing to their plans, and they lack the self-confidence and discipline to conduct the project based on its plan.

Another reason a plan is ignored is because of a lack of clearly defined deliverables that the project team can create, manage, and understand. One of the first quality assurance points during a plan review is to check that there are clear deliverables defined for all tasks of a project.

Although this may sound pedestrian, one of the obvious signs that problems are on the way is a plan that has such tasks as "Develop understanding of user needs," or "Coordinate liaison activities." Because these tasks have no explicit deliverables associated with them, project management and control become very difficult.

A comprehensive systems development methodology can be valuable in defining deliverables. IS managers must exert management control by insisting on timely and accurate delivery of quality deliverables. A project cannot be controlled solely on good intentions.

EVALUATING THE PROJECT

Nothing reveals basic human nature more than watching a manager confronted with the evaluation task in the management cycle. Essentially, this task requires IS managers to evaluate their project's and staff's performance.

Several common errors occur during this activity. The first is not conducting an evaluation at all. The most common way IS managers can avoid reviewing a systems project's progress and results is to delegate this responsibility. As a result, IS managers may only get status reports on the project; then they must rely on these reports for an accurate account of the project's progress. In some cases, even this formality is absent.

When an IS manager delegates this responsibility and is asked by senior management about the project, a common response is, "Everyone tells me it's going all right." This leaves senior management with no sense of the project's progress.

Although this tactic may result in less anxiety in the short term, managers cannot effectively manage if they are not directly involved with the project. This does not mean or imply that the managers must be actually performing and/or reviewing the work. However, they must be involved and must establish a presence with the project team.

IS managers who simply walk around, observing work proceeding on a project, have a more concrete basis with which to make an evaluation. This technique is one way to avoid delegating the responsibility for the evaluation of results.

Managers may occasionally be criticized for being "Big Brother" (e.g., when they are out observing). However, project teams quickly learn to recognize when a manager is truly fact finding for the good of the project, and not simply looking for mistakes. Clearly, project managers cannot be expected to examine each member's performance; that is why there is a hierarchy of management. Instead, managers should focus on monitoring and delivering key deliverables.

Quantifying the Work

The other aspect of project evaluation is the more analytical process of collecting counts of deliverables and time, comparing them with the plan, and assessing the project's status from these counts. This is the more quantitative aspect of evaluation work; the previous project review is more qualitative. However, both types are essential.

In the quantitative work, IS managers tend to react to the overall numbers without analyzing them. This causes the managers to focus on the symptoms rather than the underlying problem. The analysis should focus on whether variations arise out of volume, staffing, or estimate variances (e.g., unplanned activities, underestimated activities, shortfalls in staffing, and overestimated activities).

Variance Reporting

Volume variances often indicate that there is more work to be done in terms of units of design. Is the project's scope underestimated in this case? Is the trend a one-time blip or an ongoing problem? If it is an ongoing problem, can it be addressed? (For example, can the scope be trimmed?)

If the variance is due to a shortfall in staffing, it often means that IS management is not meeting its commitment to the project by arranging for adequate staffing. Again, managers have several options. Can temporary workers alleviate the problem? Does the lack of staffing reflect a changing commitment to the project by the organization? Finally, can the old standby of overtime work address the issue? If so, for how long?

Estimate variances present a more difficult problem. If the estimates used are proving unreliable, there is a tendency to say that the project plan as a whole is wrong and should be discarded. This is not desirable. In this case, IS management must be firm. The plan still states what needs to be done; the problem is with the time estimate. The correct reaction for managers is to adjust estimates and evaluate their impact, not to throw out the plan.

REVISING THE PLAN

Revising the plan is a difficult task in the management cycle. Clearly, it is a mistake to change a systems project plan every time a variance arises. However, it is also a mistake to cling resolutely to a plan that no longer has any relevance.

The most difficult aspect of revising a plan is finding the initiative to do so. In many cases, even when a project is behind schedule, IS management may have little inclination to act. In these cases, it often seems as if the perceived failure of the plan was a fulfillment of an unspoken wish by management.

The failure of the plan "proved" that there was no point in planning the systems project and that, as a result, there was no point in managing the effort. The downward spiral of planned results, actual results, and expectations seems to leave management in a state of relieved defeat, or, even worse, it may lead to an effort to hide the actual project results.

This is clearly the path to disaster. The only advice for IS managers is to find the energy and creativity to overcome these problems. The scope of the change, and the amount of time that managers should devote to changing the plan, depend on the situation. Most often, due dates are fixed but budgets have a little more flexibility. Usually, there is also some flexibility in the type of system that is to be delivered to the users.

Staffing

In this context, IS managers dealing with a project that is behind the plan's schedule should first consider additional staffing. *The Mythical Man-Month*, perhaps the best book on the issues of software development (because it is based on the experience of failure), cautions against overstaffing a project. Certainly, employees simply thrown into the project often do not help. They may even push the project further behind. However, employees carefully selected for the project present different possibilities.

A key point in *The Mythical Man-Month* is that the management process of handling additional staff can break down. The solution is, first, to revise the plan to show the impact of additional employees and their roles before adding them to the project team. Then, bring them in and let them begin working on specific tasks according to the revised project plan.

Adding staff is just one technique. Another is to revise the level of the system's capability — in other words, manage the scope. Almost all project managers have altered a project's scope to meet scheduled dates. However, a reduction in scope represents a negative rather than a positive management action. The first critical factor controlling the successful management of scope to a date is the active commitment of the system users to the long-term value of the system vs. the short-term capability delivered.

If a function is to be delayed, the expectations of the users must be managed. The users must have reason to trust IS management. That trust cannot be built during the last 3 months of a project, when management suddenly arrives to declare a problem. Trust is built by involving the system users throughout the project and helping them understand what is being done, where problems are coming up, and when the delays might begin to develop.

Most business users deal with changes and delays in their daily work. They can understand that the same types of problems arise daily in systems development. However, IS managers must take the time to make the explanation intelligible to nontechnical professionals. Often, IS professionals want to hide problems from the users, and maybe from themselves. Doing so makes their jobs and the users' experience with systems development far more difficult and trying.

MANAGING RISK

The greater complexity of a netcentric development project means greater risks, as well. These risks are organized and discussed in terms of the four-part systems management methodology illustrated in Exhibit 1.

The risks are not necessarily unique to client/server development projects. Experience has shown that these risks can lead to failure of the project if they are not properly managed and addressed.

Information Planning Risks

Several risks need to be addressed when planning for the use and implementation of netcentric technology.

Failure to Sponsor the Change. A netcentric development project affects an organization at all levels. Change ripples through the organization, altering processes and the jobs of the people who perform them. The organization must have a champion or sponsor — beginning at the executive level — to promote the new system, its benefits, and its effects. Without such a sponsor, the organization risks implementing a system and a solution that is resisted and not effectively used by its users.

Typically, this role is a full-time, participative role. Its purpose is to ensure understanding of the system and the solution with all affected individuals and at all appropriate levels of the organization (user, management, and IS). The initial champion, once established, can then be used to develop additional champions, who will be critical during later project phases. This process is sometimes referred to as the cascading sponsorship of change.

Extending Outside the Envelope of Technology. Because specific technologies change rapidly, it is generally best to limit an organization's scope to relatively stable and proven technologies. More important is to make sure that the organization is is driven by actual business needs, not simply technology that sounds innovative. For example, many companies invested in imaging technology but derived no benefit from it because their organizations were not primarily paper driven. A company should choose a technology path and pick the technologies and components that it wants to build on. It should plan for the obsolescence of technology and assume the company will be changing, growing, and upgrading. If it plans for change from the beginning, change is easier when the company has to implement it.

An organization must know its vendors and their products and establish relationships with them. In the world of new technology and new solutions, an organization may find itself dealing with many vendors and technology providers, and it is wise to involve them formally in the delivery of the company's solutions. Companies should beware of beta products, which may be quirky and unreliable and not worth the time and effort. Quite often, it may be more desirable to go with a less capable product if the organization can at least be sure of its strengths and weaknesses.

An organization must understand the technologies and techniques it wants to use. It is not wise to go outside or plan to go outside of what technology can do for the organization. The company must know the technologies it wants to work with and understand its business, its problems, and where it is trying to move the business. An organization must understand the characteristics of the business community to which it is delivering the technological solution. It must weigh and carefully analyze the costs of the technologies against the benefits to be derived from them.

Limited Experience with the Relevant Technologies. Any new technology or technique involves a learning curve for those designing and implementing it. An organization needs to be sure that it has adequately planned for training for all personnel involved with the project. It must beware of overconfidence: netcentric technology is not easier to learn or apply. Organizations must plan for extensive training programs. If possible, it is wise to use hands-on training to begin to build experience with the new technologies and techniques. To relieve the anxiety associated with learning and building new skills, the company should allow people to experiment and to make mistakes. It should use pilot or prototype projects to build skills early on and it should keep focused on skills.

Inadequate Project Planning. Many systems projects fail because of inadequate upfront planning and then a lack of tracking and revising that plan. New methods, discussed in the section "New Methodology Perspectives," must be used and followed in client/server and netcentric developments.

Even though organizations are striving to develop systems more rapidly and more iteratively, structure and planning are still necessary as well as increased involvement across the organization, management, users, and the IS departments. New estimating models, metrics, and methodologies exist to help organizations begin their transition to new solutions.

Above all, an organization must plan for change, not for stability. It must assume that all its assumptions will change and must constantly monitor and revisit those assumptions.

Systems Design Risks

Several risks need to be addressed during the design phase of client/server development.

Redoing the Old. Organizations will be making large investments in their client/server and netcentric technologies. They must ensure that they are deriving new and improved business benefits, not merely automating the old ways of doing business. An organization should use external experts to check on its plans and designs to ensure that it is properly utilizing the new technologies, architectures, and techniques and realizing the benefits they can and should provide. Everyone is susceptible to the problem of doing what worked before rather than doing things different and better.

Designing for the Future. A company must make sure that it is positioned, both from a business and a systems perspective, for the changes that accompany the new system. Developers must not just design for today; they must plan immediately for the transitions that their organization will make in the years to come. In short, an organization must strive to "future proof" its system to accommodate changes to both business and technology in the future. Future proofing can result if developers are careful to follow the model, emphasized several times in this book, that separates business function from the technology that supports that function. If a developer designs so that the technology itself becomes the point of the business, technological change may have adverse effects on the entire organization and business change may not be enabled.

Silver Bullet Solutions. There are no silver bullet or "canned" solutions in a netcentric environment. Regardless of what the vendor community may advertise and communicate, netcentric solutions delivery requires time and effort to implement effectively. An organization must be willing from the beginning to innovate, create, customize, and integrate the technological solution to fit its particular business needs.

A healthy approach is to look at all technology with a kind of skepticism, trying to understand its limits. Such information may be available from reference sites and from outside expertise. If an organization cannot determine where the limits are by information sources, it should plan on testing early to assess the limits.

New Methods, Tools, and Techniques. Netcentric methods and tools are new and unfamiliar to many users, designers, and developers. For example, many organizations have trained and built skills around the mainframe environment, COBOL, CICS, DB/2. In the new development world the language may be C, the database management system (DBMS) Oracle, and the transaction processing monitor Tuxedo. All require new skills and, more important, new methods to use successfully. Project management must be sure to provide project team members with extensive training on the products used in the architecture as early as possible in the project timeframe.

Many techniques are theoretically sound, but they may still be unproven in a real business environment, or still be incomplete and incapable of addressing all aspects of delivery. Developers must strive to pick the set of methods, tools, and techniques appropriate to their problem and their organization. In addition, design standards and program templates are required that immediately lead to consistency across developers.

Unstable Technology Providers. The definition of a stable technology vendor has changed dramatically in recent years. Indeed, it might be argued that there is no such thing as a stable vendor anymore. However, there are still at least *degrees* of stability at work in the marketplace, and organizations need to focus on how to make these vendors a part of the design team. They must be sure to execute clear and precise contracts with vendors that specify deliverables, time frames, costs, and quality of what the vendor will provide. They must build in options within the contract to upgrade or change the technology so they do not lock in to today's solutions at the expense of tomorrow's requirements.

Managing the Scope. As discussed previously, one of the risks is going outside the organization's "envelope" of technological competence. Monitoring the scope of the project to guard against overreaching is particularly important in the systems design phase of an organization's systems development project. Organizations must be sure they can deliver what they promised with their available resources. They must constantly match their business requirements to their technologies and their resources.

An important aspect of managing scope during the design phase of a systems development project is to manage the expectations of management, IS, and the user community. The organization must involve the users at every point by making them a part of the design team. The organization must not make the traditional mistake of contacting the users only at the beginning and at the very end of a project.

Another scope management technique is for the organization to use functional prototyping as an aid to communicate what it is delivering. It must beware, however, of overdesign and overcommitment at the prototype stage.

Occasionally, prototypes contain flashier features than the installed system can or will deliver, giving users false expectations of what the system will do. On the other hand, there is also the risk of underdesigning the system, and users will let the organization know about that at the prototype stage also.

Communication Barriers. In the netcentric environment, an organization is managing many different types of skills, technologies, and methods. These can lead to many problems if the project team is not well organized and if it is not communicating on a constant basis.

In traditional systems design, the technical and functional people were generally separated. With netcentric, the organization should consider having them work together on teams at all levels, sharing knowledge and experiences. Generally, an organization should look for hands-on people. It wants personnel who will get involved with all aspects of the project, not those who "manage by managing." Also, the organization should look for people who will encourage and support the new team structures necessary to design and deliver a client/server or netcentric system.

Increasing the skill base of an organization is an effective way not only to improve its ability to deliver but also to ensure that its people are speaking the same language.

Systems Installation Risks

An organization needs to identify and address several risks during the coding and testing of systems.

Lack of Acceptance of the System. The risk at the end of installation is that no one will be there to accept the new system. Here, the fruits of cascading sponsorship should become apparent. Traditionally, change management experts have been called in only at the installation phase of a project to assist with user training. However, the development of sponsors and champions is a change management effort that must begin early in the project life. Acceptance of a new system is also dependent, naturally, on its usability. Here the integrated performance support aspects of our execution architecture become crucial. Built-in help and navigation aids present a more natural or intuitive system to users, one that blends in well with their overall new job tasks. The system should adapt to its users, how they work and how they want to work. It should not require that the users adapt to it.

Inadequate Integration. With a netcentric development project, an organization is often in the integration business: piecing together technologies, vendors, and business organizations into a single, integrated, deliverable solution. Achieving that end, however, is difficult and risky. Vendors and all third parties must be pulled in and made part of the team. An organization should build the infrastructure first (e.g., the architectures) and then build the solutions on top of that. Above all, it should test as early and often as possible.

Project management should try to organize the application development teams by business functionality instead of by technology component. This will allow teams to work on design and development from end-to-end vs. only on front-end or back-end components. Subsequently, the team members will have a complete view of a business function and will be able to see how design and development decisions for one portion of the business function will impact other portions of the same business function. This approach will minimize the many integration problems and issues that usually occur between the front-end and back-end applications.

Missing the Forest for the Trees. During implementation, it is easy to for an organization to become so immersed in details that it loses sight of the more important, overall objectives of the system. The organization must make sure it is doing regular quality assurance checks and bringing in experts from outside the project to check progress, plans, and results. It must ensure that an effective communications program, initiated earlier in the project, is still operating effectively during installation so that everyone understands the what, why, how, and when of the project.

Inadequate Site Preparation. The details of preparing the physical facilities for the new system must be addressed early in the project. Quite often, netcentric technology is being deployed to sites and locations that have never had to deal with technology before. The organization should use a phased rollout approach and stay close to the users at all times to ensure that they are using the new system correctly and that problems and concerns are identified and addressed as early as possible. (More information about site preparation is provided in that chapter in Section III.)

Production Systems Support Risks

After the organization has converted and delivered the new systems, risks still remain that need to be addressed.

Coping with Ongoing Change. Support for the installed system involves reacting both to technology and to business change. The organization must continue to iterate. It must go back to earlier development activities — planning, design, and implementation — to meet the new needs of the business or to take advantage of new, proven technology capabilities. Ongoing monitoring of the technology and of the business is vital. Migration and upgrades should be focused on real business benefit, not change for the sake of change.

Losing Touch with Users. User involvement is vital during the entire project. Sometimes, however, organizations neglect to capitalize on user feedback following installation and conversion of the system to assist in iterative development. A form of logging or tracking must be put in place to monitor what is going well and what is not going well from the users' point of view.

NEW METHODOLOGY PERSPECTIVES

The techniques, methodology, and practices required to deliver applications in a netcentric environment are in most cases quite different from traditional approaches. The existing methodology for most IS organizations therefore require at least some changes and extensions to practices and deliverables to serve the needs of netcentric projects. These changes are driven not by any specific technology platform but by a change in the approach to developing and packaging applications and the need to apply new technologies to provide optimal solutions.

In general, netcentric development efforts should be done in an iterative fashion, meaning that the business/application delivery components should be defined as a series of distinct, yet related functions that can be developed and delivered independently. This iterative development and delivery approach allows an organization to better manage the project(s), react more quickly to technology change, and, most important, react more quickly to business change.

The remainder of this section provides an overview of the major new and changed development activities in a client/server or netcentric development environment. The development activities addressed here include the following

- User involvement
- Graphical user interface (GUI) development
- Prototyping
- Data architecture selection
- Application architecture
- Networking
- Standards testing
- Rollout
- Operations support

User Involvement

Because netcentric application development is typically a part of the delivery of new (reengineered) business processes, it becomes increasingly important to involve real business users in the development process.

Program and project managers need to identify and plan for the business users to actively participate in the solution development and delivery process. This participation should focus on having the users actually assigned to tasks and deliverables, while remembering that users are not systems developers. Typical activities for users can include business process design, prototyping, GUI design, testing, and acceptance testing. An added benefit of this user involvement is that typically these users return to their respective business organizations and become the champions for the new applications.

Graphical User Interface Development

The world of the GUI introduces new challenges to the applications development process. First, GUI programs are "event driven" as opposed to purely procedural. This means that GUI applications must be designed and developed to respond to events related to users, messages, and business changes. A conventional structure chart or flow diagram is insufficient for representing this type of program with these types of events.

Another important GUI issue to be addressed is the level of detail of the design. Because most programmers are unfamiliar with coding in this new environment, more detailed design documents and training are usually required. To properly design and deliver a GUI, new deliverables (e.g., control action response diagrams), new tools (e.g., window painters), and new techniques (e.g., prototyping) may be required to ensure successful delivery.

Prototyping

Prototyping becomes far more important in a netcentric environment. For example, many users, even at this time, have had little exposure to a GUI, so prototyping is a valuable activity early in the design process to gather user feedback on new business processes and new applications.

In addition, an organization might choose to prototype new business application capability (in addition to the user interface to that capability) early in the design process. This functional prototyping can be used to clarify and refine with users and management new business processing activities and the work flow supported by the new applications. Finally, prototypes can also be used to educate and train users and management in the technologies and possibilities of the new world of client/server.

The major risk with prototyping is overselling the user; a prototype often looks and performs better than the actual implemented system does. The organization needs to ensure that the prototype emulates the targeted real-world environment and characteristics as much as possible. Additional time, effort, and, complexity are necessary for preparing, installing, and utilizing a prototype within a netcentric environment.

Data

In the netcentric world, both the logical and physical aspects of delivering and managing data require changes. During the logical data design activity, time and effort must be allocated to ensure that the logical data deliverables properly reflect and support the new business process design and the data requirements of the system inputs and outputs (e.g., windows and reports). In addition, the logical data design activities should start to identify and address data sources and integration points with existing, installed systems.

Physical database design requires additional tasks and considerations (primarily in the physical DBMS design steps) to address the needs of workstation-based systems. The issues of distributed information and data, data replication, data synchronization, and the appropriate use of workstation and/or midtier DBMS products need to be addressed.

An appropriate physical database design and topology is crucial to the performance and integrity of the implemented system. Significant benefits are to be found in using innovative approaches, topologies, and products, but these opportunities are not without risk. There are also many relational database management system (RDBMS) products available with extended features not found in traditional environments.

The final data consideration relates to the objective of keeping data distinct from process. This objective typically leads to designing, coding, and testing data access logic separately from application or business function logic. Time and effort are required to develop the data access components and then to test those components with the related business functions that use the data.

Architecture Selection

Unlike traditional mainframe systems, which have limited and well-known alternatives, the netcentric environment presents difficult choices in many hardware and systems software categories, including workstations, work group servers, bridges, routers, gateways, converters, development tools, DBMSs, user interface, and communications. Chapter 1 also deals with the greater complexities presented by the increased number of options in netcentric computing.

For example, there are numerous RDBMS vendors to be considered, each with its own strengths and weaknesses. In addition, the user interface software direction can be a major decision effort in itself. It is easy to identify three popular operating systems, three popular DBMSs, three popular network approaches, three hardware providers, and three development tools that might be considered for a netcentric architecture. This simple example leads to 243 possible architectures, and the number could be far greater.

To complicate matters further, the pace of technology, competition, and product introductions and upgrades is staggering. A proper choice made today has a significant probability of being "leapfrogged" by its competition tomorrow. The variety of vendors and vendor offerings in the workstation marketplace, coupled with a general lack of experience with these products, combines to increase substantially the amount of time and effort needed to define, implement, and deliver a netcentric architecture.

In summary, the good news with netcentric is that it provides numerous architectural options. However, the bad news is that with these options, an organization must address the time and effort necessary to make technology decisions and choices. Therefore, activities must be planned early (and sometimes often) to perform architecture (technology) selections.

Application Architecture

In a netcentric environment, processing can be divided between the client and the server in a number of ways. At one extreme is the front-end intensive or "fat client" way. The application runs almost entirely on the workstation using the back-end machine as a shared database server. At the other extreme is the back-end intensive or "thin client" way. The application runs almost entirely on the back-end machine, using the workstation as only an input/output presentation device. In between these two extremes is a wide variety of logic/processing allocation strategies.

Experience has shown that no single strategy, regardless of how conceptually pure it may seem, is truly appropriate for all application types. An application architecture framework and logic allocation guidelines must be defined and delivered early in development.

Technical Architecture. Identifying standard application module types in a netcentric environment is substantially more difficult because of the wider variety of implementation options and new and unique application requirements. A natural friction exists between trying to identify and standardize on as few module types as possible and fully exploiting the client/server and netcentric environment for each application. Using personnel without client/server or netcentric implementation experience in this step can have grave consequences. In tackling netcentric architectures for the first time, project management should try to seed the team with personnel proficient and experienced with client/server architecture and development and legacy systems integration.

The system documentation requirements practice needs to be augmented not only to address the location of processing for a module (in the distributed computing sense) but also to provide guidelines for how, where, and why to break what was previously thought of as a single module across multiple processors.

The process of identifying utilities, functions, and common routines is also expanded in scope. The number of common routines rises significantly for the GUI and interapplication communications. The proper identification, early development, and management of these routines are crucial to installation productivity and application consistency.

An extensive set of common routines reduces application programmer training requirements as well as the amount of application code to be developed and tested. The design standards deliverable should be expanded to include technical architectural considerations, and should be language independent.

Networking

Network design and network management issues and considerations should be resolved early in the design process. With netcentric, reliance on networks is greatly increased and, therefore, the importance of getting the network right increases. The following issues should be addressed early and continuously through the development process:

- Reliability
- Fault processing
- Rollback fallback (disaster recovery)
- Performance
- Capacity planning

Based on the complexity of developing a client/server or netcentric application, system modeling should be performed before application development and implementation. A new practice and deliverables describing the steps required for distributed system modeling should be defined and executed.

Naming/Programming Standards

Given the pace of change, both technology and business, the need to train and retrain IS personnel, and the wish to standardize efforts, development standards become a key success factor in systems development.

For example, the client/server and netcentric environments support a directory file structure that allows for flexibility in file, library, job (process), and data set names. Standards and guidelines should be developed or extended to address client/server file system and directory naming.

Activities need to be planned to allow for the creation, delivery, maintenance, and training in the use of appropriate development standards. These standards should be additional practices or extensions to address the following activities:

- GUI design
- Prototyping
- Testing
- Coding
- Quality file/directory naming
- File/directory usage
- Architecture usage
- Test job classes (client/server test processes)
- Library naming conventions (library names and location)
- Database naming conventions (support for database-specific conventions)
- Data set naming conventions (client/server data file names and locations)
- Job classes (process and user classes)

Directory structures (directory file structures for unit test, linkage test, system test, and integration test code; libraries; test data files; etc.).

Additional future technologies and techniques such as object-oriented development, team-oriented applications, and multimedia applications (voice, video, and image) also have an impact on development methodologies. These subjects are discussed in subsequent chapters of this book.

Testing

Testing takes on an added dimension of complexity because of the distributed nature of netcentric applications. Program-to-program communications, distributed data, and GUIs all present new testing requirements that are not well met by existing tools and techniques.

The following discussion describes additions and modifications to testing practices. In general, netcentric applications require far more extensive testing than traditional centralized applications to ensure successful delivery and support.

The programming activity from a methodology perspective is largely unchanged. However, the definition of unit test in the client/server and netcentric environments may be somewhat ambiguous. It has proven difficult to unit-test a workstation program that relies heavily on frequent interchange with a host computer (for data, perhaps). The use of stubs involves a substantial amount of extraneous code development because of the frequency of interaction. Extensions should be made to the unit-testing practice to account for client/server and netcentric considerations. This may affect the following deliverables:

- Common unit-test scenarios
- Unit-test scripts
- Unit-test scenarios
- Unit-test cases and databases

Developers may note an increase in program bugs discovered at integration or linkage test. These linkage-test tasks typically take much longer to complete for client/server and netcentric workstation-based systems. The additional time needed is traceable to three factors:

1. An increased number of components to integrate (each smaller in size)
2. The frequency of interaction among components
3. The complexity of intermachine communications

In addition, the verification of results for GUI applications has proved to be both time and resource consuming. Extensions should be made to the linkage-testing practice to account for netcentric considerations. This may affect the following deliverables:

- Linkage-test scripts
- Linkage-test scenarios
- Linkage-test cases and databases

Stress and volume testing become more complex because of the distributed nature of the target applications. Stress and volume testing should be performed on each target environment and across the network. In addition, benchmarking must be performed at various levels — at each workstation, at each server, and across the network.

The following deliverables use the stress and volume testing practice extensions:

- Stress and volume test script
- Stress and volume test scenarios
- Stress and volume test cases and databases

Rollout

The final major activity related to the successful delivery of netcentric solutions is often rolling out the technology, support structures, training, and applications to the organization. This often is a new concept and activity for most organizations. Many activities and deliverables are associated with site preparation and rollout.

Rollout is the major activity that brings everything else together before going live with the system. Everything includes the technologies (e.g., workstations, servers, networks, and DBMSs), the new business processes and procedures, the new applications, the new support organization, the new support procedures, and the newly trained users. In summary, it is a new business.

Activities and deliverables must be planned that address the integration of the aforementioned components, and verify that all is well with those components prior to declaring a new system live.

Operations Support

Netcentric applications by their very nature tend to be more distributed; the number of intelligent devices in the network increases, and it becomes increasingly difficult to identify and resolve system discrepancies. As a result of these issues, several aspects of system operations and support become more important and more complex. Areas that need to be addressed through practices and procedures include the following:

- Distributed software and data synchronization
- Application support
- System fault identification and resolution
- Hardware operations and maintenance
- Ongoing vendor and contract management
- Network management
- Release management and coordination

PLANNING A NETCENTRIC PROJECT

Planning and estimating a client/server or netcentric development project can be particularly challenging. Client/server and netcentric technologies are still relatively new. A different planning approach is necessary for such development activities as GUI design and development, data distribution, and process distribution.

The GUI and multiplatform characteristics of architectures tend to result in programming work units that are more modular and more granular than conventional applications. The units also tend to be distributed throughout the network, which in turn creates more complex testing requirements.

In addition, a stable, historical estimating base for netcentric may not yet exist, so it is critical that all estimates be sufficiently reviewed by personnel who have experience with similar development efforts and technologies.

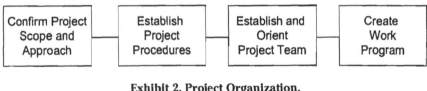

Exhibit 2. Project Organization.

The planning dimension of a netcentric development project has the following objectives:

- To achieve consensus among the project team, users, and management about the objectives, scope, costs, and approach to the project
- To develop a common framework against which the project will proceed and be managed
- To put in place the mechanisms necessary to manage the project and control and monitor its progress
- To organize, assemble, and enable a skilled project team
- To obtain management's commitment and approval to begin the core development and infrastructure activities

Project Organization

Appropriate project organization is fundamental to effective project management and execution. Project organization encompasses the planning, organization, and control processes that must be in place for the project to succeed. Project organization can be divided into four phases, as shown in Exhibit 2.

Confirm Project Scope and Approach. This task enables the project team, users, and management to achieve consensus on the goals of the project (e.g., deliverables or schedule). The project manager establishes the project advisory structure to provide direction and sponsorship to the project. This includes confirming the project's scope, objectives, and assumptions. The next step is to develop the project's going-in design assumptions, specifically the conceptual functional design, technical design, and implementation plan. A high-level work plan, organizational structure, and preliminary project timetable are created. It is important to obtain user, IS, and management's commitment to support and participate in the project.

Establish Project Procedures. This task addresses the implementation of project control standards, procedures, and systems to ensure an effective and efficient approach to completing work. Mechanisms are established for status and time reporting, user review and sign-off, issue resolution, scope control, and project communications. Then the team develops automated (or manual) project control systems to support these procedures and other administrative needs. Also, the team must establish sufficient project work space and facilities.

Establish and Orient Project Team. This task involves identification of project team structure, roles, and skill requirements, and organization of the resources needed to fill the roles. The project team structure must be appropriate for the type of work being performed, the organizational considerations, and the degrees of risk. Project management must finalize the skill and experience requirements and secure the needed personnel. An orientation package should be prepared for the project team to provide the project's background and objectives. It is important to orient team members to both the project and their specific roles and responsibilities. A couple of additional points are important here:

Project management should look to divide distinct roles among different teams on the project. For example, a modeling team should perform business modeling and a technical team should develop application frameworks.

Project management should also plan for and take time to build redundancy of knowledge throughout the project team, so that no one person's absence, be it temporary or permanent, can bring progress to a halt when problems arise in that person's area of expertise. This technique is particularly important in a multitiered application, because the natural tendency for a developer is to build deep, narrow skills in the layer of the architecture that he or she is working on due to such things as time pressure and complexity.

Create Work Program. This task involves the finalization of the project plans and the assignment of project team members to specific tasks. Project management must finalize the project's work activities and define the experience and skill levels needed to perform those activities. The project management function identifies the work packages and workday budgets associated with each activity and then assigns specific individuals to the roles and tasks. Work loads should then be balanced and the due dates finalized for each task. Management's approval and commitment to the final project plans must be obtained.

Project Scope

Confirming and controlling scope are crucial to the success of a netcentric project. Given the new tools, techniques, and project organizations, it is easy to continuously add new business functions and/or technical capabilities during design and prototyping activities and then never get to actual implementation. Work performed outside scope may be inconsistent with management and user expectations and can cause schedule delays and budget overruns. Management must approve the defined scope, and the entire team must understand that scope and adhere to it.

A crucial component of managing scope is to put in place the project advisory structure: typically a management advisory committee, a steering committee, and a project sponsor. These groups are responsible for providing overall direction to the project and for championing it throughout the corporate organization. No decisions about the project's scope and approach should be made until these groups are established.

Specifically, the management advisory committee is composed of an organization's senior executives who are going to be impacted by the project. This committee is responsible for understanding the overall scope of the project, the development approach to be undertaken, and the impact of the new system to ensure that the entire organization is committed to success and is ready for the change. The steering committee is composed of management representatives from each department or group affected by the new system. The steering committee is responsible for overseeing the detailed project status, scope, and approach. This committee also assists the project management team with addressing and resolving and project-level issues. Finally, the project sponsor should be the overall champion for the project, responsible for delivering quality and success.

By setting scope, an organization establishes boundaries for what the project is to address: This creates a clear picture not only of the target system but also of the responsibilities and constraints faced by the project team and the entire organization. For this reason, no significant project activities should be undertaken until management has confirmed the scope and approach.

Defining the Scope. Defining project scope involves identifying and understanding the following items:

- Business and project objectives
- Business benefits to be achieved
- Specific business functions to be implemented
- Key project success factors and success measures
- User constituencies and specific user locations involved
- Activities to be performed by the project team
- Overall schedule
- Expected results in terms of work packages and deliverables
- Extent of personnel involvement from all required organizational units

The level, depth, and detail of the project scope definition vary depending on the phase of the project:

- During information planning, the scope is very broad, outlining the high-level business areas to be addressed and the project's overall constraints.
- During systems design, the scope defines the project's overall size and the specific functional and technical functions, features, and assumptions.
- During systems installation, the functional and technical scope is fairly well defined, based on the results of the systems design phase. The focus of the scope is more on the project team's responsibilities and on the amount of work required to test and convert the system. In addition, if the implementation represents a subset of a more comprehensive design (a particular release of the system), the scope defines, for example, which functions, locations, and interfaces are to be implemented during this project phase. The initial definition of project scope is subject to revision and may not be finalized until the detailed work effort estimates are complete. As the work plan is developed in more detail, assumptions about project goals and required resources may change. Therefore, the scope should be outlined in as much detail as possible, including all functional, technical, and architectural assumptions. Once the final scope and approach are approved at the conclusion of project organization, subsequent changes to scope should be controlled through mechanisms such as change request management (change control) and business case management.

Defining the Project Approach. The project approach differs from the scope in that it outlines how the work is to be done rather than what particular work is to be done. The initial approach is stated in broad terms, focusing on items such as the specific methodology and methods to be used, the high-level work segments, the development environment to be used, the work locations, the high-level project organization structure, the project time line, and sign-off procedures.

The approach should also contain a set of assumptions. A scope-and-approach memorandum can document the approach and add further detail as part of the work-planning step during each client/server or net-centric development phase.

Developing the Work Plan. After confirming the project scope and approach, project managers should develop the work plan, a high-level staffing plan, and the preliminary project timetable. These plans may have been prepared in the previous phase or as part of the project approval process. Nevertheless, they should be reviewed and refined in light of any changes to the current project scope or approach.

The work plan breaks down the confirmed project approach into greater detail. It identifies the segments, tasks, and steps to be performed: the type of work packages, work objects, and deliverables to be produced; the estimated effort; and the key completion dates.

The work plan should be defined at a sufficient level of detail for work to be accurately estimated, scheduled, assigned, managed, and controlled. The work plan's organization should facilitate administration and reporting requirements for both project management and the organization's management. It should highlight major milestones and deliverables that can be precisely defined and easily verified, such as completion of source code or approval of unit-test results. Project management should use these milestones and their associated completion dates as a basis for sequencing tasks and for specifying which tasks occur concurrently or which tasks must occur sequentially. Project management should define a common set of estimating factors and carefully review the estimating assumptions for each activity.

On larger projects, a single project manager may not be able to perform all the work plan development activities. In such cases, project management should develop the overall work plan structure and then give individual team leaders the responsibility to develop detailed work plans for each project area.

Project management must ensure that the structure of these work plans corresponds to that of the overall work plan and that team leaders use a common set of assumptions and guidelines. It must ensure that the team leaders fully understand each step of the work plan and that they are prepared to take ownership of their estimates.

The project manager should carefully review the overall project work plan for completeness, appropriateness, and reasonableness.

Simply put, project managers should assume the following jobs: Verify that the work plan properly reflects the defined scope and approach. Ensure that project management, supervisory, support, and user activities are adequately identified and estimated. Recognize that a greater percentage of time is required to support these activities on larger projects, or projects that are complex in terms of technology and/or business functionality, especially when multiple levels of project management are required. Allow enough time to establish and maintain communication between the various management levels and project areas and/or teams. Recognize that additional elapsed time may be required between the identification of a problem and its resolution.

Additional effort may be needed to communicate information to a large project team. A significant amount of time must also be allotted for meetings between the various levels of project management and across the various project areas.

For these reasons, project management should develop the project organizational structure in conjunction with the work plans, identify the various project teams and determine the appropriate levels of supervision and support, and use the organizational structure to confirm that the task budgets are adequately accommodated.

Staffing Plan. The staffing plan describes the high-level organizational structure and identifies the skills, roles, responsibilities, and number of personnel required for the project. Project management should prepare the staffing plan in conjunction with the work plan and project timetable. Project management should propose initial start and end dates for each segment and then determine the skill requirements and number of personnel for each segment. This information should be consolidated to create an overall loading of personnel, by skill classification, over time (by week or month, depending on the overall duration of the phase). Project management should adjust the task and segment durations as necessary to balance the staffing levels, taking into account the following:

- Dependencies among the activities
- Reasonable ramp-up, ramp-down, and peak staffing levels
- Effects of learning curve issues and training on staffing rate
- Effect of any intended piloting on staffing rate
- Available staffing resources

The results of the staffing plan activity can be documented in the following forms:

- A preliminary organization chart, identifying the intended project team structure, proposed project team members, and project management levels.
- A bar chart, showing the segment durations and the anticipated staffing levels for the work segments by category, over time.
- A set of skill requirements, defining each skill category and identifying the specific experience levels and skill sets required for each.

Project managers must be sure to consider the requirements for user and support personnel when creating the staffing plans. They should focus the staffing plan on the current phase of work but also prepare a projected staffing plan for subsequent project phases. This is necessary to ensure the continued reasonableness of the overall system delivery plan.

An approximation of the work effort for the subsequent phases should have been prepared as part of the previous phase or as part of the current planning effort. They should prepare a high-level loading of personnel to correspond with these efforts. They must analyze this long-term staffing plan, considering the following:

- Is the ramp-up of personnel from the end of this phase to the beginning of the next phase reasonable?
- Is the peak personnel level of the subsequent phase manageable, in terms of total numbers, ramp-up and ramp-down, available skill base, work space capacity, and technical capacity?

If a long-term staffing plan is not feasible, developers should work with management to address the issue here rather than at the onset of the next phase. They should consider such techniques as the following:

- Accelerating the duration of the current phase to meet the overall target end date
- Reducing the project scope
- Adopting a revised approach (e.g., using applications software packages or available technical architectures)
- Implementing the system in multiple releases

Obtaining User Commitment. The staffing plan should indicate the user staffing and user skill levels required to successfully deliver the system. Project managers should work with the project sponsor and user management to achieve agreement on the project's resource requirements and time frames and obtain their commitment to provide the resources in accordance with those requirements. It is not necessary to identify the individual user participants at this time. As with the IS team members, the final project organization and staffing occur in a subsequent project organization activity.

To facilitate the process of obtaining user commitment, project managers should supplement the staffing plan by representing user skill requirements in terms of level, position, and functional area of expertise. They can further assist the process by specifying what each class of user representatives is expected to do, that is, the tasks in which they will participate and the types of work package they will produce.

Although some of these details do not become finalized until the project work programs are completed, it is important to provide as much detail as possible at the start. This provides a rationale as to why the user resources are required, and it helps user management to understand the necessary qualifications so they can begin identifying specific candidates. This educational process is particularly important in organizations in which the users have not typically been involved in systems development projects. User involvement, commitment, and ownership are key success factors for delivering client/server solutions that enable business change.

Project managers should strive to set proper user expectations: They should forecast total user requirements and set realistic targets as to when the resources will be needed and when the user resource involvement will be concluded. Some users may participate part-time, depending on the work segment; other project team members are typically involved on a full-time basis. In other cases, users may be required on an ad hoc, as-needed basis.

Typically, the largest user involvement is during the systems design phase and during the system test activities in the systems installation phase. Project management should work with the project sponsor and other members of user management to determine the most appropriate method of participation from the standpoint of both the project development team and the supplying user organizations.

Creating a Risk Management Plan. Planning activities associated with project risk management typically expose areas of potential risk to the development effort. (See the section "Managing Risk" for more discussion of risk in a netcentric development project.) Each project manager or team leader should prepare a risk memorandum for their area of responsibility, identifying the specific risk areas and proposing risk mitigation and management strategies for each risk. If the project is large enough to require the development of multiple memoranda, they should prepare an overall consolidated risk memorandum for the entire project and reference the more detailed risk assessments as necessary.

Developers should consider the following key potential risk areas when preparing the risk management plan:

Impact. Will the system being developed affect the company's main business functions? How significantly will it affect the users' daily operations? Are external customers or other public entities affected? Are the scheduled completion dates absolutely fixed, or are they flexible enough to accommodate unforeseen delays or changes?

Acceptance. Has a true business case been made for the system? Are the users, management, and rank-and-file committed to the project and willing to support the resulting changes to their operations? Have the user organizations committed resources to sponsor and support the systems development effort?

Project Plans. Are the project plans reasonable, and do they contain adequate cost and schedule contingencies? How significant is the critical path and the overlap among work segments? Has the project been estimated based on historical experience within the current environment? Have the project plans been reviewed by experienced netcentric project managers and developers?

Organization. Has the project management team been assembled, and does it possess the right qualifications in terms of experience level and skills? Have the project team skill sets been identified, and can they be obtained? Is there an adequate level of management, supervision and support? Will there be a need to coordinate with a significant number of organizations, both third parties and other corporate departments?

Innovation. Are the following project aspects consistent with the experience of the organization's systems and user personnel: project magnitude, project approach, development time frame, development environment and tools, technical architecture, and the use of proven, stable technologies?

Establishing Project Procedures

The objectives of establishing project procedures are as follows:

- Improve project communication, control, and efficiency.
- Establish a method of evaluating the project's progress.
- Ensure effective and efficient work practices and procedures.
- Promote quality and improve the ability to manage risk.
- Establish a standard framework for managing and executing the project.

Technical standards improve the quality and effectiveness of the design and development process. In the same way, project procedures and administrative and control standards improve project operations and communication, both inside and outside the project team.

To improve communication, operating efficiency, and overall control of systems development projects, developers should establish standards and procedures early on. They should develop policies and procedures to address the key project control functions, including

- Time reporting for all project team members
- Status reporting at all appropriate levels (individual, team, and project)
- Issue management (tracking, monitoring, and resolution)
- Scope control and management of scope change management
- User sign-off
- Documentation control and management
- Personnel management
- Vendor and contract administration
- Project communications

Developers should determine the requirements for managing each of these aspects of the project and develop corresponding standards (written, communicated, and understood) describing how the project team should perform these functions and how management should control them. Obtain the consensus of project management on these standards and then include them in the project orientation material and initial project team training to ensure that all team members are aware of and understand the relevant procedures.

The larger the project and the higher the risk it carries, the more critical these standards and procedures are. Projects with tight time frames or multiple physical locations also require increased emphasis in this area. Developers should tailor the detail and formalization of these procedures to the needs and the culture of the project but ensure that each area is adequately addressed.

Establishing and Orienting the Project Team

The objectives of establishing and orienting the project team activity are to do the following:

- Finalize the detailed project organization structure and assemble a skilled team.
- Orient the project team to the project organization, objectives, background, scope, approach, expected outputs, and standards.
- Ensure that the project team members understand their roles, responsibilities, and performance expectations.
- Introduce all the project team members to each other.

The primary activity here is to develop a plan for orienting project members to the project's history, purpose, vision, goals, objectives, methodology, scope, organization, standards, business applications, technical environment, and industry background. Team members need general orientation to the project as well as a specific orientation to their team, their role and responsibilities, and their relationship to overall organizational structure. Orientation should excite and enthuse the team members and inspire them to take ownership in the project. A productive orientation process requires structure, commitment, and leadership. Developers must structure an orientation program that can both launch the project and also accommodate new team members who join the project later in the phase. They can use the orientation package and training as the primary focus and supplement it with any additional material specific to the target audience.

Orientation may also address new techniques, new technologies, approaches, and architectures. Developers should provide project personnel with a sufficient understanding of the basic domain concepts of the project. The domain concepts form the project vocabulary and are indicative of the way the team members may organize and perform their work and communicate results and status. Domain concepts may include technical terms, acronyms, abbreviations, and buzzwords. These concepts may be standard within the industry or specific to the organization.

Depending on the size of the project, and on whether the team members arrive in groups or in a more staggered fashion, orientation sessions may be either formal or ad hoc. In formal sessions, the project manager or a senior project member may address the group to present the project overview and to answer questions. Alternatively, the team members may read through the orientation material in a less structured manner, asking questions of their supervisor as they arise.

Early in the orientation process, team members should be individually briefed on roles and responsibilities by their targeted supervisor. Their duties and deliverables should be placed in the context of the project as a whole. This helps to give them direction and focus throughout the rest of the orientation and their participation on the project.

As part of the overall orientation process, team members should be introduced to the project methodology and development environment. This training occurs as part of the development environment preparation activity. As necessary, developers should provide technical training in specific tools, programming languages, and basic techniques. They should educate the team members about the methodology and work objects that will be used and describe the relevant project, technical, and documentation standards they are be expected to follow. They must recognize that although the orientation process may take only a few days, significant lead time may be necessary to complete the technical training, especially if the project involves significant technical innovation and customized architectures.

After orientation, team members should have an understanding of the project and what is expected of them. Team members must understand their specific responsibilities, whom they will interact with and report to, and how their performances will be monitored and evaluated.

After the initial orientation training, periodic briefing sessions should continue to reinforce training concepts and describe lessons learned, what to expect next, and how the work objects created in earlier stages will be used.

Creating the Work Program

The activity of creating the work program has the following objectives:

- Translating the work plan into a specific assignment of tasks, budgets, and deadlines
- Confirming the feasibility of the project work plans and address any issues or modifications
- Balancing the work load sufficiently to maximize the effectiveness of project team members and minimize the project risk

- Developing a means for adhering to the project scope and objectives and for monitoring and controlling the project's progress
- Receiving management's approval to begin the development activities

This phase begins by refining the work plan, developed earlier, into a work program by further detailing the tasks and budgets, by assigning specific project personnel to tasks, and by defining specific start and end dates for tasks. The work program can then be used to monitor and control the project's activities throughout the life of the project. It serves as a tool for examining the project's progress and adherence to deadlines and helps to ensure that the work load is properly balanced and distributed among project personnel. It identifies all tasks to be accomplished during the project and reveals all work packages, deliverables, due dates, and personnel requirements.

Detailing Tasks and Budgets. The usefulness of the work program depends on the accuracy of the workday estimates. The program should also be detailed enough to allow prompt recognition of deviations from schedule and budget. As necessary, developers can further break down work tasks into steps (lower-level activities) or work packages (groupings of work objects to be produced or acted up).

A general guideline is that no individually scheduled task or work package should take longer than two weeks to complete. Developers should identify intermediate milestones for longer tasks to better monitor and manage their progress. When tasks are broad in scope, such as the programming activity, developers should make assignments at the work package (programming work unit) level.

To the extent possible, developers should consider shifting more time toward the analysis and design activities. Well-considered and welldocumented designs improve the efficiency of the implementation tasks and significantly reduce the amount of rework. It is also more cost- and time-effective to detect and correct errors or misunderstandings in design now than later in the development process.

When finalizing budgets and schedules, developers must consider the effects of the learning curve. Adjusting the duration of a segment due to training and learning curve issues may change the number of team members needed to perform a task.

Because each team member may have a learning curve, the size of the team may dictate how much time is budgeted for learning curve. Carefully consider the one-time learning curve that task supervisors and the project team as a whole may experience (especially when pioneering a new technique or technology) as well as the individual learning curves that may be experienced by each team member performing the task.

The following options may help to control the extent of individual learning curves: using personnel with more skills, teaming unskilled personnel with more skilled personnel, piloting the process first to reduce the impact of the project wide learning curve, building adequate time for skill building, and redundant skill building, into the project work plans, or extending the time frame of the task to reduce the total number of people experiencing learning curve effects.

Contingency in the work program should be included by allocating time and resource capacity explicitly for the unexpected, such as for correcting problems or deficiencies identified during a review. Developers should not assign the contingency to individuals or tasks but rather should keep it as a separate item to offset unplanned variances across any and all project activities. If contingency was not previously identified, or if it was not sufficient to cover the risk areas, developers should consider reducing some of the task budgets slightly to create some additional contingency budget.

Developers should not perform a significant amount of detailed planning for tasks more than two to four months into the future as changes over time inevitably cause rework to these long-term plans. Instead, developers should maintain a rolling two- to four-month detailed planning horizon and update the detailed plans.

Balancing the Work Load. As the detailed work program is prepared, it may become evident that the available resources are inadequate or that there is a surplus of certain resources at various stages. Developers should adjust the activity durations, activity relationships, or staffing levels as necessary to create a balanced schedule. They must be sure to inform management of any significant adjustments to the original plan because changes can affect the critical path as well as the requirements for work space and support resources.

Balancing the work load should be driven by the work package-oriented tasks — those tasks that produce the project work objects and deliverables. Once they schedule these tasks, developers should fill in the corresponding elapsed time-oriented support tasks, such as programming supervision, technical support, and project management.

For these tasks, developers should determine the appropriate staffing level to support the related tasks and load their resources accordingly. Then they should check the total resource allocation against the budgets and organizational charts in the original work plans and reconcile deviations by adjusting the durations of the work package-oriented tasks or by adjusting the support levels of the elapsed time-oriented tasks. If the support resources are still insufficient, systems developers must alert management and determine whether adjustments can be made to the overall project plans.

The final balancing of the schedule occurs when the staffing plan is broken down into greater detail, resulting in the staffing schedule. Developers should assign specific individuals to the roles identified in the staffing plan and then compare the staffing schedule to the work program to ensure all staffing requirements are fulfilled and that all tasks are assigned. If specific individuals have not been identified for all positions, especially those that will not be staffed until later in the phase, developers should assign placeholder names (such as Programmer1 and Analyst2).

Developers should load in specific holidays, vacations, training commitments, and other non-project-related activities for each team member. If this information is not yet known, they should assume a less than 100% availability (typically no more than 85%) to accommodate the inevitable time away from the project. Failure to do this produces an unrealistic staffing plan and is likely to result in excessive overtime or missed deadlines.

For each team on the project, developers should create a revised organizational chart that corresponds to the staffing schedule. Developers should identify reporting relationships and project start and end dates, if applicable. If the organizational charts are likely to change significantly throughout the phase, developers should produce separate charts for each significant activity (e.g., detailed design, programming, and system test).

Finalizing the Schedule. Developers should use the balanced work load and detailed staffing plan to assign specific start and end dates for each task performed by each team member. Developers should consolidate these to produce overall start and end dates for all project segments and tasks. To allow for more efficient management, all start and end dates should be scheduled by week (e.g., all dates should be assigned to either Mondays or Fridays).

Similarly, developers should create a detailed schedule for all project work packages. Often these work packages have been identified as the lowest-level tasks on the work program. If specific work packages are not identified, developers should create a separate schedule to indicate the number and type of work packages expected by person and by week.

Coordinating Multiple Work Programs. If the project consists of multiple applications and project teams, each manager or team leader may develop their own work program. Just as they are being balanced individually, they will also have to be balanced against each other. Developers should Ensure that activity and task schedules are consistent across teams, that the overall critical path and dependencies are maintained, and that the projectwide support tasks, such as technical support and project management, are properly staffed.

Consider the staffing plans for each team, as well as the need to move resources from one activity to another over time. Additional adjustments to individual work programs and staffing schedules may be necessary to smooth the overall consolidated project loadings.

Obtaining Management Review and Approval. Finally, developers must obtain approval of the final work program, project organization, and overall timetable from the steering committee, project sponsor, and other applicable user and IS management. If the detailed work planning process resulted in changes to the project scope, approach, or assumptions, these should be highlighted. If costs have changed significantly, approval by the management advisory committee may also be required.

Developers should update the project scope-and-approach memorandum and any other relevant going-in design objects. These plans and objects now become the baseline for scope management and serve to confirm the agreement between the project team and the system's sponsors.

MANAGING A CLIENT/SERVER OR NETCENTRIC PROJECT

The ultimate goal of effective project management is to ensure the delivery of a high-quality system that meets user requirements and is completed on schedule and within the approved budget. This goal contains inherent conflicts, however, which project management must resolve.

Although the guidelines and tasks of project management address techniques to effectively control most projects, each project has unique characteristics that may reduce or enhance the effectiveness of those techniques. The management process must constantly weigh trade-offs between schedule, budget, available resources, capability, user satisfaction, and quality. It is critical that in assigning priorities, project management is guided by the business case and by quality requirements.

Guidelines for Project Management

The degree of project management required is directly related to the size of the project and to the associated risks. For large, high-risk projects, several full-time project management personnel and possibly a separate team may function as support for some of the management activities. On smaller projects, a single project manager may bear these responsibilities or they may be distributed across the project teams. For example, the business systems development team leader might maintain the user relationships while the architecture team leader manages the vendor relationships.

Senior project management personnel and the project's primary team leaders perform the majority of project management activities. However, some work, particularly within the time tracking and issue tracking activities, may be delegated to administrative support personnel.

Project management personnel should have a project management background as opposed to a line management background. They should be driven by goals and products and possess a thorough understanding of the project methodology. Project managers need a mix of functional and technical skills. They do not have to be experts in either area, but they must be able to understand the issues and know where to go to find the necessary detailed information. In addition, they need a clear understanding of the approaches and techniques to be used. The more innovative the project and the higher the risk, the more critical it is to have experienced project management personnel.

A full-time manager can typically manage the activities of six direct reports. On projects of five team members or fewer, the project manager (or team leader) can perform administrative responsibilities as well as some of the core process tasks. When there are more than six members on a project (or team), project management should establish subteams, each with its own supervisor or team leader.

Managing and Reevaluating the Process. The key challenge of project management is to think ahead, anticipating potential problem areas. One way this can be done is to monitor the development process continually for areas of inefficiency, poor productivity, misestimated activities, inappropriately defined requirements, misunderstandings, or insufficient training.

In addition to individual performance indicators, project management must look for trends that might indicate a need to streamline the process. When they identify such a need, supplemental training and the involvement of outside experts or vendor personnel can often improve performance. At other times, it may be necessary to pilot a new process or to pilot an old process in a new environment. This can help people to understand the process better and to work out any problems in a controlled setting before the majority of the project team embarks on the task, thus streamlining the process, building skills, and reducing the learning curves. Prototyping and early architecture development are important, as are the ongoing reviews of the project standards to ensure that they are, in fact, meeting the overall business and project objectives.

Although it is important to minimize the disruption caused by changing the process or standards midstream, this is sometimes justified if the change avoids more costly problems that would otherwise occur later.

Managing Multilocation Projects. If the project team is in more than one location, project management is more difficult and requires a far greater amount of effort. The problem increases along with the degree of separation:

different areas on the same floor, different floors in the same building, different locations in the same city, or multiple geographic locations. The greater the distance, the greater the need for formal communication mechanisms and for additional coordination and management time.

Technology can help with this problem in a variety of ways. Electronic design repositories and electronic mail systems can be connected via local or wide area networks. Facsimile machines can transmit other types of documents instantly. Audioconferences allow people in multiple locations to participate in the same meeting. Videoconferences, which can extend those capabilities to allow face-to-face and image communication, are an effective and cost-effective way of performing long-distance design reviews.

A company can overcome the problems of distance by exploiting technology to the extent possible, but it must recognize that additional time is necessary for a more formal coordination between locations. The organization must recognize, too, that standards and written communications assume a heightened importance because they ensure that team members in all locations are working consistently. For critical tasks, such as the start of programming or the end of system test, the organization should consider relocating some individuals so that groups that must work together closely are physically co-resident. For example, the organization should consider placing on-site technical support personnel with the programming teams and on-site technical support and user personnel with the system test execution teams.

Issue Tracking and Scope Control. Rigorous issue tracking and scope control are keys to successful project management. Formally tracking issues and open points helps to control the analysis and design process by maintaining documentation of all issues and their resolutions. In addition to tracking, project management must also help to facilitate the resolution process by setting forth a procedure to review, act on, and resolve issues in a timely manner. By circulating issue documentation to all affected parties, management can minimize the risk of misunderstandings being detected later, during detailed design, programming, and systems testing. In addition, the issue documentation serves as an audit trail to justify future design and implementation decisions.

Similarly, formally tracking change requests helps to improve communication between developers and users and to eliminate misunderstandings in later stages of the project. By documenting all potential scope changes and enhancements in the form of change requests, the project team can continue to meet deadlines without the users feeling their requests have been ignored. This process also ensures that management can allow for the prioritization and incorporation of these changes after thorough analysis of the business benefits and of the resulting effects on the project's cost and schedule. It allows for justifiable changes to be made, with less critical requests deferred until future enhancement releases. This approach keeps the project on the course set out by management and ensures users that their requests are are being addressed and not disregarded.

User Sign-Off. User understanding, acceptance, and approval are critical to the success of any systems development project. An organization must be sure to obtain user and management commitment in the early stages and to identify and obtain the participation of key individuals from the affected user departments. The organization should define a formal sign-off process that ensures documented feedback and approval on the system scope, system schedule, system designs, issue resolutions, system test plans and results, and conversion plans.

The organization should educate user participants and management about the importance of their input and stress the importance of timely participation and feedback. It should consider setting up default approval guidelines to ensure that the project does not fall behind due to the inability of users to provide timely review. For instance, the default might stipulate that all designs not receiving feedback within five business days are assumed to be approved.

Specific development techniques, particularly prototyping and joint application design (JAD), can also contribute to effective user approval of the system design. Prototyping allows users to see, touch, and experience the system early in the development process and to review it more naturally than by inferring it from abstract or technical documentation. Similarly, JAD provides a forum designed to build immediate consensus. Concentrating all the key stakeholders on a design or issue at the same time helps to develop a common understanding and approach and to achieve a high-quality, workable solution.

Quality Management. Project managers should ensure that an effective quality management process is in place and is followed. Qualified quality reviewers with experience in similar project management, functional, and technical environments should be identified during project organization and should participate throughout the life of the project. They should schedule and conduct quality reviews on a regular basis. The frequency of the reviews should be commensurate with the duration and risk of the project. Project management should ensure that the project team is prepared for the reviews, that the reviewers document their findings in a timely fashion, and that the project team follows up on any identified review points.

The organization should encourage project managers and team leaders to further benefit from the quality plan by frequently consulting the quality management documentation when planning and executing tasks, as this makes the quality program a more proactive part of the management process.

Design Issues vs. Change Requests. Another management challenge during the systems design phase is to distinguish issues from change requests. Management should address this challenge by defining scope as specifically as possible early in the systems design process.

Project managers should prepare a complete list of the functions, features, and interfaces that the system requires as well as a list of the assumptions about the technical environment. They should estimate the counts for each key system component (e.g., dialogs, windows, screens, and reports), being as specific as possible (three customer service dialogs, two sales dialogs). The more precisely program managers state the scope, the easier it is to distinguish between design decisions that fall inside, or outside, the approved scope.

An organization should consider budgeting a contingency to cover the inevitable omissions. This will allow the critical change requests to be approved without requiring further project funding authorization.

Scope control becomes particularly important during prototyping tasks, especially when working in a newer environment such as the world of GUIs. During prototyping tasks, project management must guard against overdesigning, overimplementing, and overpromising more than can reasonably or technically be delivered. Project managers must be sure to properly set the expectations of users participating in the prototyping tasks.

Meetings and Communication. The systems design phase of a project tends to require many meetings to interview users, discuss issues, review ideas, and coordinate activities. Although these are critical components of the process, they also are time consuming. Designers should try to maximize the effectiveness of meetings by

Creating an agenda (or interview questionnaire), developing meeting objectives (exit conditions), and preparing participants before actually conducting the meeting

Limiting attendance to the required individuals to ensure proper coverage and focus (using minutes, interview notes, issue write-ups, or other forms of documentation to communicate the results of the meeting to others)

Considering JAD techniques that involve several user constituencies at once rather than performing a series of individual interviews

Recognizing that issues may arise that cannot be immediately resolved and that they should note these points for later follow-up and assign appropriate due dates to prevent the wrong personnel from dealing with them at the wrong time

Using electronic mail to communicate more effectively (including management and users in this process as well)

In conjunction with these techniques, designers should incorporate meeting time into the project plans and track actual vs. projected time for all meeting activities. They should monitor this variance to identify and address particular areas of concern as soon as possible.

Iterative Nature of Design. Analysis and design tasks are inherently iterative, especially when significant change is involved — as in the case of GUIs, business process reengineering, or custom architecture development. It may not be possible to perform all tasks sequentially, to complete everything that could be done, or to complete a task without revising it later.

Systems developers should recognize this tendency and adjust project plans accordingly. They can consider holding a percentage of the task budgets and durations for later revision, and they can use the mechanisms of issue, open point, and sign-off aggressively to minimize inefficiencies that are a result of information or untimely feedback.

Developing Detailed Work Schedules

Long-Term vs. Short-Term Scheduling. Although the work planning activities within the project organization activity break down the work into detailed tasks, schedules, and assignments, project planning is nonetheless an ongoing, iterative process. There are several reasons for this.

It may not be realistic or efficient to plan detailed work assignments for a horizon of longer than three months. Although positions may be identified from the start, specific staff may not be available or identified, so designers should consider waiting to assign the individual work packages until they know the specific range of skills and experience and their availability.

An initial task may have to be completed before a subsequent task can be planned in detail. For example, if a project is based on an estimate of 50 programming work units, specific programmers will ultimately be assigned to each of those work units and given specific budgets and due dates. However, this may not be feasible until detailed design is well under way and each of the modules and their relative complexities and relationships have been firmly identified.

Various other circumstances may prevent the project from proceeding exactly as planned, causing reassignment of work and short-term rescheduling despite efficient planning. These circumstances include underestimating or overestimating a particular task, overruns that result from performance or training problems, or changes in the approved scope. For these reasons, even the most farsighted project managers must be willing to react responsively to events and changes as they occur.

Because detailed scheduling and loading are time-consuming processes, it is more efficient to perform broader, higher-level scheduling at the start of the project, followed by detailed scheduling when preparing for each significant phase of work. This avoids costly revision of schedules and assignments and allows project managers to use the most recent project and system information to more accurately create and refine their schedules and assignments.

Recognizing Different Types of Tasks. In planning detailed work, it is important to recognize that there are different categories of tasks. Some tasks, such as designing windows, designing work units, or coding work units, are driven primarily by the development of work packages. Others, such as requirements analysis, are more decision oriented. Still others, such as managing issues, supervising programmers, or managing the development environment, are based on elapsed time.

The nature of these three categories of tasks affects the way the tasks are scheduled, budgeted and managed. Program managers should

- Focus the work package-oriented tasks on the delivery of the work packages. Budget, assign, manage, and control work by individual work package.
- Focus the decision-oriented tasks on objectives and goals. Organize work by logical groupings of responsibility and let the objectives, time frames, and budgets guide the control of the task and level of detail of the work. Define objectives for the timeliness of decision making and issue resolution and monitor task progress against these goals.
- Make sure the duration of elapsed time-oriented tasks corresponds to the tasks they are supporting. Therefore, assign sufficient resources to elapsed time-oriented tasks to complement the resource levels of work package-oriented tasks. Recognize the dependencies between the categories and adjust each one accordingly.

In addition, when staffing and managing each type of task, program managers should recognize that the skills and motivational techniques used in each of the three cases may be different.

Managing Day-to-Day Activities

Supervising Personnel. Supervising personnel is a key day-to-day activity of project management. Following is an overview of key techniques to perform the activity more effectively. Program management should:

- Identify tasks that team members can reasonably perform and that are consistent with their level of skill and experience. Try to carve out overall areas of responsibility for each team member rather than sequentially assigning them random tasks. This promotes task ownership and provides improved motivation. Use personnel resources efficiently, but guard against delegating too much. This can adversely affect work quality, team morale, project schedules, and cost. Clearly communicate project objectives, goals, and quality levels. Instill a set of common values (such as quality) in all team members and recognize achievement in terms of those values. Clearly communicate specific objectives and expectation levels for each task. Make sure team members understand the budget and schedule constraints as well as the nature of the products they must produce and any special techniques they must use. Encourage them to develop their own individual work programs or to-do lists to ensure they understand the activities to be performed. Review these plans to ensure a mutual understanding, and measure progress against them.
- Adjust the degree of supervision and review it periodically during the project to match the complexity of the task as well as the skill and experience level of each team member. Confirm that the work is being done within the proper scope and that the work produced is of acceptable quality. Ensure that all open points are being addressed and that external review is being sought and utilized when necessary.
- Keep tasks to a manageable size. Identify intermediate deliverables and checkpoints for long-term tasks to ensure that the project is progressing properly. Failure to review work properly and catch problems early have more serious consequences as time goes on.
- Maintain a longer planning horizon than that of the team members. Anticipate problems and develop contingency plans. Strive to balance the work load and make the most efficient use of all team members' time.
- Keep an open line of communication with team members. Encourage them to work independently but also to seek assistance when necessary. Provide direction rather than prescribing what to do, but watch for work that is outside the project scope or for too much time spent investigating superficial items.

Budgets: A Self-Fulfilling Prophecy. Project budgets are often the make-or-break item for a successful or failed client/server or netcentric development project. Following is an overview of techniques to create more accurate and successful budgets. Project management should:

Be aggressive when assigning budgets to individual tasks, but should not overlook the impact of learning curves. The first in a series of repetitive tasks (e.g., the first window designed or the first module coded) takes a team member longer, but productivity should subsequently improve as that team member performs similar tasks. If the learning curve is substantial (as in the case of a new programming environment), consider redistributing budgets so that initial items take longer than the later ones. This avoids demoralizing team members at the beginning of a task and encourages productivity improvement as the project progresses. If the learning curve is less significant (e.g., for screen design), use average budgets and expect some slight variances.

Recognize that budgets can become self-fulfilling prophecies, especially if they are overly generous. Remember to give praise for work completed under budget, in addition to focusing on overruns. Encourage excellence by setting aggressive but reasonable budgets. Allow for minor overruns on initial tasks and challenge team members to improve their productivity over time. For example, the project manager might target tasks to be completed in 90% of the originally budgeted time and retain the remaining budget as additional contingency. This is generally an effective technique, but it can backfire if the revised budgets are truly unreasonable. Monitor the use of this technique to ensure that team members are not overly pressured, as this can prove even more detrimental.

Resolving Routine Issues. In the course of day-to-day project management, routine issues arise that require the attention of supervisors and managers. These issues may involve an inefficient allocation of resources, an individual performance or training problem, or a need to reschedule a short-term activity. It is important to distinguish these routine items from the project's design, technical, or management issues because these issues typically do not require a high degree of formality. Items that can be resolved within a supervisor's or manager's scope of control, with no impact on the project scope, budget, schedule or quality, should be handled swiftly. Generally, no formal administration is needed. If these items linger, however, or cannot be resolved, project management should escalate them and address them through the formal issue resolution process.

Managing Risk. One of a manager's most important day-to-day responsibilities is managing risk. Management identifies the key potential risk areas during project organization, and also formulates risk mitigation strategies at that time. These risks are discussed in more detail in Chapter 15. Managers must ensure that these risk mitigation strategies are followed and that they successfully address the project risk areas. In addition, they should routinely reevaluate the status of the project against the risk criteria to confirm that additional risk areas have not surfaced. In particular, project managers should revisit the following areas.

Organization. Are the project, user, and management organizations stable, and do they work well together? Is the area of communications adequately and accurately addressed?

Innovation. If there is significant innovation on the project (in terms of business process change, technical environment, or development process), is that work managed properly and progressing as expected? Are the appropriate experts (both inside and outside the organization) being consulted as necessary for review and confirmation?

Project Scope. Is the project progressing within the approved scope, and does that scope still support the business case? Is the scope control process effective?

Project Staffing. Is the project receiving the required level of qualified staff within the required time frames? Are the skill and experience levels of the project team, management, and user representatives appropriate to the tasks they are asked to perform? Are there any significant performance or learning curve areas that could be addressed by additional training or piloting? Are there any skill areas in which the project is weak or deficient? Should outside experts be consulted? Is the project training meeting the skill needs and requirements?

Project Progress. Is the project progressing as expected? Are there particularly troublesome areas that should be addressed by changes in organization, approach, staffing or skill mix?

Support. Are the external and internal support services (clerical support, local area network management, computer resources, legal, and purchasing) being provided at an adequate level and quality? In particular, are any areas on the critical path adversely affected by support problems?

Quality. Does the work being produced meet or exceed project quality objectives? Are reviews (both internal and user) generating significant amounts of revision? If so, have the causes been investigated and addressed?

Managing People

Motivation and Team Building. Motivation and satisfaction among team members are critical elements in the success of any project. Team members feel motivated when they see their work as worthwhile or important.

The work must challenge their skills, and they must make a noticeable impact on the project. Because team members may not understand the big picture, managers can provide additional motivation by explaining how individual assignments contribute to overall goals. Project managers can take advantage of the orientation process to clarify roles, interdependencies, and management expectations. Also, they use periodic project or team briefings on various aspects of the project to help the entire project team understand broader areas of the work being conducted.

The following techniques can be used to better motivate project teams:

- A leader's management style must promote ownership and personal integrity.
- Project management must make clear that team members may take the initiative but the project managers are accountable for the outcome of team's efforts.
- Project managers should provide feedback on a team member's overall performance, in addition to the results of individual incidents.
- Project managers should further enhance the sense of ownership by structuring teams as a representative cross-section of the work force. For example, a team might contain both user and IS personnel.
- Recognition and reward are keys to establishing and maintaining morale. Rewards may be tangible, such as bonuses or prizes, or intangible, such as positive feedback or team recognition.
- Informal gatherings and team competition are other ways to boost team morale.

Particular accomplishments, such as completing work units and achieving goals, also help to build team morale. Keep work units to a manageable size — typically 2 weeks or less — so that progress can be achieved in steps.

The team management approach rewards team members with many successes throughout the project, and enables them to see the whole team progress. Project management should adapt the team management approach to the characteristics of the team. Specific motivational factors such as praise, advancement, team identification, and competition may not apply to all cultures. Project managers should become acquainted with all the team members to learn what motivational style may be most effective for each of them.

Managers and supervisors should facilitate and monitor the progress and professional development of their team members. They should give informal, constructive feedback frequently and conduct formal progress reviews on a regular, timely basis. They should assign work as appropriate to team member skill and experience levels and identify areas for training or additional skill building. Within the constraints and objectives of the project, managers should strive to satisfy team members' personal career objectives.

Monitoring Progress

Finally, project management entails monitoring the progress of the project. Five key categories of progress measurement are useful for monitoring a project's progress:

- Budget variance
- Resource variance
- Schedule variance
- Work package variance
- Cost variance

Although not every project requires that all five categories be monitored or that they all be monitored to the same degree, they are typical of the type of information most projects monitor. Managers should determine at the onset of the project which measures will be monitored and to what degree. Then they should ensure that the work planning and time reporting procedures capture the necessary information. Finally, managers must be sure to address and define the reporting requirements for the project progress measures.

Budget Variance. Budget variance (also known as productivity or efficiency variance) indicates the project progress as measured against the budget. Budget variance provides a sense of how closely the project will meet the estimated number of workdays. An unfavorable budget variance, without any offsetting variances in other areas, generally indicates that the project will finish later than scheduled and at a higher cost.

To determine budget variance, managers should track actual time against the budget. As actual time is incurred, managers should provide a revised estimate to complete that indicates how much effort is required to complete the task. The sum of "actual-to-date" and "estimate-to-complete" yields the projected estimate at completion. The difference between this calculation and the original budget becomes the budget variance.

Resource Variance. Resource variance (also known as staffing, utilization, or expenditure variance) indicates whether anticipated staffing levels have been met. An unfavorable resource variance without any offsetting productivity gains in other areas generally indicates that the project will finish later than scheduled. This, in turn, may contribute to budget and cost variances in other time-driven tasks (as opposed to work package-driven tasks).

To determine resource variance, managers must identify the scheduled hours per week per team member. As actual time is incurred, they must compare the time spent on all productive project tasks with the time originally scheduled. This difference represents the resource variance. Resource variance calculations become even more accurate when projections of future resource availability are combined with the variance experienced by the project to date.

Schedule Variance. Schedule variance indicates whether the project will meet its completion dates. This variance is the combination of the budget and resource variances coupled with any additional impact due to critical path and task dependencies. A simple schedule variance is a straight sum of the budget and resource variances. Budget and resource variances may offset each other (less available time may be compensated by more productive time), but two unfavorable variances have a cumulative effect (less available time is further exacerbated by reduced productivity).

In more complex situations, dependencies between tasks may require more sophisticated extrapolation to determine the full effects on the project's schedule of variances in the schedule of each individual task. Although a schedule variance for a task on the critical path forces a corresponding schedule variance for the project, it may be possible to compensate elsewhere for schedule variances that do not occur on the critical path. Similarly, a schedule variance for a task on the critical path may result in additional budget variances for related, time-driven tasks. For example, delays in extending the schedule for the coding task incur additional programming supervision and technical support time.

Work Package Variance. Work package variance (also known as product, deliverable, or earned value variance) tracks whether work packages are being delivered as scheduled. As with schedule variance, work package variance is a key indicator of whether the project will finish on time.

Work package variance can be used as a reasonability check against budget variances and estimates to complete. For example, if 60% of a task budget (such as design work units in the detailed design segment) has been expended but only 25% of the expected work packages are complete, a problem is indicated. Although some of the variance might be attributable to a learning curve, it is likely that the estimates to complete and the resulting task budget variance have been understated.

Cost Variance. Cost variance translates the budget and schedule variance into dollars. It converts actual days spent and days projected into payroll dollars and then compares them to the original plan. This variance reflects the overall cost-effectiveness of the staffing mix and productivity levels. Cost variances may also reflect planned vs. actual levels of outside (nonlabor) expenses.

A cost variance may occur independently of the budget variance or of the resource variance. For example, a task may be over budget by 10%, but the overall cost variance may actually be favorable because the budget variance is due to lower productivity caused by staffing the task with less skilled and less costly resources. Another example of a cost variance occurs when a more expensive resource is used to cover a shortfall in a less expensive resource, increasing the overall project cost. In this example, however, there is no budget or cumulative resource variance because the task takes the same number of workdays.

CONCLUSION

One of the most important things to bear in mind when managing a netcentric project is that the new business/technology solutions are not faster, easier, or cheaper. However, an organization can obtain major business change and benefit with the delivery of client/server-based and netcentric-based solutions. Organizations should proceed with caution, always weighing the benefits against the costs of the application of the new technology.

The world of netcentric applications development and delivery is a new and challenging environment. One of the critical key success factors to prospering in this world is to make sure that development activities are adhering to a sound, complete set of methods, procedures, techniques, and deliverables. There is no one right or complete answer to this issue. In fact, numerous interrelated methodologies and techniques (such as object-oriented and information engineering) often must be integrated into a cohesive development approach and methodology. Experience has shown that even the definition and delivery of an iterative approach to netcentric development is *itself* an iterative process. Systems designers always need to be assessing what they are currently doing and what they might be doing with a methodology.

This chapter has discussed the major activities, techniques, and issues associated with planning, estimating and managing a project for client/server and netcentric implementation. Although most of the activities are not inherently unique to client/server or netcentric development, these development environments require sound project management skills and techniques.

Chapter 27
Change Management

For some time, information systems (IS) professionals operated under the assumption that the focus of change was on the system *user.* Developers designed and implemented systems and then trained users — a week or two before conversion — to use the system, believing, "If you build it, they will come."

However, the real world of the business user is hardly a field of dreams. One large bank converted to a new system that made use of imaging to cut down on the reams of paperwork generated each year. Soon after conversion, the IS department realized that employees were calling up document images and sending them to their printers, so they could have a hard copy anyway.

Consider the large utility that developed a new customer service system. By every conventional measure, the project was an enormous technological success: on time, on budget, with on-line performance measured in the low fractions of a second. However, the impact on the manner in which employees performed their jobs was huge and not predicted adequately. The utility staffed its customer service center on the presumption that an average telephone episode with a customer would take four minutes. However, for the first 3 months after conversion, the average was 6½ minutes. If that customer time could not be reduced, the economics of the entire multimillion-dollar investment would have been undermined.

INTEGRATING CHANGE MANAGEMENT WITH SYSTEMS DEVELOPMENT

There are numerous examples like these: examples not just of making change happen, which is relatively easy, but of making change work, which is very difficult. IS professionals must now expect to initiate a change management program that is integrated with their systems development projects. There are a number of approaches to planning and managing such a change program, and this chapter discusses several.

Change management is a relatively new management dimension and a great deal of innovation has recently come from many different sources. In no way should this chapter be considered a comprehensive discussion of change management principles. Today, opportunities to dramatically improve the performance of businesses are being found by focusing on human performance within companies. New forms of human resource management, new forms of enablement and training, organization design, journey navigation — all these are important developments in recent management theory. Change management has implications that extend well beyond information technology projects, though that is the primary focus in this chapter. This chapter will look at change management in terms of its ability to help the people of an organizations assimilate — accept and take advantage of — new technology.

THE PROJECT TEAM AS A CHANGE AGENT

A netcentric or client/server development team is a change agent in itself. For the system to bring benefits, the project team must convince its users that the system will make them more effective in performing their jobs and in achieving the organization's business objectives. The project is of no value if the users do not accept and implement the changes implied by the system.

Involving Users

User involvement helps ensure that the system satisfies management expectations. In the long run, the involvement and active participation of qualified, empowered users prevents serious problems, rework, conflicts, and delays. User involvement in the systems development process has the following benefits:

- It facilitates acceptance at an early stage.
- It helps to champion and gain support for the project throughout the organization.
- It maintains a realistic level of expectations.
- It ensures that the true business requirements are being addressed.

Choosing a Project Sponsor

The project sponsor is a key part of the project advisory structure. In the context of change management, the project sponsor plays a crucial leadership role in ensuring the success of the system. Effective sponsors can help achieve buy-in from the user community, ensuring that users "own" the change being caused by the new system.

The project sponsor is responsible for demonstrating the organization's overall commitment to a specific systems development project and for ensuring that user and IS organizations remain interested and committed. The sponsor is typically an executive from the user organization who will benefit most from the system and will pay for its development. The sponsor must have a genuine interest in the project and must be able to convey this commitment to both the steering committee and the rest of the enterprise.

If possible, the sponsor should be the steering committee chair and a representative on the management advisory committee. This allows the sponsor to better emphasize the project's importance during meetings and to take appropriate action if progress slows down because of reduced commitment from users or IS personnel.

Despite the heavy involvement of the project sponsor in the system's development, an organization should avoid the tendency to place a senior IS representative in this role. Such an individual may not be a true representative of stakeholders and their interests. Placing a user representative in the project sponsor role helps to ensure that its users accept the system and integrate it with the business process. The organization should complement the project sponsor by giving an IS representative the lead role in managing day-to-day the project development effort.

Managing User Involvement

The greater the impact of the system on the business organization and its structure, the more complex the challenge to the project team becomes. The change agent role becomes more difficult and requires more interaction with users when the project modifies many facets of organizational infrastructure (e.g., numerous organizational units, processes, culture, and reporting relationships). It is critical that users are given the tools and the motivation to change. This is accomplished by involving users in system design and having them help determine the expected benefits.

The development of the system could also require a significant change in IS's skill base and in its investments in network and operations support infrastructure. Involving users early and demonstrating management's commitment help to build the case for significant change in IS. It is also important to ensure that both IS and the user department agree on direction.

Complex netcentric or client/server applications are more likely to affect white-collar professional positions. Because the related business functions may not have been automated previously, more user involvement may be necessary, especially in the early stages. In addition, this group is likely to have a stronger influence than clerical workers on the look and feel of their system.

Users should play a key role in analysis and design, providing insight into the business, functional, and operational objectives, and details of the target application. Some effective techniques for involving end users in specification and design of systems are joint application design (JAD), focus groups, facilitated meetings, prototyping, usability tests, and participation in issue and business case analysis. During installation, users should participate in detailed design issue resolution, test planning, data

Can the workforce perform optimally?

Will the workforce perform optimally?

Exhibit 1. Optimum Human Performance Results from Attention to Context, Ability, and Motivation.

purification, test execution, rollout planning, procedure development, and training.

TECHNOLOGICAL CHANGE IN CONTEXT

User involvement is a practical approach to coping with technological change. However, technological change must be placed in its larger context. An overall change management program sees human performance — not an information system — as its primary focus. What are the tasks and goals that employees are charged with accomplishing, either individually or as members of a team? How do the information systems of an organization relate to those goals? What kinds of performance support, especially support delivered technologically, do workers need to perform optimally?

This human-centered viewpoint of technological change illustrates technology in its larger context within the organization and works toward the goal of creating an environment in which every worker can perform optimally (Exhibit 1).

The first issue to consider in empowering workers to attain and sustain optimum performance is "Can the individual perform the necessary tasks?" This question primarily involves matters of ability: the aptitude, knowledge, and skills of the work force. The second issue, however, relates to motivation as well, "Will the individual perform the necessary tasks?" Here an organization must concentrate on issues of the needs, values, and attitudes of the work force. The third component of the performance model, context (or environment), spans both performance questions. An organization's self-understanding, its technology, and its processes should ensure that adequate support is provided to the worker to ensure optimum performance.

Organizations cannot overestimate the motivational value of that orientation. The employees of a performance-centered enterprise are more satisfied, more fulfilled. Ingvar Petursson, chief information officer of McCaw Cellular Communications, notes that "employees feel frustrated when they do not have supporting resources available to them when they need them. That frustration increases as they get into a more dynamic and fast-changing environment. And frustration leads inevitably to dissatisfaction."

REENGINEERING AND ADVANCED CLIENT/SERVER CONCEPTS

The cost and difficulty of netcentric and client/server computing can be justified only if the organization is fundamentally changing its business processes. Business process reengineering reflects changes in the roles, responsibilities, and rules that define a business. New processes are essential for any organization attempting to implement netcentric computing.

To define the reengineered business process, it is first necessary to understand the business and the information technology and what the technology can do for the business. The organization must analyze the business process and each of its steps, asking why and how they contribute to the business. Only then can a reengineered process emerge.

However, how can people be empowered and supported actually to perform the new process? Traditional computing solutions often unintentionally interfered with natural performance of job tasks by making the system itself the focus of work. One of the dramatic ramifications of client/server computing is that, because of its inherent flexibility and adaptability, information technology can now be designed around the actual performance needs of the business community. Several important facets of advanced client/server computing can, if properly designed and managed, facilitate the management of change:

- Distributed information
- Graphical user interfaces (GUIs)
- Advanced usability principles

Distributed Information

The distributed character of information and processing in a netcentric or client/server environment implicitly empowers employees. Processing power is placed at the workstation, and — within certain well-defined boundaries — workers are given instantaneous access to information for which they previously had to wait hours or days.

With the opening up of an organization's information flow, and with the coming of new kinds of users — from clerical workers to professionals — the "usability gap" drastically increased. It may well be that the well-documented failure of information technology to return on its investment for many organizations over the last decade is traceable to an increase in system complexity accompanied by an enlarged user pool.

To counter this development, systems professionals have increasingly been turning to advanced research in human–computer interaction to increase efficiency and effectiveness of people interacting with systems.

Graphical User Interfaces

GUIs are usually discussed simply in terms of how they enhance system usability. However, the importance of GUIs goes beyond usability. A GUI can mimic the work world of an employee; it can represent pictorially the mental model of how a person perceives his or her work. By extension, then, an organization can facilitate change by representing a new work process in a graphical mode for its employees. (Remember, however, that a GUI does not mean a simplistic interface. Some interfaces, such as for factory or refinery applications, can be extremely busy and complex in order to present the work environment just as the users see it. Engineers can then plan, monitor, and control with the aid of the system, which supports their work in a natural way.)

Change, however, can be managed more effectively with an effective GUI. A process change can be reinforced for workers by altering the system interface (and its capability, of course). New kinds of help and performance support, delivered through the system, can then be designed to further facilitate performance of the changed process.

Advanced Usability Principles

Usability of a system goes beyond interface design. Usability is a dynamic quality and relates to every aspect of the interaction between a person and a system. Interaction has many dimensions, but this section focuses on four of them: presentation, navigation, manipulation, and integrated performance support.

Presentation. A GUI is the most obvious tool with which systems now provide more powerful aid to users. But presentation involves more than the primary interface. Effective presentation in client/server computing means that the user is able to recognize and choose rather than having to remember. The system should not force users to remember things the computer already knows. Technical details should be masked from users — users should not be distracted by or expected to understand technical details.

Navigation. How does a worker discover and then take advantage of all the capabilities, all the functions, of the information system? For example, with what percentage of the full options of their major word processing software packages are users familiar? If the percentage is small, users must ask themselves why. The answer is because it is difficult to navigate through the application and find everything that a user is able to do.

Options are not dynamically presented in the context of what the user is trying to accomplish, and there is no feedback to let users know they have successfully performed an action. There is little or no advice provided to help users perform, icons and menu options are grouped or labeled in a way that makes it difficult to locate and understand information, and the cost of changing or standardization to a new application package is significant.

The traditional response of organizations to these design problems has been user training. However, traditional training is costly, time consuming, and takes the worker away from the job. Advanced usability principles implemented in client/server systems make navigation through a system more natural and intuitive. Context-sensitive help and advice from the system coach workers through their tasks and point them toward additional system functions that can support their work.

Manipulation. How does a user work with data and information, and move that information around? Until the advent of GUIs, manipulation of data was a labyrinthine process. Consider the amount of effort necessary with older word processing programs to do a simple task: copying a document from the computer's hard drive onto a diskette.

When Apple revolutionized the marketplace with its GUIs, the process became intuitive and obvious. An icon, or symbol, of a piece of paper represented the document; it was located in a file, represented by an icon of a file folder. With the handheld mouse, users pointed at the file, clicked on it, and "dragged" it over to another icon representing the diskette.

Integrated Performance Support. Integrated performance support (IPS) involves creating a system that includes for users a proactive suite of advice, tools, reference, and training available to workers whenever and wherever they need it. IPS has begun to make an impact in its most important area: letting system designers know that training can be built into a system rather than administered to users after the system has already been implemented.

ABILITY AND MOTIVATION: AN INCREMENTAL APPROACH TO ACHIEVING USER ACCEPTANCE

In an ideal development world, trained change management professionals are involved from the beginning in an organization's reengineering initiatives, in

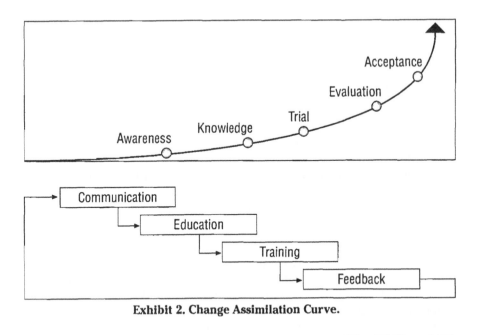

Exhibit 2. Change Assimilation Curve.

developing both the business and technology visions prior to systems development, and in helping with system usability issues. However, this is not always an ideal world. Indeed, budgets are often tight, and management is still prone to make its first cuts in change management and training line items in the budget. In fact, this point of view places the entire development process at risk. The following discussion presents an approach to change management during systems development that can help your project to succeed.

The traditional mind-set regarding system users focuses only on the "ability" aspect of the change model noted earlier. User training tends to be knowledge based. Put users in a classroom with a collection of reference binders and an instructor and then give them some training at the system. In fact, there is a spectrum of activities needed if system users are truly to be motivated to work in new ways, and enabled to perform optimally.

Business users move through several stages over time until they attain acceptance of a reengineered business process and a new information system. As the curve in Exhibit 2 indicates, change management begins well in advance of user training.

User Awareness

The first stage is to build awareness of the reengineered business process and any new technologies. This means helping the business user understand what the system is about, why it must be changed, and — at least in a preliminary way — how the reengineered process will work.

Relentless communication is a vital part of this stage: presentations about the new process, prototype demonstrations, and various written and verbal communications. These early communication efforts must be led by a business user who has the respect of the business organization, particularly the users of new systems. Without this, the typical IS person may have a credibility problem in advising business users on the need to do things differently.

User Knowledge

Awareness building is followed by an effort to build real knowledge of the proposed reengineered business process and the new technologies being proposed. This stage involves a more intensive effort to ensure that the user understands how the new process and system behave and how the user will perform with the aid of the system. A model office, including a complete simulation of the proposed work environment, is useful at this stage. The business user can go through significant parts of the workday and deal with specific parts of the new business process.

Trial and Evaluation

Business users need to test the reinvented business process and new system in real time. Do the users have an adequate knowledge of the business? Do the new process and system make the business more effective? It is imperative that the change management and systems building teams listen to the business users' concerns about the new processes, work flows, and new technologies, anticipating potential problems. The teams must carefully consider whether the issues raised by users point to a deficiency in the new process or whether these issues simply reflect a natural reluctance to change.

If the problem relates to users' reluctance, systems builder must make a greater effort to explain why the new way is the answer for the future. However, if the systems builders determine that there is a need to change the planned reengineered process, the organization must undertake more reengineering work. The business users who wanted the change must review and evaluate it to ensure that it addresses their concerns. This is a way for users to see that they are a part of the systems-building process and can have an impact on results when they have real concerns. This perspective may be invaluable in enhancing the credibility of the systems-building team.

Although strategies vary depending on the size of the user population, the change management effort should attempt to move as many business users as possible through this process. Even if that can be done, however, it is vital to promote champions or change sponsors within the organization. Sponsorship must begin at the highest level within an organization and then ripple or cascade down as successive people become convinced about the importance of the business change and the system that will reflect that change.

The goal, ultimately, is acceptance of the system by those who use it. The larger concept here is increasingly being referred to as ownership of the change. As one executive has been quoted as saying, "Change is a door that can only be opened from the inside." Sponsors or champions are important to push change through an organization, but change has to be pulled from within as well.

User Training

Once testing, revision, and additional changes to process and system eventually begin to stabilize, the training effort can begin. It is important to remember, however, not to start training too soon. If it is begun too soon, the system may change significantly enough to require retraining — even "untraining" users in aspects of the system that no longer exist.

EFFECTIVE COMMUNICATION

User participation is probably the most effective means of communication with the user community. However, an organization should also employ other formal mechanisms. An organization should plan to communicate status formally to user management on a regular basis, as described below.

Project Sponsor

The project manager should hold regular meetings with the project sponsor to report status and resolve issues. The frequency of these meetings (weekly, semimonthly, or monthly) depends on the involvement of the project sponsor, the pace of the project, and the degree of risk. However, these meetings should occur at least as frequently as the steering committee meetings, and probably more often. If possible, the project manager should not combine these status meetings with the (weekly) project status meetings, as it may intimidate the project leaders and prevent them from communicating freely.

If necessary, the project manager should meet with the project sponsor on a regular basis to discuss proposed change requests, either in regular status meetings or separately. The project manager should maintain a close working relationship with the project sponsor. Because they share the responsibilities and the risks associated with the project, they must be able to communicate well and work together effectively.

Steering Committee

Project managers should hold regular meetings (typically monthly) with the steering committee to update members on project progress. Project managers should advise steering committee members of progress as measured by key project milestones and highlight any significant developments. Project managers should discuss major issues — resolved, unresolved, and those requiring the immediate attention of the steering committee. They should review any recommended scope changes (change requests) and obtain steering committee approval.

Project managers should base the frequency of the regular meetings on the degree of project progress and risk. They should convene special sessions of the steering committee when time-critical issues arise and brief the participants prior to the meeting so they will be prepared to resolve issues swiftly. Project managers should consider seeking the counsel of individual steering committee members when specific issues arise that fall within their area of expertise or directly affect their area of responsibility.

Management Advisory Committee

In contrast to the steering committee, which is formed specifically for the project, the management advisory committee (MAC) typically oversees more than one project. For this reason, it has a more limited involvement, usually only at key project milestones. Project managers should invite the MAC members to the initial steering committee meeting or should consider holding a separate kickoff meeting exclusively for them. Project managers should meet with the MAC near the end of the project when management approval is required to proceed to the next phase. In between, project managers should meet with the MAC either at significant project milestones or on a quarterly basis.

Between scheduled MAC meetings, project managers should keep MAC members informed of project status. Typically, they do this by sending them copies of the steering committee status reporting packages and by encouraging them to attend the steering committees if they wish. Project managers should copy MAC members on all significant correspondence to the steering committee members.

As with the steering committee, project managers should convene special sessions with the MAC when significant issues arise that require MAC members' input or approval.

Other User Management

Project management, in conjunction with the project sponsor, should decide on the mechanism for updating any other user management personnel involved with the project. In some cases it may be appropriate to copy such personnel on the status reports that go to the project sponsor or the steering committee.

At a minimum, any user management personnel involved in the sign-off process should also be involved in the issue-resolution process. Such personnel should regularly receive reports documenting outstanding issues and the resolution of closed issues as well as reports indicating the disposition of approved and outstanding change requests.

As appropriate, project management should include full-time user project personnel in all project team meetings and communication. This reinforces their status as true members of an integrated project team. Also, project management should consider the need for less formal types of communication or other creative approaches, to garner attention and foster better overall communication.

MANAGING EXPECTATIONS

Managing expectations goes hand in hand with communication. This is especially important for systems development efforts and applies particularly to projects of extended duration. Project management must maintain a delicate balance between users' enthusiasm and realistic expectations.

Management

First and foremost, project management should manage the expectations of the project sponsor, steering committee, and MAC. These are the project's leading advocates and they must be able to sell the project in realistic terms.

Project managers must make sure they clearly communicate the scope of the project. They must stress the benefits but make sure that everyone understands what is not included because misunderstanding and creative marketing eventually backfire. Project managers must make sure, too, that the project sponsors, steering committee, and MAC understand the development methodology and milestones; only when they know what to expect and when to expect it can they effectively evaluate the project's progress and management's effectiveness.

Project managers must work closely with the project sponsor to determine how to sell the project. They must consider what is necessary to achieve buy-in from the affected user departments, both management and the rank and file. They must consider how the IS department views the development project. Is it an attractive project, for example, in terms of exposure, technical challenges, and pioneering techniques?

Project managers should develop a consistent message about the system's benefits and scope. They must depict the project's time line in a way that makes progress easy to track. As the project progresses, they should provide further detail and examples of the benefits and high-level scope items. This focus on the business case improves users' understanding and encourages them to buy into the new concepts.

When developing netcentric systems, an organization should acknowledge the professional status of the users, who tend to be in more powerful positions than the rank-and-file users of conventional systems. Project managers should welcome their feedback; they must avoid condescension or the appearance that they are telling users how to perform their jobs.

Project managers must work carefully to achieve users' buy-in and enlist their support as advocates throughout the organization. Project managers should exploit users' knowledge by encouraging their participation in areas such as JAD, prototyping (business process, GUI, and application capability), design of new methods or processes (e.g., an improved credit scoring algorithm), change management, and system pilot and rollout.

In client/server and netcentric environments, project managers must also recognize the inherent complexities of GUIs and message-driven architectures and must set appropriate expectations. They must acknowledge that it may not be possible to test the infinite number of system software interactions and combinations and prepare users for an occasional glitch. They must consider rolling the system out slowly, in a more controlled fashion, to further limit the impact of such complexities.

User Participants

Project managers should be particularly sensitive to the expectations of users directly involved in the project, especially those who are interviewed or who provide review or sign-off. They should orient newcomers by providing the objectives and context of the project, but they should not provide guarantees for any specific capability, especially early on. Project management should solicit as much input as possible during the early stages of requirements gathering but guard against the impression that users and interviewees will have all their wishes satisfied.

Even for items clearly within scope, project managers must make sure that users understand the time frames in which they can expect to realize the benefits. When reviewing designs with users, project managers should be sensitive to their concerns and note their points but avoid scope creep — they should not agree to changes without approval from management within the user department.

Prototyping Is a Double-Edged Sword. Project managers must recognize that prototyping is a double-edged sword. A system may have a no more effective tool to demonstrate its capability and its look and feel, especially in a netcentric environment where users may be unfamiliar with GUIs. However, there is also no more dangerous tool than a prototype because the more realistic it is, the more likely users are to believe they have a working system.

When reviewing a prototype with users, project managers should stress positively its ability to be representative of the system but also must make sure the users understand the limitations and what it takes to get from here to there. Project managers must recognize the danger of generating tremendous enthusiasm from a prototype's review only to squelch that enthusiasm and do even more damage when users find out how long it will be before the system is actually delivered.

Project managers should emphasize the system's benefits but ensure that users understand that there will be a transition from their current state to the new process, and that they will experience some learning curve before they realize the benefits. Project managers should attempt to minimize the disruption of the conversion through good training and realistic preparation of target users. They can employ change management techniques to plan and achieve this transition.

External Customers

External customers are another class of users whose expectations may need to be managed. This is important for systems that have public or supplier access (such as automated teller machines or voice-response systems), systems that generate output that goes directly to customers (such as billing systems), or systems that closely serve customers (such as customer service applications).

In these cases, project managers should work closely with marketing specialists to determine how to publicize the change and how to prepare customers for the transition. They should not underestimate the lead times needed by marketing for these efforts (3 to 12 months is not unusual). Project managers must be extremely careful not to misrepresent the system to the marketing representatives. They must be sure that they clearly understand the scope and details of the system, and that they do not make any premature claims as to its capabilities or availability. Project managers should involve the project sponsor as the primary liaison in all significant marketing communication.

CHANGE MANAGEMENT AND TRAINING FOR IS PROFESSIONALS

Change management is just as important for the IS person as it is for the business user. The objective of IS change management is to complete the learning curve in the application of netcentric computing. This effort tends to be overlooked or treated in an ad hoc fashion. This is unfortunate because client/server and netcentric technologies can succeed only if systems personnel are well informed, trained, and experienced.

Rules, Schools, and Tools Method

One approach to developing training for IS personnel is dubbed the "rules, schools, and tools method." The first step to building new skills for IS personnel is to establish the overall methodology used for development. This methodology defines the tasks, steps, and deliverables within client/server development. It defines the roles of designer, programmer, architect, and project manager. This can be built on a custom basis, but often it is more cost-effective and timely to acquire one from an outside vendor, if necessary.

Once the rules are in place, systems developers can then define the training required for each role. Based on these requirements, developers can then select, purchase, or design the training and deliver it to the IS personnel.

The amount of training depends on the individual's background, the rules and technologies selected, and the architectures in place. It is reasonable to expect programmers to need 2 to 4 weeks of training; designers may need 1 to 3 weeks and architects 1 to 4 weeks. Project managers may need 1 to 2 weeks of training.

Following this training, systems developers should count on an additional period of time for the trainee to work with an experienced person doing job-related work. Building real proficiency comes both from classroom training and on-the-job experience. With all these factors considered, training can run from $1,000 to $4,000 per person. When going forward with client/server and netcentric technology, IS management should plan on one to two weeks of skills upgrading each year for each individual.

With regard to tools, as the rules are established, it becomes more logical to define criteria for selection and opportunities for building the tools to be used as a part of the systems-building effort for future netcentric environments. If the rules are not well defined, the selection process can lead to a set of discrete tools that are difficult to integrate and share across the entire development process.

Training Costs

Another issue is how to account for training costs. Companies use several strategies. Many sites simply try to ignore the costs and hope that they go unnoticed. That is not a wise choice. Inevitably, the training either does not happen or is done inadequately, with subsequent loss of effectiveness of the personnel.

A second approach is to have a formal training budget that treats skill upgrades as part of doing business. The advantage to this method is that it allows the IS department to focus on and control the cost of skill upgrades. It allows the organization to implement a program for the IS department, which can ensure a consistent and high-quality training program. Such an effort also creates a sense of the IS department working as a team to meet the shift to a new technology.

The problem with this approach is that when the organization undertakes the large technology shift to netcentric, the costs to build skills in the IS department can be so high that they may be questioned and perhaps denied.

Making the Business Case for Learning

A third strategy is to make the cost of learning a part of the business case for the application that is prompting the move to netcentric computing. Because these costs are typically only for the team members committed to the project, they are often smaller and more acceptable as an overall amount. In addition, the costs can be made a part of the business case for the application and thus have a direct payback. This approach also has its potential drawbacks. It may not be fair to ask one project to absorb all the costs associated with training people when that knowledge can be used across subsequent projects. In addition, the training received may be project specific and may not address the full range of training required for netcentric and client/server competence. The fact that only team members are trained can also create an "us vs. them" situation in which some people seem favored and others do not.

Decisions on how to pay for training depend on the site specifics. A site committed to upgrading the skills of its personnel continuously may value and measure a training budget that shows proof of commitment. A site focused on return on investment for each dollar may insist on the project justifying cost. The key point is that significant training is required for the move to netcentric technology. To succeed with this technology, the enterprise must invest in its personnel development.

Section IV
Special Topics

Chapter 28
Netcentric Security

A hacker penetrates the Web site of the Central Intelligence Agency and defaces it. The Chaos Computer Club writes an Active-X based Trojan horse that is downloaded to a user's PC and then enacts a funds transfer from Quicken. A disgruntled systems administrator commits acts of sabotage that causes a company to lose fifteen million dollars of business after he leaves. Hidden form fields present in numerous corporate Web sites leave sensitive information open to major security risks. These are a few examples of potential dangers in the netcentric computing environment.

Preserving security of information as it travels across the Internet, or even within an intranet, is complex. The Internet is a public resource accessible worldwide, comprised of heterogeneous nodes that are managed locally with minimal systemwide policy. However, businesses today rely on the Internet for the transfer of increasingly sensitive information. The interaction between diverse components (e.g., databases, operating systems, firewalls, routers, and application servers) makes it difficult to ensure that fundamental security requirements are met throughout the system. Implementing effective security in the netcentric computing environments often means finding and dealing with the weakest link in a large system of complex and dynamic links. However, the challenges are not insurmountable. By designing security into a netcentric solution and implementing the appropriate application, infrastructure, and procedural controls, security can be appropriately aligned with business risk.

Exhibit 1 illustrates several potential areas of weakness in a basic netcentric application.

The following explains the exhibit, starting on the right side and moving to the left:

1. The first vulnerability is from someone authorized to use the corporate network. After the insider attack, the next potential breach is through the corporate firewall. If the firewall is circumvented, a primary line of defense is lost, and attackers can launch a series of attacks against the internal network.
2. Assuming the firewall is secure, a second and potentially more likely target is the application (i.e., Web) server outside of the firewall. A number of possibilities exist, including unauthorized access to a

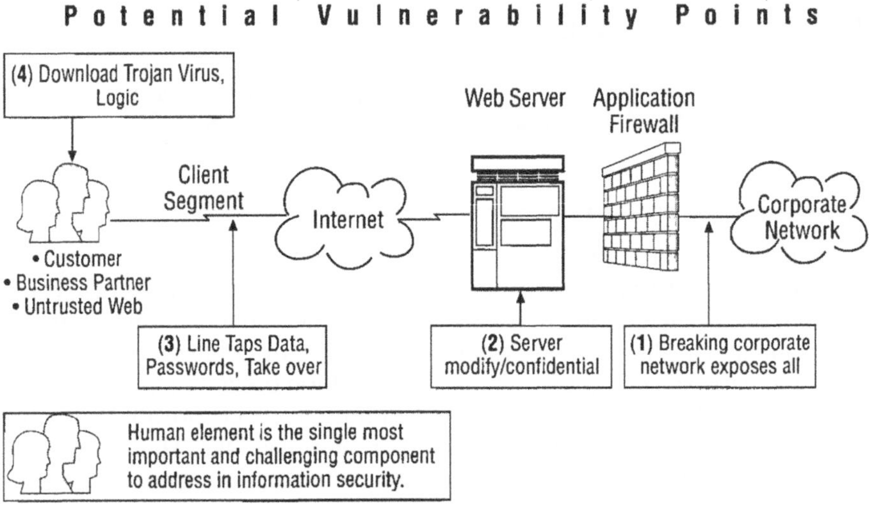

Potential Vulnerability Points

Exhibit 1. Vulnerabilities in Network Environments.

user account in order to withdraw funds from an investment account. A more serious breach may involve access to the operating system on the Web server: here, all user passwords can be intercepted, data can be captured and modified, and attacks may potentially be launched through the firewall against the internal corporate network and other supporting application servers, database servers, and other connected systems. Perhaps even more damaging is the use of such a Web server to represent the organization in a bad light or to conduct business transactions without the approval or knowledge of the organization's management. Liability for such transactions might be avoided, but the lasting damage to reputation may never be overcome.

3. A third risk involves interception of packets as they traverse the network between the client machine and the Web server. Fairly common are attacks on the Secure Sockets Layer (SSL) protocol, which is the protocol most often used to encrypt data across the Internet. Brute force attacks involving a number of computers in parallel have been successful when shorter key lengths, such as 40 bits, are used.

4. The most insidious technical risk of all is that of unauthorized code being downloaded to the user's computer and executing a harmful command. The Trojan horse written by the Chaos Computer club mentioned above is an example of this type of attack. Such code is acquired unwittingly either from sites run by individuals with malicious intent or from sites that are themselves victims of attack.

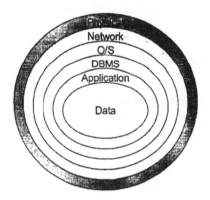

Exhibit 2. Layers of Security.

Although the sophisticated attacks, such as those against SSL, tend to get the most attention, it is actually the simple ones that are most often successful. The weak point is frequently a user who doesn't protect a password, a developer who doesn't code an application securely, or a system administrator who doesn't implement the necessary measures on a machine.

SECURITY LAYERS

The security objectives and requirements discussed in this chapter are applied to a variety of layers that exist in the physical computing environment. As shown in Exhibit 2, these layers are physical, network, operating system, database management system, application, and data.

The physical layer is the first line of defense. It represents basic controls like access to buildings and computer rooms. Physical security is one of the most critical layers since anyone with physical access to a machine may turn off any other security measures in place. Network security includes controlling access by firewalls, using subnets, and routing. Network security may be augmented by or include cryptographic assurances of correct data flow, data integrity, and confidentiality of data distribution. Operating system security has controls which provide authentication and access control services. The database and application layers provide additional controls on accessing data. One additional potential layer, not shown on this diagram, is middleware. Middleware products such as Tuxedo often mediate access between the netcentric system and legacy applications. In the future, some of the greatest issues will be those associated with the relationships and interdependencies that are formed or that breakdown between these layers.

NETCENTRIC COMPUTING AND THE HEIGHTENED NEED FOR SECURITY

Networks are increasingly replacing individual computers, and access to all kinds of computing resources — such as CPU cycles, disk storage, and RAM — are being mediated by the network instead of individual boxes. This change is significant because the most pervasive computer networks and networking protocols were never designed to be secure. The following are several beliefs that IS managers have held:

- Security is done in the operating system (e.g., RACF and ACF2).
- Security primarily involves creating IDs and passwords, and is a relatively simple matter.
- We can implement the system with a low level of security and then increase it later.
- Data inside the corporate network are secure.
- We will start thinking about security when we begin to plan the system rollout.
- Security is managed by the "security group" and they often restrict access too much.

The following discussion looks at the important features of netcentric computing environments that lead to increased reliance on heightened security measures.

THE NETCENTRIC WORLD IS VIRTUAL

The Changing Meaning of Location

In the past, organizations relied on the physical security of a location as a means of controlling access to systems; this is still true to a lesser extent today. Access to the data center is strictly controlled. Physical access to PCs is controlled through building access security. Network security often involves the establishment of "trusted" network boundaries, which in the past have corresponded to a company's officially designated places of doing business. However, telecommuting, virtual corporations, outsourcing, wireless networks, portable computers, and partnering arrangements are extending the boundaries of the network in increasingly complex ways. It is becoming increasingly difficult for security measures to rely on location as a means to validate the security access of a user.

Blurring Lines Between Internal and External Users

In the netcentric world, it is more difficult to distinguish clearly between internal and external users. Some of the greatest benefits in netcentric computing are achieved when we extend access to corporate systems to business partners and customers, creating more insiders. Why is this a security concern?

In testimony before the U.S. senate, FBI director Louis Freeh said, "A large portion of the computer intrusion reports that the FBI... receive have at their core an employee, or a former employee, who has exceeded his or her access, often in revenge for a perceived offense or wrong. These individuals have the knowledge of where the most sensitive information is stored, how to access the information, and, at times, how to steal or damage the data."

As more users become insiders, the levels of access and knowledge of systems expands towards a larger number of people with diminished loyalty to the organization. Consulting and outsourcing arrangements, telecommuting, vendor access, and virtual corporations all combine to make it difficult to draw concrete lines. Companies that maintain very strict security policies for external access will inhibit the formation of productive business partnerships and those who aren't careful enough may open up their network to intrusion from connected networks.

Less Permanence of Access

Permanence of access to systems is decreasing. Today, ad hoc partnering relationships are formed and then dissolved; an organization may have temporary needs for project resources, bringing in skilled people for short periods. Some consulting firms, for example, use development centers to support systems development activities. Several different development centers may be involved in a development effort, each communicating across a network with each other and with computing resources on the client's network. The project may be staffed at any combination of sites — either client or development center — and personnel may need varying levels of access to solution center and client systems for varying periods of time. After deployment, some of the maintenance activities may be outsourced and some of the company's employees may accept positions with the outsourcer. The project team access requirements must be met so that the job can get done, but access must be removed when it is no longer needed. In this transient environment, security must be flexible, timely, and address the complex issues that are present.

The Need to Establish Trust in Absence of Physical Observation and Contact

Most of today's retail purchasing involves a trip to the store and a face-to-face purchase. Customers know that the store is a legitimate store because they can see it, walk into it, and carry out the physical merchandise. The store clerk will accept cash, validate a credit or debit card, or accept a check with validation of some form of identification. Even in the case of telephone-based catalog sales, customers are generally assured that that they are talking to a bona fide merchant, because they initiated the calls to the well-publicized toll-free number, and the merchant is assured of payment by the credit card company.

In an eCommerce environment, it is more difficult to establish trust. The Web site that looks legitimate may exist only for the purpose of acquiring credit card numbers. Merchants and banks are affected because there is a lower level of assurance that the credit card number being provided is actually valid without the presence of a physical card. People are more likely to initiate fraudulent transactions when they do not come into physical contact with those whom they defraud.

Companies are rapidly discovering new types of consumer fraud that are unique to the netcentric environment. These types of fraud are not addressed by standard credit card authorization mechanisms or methods, such as Address Verification Screening (AVS), that have been used to combat fraud in the mail order environment. The stakes can be even larger in business-to-business transactions because the risk goes up as the number and value of those transactions increase.

ORGANIZATIONS ARE INCREASINGLY DEPENDENT ON KNOWLEDGE AND THE SYSTEMS THAT MANAGE IT

Increasing Importance of Knowledge Capital and Information as an Asset

The terms "information age" and information superhighway" are already cliches, even though we have only begun to realize the power of knowledge management in the organization. Information and knowledge will be primary currencies of this coming century, and organizations will need to manage information efficiently to compete effectively. One has only to observe the success of eCommerce enterprises to be convinced of the diminished importance of hard assets, such as plants and equipment, for some industries.

Knowledge management systems, data warehouses, and other types of information access will continue to increase in importance. A greater need to make knowledge capital and corporate databases available inside and outside the enterprise and the increasing value of that information serve to make protection of knowledge capital and information a significant challenge as organizations attempt to achieve a balance between security and the need to share information.

Increasing Dependence on Computers and Networks

Netcentric computing and client/server technology continue the trend toward increasing dependence on computer networks, as mission-critical applications are developed and new potential points of failure are created. When businesses use this technology to collaborate with one another, forming intricate relationships, this complexity is multiplied. When communication with vendors, partners, and customers depends on computer technology and when that communication becomes integral to the delivery of customer products and services, integrity and availability become the essential ingredient for success.

THE TECHNOLOGY IS EVOLVING WITH EVER-INCREASING SPEED

Increasing Intelligence of Devices and Communication with Those Devices

In the past, security was often under the purview of a small group of specialists who were experts in securing the centralized mainframe environment. With the move to client/server, this has been changing dramatically as more and more critical processing becomes distributed. Netcentric computing continues this trend with more complex functions and the corresponding distribution of security mechanisms throughout an organization, together with its business partners.

Furthermore, fewer than three percent of the microprocessors produced today go into traditional computers. The rest go into a host of other products and devices including medical equipment, appliances, stereos, environmental control systems, process controllers, navigation equipment, and network communications devices. As these products and devices become more sophisticated, more interactive, and ubiquitous, the paths of access among these devices and computers will be increasingly complex.

For example, Sun Microsystems unveiled a product called Jini, which uses the Java programming language to harness the power of potentially millions of computers, ranging from giant mainframes to tiny palm-sized devices. These kinds of developments, as one press report wrote, have "encouraged developers to proceed on the assumption that every home, car and other personal environment will eventually be part of — and empowered by — a universal network ... a world in which millions of small programs, called objects, seamlessly flit back and forth between tens of thousands of devices that have been enabled to recognize and be recognized by the network."

In a world of ubiquitous computing, security provisions must keep pace and yet not be too intrusive. Traditional ways of securing access, such as an ID and password at the device level, will not scale well in this environment.

Increasing Concerns Over System/User Privacy

The dark side of the visionary accounts of the world of ubiquitous computing is the growing concern for personal privacy. The ubiquitous network means, for example, that as we drive our cars, devices in the cars will communicate with systems to tell us our location, give us traffic and weather reports, and advise us on best routes. That capability also brings with it, however, the capability to be constantly tracked by "Big Brother." The speed with which data can now be aggregated and the use of focused intelligent agents to isolate data of interest means that everything from buying patterns to sensitive medical histories are possible targets.

Privacy is often confused with security; however, privacy is a somewhat different issue which is focused more on protecting information associated with individuals. Many countries have laws involving privacy of certain types of personal data such as medical records, addresses, and phone numbers. These laws and the rights of individuals will have increasing importance in the future.

Several concepts are important when considering privacy:

1. People should know what information is on file about them and should know how that information is used.
2. People should have the right to challenge and correct any erroneous information.
3. There should be no secondary use of the information without the person's consent.
4. The custodian of the information has an obligation to maintain security and quality of that data.
5. Some type of public notice should occur in cases where systems store private information about individuals.

Increasing Rate of Change in Technology and Its Deployment

Every new program and every new major enhancement to an existing program introduces the potential for software bugs. Some of the bugs may ultimately affect security. Examples of this have been found in browser software as well as in Windows NT and UNIX operating systems. In some cases, new technology is developed without sufficient consideration of the required security. In still other cases, the security features are there but people responsible for implementing them do not know how to use the security features. In other cases, people may know how to use the features, but they have difficulty in managing them across the plethora of environments.

It is common for IS managers to wait to expend resources on security because they are waiting for the technology to mature. However, in fact, products never really "mature"; they will just keep enhancing features and functionality to keep pace with new challenges. In fact, it is critical to select solutions that will keep pace with new versions of the technology, new standards that are being developed, and new industry directions so those solutions will integrate well with products under development.

Increasingly Sophisticated Attacks on Security

Easy-to-use software tools that automate sophisticated attacks on networks circulate freely on the Internet, so these tools are accessible to a broad range of unskilled intruders. Some examples of these tools include sophisticated programs that take advantage of weak points of the TCP/IP protocol and perform activities such as taking over an established user's sessions (also called a session hijacking). Such attacks have always been possible, but the technical complexity of performing the attack has prevented widespread abuse. Commercial and public domain software such as Satan and password crackers can also be used to look for security holes on devices attached to networks. Although these tools serve a valid purpose in the hands of a responsible party, they can also be used by attackers.

One of the most significant issues with netcentric security involves weaknesses at the client (a PC, PDA, etc.). Client operating systems often do not implement strong security. The fact that codes and files are downloaded to the client from a source that is often untrusted, raises all types of security concerns. Although there have been some attempts to combat these issues in browsers and in popular programming environments such as Java, these methods are far from foolproof. Malicious applets can redirect the PC to a phony Web site, steal passwords and certificates, and even launch attacks against the internal network to which the client is connected.

In the future, some of the most serious attacks will be directed against weaknesses in the client, because it has some of the most serious inherent security weaknesses. In addition, the greatest vulnerability will lie in network management systems, system management platforms, and key management/key recovery infrastructures. These components become the "keys to the kingdom"; once compromised, they grant access to a great number of machines on the network.

WHY SOLVING THE SECURITY PROBLEM IS IMPORTANT

As this book stresses, netcentric computing leads to immense business opportunities, which include

- *Lower cost.* The cost of performing a transaction through electronic media is an order of magnitude lower than the cost for a face-to-face transaction.
- *Increased efficiency.* Businesses and consumers can be in touch with resources around the world at a moment's notice.

SPECIAL TOPICS

- *Speed to market.* Netcentric technologies are more compartmentalized and reusable than older client/server counterparts, and also facilitate knowledge sharing from developers around the world, radically reducing development time.
- *Improved customer service.* Netcentric technology goes beyond simply improving customer service. Through media like the Internet and kiosks, technology solutions enable customers to serve themselves
- *Creates new services.* Netcentric computing does more than permit new channels to offer services; it adds a service dimension to physical products. Netcentric computing enables new products that meet new market needs.

If security issues cannot be solved, the technology cannot be implemented safely. To realize the potential benefits of netcentric computing, security issues must be addressed in a thorough, dynamic, and flexible fashion. New threats and risks evolve quickly in the netcentric environment, and security programs will become ineffective and obsolete if not reviewed and updated regularly.

A FRAMEWORK FOR IMPLEMENTING SECURITY

Today's netcentric computing infrastructure requires a complex mix of operating systems, Web servers, database servers, firewalls, management tools, routers, and underlying network components. Each different component of this infrastructure has specific security considerations that need to be addressed. Each component supplies some level of security protection, at the same time offering a target to an attacker.

How can organizations bring a set of components together to form a system and then determine the security attributes of the system from the analysis of the properties of the system's components? Companies are faced, on the one hand, with a set of high-level, abstract, system requirements and, on the other hand, with a combination of commercial products that may be configured in a multitude of ways and special-purpose devices and/or software developed by the system integrator. There is a substantial intellectual gap between the high-level statement of requirements and the realities of the implementation.

To bridge this gap, companies must start with a set of *security policies.* A security policy is the set of rules, directives, and practices that regulate how an organization manages, protects, and distributes sensitive information. A security policy is translated into access control rules that are enforced by the system. The desired attributes of the environment are realized, in turn, by the implementation of a set of "mechanisms" — functions that can be shown to provide the requisite attributes. The critical point is that one proceeds from policy (i.e., a high-level statement of the desired global properties or characteristics of the system) to a set of specific mechanisms.

Understanding fundamental security objectives and requirements is a prerequisite to the implementation of a good solution.

Policy Objectives

Many high-level policies begin by articulating broad objectives for the system under consideration. Frequently, these can be gathered under one of three general categories, sometimes referred to as "CIA":

- Confidentiality: data should be accessible by only those properly authorized.
- Integrity: systems, and the data stored on them, should be immune to unauthorized modification.
- Availability: systems should be immune to denial-of-service attacks and should be able to meet the service levels they were designed for.

As information systems have matured, the body of laws and corporate regulation governing their use has expanded. As a result, many policy statements include objectives concerning *laws and ethics*, which insure that network, system, and security operations function within applicable laws, regulations, mandates, licenses, contracts, and "codes of conduct."

Although technology-based mechanisms play an important role in the enforcement of security policies, day-to-day procedures and management vigilance by management are required to achieve these objectives. For example, operational procedures and disaster recovery plans help ensure availability. Manual controls may help to ensure the integrity of data at certain key points in processing.

Requirements

Policy objectives are met by aligning people, processes and technologies to meet four fundamental security requirements: Identification and Authentication, Access Control, Audit, and System Integrity, defined below.

Identification and Authentication (I&A). An identifier is a piece of data used to uniquely identify an entity in a transaction. Real-world examples of identifiers include a drivers license or a national identification number. Identifiers must possess the following characteristics:

- *Uniqueness.* Each entity must have one unique identifier. No two entities have the same identifier.
- *Association.* There must be some way to bind the identifier to the entity (e.g., tying a social security number back to an actual person.)

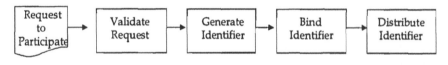

Exhibit 3. Synergy Between Process and Technology.

Exhibit 4. Authentication Methods

Authentication method	Examples
What the user knows	A secret password, PIN number, credit card number and expiration date, mother's maiden name
What the user has	An ATM card, credit card, smart card, private key stored on an encrypted file on a PC
What the user is	Biometric verification such as voice prints, iris scan, signature verification, thumb scan

I&A provides a good example of the necessary synergy between process and technology (see Exhibit 3). Policy may mandate, for example, that requests for new accounts may be issued only by Human Resources managers and that each request must be properly logged. Identifiers are issued to entities during part of a registration process that validates an entity's request to participate in a system, generates a unique identifier, binds that identifier to the requesting entity, and distributes the identifier to the now participant entity. The technology is invoked at several points to support this process.

Similarly, once participating entities have been registered, an authentication mechanism validates the identifier during a transaction. Authentication is the process that validates that the entity requesting access, whether that is a human or automated process, is the true owner of that identity.

Authentication is performed by three primary methods, by validating

- What the user/entity knows
- What they have, or
- What they are

Exhibit 4 describes examples of each of these methods.

Access Control. Once identity has been established, access control rules determine what resources the entity may use. In one frequently used model of secure computing, the entities of interest in a system are "subjects" and "objects." A subject is an active entity, loosely described as a program in execution, and the surrogate of a person. A subject has an identity and attributes. An object is a passive entity, usually a repository of information.

The goal of the access control requirement is to reliably mediate the access of subjects to objects. On each attempted access of an object by a subject, the system determines whether or not the access is to be granted. It does this by applying a set of access control rules along with information it has about the subjects and the objects.

Access Control is used to permit or deny a specific type of use of system resources. For example, a user may be authorized to access a resource, but only for reading. Access control can be used to arbitrate access to files, processes, operating system ports, application functions, database tables, portions of a network (such as through virtual or dedicated circuits and firewalls), and other types of resources. This is accomplished most frequently through the use of Access Control Lists (ACLs). An ACL for a resource specifies the user or group and the type of access permitted (read, write, etc.). ACLs may optionally include date and time restrictions and program restrictions.

A refinement of traditional access control is referred to as "Role based access control" (RBAC). RBAC associates a job function/role to a set of resources, and then assigns the user to a particular role. Therefore, for example, the role of junior bookkeeper may have read and write access to the petty cash account, but read-only access to the general ledger. The advantage of RBAC is that it facilitates the management of access control and prevents users from retaining access to data that is no longer needed as they move from role to role.

Resource access control may be either restrictive or permissive. Restrictive resource access control is based on the policy that "whatever is not explicitly authorized is denied." Permissive resource access control is based on the policy that "whatever is not explicitly prohibited is allowed." Each of these methods has a use. For network and firewalls, restrictive access control is commonly used. For most servers, permissive access control is the norm.

Audit. Auditing is used to record accesses to resources and may be implemented at a number of layers, including operating system, database, application, and middleware as well as in network devices such as firewalls and routers. Auditing is typically implemented in combination of these layers to allow reconstruction of events after a security problem is detected. Good logs should be searchable for known or suspected patterns of abuse, and should be protected from alteration. Logs can monitor a variety of data, including access times, user IDs, locations, actions the user performed, and whether or not those actions were successfully completed.

A widespread perception is that logging is a post hoc security measure; it only has benefits after disasters, or hackers, have struck, and even then

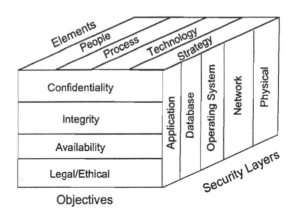

Exhibit 5. Security Framework.

---

it will only help assess the damage done. Logging *will* do those things, but good logging capability, wisely used, is like the TV cameras hiding behind the smoked plastic domes on the ceiling at the mall: unobtrusive but potent deterrents to roguish behavior. When people know that somebody *might* be watching, they tend to behave better. If the unwanted behavior is not the result of malicious intent, proper auditing allows administrators to determine the cause of the problem. It is an excellent "lessons learned" tool. Well-designed log strategies allow the employment of power forensic analytical tools for determining the source cause for poorly-behaving systems. As such, auditing is a strong risk mitigation mechanism.

Integrity. Integrity refers to the property that any system must have if it is to protect itself and enforce the security policy. Integrity is the assurance that a system's implementation (or a component's implementation) conforms to its design. Of the four requirements, it is the most nebulous but perhaps the most important. Systems breached by buffer overflows, faulty parameters, or attacks on improperly configured network ports have failed to meet the integrity requirement. Viruses constitute what is probably the best known attack on integrity. Such faults appear at the boundaries of a system, and must be removed by a thorough analysis of those interfaces, as well as the use of mechanisms use to ensure that system files are safeguarded.

SECURITY FUNCTIONS

The appropriate combination of people, processes and technology should be applied to implement security requirements across all layers of the physical environment to achieve the objectives described above. This is illustrated in Exhibit 5.

People: Security Roles and Responsibilities

Neither the most advanced technology, nor the most careful procedures, will serve to secure a netcentric environment if the people who use and manage it lack the understanding and training to do their job properly. The failure of people to do what is required to secure the system is the most common failure in security. Some of the most significant barriers to security are

- Mismatched customs, cultures, and values
- Conflicts of divisional objectives and strategies
- Poorly defined and implemented roles and responsibilities

All of these can derail the best security architectures, models, and plans.

Several actions should be undertaken when planning and executing netcentric efforts:

1. A program of training and security awareness should be undertaken to sensitize responsible parties to security issues and to their basic responsibilities. Because security is implemented in many different places, and a breach in only one can result in failures in security, a well thought-out communication plan is critical.
2. Roles and responsibilities for security should be identified for all facets of the design, build, and run phases. Mechanisms, responsibilities and budget for proper operation should be clearly delineated for each phase of the effort. In addition, responsibilities should be established at the infrastructure level to complete necessary processes (described in the next section).
3. Required organizational changes must be planned and executed to support the netcentric environment.

Process: Administration and Management

Several processes are essential to secure a computer environment (Exhibit 6). These include

- Policy development
- Risk assessment
- Plan and Build
- Administration
- Compliance
- Change management

Security Policy Development. It is imperative that a well-constructed statement articulate the organization's goals and policies with respect to the use of computers and networks and the protection of the information they contain.

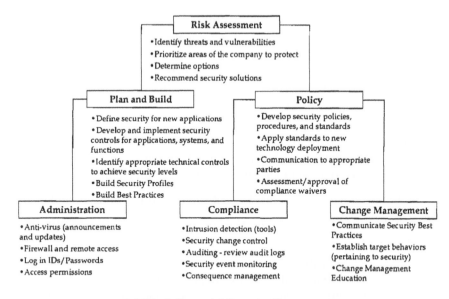

Exhibit 6. Essential Security Processes.

A number of issues must be addressed when developing a security policy. Example issues that may be covered include

- Who is allowed to use the resources?
- What is the proper use of the resources?
- Who is authorized to grant access and approve use?
- Who may have system administration privileges?
- What are the users rights and responsibilities?
- How is sensitive information classified?
- What happens when the policy is violated?

Supporting standards, guidelines, and procedures should be developed to provide direction to security implementation. These supporting documents may cover specific technologies and platforms. Change management helps to facilitate the adoption of the directions, and compliance processes are used to verify that the directions are being followed.

Risk Assessment. This is the process of identifying business risks, identifying system vulnerabilities or weaknesses that can affect those risks, and recommending mechanisms to control those vulnerabilities. The risk assessment process determines what is to be protected, something that is the cornerstone of any effort to secure a system. The assessor examines the organization's security policies and the infrastructure of processes and mechanisms to find gaps in the fundamental security requirements. (If there are no policies in place, that is itself a risk.)

By determining what corporate assets are most in need of protection, the assessor gains a good understanding of the assets critical to the business. These assets can be

- Physical (e.g., systems, networks, facilities, customer data, or revenue stream)
- People (key employees)
- Intangible (e.g., reputation of the business)

The risk assessment involves a thorough appraisal of the environment from a technical, procedural, and business standpoint. The result is a set of measures designed to mitigate the risks in a cost-effective fashion.

Because no system can be made perfectly secure, the challenge of the risk assessment is to balance the tradeoffs between increased security and cost. Some assets may warrant large expenditures; others may not. A result of the assessment is a "residual" risk (meaning the risks that will exist after all recommended countermeasures have been implemented) that is consistent with the organization's needs and policies.

Plan and Build. This involves the integration of security into new technology design, development, and deployment processes. As described above, netcentric environments may provide control mechanisms in many different places, because security is integral to the application. For these reasons, it is essential to take the appropriate steps to design in security up front. In fact, the impact of implementing and maintaining security mechanisms can be so significant as to effect the entire value proposition of a system capability being considered.

If, for example, the solution will require costly smart cards and an infrastructure of readers, it may dramatically affect the cost per transaction. In addition to hardware cost, it is not uncommon to have significant resources on a project dedicated to implementing firewalls, developing public key infrastructures, integrating security into the application, locking down operating systems and Web servers, and implementing intrusion detection and audit tools. Such tradeoffs need to be considered carefully during the risk assessment.

It is also important to note that the Plan and Build environment is subject to business and technical risk itself. Consequently, it requires the development of an appropriate security policy to govern itself. If, for example, the test system is broken into and back doors are introduced, it may lead to later compromise of the production system.

Administration. This includes the processes to administer the environment securely, such as maintaining user accounts and security profiles, certificate issuance and revocation, configuring servers for proper security, and changing access rules. It is helpful if security administration is separately monitored. All administrative functions should be defined with proper attention to separation of duties to provide proper accounting and control of business processes. Metrics for service level monitoring should be collected and distributed to the proper accounting or monitoring function. Data collected for service level monitoring should be protected from tampering to ensure proper accountability and accuracy. Security administration must be separated from the Operations and Help Desk functions to provide segregation of duties and to ensure that the metrics of the organization responsible for the function are aligned with the need for security.

Technology: Security Mechanisms

Although rapidly changing technology represents a security challenge to the netcentric world, these same advances have provided valuable tools for the security architect. Among the most important of these new technologies is public key cryptography. Its chief merit lies in its ability to permit total strangers to communicate spontaneously and in secret without going through an elaborate preparatory process to establish secret keys. Without this form of cryptography, many of the benefits of netcentric systems could not be realized. The following sections provide an introduction to this important technology as well as the enabling technologies of Firewall, Audit Tools, and Intrusion detection software.

Cryptographic and Certification Services

Public key cryptography is one of the most important enabling technologies in the netcentric environment. Along with the Certification Services provided by a Public Key Infrastructure (PKI) this technology provides fundamental capabilities that are essential to the netcentric world:

- *Confidentiality.* As defined above, cryptography ensures that messages are accessible only by those properly authorized — even when they traverse insecure networks. (Note that the term "message" here can refer to an e-mail dispatch, or the more dynamic transactions of Web sessions.)
- *Authenticity.* This is the assurance that a message was actually sent by the purported sender.
- *Integrity.* This is the assurance that the message has not been modified in transit.
- *Nonrepudiation.* This is the assurance that a sender cannot disavow a message (see later section).

Cryptography relies on the use of "keys" to encrypt communications. There are two types of keys:

1. A *secret* key is shared between the two entities in a transaction. Because the same key is used to encrypt and decrypt data, this is referred to as *symmetric* key encryption. For the parties to communicate, they must establish the secret key in advance, using a secure channel. The most common implementation of a symmetric key algorithm is the Data Encryption Standard (DES.).

2. A *public/private* key pair or *asymmetric* key uses a pair of keys to encrypt and decrypt messages. Messages encrypted using one of the keys can only be decrypted with the other key. Each party possesses a pair of keys, one public key accessible to all participants in the system, and one private key accessible only to the party that owns it. The most common implementations of public key algorithms are supplied by RSA Data Security, Inc. In the most basic implementations, data are encrypted by the sender with the public key of the recipient and decrypted by the recipient with their private key.

Symmetric key systems can provide secure communications between two entities, but they have significant key management problems. "Key management" refers to those processes necessary to issue, maintain, and revoke keys as appropriate. Because a different symmetric key must be exist for each pairs of users, in a community of N participants there are approximately N^2 keys to track. Additionally, the life span of a symmetric key is short (1 day is common for a 56 bit DES key) so symmetric keys must be changed frequently. Tracking up to N^2 keys per day adds significantly to the complexity of key management.

Although public key cryptosystems do not require users to share a common secret key, key management is still a serious problem. Public key systems require a binding between a specific public/private key pair and an entity that is participating in the system. When using a public key to protect information destined for a specific entity, the user assumes that the public key he or she uses is really the one belonging to the entity. The only way to assure this binding is through the use of a trusted third party (TTP), called a "Certificate Authority," or CA.

Recall that the method for transmitting a message using public key cryptography is to encrypt the message with the receiver's *public* key. The benefit is that a user's public keys can be sent as clear text, or even published in a directory. Therefore, if Alice wants to send a message to Bob, but is tricked into using Eve's public key, then Eve will be able to intercept the message. (Eve can then, if she chooses, reencrypt the message using Bob's actual public key, and neither Alice nor Bob will be the wiser.) In a global

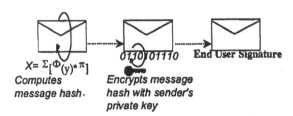

$X = \Sigma_{[}\Phi_{(y)*}\pi_{]}$

*Computes
message hash.*

*Encrypts message
hash with sender's
private key*

End User Signature

Exhibit 7. Digital Signatures.

network lacking face-to-face contact, users must be assured they are using the right key. The CA provides this.

The CA serves a function analogous to that of a passport or drivers license. The CA binds public keys to users and services similar to the way a passport agency issues you a passport that ties your name and relevant personal information to you with a picture. CAs deliver public keys through "certificates," which are generally compliant with the X.509 standard. The CA will publish information to a directory, which contains an entry for each entity with a certificate. It is not too far-fetched to think of the CA as a sort of rigorously maintained cryptographic Yellow Pages.

Public key cryptosystems provide transaction authentication through the use of "digital signatures." Digital signatures are created by the application of a hash function to a piece of data (e.g., a message). This message hash is then encrypted with a sender's private key, as shown in Exhibit 7. The message recipient can use the sender's public key to decrypt the message hash, and rerun the hashing algorithm to make sure the hash has not changed. If the two hashes match, the sender has been properly authenticated. Note that for authentication, the pattern of public/private key use is the reverse of that for confidentiality. For confidentiality, the sender encrypts with the receiver's public key. To provide authenticity, the senders encrypt with their own private key.

Public key cryptography is computationally expensive. For this reason, most modern systems use a combination of public key cryptography and symmetric key cryptography for performance reasons.

Certification services are the support activities needed to verify that the certificates are properly used, to ensure the authenticity and confidentiality of communications and stored data.

The binding of a public key to an entity by a CA does not address all the key management problems associated with asymmetric cryptography. "Key recovery" is another challenge. Data encrypted under a public key cannot be recovered without the private key. If the private key is rendered inaccessible (through file corruption, token destruction, or failure), it is essential that the cryptosystem owner/operator provide a means for recovering that data.

Another chore associated with key management is *revocation*. In any public key cryptosystem, keys will eventually be compromised, either because they are lost or stolen. Procedures must allow participants to notify an administrator if their keys are compromised, to disseminate the list of compromised keys to all participating entities, and to issue new keys to replace the compromised keys. Because public key binding is typically carried out using x.509 compliant certificates, this process is called *certificate revocation*.

Using public key cryptography requires a "public key infrastructure" or PKI. A PKI provides the administrative structure to manage public key pairs effectively. The PKI functions include key recovery, certificate reissue or renewal, key registration, and key distribution. More complex (and more complete) systems include directory services for registration of participants, distribution of the certificates, a key repository, and a CA hierarchy. A PKI provides the necessary support systems and processes to ensure that all entities are properly bound to their public/private key pairs.

Exhibit 8 illustrates one potential implementation of public key cryptography. The *End User* has a personal private key stored on an encrypted file in the PC or possibly on a more secure device such as a smart card. The client has access to a repository used for *Public Key Storage* to obtain public keys of other entities. The *Web Server* has its own private key stored in a secure file or cryptographic device in the server. The combination of a public and private key pair associated with the *Web Server* and *End User PC* along with cryptographic software on either end enable the two entities to authenticate to each other, send encrypted data, and digitally sign documents. In some cases, an *Authentication Server,* or directory service such as LDAP, can be used to validate the user's current access rights to the system. Authentication services and directories are often used to supplement Certification Revocation Lists to provide faster and more granular authorization. The technology to support directories, certificate revocation, certificate issuance, and other components of the PKI are rapidly advancing and common architectures and methods are still evolving.

A number of specific technologies are available to implement cryptography and certification in today's netcentric environments. If an organization is running a Netscape Web server, it may want to consider Secure Sockets Layer, or SSL, which provides data encryption, server authentication, message integrity, and optional client authentication for a TCP/IP connection. Secure Mime and Pretty Good Privacy, or PGP, are common encryption

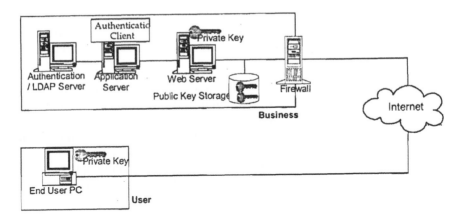

Exhibit 8. Implementation of Public Key Cryptography.

solutions for electronic mail. PGP will both authenticate the sender of the message, and encrypt the contents of the message through the use of a public key/private key pair.

In eCommerce solutions, the Secure Electronic Transactions (SET) specification jointly developed by Visa and Mastercard may be considered. SET will require authentication of all parties involved with a credit card transaction through the use of digital signatures and certificates, and will use a separate encryption handshake in order to guarantee both confidentiality and integrity. A number of options are available to implement a PKI, including service providers such as Verisign, and a number of CA products that can be implemented and managed in-house. Elliptic key cryptography can be used to increase the speed of cryptographic functions. The technology choices are rapidly developing, so what was a good solution six months ago may be out of date today. A variety of toolkits that implement these technologies are being rapidly advanced in the marketplace, and the options are evolving as some features are incorporated in to new versions of Web browser, server software, and development environments.

Two useful capabilities provided by cryptographic system include integrity preservation and nonrepudiation:

- *Integrity preservation.* Integrity controls ensure that data maintains a level of quality commensurate with the business needs, and that data is not modified by unauthorized parties or in an unintended fashion. Integrity controls can apply to a single message, an entire transmission, or a piece of data in a database. Digital signatures, message authentication codes, input edits, check digits, checksums, hash values, headers/trailers, and control totals are several methods that are used to ensure integrity. Access control helps to ensure integrity by allowing access to modify data only by authorized parties. Many controls that assure integrity are outside the scope of this chapter because they would not be classified as security controls. (See the chapter on controls in Section III). The primary controls that are directly related to security are those that involve the implementation of cryptographic functions and those involving access control.

- *Nonrepudiation.* Nonrepudiation means ensuring that one's actions are properly attributed and cannot be denied. This is done with strong audit methods, with entities whose identities have been strongly authenticated. Digital signatures, if properly implemented, can be used to provide nonrepudiation.

Firewalls

Firewalls are used to restrict traffic between networks. They can include a number of features. More conservative firewall technology involves the use of a proxy server that mediates all access through the firewall through a proxy application that is a small, highly trusted piece of code to mediate access through the firewall for a specific service. Less secure, but more flexible approaches use packet filtering to restrict access. These approaches are more flexible because packet filtering rules are extremely flexible; one can write rules to allow or disallow any service, type of packets, etc. Packet filtering is less secure because an organization may allow insecure services through its firewall. Firewalls may also provide authentication based on source location or userID, password, token, or public key authentication. All firewalls have extensive access control, audit logging, and alerting capabilities. Virtual private networks can be created by using encryption-enabled firewalls to establish a secure pipe between several locations over the Internet.

Audit Tools

Compliance auditing is often enforced through a combination of manual and automated procedures. Automated methods are especially important in the netcentric environment because the threats evolve so rapidly that it is only through automation that an organization can truly get a handle on all of the vulnerabilities that may be present across the increasing number of computers involved. These audit tools may scan the network for insecure machines, assess operating system security provisions across a large number of machines, assess the security Web server, or perform other similar functions.

Intrusion Detection

Intrusion detection software is relatively new. Intrusion detection takes audit logging services one step further by monitoring the environment in

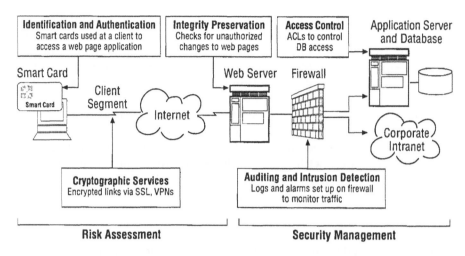

Exhibit 9. Components to Secure a Netcentric Solution.

real time, and actively warning of suspicious activity. Processes continually monitor the system using a set of heuristics, looking for signs of intrusion, such as attempts to take advantage of common security holes, repeated attempts to guess a password, or large concentrated numbers of access list violations. Other intrusion detection devices attach to a network and inspect passing packets for attacks on networking protocols.

Active Security Feature Enhancement Tools

A variety of tools are available to improve security of operating systems and PCs. Some tools, such as HP Virtual Vault and Memco's SEOS, actively improve the security of the UNIX operating system by increasing file protection capabilities, improving sign-on security, and improving segregation of duties. Other tools, such as Finjan, work to combat mobile code threats presented by Java, JavaScript, and Active-X. Still other tools are used to combat viruses and other types of threats. Fraud detection services may be used to catch unauthorized use of credit cards.

Exhibit 9 illustrates a number of components that may be used to secure a netcentric solution.

CONCLUSION

The Internet presents almost limitless opportunity, but comes with a price of almost limitless risk. The security challenges are among the most difficult an organizations will face as it moves into the netcentric environment. The lack of generally accepted methods, the difficulty in integrating consistent security into the plethora of environments to be protected, and the netcentric characteristics outlined previously will continue to pose significant challenges in the future.

Netcentric technologies are always changing and evolving. On the horizon today we have the next generation of IP (IPng or IPv6), a growing and more complex public key management problem, new types of development environments, and many others. Similar to the development of current Internet technologies, some of these will evolve after a long slow process, and others will burst quickly onto the scene.

Although the enumeration of the security challenges faced in the netcentric world may seem daunting, this technology holds out the promise of better security and enhanced privacy. It is, after all, far easier to forge a written signature on a paper check than it is to forge a digital signature. The eventual universal availability of strong encryption will put even mundane communications beyond the reach of most determined snoops.

Security is only as strong as the weakest link. It is vital that organizations think of security in all its facets, including people, process, and technology components. One key will be to stay abreast of the new technologies and to continually reevaluate the security of the evolving netcentric environment. Security must be considered at every stage of netcentric systems integration. It will be especially important to plan for security upfront, to design security into the architecture and application, to invest in security solutions that will enable the entire enterprise, and to have people with the correct skills developing the security solution.

As an organization selects tools and strategies to maintain its security, it is important to evaluate both leading-edge technologies as well as traditional solutions. The solution that is right for a given circumstance will probably be a mix of the two. To maintain security, it is critical not only to watch out for security bugs in new technologies but for new problems discovered in old technologies, and, in all cases, it is the risk assessment that should drive the efforts.

Chapter 29
Knowledge Management

There is a good deal of interest these days in the topic of knowledge management. The valuation of intangible, intellectual assets is becoming an accepted part of business today. Thus, it makes sense that managing those assets effectively is now looked at as a vital aspect of maintaining competitiveness. This chapter looks at the following issues:

- What is knowledge?
- What is knowledge management?
- Why implement a knowledge management capability?
- What are the essential elements of an effective knowledge management capability?
- What is the required technology framework?

DEFINITIONS: KNOWLEDGE AND KNOWLEDGE MANAGEMENT

Providing a definition of knowledge on which everyone can agree may be impossible. There is a wide spectrum of definitions, ranging from the inclusive to the exclusive. Some hold that knowledge is simply the content provided by organizations within the convergence framework discussed in this book. Others hold a more precise sense that knowledge must attain a quality far beyond traditional data and information.

For the purposes of this chapter, knowledge is "complex content," that is, the fact that IS staff even use the word *knowledge* means that the content in aggregate has attained a level of complexity beyond that of traditional transactional data. Knowledge is captured not only in figures and text, but also in voice, images, video, and other mediums. To prevent the discussion from becoming too metaphysical, it is best to remember that content cannot be called knowledge unless it can be captured in some way, stored, and then delivered.

Since Alvin Toffler and Peter Drucker first began to talk about the "third wave" and the "knowledge economy," even academic economists have begun to accept and write about knowledge as the new form of capital in the postindustrial economy. Economist Paul Romer, for example, writes,

"Instead of just capital and labor and raw materials producing output, it is the ideas themselves and the economic incentives that lead to their creation and diffusion that are the fundamental determinants of economic well-being."

If knowledge is a form of capital, however, it must be able to move from one person to another, and it must be able to grow. "Knowledge management" is the group of activities that performs these functions. Given the criticality of knowledge in today's economy, attention must be paid to the effective management of knowledge: identifying, capturing, and making knowledge easily accessible at the point of need. Although this seems simple and obvious, in practice it is quite difficult and presents several new concepts to master.

Perhaps the clearest way to understand the potential impact of knowledge management is to illustrate how one company is pursuing initiatives to improve its knowledge management capability in the field of insurance.

An insurance brokerage places risks in the insurance marketplace on behalf of its clients. The reason that a company uses the services of an insurance brokerage in the first place, rather than going directly to the insurance marketplace itself, is the brokerage has superior knowledge about the insurance marketplace and is able to leverage that knowledge to provide its clients with more efficient service and more cost-effective coverage. In other words, the brokerage adds value through knowledge. Its only competitive advantage lies in its ability to apply knowledge effectively to provide client service during the actual risk placement process, a process that is highly complex and can take up to 12 months to complete.

One global insurance brokerage realized that it needed to decrease the elapsed time required to place risks and also to reduce the number of errors and omissions that typically occurred during the placement process. This company realized that, although knowledge and valuable experience were being created with each risk-placement deal, this knowledge was not being captured during the placement process and thus could not be leveraged effectively on subsequent risk placements, either by the same or different brokers. The only recorded information happened at the very end of the placement process, when the basic structured data elements that defined the placement transaction (e.g., client name, risk coverage amount, and premium amount) were recorded to feed the traditional back-office data processing systems, such as billing and accounts receivable. None of the real essence of broking a deal (i.e., the nuances, the negotiating techniques, or the creative approaches to handling unusual client needs) were being captured electronically. Thus, information technology was being used only for recordkeeping, probably the least important part of the company's value proposition to its clients.

Another important issue is that, from the perspective of the insurance brokerage, the placement process calls for constant interaction and collaboration among people from other companies: the client company and the multiple insurance carriers that might be participating in the deal. Thus, the knowledge that is created during the placement process cannot, by definition, be confined to inside the walls of the brokerage and among the brokers only.

This particular insurance company embarked upon a significant set of initiatives to try to attack the real opportunity: the entire life cycle of the broking process. Included in the entire life cycle is how knowledge could be identified, captured, and made available during the process to increase the speed and quality of client service. These initiatives are addressing not only the technology challenges but also the process improvements (i.e., the flow of information and responsibility) and the resulting organizational changes (i.e., the measurements and rewards) required, including the cross-company aspects so important to the broking process. This chapter focuses on all of these critical aspects of knowledge management.

ESSENTIAL ELEMENTS OF KNOWLEDGE MANAGEMENT

As the previous example demonstrates, effective knowledge management is a complex proposition that involves a multitude of competencies to execute. This section examines each of the primary competencies required for knowledge management: strategy, process, people, and technology, paying particular attention to the technology aspects.

STRATEGY

A company strategy should set an overall framework for knowledge management. In many ways, knowledge is content that has the potential to affect behavior. This is very powerful, but it can also be very dangerous if the behavior change is not in accordance with a company's overall strategic vision and mission.

One of the key management issues associated with knowledge management is that a commitment to an effective knowledge management capability is indeed a strategic commitment. Knowledge management pertains to opportunity enhancement rather than cost control; its goal is to make a quantum leap forward rather than incremental adjustments. Many companies embark upon knowledge management initiatives without any type of formal, quantitative cost-benefit analysis because it is simply the appropriate action to take.

This does not mean that a knowledge management initiative should be undertaken without the proper thought and planning. It does mean that, to most companies, knowledge management is and should be considered a strategic imperative that must be addressed in some manner. There is no formula that "proves" whether knowledge management is worthwhile to an organization.

PROCESS

Knowledge management is a means rather than an end; it enhances a company's ability to execute its core processes in a manner that gives it a competitive advantage. The linchpins are the actual core business processes themselves, for they provide the context for both the original creation of knowledge and its effective application.

The insurance brokerage mentioned in the previous section highlights the importance of process to knowledge creation and application. This example also demonstrates the criticality of the interdepartment and interenterprise element to the overall process. A chain is only as strong as its weakest link. Likewise, a process is only as strong as its individual participants, regardless of which department or company for which the individual participants happen to work.

Numerous companies have implemented knowledge sharing systems out of context, or at least out of synch, with underlying core business processes. Such knowledge-sharing solutions that treat knowledge management as a separate and distinct process are typically easier to implement and can definitely add value, but in a suboptimal fashion. The most notable problem is that of knowledge capture. Capture simply does not happen consistently and with high quality if it requires significant additional effort above and beyond a worker's normal processes. Without effective knowledge capture, all other aspects of knowledge management are moot.

It might seem that the typical worker does not have the time to capture knowledge while completing business processes, and that, as a result, a separate process and a separate group of people should be responsible for knowledge capture. In fact, this section discusses some special roles and responsibilities that can greatly assist and support the knowledge management efforts, but those outside of the process cannot, by themselves, constitute effective knowledge management. The key is how to provide appropriate knowledge management support mechanisms together with the actual knowledge workers in the process, so knowledge can be captured and used with the greatest ease and efficiency.

A complete life cycle for knowledge management must address the following:

- Capture of knowledge from external or internal sources
- Classification of knowledge
- Valuation of the knowledge

- Access to the knowledge
- Use of the knowledge
- Improvement of the knowledge
- Retirement of the knowledge when it has outlived its usefulness

The field of library science makes clear that there is an essential role for the librarian. This role is responsible for managing the process of classification and providing assistance to people when the "least effort" access models to the knowledge do not work. This role manages the content created in the actual work process and helps to provide access to wider sets of knowledge that may not otherwise be known to the average worker.

The librarian cannot act alone, however. A librarian is primarily concerned with the acquisition, classification, and accessing of knowledge. This role does not address the initial valuation as well as improvement and retiring of knowledge. Put another way, although librarians like to purchase books, they do not like people inserting improved ideas into existing books, nor do they like people tearing pages out of them. The initial valuation and continual enrichment of knowledge is a key aspect of knowledge management, but it can only be performed by those with the knowledge and the context of how this knowledge relates to the business processes. This synthesis role is the role of a knowledge manager. The knowledge manager represents the actual knowledge workers conducting the core business processes and has an obvious symbiotic support relationship with librarian. The following section examines the knowledge manager role in more detail.

Definition of a Controlled Vocabulary

Effective knowledge management requires a classification scheme by which to find knowledge components. Such an approach is achieved in the field of library science through the use of a controlled vocabulary. This vocabulary would be a basis for accessing the knowledge components found in a knowledge repository. The controlled vocabulary is a key step to organizing knowledge and making it available to people. If we are to provide one-stop shopping for knowledge components, the controlled vocabulary is the point where the knowledge shopping begins.

Creating a controlled vocabulary requires one to go through long lists of terms, adding, deleting, and modifying each controlled list. The field of library science suggests that such lists consist of the following:

- The primary term itself
- Related terms that might be used in place of the primary term
- Broader terms that encompass the primary term
- Narrower terms that refine the primary term
- Context terms that describe in what different contexts the primary term is typically used

Exhibit 1. Controlled Vocabulary List

Primary term	Related terms	Broader terms	Narrower terms	Context terms
Asset management	Configuration management Inventory management	Distributed systems management Managing change	Hardware management Software management	Requirements Benefits Design Architecture Implementation Tools Products Experiences Best Practices Futures Economics Contacts

Exhibit 1 is an example of one such controlled vocabulary list for a technology knowledge repository.

The term *controlled vocabulary* does not mean that there are no changes to the vocabulary. Rather, it means that changes occur under controlled conditions. A controlled vocabulary is likely to need reassessing on a regular basis (e.g., semiannually).

Many sources of changes are possible. One is to monitor the use of search engines and then to report those cases when the controlled vocabulary does not meet needs but when the searches found hits for requested terms. Change requests from knowledge managers would be another source of change. In addition, monitor usage is necessary to watch for cases when certain terms are no longer in use. These terms can be marked for possible removal from the list because of lack of use. All of these potential changes will need to be fed into the twice-yearly update of the controlled vocabulary.

Accessing, Using, and Creating Knowledge Components

Once a controlled vocabulary list is defined, how can it be used for one-stop shopping for knowledge components? The essential idea that of a knowledge directory, which users search using the terms in the controlled vocabulary. This directory identifies, for a given term or combination of terms, the knowledge components that have been identified for the terms. The directory also includes a knowledge descriptor for each component. The knowledge descriptor is typically sufficient to determine if the component is of value to a given user in a given situation. The descriptor thus prevents the user from having to actually access the entire knowledge component before determining its relevance.

As an example, the following are questions that one would be able to ask with a controlled vocabulary. The words in italics are controlled vocabulary terms.

Find all knowledge components on *Architectures* for *Client/Server.*

Because of the capability of the underlying relational database technology required for an effective knowledge directory, one could also ask more complex things, such as

Find all knowledge components on *Designs* of *Architectures*
for *Agents* on the *Internet.*

What would come back would be a list of all such knowledge components with sufficient networking and resource information to make it feasible to get them. It should not matter whether the components were stored in Lotus Notes (i.e., .NSF files), in Word (.DOC files), or some place on a corporate intranet or the Internet. This is the point of one-stop shopping. The ability to do this would free workers from having to learn about the physical storage and format of the individual knowledge components.

The Point of Knowledge-Component Creation

To enable such a usage scenario, an understanding of how knowledge components get created in the first place is required. At what point is a knowledge component created? What is the creation process?

As discussed earlier, the integration of knowledge management with core business processes is very important, because the processes themselves provide context for both the use and creation of knowledge. The business processes produce results (e.g., a design, a spec, or a document) that are all candidates to become knowledge components. A knowledge manager is responsible for determining which particular process results should become knowledge components. The knowledge manager must identify the appropriate terms from the controlled vocabulary that properly describe the knowledge component. He or she must also develop a descriptor of the component. The descriptor gives an overview of the knowledge component in sufficient detail so one could determine the value of the knowledge component without having to actually access it. The knowledge manager also places a valuation on the component (i.e., is the content based on someone's opinion or has it gone through levels of official authorization?). Finally, the component must be made available to the appropriate personnel, both inside and outside of the enterprise. To enable this, the knowledge manager must provide a link to the actual physical technical storage location of the component (e.g., a Web page URL or a Lotus Notes database.) and ensure that the proper security mechanisms are in place for the component.

SPECIAL TOPICS

Content-Based Index Searches

In addition to the search-and-classification capabilities that the controlled vocabulary and directory provide, powerful content-based search engines can also be helpful for situations in which the provided controlled vocabulary framework does not provide the appropriate retrieval framework for the end user. Such search engines construct a content-based index based on all the words actually contained within the knowledge components themselves. The end user can specify a word or combination of words in which he or she is interested, and the search engine retrieves all components that contain the desired word or combination of words. Several examples of this technique can be found today on the World Wide Web, such as AltaVista, Excite! and Lycos.

This approach has both advantages and disadvantages. One advantage is that the search does not depend upon the creation and maintenance of either a controlled vocabulary or knowledge directory, as these were defined previously. With content-based searches, the user merely enters words or word combinations he or she is interested in and receives a list of all components that contain the desired word. Because the creation of content-based indexes is fully automated, they can be kept very current and are rarely out of date. This is different from a controlled vocabulary-based directory that probably cannot be updated for new terms or term usage more frequently than semiannually.

The primary disadvantage to the content-based index approach today is that the typical user is often inundated with an excessively large number of items that meet his or her search criteria, most of which are not necessarily in context of the original search request and are therefore useless. This problem should improve as search agents become more sophisticated, but today such an approach should not be considered as the only knowledge access technique.

An example of these two access techniques is to compare the popular Yahoo! catalog on the World Wide Web (www.yahoo.com) with the various search engines mentioned above. The Yahoo! catalog classifies hundreds of thousands of Web sites based on a taxonomy (i.e., the controlled vocabulary) consisting of over 25,000 different categories. The user starts with the Yahoo! top-level category list and continues to drill down through various levels of subcategories until the desired information is found. This approach has proven to be accurate and easy to use.

However, the user must understand key aspects of the taxonomy hierarchy. For example, Yahoo! considers *Movies* to be under Entertainment rather than under Art. In essence, this categorization decision represents a particular point of view (i.e., that of the people at Yahoo! who control the taxonomy) that must be understood by the user. If this is understood, the user can drill down and find knowledge that is likely to be highly relevant to his interest. On the other hand, the user of a search engine such as Excite! is not constrained by having to understand whether movies are considered art or entertainment; he or she can merely search for a particular movie by entering "movies AND Godfather" and receive pointers to all Web documents that contain both words. However, this user is likely to receive thousands of references, many of which may be nothing more than peoples' personal home pages stating that the Godfather was one of their favorite movies, not exactly what the user had in mind.

The point is not that one technique is necessarily more effective than the other, but that both techniques have their strengths and weaknesses, and both should be considered for usage. In fact Yahoo! now combines both capabilities together in that it provides content-based searches within a particular classification category. If a content-based search can be narrowed using controlled vocabulary and classification scheme, then the number of useless hits can be kept to a minimum.

PEOPLE

Effective knowledge management requires a fundamental change in the way most companies do business, and people are at the heart of any effective change. Significant changes to measurements and rewards are typically required to support knowledge management. This chapter examines the issues for four distinct sets of people:

- Knowledge users
- The line knowledge manager
- The competency knowledge manager
- The chief knowledge officer

Knowledge Users

Several important considerations for the average knowledge user center around effective contribution and reuse of knowledge. Although the roles of the various knowledge managers are important ones, an effective knowledge management capability is heavily dependent on the users, for the users themselves are actually involved in the day-to-day core business processes that provide the primary context for knowledge capture and reuse.

This, of course, presents a natural conflict. Taking the time to capture knowledge and best practices about a given core business process typically does not contribute immediately to the successful completion of that process. Through an effective knowledge management capability, such captured knowledge is likely to contribute significantly to subsequent activities performed by other users, but because this knowledge capture does not provide immediate payback to the original contributor, it is a significant challenge to encourage knowledge capture behaviors as the norm. Managing this challenge is the responsibility of the line knowledge manager and the competency knowledge manager.

Knowledge users

- Are trained in the controlled vocabulary so that it can be used intuitively.
- Provide feedback on the vocabulary usage for its evolution.
- Use automated tools to find and access knowledge, including tools based on the controlled vocabulary and search engines.
- Work with both the line knowledge managers and competency knowledge managers to ensure that the users are contributing effectively to the objectives of both line and competency knowledge development.

The Line Knowledge Manager

A line knowledge manager has responsibility for the management of everyday line activities within his or her area of responsibility. As it pertains to knowledge management, the line knowledge manager is also a knowledge user, but he or she also must

- Identify the results of normal, everyday line activities in his or her responsibility area that are candidates for classification as knowledge components.
- Identify the correct controlled vocabulary terms to apply to the candidate knowledge components and develop a descriptor for each.
- Provide feedback on the controlled vocabulary for its evolution.
- Define the initial valuation of new knowledge components.
- Implement the measurements and rewards system developed by the competency knowledge managers.

The Competency Knowledge Manager

Every organization has key competencies, or skills and capabilities, that it must excel in to succeed. These competencies typically transcend individual situations or projects but ideally are enhanced as a natural part of carrying out daily work activities. For example, in the insurance broking example, some competencies are fundamental to the broking business (e.g., managing client relationships, financial services trends, industry acumen, and risk strategies). Ideally, these competencies are established in the broking professionals before they begin a specific risk placement, even though the broker can learn a lot from the knowledge that gets created during each and every placement. The role of the competency knowledge manager is to manage the knowledge for a given competency area, independent of the individual instances where those competencies are used in carrying out work activities. Competency knowledge managers:

- Define and develop a measurements and rewards structure that encourages contribution of knowledge capital from daily line activities.
- Define and maintain the controlled vocabulary framework.
- Identify overall executive sponsor for each broad yet clearly defined competency scope.
- Determine the new or changes to existing knowledge components required to support the competency scope.
- Identify the correct controlled vocabulary terms to apply to the candidate knowledge components and develop a descriptor for each.
- Provide feedback on the controlled vocabulary for its evolution.
- Define the initial valuation of new knowledge components.
- Set security and ownership specifications for content and provide guidance on the content accessibility as a function of the value of intellectual property.
- Perform any needed analysis or synthesis of a particular subset of knowledge.
- Approve the modification of knowledge base content within area of responsibility.
- Monitor any electronic discussions related to area of responsibility.

The Chief Knowledge Officer

The chief knowledge officer (CKO) is responsible for the overall knowledge assets of a company. The CKO is responsible for defining the areas in which the knowledge capabilities of the organization should evolve, based on its ongoing mission and vision. The CKO has the ultimate enterprisewide responsibility for the controlled vocabulary and knowledge directory and tackles the difficult issues associated with cross-department or cross-enterprise processes that have unique knowledge sharing requirements. The CKO also is responsible for ensuring that an appropriate technology infrastructure is in place for effective knowledge management. This responsibility is largely a coordination role, as the technology infrastructure needed for knowledge management is likely to be managed outside of the CKO's jurisdiction. This is because the required technology infrastructure should be used for more than knowledge management alone, as will be discussed in subsequent sections.

TECHNOLOGY

Knowledge management represents some new challenges from the technology perspective. There are new application characteristics that are typical of knowledge management solutions. In addition, some new technology architecture components are required to support these new characteristics. The remainder of this chapter will be devoted to these technology issues. Exhibit 2 illustrates some of the newer technology components that must be considered and brought into overall technology architectures for knowledge management.

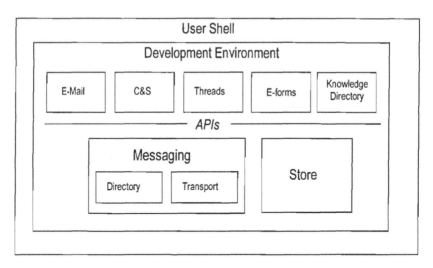

Exhibit 2. Knowledge Management Framework.

Knowledge Management Key Characteristics

Knowledge management solutions have the following characteristics that are typically not found in traditional client/server solutions:

- *They manage rich information objects.* Teams work with a wide variety of information, far beyond the simple fixed-length data elements managed in relational DBMS products. Image, voice, video, and large amounts of unstructured text are what teams share, in addition to more structured, quantitative data.
- *They are externally aware.* Today's virtual teams focus on end-to-end business processes that span individual functional departments, and often even extend outside the enterprise. As described previously, these interdepartment and interenterprise processes must focus on external sources and destinations of information, rather than assuming that all information can be housed within internal proprietary databases.
- *They transcend time and place.* Today's virtual team members are often mobile and must be able to participate in team processes regardless of time and place. This requires the ability to work off-line with a store-and-forward, "deferred update" scheme.
- *They are satisfying to the end user.* IT professionals have always worked to achieve a high degree of usability in their applications, but they have traditionally been creating single-function applications for more clerical, single-function users. Today's professional users demand more from application usability, and they will shun the automated solution if this demand isn't met.

Some relatively new infrastructure components are required to support the above application characteristics. These components break down into two types: lower-level infrastructure services and infrastructure applications that use the lower-level infrastructure services.

Key Infrastructure Components

Core infrastructure services are the underlying technology components required to enable the knowledge management characteristics referred to in the previous section. They also provide support for the infrastructure applications covered in the next section.

The User Shell. The user shell is a user's cross-application operating environment; it is the user interface (UI) that the user sees and interacts with. Ideally, the user shell should provide consistency across all of a user's activities, rather than having unique user interface characteristics for each specific application used. An example of a user shell is the Lotus Notes desktop: tabbed folders, database icons, views, and forms. This shell provides a consistent set of user constructs for all Notes applications. Another example of a user shell is the Microsoft Windows 95 desktop and Explorer UI. HTML-based Web browsers are beginning to emerge as a separate user shell with a certain level of consistency between all Web pages.

The Messaging Architecture. A necessary function for a team is communication. This typically requires a messaging architecture to serve as the infrastructure for communication and sharing of information among the team members. Because of the mobility characteristic identified above, a store-and-forward capability is paramount to supporting work flows or collaborative activities. A messaging architecture is the primary technology beneath any e-mail product, but a robust offering also serves as the infrastructure for additional functionality such as group scheduling, work flow, bulletin boards, and other collaborative functions and also provides application programming interfaces (APIs) for all functions.

At the core of any messaging architecture is the directory services component. Directory services are the foundation for distributed computing systems, as they essentially define the network and its resources (both people and information objects). Today's generation of directory services typically provide only application specific administrative support (e.g., Lotus Notes Name & Address Book only provides basic resource and security services to Notes itself). In addition the Notes Name & Address Book, another example of today's directory services is Novell NetWare Directory Services (NDS) and the Microsoft Exchange Server directory service. Directory services offer APIs to facilitate the development of custom solutions that use directory information.

Another important aspect of messaging is transport services. A transport service enables information to get from point A to point B. It provides queuing, store-and-forward communication, intermediate storage, routing, and generalized procedural and management interfaces. Examples of message transport would be the proprietary native Lotus Notes transport protocol, the X.400 protocol, and the Simple Mail Transfer Protocol (SMTP). Microsoft's Messaging API (MAPI) is a good example of a programming interface to messaging transport services.

A messaging architecture is a key strategic resource of the enterprise. This is becoming more and more true as virtual teams span traditional departmental and organizational boundaries. Any products that utilize messaging and directory services must be considered in the context of enterprise strategy, rather than individual workgroup needs alone.

Store. A generalized information store provides a server-based repository for storing unstructured and semi-structured information created by users, such as e-mail, attachments, electronic forms, images, and voice messages. Ideally, information stores allow for granular security, the establishment of storage limits and age limits, advanced information retrieval capabilities, and replication capabilities to manage distributed copies of information. Lotus Notes databases and Microsoft Exchange folders are good examples of a general-purpose object store. HTML/HTTP Web servers are examples of simpler, file system-like information stores. Information stores should provide programming interfaces for all information management functions.

More traditional information stores (e.g., relational DBMSs, image management products, etc.) are still required for many information management needs. These products should not be ignored just because they do not come prepackaged along with the other infrastructure services in a single product.

The Development Environment. An integrated development environment is required to support the development of end-user solutions based on the above component services. For example, Lotus Notes provides integrated development capabilities that produce Notes database applications that use the Notes user shell "look and feel," leverage the Notes Name & Address Book directory, store information in Notes database stores, and use the Notes transport protocols to route information.

In addition, because of the APIs provided for each individual component service, more customized solutions can be developed that use alternative or additional services. For example, a developer could write a Visual Basic or Visual C++ application for a more Windows 95-like user experience that stores information in Notes databases but uses Microsoft's MAPI as the transport mechanism. This "mix and match" approach is much more complex but does allow for more customized solutions than the "standard" development environment.

These are the component building blocks from which vendor shrink-wrapped solutions are built and on top of which build custom knowledge management solutions can be built. Up until now, vendors have tended to offer vertical application solutions using only their own proprietary component services, and they have encouraged their customers to do the same. Although this is the higher productivity approach, it is also the lower capability approach, and the Internet oriented, open style of computing is already beginning to render this vertical approach obsolete.

Infrastructure Applications

Several generic infrastructure applications typically make up part of an effective knowledge management technology environment. Although some of these applications are theoretically ready to use "out of the box," they typically require the development of significant policies and procedures and training before they can be used effectively. In addition, custom functional solutions can be built on top of or around these generic applications, and on top of the underlying infrastructure services.

E-mail. E-mail is nothing more than a correspondence application written by a vendor that typically uses that vendor's messaging, directory, transport, and store. Often, the vendor provides additional value-added features such as administration tools and end-user agents. Examples include Lotus Notes mail databases and the Microsoft Exchange in-box application.

Group Calendaring and Scheduling. Group calendaring and scheduling provides group activity and task management capabilities to the team-based activities associated with knowledge management. This application uses a directory and information store to manage resources and schedules, transport to route meeting and task requests, the e-mail application to present request information to users, and a calendaring interface to present scheduling information. Example products include Lotus Organizer and Microsoft Outlook.

Threaded Discussions. Threaded discussion or news reader applications enable the creation of what are commonly known as electronic bulletin boards or discussions. They enable a user to follow the history of discussion on a subject (e.g., the original item, responses to the original item, responses to responses) and to build up increasingly robust knowledge about a topic. Threaded discussion applications typically use directory services for user information, store services to manage the discussion items, and present a hierarchical drill-down user metaphor that is in concert with the overall user shell. Examples include Internet Usenet newsgroups, Lotus Notes discussion databases, and Microsoft Exchange folder posts.

E-forms and Workflow Applications. E-forms and workflow applications enable end-users to develop simple forms-based (with or without basic routing) solutions without programming that adhere to the overall user shell metaphor. This is typically achieved through both e-forms generators and sample applications (e.g., templates). Ideally, the end-user solutions created with the e-forms generator are extensible with professional developer tools such as Visual Basic or Visual C++. These solutions typically use the information store for forms management, and directory and transport for forms routing. Examples here include Lotus Notes database templates and Microsoft Exchange Forms Designer and sample applications.

The Knowledge Directory. As discussed above, the knowledge directory is a key component of an effective knowledge management capability, as it contains critical information on and pointers to the individual knowledge components, regardless as to where these components might be physically located. Based on a controlled vocabulary, the knowledge directory provides a needed framework for knowledge usage.

The document management model is probably the best model to consider when describing the underlying technical architecture required for an effective knowledge directory. Document management products, such as Documentum or Saros Mezzanine, provide for a control record for each document or object being managed by the product; each control record contains key data attributes about that object, as well as a pointer to the actual object itself. The data attributes are used for subsequent attribute-based searches. Check-in and check-out security as well as version control capabilities are built around the control record.

The knowledge directory is an excellent infrastructure application for a document management engine. Each knowledge component has an entry in the knowledge directory. Among the attributes stored for each knowledge component are the knowledge descriptor and the categorization terms, based upon the controlled vocabulary.

CONCLUSION

Knowledge management will continue to grow in importance in coming years. One key to watch is the extent to which knowledge assets and other intangibles become an accepted part of most companies' financial reports. Many companies already report these intangibles.

As for the knowledge management applications themselves, the types of knowledge contained will broaden, and the applications will move beyond capturing, storing, and displaying knowledge. They will begin to provide more sophisticated ways to organize knowledge and will incorporate agent technology so that users can find a wide range of useful knowledge. The knowledge component will have the ability to detect similarities and patterns in knowledge and provide analogs and related knowledge components based on these patterns.

Chapter 30
Collaborative Computing Solutions

This chapter builds on the netcentric architecture concepts and framework by discussing the issues and future scenarios associated with collaborative computing solutions.

THE POWER OF COLLABORATION

Collaboration focuses on supporting the nondeterministic, interpersonal, people aspects of complex business processes. Such aspects typically deal with highly unstructured and incomplete information and the often random, spontaneous nature of people. This is in stark contrast to traditional information technology (IT) systems, which assume that all data and processes are definable and orderly. Because of their training in the structured, linear analysis of building these traditional transactional systems, most IT professionals are ill equipped to understand the dynamics of collaborative application development and deployment.

Many people believe that the future belongs to flat, nonhierarchic, marketlike, flexible enterprises that enable autonomous knowledge workers to instantly form flexible teams to conduct business processes, respond to opportunities, and solve problems. Such enterprises have several decisive advantages over the traditional hierarchical command-and-control organizations: efficiency, flexibility, agility, and price.

However, these new organizations have much greater needs for collaborative interactions. When interaction is expensive, it is cheaper to move information through an organization via a hierarchy. When interaction is inexpensive, the hierarchy loses this advantage. Therefore, if information technology can enable interactions to be made inexpensively and flexibly, an organization can operate in a more effective fashion without the overhead of a large hierarchy. Collaborative solutions can enable an organization to reap the benefits of flattening without increasing costs.

One excellent example of a collaborative computing solution comes from a pharmaceutical company. One of the strategic imperatives of a pharmaceutical company is to bring new drug products to market quickly and continually. The new-drug development process is highly complex and can take literally dozens of years. Conversely, reducing a single month from this process and introducing a product to market more quickly can mean millions of dollars in added revenue.

There are several outside entities with which a pharmaceutical company must interact constantly in order to bring a new drug to market, particularly government agencies. In the United States, the Food and Drug Administration (FDA) is responsible for approval of new drugs and is intimately involved with the entire drug-approval process. The FDA review team itself consists of a wide variety of specialists, each with his or her own particular technical expertise: chemists, pharmacologists, physicians, pharmacokineticists, statisticians, and microbiologists. In addition, numerous clinical trial research companies are also heavily involved with the pharmaceutical company and the FDA throughout the process. A pharmaceutical company is thus dependent upon people outside of the organization, as well as on a variety of disciplines inside the organization (i.e., research, production, finance, and sales), to create new drug ideas and streamline the drug-approval process. The effective and efficient sharing of experiences and knowledge among all of these entities is what leads to new products and reduced time to market.

COLLABORATION DEFINITIONS AND FRAMEWORKS

Despite the growing importance of technology-enabled collaboration, the information technology community has paid insufficient attention to it. This is partly because collaborative activities, being primarily unstructured and nondeterministic in nature, are so very different from the classic, precise, if-then-else character of information technology solutions. Now that the need to enable collaborative activities has been more clearly identified, it is still the unstructured nature of collaboration that causes it to be overlooked by the IT community. After all, how can something so unstructured and nondeterministic be a candidate for improved effectiveness?

A collaborative activity has a single focus of attention and produces a well-defined output, even though the activities leading up to the deliverable are not predictable nor well defined. This focus on the deliverable distinguishes collaborative activities from other social and professional interactions, and the focus on unstructured activities distinguishes them from procedural workflow. In workflow, the mutual influence and interactivity of workers on each other is often minimized by the existence of well-defined and compartmentalized tasks. In a "pure" workflow system, the input/output relationship is dominant and, in a sense, the goal is to eliminate mutual influence by perfectly streamlining the process and thus eliminating any need for flexible and thus unpredictable, uncontrollable human interaction. In reality, workflow alone is a poor model for the majority of business processes that involve teams of knowledge workers.

One way to begin to understand how to enable more effective collaboration is to understand the nature of a particular type of collaborative activity. Collaboration covers a very wide area, and it is necessary to further refine different collaborative scenarios if it is to be seen how technology might be applied to improve the overall effectiveness of a given scenario.

Dimensions of Collaboration

Collaborative interactions can be classified according to numerous different dimensions.

Size. The size of the group has a significant impact on collaborative processes. What is possible in a small group can be impossible in a large community. Not much can be achieved in a meeting with a thousand people except a speech and a round of voting.

Location. Collaboration has typically been accomplished through in-person meetings in which all participants are located in the same physical location. However, technology is increasingly being used to facilitate collaborative interactions among individuals who are not co-located.

Impression. Media used for collaborative activities have different levels of impression. Video gives the highest level of impression, whereas audio and text have successively lower levels of impression.

Interactivity. Different collaboration scenarios exhibit different levels of interactivity or intensity. For example, a collaborative session to initially engage someone in a subject or discussion requires a lower level of interactivity, whereas a session to persuade or solve a problem requires a very high level of interactivity.

Anonymity. In a typical meeting, when a person speaks, everyone knows who that person is, so all comments are attributed. However, in military organizations and other highly hierarchical rank-conscious structures, this attribution may restrict freedom of response; everyone may line up behind the highest-ranking member of the group. Such situations may call for technologies that allow for anonymous contribution from participants in a collaborative exercise.

Several factors greatly influence collaborative activities. This chapter focuses on collaborative situations that are remote and attributed, supporting a group size between two and ten. This leaves the dimensions of impression and interactivity for segmenting the different types of collaborative support, as depicted in Exhibit 1.

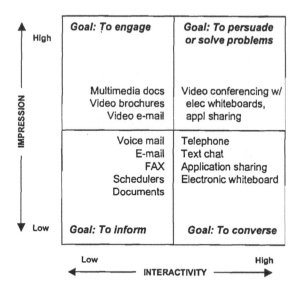

Exhibit 1. Interactivity and Impression Matrix for Collaborative Support.

Collaboration Technologies

Using Exhibit 1, this section describes different types of collaborative tools by starting with the goal of the collaboration.

Quadrant 1: To Inform. Quadrant 1 represents a collaborative situation that is both low impression and low interactivity. Quadrant 1 tools are useful for routine asynchronous collaboration, in which the context of the information being exchanged is well understood. Situations include question and answer, status, and review of work. Technologies include voice mail, e-mail, fax, schedulers, and document repositories.

Quadrant 2: To Converse. Quadrant 2 covers collaborative activities that are low impression and high interactivity. Quadrant 2 tools are effective when the people collaborating are familiar with each other and already have a working relationship or when the purpose and goals of the collaboration are clear to all parties. Situations include revising a process flow, discussing an installation plan or monitoring progress in real time. Technologies include the telephone, text chat, application sharing, and electronic whiteboards.

Quadrant 3: To Engage. This covers collaborations that exhibit high impression and low interactivity. Quadrant 3 tools are useful when a rich communications medium is needed to convey the information, but the information is static or can be shared asynchronously. Situations include annotating documents, explaining a concept or product, giving presentations, or conducting training. Technologies include multimedia documents, video brochures, and video e-mail.

Quadrant 4: To Persuade or Solve Problems. Quadrant 4 covers situations that call for both high interactivity and high presence, those that simulate face-to-face meetings. This is needed when the content of the meeting is dynamic and subject to change during the meeting, forcing people to make quick adjustments. Situations include early stages of a project when people do not know each other, as in design work and project planning. Technologies in this quadrant include video conferencing in conjunction with real-time collaborative tools, such as electronic whiteboards and application sharing.

Collaboration Approach

A generalized approach for collaborative activities can be used regardless of the type of collaborative scenario outlined above. This approach starts with a simple observation that many collaborative activities consist of three steps:

- Generating ideas for what to do
- Reaching consensus on what to do by identifying and resolving potential issues
- Planning and executing coordinated actions

One example is the process of requirements definition for a system development project. There are many approaches to this process, JAD (Joint Applications Development) being one of the most popular. The first step in JAD is to make sure that nothing relevant is forgotten, that all ideas for requirements are considered. To achieve this, all constituencies potentially affected by the contemplated system are asked to send a representative to the JAD session. In a brainstorming session, the participants generate, discuss, and rank the initial set of requirements according to priority. Representatives of various constituencies raise potential issues with the proposed requirements. These may include dependencies, constraints, and outright contradictions. The group negotiates and resolves the issues. Once the synergy is achieved, the group divides the work of creating the requirements document. Because different parts of the document depend on each other, the group decides how the work should be coordinated. This may include status meetings, draft reviews, etc. Finally, the group executes the plan and produces the requirements document.

In reality, the above process is rarely linear. Teams may go through several rounds of brainstorming and raising issues before converging on a plan of action. Even after the requirements document is created, groups may go back to the issues step to make sure that nothing was overlooked.

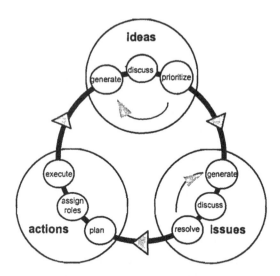

Exhibit 2. The ICAA Model.

These steps are not limited to requirement definition but are common to many team activities. In addition, when these steps are not all made explicit — when teams skip some of the steps — breakdowns, miscoordination, and floundering begin. For example, when the group skips issue raising, it may fail to achieve synergy and leave hidden contradictions unresolved, only to discover them too late during the execution stage.

IDEAS, ISSUES, AND COORDINATED ACTIONS

This section presents a formal model of collaboration called IICA (ideas, issues, coordinated actions), which follows the belief that collaborative team activities in business can be modeled as a combination of a few elementary actions. Understanding the elements and how they combine to form collaborative activities helps in the understanding of support and the improvement of current forms of collaborative work, and possibly to devise new forms.

The three steps of the IICA model are depicted in Exhibit 2 as large circles. The following sections examine each of these elements in greater detail.

Ideas

When a team is facing a task such as design of a system or developing of a business plan, the first step is usually to establish a shared understanding of what needs to be done. Without such an understanding, individual members may misinterpret the task or, worse, they may pull in different directions or

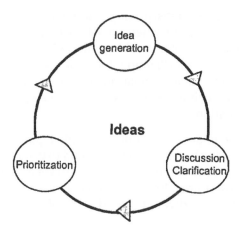

Exhibit 3. The Three Steps of Idea Processing.

work at cross-purposes. Valuable approaches may remain unexplored. To build a shared understanding, meeting facilitators in a wide variety of situations often use a three-step process, as shown in Exhibit 3.

Step 1: Idea Generation. Traditionally, the idea-generation process has been conducted in face-to-face brainstorming meetings (i.e., co-located, same time, attributed). The participants take their turns proposing one idea at a time (i.e., sequentially). The facilitator often goes around the table asking for a contribution (i.e., mandatory participation). Depending on the size of the meeting, usually, there is time for two or three rounds of contributions. This approach to idea generation is beginning to change. Increasingly groups are taking advantage of electronic support systems, such as Ventana's Group System 5, to make their meetings more productive. Busy groups are using the on-line discussion facilities of products such as Lotus Notes to conduct brainstorming without bringing everyone into the same room. These new forms of collaboration use different modalities that have a significant effect on mutual influence and, ultimately, on collaboration results.

With the electronic support, the sequential mode of contributions can be replaced with the parallel mode. All participants can type their contributions into the electronic brainstorming system at the same time. This leads to an order of magnitude increase in the quantity of contributions. This is the good news. The bad news is that a great deal of mutual influence is lost in the process: In a sequential mode, participants tend to react to each other contributions, while in parallel mode, each participant is focusing on his or her contributions paying little attention to the others.

The result of parallel brainstorming, anonymous or otherwise, is very "dirty." In a traditional setting, when a participant makes an unclear contribution, the person taking notes would usually ask for clarification. In a parallel mode, this "instant" clarification does not take place. In addition, the parallel mode results in many similar ideas that need to be consolidated. This necessitates a much more extensive second step of the process: discussion and clarification.

Mutual influence is a powerful factor in idea generation. By limiting mutual influence during brainstorming, we tend to get a greater diversity of ideas. By increasing mutual influence, we tend to get a "denser" and deeper coverage of a narrower area. Experienced facilitators select from a variety of modes to achieve both diversity and density of ideas.

Step 2: Discussion. The second step of the idea process is important, even if the first step is skipped. For example, there are many situations when what needs to be done is well-known in advance. Even in these cases, the discussion may reveal critical misunderstandings that can affect the process later.

Step 3: Ranking According to Priority. The goal of the third step is to reach joint understanding and consensus on what is important. When a group skips this step, each member may rank the ideas differently. This can lead to a serious breakdown of the teamwork later. Although small groups can rank their ideas informally, larger groups need a more formal approach. There are several techniques for achieving this goal. Some of the most common are

- *Everyone orders all the items.* For each item we compute the sum of all positions assigned by each participant and divide it by the total number of participants. The list is then ordered according to the resulting weights.
- *Everyone selects five most important items.* Each item gets the number of points equal to the number of participants who selected this item.
- *Everyone is given 10 votes that they can distribute among the items.* For each item, the sum of all votes assigned by each participant is computed and the list is ordered accordingly.

"Delphi" is a well-known variation of the first technique in which the ranking is conducted in several rounds. After each round, participants can compare their ordering with the group ordering. In this way, the emerging group opinion influences individual participants and leads the group to a consensus if a consensus exists. This technique was developed at Rand Corporation during World War II and was considered so powerful as to be classified as a military secret.

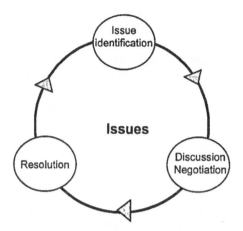

Exhibit 4. The Three Steps of Issues Processing.

Shared Knowledge. Mutual influence without shared knowledge is dangerous. It often leads to a battle of unsubstantiated opinions, guesswork, or the "follow the leader" syndrome. When a team member proposes an idea, it usually comes from one of the two sources:

- Packaged knowledge (e.g., textbooks and methodologies)
- Previous experience (e.g., cases)

Even very novel ideas usually have some relationship to prior experiences (e.g., modification or synthesis of prior cases). To help teams ground their discussion and stimulate their creativity, easy access must be made to the company's knowledge capital relevant to the present discussion. Electronic knowledge management systems can be of great help in this task. They can augment the individual experience of team members with the collective experience of the whole enterprise.

Issues

Once a team has determined what needs to be done, the process of synergism or consensus building is not finished. The team needs to examine the list for possible omissions, pitfalls, contradictions, incorrect assumptions, etc. This is done through the process called *issue resolution*. This process contains three steps, as illustrated in Exhibit 4.

Although small groups can go through this process informally, larger groups need a more systematic approach. The pitfalls of an inadequate approach to issue processing include missing an issue, endless discussion without a resolution, and a lack of "buy-in" by the team members.

This section proposes a fairly formal approach to issue processing that contrasts sharply with some existing approaches.

Step 1: Issue Identification. During the first step, the participants are asked to raise issues with the proposed list of ideas. There is a fundamental difference between an issue at this step of the process and clarification requests during the idea discussion. The person who raises an issue has to specify three things:

- A problem statement
- A set of alternatives for issue resolution
- A procedure by which the resolution will be reached

A prototypical example of an issue (as defined here) is the instructions a judge gives to a jury: "You have heard the arguments and now you must decide whether the accused is guilty of a first-degree murder, second-degree murder, manslaughter, or is not guilty. You will reach a decision by unanimous vote." These instructions refer to a problem statement, give a set of alternatives, and specify the resolution procedure, namely unanimous vote. In a business situation, an issue may be the choice of an operating system — the alternatives being Windows NT, OS/2, or UNIX, and a resolution procedure a majority vote.

Although this definition of an issue may seem a bit too formal, it has considerable advantages:

- The person who proposes an issue has to think it through so as to define a complete set of distinct positions that one might reasonably take on the proposed issue.
- The amount of "flaming" is reduced and the discussion focuses on the differences between the proposed positions.
- Team members spend less time talking to people with whom they are in agreement and more time talking to people with whom they disagree.
- The clearly specified resolution procedure encourages negotiations and compromise and discourages posturing.

This formal definition of an issue contrasts sharply with the treatment of issues in the Issue-Based Information Systems (IBIS) framework. In IBIS, issues are arbitrary statements on which people can take positions, which are also defined as free-form statements. Positions can be either supported or refuted by arguments. In this free-form definition, positions are not forced to be distinct and represent a set of alternatives, and resolution procedures are not specified. In lieu of a more formal definition of issues and positions, the IBIS framework can still be useful in documenting issues, their discussion, and resolution. The best-known implementation of IBIS is

MCC's gIBIS system and its commercial successor CM/1 from Corporate Memory Systems.

Step 2: Discussion and Negotiations. During the position-taking and discussion phase, participants take positions on the issues and try to influence participants who take different positions. There may be several reasons why two people take different positions on an issue. Different types of disagreements require different approaches to their resolution. Inappropriate approaches to disagreement resolution can lead teams to conflict and loss of trust and productivity. This section proposes a procedure for the analysis and resolution of several common disagreements.

When two people take different positions on an issue, the first thing that needs to be established is whether there is a disagreement at all. People may simply interpret the issue differently or assign different meanings to the terminology, or they may use different value scales. For example, when the suitability of a particular manager to lead a project is considered and assessed on a 1 to 5 scale, some people may give that manager 3 points and some 4 points (5 being the best). The problem may be the use of different standards. Standards are set either by rules or by prior cases. Teams need to have an easy access to the relevant rules and to help teams establish standards for position taking.

Sometimes the normalization of standards is not sufficient to resolve an issue; there may be a genuine disagreement. What often helps in these cases is to try to isolate specific areas of disagreement. To continue the above example, the team may list the qualifying criteria for the job and then treat them as separate sub-issues. Everyone may agree that the manager in question has good technical skills but disagree on the extent of his supervisory experience. This process of issue decomposition should continue until the parties have a clear and precise understanding of their disagreement. Here again, access to precedents and specific cases can greatly facilitate issue resolution.

Finally, an apparent disagreement may mask other problems, such as insufficient information to resolve the issue. Some members may consider themselves unqualified, or the team may lack interest in the issue itself and treat it as unimportant. It is important to identify these problems during the discussion phase. An issue resolution system developed at Accenture's Center for Strategic Technology Research (CSTaR), called "OMNI," addressed this problem by asking the participants to indicate the importance they attributed to the issue (low, medium, high), and the degree of their confidence in the position they were taking (low, medium, high). Low confidence for highly important issues usually indicated the need for further investigation. The confidence and importance indicators help team members identify good candidates for persuasion and make the consensus building process more efficient.

Step 3: Resolution. A number of different resolution procedures are possible. Unanimous vote is one of them. Simple majority vote is another. Alternatively, a team leader may allocate a specified time limit for the discussion and then make a unilateral decision. Many other resolution procedures are possible. What is important is to have one.

Shared Knowledge. Previous cases and packaged knowledge are reliable sources of potential issues. For example, internal investment. Many issues that need to be examined in this context are known in advance: return on investment, alternatives, and available resources may be a problem. In fact, the whole process of due diligence is designed to uncover all the important issues of a proposed investment. Teams can use these knowledge sources to ensure efficiency and completeness in issue raising.

As previously discussed, it is critical that people support their positions by pointing to specific prior cases, policies, or best practices rather than engage in battles of opinions. Here again, electronic support can provide instant access to the relevant knowledge capital.

The two key results of the issue processing step are

- A common understanding of the task and team consensus on what needs to be done
- A list of dependencies between various parts of the task

Both the consensus and the dependencies are critical during the next step: the action part of teamwork. The first of the above items is fairly obvious: When teams lose the common understanding of their task, the risk of failure is high. The second item is more subtle. Issue identification, discussion, and resolution help teams identify various dependencies among the proposed tasks which will generate the need for coordination. After all, if there is no dependency between tasks, there is no need for coordination during their execution. Many projects fail because some dependencies were not identified and provisions for the appropriate coordination were not made.

Actions

Once all important issues have been successfully resolved, it is time to act. This is done in three steps. First, it is necessary to plan the team's actions taking into considerations the dependencies discovered at the previous step. Second, specific actions need to be assigned to specific individuals and, third, these individuals need to carry them out in a coordinated fashion.

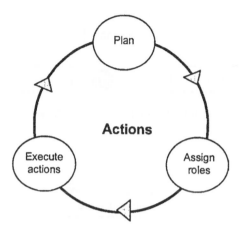

Exhibit 5. Coordinated Actions Steps.

The key to successful teamwork at this stage is coordination, which this section defines as a relationship among actors, tasks, and objects. This relationship reflects dependencies among planned actions and represents a commitment by actors with respect to these dependencies.

The following are the five dependencies: goals and deliverables, sequencing and flow, constraints, shared resources, and synergy. The existing planning and project management techniques focus primarily on the first two types of dependencies. The other three dependencies often remain implicit in the work plans. These dependencies are coordinated primarily through mutual influence among the team members and need explicit representation in the team's plans, and teams need explicit mechanisms for dealing with them (Exhibit 5).

Goals/Deliverables. One actor can commit to deliver to another actor a deliverable with certain characteristics. Usually, there is some form of handshake, during which Actor 1 announces the delivery of the product and Actor 2 acknowledges that the product is satisfactory and that it has been delivered. Winograd and Flores discuss various forms of such "speech acts," which could be quite elaborate. This dependency is illustrated in Exhibit 6.

Sequencing/Flow. This is the traditional work flow. Task 2 cannot start until Task 1 is completed. For example, a company may not want to initiate the shipment of goods until the payment is received. The traditional treatment of workflow and project management is usually limited to goals and sequencing of tasks. The following three types of dependencies are just as critical.

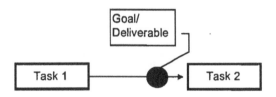

Exhibit 6. Goals and Work Flows.

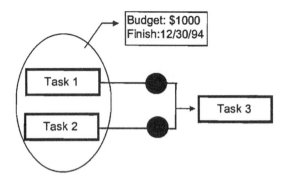

Exhibit 7. Constraints.

Constraints. Constraints on money, time, space, and form create the need for coordination. For example, there may be only a limited amount of money and time allocated to a combination of tasks. Team members may also be constrained to a certain form of deliverables (Exhibit 7).

Resource Sharing. Several actors may be sharing the same piece of equipment or access to the same knowledge source. The shared resources need to be scheduled and may be subject to various constraints.

Synergy. This is the most important factor, as well as the least appreciated form of coordination. When team members begin to execute their assignments and confront real world problems they may develop divergent ideas about the problem and its solution. This is a frequent cause of failure of team work. It is extremely important for the whole team to maintain shared understanding of the problem. To achieve this, teams have to set up explicit mechanisms to keep the team members informed about their actions, the information they gain during these actions, and of any changes in their understanding of the task. Synergy is usually maintained through status meetings (Exhibit 8).

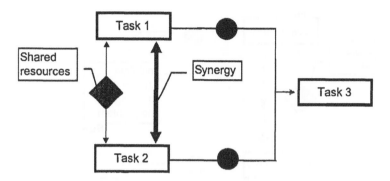

Exhibit 8. Shared Resource and Synergy Maintenance.

For example, a team consisting of a manager, Sue, and two assistants, Jim and Bob, is doing a study. The study is for a client located out of town, and requires frequent interaction with client personnel. The plan is to send Jim and Bob to the client's location, while Sue continues her usual hectic travel schedule supervising several projects.

Jim's first task is to get additional client information, while Bob is getting information from the relevant vendors. It is critical that Jim and Bob keep each other informed while pursuing their separate tasks, because many of the questions Bob ask vendors depend on what Jim learns, and vice versa. In addition, during the first phase, Jim and Bob msut share one car and arrange their schedules accordingly. At the end of the first phase, both Jim and Bob are expected to produce reports on their findings (Exhibit 9).

During the second phase of the plan, Jim writes the technical part of the study, while Bob writes the business part. To enable and encourage information sharing, they use some specific groupware forms for their work in progress. Sue accesses these forms from the road and conducts status meetings. Jim and Bob communicate with Jean-Claude, who is a very busy technical specialist. They batch their questions together, so as not to bother this resource too often. Finally, in two weeks, Sue is supposed to receive the technical and business sections of the study from Jim and Bob and synthesize them for the final report. The notation makes a first step toward concisely and explicitly depicting the many complicated dependencies involved in coordinating the team's actions.

SUMMARY

The IICA approach for team collaboration attempts to provide an integrating approach to guide the analysis and design of team processes. It focuses on mutual influence, knowledge management, and coordination, and it proposes

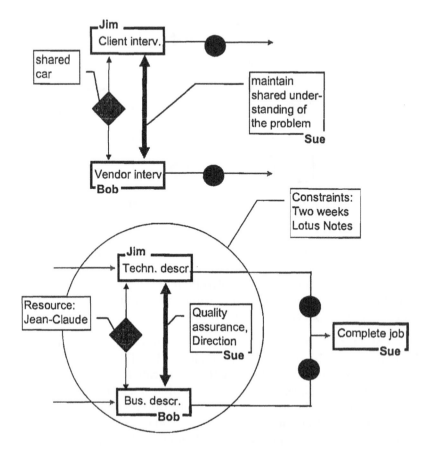

Exhibit 9. Dependency/Coordination Links.

an explicit mechanism for their implementation. The approach bridges the two ends of collaboration: reaching consensus on what needs to be done and executing the agreed-upon actions in a coordinated manner. The missing link between the two ends is the systematic identification, discussion, and resolution of issues. This process reveals the hidden dependencies among the proposed actions; coordination manages these dependencies. The IICA model consists of nine steps:

Ideas

1. Idea generation
2. Idea discussion and clarification
3. Idea ranking according to priority

Issues

4. Issue identification and generation
5. Issue discussion
6. Issue resolution and dependencies identification

Actions

7. Action planning
8. Role assignment
9. Coordinated execution of actions

This approach can be useful for different collaborative processes and can help set the stage and define requirements for the increasingly large numbers of collaborative tools and technologies that are emerging in the industry.

Chapter 31
Data Mining

Organizations have been accumulating large amounts of data through their transaction systems for the last 2 decades. Although this data has a great deal of potential value, organizations have lacked the resources and the ability to process it to recover that value. Most of the time, the data have simply languished in dusty archives until lawyers or regulators pronounced the data safe to purge.

New tools and techniques, called data mining, are allowing organizations to sift through their data archives to find previously undiscovered "golden nuggets." In fact, the ultimate goal is to find more than just nuggets; it is to tap into a mother lode of knowledge that can help an organization understand its customers, markets, and business better. One of the key distinguishing feature of data mining is the high degree of automation involved in discovering hidden relationships and patterns existing in data.

Although enterprises from any industry sector can take advantage of advanced techniques in data mining, many early adopters have been organizations in the retail, finance, and health care industries. A few success stories can also be found in insurance, chemical, petroleum, manufacturing, security, aerospace, transportation, and the environmental industry sectors.

Data mining is becoming attractive to business organizations because it can provide a competitive edge. It is now gaining more momentum because of the availability of tools such as neural networks and massively parallel processors, which provide large computing power at relatively lower cost.

This chapter describes data mining concepts, discusses a framework for understanding data mining, and explores specific tools and techniques.

WHAT IS DATA MINING?

Data mining is the process of extracting valid and understandable, but previously unknown, information from large data stores in a format that supports making useful business decisions. Mining makes sense out of huge data stores by unveiling implicit relationships, trends, patterns, exceptions, and anomalies that were previously transparent to human analysts. Data mining begins by organizing and storing data in an appropriate fashion. It then sifts through this large data volume using pattern recognition algorithms as well as statistical and mathematical techniques.

The process is data driven, an extraction and presentation of data and information to a knowledgeable user for review and examination. Although the process is data driven, however, users play an important and essential role. Ultimately, only they can decide if the information is interesting, relevant to the business, and useful to the organization. Therefore, data mining requires substantial human effort and interaction throughout the process.

BENEFITS OF DATA MINING

Data mining enables organizations to leverage data stores for strategic advantage. For decades, corporations have been storing enormous amounts of data about customers, sales, finances, inventories, and operations. These data stores are primarily designed to streamline and facilitate day-to-day operations. During the last 15 to 20 years, these data stores have reached varying levels of maturity; in some cases, they are quite robust and stable. A number of organizations are in the process of transforming this data, ensuring its accuracy, and making it available to the business analyst for strategic information processing by implementing an information delivery facility (i.e., a data warehouse).

When organizations reach the level of sophistication at which they view data as an asset and make it available for business analysis purposes, they have yet another opportunity to leverage it for additional strategic advantages. From this realization, the leading-edge technology exploiters are putting data to a secondary use, over and above the traditional information delivery facility, for untapped knowledge.

With data mining tools, organizations can comb through their data looking for patterns and relationships that predict customers' buying behaviors, that identify consumers likely to default on loans or perpetrate fraud, or that anticipate unusual demands on inventory. Business analysts can use this information to develop strategies to increase return on investment, minimize risks, and adjust inventory levels.

EXAMPLES OF DATA MINING

Data mining techniques find applications in almost all industries, including insurance, finance, manufacturing, health, and environmental science. There are many examples where data mining can yield useful patterns that can be applied beneficially for business.

In the supermarket and retailing industries, for example, data mining has been used to gain knowledge about shoppers and their purchases. Knowing and analyzing a market basket makeup can affect strategy and operations at various levels. At one end of the spectrum, it permits serving the customer as an individual; at the other end, it allows for development of marketing strategies for a group of stores in a region. In between, it helps in designing efficient store layouts and making profitable operational decisions.

In the highly competitive airline market, data mining tools can be used on data from reservations, travel, ticketing, and operations to discover patterns, relationships, or associations to improve a number of important factors ranging from customer satisfaction to flight yield management. Fliers can be grouped and classified into categories, and appropriate frequent flier program features can be developed for the various groups to maintain the fliers' loyalty and improve the margins. New marketing channels can be developed to increase the market share. In the banking and financial services industry, data mining can provide benefits in several areas, with applications varying from one-to-one marketing to branch profitability to predicting stock and bond prices based on the rules determined from the historical trading patterns. Such patterns may not be intuitively obvious because of the massive amount of data. Of all the applications, those associated with credit card operations have received most attention.

Grouping credit card holders into different categories based on their spending and payment histories is the basis for several business strategies. Predicting future behaviors of the existing and new card holders using pattern-based groupings can significantly help in this business where the customer base is essentially flat and the gain of a new card holder is at the cost of another company. Classifying a card holder according to one of the following categories can lead to some precise and cost-effective target marketing:

- *Attriters.* These are customers who are likely to be lost to competitors because of their marketing programs. In the United States, where the credit card business is now a zero-sum game, companies typically lose 1 to 10% of their customers to competitors.
- *Revolvers.* These are typically the best customers who do not default on payment, yet keep high revolving balances and are not constantly shopping for the lowest interest rates.
- *Transactors.* These customers neither keep balances nor pay interest. They pay their monthly balance on time but generate fees through transactions.

Finding and acquiring the lucrative customers from hundreds of millions of potential consumers is expensive. Keeping the existing customers is relatively less expensive. Data mining techniques have been particularly effective in target marketing to both existing and potential customers.

Fraud detection is another example of how data mining techniques can find applicability across several industries. In the automotive industry, one company used data mining techniques to replace manual auditing of claims for warranty work. Because of the time-consuming nature of the auditing process, less than 10% of claims were actually being audited. Data mining allowed the company to reduce the time for selecting claims for review, increased the probability of identifying dealers or claims needing investigation, and ultimately reduced the amount of payments in warranty claims, resulting in an annual savings of about $3 million.

Although one might argue that these applications could be implemented without the use of data mining tools, that is actually unlikely. Data mining brings to bear new techniques of statistical analysis. An analyst following hypothesis-driven methods are unlikely to find the patterns turned up by data mining.

INCREASED INTEREST IN DATA MINING

Why is data mining gaining more visibility now? Two reasons: business is driving the technology, and technology is enabling a new way of doing business.

Business is becoming more and more competitive every day, and the leading companies are looking for every tool that provides an extra edge. Data assets, when mined for new knowledge, provide that edge. The cases discussed in the previous section show the driving forces in the business world that require technology to step up and enable the solutions.

At the same time, data mining algorithms, such as inductive reasoning and artificial neural networks, are reaching a level of sophistication and maturity, where they can now be applied to discover data patterns for commercial applications, some of which can require large computational resources.

Coincidentally, after years of promising potential, parallel processing hardware technology has now reached a stage on the technology take-up curve in which is it commercially viable to deploy it with the new data mining software algorithms. (Parallel processing is not required in all data mining solutions.) This combination of parallel processing hardware technology and data mining software algorithms is now poised to enable businesses to uncover the hidden value in their data.

At the same time, the emphasis on the information delivery facility (i.e., data warehousing) applications have helped data mining in two ways:

- Information delivery facilities have raised the awareness of the value of the data asset. Businesses want to deploy data assets as a competitive advantage.
- Some of the implementation steps required for information delivery facilities and data mining are common. Gathering of the data for mining requires understanding its sources, currency, accuracy, cleansing,

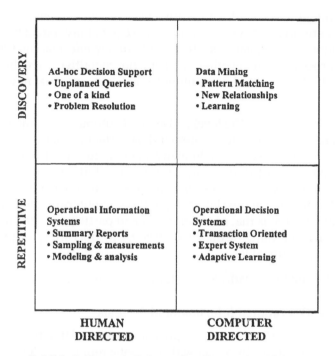

Exhibit 1. Strategic Information Processing Matrix.

---

extraction, and reformatting. These steps are also part of the processes involved in the information delivery facility, which has been a catalyst in the development of tools and skills for data preparation. An information delivery facility is not a prerequisite for data mining, but it can facilitate it by making reliable data available more quickly for mining purposes.

DATA MINING AND THE STRATEGIC INFORMATION PROCESSING MATRIX

Data mining is part of an organization's overall strategic analytical information processing, in which data-driven discovery of patterns is paramount. It can be distinguished from other strategic analytical processes by the type and the extent of automation and human interaction involved.

Exhibit 1 shows the strategic information processing matrix, which organizes types of systems and processes according to a number of criteria.

This chapter uses this matrix as a framework to organize the discussion of alternatives when attempting to use corporate data resource for strategic information processing. Alternatives along the y-axis of the matrix are whether the process used is repetitive or discovery oriented. Repetitive processes are prescriptive in nature and are generally parameters driven for execution on a regular basis to provide timely information. Discovery-oriented processes, on the other hand, are not repetitive. Here the data are examined by humans and computers to discover or reveal new information.

The x-axis represents the level and style of automation — the manner in which humans and computers interact during the information processing. Of course, there is always both human and computer involvement. It is the style of involvement that is different. On the left side, in the human-directed arena, the user raises specific queries to solve a problem or to gather information. On the right side, in the computer-directed arena, the human involvement is that of observation and participation to ensure that the problem is relevant, the data is accurate, the tools are appropriate, and the solution is actionable.

The following four quadrants are formed by the two-by-two matrix.

Quadrant 1: Operational Informational Systems

This represents work that is prescriptive in nature and that requires coding of queries or programs by a user with a specific report or solution in mind. Examples of such work include summary or detail reports produced on a regular basis for business measurement, analysis, modeling, and management. These reports are generated on a repetitive basis and are generally parameter driven. One obtains the information that has been preplanned.

Canned queries are generally the basis for quadrant one work, including "What are the sales in New York?" and "Are the new products better received in urban or suburban markets?" Sophisticated multidimensional programs and tools may be used to generate queries and output displayed in attractive graphical reports. In such cases, these programs or tools become the proxy for humans for developing the actual query, but the paradigm remains the same.

Quadrant 2: Ad Hoc Decision Support

This represents work that is discovery oriented. The queries are not repetitive or prescriptive in nature. A user codes these queries to find information in order to solve a specific problem. The queries are one-of-a-kind and not preplanned. Although the work in quadrant two is very different from that in quadrant one, in one respect the work is very similar. In both cases, user-initiated queries are the basis for information processing. The computer is a facilitator, responding to the questions that the user already knows to ask.

In this quadrant, ad hoc queries are generally created to analyze a problem. For example, an organization's sales in a specific region during the last quarter did not meet the forecast. Queries may be developed to examine the sales by cities, comparing actual vs. forecast, revealing one particular city as the culprit. Additional queries may indicate that sales were very low in certain localities during one month. Further investigation may reveal that the cause was an aggressive sales campaign by a competitor. Strictly speaking, this style of processing, although discovery oriented and facilitated by automation, is not data mining.

Queries such as those issued within quadrant two return an answer set that satisfies the query predicates. Whatever new information is discovered either supports or nullifies the hypothesis that the analyst started with. The successive iterations of queries and the examination of the retrieved data is driven by the analyst based on his or her hypothesis. The iterations of the queries end when the hypothesis is either proven or rejected in the analyst's judgment. This is the essence of the user-created-hypothesis verification model.

From the analyst's viewpoint, new data facts are being discovered. The queries may be either user generated or formulated by some query tool, which has a point-and-click graphical user interface. Multidimensional products are examples of such tools that make it easier for the user to drill down into the data. However, these are still manifestations of the verification model.

Many vendors offer products to facilitate such analysis. They often call these verification model "data mining tools" to garner a share of this emerging new market and to benefit commercially from the increasing expenditure for data mining.

Quadrant 3: Data Mining

With data mining, computer algorithms, rather than the analyst, examine data to discover patterns. Unlike quadrant 2, where the analyst started with a hypothesis, computer algorithms create hypotheses based on data patterns. This is the discovery model, as opposed to the verification model discussed above.

This is significantly different from traditional computational work, in which the computer is used merely to respond to predefined queries, or crunch the numbers to arrive at answers rapidly. Here the data are being examined by a computer to generate new hypotheses.

It may be argued that an analyst using the same data and collective experience may generate the same or a very similar hypothesis to the one that a data mining tool may discover. However, for data with many variables and a large number of records, the possibility is low that the analyst will determine the pattern, for several reasons. It is impractical to run repeated ad hoc queries against large data stores due to the required elapsed time and computer resources. In addition, the analyst's time is expensive. Finally, and most important, an analyst may not be able to conceive a hypothesis because of prior biases or the large number of variables involved. Traditional queries provide responses to the questions that a person thinks of and decides to ask; they do not, however, seek for patterns in data that can lead someone to discover hypotheses that exist but have not been thought of or that even contradict the analyst's views and judgments.

Patterns can be associations, sequences, and classifications. Classifications are sometimes also called "clustering" or "segmenting." Associations occur when occurrences are linked. For example, a study of supermarket baskets may reveal that 50% of potato chip purchases are accompanied by a soda purchase. When there is an associated marketing promotion, soda is purchased 75% of the time. This association can be used to adjust promotions or pricing.

In sequences, events are linked over a time period. For example, data mining might determine that, when a customer buys a sleeping bag and a backpack, in 65% of cases the same person also buys a camping tent in the following 2 months. For this sequencing pattern to be identified, the customer identification must be maintained along with the record of purchase. Many supermarkets have initiated a frequent buyers reward program, in which the buyer is offered an incentive to provide a linkage between their purchases over a period of time.

Classification is probably the most commonly used data mining process today. It identifies patterns that can be used to classify items into segments with similar characteristics. For example, the financial industry uses classification to determine whether or not a particular customer is a good credit risk.

Data mining techniques currently being used with some frequency can be classified into several categories, including

- Inductive reasoning
- Neural networks
- Memory-based reasoning

Some methodologies and tools for data mining are based on a combination of these methods, including statistics-based algorithms, which have been widely used in the business in the past. Some of these data mining techniques are discussed in more detail later in this chapter.

Quadrant 4: Operational Decision Systems

These systems are repetitive, rather than discovery oriented. They are prescriptive in nature and may apply the patterns and knowledge discovered by data mining to business use. (Of course, such applications can be implemented using other knowledge, which has nothing to do with data mining.) An example is the automated underwriting of an insurance policy to a new applicant, classified into a segment based on a pattern discovered by data mining. Another example is granting a mortgage loan to a prospective home buyer based on the classification of the applicant.

Such applications can also assist in real time. For example, a particular cellular phone number, usually used to make only domestic calls, is suddenly used for making a series of overseas calls. This may indicate fraud and necessitate corrective action.

DATA MINING TECHNOLOGY COMPONENTS

The next few sections discuss the significant technology components of data mining. The discussion is organized as follows:

- Common types of information
- Supervised and unsupervised mining
- Data mining tools
- Data mining techniques

The first section discusses the types of relationships and patterns that can be discovered, namely: associations, sequences, and clusters. This provides the basic understanding of important data mining concepts . Before the section discusses the actual data mining tools and techniques, it introduces the notion of supervised and unsupervised mining. This is necessary because the tools (i.e., algorithms based on data mining techniques) must first be trained to work with the available historical data. This training is generally classified as "supervised" or "unsupervised." The third section, techniques and tools for data mining, discusses the actual techniques, such as induction trees and artificial neural networks. It begins with a short discussion of the preparation process that a tool typically goes through before use for prediction in the actual use environment. Then the actual techniques are discussed.

Common Types of Information

There are three common types of information that can be discovered by data mining:

- Associations
- Sequences
- Clusters

Some other terms are frequently encountered in discussions of information types. Classification is sometimes considered another type of information discovery. However, classification is really just another aspect of clustering; it determines the cluster to which a new item belongs. Forecasting, yet another concept related to data mining, is about predicting the value of an unknown field or variable. Both classification and forecasting indicate something about an unknown: classification indicates a cluster to which a new item or record belongs, while forecasting estimates a value of the unknown field or variable in a new record.

There are no clear-cut and agreed-upon definitions to many of these terms, and vendors and their product literature often use these terms interchangeably.

Associations. Associations are occurrences that are linked in a single event. The supermarket baskets are examples. In the first example, basket analysis indicated an association between cosmetics and greeting cards. In the second example, there was an association between potato chips and soda. Such associations can be used for store layout design and promotions.

Sequences. In sequences, events are linked over time. Recall the example of the link between the purchase of a backpack and the purchase of tent. This link is discovered through analysis of a sequence of sales records.

The concept of similar sequences is somewhat related to sequential patterns. Given a series of events, similar sequences discover patterns similar to a given one. Typical examples include finding stocks with similar price movements, products with similar sales patterns, or stores or departments with similar revenue streams.

Clusters. Clustering discovers patterns that recognize the grouping within data. This is perhaps the most common activity in the data mining field today. An example is the clustering of credit card customers (i.e., an attriter, revolver, or transactor) discussed earlier in this chapter.

The clustering process forms the groups. The algorithm, or tool, discovers different groupings within the data, such that each group is made up of similar objects but is distinctly different from other groups.

The matching of the profile of a new item with that of an appropriate cluster group is known as classification, which presupposes the existence of such clusters.

Forecasting is a concept similar to classification. It estimates the future value of a variable, such as revenue. Both forecasting and classification are about predicting something about a new item. Classification identifies the cluster to which a new item belongs, whereas forecasting estimates a value of a variable for a new item.

Supervised and Unsupervised Mining

The concept of supervised and unsupervised mining relates to whether a set of historical records can be used for focused learning or training of a tool. For example, if a set of records containing existing customer profiles with indicators for good or bad credit risk exists, a tool can be trained to discover patterns for predicting credit worthiness of future new applicants. In this case, the process of discovering the pattern and tool training is called supervised learning or mining.

On the other hand, if there is no identified target field of interest and the data mining process results in segmentation of data, the process is known as unsupervised learning or mining. For example, a set of auto accidents and related repair records can be mined for patterns, which may result in two segments, one containing 98% and the other containing the remaining 2% of records. Further manual auditing may reveal interesting facts about the segments, such as excessive charges or fraudulent behavior for the smaller set. This is unsupervised mining, because there was no interesting (or target) field in the record on which the tool could focus initially.

Data Mining Tools

Commercially available data mining tools use stand-alone data mining techniques, such as induction reasoning or artificial neural networks, or combine several of them to provide a useable product. New phrases, or "jargon," depending on the perspective, are being coined and introduced at a rapid rate as new tools and techniques, or variations of old ones, are being introduced.

Before a tool can be put in "production" for actual use, however, it needs to be prepared. Preparation includes training, evaluating, and assessing the likely accuracy of the prediction results. Put differently, during the preparation process, tools figure out the answer or the pattern by examining a subset of the data where the outcome or result is already known from the historical data. Then, during production, they apply the pattern knowledge to other data records to predict the answer or response for the unknown field or records. Tool vendors use different names and steps for the preparation process. For ease in understanding this process, Exhibit 2 illustrates a scenario that uses three steps or phases.

Tool users designate some field of interest in the historical database as the response or answer field. This is the field that the user desires to predict (i.e., supervised mining). Sometimes it is also called the target or

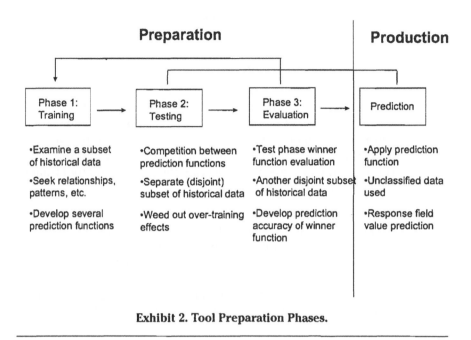

Exhibit 2. Tool Preparation Phases.

dependent field. The other fields in the record are known as independent or variable fields.

The Training Phase. In the training phase, tool modules examine a subset of historical data, seeking patterns and relationships between the values of variables and response fields to establish functions that would enable the tool to predict the value of the dependent field based on the values of the independent fields. The output of the training phase is a family of prediction functions, which are candidates for further investigation in the subsequent phase for the selection of the best one.

The Testing Phase. In the testing phase, the candidate prediction functions are applied to a test subset of the historical data. This subset consists of records which are distinct from the ones used previously for training purposes. Candidate-prediction functions use the new variables to predict the related response. The winner is the function that statistically best approximates the answer. This approach also minimizes the effects of over-training of the function. It is likely that in the training phase, functions may have adopted, or overtrained, themselves to the unrepresentative idiosyncrasies of the training subset of the historical data.

The Evaluation Phase. The winner from the testing phase will be used for the actual prediction during the production process. However, it first goes through the evaluation phase, where it is applied to yet another set of historical records to estimate the accuracy of the prediction function. Because the answer or the outcome in the historical data is already known, the ratio of prediction function answer to the actual outcome gives a degree of confidence in the predictability of the selected function.

The actual steps and preparation process varies with vendors. Also, the degree of automation, process control, and amount of manual intervention required are some of the distinguishing features of the tools.

Finally, during production the prediction function is applied to unclassified data for which the value of the response or dependent field is not known.

It might become necessary to go back and start from the training phase again for several reasons, such as the use of a different technique or tool, changes to the parameters, changes to the historical data, or changes to the business environment. A prediction function that works well in a 3% inflation environment, for example, may not be equally applicable in a 9% environment.

Data Mining Techniques

There is no commonly agreed-upon classification scheme for data mining techniques. This is not surprising, because this is a new and emerging computational arena in commercial processing. For discussion purposes, the more popular techniques are classified into the following types:

- Inductive reasoning
- Artificial neural networks
- Memory-based reasoning

Although this section discusses these techniques individually, typically commercial products combine these techniques along with statistical analysis and other advanced techniques such as fuzzy logic and genetic algorithms to produce hybrid tools.

Inductive Reasoning. Induction is the process of starting with individual facts and then using reasoning to reach a hypothesis or a general conclusion. By contrast, deduction is to start with a hypothesis and trying to prove or disprove it by specific facts. In data mining inductive reasoning, the facts are the database records, and the hypothesis formulation usually takes the form of a decision tree that attempts to divide or organize the data in a meaningful way. The tree can then be used to create rules, generalities, or hypotheses, with the nodes serving as decision points.

Decision trees divide the data into groups using the values in the fields or variables. It resembles the game of "20 questions." The tree is a hierarchy of if-then statements that group the data. These tests are applied at

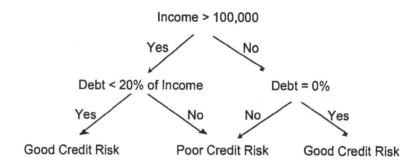

[Confidence Factor: 0.97]

Exhibit 3. Sample Decision Tree.

each node to a record (e.g., is income greater than $100,000, is debt less than 20% of income, and so forth). The result of each test indicates the choice of which test to perform next. The tests are designed to extract a set of characteristics that reliably predict the value of the response (i.e., answer) field. Exhibit 3 shows a very simple decision tree for classification of individuals as sound or poor credit risks. To keep the example simple, the response at each node is assumed to be binary valued. In actual cases, multivalued responses are encountered.

One of the key advantages of tools based on decision trees is that in addition to using a decision tree to make a prediction, the user may examine the tree itself. Looking at the tree allows one to observe the prediction criteria or rules that the tool has induced for a particular set of records in order to discover the pattern. There has been a surge in decision tree-based products because of this visibility to the induction rules and because such tools tend to be faster than those based on neural networks.

A variety of parameters are used to control induction functions or rules, including the rule length, an importance factor, the maximum or minimum number of rules to generate, rule confidence factor, error margins, and training and validation data set size. Tools provide default values for these parameters. However, user analyst's input based on the type of problem and business knowledge is critical.

Decision trees are not suitable for all kinds of problems and may not work with some types of data. Some decision tree-based tools have problems dealing with continuous sets of values, such as revenue or age, and may require that these values be grouped into ranges. In addition, the way the ranges are specified may inadvertently hide patterns. For example, grouping customers aged 16 to 23 together may hide a significant break

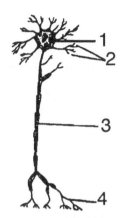

Exhibit 4. A Neuron.

---

that might occur at age 20. Tools such as Darwin from Thinking Machine avoid this problem by using techniques to best cluster the data first. Information Harvester from Information Harvesting Corporation solves this problem by assigning values to groups based on fuzzy logic. Each instance of the same value is assigned to a different group.

Also, there is a limitation that the questions must generate discrete responses such that a record can traverse only along a single branch at each node. More important, a significant segmentation opportunity could be missed if analysis is based on the sequencing of the earlier questions. For example, if questions are based on sex, age, and education level, the segmentation may not be as revealing if the sequence were to be reversed. Tools use a variety of techniques to overcome this limitation.

Another problem is that a set of if-then statements can get very difficult to understand, particularly if the condition list is long and complex. In many cases, the tree created through induction may not be hierarchical and may have overlaps. Different tools resolve such issues differently. Tree pruning and partial tree generation are some of the remedies.

Neural Networks. Neural networks simulate the way the human brain works, and apply the research done in the field of artificial intelligence to business problems. A neural network is a computer implementation to simulate the biological process of the millions of neurons, which comprise the brain.

These networks can be better understood by considering the makeup of a neuron and how pulses are emitted and propagated along the neural paths (i.e., nerves) in the brain (Exhibit 4).

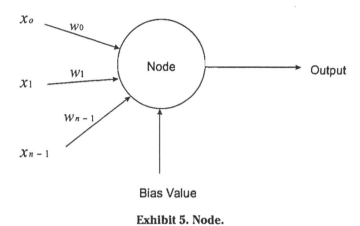

x_0
w_0

w_1
x_1

Node

Output

w_{n-1}

x_{n-1}

Bias Value

Exhibit 5. Node.

1. The soma is the center of the nerve cell where the collection of inputs from dendrites are combined and processed.
2. Dendrites receive input from other neurons.
3. Axons are the parts of the nerve cell that produce the pulses emitted by the neuron.
4. The synapse is the location where electrical pulses are transmitted.

In neural networks, the idea is to map computation jobs to each of the parts of a neuron. The basic unit of a neural network is called a node (see Exhibit 5). The node has a series of N inputs. Associated with each input is a corresponding weight, which are applied to each input, and the result is summed. This is the weighted sum that serves as input to the node and corresponds to the synoptic weighted sum of the human neuron.

A function is then applied to the weighted sum, adjusted using a bias value. The resulting output value is then released and passed as input to other nodes. This can be represented by the following equation for the output:

$$i = n - 1$$

$$y = F(h)\{S \; Wi \times xi + b\}$$

$$i = 0$$

How, then, are neural networks applied to solving business problems? Neural networks are multilayered networks that learn how to solve a problem by examining and processing data values. They are essentially a collection of nodes with inputs, outputs, and simple processing at each node. Between the visible input and output layers, there may be several hidden intermediate layers.

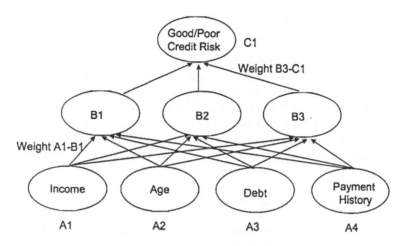

Exhibit 6. Example of a Neural Network.

In general, neural networks provide a method of predicting output values from input values. In the data mining context, the input values are the values of the independent (i.e., known) fields, and the output value is the predicted value of the response (i.e., unknown) field. Exhibit 6 is an example of a simple neural network created for identifying solid and poor credit ratings. This neural network of nodes learns by taking the input fields (A1 to A4) and processing their values such that the output field (C1) indicates the answer (Good or Poor Credit Risk). Layer B is known as the hidden layer, and there can be multiple hidden layers, though normally one to two suffice.

Each node processes the input from the nodes from the previous layer and outputs a value, which becomes input for the nodes in the next layer. Values are modified by the weight factors, which are unique between any two nodes. Each record in the training set is processed and the outcome compared with the known value of the response field. If it disagrees, a correction to the weighting factors is calculated and applied such that the output agrees with the known value in the response field. The process is repeated until the output agrees and corrections become less than a given amount. After the neural network has been trained, it can be used to predict values for the unknown set.

Neural networks are an opaque tool, which means that the model produced does not have a clear interpretation. It is usually applied to the business problems without the user fully understanding the reasoning behind its results. This is one of the key reasons why induction-based tools are often preferred for those applications where legal or business needs require clear interpretation.

Some algorithms attempt to translate a neural network model into a set of rules that the business analyst can understand. However, it is generally very difficult, because the function applied at the various nodes can be nonlinear and the bias introduced to achieve a solution can be quite significant. Many applications for neural networks are beyond the typical commercial arena. For example, neural networks may be applied to interpret electrocardiograms, voice recognition and synthesis, and handwriting recognition.

Memory-Based Reasoning. Memory-based reasoning is another artificial intelligence technique used for classification in a fashion similar to what people may do to classify objects by comparing attributes with those of other objects recalled from memory.

Tools that use memory-based reasoning classify records in a data base by comparing them with similar records that have already been clustered or classified. Also called "k nearest-neighbor" (kNN) technique, the following algorithm is used:

1. Find k cases nearest to the examined case.
2. Use a weighted average vote to select a classification or cluster.

When an examined record falls within a group of neighbors that have the same classification, the new record is directed to that class. Otherwise, it is classified with its "closest" neighbors. Closeness is measured by weighted relative importance of the different attributes of the records. For example, StarMatch from Thinking Machine Corporation uses weighted n-dimensional Euclidean distance of the normalized values of the attributes, where each attribute is assigned an axis. Weights for each attribute can be either prespecified by the analyst, or derived by the tool as a part of the training process.

A consideration here is that a single record can influence the classification of the examined record. This can be an advantage or disadvantage, depending on the problem. This consideration does not apply with other techniques such as Neural Networks.

This chapter examines in subsequent sections some of the criteria that can be used to narrow the list of available tools for any particular organization.

Statistics and Data Mining

Statistics have been used over the years to analyze business data to derive value and to perform many functions, such as factor analysis, linear regres-

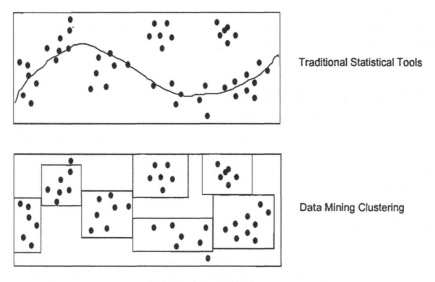

Traditional Statistical Tools

Data Mining Clustering

Exhibit 7. Clustering vs. Traditional Statistical Tools.

sion, and prediction. Frequently used in combination with other techniques, statistics have often been the tool of choice. Statistics-based
algorithms will probably continue to play an important role in the future,
even as the new data mining algorithms become more popular. Hybrid
tools judiciously combining the power of new data mining algorithms with
statistical analysis will find increasing demand. Standalone statistics-based
tools are at times difficult to apply; they bog down when a large number of
variables and nonlinear functions are involved. Most important, statistics-
based tools require up-front assumptions and can mask the subtleties of
data. It is said that "In statistical analysis, you will never find what you are
not looking for."

Exhibit 7 shows an example. Traditional statistical tools (at the top of
the diagram) attempt to fit the data to an expected function or pattern (in
this case, a sine curve) and do not account for data points that lie outside
of the function. These unusual data points outside the pattern, often
referred to as "outliers," are typically discarded from the analysis. Nevertheless, given a function and the data points, these tools are very good at
finding the best fitting function.

The new data mining tools are likely to begin by clustering the data
points and finding the best fitting functions for each cluster without requiring the analyst to provide a function. In the traditional statistical techniques, these functions may be difficult to estimate or, worse, may be
missed completely because of one's preconceived notions and biases.

In summary, it is likely that the new data mining tools will include not only the techniques such as Induction Trees and Artificial Neural Networks but also the traditional statistics-based algorithms to address business needs.

CRITICAL SUCCESS FACTORS IN DATA MINING

The key to successful data mining is to focus on the business processes, data, and technology. A good understanding of the business problem domain is essential; without it, the misuse of the data and technology is possible. Emphasis on the technology or the tool by itself is likely to lead to failure.

Quality of Data

The quality of data used for data mining is paramount. The old adage of GIGO (garbage in, garbage out) certainly applies here, because the raw material that is being mined is data. If the data are incorrect, inconsistent, or missing, the results are going to be unreliable. The impact of incorrect and inconsistent data is easy to see. Missing data or records can have an equally significant impact. If some records either have never been collected or were discarded during the editing phases in the operational systems, the patterns and relationships developed based on the partial data by the mining tools can be significantly flawed. The problem becomes compounded if the business analyst, who is trying to apply the knowledge gained for effective solutions, is not even aware of the missing records. People responsible for "sourcing" the data and using the data must communicate to avoid this problem.

Another aspect of the missing or incorrect data can manifest itself when some variables in the existing records being mined are defaulted to some values (e.g., zeros, blanks, or high values) or computed to reflect values of some other fields. The impact on the discovered patterns because of the computed field may be very well disguised. In some cases, it may result in the discovery and development of patterns so perfect that it may just reflect what has already been coded in the data in the first place.

The problems and solutions for "sourcing" well defined and consistent data from operational systems is similar to those discussed in the chapter on Information Delivery Facilities in this section. It makes sense to use the data that has already been cleansed and stored in the warehouse. In this sense, having implemented an information delivery facility eases implementation of data mining success. However, it is not necessary to implement the information delivery facility first to use data mining.

Technology and Tools

From a technology and tools perspective, several tools available in the marketplace as of this writing are unable to process large amounts of data and require the user to provide a representative subset. The subset may be horizontal (i.e., a number of rows that represent the entire set), or the subset may be vertical (i.e., including only columns of interest). It may be possible to do this effectively, provided that one fully understands the problem and the data. Several other tools sample the data on their own without user involvement. In any case, the user must understand the implication of sampling and deal with the results cautiously because the results may be tainted by the selected sample.

Furthermore, not every data mining technique is appropriate for every business problem. It is necessary to understand the algorithm used by the tool, and its limitations and to understand the data sampling technique, prior to applying the results to the business situation. If the model developed is very sensitive to a particular variable, one must ensure that minor errors in data values or missing values for that variable haven't resulted in skewed results.

Business Processes

The social issues concerning the use of data is another key consideration. Concerns regarding privacy and use of data for purposes other than what it was initially gathered for should be considered. In the European Common Community, issues regarding the use of data are particularly sensitive.

Successful application of data mining techniques and other computer-based algorithms demand that appropriate processes be put in place to avoid embarrassing business publicity and to meet legal obligations. Recently, a major bank that issues credit cards for a famous toy company denied a card to an individual with apparently excellent credentials: The individual is 41 years old, earns $123,000 a year, has excellent job security, pays his mortgage on time, and has a clean credit history ("A Man Who Governs Credit Is Denied a Toys R Us Card," *The Wall Street Journal*, December 14, 1995, p. B1). The process that rejected the individual uses a computerized scoring system to rate applicants. The bank process ensures that a human checks every application before it is approved, but not every one that is rejected. Examples such as this have legal and social ramifications. However, from a pure business perspective, it is indicated that, if practical, procedures be put in place to review computer-generated recommendations to avoid such incidents.

The rejected candidate said in a speech to the Boston Bar Association, "I would expect credit-scoring type procedures to be overwhelmingly dominant by the end of the decade. We will obtain the fairness of the machine, but lose the judgment, talents, and sense of justice that only humans can bring to decision making."

Besides being instructive, the case is interesting because the rejected individual happens to be a governor of the Federal Reserve Board in Washington, the agency that sets interest rates and regulates banks. As it turned out, the application was rejected because eight other companies had requested copies of his credit history recently. A proliferation of inquiries by potential lenders is a sign that people are really looking for a lot of credit and is not considered a good thing by financial institutions. However, in the case of the governor of the Federal Reserve Board, five of the eight requests appear to have been prompted by the fact that he refinanced his mortgage and shifted his home-equity line to another bank.

Another key success factor is to remain cautious in using the data mining output. An interesting recent story in this regard deals with how a super-regional bank applies this concept and the business and technology implications of "predictive computer modeling" ("To Make More Loans, Banks Use Computers to Identify Candidates," *The Wall Street Journal*, March 15, 1996, p. A1). Part of this bank's strategy is to increase its share of the consumer loan. For the banking industry, facing all the outside competition that it does, "a couple of years and it's too late to regain market share," the chairman says. The bank's strategy includes taking on lower-quality accounts. As long as there is automotive or real estate collateral to tap, the bank books auto and other loans of less than A-quality credit in its finance-company unit.

The main reason these bankers are not lying awake nights is that they are using powerful computers to analyze large amounts of information about potential borrowers. This helps them spot both the good customers who can afford to take more debt and the marginal consumers who actually are better risks than they seem at first glance.

Using computers for database marketing by mail, the bank aimed one promotion at new auto loan customers. Armed with research showing that car loan customers are more likely to respond to a preapproved credit card offer if they are approached right after buying the car, the bank sent 7,000 preapproved credit offers to such prospects. It got 1,000 acceptances, which it says is a rate six times the normal response rate to mail solicitations of its customer base.

One of its analysts says, "Point and click. That is all there is to it," as he starts tapping away at his terminal. By the time he is finished, he has constructed a diagram that looks like a family tree. On it are boxes representing 30 variables weighted to reveal the six most common characteristics of existing home-equity credit line customers. Those characteristics–the ones most predictive of loan acceptance–include a high number of existing bank relationships, such as a gold credit card, at least 12-year relationship, and a home value of less than $350,000.

Another interesting observation related to risks associated with loan applicants was that at some locations, customers who had held a job less than two years were more likely to pay back loans than some others who had longer tenures on the job. The speculation is that this is because many new fast-growing companies had started up in that particular locale, while downsizing was going on among older, established companies.

To reduce the risks on predictive computer models, the bank measures every single mailing to see if it will meet a financial rate of return. Further, the bank says it is taking a cautious approach. "We do not drop one-million-piece mailings," says its analyst. "If one of those monthly mailings goes bad, it is not going to ruin our balance sheet." A monthly monitoring program tracks the progress of each mailing to see if refinements in the selection process are needed for subsequent solicitations.

In summary, critical success factors require one to keep focused on the business procedures, data, and technology to ensure success and to minimize exposure due to errors in predictive data mining.

TOOLS SELECTION CRITERIA

Data mining is an emerging commercial arena. Thus, there is limited practical experience, and classification schemes for tools have yet to be defined adequately. Listed are some criteria that can be considered when selecting a tool and when evaluating it as to how well it solves the problem and integrates within the environment.

- What kind of problems does it solve? Is the tool relevant to the problem at hand?
- What type of user interface does it use? Does it explain the induced rules? Is it easy to use? How does one provide input parameters?
- Can it handle the number of records and variables that need to be processed to solve the problem? Generally, the larger the number of records and variables the tool can handle, the better.
- Can the tool extract the data from the existing store or must customized programs be written to meet its requirement?
- Does the tool guide the user through the multiple steps of data mining and keep track of his progress? Or is the user required to figure it out for himself or herself?
- How is the performance of the tool? Will it take too long to be useful for the problem at hand? Does it exploit parallel processing to provide adequate performance? If direct mailing must be completed within a few days, will the tool be able to process the input in time?

Data mining is an ideal application for parallel computation. In many cases, it is an "embarrassingly parallel" problem, lending itself to parallel execution. Generally, there are two separate challenges in exploiting parallelism: the parallel processing of the set of records and the parallel execution of other remaining processing.

In data mining, if the tool uses SQL queries, the first challenge may easily be met by the use of the relational data base management system. The second challenge, in general, requires more work. However, in the case of data mining, the solution is comparatively easy. The pattern recognition engine usually has several hypotheses and possibilities to consider, and it needs to evaluate many options. Many of these tasks are quite independent, and can be processed in parallel without needing too much synchronization and communication, the two difficult problems associated with exploiting parallelism. The performance of search engines can be significantly enhanced by use of such computational techniques. Some of the questions that need to be answered are

- What resources does it require? Are resources available in house? What hardware and software requirements are imposed by the tool?
- What techniques does the tool use for pattern recognition: induction rules, neural networks, memory-based reasoning, data visualization, or traditional statistical analysis?
- What are the training requirements to use the tool effectively ? Does the vendor provide good technical and marketing support to help train the users and provide help if needed? Does the vendor have a good reputation for quality and technology?
- How does the tool deal with variable continuous data, like age and alphabetical data?
- Is the tool very sensitive to data "noise"? How does it deal with it?

However, the emphasis must remain on the business problem and not on tools or the technology, because the benefits that can accrue from discovering the hidden information about customers can be so significant that it may dwarf other considerations.

SUMMARY

Data mining techniques are allowing organizations to uncover significant value in their own data stores. Techniques and tools will become increasingly sophisticated over the next few years, permitting an organization to understand its customers, markets, and business better. However, one must be cautious in applying the newly discovered knowledge. As powerful and sophisticated as the technology is, common business sense must prevail.

Chapter 32

The Information Delivery Facility: Beyond Data Warehousing

Data warehousing has become a key technology in a client/server environment, and it promises to become even more important in the age of netcentric computing. Decision makers, knowledge workers, stakeholders, and customers all derive enormous benefits from a software's capability to locate meaningful knowledge about an organization. The data warehouse is still in its infancy, and early expectations have yet to become reality. The picture today is not quite, as one analyst has it, one of "managers easily gathering up valuable nuggets of business intelligence as they romp through gigabytes of suddenly understandable corporate data." The potential does exist, however, to gain competitive advantage through knowledge that is quickly located and retrievable.

The discussion in this chapter begins with basic definitions, because the term data warehouse has already become overused and misused. A data warehouse is not simply any system that stores data for subsequent retrieval. Data warehouses are defined more specifically as read-only, time-based collections of data that support on-line analysis. The notion of read-only helps to clarify the distinction between data warehouses and transaction processing systems.

The focus on time-based data highlights the fact that data warehouses are particularly valuable when they are used to analyze trends over time. The idea of on-line analysis highlights the fact that data warehouses are not the general solution to the general problem that users need access to data.

Successful data warehouses deliver focused solutions for specific user groups of analysts. In fact, it is probably useful to go beyond the idea of a data warehouse. Warehousing does not alter the nature of the goods being warehoused but raw data from operational systems delivers marginal value to business users. Real value comes only if the data is transformed into content-rich information. This leads to the concept of a "data refinery," in which the product delivered to end-users has been refined from data into information and knowledge that is useful for strategic decision-making and for tactical decision making. Accordingly, from this point forward, this chapter refers to the pool of data as the data refinery, not the data warehouse. This chapter also refers to the process that transforms data into information as the refining process.

FROM DATA REFINERY TO INFORMATION DELIVERY FACILITY

It is not enough simply to build a data refinery. A company might easily believe that, because users need access to data, it can merely build a data refinery that contains all the enterprise's data and then let the users do whatever they want with the data.

This belief is unfounded. Users are rarely knowledgeable enough about the ways of information technology to be able to take even content-rich information and manipulate it to support decision making. Furthermore, it takes too much time and distracts users from their real missions within the ongoing life of the enterprise. The responsibility of IS departments is to deliver a data refinery, not just a data warehouse. Further, the responsibility is to deliver that content-rich information within a meaningful context to the user. The delivery of a meaningful context normally requires the development of an application that places the information within a user-oriented context.

IS departments need to go one step beyond the idea of a data refinery. Users need a complete "Information Delivery Facility" (IDF). An IDF (see Exhibit 1) is an information management architecture comprised of four major components:

- End-user access applications
- A business directory
- A data refinery
- A collection of refining processes

The IDF delivers a complete architecture. The most important component of architecture is the delivery of high-value information to end users. The IDF is supported by specific data designs and robust processes for the extraction and transformation of source data. IDF solutions are custom systems. Vendors offer many products, each of which claims to be the ultimate data refinery solution. No product, however, can deliver more than a piece of the puzzle. The real value comes with the understanding of the specific business benefits to be delivered and the ability to develop unique ways to deliver those benefits. This chapter describes each component, as well as

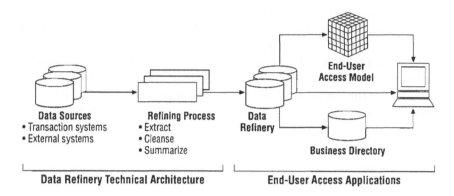

Data Sources	Refining Process	Data Refinery	End-User Access Model		

Data Sources
• Transaction systems
• External systems

Refining Process
• Extract
• Cleanse
• Summarize

Data Refinery

End-User Access Model

Business Directory

Data Refinery Technical Architecture   **End-User Access Applications**

Exhibit 1. The IDF Architecture.

a framework that is useful for planning the development of such an information delivery facility.

WHY BUILD AN INFORMATION DELIVERY FACILITY?

The IDF is most appropriate as support for making major business decisions, which must be supported by bringing together both internal and external data from multiple source systems and then transforming that data into accessible and usable knowledge. IDFs are the way to do this, but they are multimillion-dollar solutions, best applied to multimillion-dollar problems.

The primary industries to benefit from IDFs are products, consumer products (especially such areas as pharmaceuticals), retail, telecommunications, insurance, and health care. Almost every industry, however, appears to be interested in IDFs.

What are the applications that are justifying these investments? Product companies are using the IDF to help monitor expensive manufacturing processes, by monitoring the trends in resource consumption through the process. An IDC study published in 1996 found an average 400% ROI across 59 companies. The stars of the study raising that average, however, were major heavy metal companies. They reported extremely high ROIs, including one that reached 16,000%. These applications can be categorized as asset management processes.

Consumer products provides a powerful example of the convergence of computing, communications, and knowledge on the customer. These opportunities lie more in the category of opportunity discovery than in asset management. Manufacturers have long purchased external data from providers, who survey samples of consumers to estimate buying patterns for types of products. Today, manufacturers would like more detailed information about who their customers are and what they are buying. However, their own sales data do not answer those questions because most manufacturers sell to distributors and wholesalers, not consumers. Manufacturers that can work out partnerships with their distributors to acquire the sales data of the distributors are much closer to understanding consumer buying patterns. Distributor sales to retail outlets can be analyzed for neighborhood demographics, producing a much richer analysis than can be obtained from the manufacturer's sales data.

Alternatively, convergence may lead manufacturers to go beyond the notion of purchasing consumer data from such companies as AC Nielsen and downloading the data to their own IDF. Future providers of consumer information may become the marketing department for manufacturers. Manufacturing personnel may reach through cyberspace to access the IDF of the provider of consumer information; conversely, the provider may reach through cyberspace to access the IDF of the manufacturer, as increasing convergence blurs the lines of corporate entities.

In an entirely different vein, manufacturers and retailers merge warranty or sales data with weather information from cyberspace to analyze the effects of weather on warranty claims or sales results.

Retailers have been the leading lights of the information delivery facility trend. Their direct access to consumer sales data allows them to conduct detailed analyses of buying patterns over time and location. Such analyses allow them to improve discounting approaches during holiday seasons to maximize profits while minimizing leftover inventory at the close of the holiday season. Such analyses also allow them to maintain much smaller in-stock inventory levels and to replenish them in patterns that match consumer demand.

Utilities use IDFs to determine resource consumption patterns, as an input to decisions about future plant construction or retirement. For example, NICOR, a gas utility in northern Illinois, now provides annual consumption trends in its monthly consumer invoices. Might an IDF allow consumers the option to monitor consumption online? Insurance companies use IDFs to identify long-term expense patterns and trends. Credit-card processors use IDFs to search for fraud. Health providers use IDFs to search for both fraud and trends in diagnoses and treatments that may suggest a need for action by health providers or regulatory agencies. Universities use IDFs to detect trends in enrollment to project faculty staffing requirements, construction requirements, and course development requirements. In addition, most enterprises that have IDFs use them to standardize reporting. This addresses the age-old problem of reports from different departments that do not use a common base of information for enterprise reporting.

The most compelling reason to build an IDF harks back to the point made at the beginning of this book: that there is no longer a sustainable competitive advantage available to companies. Astounding solutions require divergent thinking. They require the ability to look at the marketplace and to turn the world upside down. An IDF can deliver a view into an enterprise's marketplace that is not available to any of its competitors. An IDF may result in a new offering in the market that has not even been dreamed of by the competition.

IDFs also support today's demands for analysis and strategic decision making. Strategic decision-making requires information that goes well beyond that typically found in operational systems. These requirements include

- A mix of consistently defined corporate data and external data
- Data that spans more time periods than typical operational systems retain
- Integration of data from many sources, both within the company and without
- Transformation of the data from those various sources to a common semantic understanding, called information

WHO USES AN IDF?

Because everyone within the typical enterprise needs information, one prevalent misconception is that the IDF should be built to be accessible by everyone for any information need. In fact, it is not practical to develop such a resource. As mentioned earlier, IDFs are expensive solutions and need to be solving expensive problems. There is little justification for providing expensive solutions for people who would only use the information occasionally and who would find little measurable benefit from having it available. This is not to say that such user communities should be restricted from accessing an existing IDF, but their need alone is typically not enough to justify the original cost of construction.

The more sensible approach is to identify groups of individuals who would experience great benefit from access to an IDF, then tailor the IDF to their needs and deliver it to them. Such individuals are typically knowledge workers responsible for analyzing information in support of strategic or tactical decision making.

How does the organization begin to determine which groups may or may not need an IDF? Most salespeople, for example, need to be spending their time visiting with prospects, not surfing the data refinery. They may need additional systems support, but those systems are more likely to be customer information systems or automated sales force systems than IDFs. Customer information systems and automated sales force systems are much more like operational transaction processing systems, supporting both data entry and data retrieval. A salesperson is likely to use it briefly for simple queries, such as, "What product has the customer ordered recently?" and "What items in the product line have they never ordered?" An exception to this general rule would be the salespeople who deal in very high-value items and have very long sales cycles. Under such circumstances, extra information about the customer or the competition may provide the added margin of victory in making the sale.

The knowledge workers who benefit from IDFs are people who have a primary responsibility to massage data. Such individuals tend to have little customer contact and little contact with operational systems. Instead, they are individuals who provide the analyses that form the basis for strategic and tactical decisions, such as product design and marketing, buying, fraud or abuse detection, rate making, and usage analysis. They spend too much time gathering data and transforming it into something useful. Access to an IDF that performs those tasks automatically frees these knowledge workers to concentrate on analyzing results instead of preparing for the analysis. This is one of the promises of today's technology: knowledge workers will spend more time analyzing information than they spend gathering information. An IDF supports that kind of work.

With the convergence of computing and communications on customers, organizations can look forward to a day when online access for customers enables similar facilities. Such customers are likely to be corporate customers, such as financial analysts in companies that use service bureaus, health care specialists in customers of group insurance companies, and other linkages between information providers and their customers.

SUCCESS FACTORS FOR THE DEVELOPMENT OF THE IDF

Many approaches exist for building an IDF. One is the "build it and they will come" approach. This approach replicates most of the data in operational systems and stores it on parallel processors for use by anyone who needs it. Some enterprises have used this approach successfully, but it has not worked for most that have tried it.

One might compare this approach to the idea of General Motors opening their parts warehouses to customers, and telling them that they can build any kind of car they want. This raises a number of concerns. First, most people do not know how to build a car and do not want to learn. Second, there is no reason to think that the warehouse is stocked with the parts one particular consumer would want, if none of the company's production car models provide what that person wants. What the customer really wants from General Motors is for the company to accept the responsibility for determining what the customer wants and to provide the facility to tailor the product, not to build the whole product from scratch.

In a similar vein, IDF users want information and knowledge, not data. They want it presented in a format that is easy to acquire, easy to tailor and easy to use, so they can concentrate their energies on their jobs, not on doing IT's job. The data from most operational systems is too fragmented for users to be able to transform it into accurate and meaningful information. The data from operational systems is also incomplete and needs to be supplemented with data from external sources or from nonintegrated sources like manual files or PC systems.

Seven factors are particularly key to a successful IDF:

1. A focused audience of users who have a critical need for personal access to information that describes business trends over time
2. A committed executive sponsor
3. A specific delivery vehicle that provides information needed by those users in a format they need and understand
4. Extraordinary ease of use
5. Transformation of source data to a data structure and level of data quality necessary for users
6. A strong support organization that maintains and extends the refinery and provides direct support to users
7. A business directory that allows business users to identify the contents of the refinery, its sources and transformations, and its currency

A Focused Audience of Users

Early notions of data warehousing assumed that the warehouse should contain all corporate data, which different end users would transform for their own purposes. However, most workers in an enterprise have plenty of work to keep them busy; transforming data into useful information is very time consuming. Learning how to use an IDF, even a well-designed one, takes time that interferes with each worker's primary task. If the old task successfully gets done the old way, then there is little incentive to take the time to learn a new way of working. It is easier and safer to ignore the new system and to keep working the old way. This has been the downfall of many IT projects dealing both with transaction processing and query. Instead, successful IDFs focus on the information needs of specific user communities and provide all the transformations. Furthermore, the user community feels an urgency for the information because the business value is so great; this urgency overcomes the natural impediment of the learning or uptake curve.

Committed Executive Sponsor

A committed executive sponsor can overcome many potential difficulties. For example, the IDF runs the risk of being viewed as just another source for conflicting data. In enterprises that successfully install data refineries, a senior executive declares that the refinery is the official book of record. If other sources generate reports with conflicting results, then those other sources are, by definition, wrong. This clear directive from senior management is a key ingredient in the success of data refineries.

Specific Delivery Vehicles

The delivery vehicle refers to the application that is placed on users' desktops and allows them to view the information in the refinery. Many refineries start with a simple ad hoc query tool on the desktop, which allows users to compose their own queries. Such a solution, however, limits the value of the refinery to the sophistication of the user, because such tools expose the user to the raw data structures. Such tools are necessary but too cumbersome for everyday use. They are analogous to having to use jumper cables to start your car instead of the ignition switch.

Extraordinary Ease of Use

Extraordinary ease of use is absolutely necessary if users are to accept the IDF as a natural part of their work environment. A number of hurdles traditionally stand in the way of ease of use. The structured query language is one example. Clumsy data structures (from the users' viewpoint) and especially normalized data structures are a second. Inconsistent data is a third. As a general rule of thumb, users tolerate two or three such hurdles; by the fourth, however, they quit trying and revert to older, known techniques for getting their work done. Thus, the data structures and the tools that deliver information to the desktop must reflect the users' view of information, not the IS view.

Transformation of Source Data

The transformation of data is a major function within the IDF. Two major classes of transformations are syntactic and semantic. Syntactic transformations include such items as transforming data to conform to IDF encoding standards. Semantic transformations are those that adjust data from different sources that were defined differently in the various source systems to a standard definition in the IDF.

For example, in auto insurance, one source system may define a "claim" as an incident, such as a car accident; another source system may define a claim not as the incident but as the administrative step when someone files an injury claim from the incident. These are quite different views of a claim, and the differences must be reconciled before the data can be stored in the IDF. Without reconciliation of the differences, users will perceive the IDF as containing poor information and will refuse to trust any report based on its contents.

Strong Support Organization

Like most production systems, an IDF requires a support organization. Two key aspects of such an organization are user support and systems support. User support requires personnel who understand the contents of the IDF and also understand the tools available to users. They are the ones who can answer the questions about where information can be found in the refinery, and how to use the tools to get it. Systems support includes all the usual aspects of supporting a production system: DBA support, technical tool support, and production support. Systems support personnel are the ones, for example, who ensure that night-time batch processes to populate the IDF execute to completion and are rerun when needed.

Business Directory

A business directory tells users what information is available, where it came from, and how it was transformed. An active directory may also define the currency of the information, that is, how recently it was updated. However, most effective directories are not active. The publication of paper-based definitions is often the most effective way to get the directory into the hands of any user who wishes to examine its contents and seems to be a popular solution, given the current state of technology and users' comfort with it.

The rest of this chapter discusses in turn each of the four major components of the IDF architecture:

- The data refinery
- The refining process that populates the refinery
- The end-user applications
- A business directory

DATA REFINERY

The data refinery itself is usually a relational database containing information extracted from other systems and transformed under the syntactic and semantic transformations mentioned earlier. A great deal of discussion has taken place in recent years about whether the data refinery needs to be a separate database with extracted data. Why not make it a virtual database, physically supported by pointers back into the source systems, so extraction and duplication is avoided? Practical experience to date has shown that there are two significant problems with the virtual database approach.

First, most operational systems operate under significant load. The additional load imposed by online queries typically cannot be tolerated by the operational system. The prospect of creating additional load, which slows down the machine response to operational processing, is usually unacceptable. It may be, however, that the advent of massively parallel processors (MPP) will allow queries to complete so quickly and to provide so much processing power that concerns about operational systems become obsolete.

However, this leads to a second problem. Operational data is typically highly fragmented under the rules of normalization. Normalization of data allows data to be highly fragmented, which then allows application programs to be modified in significant ways as the business changes, without mandating a corresponding change in the data structures. This works very well for operational programming, which permits multiple levels of testing of the data reconstruction before the program is put back into production. However, for IDF queries, there is limited opportunity for testing. This imposes a requirement that the data structures be much simpler than those used for operational systems. Furthermore, pointers back into the source systems ignore the transformation needs discussed earlier. Thus, effective IDF systems extract data from source systems, transform it to be more usable by business personnel, and store it in a data refinery.

To address the issues of usability, the data in the data refinery is not stored according to the rules of normalization. Instead, it is stored under the rules of dimensional modeling. The dimensional model is often called a star schema. Dimensional modeling is used heavily with multidimensional tools that use their own proprietary data stores. However, it was originally developed for use with relational DBMSs, and it is highly recommended for use with RDBMSs in decision support systems.

Data redundancy is often a concern when data are extracted from operational systems and stored in the data refinery. In fact, there is little data redundancy between the data refinery and operational systems. This is because operational systems and the data refinery have different perspectives on content and time. Operational systems contain two kinds of data: (1) business data and (2) system data, which are necessary for the operational system to operate but have little to do with the business from a tactical or strategic decision-making standpoint. System data are not extracted and copied to the refinery.

Furthermore, most operational systems impose strict limitations on the duration of data held in the operational system, because large data volumes can place a serious drag on the performance of the operational system. Operational systems usually have much higher performance demands than do data refineries. Therefore, data that must be kept for several years are placed in the data refinery, and the refinery becomes the book of record for historical information. Furthermore, the data refinery is often enriched by the inclusion of external data, purchased from external providers or downloaded from cyberspace.

Data refineries are often very large databases. Much of the value of today's IDF was delivered in the last decade through decision support systems built on multidimensional databases. However, today's requirements have exceeded the capacity of those systems. Thus, today it is more common to build the data refinery on a relational database system (RDBMS) on a parallel processor that is capable of supporting very large systems. It is this requirement for very large databases that has driven the IT community to view the data refinery as a separate component from the user tools that deliver value to the business community.

The strategic nature of IDF queries, coupled with the large size of the refinery databases, makes interrelations among information and a historical perspective much more important in the data refinery than in OLTP systems. Multidimensional business views of the data are critical to the effective use of a data refinery. The following two sections highlight two important features of IDF systems: multidimensional analysis and hierarchies.

The Multidimensional Business View

Multidimensional analysis is the backbone of decision support. It is easier for the user to visualize multidimensional data because it more closely resembles how users analyze data than do normalized tables. Users analyze data with the questions Who?, What?, Where?, and When? With multidimensionality, users can answer multiple questions simultaneously. Also, it simplifies the analysis process because users do not have to formulate complex queries to obtain the information they desire.

IDF analysis is multidimensional (i.e., sales by product by location by month in an array). The multidimensional views allow users to view numerical totals at different levels and facets of the organization. The following questions are easily answered by multidimensional business views:

- Which individual products have had poor sales and in which months? (Sales by month and product, ranked by ascending sales)
- Why have sales in Product Group A fallen below target levels? (Actual vs. target sales, by month and subproduct groups)
- Are there specific weeks to which the product's slump in sales can be attributed? (Sales by week and product)

SPECIAL TOPICS

Much has been written in recent years regarding the merits of multidimensional databases (MDBMSs). A multidimensional database, however, is
not required to provide a multidimensional view of the data. Dimensional
data design techniques allow effective use of relational DBMSs.

Hierarchies

Typically considered an integral part of multidimensionality, hierarchies
show the parent–child relationships between elements of the dimension.
Hierarchies are natural structures within organizations, particularly for
how organizations are analyzed and managed (e.g., an organizational hierarchy is Region > District > City; a product hierarchy is Division > Brand >
UPC). Hierarchies are used to logically group and analyze information
within one dimension.

Considering the distinct characteristics of OLTP systems and IDF systems, the requirements for each are different. They have different types of
users. IDF systems are used by knowledge workers and decision makers to
analyze the business activity and determine what future activities should
look like. The success of the project depends on supporting these requirements.

Characteristics of the Data Refinery

Four critical characteristics of a data refinery are performance, flexibility of
analysis, ease of access and confidence in the data integrity.

- *Performance.* IDF systems typically process large data volumes, which
  presents unique performance problems. Although IDF systems do not
  require the sub-second response time of OLTP systems, even moderate performance can be difficult to attain in an IDF system. Acceptable
  performance means allowing users to ask all relevant questions and
  eliminating locked-up keyboards while users wait for an answer.
- *Flexible analysis.* All users must have the ability to analyze the data in
  a manner that enables them to answer pertinent business questions. If
  the information is not available using the IDF system or the analysis
  cannot proceed to the full extent of the user's information needs,
  users become dissatisfied with the system and return to the traditional means of generating reports.
- *Access.* Whereas dedicated users, such as data analysts, would adapt
  to forming complex queries for common business questions, casual
  executive users cannot be expected to perform complex query analysis. Executive jobs need to be focused on analyzing the information
  and decision making, rather than spending their time determining how
  to get the information. Therefore, the value of the IDF system is getting
  users beyond gathering and massaging data by using the IDF system to
  perform the gathering and massaging. Although end-user access tools

can provide the multidimensional view and query writing facilities necessary to provide easy access, proper database design is required to provide acceptable performance under these circumstances.

- *Data integrity.* Because users make tactical and strategic decisions based on the perceived integrity of the information contained in the data refinery, they must have the same confidence in the results obtained through the data refinery as they would from manual analysis. Because the data refinery places an intermediate step between the transaction systems and the end user's analysis tools, the results obtained from the cleansed and organized IDF data may disagree with reports generated before the IDF was implemented. This may cause a confidence crisis for the user. It is important to build the user's confidence in the new system by ensuring there is consensus on the data definitions and data transformations.

If the previous requirements are not addressed to user satisfaction, the IDF will not be used by the knowledge workers. The data refinery should be designed to meet the requirements of the IDF system and enable the use of IDF data analysis. The logical model of the data provides multidimensional data views, including hierarchies. The physical design of the database provides data structures that meet the four requirements for an IDF system: performance, flexibility of analysis, ease of access, and confidence in the data integrity. There are three significant data refinery design issues:

- Architecture of the data refinery
- What data are stored
- How the data are structured

The design of the refinery architecture is completed as part of system analysis and design, but it must fit into the conceptual architecture created during the preceding conceptual design phase. For this reason, architecture decisions for the data refinery will become important early in an IDF project.

The data refinery architect has several options from which to choose. The data refinery architecture is interdependent with the architectures of the refining process and the end-user access applications.

The data refinery architecture is the basic or centralized architecture. The centralized architecture is applicable for most nonenterprise IDFs. However, when the data refinery is used to store corporatewide data, a distributed refinery may be a more appropriate solution.

A fully distributed architecture distributes the data over multiple databases or locations without maintaining a complete copy of corporate data in a central warehouse. This configuration is more than the combination of many departmental IDF's, in which data are not shared across nodes but allows corporatewide access to data regardless of location. The design and management of a fully distributed refinery is too complex for most IDF solutions; however, the information presented in this section applies no matter what the architecture of the data refinery.

Often, a partially distributed refinery is an appropriate solution when a distributed data refinery is being considered. Again, a partially distributed refinery only applies when enterprise data are to be supported in the refinery. A partially distributed refinery consists of a central repository of corporatewide data and several departmental data refineries (often called data marts). This architecture is generally implemented for performance reasons.

Finally, some projects may decide to implement an architecture construct separate from the data refinery for operational reporting. Whereas the data refinery is intended for strategic analysis of information, the operational data store (ODS) satisfies operational information needs. The ODS derives primarily from the need to further reduce the workload on legacy systems and to make use of the extract files that were being produced for the data warehouse. The text *Building the Operational Data Store* by Inmon, Imhoff and Battas (John Wiley & Sons, 1996) contains more information on the techniques for building an ODS.

A centralized architecture is the most straightforward to implement, because there is one source of data for all applications. A centralized refinery is appropriate when the volume of data and number of users does not degrade the performance on one system. Generally, as the refinery or information requirements grow, either a distributed architecture will be adopted, or multiple IDFs will be established.

Advantages of distributing the data refinery are

- It better reflects the structure of the organization. Only the data relevant to each department or region is on its server's data mart.
- It provides improved performance because the data mart is smaller and can be queried more rapidly and is closer to the end users and typically accessed over higher speed networks.
- The availability of the data is improved, because if the server fails at one site the other sites are unaffected.
- It allows for easier growth towards an enterprisewide IDF. The organization can start with one department, then add others as the process is perfected.
- There is a reduced communication cost, because there is no need to maintain a constant link between every end user of every department and a central server.

Disadvantages of distributing the data refinery are

- Data integrity is more difficult to maintain, as some of the same data is in multiple sites.
- There is a more complex update process, because the data need to be divided and distributed to the appropriate data marts. The process must be coordinated so there is no possibility of receiving two different answers from different servers (e.g., a central summary server provides an answer that is inconsistent with the distributed detail server).

IDF developers often ask whether they should use a relational DBMS or a multidimensional DBMS for the data refinery. As a broad guideline, it is preferable to think of the data refinery as an RDBMS and the data mart as an MDBMS. The major RDMSs offer the advantage of scalability into the hundreds of gigabytes. The MDBMSs offer the advantage of performance for rapid drill-down, surfing, and statistical analysis. Not all data marts need the OLAP capabilities of an MDBMS. Conversely, only very small data refineries are able to use an MDBMS.

REFINING PROCESS

The refining process populates the data refinery. This is the component that requires the most effort from those who build an IDF. If this component is not well done, the IDF will fail to deliver the value it promises. The combined refining process is a major contributor to the ability of the IDF to support decision-making in ways that have not been possible under the techniques used in the past. This process is extremely challenging and often is not given as much weight as it should be when organizations are planning their IDF. The data often undergo a major transformation in form and size on its journey through the data refinery. One medical diagnostics equipment company had an estimated 70 gigabytes of production data on its operational systems. After refining, the amount of data finally loaded into the refinery was 20 gigabytes. This is not to imply that the size cannot increase; if the database has many aggregations, the data refinery process can actually expand the amount of data.

The refining process contains several major functions:

- Extraction
- Cleansing/transformation
- Summarization
- Load

Each of these functions offers significant challenges which, combined, makes the refining process the most difficult component of the IDF architecture.

Extraction addresses the question of how to source the data. Mapping data requirements against existing systems is a major challenge with most systems in business. Few systems are well documented. Original naming standards may have changed over time to ad hoc definitions that are poorly understood. Data fields will have different usage over time — all undocumented. Multiple source systems offer multiple opportunities to source data, and deciding between different options may prove difficult. Trying to bring data together from multiple sources may encounter incompatible cutoff dates, which means that the data from one system does not integrate with data from another over time. The data refinery may need transaction data that passes through operational systems but is not explicitly saved as a transaction. System loads on operational systems may mean that there is no spare capacity for running extract programs. The difficulties and resultant opportunities are numerous.

Key principles for successful extraction include

- *The data should be accurate.* The budget department may keep slightly different versions of the same period's data. The architects should be sure to extract the appropriate version.
- *The data should be the most recent.* For example if extracting marketing statistics, the architects should get the most current data.
- *The data should be finished.* It is advisable to wait until all the day's sales have been logged in the operational system before starting the day's extraction. With monthly updates, the month should have been closed before the data is extracted.
- *The data should be the most complete.* For example, one department may have been analyzing data from all accounts; another may have been analyzing data from all major accounts. The unabridged data should be extracted.
- *The data should be nearest to the originating source.* As data spreads throughout an organization, it goes through a limited extraction process each time it passes from one department to another. Each time this happens, the likelihood of discrepancies in the data increases.

Cleansing and transformation are also significant challenges. The data refinery often requires data that is captured in operational systems but is considered anecdotal only. As anecdotal data, it often is not structured or validated. Data that were not validated are almost guaranteed to have data quality problems: data values will have an extraordinarily high error rate, and data items will have inconsistent structures. What should be done? If the data refinery is to have integrity, the data need to be cleaned up before it goes into the data refinery, and the source system itself should do the cleaning. The refining process needs to perform well-documented transformations but should not be otherwise altering data passed to it from source systems. It becomes too difficult to trace information back to its source.

Cleansing data in source systems that do not presently validate it, however, requires programming changes to those systems. Because the source system has never found it necessary to validate the data before, support personnel are unlikely to give such changes much priority. This issue restates the importance of an executive sponsor who has the authority to prioritize such system enhancements. The difficulties of achieving consensus in this area makes it one of the major challenges of building a data refinery. Difficulties aside, there is a right answer for the majority of data refineries, and that right answer is that the source systems need to validate any data which is needed in the data refinery.

Transformations need to be performed in the data refinery. Transformations differ from data cleansing because transformations deal with converting valid data to standard enterprise definitions of the data. In general, there are two types of transformations: syntactic and semantic. Syntactic transformations deal with changing the encoding of the data or the structure of the data. Examples of syntactic transformations include converting dates from MMDDYYYY format to YYYYMMDD format, or converting 0/1 indicators to Y/N indicators. Some authors further subdivide this category between syntactic and structural, but I find the further subdivision to be unhelpful.

The second type of transformations are semantic. Semantic problems occur when the user's interpretation of the data may differ or when the disagreement among source records requires a human to resolve. These are much more difficult problems than the syntactic problems. Examples of this type of problem include

- *Inconsistent definitions.* Sales figures from one system include returns, whereas sales figures from another system exclude returns.
- *Old information.* Two sources may have records with the same customer ID but different addresses and phone numbers. Which record is current?
- *Optional fields.* Optional fields extracted from operational databases are often difficult to cleanse. There is no way to constrain these fields to apply rules for cleansing because there is no guarantee that the fields will contain data.
- *Free-form text fields.* A source field contains the customer's full name, but the target field accepts only the customer's last name. For example, an insurance company used the term *claim* to communicate different meanings, resulting in confusion across the divisions. To rectify this, new terms were created to uniquely identify the uses of this multipurpose term. These consistent definitions benefit internal communications across divisions.

In the corporate data model, three levels of claims were defined: policy, coverage, and claimant.

A policy claim is the demand against a policy for a single loss event, which may result in multiple coverage claims and claimant claims. At the policy claim level, underwriters evaluate their underwriting performance.

A coverage claim refers to the demand against the policy coverage's affected by a policy claim. For example, if an insured's car collides with another car, both cars are damaged, and the other driver and a passenger are hurt, there would be one policy claim (a single event) but three coverage claims: property damage for the other car, bodily injury for the other driver and passenger, and collision for the insured's car.

A claimant claim is the demand by a claimant against a policy coverage. In the example above, there would be four claimant claims: property damage for the other driver's car, bodily injury for the other driver, bodily injury for the passenger, and collision for the insured's car. The bodily injury coverage claim was expanded to two claimant claims.

The divisions had stressed the need for viewing and counting claims at all three of these levels. In some cases, by seeing the different levels of claims, the divisions identified new, more useful ways to look at the information.

To realize this, the following business rule was applied to the data as it was being cleansed. If different claims were made against the same policy on the same day, they were for the same loss event (i.e., there was one policy claim). Although this is not true in all cases, it was believed to be correct more than 99% of the time. The few exceptions to this rule were deemed insignificant. This is often the case when applying such business rules; there is a trade-off between absolute accuracy and efficiency.

As the example illustrates, the cleanse phase can also be used for applying business rules to the data. The application of business rules is one means of resolving several of the issues of the cleanse phase.

There are knowledge-based reasoning tools that construct logic-intensive applications. They can be used to apply business rules to the data to help transform it into the desired model.

The cleansing and transformation portion of the refining process consumes the bulk of the implementation effort. Insuring the integrity of the data is vital. Major decisions may be made based on the information in the data refinery; it should be irrefutable.

The extract process is an interface process. As such, it faces that unique interface problem that it may be unaware of changes to the source systems. Such changes can cause the extract process to fail or, worse yet, to unknowingly deliver bad data to the warehouse. Therefore, it is extremely important that the extract process be supported by controls to catch such errors. Oftentimes, simple trending of record counts is sufficient.

Procedural controls should be the IDF's first line of defense. Procedural controls should ensure that the IDF personnel are notified during the design of such changes to source systems. However, because such controls are usually only about 80% effective, automated controls are needed, even when effective procedural controls are in place.

The third function is summarization, the creation of summary data. Most refineries do not store base transactions. Instead, they store lightly summarized transaction data. For example, a retailer may store the summarized transaction by hour by SKU by store. This lightly summarized data is likely to create very large volumes by itself. The large volume is the reason that most refineries do not store actual transactions. If higher summaries can be avoided, there are substantial benefits to be derived. Higher summaries make assumptions about the product hierarchy or store hierarchy, which are highly subject to change. Change in the hierarchies mean that the summaries have to be recalculated. The flip side of the problem is that summaries may be required to allow queries to complete in reasonable amounts of time. This is the area in which MPP can provide enormous benefit. If MPP can place enough processing power at the disposal of the queries, higher summaries may be avoidable. As yet, however, MPP is considered too expensive and risky by most companies. Therefore, higher-level summaries are the reality today.

Computing sums among records based on a hierarchy of attributes the data have in common is called aggregating. Aggregating records produces roll-ups or summary data, which can be stored in separate tables in the refinery, or in the same table.

The issue of storing aggregation records in the refinery is not the same as the granularity of the data discussed earlier. The sales data is still stored at the daily level in the refinery, but there are also separate records for monthly, quarterly, and yearly sales figures.

Beyond simple sums, the summarize phase can be used to compute derived data by applying mathematical formulae to fields to create completely new fields (e.g., computing margin from net sales, returns, and cost of goods sold).

By performing the calculations shown earlier (where all the data are together), everyone will be using data resulting from the same calculations. Departments can avoid using different methods for calculating values, thereby avoiding contradictory results.

Balancing is important when performing summaries, roll-ups, and other calculations. Be certain that the information is not changed or lost during the summarize phase. Whenever possible, the data computed during the summarize phase should be compared and aligned with existing reports.

Another issue that may arise is how changes in history affect previously loaded summarizations. There are two methods one can use to accomplish these adjustments. If the changes in history are rare, they can be completed from within the data refinery. The lowest level of data is manually updated, then select and insert statements are used to update the roll-ups. This would likely be faster, but the user must remember to perform the update. The most efficient method is to use a mechanism which notes changes in the operational data, either by monitoring the data or by reading a log file, and automatically determines what updates need to be applied to the lowest level data. The changes are extracted, cleansed, and summarized with the new data during the refining process. Thus, the aggregations and other computations are automatically amended. This is a more complicated process, but it will work much better if changes in historical data are common.

Major changes in the data model and its hierarchy can result from an adjustment to the basic structures of the organization. Businesses change over time, and these reorganizations need to be reflected in the data refinery and refining process. Because decision-support systems rely heavily on hierarchies to provide drill-down and other analyses, these reorganizations create special problems.

Note that realignments need to be addressed during the refining process only if summaries are stored in the data refinery. If summaries are only applied by a multidimensional end user application, then the data in the refinery is unaffected. In such cases, the data in the refinery are stored only at the lowest level, and reorganizations do not affect it. Because the end user application calculated the aggregations, it must be changed to reflect these changes.

There are three main methods for resolving realignments. The historical data should not be changed. The historical data should be modified to conform to the current organizational structure. Finally, these two approaches can be combined. When an organization changes, the historical data is realigned to reflect the changes, as in the second approach. In addition, historical metadata tables are created and maintained with effective dating of the dimensional structure. This allows the historical data to be retrieved as a snapshot of the past data (e.g., "What were sales by product based on the product hierarchy of 31 December 1994?").

Usually, the records extracted from the source are sorted early in the refining process, as this facilitates the cleanse and summarize phases.

However, if this is not the case, a final step before loading the data into the refinery should be to sort the rows of the file to be loaded. If sorted in the way the RDBMS expects (e.g., by date first, then product, then market), the load will go faster. Sorting may be done by the data refinery management software, or using high-performance sorting tools.

The fourth and last function of the refining process is the load process. Load is the process of getting data into the data refinery after the refinery has completed transformation and summarization.

There are three options for loading the finished data into the data refinery:

- Load by the data refinery management applications
- Load by the RDBMS
- Load by a third-party utility

Most enrichment tools provide the option of loading the data directly into the refinery. The specifics of the refining tool will describe if it supports the target RDBMS. If an enrichment tool is not used, the customized applications can be designed to perform the load.

There are two advantages to this approach. The first is that it saves the time that would otherwise have been spent writing and reading the data on an intermediary store, such as an ASCII file). Second, it requires less human interaction, and one less tool.

A second method is to have the data refinery management software or the enrichment tool, if one is used, create a flat file with the finished data and then use the RDBMS's own load utility. The advantage of this approach is that many RDBMS vendors provide enhanced load utilities which employ fast loading or specialized loading techniques.

As an alternative to having the load performed by the data refinery management software or the data refinery, there are third-party loaders that can be even faster on certain platforms.

When data are first loaded into the refinery, the database will be empty. When the source data is changed or has new data, there will be periodic updates to the refinery (e.g., daily or weekly). There are two options for performing these updates:

- Total load: reloading the entire set of data into the refinery
- Incremental load: inserting only the changed or new data to the refinery

If much of the information has changed, or the information currently in the data refinery is outdated and needs to be disposed of or archived (perhaps for storage space reasons), it may be beneficial to perform a total load into the refinery (completely replacing the previous information). However, a disadvantage is most refineries exist for the purpose of storing historical data, and regular updates are used to add recent information to them. Also, even total loads into modest-sized refineries (50 to 100 GB) can take a long time.

On the other hand, if the size of the data refinery is in the range of 2 to 5 GB or smaller, a total load could take an hour or two. Nevertheless, it is more desirable to perform incremental loads. An incremental load inserts new data into the refinery without replacing the old (e.g., adding the newest week's sales figures). Also, it can be used to update the old data as well, when changes in the source data impact existing records in the refinery.

In an incremental load, the task is to keep track of what information has been changed in or added to the source data applications. Enrichment tools can offer limited assistance in this area. However, there are performance and integrity issues involved with incremental loads.

While straight inserts (of new data) are fast, updates that require extra processing (changing existing data) can be extremely slow. Most RDBMS load utilities cannot do incremental loads. Most bulk load utilities do not support restart and recovery. If this is a necessary feature, bulk load utilities cannot be used.

There are three ways to add to existing data refineries. Some tables in the refinery are reloaded completely every time an update is required. Others use a load-append approach, which just adds more data to the end of the data that already exists. Yet a third set of tables are updated by inserting new rows. Most organizations find that they need to use all three techniques, depending on the volumes and volatility of the data being added to the refinery.

END-USER APPLICATIONS

End-user applications provide the delivery vehicles to astound the business community with the effectiveness of an IDF. The application that sits between the user and the data refinery is what delivers value. Successful IDFs have demonstrated the importance of knowing what analyses need to be performed, and then delivering applications that provide those analyses. General-purpose solutions that allow business personnel to compose their own queries offer only marginal value compared to the value derived from sophisticated applications supporting known analysis needs. Such applications can be built rather easily by IT professionals using advanced multidimensional tools.

Multidimensional tools are pricey, however. There is a common notion that a safer approach is to build the data refinery, give end users ad hoc query tools that generate SQL, and then wait for a period of time to see if the data refinery is useful for ad hoc query before investing in expensive tools. Such an approach is a self-defeating strategy, however, because it does not deliver enough value for the data refinery to be viewed as a success.

End-user access applications provide windows into the data refinery with intuitive graphical user interfaces (GUIs) and access to enterprise-wide data for analyses, report generation, and decision making. There are many different types of end user access, distinguished by their various capabilities. The specific type used depends on the various requirements and knowledge levels of each end user. Because user requirements vary greatly, it is uncommon for one end user application to satisfy all the user and business requirements. Therefore, an organization commonly uses more than one application to meet these requirements.

In the world of convergence, many users are remote users of the information delivery facility. As remote users, they face many unique problems not shared by local IDF users, such as security, data structuring, homogeneity of equipment, and system performance. The true value of the IDF, however, is evolving to be the ubiquitous access to critical business information for remote users, whether it's the store manager in Wal-Mart, helping a customer determine what other stores have that special Christmas gift item, or a salesperson on the road getting a flash report on the most recent activity against a customer's account, or dealers examining what other successful dealers are doing and improving their own performance through emulation.

There are several categories of tools designed to access and analyze data. They offer different advantages and disadvantages, depending on the needs of the user. These categories are ad hoc querying, ad hoc aliasing and reporting, decision support systems (DSS), executive information systems (EIS), enterprise intelligence systems, data mining, and data visualization. However, as vendors try to provide tools that serve multiple types of customers, many tools are adding capabilities that place them in more than one of these categories. Identifying a tool as a single type is usually not possible. Exhibit 2 summarizes how each end-user access category uses information and the typical users for each access category.

Each category of end-user access is designed for different functional capabilities and user levels. A large organization might have many users with various requirements and abilities. In this situation, it is possible to have several tools accessing the same data but performing different functions. It is important to select an end-user access application that closely matches the user's functional requirements and abilities. However, the focus in today's IDF solutions tends to be oriented to one of two solutions:

- The use of "fat client" products that support multidimensional analysis
- The use of browsers to support multidimensional analysis

Exhibit 2. End-User Access

Access category	Information usage	Users
Ad hoc query	Fact finding	Power analysts
	Querying	Specialists
Ad hoc aliasing and reporting	Fact finding	Analysts
	Reporting	
Decision support systems	Issue resolution	Analysts
	What-if analysis	Planners
	Multidimensional analysis	Specialists
	Exception management	
Executive information systems	Status reporting	Executive
	Summarizing data	High-level
	Drilling capabilities	Management
	Projection	Executive
	Planning	High-level
	Proactive	Management
		Planners and analysts
Data mining	Rule discovery	Specialists
	Pattern identification	Analysts
Data visualization	Interactive graphics	Executives
	Pattern recognition	Managers

Therefore, the bulk of the discussion of end-user access issues focuses on these two areas.

The following paragraphs briefly introduce the different categories of end user access listed.

Ad Hoc Query. Ad hoc query capabilities are used to support the retrieval of basic information through Structured Query Language (SQL). The ad hoc query returns a basic list of the requested information to the user. This capability requires users who are knowledgeable in SQL and database structures. As a general rule, users find SQL difficult and tedious and experience a high frequency of bad data generated by incorrect SQL.

Ad Hoc Aliasing. Ad hoc aliasing capabilities are used to support the retrieval of basic information when the SQL is transparent to the users. Ad hoc aliasing techniques are accomplished by using common business terms in menus or objects that can easily by selected by the user. This capability requires not only users who have some knowledge of query languages and database structures but also users who are familiar with the business functions. The advantage of this class of tools when compared to the ad hoc tools described above is that the level of required SQL knowledge is diminished.

Decision Support Systems. DSSs are used to support multidimensional analysis of data and in many cases provide advanced capabilities such as statistical and financial modeling. DSSs are typically used by analysts, planners, midlevel managers, and other knowledge workers to carry out day-to-day operations and decisions. The modeling and manipulation capabilities enable users to create and maintain specific data sets of information from the result set generated by a query accessing the data refinery database. The analysis and presentation capabilities enable users to view data from different levels and viewpoints and the flexibility to display data through vehicles such as graphs, reports, and charts, among others.

Executive Information Systems. EISs provide graphical user interfaces for more intuitive access to data. Many EISs also provide capabilities to summarize data and generate a variety of text, graphical, and/or tabular information for the user. EISs are typically used by high-level executives, such as CEOs, VPs, managers, and directors to do strategic planning and view enterprisewide data. There tends to be minimal functionality for drill-down, under the assumption that the executives who use such systems delegate investigative work to others, who have access to the greater functionality of DSS.

Enterprise intelligence systems is a term that encompasses features included in both DSS and EIS such as data modeling, manipulation, analysis, and presentation capabilities and includes additional features, such as intelligent agents, proactive alerting, and exception monitoring. These systems provide specific focus on detection of abnormal conditions.

Data Mining. Data mining differs from traditional decision support systems in that these tools attempt to interpret the data by using pattern recognition technology. Discovering relevant patterns in large data stores at atomic levels can be important for more effective decision making. Primitive data mining searches for patterns requested by the end user. More advanced data mining detects patterns in the data that are unknown to the end user. Primitive data mining can be conducted using the ad hoc tools described previously. Advanced data mining requires special artificial intelligence products.

Data Visualization. Data visualization enables users to view and understand complex information and gain insight into data patterns by using interactive graphics and imaging to represent and manipulate volume data. Presently, most applications have been scientific in nature. The benefits of data visualization to the business environment are being researched with increasing interest. Data mining vendors have made significant strides in using data visualization techniques to present data mining results.

Multidimensional Data Structures

Presently, the trend for end user access is toward on-line analytical processing (OLAP), the term used to indicate that a system's primary focus is on interactive data access rather than batch reporting or transaction processing. OLAP indicates a type of design or architecture that optimizes the ability to query the data. Many vendors have added OLAP functionality to their products as an OLAP extension or an OLAP engine, which can be purchased separately or as an add-on.

Multidimensional Tools

In today's world of end user access applications, there is a plethora of options to choose from when developing an application to solve business problems. To this point, only packaged tools with ad-hoc querying and DSS/EIS capabilities have been described. General purpose developmental tools such as Sybase's PowerBuilder, Microsoft's Visual Basic, and SQLWindows from Centura Software Corp. must also be considered when selecting an end-user access application. These developmental tools have also been used successfully for developing customized end user access applications.

Advantages of Development Tools. Advantages to choosing a general purpose developmental tool include the following:

- Leveraging existing skills
- Flexibility in design
- Less expense than packaged tools

Disadvantages of Development Tools. Reasons not to use development tools to create an end-user application include the following:

- Development time
- Consistency of user interface
- A lack of multidimensional analysis capabilities and therefore less analytical functionality
- Built-in functions must be created
- Limitations in reporting capabilities because data is accessed through SQL

Development tools are very powerful depending on the circumstances in which they are used. They tend to be most effective when an organization is developing a simple data access system, and has significant expertise in using the chosen tool. If an organization requires a more complex system (requiring multidimensional analysis, statistical functions, extensive reporting capabilities, etc.), using a development tool as a complement to a DSS/EIS tool can add flexibility for both developers and users.

Other Architecture Issues

Throughout this chapter, a basic architecture has been assumed. However, it is common for several architecture issues to arise. These issues arise for several reasons, including performance and stability claims of tool vendors and the needs of remote users. There are two key issues:

- Two- vs. three-tier application architectures
- Remote access and take-away use

Two-Tier vs. Three-Tier Architectures. Many of the DSS/EIS products allow two different configurations:

- *Two-tier configuration.* The data refinery (RDBMS) is on one machine, and the end user access application runs on the PCs. Almost all ad hoc query tools use this architecture.
- *Three-tier configuration.* The data refinery is on one machine, and the end-user access application has both a client and a server piece. Most browser-based products use this architecture.

With the three-tier configuration, the analytical engine can be on a separate platform or the analytical engine can be on the same platform as the RDBMS. This is an important issue, as both the analytical engine and the RDBMS tend to be resource gluttons. The response times of the IDF in the two configurations should be benchmarked to see if the increase in performance of using separate platforms is worth the cost of purchasing and maintaining the extra machine.

In the two-tier approach, the DSS/EIS client application can access either the RDBMS or a multidimensional store directly. In the three-tier approach the DSS/EIS client must go through the multidimensional engine to access the RDBMS or a multidimensional store. The following lists highlight some of the advantages and disadvantages of each configuration.

Two-Tier Configuration

- Heavy client processing. All application logic is on the client.
- More powerful (more costly) client PCs.
- More suitable for takeaway use.
- Heavier network traffic. All the data are brought to the client for processing.
- Could be slower if the less powerful client is required to do a large amount of processing, such as heavy multidimensional analysis.
- Application distribution problems. Modifications in the end-user applications must be updated on every client.

Three-Tier Configuration

- Light client processing. The application is split, with the client only doing presentation plus perhaps limited processing.

- Background processing. Reports and functions such as agents and alerts can run in the background on the server. In some applications, these can be set to run at certain times (e.g., every Sunday).
- Remote use requires a connection to the server. If the laptop cannot communicate with the server, the end-user application is unusable.
- Lighter network traffic (between the server and the clients) — the more powerful server does most or all the processing and only sends back the results.
- Could be slower if many clients are competing for the server's resources or if the server and RDBMS are on the same platform and competing for processing time.
- Updates to the application can usually just be made to the server piece.

Remote Access and Takeaway Use

Remote availability of the end-user application is often important in designing an IDF. In such cases this issue is a major factor in the choice of an end-user application. Two techniques make the data available to remote users:

- *Remote access.* The users dial in to the server for live access (probably browser based).
- *Takeaway use.* The users take the application and part of the data with them.

A three-tier architecture is better suited for remote access. In this setup, a remote user with a laptop dials in to the end user access application server. The server does most or all the data retrieval and number crunching and just sends the results to the laptop. The client piece of the end-user application is primarily concerned with the presentation of these results.

Because only the results are sent back to the client, the network traffic (a major bottleneck) is lower and the remote laptop does not need to do much (if any) application processing and can therefore be a less powerful machine. The main disadvantage of this is availability. The remote user (e.g., a traveling salesperson) will be required to dial in to the server and remain connected for as long as the data are used. If the remote user does not have a connection to the server, the end-user application is unusable.

Remote access is important when an organization's remote users need frequent access to a large portion of the data, the updates to the data refinery are frequent (e.g., daily), and the remote users need the most recent data. As an alternative to live remote access, takeaway use is handled by replicating part of the data refinery to the laptop. The end-user application then runs entirely on the laptop, requesting data from its local store.

There are a few ways this can be done:

- Using a powerful DSS/EIS application with multidimensional data stores. An organization with a large traveling sales staff may want its salespeople to be able to take a small multidimensional data store with them on their laptops. They could occasionally dial in for updates. The two-tier approach is necessary for this because all the application logic is on the client.
- Using a smaller database on the client. For applications that must go directly against a database, the laptops can contain a portion of the data in their own RDBMS. For example, some vendors will run against Microsoft Access on a laptop.
- Using flat files. Some ad hoc query applications also allow remote users to take part of the data away. Two-tier products bring the data down to the client for manipulation. The remote user can just take these files away on the laptop.

BUSINESS DIRECTORY

The business directory is the medium for apprising end users of the contents of the IDF. At a minimum, it describes the data contents in business terms, and the transformations that have changed that data from the way the end users may be used to seeing it in the operational systems.

If the business directory can serve more than the minimum requirements, it also provides information on the currency of the data presently in the IDF (i.e., when the last update was run). For example, knowing that the data are supposed to be updated every weekend is not the same as being able to confirm on Monday morning that the update actually ran successfully.

Ideally, the business directory will be electronic. In fact, the theoretically best technique is to use the enterprise data dictionary for this function. This strategy is not generally possible. Data dictionary products are not designed for use by end users and lack the usability characteristics needed. Furthermore, the licensing of the number of copies needed for all end users to have access is often prohibitive.

A more common solution is to build a simple, minimalist business directory. Occasional success stories are found from users of such products as Information Builders Focus, or Lotus Notes. The most common success stories describe paper directories, published as pocket guides to the IDF. Despite its inherent update problems, paper continues to be ubiquitous and readily duplicable for new users, who need it the most. Furthermore, for most companies, the business directory is a reference that supports their use of the IDF, but is not used continuously. Therefore, many users find it more convenient to use the real estate of the PC screen for doing the main work of data slicing and analysis and keep the directory off to the side of their work space.

The primary success factor for the business directory is the quality of the business definitions of the data. A major contributor to the success of these business directories is the effort put into the development of the definitions themselves. Focus groups of users from different organizations who need to share the data serve to elevate the differences in data definitions that exist across every organization and to educate the participants. These efforts sometimes grind to a halt when it becomes clear that there are different definitions, and consensus cannot be achieved on single definitions. These efforts achieve success when the participants recognize the validity of different business definitions and find ways to incorporate multiple definitions into the IDF. Clearly, the definitions of similar but different data items must highlight both the similarities and the differences, to clear away the natural confusion. Oftentimes, companies discover that the IDF delivers, for the first time, a clear analysis of important business data and the subtle variations required to support the business properly.

The natural desire for consensus on single definitions is not the only impediment to success. A second impediment is the MIS desire to standardize terminology and to homogenize the granularity of the data, but the definition must be meaningful to the end user. The definitions must continue to relate to the information that users know about in the source systems, which are not standardized or homogenous. Thus, user participation in the development of definitions is absolutely critical. It is often necessary to use aliases extensively, to ensure that communication about the IDF data is clear and understandable to all users.

Rather than paper-based pocket guides, most companies prefer an electronic solution because maintenance of definitions is so much easier electronically. Whereas electronic business directories certainly make maintenance easier, it is vitally important that the delivery of an electronic solution does not dilute the effort required to develop good business definitions. An exotic electronic delivery vehicle with casual, incomplete definitions of the business data is likely to fail.

Many end-user tools require metadata to function. This metadata is more closely linked by its nature to the MIS data repository than the true business directory we have been describing. Multiple tools are likely to require multiple metadata stores. Because of the redundant nature of this metadata, it is best to think of this as ancillary to the real business directory. It should be considered to be MIS technical data that supports the tool rather than business data that supports the user. The challenge is to ensure that there are enough linkages between the technical definitions which the users will see and the business definitions in the business directory to allow users to move easily between them.

The MIS data repository is a key resource to help the IDF support organization maintain the IDF. They need the technical definitions of the IDF data, the sources of the data, the transformation rules, the interrelationships between data items, the relationships between tables and columns and between applications and the data the application presents, and the timing of data refreshes.

The MIS data repository is normally electronic. It may consist of a custom solution, using the native capabilities of relational DBMSs to craft a custom solution, or it may use one of the commercially available data repository products. Typically, it is not centered on a commercial product that provides extract-and-transform capabilities for extracting data from the source systems. Such products need metadata to perform those extractions and transformations. However, the metadata are often highly proprietary and not extensible.

One of the pleasant trends emerging from the extract tool vendors is the ability to export the metadata from those tools to populate the end-user tools and to populate stand-alone corporate data repositories. This is a significant development that should be enthusiastically explored.

SUMMARY

Successful IDFs focus on specific business problems that require analysis, and then deliver a high-value application to a focused group of users to help them solve that problem. Additional applications can then be added to support other user groups based on the value received by the first group.

An IDF is most useful when it is used by personnel whose job descriptions require that they spend much of their time analyzing information as a basis for tactical or strategic decision making. Retail buyers use the information for determining what and how much to buy; insurance underwriters develop risk management strategies; utilities study repair trends to determine capital investments. If the purpose of the IDF is to allow users access to data, but there is no understanding of the kinds of access needed or the use that will be made of the data retrieved, then it is unlikely that the IDF will be successful.

Chapter 33
Componentware

The complexity of netcentric technology means that today's information systems have become more difficult and time consuming to build and maintain. Long custom development cycles imply that a system designed in one business climate may be deployed in a radically changed climate, losing the window of opportunity to take advantage of the competitive benefits embedded in the system. The goal of designers today is to design systems that are quickly built, robustly tested, and easily maintained as market conditions shift.

Componentware promises to enhance an organization's ability to build robust systems quickly through the use of reusable prebuilt software components. Componentware is an approach to software development in which expert software engineers encapsulate core business and technical processes and knowledge into black-box segments of code. These prebuilt pieces of code are then assembled together by less experienced developers to rapidly build robust and flexible systems.

Properly leveraged, components can provide the foundation upon which organizations meet and exceed the demands of a global marketplace that increasingly uses technology as a primary competitive advantage.

COMPONENTWARE DRIVERS

Four major drivers are contributing to the trend toward component-based systems development: a crisis in software engineering, the continued evolution of object-oriented (OO) technology, entry into the market by major industry players, and a burgeoning marketplace for components (Exhibit 1).

Software Engineering Crisis

Over the years, technological advances in computing equipment have outpaced the science of software engineering. Whereas computers have gone from giant room-sized boxes to lightweight laptops and modems have advanced from 300 bps to 56Kbps and beyond, systems development has remained largely unchanged. Granted, several systems development approaches (including CASE and Information Engineering) have been proposed as solutions for quick and robust systems building. Although these

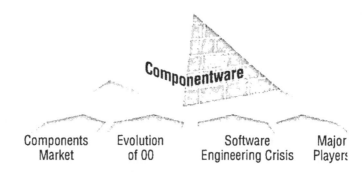

Components   Evolution   Software   Major
Market   of OO   Engineering Crisis   Players

Exhibit 1. Major Drivers Behind Component-Based Systems Development.

have had success in specific areas, they typically require significant up-front investment and have not seen widespread acceptance.

In the 1970s and 1980s, business systems supported the back office by processing accounting data and periodically sharing data with other internal systems. Although necessary for the business, these systems did not provide any significant competitive advantage. It was acceptable to take three years to build a system, and reasonable life spans for software reached to 10 or 15 years. Today, business systems can be a significant factor in a company's competitive advantage. Having the right software at the right time can allow a company to leap past its competitors and gain market share. Early on-line banks are one example. As a result, organizations are beginning to look for systems that can be built very rapidly and that can evolve quickly to meet the changing conditions of the marketplace.

To resolve the software engineering crisis, a development technique is needed that greatly reduces the time required to build a system and increases system quality. Several complementary approaches have been developed to address these needs, as shown in Exhibit 2.

For a development technique to gain widespread acceptance in the marketplace, it must include the following characteristics:

- *Provide for reuse.* Provide the capability to use a toolbox of pre-built code segments across projects, business units, and corporations.
- *Minimize complexity.* Break code into smaller pieces and reduce the number of interfaces between units, using encapsulation to hide internals.
- *Provide for solutions that can be tailored.* Allow the use of off-the-shelf code that can be "glued" together to build a variety of products.

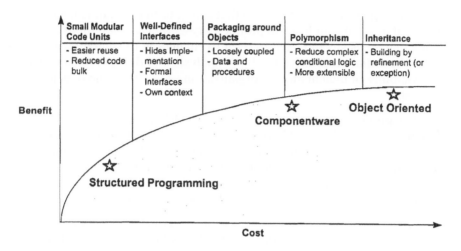

Small Modular Code Units	Well-Defined Interfaces	Packaging around Objects	Polymorphism	Inheritance
- Easier reuse - Reduced code bulk	- Hides Implementation - Formal Interfaces - Own context	- Loosely coupled - Data and procedures	- Reduce complex conditional logic - More extensible	- Building by refinement (or exception)

Exhibit 2. Development Techniques.

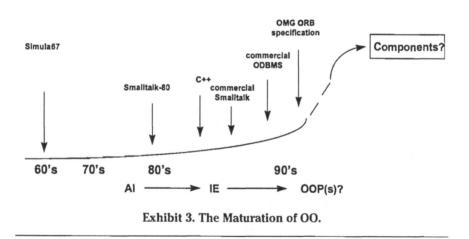

Exhibit 3. The Maturation of OO.

- *Lower learning curves.* Minimize the number and types of specialized skills required from the development team.
- *Increase productivity.* Allow quicker construction of applications than with other development techniques

The Evolution of OO

Over the past several years, OO methodologies and technologies have matured sufficiently to provide the foundation for complex, mission-critical applications (Exhibit 3).

Many organizations have found that a long-term commitment to OO has resulted in significant leaps in productivity as well as more robust applications that are easily modified to react to changes in the marketplace. However, the initial investment in object analysis and design typically delays the visibility of benefits to the organization until late in the development process.

Also, properly designing and building an OO system requires advanced functional and technical skills on behalf of the entire project team. Few people have the breadth of knowledge to design and develop both application-level and infrastructure-level objects. This often results in an intensive effort to retrain existing developers as well as recruiting or contracting hard-to-find specialists to assist with the development process.

For OO to become successful in the mass market, a new paradigm must emerge in which its benefits can be exploited while simultaneously insulating the majority of developers from the intricacies of OO development. With componentware, individuals with OO skills can be focused on the task of designing and building the components themselves. Then, application architects can design applications on top of existing infrastructure frameworks, which less-experienced developers then build by gluing together a set of components. In this manner, OO can be scaled up to massive development efforts when sufficient OO resources are not available.

Major Players

Another of the drivers behind a broad acceptance of componentware is broad availability of the necessary software infrastructure. By building this infrastructure into widely distributed products, organizations such as Microsoft, OMG (the Object Management Group), Sun, and IBM have significantly reduced the amount of work required to build a component-based solution. As a result, software developers can build upon these platforms using standardized frameworks and tools, such as COM(Microsoft), CORBA (OMG), and JavaBeans (Sun).

As these infrastructure pieces have become available, vendors are beginning to build development tools that take advantage of them. These tools provide for rapid application building and deployment based partially or wholly upon component technologies. For example, Microsoft Visual Basic provides developers who only have a basic understanding of OO with access to a tool that can be used to build component-based applications.

Components Market

Now that the necessary infrastructure and tools are becoming available, the market for components, which originally was concentrated on reusable technical components such as grid controls for user interfaces, is starting to expand to include real business components. An example is SAP, where the SAP software is being packaged using component technology, enabling application developers easier access to SAP's functionality. For componentware to reach widespread acceptance, the market needs to expand past technically oriented components into business components.

COMPONENTS DEFINED

To best describe componentware, it is necessary to define the concept of a component. A component is a packaged piece of software that exhibits the following characteristics:

- *Encapsulated.* A good component is a black box with predictable, well defined interfaces. Requestors of its services know what it does, but not how it does them. Its internal workings are both hidden and isolated; they can be implemented using any technology.
- *Nearly independent.* A component should be loosely coupled to other components. In other words, the dependency between any two components should be minimal. If a component changes, the impact on other components should be minimal and vice versa.
- *Highly cohesive.* Cohesion is the "state of sticking together tightly." A component exhibits this characteristic if its purpose is clearly defined, unmistakable, and precisely focused. All of its services should contribute to this purpose.
- *Trusted and marketable.* An *existing* component should be proven in a prior implementation, and it should perform without any undocumented side effects. A *new* component should strive for this characteristic. It should provide functionality that is desirable to consumers other than the original developers.
- *Reusable.* After an organization has designed, built, or bought a component, anyone can use it to perform its specified services. This promotes the assembly of applications from components. To achieve this goal, components must be developed to be used in unpredictable combinations.
- *Replaceable.* It should be simple to replace a component as long as the new component offers, at a minimum, the same set of services through the same interfaces. Of course, the new component will probably offer an expanded set of services.
- *Executable.* A component can be executed by anyone, without having to make its source code available.
- *Distributable.* Components can be distributed for execution using standards for component interfaces and middleware services (e.g., COM, JavaBeans, and CORBA).

- *Scalable.* A component can be configured to execute on any number of servers. Consequently, an application can adapt more readily to changing transaction volumes.
- *Interoperable.* As long as a component adheres to standards for component interfaces and middleware services, it should be possible to request the component's services from any platform.
- *Self-describing.* A component should be able to describe its public interfaces, any properties that are customizable, and the events that it generates.

In addition to these characteristics, components are also defined by their granularity, or the relative size of components when compared to the application as a whole. Granularity can be broken down as follows:

- *Small grained.* A piece of code containing few internal data structures and comprising minimal functionality, such as an entry field or a collection object.
- *Medium grained.* Code containing several complex internal data structures and providing a number of complex functions, such as an invoice or a mortgage loan form.
- *Large grained.* A component providing significant functionality encapsulating a business function (e.g., accounts receivable) or an architectural concept (e.g., distributed transaction processing), although smaller than a complete application.

TYPES OF COMPONENTS

Experience has shown that it is quite common for people to view components from different perspectives.

- Some of them — typically designers — take a *logical* perspective. They view components as a means for *modeling* real-world concepts in the business domain. These are *Business Components.*
- Others — typically developers — take a *physical* perspective. They view components as independent pieces of software, or application building blocks, that *implement* those real-world business concepts. These are *Partitioned Business Components.*
- Developers also emphasize that Partitioned Business Components can be built from other independent pieces of software that provide functionality that is generally useful across a wide range of applications. These are *Engineering Components.*

Business Components

Business Components represent real-world concepts in the business domain. They encapsulate everything about those concepts, including name, purpose, knowledge, behavior, and all other intelligence. Examples include: *Customer, Product, Order, Inventory, Pricing, Credit Check, Billing,* and *Fraud Analysis.* One might think of a Business Component as a depiction or portrait of a particular business concept, and, as a whole, the Business Component Model is a depiction or portrait of the *entire* business. It is also important to note that, although this begins the process of defining the application architecture for a set of desired business capabilities, the applicability of the Business Component Model extends beyond application building.

Partitioned Business Components

Whereas Business Components model real-world concepts in the business domain, Partitioned Business Components *implement* those concepts in a particular environment. They are the physical building blocks used in the assembly of applications. As independent pieces of software, they encapsulate business data and operations, and they fulfill distinct business services through well-defined interfaces. Business Components are transformed into Partitioned Business Components based on the realities of the technical environment: distribution requirements, legacy integration, performance constraints, existing components, and more. For example, a project team might design an *Order* Business Component to represent customer demand for one or more products, but, when it is time to implement this concept in a particular client/server environment, it may be necessary to partition the *Order* Business Component into the *Order Entry* component on the client and the *Order Management* component on the server. These are Partitioned Business Components.

Engineering Components

Frequently thought of as "all other components," Engineering Components are independent pieces of software that provide functionality that is generally useful across a range of applications. They come in all shapes and sizes, and they are typically packaged as black box capabilities with well-defined interfaces. They are the physical building blocks used in the assembly of Partitioned Business Components. Examples include a workflow engine, a JavaBean that encapsulates a reusable concept such as address or monetary unit, a complex widget that allows users to edit a list of order lines, a group of objects responsible for persistence, a JavaBean that sorts a collection of objects, and a multiple column list box coded as an ActiveX control.

CRITICAL PIECES

The infrastructure necessary for componentware to become widespread is made up of several smaller pieces. These include a development process and tools, a component assembly language, broker services, components, and component services (Exhibit 4).

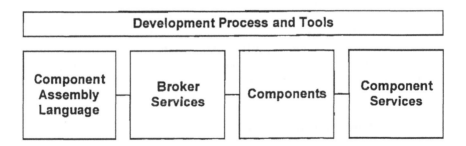

Exhibit 4. Componentware Infrastructure.

Development Process

Assuming a marketplace of widely available off-the-shelf commercial components that match the development effort, the focus of the software development process becomes the location and assembly of preexisting components. As a result of this shift in emphasis, several new processes need to be performed:

- *Searching.* Researching the current marketplace for components that match application requirements.
- *Selection.* Choosing a component and component vendor based upon a variety of criteria such as vendor stability, special component features, and component cost.
- *Integration.* Reviewing a component's documentation and interfaces to determine the best manner for integrating it into the system; developing an approach for integration.
- *Adaptation.* Because it is unlikely that components from different vendors will work together directly, especially while the industry is still immature, components may need to be enhanced. The two most common enhancement techniques are wrapping (i.e., providing a layer of code which isolates the component from the remainder of the system and variously hides, adds, or modifies the characteristics of the component interfaces) and aggregation (i.e., combining two or more components together so that they appear as one logical unit to the component consumer) to make it work within the system).
- *Testing.* Conducting thorough testing of the component to ensure that it performs as specified.

Because of similarities between componentware and object-oriented development, it is possible to leverage many of the existing OO processes and tools for component development. However, there still exists significant opportunity for growth in this market, especially on the side of tools for the developers who assemble components.

Component Assembly Tools

Component assembly tools are not necessarily the same tools as those used for constructing components themselves. Typically, they are less complex third-generation languages, which emphasize rapid application construction over run-time speed or efficiency. The market for component assembly tools currently has a number of entrants, such as ParcPlace/Digitalk PARTs, IBM VisualAge, and Microsoft Visual Basic. These tools provide at least the minimal functionality required for component assembly tools — the ability to include prebuilt components into applications and glue them together.

However, to reach a wider audience, component assembly tools need to move away from extensions to current procedural languages and towards easy-to-use, integrated development environments. A partial listing of the features of an ideal component construction language includes

- *Component catalog.* Tool used for browsing in-house and third-party brokerages and selecting components.
- *Component inspector.* Tool that allows viewing the various characteristics of a component, such as interfaces, documentation, and file size.
- *Component installation.* Interfaces with brokerage services and the operating system to properly register components on the local machine or the appropriate server machines.
- *Component tester.* Tool used to automate the testing of components and their integration
- *Semiautomated wrapping.* Assists with the development of wrappers around off-the-shelf components.
- *Semantic transformation.* Allows components with different application-level semantics to be able to collaborate, e.g., "the customer I am passing to you means the same thing to both of us."

Component Broker Services

Collaboration between components that are potentially sold by different vendors, built in different languages, and located on different machines requires standards. A "component bus" is the common infrastructure for this interoperability. Minimally, such a bus provides protocols for

- *Component instantiation.* Creating or asking for a particular component without knowing its location.
- *Component access.* Providing access to a component, even if it is on another machine, which can be used to manipulate it.

- *Service discovery.* Identifying the services that a component provides at run time.
- *Component release.* Telling a component when it is no longer needed so it can release resources as necessary.

Applications discover and invoke a component's available methods using a common protocol. Methods are specified with an interface definition language (IDL), which is independent of the programming language or tool used to implement the component. Then, the methods on a component can be invoked via one of three techniques:

- In-process, similar to a DLL in Windows
- Across process boundaries but on the same machine, using a Lightweight RPC (or LRPC) mechanism
- Across machine boundaries, through RPC, Message-Oriented Middleware (MOM) mechanisms, or Object Request Brokers (ORBs)

Once a component is invoked, the bus infrastructure marshals requests between components. Marshaling bundles the parameters for a request in a format for efficient translation and transmission, potentially across a network. The server component receives the request, unpackages the parameters, and dispatches to the appropriate function. Finally, any return value must be marshaled back to the client. In this manner, standardized marshaling hides the details of another component's location, operating system or implementation language. The service that locates components and manages their communications is an ORB.

Brokers provide additional roles in the component environment, such as management of concurrent requests to a given server, transaction management, and security auditing.

DEVELOPMENT MODEL

At a high level, component-based software development involves two parties: the component producer and the component consumer. The producer is responsible for creating components and ensuring that they perform as specified. Producers can be either third-party vendors — mass-market or contractual — or internal component development teams. Components may be developed from the start as components, or they may be harvested from new or existing solutions. For example, a retail company may extract bar code scanning out of an existing application and repackage it as a construction component for internal or mass-market use.

Component consumers, on the other hand, build applications by assembling components. These components are purchased from a third-party vendor, acquired from internal asset repositories, or contracted out to a component builder. Feedback from the consumers is used to refine existing components and identify additional components to be built.

When using business components, the software development process focuses on the business domain or business model. Instead of dealing with the mechanics of process-to-process communication and calling conventions, developers are able to describe systems in functional terms. By using entities that map to the business model and the information flow within it, development can become less complex and less error prone, and new code creation is minimized.

By packaging code into cross-application units, business software becomes a collection of reusable assets. Proprietary assets can contain internal intellectual property that can be leveraged from one application to another, for example, a company's policy component or its code for loan approvals can be built into a back-office client/server system, an Internet customer service system, and a multimedia kiosk.

BENEFITS OF COMPONENTWARE

Business Components and Partitioned Business Components represent a major improvement in design capability — some might argue the first major change in design thinking since structured design. There are several benefits arising from this breakthrough:

- Business Components model entities and processes at the *enterprise* level, and they evolve into Partitioned Business Components that are integrated into applications that operate over a network. Consequently, they serve as an excellent first step in the development of scalable, distributed enterprise applications that map closely to the business enterprise itself (i.e., the way it operates and the information that defines it).
- Business Components model the business, and thus they enable applications to more completely satisfy the business needs. They also provide a business-oriented view of the domain and consequently a good way to scope the solution space. This results in a good context for making process and application decisions. Additionally, Business Components provide a common vocabulary for the project team. They educate the team about what is important to the business.
- When modeled correctly, entity-centric Business Components represent the most stable elements of the business, while process-centric Business Components represent the most volatile. Encapsulating and separating these elements contributes to the application's overall maintainability.
- To manage the complexity of a large problem, it must be divided into smaller, coherent parts. Partitioned Business Components provide an

excellent way to divide and conquer in a way that ties the application to the business domain. They provide the ability to "package software capabilities into more manageable (and useful) chunks." By contrast, traditional modules are too cumbersome to be reusable in multiple contexts. On the other end of the spectrum, objects are too small to effectively divide and conquer — there are simply too many of them.

- Partitioned Business Components provide a greater emphasis on application layering — a well known, but often neglected concept in application development.
- Partitioned Business Components are application building blocks. As an application modeling tool, they depict how various elements of an application fit together. As an application building tool, they provide a means for systems delivery.
- Proven processes, patterns, and frameworks offer a higher level of reuse. This is one of the key advantages because it means greater agility. These mechanisms make it possible for hundreds of developers to do things consistently and to benefit from previously captured, reusable knowledge capital.

CHALLENGES OF COMPONENTWARE IMPLEMENTATION

Identifying Components and Achieving Reuse

Business Components model the business. That sentence may sound straightforward, but even with experience it is a challenge to identify the *right* components and to design them for flexibility and reuse. Flexibility and reuse are certainly more achievable with Business Components, but they are not inherent to Business Components. To accomplish these goals, project teams must understand what is happening within the enterprise and across the industry. Project teams must work with business experts who understand the factors that will influence the current and future evolution of the business domain. By accounting for these factors, the Business Component Model will be more flexible and reusable if it is challenged by scenarios that are likely to take place in the future.

Reuse becomes a reality more quickly if it is planned for from the start. Reuse endures if it is managed over time. However, both of these things are difficult to do, especially for large projects and large enterprises. First, it is easy for communication across one or more projects to break down. It is also common for individual projects to pay more attention to their requirements and deadlines than to project-wide or enterprisewide reuse. After all, their most important objective is to deliver value to their customers. Reuse must be ingrained into the culture. This could mean teams responsible for projectwide and enterprisewide reuse, but, no matter how it's done, reuse must be one of the most important technology objectives.

Too much focus on low-level (i.e., code) reuse can be a trap. To draw an analogy, take a look at the auto industry 10 years ago. Some auto makers were focused on interchangeable parts and low-level standardization. For example, they decided to use the same body style for all of their cars. Unfortunately, when the industry began to move away from the boxy body style, they were not well prepared, nor were they agile enough to react in a timely fashion. They had invested too much in low-level standardization. Conversely, other auto makers were focused on quality processes and frameworks (i.e., high-level reuse). As a result, they were able to respond more quickly to the changing requirements. Engagement experience has shown that the same thing can happen with components and objects (e.g., too much emphasis on low-level inheritance). That is why it is important to focus appropriately on the high-level reuse enabled by processes, patterns, and frameworks.

Standards Wars

Although Business Components and Partitioned Business Components represent a significant breakthrough in design capability, the architectural frameworks to support this breakthrough are still maturing. Standards come to mind first. Will it be Microsoft's COM, Sun's JavaBeans, or OMG's CORBA? The answer is still not clear. Likewise, with languages. Will it be Visual Basic, Java? Tools and repositories offer another challenge. Clear winners have yet to emerge, and newcomers are constantly appearing with promising products. Finally, the legal and commercial market for buying and selling components is not mature. The market for high-level common business objects is just emerging, while the market for low-level components is still somewhat chaotic.

Training

One of the most important challenges is teaching a new application development style. Although components and objects have been around for a while, they are new to most people. Furthermore, component-based development requires a change in the way one thinks about designing and building applications. Real project experience has shown that it takes a couple of months to feel comfortable with this paradigm — and longer for those pursuing deeper technical skills. However, this challenge is certainly not impossible to overcome. A combination of training and mentoring has proven to be the best way to teach these concepts, and the more rigorous approach that results from this education is well worth the journey.

Interoperability

Interoperability includes two major facets: the ability for components from a variety of sources to coexist in a single solution and the ability to substitute one vendor's components for those of another. Specific requirements for interoperability include

- *Common interface across vendors' components.* Similar components from different vendors, such as grid controls and customer objects, must have common interfaces so one can be substituted for another; standards groups have begun work on this field, but it is still unclear if these standards will be widely accepted.
- *Language independence.* The interfaces between components must not be dependent on the languages in which they were written.
- *Platform independence.* Components on differing platforms must be able to communicate with each other, without needing to include custom data type translation code into the components themselves.
- *Communications infrastructure.* Components must be able to communicate across machines without the inclusion of communications-specific code in the components.
- *Location independence.* Services must be available that can be used to provide location-independent component communications.
- *Glue language specifications.* A standard set of interface constructs is required that can be used to "glue together" components from various vendors.

Many of these challenges have been met within the CORBA and COM standards. However, the resulting products have yet to reach maturity, such as distributed computing with OLE and CORBA under the Windows platform.

Configuration Management

As systems move from single-vendor monolithic applications to multivendor component-based solutions, configuration management will become an ever-greater challenge. Originally, with single-vendor applications, configuration was straightforward. Systems were installed according to the vendor's specifications and had little interaction with other software on the same machine. Licensing was equally simple, with licenses paid according to a single vendor's terms. However, the component-based model introduces a series of challenges that are only beginning to be addressed in the market:

- *Packaging and delivery.* Traditional shrink-wrapped software packaging for monolithic applications will be replaced by electronic distribution of software; this will also spur the development of new payment and licensing techniques.
- *Licensing.* As solutions become conglomerates made up of many components, traditional licensing techniques will not always apply; the use of one-time unlimited-use payments will increase as well as new schemes, such as pay-per-use micropayments (i.e., the transfer of a very small amount of money, such as .01 cents, via an infrastructure that efficiently supports such small transactions).

- *Component repositories.* Software developers must have electronic warehouses where components can be stored along with a record of their distinguishing attributes, such as descriptions, interface definitions, and version numbers. These repositories must be extremely easy to navigate, or developers will not use them.
- *Versioning.* When a single component is used by several applications, versioning becomes significantly more complex (as can be seen in the case of DLLs in Microsoft Windows). Advanced versioning software, including system support for versioning, will be required.

Market Segment/Maturity

Although growth is expected in the componentware market, today there are currently few commercially available business components. Now that the technical hurdles have been crossed, the following issues need to be addressed by the market before business components will see widespread acceptance:

- *Business case and economic model.* The benefits of components must be that they are more cost-effective than traditional development.
- *Defined business domain.* Specific business domains where components can have the greatest impact need to be identified and well-defined; this is likely to emerge first in strong vertical markets, such as health care.
- *Domain compatibility across vendors.* As different vendors begin to make business components available, the existence of standardized functional domains will allow for plug-and-play component substitution.
- *Market momentum.* The component market needs to gain momentum through the entrance of several larger vendors, as well as high-profile success stories.
- *Strategic assets.* Corporations will need to decide which components are indeed generic, such as customer components, and which are strategic to their business, such as an insurance pricing engine.
- *Intellectual property rights.* As components are embedded in larger components and systems, royalties or other methods of protecting intellectual property will need to be constructed.

Discovery and Acquisition

Real-world experience has shown that a significant problem with component reuse is discovery and acquisition. With today's rudimentary discovery tools, once repositories grow to contain thousands of components, they are no longer navigable, and developers resort to recoding functionality already implemented in existing components.

As software engineering moves toward component-based solutions, an even larger part of the engineering process will be that of component discovery and acquisition. This will involve searching through electronic components catalogs, both internal and external to the corporation, to identify the components that best fit the requirements of the development project. This can be aided by storing metadata for each component which can then be used for both design- and run-time negotiation.

The increasing popularity of the Internet, specifically the World Wide Web, has made the location task somewhat easier; however, component search technologies are still in their infancy. Current component sales venues include

- *The World Wide Web.* Various component consortium homepages.
- *Direct from vendors.* Through catalogs or other informational materials.
- *From component brokers.* Potential future services which match component requirements with commercially available components.
- *Catalogs or magazines for component languages.* These include *Visual Basic Programmer's Journal* and the *Programmer's Paradise Catalog.*

Robust Technical Infrastructure

To enable the rapid construction of nontrivial applications using components, the underlying infrastructure must provide features over and above those available in today's tools. These additional features include

- *Transactional integrity across components.* These are especially important in distributed component environments, where it is necessary to be able to perform a single transaction across multiple components and rollback partial changes in the case of an error.
- *Cross-component trace tools.* These provide for tracing application execution across components regardless of original development language, process boundaries, or location in the network.
- *Scalability and performance.* These allow smaller solutions to be grown into larger environments while still retaining good response times.
- *Load balancing with failover.* These provide the ability to deploy a class of components on multiple servers for high-throughput transaction processing.

TARGET APPLICATIONS FOR COMPONENTWARE

Because the construction of applications using commercially available components is relatively new, there is not yet a lot of experience with these technologies. An exception to this is the proliferation of VBX and now ActiveX controls for useunder Microsoft Windows. However, a few types of applications have been identified as well-suited to the use of component technologies:

- *Highly graphical.* Programmers can use construction components, such as grid controls and specialized drop-down list boxes, to reduce the amount of time required to design graphical, highly interactive interfaces.
- *Rapid development.* These tools are prevalent in fields in which the underlying business model is stable, allowing reuse of well-defined business components, but applications evolve quickly, for example, the banking industry, as new offerings are created.
- *Throwaway.* This type of tool is useful when the business model is stable, but applications are built for single-use or limited-time use, for example, a promotional feature added by the carrier to a cellular line.
- *Multimode deployment.* These are applications that are to be deployed across multiple user interfaces, but where the core logic is the same, for example, a loan approval application which is deployed internally via a Visual Basic client and externally via a World Wide Web site.
- *Migration of legacy applications.* These are solutions that partition pieces of the solution into components which "wrap" legacy systems; components separate the interface from the implementation, providing for rehosting of the components to a new OS or language.
- *Volatile business applications.* These encapsulate application variability so that changes to the implementation (reflecting variability in the business models) are hidden from other components.

CASE STUDY: ABC SHIPPING COMPANY

ABC Shipping Co. wanted to build a shrink-wrapped application that allows customers to print out custom shipping labels on their premises. A review of their current custom applications showed that these applications:

- Shared a common core of features that made up at least 50% of the functionality for each application
- Shared very little code
- Were written using a variety of tools

A 10-person team used object-oriented techniques to create small-grained business objects, such as shipment, receiver, and invoice, as well as construction objects, such as transaction and print handler. These were then built as OLE Automation objects using Visual C++ and assembled into an application using Visual C++ and Visual Basic.

Using OLE allows the company to reuse and extend these components for other systems. The business case here included several example scenarios. For example, the company could redeploy the application on the Internet, using any Internet tool that supports OLE protocols. Alternatively, the company could extend the components for enterprise-wide reuse. The business case cited the sample work involved to reuse the components in a shipment notification system.

SUMMARY

Companies today must begin by gaining a better understanding of the consumer side of component-based software engineering, and the market surrounding it, including the following steps:

- *Performing an ongoing technology investigation.* Companies should continue investigating the use of OLE as a foundation for desktop integration of construction and business components into working systems.
- *Identifying leading projects for componentware.* Companies should identify key projects that are candidates for building systems using a producer/consumer model, using technologies such as OLE, ActiveX, or CORBA.
- *Monitoring component marketplace.* Companies should identify new trends, such as expanded offerings of business components, monitor known component vendors, and watch for new entrants in the component marketplace.

Chapter 34
Costs and Frameworks for Managing the Client/Server Environment

Client/server environments pose three hurdles to success:

- The development for client/server is more complex than for traditional systems, with steep learning curves and often challenging development problems.
- Getting the technology and new business processes introduced into the business environment presents change management and education issues.
- Just when it seems that the build and rollout problems are under control, one more hurdle appears, managing the environment from a systems standpoint.

This chapter expands on the systems management issues discussed in the chapter on management of distributed systems (see Section III), with a particular focus on the cost issue. Specifically, this chapter gives a framework for understanding what the costs of systems management are in a netcentric or advanced client/server environment. Within this framework, we give various estimates of what these costs might be.

The chapter will be of value to anyone who wants to understand what the sources of costs are and especially those people who need to create a cost accounting approach. In addition, the material may be of value when looking at outsourcing systems management of client/server environments. The framework is applied to an outsourcing example to assess coverage of the environment by the vendors' proposals and as a means to compare costs.

SPECIAL TOPICS

MODE REFRESHER

The Management of Distributed Environment (MODE) framework (discussed in detail in Section III) is the centerpiece of the discussions that follow. MODE is a comprehensive view of the distributed computing management picture. In its simplest form, MODE provides a mechanism for understanding *what* needs to be done, *why* management tasks need to be performed, and *how* the management of systems is changed with the introduction of a netcentric client/server environment. The framework focuses on four main areas: service management, systems management, service planning, and change management.

Service Management

Service Management is the fundamental area within the model. It involves

- Forming liaisons with users, developers/architects, and vendors
- Monitoring the services that are provided
- Ensuring that the services are meeting standards as defined in Service Level Agreements

The key to Service Management, and to the overall management of distributed client/server systems, is the use of a Service Level Agreement (SLA), which clearly articulates and documents the level of service the users expect to receive. The SLA represents a contractual agreements to achieve agreed levels of business performance. For example, an SLA for an insurance claims environment might identify the number of claims that would be processed in a workday. SLAs should be used to drive out the requirements for the service organization and the operations architecture, as well as to justify expenditures for tools and infrastructure.

Ultimately, the users of the system will define the service offered to the customer base through a Service Level Agreement. Where the service management concept is implemented correctly, users have a single point of contact for all systems-related problems, suggestions, and planning. The service management function in turn navigates and coordinates the needed systems personnel and resources on behalf of the user.

Service Management is also the direct interface to the Developers/Architects and Vendors for the distributed system. Each of these groups has requirements for, and introduce changes to, the distributed environment. Service Management controls the overall service to the users and handles the relationships with Developers/Architects and Vendors.

Functions within Service Management are

- *SLA management.* Involves the creation, managing, reporting, and discussion of SLAs with users.

- *OLA management.* Involves the creation, managing, reporting, and discussion of OLAs (Operational Level Agreements) with domain suppliers/vendors. These agreements represent contractual agreements to achieve agreed levels of performance in terms of information processing targets. An OLA agreement might identify the expected response time for an application.
- *Help Desk.* Provides end users with a single point of contact and controls the resolution of incidents and problems within the client/server environment.
- *Quality management.* Ensures quality in the management of the client/server environment through training, as well as through the design and execution of quality improvement plans.
- *Administration.* Handles the financial accounting and legal aspects of managing a client/server environment.

Systems Management

Systems Management involves all functions required for the day-to-day operation of the distributed system, such as event monitoring, failure control, performance monitoring, and tape loading. Regardless of the changes taking place within the distributed environment, Systems Management activities must take place in an ongoing manner.

Functions within Systems Management are

- *Production control.* Ensures that production activities are performed and controlled as required and as intended.
- *Monitoring.* Verifies that the system is continually functioning in accordance with whatever service levels are defined.
- *Failure control.* Involves the detection and correction of faults within the system, whether they are minor (a workstation is down) or major (a disaster has occurred.)
- *Security management.* Ensures that the system is accessed only by authorized users and that those users are restricted to authorized resources.

Service Planning

Service Planning encompasses all of the functions that outline the tactical and strategic planning that needs to take place to manage a distributed environment effectively. Service Planning for a distributed client/server environment requires a more integrated approach. Effective planning for any one component such as network capacity cannot be done independent of an understanding of the whole system and how it will be managed. (For example, the chosen software distribution approach may impact the overall network bandwidth required.)

Once a change has been planned, the change will be controlled and implemented in detail within either Systems Management or Managing Change.

Functions within Service Planning are

- *Service management planning.* Defines the financial and training plans for the organization.
- *Systems management planning.* Determines the strategies for day-to-day operation of the system.
- *Managing change planning.* Develops the plans for releasing new sites, services, or updates to existing service.
- MODE strategic planning. Formulates the long-term strategy for managing the distributed environment, including people, tools, and processes. It also ensures that the management strategy is in-line with the enterprise strategy.

Management of Change

Managing change includes all of the functions necessary for effecting changes to the client/server environment in a controlled and orderly way (such as software and data distribution, and license management). Due to the large number of interrelated hardware and software components in a client/server environment, assessing and controlling the "side effects" of system change is crucial to maintaining acceptable system availability.

Functions within Managing Change are

- *Controlling.* Monitors change to make sure that change is delivered on-time according to established plans, making adjustments to the plan when unforeseen issues or events arise (such as rollout management, change control, and asset management).
- *Testing.* Ensures that changes to the client/server environment will achieve the desired result and not produce unwanted side effects.
- *Implementing.* Executes change within the distributed environment with tested components and techniques according to the appropriate plan(s). Implementing includes such things as initial installation, software and data distribution, and license management.

MODE AS A COST FRAMEWORK

The at-a-glance matrix in Exhibit 1 summarizes the MODE functions; it is essentially a functional outline of what work must be done when managing a distributed environment. There are many ways to work with this matrix.

One is to think in terms of organization structure. What functions should report to other functions? What processes and procedures are required to

Exhibit 1. The MODE Functions

Service management	Systems management	Service planning	Managing change
SLA management	Production control	Service management planning	Controlling
SLA Definition	Production scheduling	Service costing and pricing	Change control
SLA Reporting	Print management	Training planning	Asset management
SLA Control	File transfer and control		Rollout management
SLAReview	System startup and shutdown	Systems management planning	Release control
	Mass storage management	Physical site planning	Migration control
OLA management	Backup/restore management	Security planning	License management
OLA Definition	Archiving	Capacity modeling and planning	
OLA Reporting		Contingency planning	Testing
OLA Control	Monitoring	Recovery planning	Product validation
OLA Review	Event management	Disaster recovery planning	Release testing
	Performance management	Hardware maintenance planning	
Help Desk	Physical site management		Implementing
Incident management		Managing change planning	Procurement
Problem management	Failure control	Rollout planning	Initial installation
Request management	Fault management	Release planning	System component configuration
	Recovery	Procurement planning	Software and data distribution
Quality management	Disaster recovery		User administraion
Quality management	Hardware maintenance	MODE strategic planning	
Training		MODE strategic planning	
	Security management		
Administration	Security management		
Billing and accounting			
Contract management			

support the work to be done and the reporting relationships of the organization?

A second option is to take the functions and use them as criteria to evaluate tools and automation approaches to support a MODE implementation. A third way to use the framework, and the focus of this chapter, is to use the functional framework as a *cost accounting framework* to define the sources of costs and estimate the costs associated with managing a distributed environment.

In addition to determining how to actually execute or perform the functions, it is necessary to determine the cost for each function. As such, the framework can be thought of as a functional breakdown, which, in turn, provides a means to define the costs associated with operating such an environment.

For example, one function in MODE is to track SLA. Although there are many subfunctions to this activity, at this level an associated cost for performing this function can be assessed. The question then becomes how costs are determined and best used to manage a distributed environment.

Determining the Costs of Managing a Distributed Environment

We have worked with several clients and examined industry sources to define these costs. The following are some key observations that come from these real-world cases; these observations may apply to other distributed environments.

- Many times it is possible to define the costs in terms of "cost per workstation per month." Cost per workstation per month is a fairly common measure used in outsourcing arrangements, for example. In such arrangements the cost per workstation per month is typically agreed to for the length of the contract.
- Using cost per workstation per month as a parameter and by looking at a variety of cost models and a set of assumptions, we can determine a reasonable cost range and what percentage of total costs the MODE function represents.
- The models that result are fairly comprehensive in their coverage and often point out cases where unexpected costs are significant and could be overlooked without the model.
- The costs are very situation specific, and it is easy to move a cost well outside of range by changing assumptions.

Underlying Assumptions About Costs. As an example, a cost for site backup can be defined on a workstation-per-month basis. Implicit in these costs is the fact that availability and speed to recovery fall in "typical" ranges, such as 95% availability. If one alters the assumptions to a much more stringent requirement of 7 by 23:50 minutes and one minute recovery time, then the costs shift dramatically.

When looking at an industry-provided standard or at the numbers discussed throughout this chapter, remember that they must be evaluated in the context of the assumptions behind them. Discrepancies in actual costs vs. industry averages can and should be justified as change in assumptions. Unfortunately, such assumptions are often not explicit.

Put another way, the specific costs identified here are of very little value without an understanding of the assumptions behind them. Some key assumptions will be explained as the discussion proceeds. The model provided here should be helpful in allowing readers to develop a model of actual costs that they might experience. However, as significant discrepancies are found in other's models and your own, the point is not to reject either but to understand what the different assumptions are that cause the shift in numbers.

Developing Cost Approximations with Activity-Based Costing

The method we employ is an activity-based approach to costing out the work associated with managing a distributed environment. In such an approach a cost is developed for each major activity that needs to be pursued to accomplish the work. In this case the MODE model can be viewed as an inventory of such costs. The challenge then becomes to define the costs associated with activities found in the MODE model.

How can these costs be determined? In a distributed environment, a first step is to develop an assessment of your own costs. In essence, you need to completely understand what each function in the MODE model means. Next you determine who is contributing to the costs found in the function. In some cases, the cost may be well managed. For example, a help desk with 20 people may be assigned to the Service Management Help Desk.

Example: Personnel-Related Activities and Costs. In doing such an analysis you must decide what costs to account for. For the purposes of our example, the costs under consideration are those associated with people costs. This is partially as a matter of simplification. Another reason is that many of the other costs, such as software and hardware, are often accounted for as indirect or overhead costs and are not always directly transformable to activity-based approaches. Finally, such costs may have been accounted for in the initial justification of costs for acquiring the software and hardware. For this discussion we look only at how to develop the personnel-related activity costs. Other nonpayroll costs will need to be accounted for in other models.

The determination of costs is not trivial. MODE functions often cut across many organizational functions, and there may be no single place where the costs roll together. In other cases, the cost may not be explicit.

For example, there is frequently an "unofficial" help desk function in many departments where there is a certain individual or individuals who know something about computers and who other people call for help, rather than wait in the queue of calls to the "official" help desk. This type of unrecognized peer support contributes hidden or shadow IT costs.

For cases such as these, an accounting level of precision may be impractical. An approximation is often adequate. For example, in this case you might estimate that in each department there is a person fulfilling this role and applying approximately 2 hours per week to the function. The focus should be on identifying sources of costs and making and documenting reasonable approximations. Inevitably discussions and argument will arise. The discussion process should lead to some revisions and broader acceptance of the proposed costs.

In other cases, there may be functions that are not done. For example, MODE differentiates between SLAs and OLAs. An SLA is a commitment on business performance. For example, an SLA for an insurance claims department might state how many claims the department will be able to process per hour. An OLA is a commitment to what the technology must do to meet the SLA commitment. For example, to meet the targeted number of claims per hour, an OLA for the department might commit that end-to-end system response time for initial claim collection will be 3 seconds or less at the 95th percentile.

For many information systems organizations there are sufficient challenges in getting OLAs defined and they choose not to define SLAs. While there are many good reasons for using both SLAs and OLAs, the reality is that often it is just not feasible to do all these types of agreements. In that case, an organization may choose to forego the development and use of SLAs as defined by MODE and instead treat the OLAs as SLAs. In this case there would be no accounting for SLAs.

In other cases, there may be costs that are not currently available but which can be anticipated to be part of the effort going forward. For example, if no one is currently doing event management, there will be no way to look to internal costs to determine an activity based cost. Instead, you need to look at external sources for some views on reasonable costs and then select one of these costs. Particularly in this case, you must understand the assumptions behind the costs. (Sources for such costs are discussed in a subsequent section.)

The act of determining costs is essentially an analytical one with approximations created wherever possible. It is often a cross-department activity, in that costs may need to be collected from many department organizations. Because the costs must come from many departments, support for this effort needs to come from senior management; otherwise, individual departments may be reluctant to report internal costs outside the normal lines of reporting. However, given the total costs associated, there is often real interest in such an effort and management support can be enlisted to help get the facts.

As these costs are being collected it is essential to normalize the costs so that there is a basis for comparing costs. Cost estimates for the MODE functions can, in many cases, be normalized according to a *cost/seat/month* basis.

The use of this normalizing factor is based on the authors' experiences analyzing services costs for several engagements of Accenture. By using this normalizing factor, it is possible to compare relative functional costs. There is also a basis for comparing functional costs that come from different sources. This, in turn, provides a basis for comparing annual costs.

Using External Sources for Estimates of Cost

External costs are sometimes needed to fill in some blanks in the cost model. In addition, as the cost model is being developed, there is always value in having additional sources of estimates to confirm your own estimates or to challenge them.

The analysis of external costs that is presented here is not exhaustive, but it does provide some insight and consistency of view of the costs. Remember that the numbers presented are for a given point in time and it is reasonable to expect them to age quickly as we learn better how to manage such distributed environments.

Furthermore, remember that the underlying assumptions are key. The factors given can serve as an initial benchmark for understanding potential cost impacts in the area of distributed systems management. They may be of value if one has no cost to go by, but in all cases such costs are best defined based on the actuals at hand.

Some common features that apply across the inputs to the analysis include the following:

- PC client workstations
- Local and remote LANs
- UNIX or NT Servers
- Mixture of TCP/IP and IPX protocols
- Systems and gateways to host mainframe processing.

None of the cases analyzed pushed the edge of the envelope in terms of demands for availability, reliability, or recoverability. For example, none of the cases addressed 24x7 (24 hours a day, 7 days a week) or subsecond response time or global processing. Also, although the networks under consideration involved hundreds of workstations, none involved thousands. It does appear that there may be diseconomies of scale in this environment. As a result, costs within a 100-workstation environment may give very little insight to the costs for a 10,000-workstation environment. In larger environments the reality is that the interactions increase geometrically and so, too, may the cost. Furthermore, in the cases presented, where the specifics are known, the costs are associated with U.S. operations.

The cost value does not include mainframe or wide area network (WAN) support services. For any particular environment, the *cost/seat/month* value may be higher if more complex processing requirements are needed, such as the ability to manage more network protocols or platforms. The cost may be lower if the target environment is simpler or there are fewer protocols to manage. Items such as software, hardware, facilities, and premise wiring are not included in the services. Voice support was also not taken into account.

Several sites were used to estimate the costs. Because of confidentiality issues, some specifics cannot be provided. Generally speaking, however, detailed costs were mainly estimated using information from a large systems management engagement client. Costs are based on the following assumptions:

- $100,000 annual salary for manager positions
- $55,000 annual salary for worker positions

For many companies, the worker position costs may be too low. Estimates were then compared against other estimates to confirm reasonableness.

For the analysis of external sources of costs discussed in this chapter, some of the results are taken from an actual outsourcing arrangement. Some of the other results discussed, such as the Gartner Group numbers, continue to be revised and improved over time and may be updated. Therefore, any of the costs discussed should be looked on as examples of how to go about finding external costs, not as final sources to do your own estimate.

Large Consumer Products Manufacturer. This site had a $500,000 help desk function. Network management costs were at approximately $400,000, and technical support costs were $700,000. Total annual cost was $1.6 million. There were 450 users at this site so the monthly per-seat cost was approximately $300.

Gartner Report on Large Enterprise Client/Server Costs. A 1994 strategic analysis report from Gartner Group showed a five-year total cost of $48,400 per user. This comes to $9,680 per year or $806 per month. When describing cost analysis without end-user labor, the following percentages were given for systems management activities: IS labor for end-user support: 14.6%; IS labor for operations: 15.7%, education and training: 5%, professional services: 2.8%. This totals 38.1%, or an operations per-seat cost around $307.

Forrester Research Report Vol. 10 No. 4: Client/Server's Price Tag. This February 1993 report showed approximate costs of $1 million over four years, plus an additional $160,000 for training, which totals $1.16 million over four years. There were 140 users in the study, so the per-seat cost comes to $169. However, the report analyzes cost on a per-application basis. Therefore, several applications will probably increase the overall per-seat cost. Page 10 of the report cites an estimate of $475 per user as an average across several applications.

Datamation Report on Client/Server Costs. A *Datamation* article from February 15, 1994 notes that $2.2 million annual costs were spent for support services for a 3,000 user application. This figure included mostly systems management tasks but not items such as systems administration, Help Desk, or training. The annual cost reduced to a per-seat cost is $61/seat just for production and control and some monitoring services. If the entire MODE spectrum of services is taken into account, it would be anticipated that a per-seat cost of $292 would be needed.

This same article references a Hyatt Hotels study in which $44.5 million was cited as a 5-year cost for their client/server systems, of which 23% represents support costs for a 500-user network. This boils down to $10.235 million over 5 years for those costs — $2.047 million per year, $4,094 per user, and $341 per seat per month.

Information Week Report. An *InformationWeek* article (January 3, 1993) described the costs over a 5-year period for personnel to support client/server systems. An examination of the PC/LAN and UNIX values shows that the costs are $17,000 per user over 5 years, or $283 per seat.

Large Communications Vendor Proposal. The proposed cost for help desk services and hardware/software maintenance services for an Accenture client, a large communications vendor, is approximately $25 per user per month. In addition, four deskside help technicians at approximately $12,000 per year are included. There are 6,500 users at this organization. Therefore, the deskside support adds about $7 per user per month in support costs. This brings the total to $30.50 per user per month for just

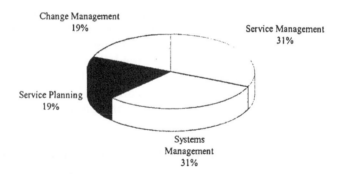

Exhibit 2. Services Cost Per Seat, Breakdown by Function.

these services. Using the projected costs for MODE services not covered under this proposal would result in a per-seat charge of around $300.

Dataquest Study. In its 1994 annual edition on software services, Dataquest reported the average dollars spent in 1994 per end user by the study's respondents. It showed a client/server expenditure of $327.54 per user per month.

In all the examples discussed, total costs were established by a roll up from the individual MODE functions. It is the cost at the function level that may be of key value in managing a distributed environment. For example, the cost for the help desk function, as defined in MODE, was estimated at approximately $35 per workstation per month across the several cases noted, where it was feasible to determine help desk functions. This was done for each of the MODE functions.

Taking the previous discussion into account, the overall *cost/seat/month* figure for all of MODE services appears to cluster around approximately $300. Once again there is a set of assumptions behind this figure that includes such things as the use of PCs for clients, local and remote LANs, and an average of 100 workstations but no global processing or 24x7 operations. An estimate of how the $300 cost is broken down by MODE functions is shown in Exhibit 2.

USING THE MODE ESTIMATES

The point of this effort to develop MODE costs is to begin to influence the costs associated with managing a distributed environment.

As a first step, a comparison must be done with external costs to see if internal costs are reasonable. This can and should be done on a MODE function basis.

Recognize that the costs are simply approximations at this point. If you determine a total cost of $600 per workstation per month, the approximation may suggest that there is a problem. Similarly, if you find a MODE function cost (e.g., the cost of the help desk) is at $100 per workstation per month vs. perhaps $35 per workstation per month, then there may be an opportunity for improvement. Go back and examine the assumptions going into the actual estimate. A discrepancy may be due to the allocation of costs that are not part of the help desk in the cited estimate.

The estimated costs may approximate actual costs within 25 to 30% for any given set of assumptions. Thus, if costs for a help desk were estimated at $40 per workstation per month, this amount is essentially comparable to the estimated costs of $35. Although there is no major cost discrepancy, the manager should be thinking about what should be done over time to move the costs down. In this case, the $40 becomes the reference and the focus is on improving it over time. The fact is that it is very hard to make such improvements without first having such a reference.

Alternatively, if a cost is significantly lower than industry averages, then it is also worth examining. For example, in the MODE cost models we have developed, the cost for production management (which addresses such functions as network, print, and mass storage management) is estimated to cost approximately $80 per workstation per month. If an individual site shows actual costs of $30 per workstation per month, it could perhaps mean that the site is doing a very good job. Conversely, it could mean that the service delivered could be greatly improved and the function is in need of further investment and personnel, and, of course, it may again mean that different assumptions apply and the differences can be justified based on the changing assumptions.

MODE COST MODELS AND EVALUATION OF OUTSOURCING ALTERNATIVES

The decision to outsource the management of distributed environments is a common one, and the MODE cost model can be applied to outsourcing arrangements.

There are many such reasons to outsource systems management of client/server networks. Often an internal systems management group may have limited skills in operating the technology associated with client/server. Outsourcing can bring a needed skill set to address the problem.

Another reason revolves around the inherently distributed nature of the work. Often the operation of the systems demands that people be on-site to do installations, and monitor and fix problems daily. A traditional systems management group may not have the personnel to do this work. Furthermore, an outsourcer may be able to take advantage of economies of scale by being able to place personnel in an area to deal with several local distributed sites.

Other traditional reasons for outsourcing revolve around controlling and perhaps reducing costs. Also, management sometimes turns to outsourcing when it has determined that the skill sets of IS staff do not represent core skill sets of the enterprise.

Leveling the Playing Field with the Outsourcer

If a decision is made to outsource a distributed environment, then the MODE functional framework can be a valuable tool. To understand this one has to begin with a key observation. Outsourcing is essentially a contractual activity. In this process, through negotiation, the enterprise and outsourcer come to an agreement on what services the outsourcer will provide. These agreements are reflected in a formal contract defining services and the associated costs.

In most cases, the contract becomes the core of any discussions between the enterprise and the outsourcers regarding ongoing services. Frequently, an outsourcer will only enter into a discussion with the contract in hand and will provide a service only when it is described by the contract or with an approved change order. Of course, associated with the change order are additional charges. This change-order process then becomes a key determinant in terms of actual vs. planned costs. It can also be the source of almost continual discussions between the outsourcer and the enterprise.

It is essential, then, that the enterprise enter into the discussion with a solid understanding of what functions it wants provided by the outsourcer. It is safe to assume that a competent outsourcer already knows what it wants to make explicit through the contract and what it would expect to deal with through a change-order process. Outsourcers often have an advantage in the negotiations simply because they have more experience in these negotiations than the enterprise looking to outsource.

In this case, the MODE functional framework can be a valuable framework for guiding contractual discussions. Functions would be excluded from a contract, then, not through oversight, but from a conscious decision not to include them. The framework can also help clarify the different parties' understandings of terms. It can be used to ask an outsourcer questions such as who will do SLA reporting and who will do such things as security management and all the other functions found in MODE.

Note, however, that the MODE framework is not exhaustive and it is not at the level of detail needed for contractual negotiations. However, it does give a good starter list of the functions required to manage a distribute environment.

Example. In the typical contractual process, the major steps would be

- Request for information (RFI)
- Request for proposal (RFP)
- Proposal evaluation
- Contractual negotiations

The RFI stage starts with the enterprise defining appropriate parts of the problem that it wants the outsourcer to address. If nothing else, this effort allows the enterprise to start off with a common view of its need. However, it also provides some advantage to the enterprise by requiring that responses be in a format that is consistent with the MODE framework. The evaluation of proposals becomes much more rational, because one starts with a common standard with which to compare.

By starting with the MODE framework, the user company can also require from the vendors the pricing of the functions as found in MODE. This information is another basis by which to evaluate proposals, comparing costs outlined in each proposal to a common standard to determine which vendor offers the most attractive pricing.

For example, if one vendor bids a help desk function at $10 per month per workstation and another bids it at $40 per month per workstation, this may be an indication of a problem. Although the tendency may be to say that the $10 bid is a better deal, the fact is that such a low bid may signal the vendor's lack of understanding of expectations, which may result in many subsequent change orders. This alone should be a source of concern in evaluating proposals.

More generally, it is remarkable how often a company will select a bid that clearly reflects charges that cannot cover costs. Sometimes an enterprise will accept a low bid with the intent of taking advantage of the vendor. However, if the outsourcer is taking on a critical function for the enterprise — such as running the distributed network — and the bid is low, it may be because the vendor does not understand the problem. Does the enterprise really want to entrust this function to them while they learn the problem?

A vendor that has misunderstood the requirements will not be an effective partner. Worse, if the vendor ends up servicing the deal with subpar personnel and commitment, the enterprise will not be well served. Also, there is always the risk that the outsourcer could simply walk away from the deal or end up in bankruptcy, which will do the enterprise no good.

A "conservation of effort" seems to exist in many of these cases. Doing a piece of work adequately is going to take a certain minimum amount of effort and associated costs. There is no magic in this business, so a cost that seems too good to be believed should not be believed. Costs truly reflecting this conservation of effort are, at best, going to differ by percentages, not by orders of magnitude. If you find large discrepancies, it is essential to understand why. An outsourcer that is not doing the job expected or that is losing money every day is not going to be effective in getting the job done. The MODE model can help with this evaluation, but it cannot guarantee that a vendor grasps the scope of the problem at hand nor can it provide guidance as to how to proceed with negotiations.

CONCLUSION

The costs associated with management of a distributed environment are a very significant part of the costs of the ongoing use of a client/server technology. Unfortunately, these costs are often not recognized or understood very well.

The MODE framework, discussed in detail in Section III and overviewed here, provides a basis for building an understanding of what the costs are. Then you can implement a program to monitor and improve the costs over time, while ensuring that the quality of service remains acceptable — whether functions in the model are being performed in-house or are being considered for outsourcing. MODE can be a basis for not only building the environment for managing distributed operations but also for improving it and reducing costs over time.

About the Authors

Mark Goodyear is the Managing Partner of the Architecture Programs within the Global Technology Integration Services organization of Accenture. He directs all firmwide competency development activities relating to the design and implementation of systems architecture for client engagements. These directly affect the training, development, and core architecture skills of approximately 40,000 consultants around the world. He is a member of Accenture's Technology Advisory Committee (TAC), a group that provides direction to the firm's worldwide Technology programs, activities and vision. In his 19-year career with Accenture he has worked with clients in both the public and private sectors, specializing in the design and implementation of advanced, large-scale systems.

Hugh W. Ryan is a partner with Accenture and the current Managing Director for a leading-edge group within Global Technology Integration Services devoted to Large Complex Systems. In his 26-year career with Accenture, he has worked on leading-edge applications of information technology, from the earliest on-line systems and DBMSs in the 1970s through today's emerging netcentric applications. He has written more than 30 articles on various aspects of computing and contributes a regular column on systems development to the journal of Information Systems Management. He has been a featured speaker at more than 50 conferences on the impact of computing on business solutions.

Scott R. Sargent is a partner in the Global Technology Integration Services organization of Accenture. He leads the Americas group, which supports Accenture's worldwide consulting organization in the planning, design, and implementation of advanced client/server systems that integrate existing data processing and office systems with emerging technologies. He has extensive experience with open systems, image systems, and data communications. He specializes in the telecommunications, transportation, insurance, financial services, aerospace, and manufacturing industries.

Stanton J. Taylor has more than 13 years' experience working with large US and European corporations in applying emerging information technology for competitive advantage. He is currently a partner with Accenture's Global Technology Integration Services organization. He leads the Internet and New Media group, which specializes in developing high-impact business solutions that leverage Internet and multimedia technologies. He has extensive experience in the planning, design, and implementation of client/server workstation-based solutions using state-of-the-market technologies and products, and has helped over a dozen organizations in the conceptualization and implementation of enterprise-wide technology strategies. He has worked with a broad range of companies in the financial services, transportation, retailing, pharmaceutical, and oil and gas industries.

Timothy M. Boudreau, a partner with Accenture's Global Technology Integration Services organization, is responsible for the Architecture Delivery and Integration group which is located in North and South America and Europe. The Architecture Delivery and Integration group specializes in the integration of emerging technologies using component system building techniques, netcentric architectures, client/server architectures, and mobile computing. He has worked with private and government organizations throughout North America and Europe in the financial, insurance, transportation, health care, and telecommunications industries.

Yannis S. Arvanitis is a partner in Accenture's technology organization. He is a member of the Products Industry Technology Architecture Group, which supports the worldwide consulting organization in planning, designing, and implementing systems using new and emerging technologies. He has extensive project experience with client/server architectures and applications, GUI design and development, object-oriented development, and Internet technologies, including HTML and Java. He is also an inventor on a patent held by Accenture for client/server architecture and tools.

Richard A. Chang, a partner with Accenture's Strategic Information Technology Effectiveness organization, is responsible for the firm's Global Architecture Planning group. He specializes in the strategy and planning of enterprise-wide information technology (IT) architectures. He has developed and is responsible for the firm's enterprise architecture planning methods, used in IT planning engagements, and has written several articles on this topic. He has extensive project experience in the strategy, planning, design, and delivery of solutions involving distributed computing, client/server, high-volume transaction processing, and database technologies, working with clients in financial services, insurance, utilities, consumer and industrial products, and government.

John K. Kaltenmark, a partner with Accenture's Global Technology Integration Services organization, is responsible for the Architecture Planning group, which specializes in the strategy and planning of large-scale, enterprise-wide information technology (IT) architectures. He also has extensive project experience in leading the development and implementation of large-scale IT architectures. He is also the program director for Accenture's Technology Architecture and Infrastructure Delivery program, which is focused on building technology infrastructure methodology, training, and tools covering areas such as networking technologies, operations architectures, security architectures, and next-generation architectures. He works with clients in the retail, electronics, government, and financial services industries.

Nancy K. Mullen is an associate partner in the Global Technology Integration Services organization of Accenture. She leads the Global Information Delivery group, which supports Accenture's worldwide consulting organization in the planning, design, and implementation of data warehouses and of complex OLTP database applications. She has extensive experience with data design methodologies, database design and tuning, and database performance management. She specializes in the consumer products, insurance, financial services, and manufacturing industries.

Shari L. Dove is an associate partner with Accenture's Business Process Management organization. She leads the Products Industry Transformation Team, which is responsible for planning and executing large scale change programs enabling large outsourcing engagements to deliver on the value proposition to the client. Previously, she served as Program Director for the Worldwide Systems Delivery Continuous Improvement Program, responsible for planning and managing the continuous improvement of the Accenture systems building capability, and as Project Manager of Accenture's "Reinventing Testing" Project, which included the development of a comprehensive client/server testing methodology, definition of testing metrics and estimating guidelines, and the development of training, practice aids and integrated tool suites.

Michael C. Davis is an associate partner with Accenture's Global Technology Integration Services organization. A member of the Internet and New Media group, he has responsibility for knowledge management and collaborative technologies, and is a frequent presenter on these topics at seminars and industry gatherings. He is experienced in the financial services, insurance, and health care industries.

John C. Clark is an associate partner with Accenture and current leader of the Security Consulting Practice within Global Technology Integration Services. He has fifteen years of combined experience in information systems development, information security, and security consulting. He is a recognized leader in the information security field and has been a featured speaker at more than 30 conferences and workshops. He has led security consulting work for over 35 different clients in a broad number of industry sectors including financial services, telecommunications, transportation, manufacturing, service industries, and health care. His expertise includes eCommerce and netcentric environments, network security, client/server security, risk assessments, and technology architecture.

ABOUT THE AUTHORS

Craig Mindrum teaches at DePaul University in Chicago. He is also a consultant and writer in the areas of organizational ethics and the effects of information technology on workforce performance and purpose, and is a regular conference speaker on issues related to human performance within organizations. He previously served as primary researcher and editor for *FutureWork: Putting Knowledge to Work in the Knowledge Economy* (New York: The Free Press, 1994), and is a co-author of *Practical Guide to Client/Server Computing* and *Netcentric Computing,* also published by Auerbach. He received his doctorate from the University of Chicago, following previous studies at Indiana University and Yale University.

Index

Index